Windows® 2000 System Administration Handbook

ISBN 0-13-027010-5

90000

9 780130 270108

PRENTICE HALL PTR MICROSOFT® TECHNOLOGIES SERIES

NETWORKING

- Microsoft Technology: Networking, Concepts, Tools
  Woodard, Gattuccio, Brain

- NT Network Programming Toolkit
  Murphy

- Building COM Applications with Internet Explorer
  Loveman

- Understanding DCOM
  Rubin, Brain

- Web Database Development for Windows Platforms
  Gutierrez

PROGRAMMING

- Windows Shell Programming for C++ and MFC Developers
  Seely

- Windows Installer Complete
  Easter

- Windows 2000 Web Applications Developer's Guide
  Yager

- Developing Windows Solutions with Office 2000 Components and VBA
  Aitken

- Win 32 System Services: The Heart of Windows 98 and Windows NT, Third Edition
  Brain

- Multithreaded Programming with Win32
  Pham, Garg

- Developing Professional Applications for Windows 98 and NT Using MFC, Third Edition
  Brain, Lovette

- Introduction to Windows 98 Programming
  Murray, Pappas

- Windows CE: Application Programming
  Gratten, Brain

- The COM and COM+ Programming Primer
  Gordon

- Understanding and Programming COM+: A Practical Guide to Windows 2000 DNA
  Oberg

- Distributed COM Application Development Using Visual C++ 6.0
  Maloney

- Distributed COM Application Development Using Visual Basic 6.0
  Maloney

- The Essence of COM, Third Edition
  Platt

- COM-CORBA Interoperability
  Geraghty, Joyce, Moriarty, Noone

- MFC Programming in C++ with the Standard Template Libraries
  Murray, Pappas

- Introduction to MFC Programming with Visual C++
  Jones

- Visual C++ Templates
  Murray, Pappas

- Visual Basic Object and Component Handbook
  Vogel

- Visual Basic 6: Error Coding and Layering
  Gill

- ADO Programming in Visual Basic 6
  Holzner

- Visual Basic 6: Design, Specification, and Objects
  Hollis

- ASP/MTS/ADSI Web Security
  Harrison

BACKOFFICE

- Designing Enterprise Solutions with Microsoft Technologies
  Kemp, Kemp, Goncalves

- Microsoft Site Server 3.0 Commerce Edition
  Libertone, Scoppa

- Building Microsoft SQL Server 7 Web Sites
  Byrne

- Optimizing SQL Server 7
  Schneider, Goncalves

ADMINISTRATION

- Windows 2000 Hardware and Disk Management
  Simmons

- Windows 2000 Server: Management and Control, Third Edition
  Spencer, Goncalves

- Creating Active Directory Infrastructures
  Simmons

- Windows 2000 Registry
  Sanna

- Configuring Windows 2000 Server
  Simmons

- Supporting Windows NT and 2000 Workstation and Server
  Mohr

- Zero Administration Kit for Windows
  McInerney

- Tuning and Sizing NT Server
  Aubley

- Windows NT Cluster Server Guidebook
  Libertone

- Windows NT 4.0 Server Security Guide
  Goncalves

- Windows NT Security
  McInerney

- Windows NT Device Driver Book
  Baker

- Windows 2000 System Administration Handbook
  Willis, Watts, Strahan

CERTIFICATION

- Core MCSE: Windows 2000 Edition
  Dell

- Core MCSE
  Dell

- Core MCSE: Networking Essentials
  Keogh

- MCSE: Administering Microsoft SQL Server 7
  Byrne

- MCSE: Implementing and Supporting Microsoft Exchange Server 5.5
  Goncalves

- MCSE: Internetworking with Microsoft TCP/IP
  Ryvkin, Houde, Hoffman

- MCSE: Implementing and Supporting Microsoft Proxy Server 2.0
  Ryvkin, Hoffman

- MCSE: Implementing and Supporting Microsoft SNA Server 4.0
  Mariscal

- MCSE: Implementing and Supporting Microsoft Internet Information Server 4
  Dell

- MCSE: Implementing and Supporting Web Sites Using Microsoft Site Server 3
  Goncalves

- MCSE: Microsoft System Management Server 2
  Jewett

- MCSE: Implementing and Supporting Internet Explorer 5
  Dell

- Core MCSD: Designing and Implementing Desktop Applications with Microsoft Visual Basic 6
  Holzner

- Core MCSD: Designing and Implementing Distributed Applications with Microsoft Visual Basic 6
  Houlette, Klander

- MCSD: Planning and Implementing SQL Server 7
  Vacca

- MCSD: Designing and Implementing Web Sites with Microsoft FrontPage 98
  Karlins

PRENTICE HALL PTR MICROSOFT® TECHNOLOGIES SERIES

Windows® 2000 System Administration Handbook

Will Willis
David Watts
Tiilman Strahan

Prentice Hall PTR, Upper Saddle River, NJ 07458
www.phptr.com

Library of Congress Cataloging-in-Publication Data

Willis, Will.
    Windows 2000 system administration handbook / Will Willis, David Watts, Tillman Strahan
        p. cm. – (Prentice Hall series on Microsoft technologies)
    Includes bibliographical references and index.
    ISBN 0-13-027010-5
      1. Microsoft Windows (Computer file) 2. Operating systems (Computers) I. Watts,
    David (David V.), 1962- II. Strahan, Tillman. III. Title.

    QA76.76.063 W559 2000
    005.4'4769–dc21   00-032404

Editorial/Production Supervision: *Nicholas Radhuber*
Acquisitions Editor: *Jill Pisoni*
Marketing Manager: *Bryan Gambrel*
Manufacturing Buyer: *Maura Goldstaub*
Cover Design: *Anthony Gemmellaro*
Cover Design Direction: *Jerry Votta*
Interior Series Design: *Gail Cocker-Bogusz*

© 2000 by Prentice Hall PTR
Prentice-Hall, Inc.
Upper Saddle River, NJ 07458

Prentice Hall books are widely used by corporations and government agencies for training, marketing, and resale.

The publisher offers discounts on this book when ordered in bulk quantities. For more information, contact Corporate Sales Department, phone: 800-382-3419; fax: 201-236-7141; email: corpsales@pren-hall.com
Or write Corporate Sales Department, Prentice Hall PTR, One Lake Street, Upper Saddle River, NJ 07458.

Product and company names mentioned herein are the trademarks or registered trademarks of their respective owners. The Electronic Commerce Game™ is a trademark of Object Innovations. Inc.

Printed in the United States of America

10 9 8 7 6 5 4 3 2 1

ISBN 0-13-027010-5

Prentice-Hall International (UK) Limited, *London*
Prentice-Hall of Australia Pty. Limited, *Sydney*
Prentice-Hall Canada Inc., *Toronto*
Prentice-Hall Hispanoamericana, S.A., *Mexico*
Prentice-Hall of India Private Limited, *New Delhi*
Prentice-Hall of Japan, Inc., *Tokyo*
Pearson Education Asia Pte. Ltd.
Editora Prentice-Hall do Brasil, Ltda., *Rio de Janeiro*

CONTENTS

PREFACE

Welcome to the Windows 2000 Systems Administration Training Course. As IT professionals, we have watched Windows 2000 slowly mature from a very rough NT5 beta 1 to a robust, polished Windows 2000 released product. As authors, we have attempted to bring you a collection of the topics most relevant to systems administration while adding insight from our own personal experiences implementing and administering Windows 2000 throughout the lengthy beta period, up to and including the final release. We hope that you will find this multimedia training course useful as you study and develop your Windows 2000 system administration skills.

Windows 2000, which initially was to be called *Windows NT 5.0*, is the newest upgrade in Microsoft's NT line of business operating systems. Windows NT was originally launched in 1993 as Windows NT 3.1. Microsoft chose to number it 3.1 rather than 1.0 to capitalize on the name recognition of its consumer Windows product line. At that time, Windows 3.1 was the current version of Windows and ran on top of DOS.

Windows NT 3.1 was upgraded to 3.5 and later to 3.51, while retaining the older "Program Manager" GUI (graphical user interface). After five service packs, Windows NT 3.51 was showing its age, and, in 1996, Microsoft released Windows NT 4.0. NT4 was essentially 3.51, updated to use the Windows 95 "Explorer" style GUI. Although there were a few new features in NT4, notably Microsoft DNS Server, the basic product was largely the same. Any administrator who had worked with NT 3.51 and knew the Explorer GUI could sit down at an NT4 console and instantly administer the system. Technology has changed rapidly since 1996, when NT4 was released, and making NT keep up with newer technologies has been difficult for both Microsoft and for third-party developers. To keep up with the times and push the NT line of operating systems ahead, Microsoft has dramatically revamped NT4 into what is now Windows 2000, finally released in February 2000.

The Audience

The audience for this book is twofold. Topics are explained in sufficient detail to satisfy readers without prior experience in Windows NT systems administration, yet will help Windows NT administrators leverage their existing knowledge to get up to speed quickly on the new features and techniques of Windows 2000. Throughout the book, we often point out changes between Windows NT 4.0 and Windows 2000 and show the new ways to do the old familiar tasks.

The Contents

It is important to note that the authors of this book are all IT professionals with extensive experience in Windows NT systems administration. While brainstorming for this book, the idea came up to present the material in a way that would provide the best benefit not only to someone reading this book for educational purposes, but also for the real-world systems administrator who needs a reference while on the job. To that end, we've taken care to add tips and insight from our own real-world systems administration experiences and have arranged the topics to cover the common tasks of a Windows 2000 systems administrator. The arrangement of subjects in this book is broken down into sections as follows:

INTRODUCTION TO WINDOWS 2000 SYSTEMS ADMINISTRATION

In this section, we provide an overview of Windows 2000 basics, starting with discussing the different versions of the Windows 2000 operating system. Although the vast majority of this book relates to Windows 2000 Server, you will learn about the Windows 2000 Professional, Advanced Server, and Datacenter Server products, as well, and how they differ from each other. Chapter 1 discusses the different versions of Windows 2000 and how they relate to their Windows NT 4.0 counterparts.

We also discuss new Windows 2000 terminology, such as *Microsoft Management Console* (MMC), *Active Directory*, *domain trees*, and *forests*. Windows NT 4.0 systems administrators will appreciate the quick overview, as well as the new features section that follows the terminology. Readers who are new to the world of Windows NT technology (Windows 2000 is built on NT technology) will gain an insight into some of the topics ahead of them in the book.

WINDOWS 2000 SYSTEMS ADMINISTRATION BASICS

With the introductory material out of the way, we dive headfirst into Windows 2000, beginning with installing the operating system. Once the OS is installed, we move on to basic systems administration concepts, such as using the Control Panel, Registry, and MMC snap-ins. We finish this section with a discussion of the boot process as it relates to systems administration and troubleshooting. Windows 2000 Active Directory

Active Directory is probably the most visible and most talked-about new feature of Windows 2000, and we devote an entire section to it. We start with an introduction that explains what Active Directory is and what it does, then we move into a discussion of the structure of Active Directory, which includes terminology, concepts, and planning issues. With a foundation built, we install Active Directory and learn about the issues surrounding single-domain environments versus multidomain environments. We finish the section on Active Directory by learning how to administer it.

WINDOWS 2000 USER AND GROUP MANAGEMENT

One of the more common tasks of a systems administrator is user and group management; thus, we devote an entire section to it. Initially, we discuss the basics of user accounts, from the type of accounts available in Windows 2000 to creating and defining options for user accounts. We then learn how to administer user accounts through user profiles, how to make changes to user accounts, and about home directories for user accounts.

With an understanding of user accounts, we expand into groups, which are collections of user accounts, other groups, and/or computers. We discuss groups from the systems administrator's perspective, including strategies for using groups and how to implement groups. We then look at using Group Policy to administer security on a Windows 2000 network.

WINDOWS 2000 DATA MANAGEMENT

Server management is another important topic for systems administrators, and we cover it in this section. We start with a discussion of managing server hard disks with Windows 2000 utilities and features and learn about the NTFS file system and its benefits for server file management. Next we learn about shared folders, because one of the most basic functions of a server is to serve files. Once we understand how shared folders work and how to manage them, we expand on that to administer data storage, including NTFS compression, disk quotas, and disk defragmenting.

No discussion of systems administration would be complete without backup and restoring data from servers and planning for disaster recovery. We discuss these subjects and provide insight into fault tolerance issues and best practices for protecting Enterprise data.

WINDOWS 2000 NETWORKING BASICS

Up to this point of the book, we have focused primarily on single server administration and functions that take place within a server. In this section we expand our focus into the networking environment as it relates to Windows 2000. We discuss network protocols supported by Windows 2000, with a focus on TCP/IP, the protocol of choice for most networking environments and the required protocol for many Windows 2000 features such as Active Directory. You will learn about TCP/IP topics such as DHCP, WINS, DNS, and how to implement and administer them on a Windows 2000 network.

WINDOWS 2000 SECURITY

Security is another important topic for systems administration, and we discuss auditing access to network resources and monitoring network resource usage. This is done from the systems administrator viewpoint, including designing policies for auditing and monitoring, why it should be done in the first place, and managing security logs. We learn how to view currently used resources and how to disconnect users from resources when necessary.

WINDOWS 2000 PRINTING

Network printing is another common function of a Windows 2000 network, so we devote a section to it. We introduce printing concepts and learn how to create and share printers, and how to administer printers and print queues. Systems administration issues, such as driver files, client and server configuration, and print pools, are discussed.

WINDOWS 2000 ADMINISTRATION PRACTICES

We finish the book with a general section on systems administration best practices. Some of the topics are about systems administration, in general, rather than being Windows 2000-specific, but all are relevant to the real world administrator. We discuss issues related to documentation, restoring workstations and servers to original configurations, and general administration practices, such as driver management and issues related to when your organization moves from one location to another and you have to move your systems.

CONCLUSION

After much discussion back and forth, we feel like we have come up with a structure for this training course that will allow the beginning systems administrator to build knowledge throughout the book as later topics build on the foundation laid by previous topics, while allowing the experienced systems administrator to find topics of interest quickly. We hope that you find this training course valuable as you study Windows 2000 systems administration and learn to apply that knowledge in the real world.

ACKNOWLEDGMENTS

*W*ill Willis would like to thank: My wife Melissa, who somehow manages to put up with me even during my worst moments. You're a better person than I am!:-) My son Duncan, who can light the world with his smile. Dad, for teaching me to be disciplined and stand behind my commitments. Mom, for the greatest gift of all … life. Alex, for being generous to a fault. Now you just need to take care of yourself! Donna, for our little "one-upmanship" game that gives me a little nudge whenever I start feeling complacent. Melba, for accepting me into your family. That means a lot to me! Bill, for giving this city kid an appreciation for the open country. I can't wait to move far away from the city! Grandma Estes, for everything you did when you didn't have to. I'll never forget it!

To Dr. Ray Bandy and the great people at Trinity Southern in Lewisville, TX … thank you for helping bring Jesus Christ back into my heart. It's been a long trip home, but I've finally made it!

Thanking people is often difficult because there are so many people who have affected my life in one way or another, and there's only so much space to fill. Inevitably, someone important gets left out. So, I'd like to simply thank everyone who has made an impact on my life … family members, teachers, friends, colleagues, teammates, public figures, musicians, artists, authors, and anyone I might have missed who fits into a different category. So many people have influenced who I am, and hopefully that concoction of influences has turned out fairly well:-) Lastly, I'd like to thank you the reader, since without you this book wouldn't have been written.

Will Willis—12 March 2000

A bouquet of endless orchids to so many different people. Writing this book has been a lot of fun for me, but an author does not write in a vacuum. First I would like to extend thanks and love to my parents, Len and Kit. I love you both, and thank you for everything (how is Vange this time of year?). I also want to thank my wife, Siobhan Chamberlin-Watts, who has supported me throughout this effort. Without her many trips to Starbucks, I don't know how this would have gotten done. To my brother John Watts I would like to celebrate his many victories, and happiness to come. Life is full of curve balls, but we're getting better and hitting them out of the park. I also want to mention my sister Catherine and her husband Jeff. I haven't seen you in a while, I hope to do that soon. To Siobhan's mother Moira and brother Peter — "Hey Guys!"

I have so many understanding colleagues. I would like to thank Jeff Hilton, Mona Reed, and Mike Stewart at Hilton Computer Strategies for their faith in my skills and their patience when I seem to move slowly. We have a great team to work with. I want to thank the trainers at Hilton—Sam Thompson, Jaime Rodriguez, Boyd Collins, and Darrell DeMartino. I have horrendously high standards, and you guys exceed them. The sales team also deserves mention—Jeanne Hromadka, Donna George, Daryl Pavlicek, and Richard Spoonts. And not forgetting Tara Gold. When I need something I can always count on Jeannie Griswold to help, and I appreciate that. And of course, not forgetting Sandy Pienkosz who has been away for a while — please come back soon! There is also a little bit of the British Isles here with David Aldridge. While I cannot imagine his beloved Scotland beating my English national team, his unquestionable talent and technical expertise allow me to worry less, and that means a lot.

I could not have done this without my co-authors Will Willis and Tillman Strahan. It is good to know that there are people at least as crazy as I am for taking these things on. I want to say thanks to Michael Cook, a great friend. I also want to make sure that Zevi Mehlman knows I have not forgotten him. Stay in touch! To Sam Rao I would say—you have done a lot since we last met and your hard work will pay off. Congratulations!

Finally, I would like to thank the people who have bought this book. We worked hard to make sure it was useful. I hope you enjoy it. A bouquet of barbed wire to all those that got in the way.

David Watts

This has been an amazing process, and I've learned much during it. I still don't know what Will and David were thinking (or maybe drinking) bringing me on to the project, but I'd like to thank them for the opportunity.

I think that any acknowledgements by a writer of any sort must begin with the family. After all, it is the family that forms the core of a writer's support. I would like to thank my wife and soulmate, Tamara, for putting up with me during this process, supporting me when I got bogged down, and providing motivation when I felt like the process would never finish. I would also like to thank my parents, Roger and Paula, for stressing the importance of a good education and for buying that first TI 99/4 way back in the stone ages of home computing. Thanks to David and Vicki and all the various inlaws, outlaws and friends for their support and encouragement, and also for just getting me out of the house from time to time.

Some of my coworkers at Insource were aware that I was working on this book at home, and I'd like to thank them for their support and for putting up with me after a few all-nighters. Thanks also to Dr. Samantha Hastings of the University of North Texas, who helped teach me to balance work and my studies. Thanks to the staff and forum contributors at www.InsideIS.com who are probably the sharpest people I know in this industry – you all helped me retain a sense of balance.

      This book is dedicated to Delaney Alton Strahan, my parent's first grand-child and my favorite niece.

Tillman Strahan

Introduction to Windows 2000

*W*ith Windows 2000, Microsoft stakes its claim as an Enterprise-class operating system developer. Previous versions of Windows NT have been viewed as less than reliable for mission-critical business functions, and Microsoft is putting everything it has into ensuring that Windows 2000 addresses the shortcomings of Windows NT 4.0. Like NT4, there are multiple versions of Windows 2000 that are targeted at different audiences, and much has changed in the last 3+ years since NT4 was released. In this chapter, we will look at the following topics as we introduce Windows 2000.

- What is Windows 2000?
- What has changed between Windows NT 4.0 and Windows 2000?
- Overview of Windows 2000 features

What Is Windows 2000?

Windows 2000 is Microsoft's latest flagship operating system, an operating system that has largely been redesigned and enhanced to support Enterprise-class computing. At one time in the beta process, Windows 2000 was officially known as *Windows NT 5.0*, but between beta 2 and beta 3, the line of NT5 operating systems was renamed. Only Microsoft knows for sure why the name was changed from the descriptive NT5 (systems administrators and IT professionals knew what NT was) to a vague Windows 2000 that sounds more like an upgrade to Windows 95 and Windows 98. Speculation, however, includes the slow convergence of Microsoft's consumer (Windows 9x) and business (Windows NT) operating system lines. Windows 2000 supports many of the features that Windows 98 users have enjoyed over NT users, such as Plug and Play and full DirectX support for games. It also supports the security and reliability features that NT users have enjoyed, compared with Windows 9x users. Other speculation is that whereas Windows 2000 is built on NT technology, the NT name has become somewhat tarnished in the high-end server and workstation market in which Microsoft really wants to play. By changing the name, Microsoft differentiates Windows 2000 from its NT ancestry. That could be considered a productive move, because although Windows 2000 is built on NT technology, it is definitely not the NT of three years ago. Some estimates have NT4 at around 3–5 million lines of code, with Windows 2000 checking in somewhere around 40 million lines of code late in the beta process.

In the process of upgrading Windows 2000's capabilities as an Enterprise operating system, Microsoft has borrowed heavily from the concepts and practices inherent in their own BackOffice line of server products. Many of these features are discussed throughout this book and are given an overview later in this chapter, but notable BackOffice apps that Windows 2000 has borrowed ideas from include Exchange Server, SQL Server, and SMS.

In developing a Windows 2000 at all levels of the company strategy, Microsoft has come up with the following distinct versions of the operating system.

- Windows 2000 Professional
- Windows 2000 Server
- Windows 2000 Advanced Server
- Windows 2000 Datacenter Server

Windows 2000 Professional

Windows 2000 Professional is the successor to the increasingly popular Windows NT Workstation 4.0. It combines some of the best features of the consumer Windows 9x line of operating systems such as Plug and Play, DirectX, a Device Manager for easy hardware management and troubleshooting, and others, along with the reliability and security of NT Workstation. Windows 2000 Professional is aimed squarely at the corporate desktop, offering a host of manageability features to reduce the total cost of ownership (TCO) of PCs and providing a more robust computing environment than its predecessor.

Windows 2000 Server

Windows 2000 Server is everything that Windows 2000 Professional is and more. In addition to providing all of the features of Professional, Server includes additional server-specific functionality, such as Internet Information Server for website hosting right out of the box. Windows 2000 Server is aimed at the small to midsize business needing a solid platform for file, print, and application serving. This is a direct replacement for Windows NT Server 4.0, with many more features. Windows 2000 Server is the primary operating system used throughout this book.

Windows 2000 Advanced Server

Largely the same as Windows 2000 Server, Advanced Server is a more scalable version with some additional features to support Enterprise-class networked environments. In addition to all of the features of Windows 2000 Server, Windows 2000 Advanced Server also has enhanced memory support and supports clustering. Advanced Server also scales to eight processors, whereas Server scales to only two CPUs. Windows 2000 is the equivalent of Windows NT Server 4.0 Enterprise Edition, with many more features and support for more processors.

Windows 2000 Datacenter Server

Windows 2000 Datacenter Server is designed for the high-end server market, a market currently dominated by UNIX and mainframe operating systems. All of the features of the other Windows 2000 operating systems are included, as well as features that optimize its use for large-scale installations supporting thousands of users, data warehousing, and other applications that require the reliability and performance that only an Enterprise-class operating system can provide. Windows 2000 Datacenter Server offers functionality not found in other Windows 2000 operating systems, such as managing the allocation of critical server resources, including processor affinity, scheduling priority, allowable number of processes, memory use amounts, and limits to the amount of CPU time used for a specific workload. Small and midsize businesses typically will not run Datacenter Server; it is designed to support businesses with very large server needs.

What Has Changed Between Windows NT 4.0 and Windows 2000?

As you will see as you progress through this book, much has changed in the almost four years between Windows NT 4.0, released in 1996, and Windows 2000. The changes are too many to cover in any detail in this introductory chapter, however, we will look at some of the following features in this section.

- Windows 2000 workgroups
- Windows 2000 domains
- Windows 2000 domain Trees
- Windows 2000 forests
- MMC
- Universal groups

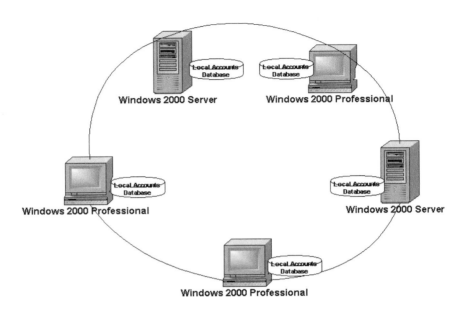

Figure 1-1   *A Windows 2000 workgroup.*

Some of the topics listed above may seem familiar to those who have worked with Windows NT 4.0. However, some of the terminology has changed. In some cases, the changes are slight, and in other cases the changes have been radical.

Windows 2000 Workgroups

Workgroups are very similar between Windows NT and Windows 2000. A workgroup is simply a decentralized grouping of network resources. Workgroups are also commonly referred to as peer-to-peer networks because of their decentralized nature. By *decentralized*, we mean that there is no central accounts database or control over all of the systems, printers, and other network resources. If you have a workgroup, such as that in Figure 1.1, a user must have a user account on each workstation in order to use it. They cannot login with the same user account on each computer. This means that while a user *can* have the same username and password for each workstation, changing the password on one computer does not change it on all of the computers. Passwords would have to also be changed at each and every computer the user logged in to.

ADVANTAGES OF WORKGROUPS

• Workgroups do not require a dedicated Windows 2000 server to hold the accounts database.

• Workgroups are cheaper to implement because there is no need for a dedicated server.

• Workgroups are easy to implement. Two computers networked together constitute a workgroup.

• Workgroups allow local control of resources for environments where that is an issue.

• Workgroups can be more convenient when there are a small number of computers on a network (10 or fewer).

DISADVANTAGES OF WORKGROUPS

• Users must have a user account on each computer they want to use; otherwise, Guest accounts must be enabled to allow other users to access a computer remotely. Guest accounts greatly reduce security and are discussed in detail later in this book.

• Changing any properties of a user account, such as a password, must be done on each machine if the user wants the change to be consistent across all of the computers they use.

• No centralized administration means users must keep up with their own resource administration.

• Workgroups do not scale well beyond approximately 10-computer workgroups, become increasingly cumbersome to manage.

• Workgroups do not offer the security benefits of domains.

Windows 2000 Domains

A domain is like a workgroup in that it is a logical grouping of network resources. However, the main difference is that a domain uses one or more servers that contain security information, such as user names and passwords, for the entire domain. A user needs to remember only a single domain user-name and password to sit down and login from any computer in the domain. Because passwords are stored on the server, changing them need be done only once, rather than on every single machine.

A server that holds the security information for a domain is called a *domain controller.* If there are multiple servers in a domain, there can be multiple domain controllers or member servers. Member servers provide network services without the overhead of handling security information. A process called *replication* allows multiple domain controllers to keep domain information synchronized between them, so that it won't matter which server responds to an authentication request. Figure 1.2 shows an example of a domain that contains multiple controllers, a member server, and a couple of workstations.

Whereas windows NT and Windows 2000 were very similar with regard to workgroups, significant changes have been made with regard to domains. One of the hottest topics of Windows 2000 has been Active Directory, which is

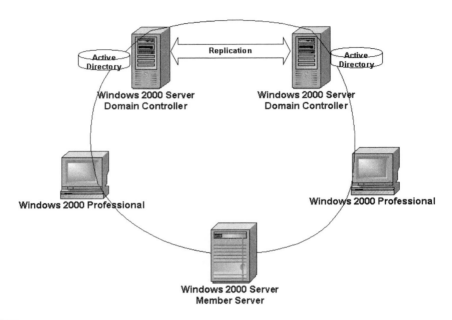

Figure 1-2   *A Windows 2000 domain.*

the name of Microsoft's new directory services. Active Directory runs on Windows 2000 domain controllers only. We talk more about Active Directory in the next section and later in the book. For now, suffice it to say that Active Directory dramatically changes the concept of a domain in Windows 2000. Domains in Windows NT and Windows 2000 share similarities only in the theory of providing centralized administration of network resources.

Domains do not have to be contained entirely in one location, which is typically how workgroups are implemented. A domain can span WAN links to cover multiple locations. This ability adds flexibility to corporations that need to share and manage network resources in different cities, states, and even countries.

An ideal Windows 2000 domain will not have any *downlevel* clients, which are legacy systems running Windows NT, Windows 9x, or non-Windows operating systems. A pure Windows 2000 network running Windows 2000 Server on the servers and Windows 2000 Professional on the workstations is able to take maximum advantage of the new features that Windows 2000 offers. Many of the features are not available to downlevel clients, and some features cannot be used at all unless only Windows 2000 systems are being used.

ADVANTAGES OF DOMAINS

- Centralized management of resources provides more consistent administration and control of network resources.
- A user needs only a single domain user account and password to login from any computer in the domain.
- Domains scale much higher than do workgroups, effectively handling thousands of user accounts.
- Domains span WAN links more effectively than do workgroups, making them more convenient for companies with multiple locations.
- Windows 2000 domains support the advanced features of Active Directory that workgroups cannot use.

DISADVANTAGES OF DOMAINS

- Windows 2000 domains are expensive to implement, compared with workgroups, requiring Windows 2000 Server software and typically at least one dedicated server to manage the domain.
- Windows 2000 domains require additional planning to implement a domain
- Centralized management of Windows 2000 domains requires the hiring of a dedicated network administrator to administer the domain, or at least the addition of network administration responsibilities to an existing employee's job duties.
- Windows 2000 domains require additional training costs if there is no one internally who knows Windows 2000 Server, and the network is too small to hire a full time administrator.

Windows 2000 Domain Trees

A *domain tree* is an Active Directory term that describes a hierarchical structure of Windows 2000 domains. At the top of the domain tree is the parent domain, and domains that branch off from the parent are called *child domains*. Figure 1.3 shows an example of a simple domain tree.

As you can see from the example, the domains are related even though they are separate. The parent domain is *InsideIS.com*. The two child domains also share the *InsideIS.com* namespace, though they are broken down further into *development.InsideIS.com* and *marketing.InsideIS.com*. The domain tree links the three domains together, which form what is known as a *contiguous namespace*. Domain names for Windows 2000 domains are DNS names and are discussed in Chapter 24.

In Windows NT, one of the most headache-inducing chores of network administration came with respect to trust relationships, especially when managing more than a few domains. A trust relationship is simply a mechanism by

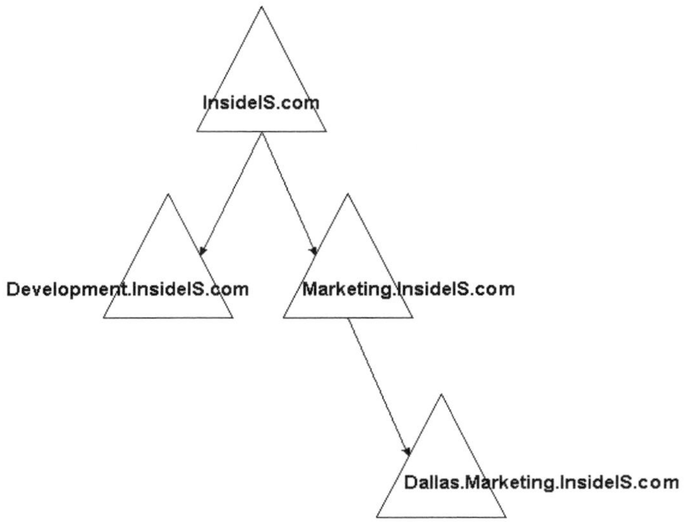

Figure 1–3   *A simple example of a Windows 2000 domain tree.*

which one domain allows users in a different domain to access resources without having to have a domain user account. For example, let's say that there are two domains, Domain1 and Domain2. By default, users in Domain1 could not access resources in Domain2, and vice versa. If a trust relationship was established, where Domain1 trusts Domain2, then users in Domain2 could access resources in Domain1. However, if you wanted the relationship to work the other way also, another trust relationship would have to be established, with Domain2 trusting Domain1. Windows 2000 solves this problem through its implementation of the industry standard Kerberos security protocol. This protocol enables Windows 2000 to use transitive two-way trust relationships that are formed automatically between domains in a tree. Transitive trusts created a situation where all child domains trust the parent domain, and all child domains within a tree trust each other. This allows users to access resources in domains in the tree other than the one they are logged into.

Domain trees form the foundation for Active Directory, which uses the tree to share a common schema and Global Catalog with subdomains. These terms and concepts are discussed later in the Active Directory chapters.

Windows 2000 Forests

The next logical extension from the domain tree is the forest. A forest enables the Windows 2000 administrator to connect domain trees together that don't share a contiguous namespace. The advantage to using a forest is that

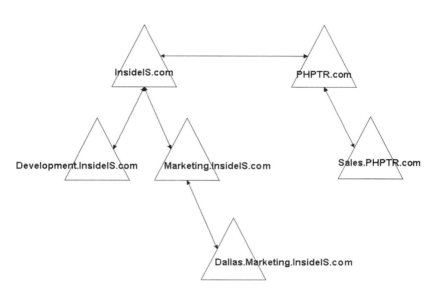

| Figure 1–4 | *An example of a Windows 2000 forest.*

domain trees within a forest are connected by transitive trust relationships and share a common schema and Global Catalog, as do domains within a tree. Figure 1.4 shows an example of a forest.

Forests exist primarily as administrative units, allowing an administrator to manage multiple domain trees with disjointed namespace.

MMC

One of the new features of Windows 2000 actually became available in Windows NT 4.0 with the release of Service Pack 4 (SP4) and may be familiar to current NT administrators. This feature is the Microsoft Management Console (MMC). The MMC is a framework that Microsoft has built for its operating system tools that provides a uniform interface for administrators and users. The MMC framework is extensible to third-party tools and easily customized to reflect your individual needs.

MMC works on the concept of snap-ins, which are the applications that are loaded into the console to be used. Windows NT administrators had to deal with the hassle of working with multiple administrative tools and switching Windows back and forth from Server Manager to User Manager for Domains to DHCP Admin, and so forth. MMC gives you the flexibility to build your own administrative consoles that contain the tools you want, arranged as you want them. This creates flexibility and improves efficiency for the administrator. MMC has a chapter all to itself later in the book.

Universal Groups

Universal groups are a new feature of Windows 2000 that have no corresponding component in Windows NT. The purpose of universal groups is to ease the administrative burden of managing domain global and local groups across domains. You can still use global groups just like in Windows NT; however, universal groups can contain global groups, other universal groups, and users from anywhere within a forest. Universal groups can be used only if a domain is running in native mode, which means that all of its domain controllers are running Windows 2000 and the administrator has manually changed the domain from mixed mode (which supports legacy Windows NT domain controllers participating in a Windows 2000 domain) to native mode. One popular use for universal groups is to combine multiple domain global groups into a single universal group and use the universal group to assign permissions and rights throughout a forest. Doing this simplifies the administrative process because the properties of the universal group will not change frequently. Global groups are infrequently added or deleted, whereas users are often added to or deleted from global groups.

Overview of Windows 2000 Features

Windows 2000 is an enormous upgrade to Windows NT 4.0, over four years in the making. There are many new features and upgrades, and in this section, we will focus on some of the more popular changes, such as:

- Active Directory
- Disk Quotas
- File System Changes
- Group Policies
- Security (Kerberos)
- Distributed File System

Active Directory

Active Directory is probably the most anticipated new feature of Windows 2000. For the first time, Windows has a directory service that is native to the operating system and not an add-on like Novell's NDS for NT. Active Directory greatly enhances the domain-based solution of Windows NT by distributing the storage of Directory information across domain controllers on a network. Windows 2000 uses a technique called *multimaster replication*, which eliminates the Windows NT concept of a Primary Domain Controller (PDC) and Backup Domain Controller (BDC). In Windows 2000, each domain controller contains a master replica, or copy of the Directory. Windows 2000 can still act as a PDC in mixed environments, though, where both Windows 2000 and Windows NT domain controllers are operating in the same domain.

Because Active Directory is much more integrated than the loose domain-based structure of Windows NT, searching for resources is much easier. Searching has become much more advanced; you can find resources based on criteria that you specify (name, phone number, location, etc.), as well as find all resources that fit into a particular classification (printers, domain controllers, etc.). Active Directory has several chapters devoted to it later in the book.

Disk Quotas

Disk quotas are a new feature of Windows 2000 that lets Windows administrators enjoy what users of other network operating systems such as UNIX and Novell NetWare have enjoyed for years. Quotas allow the administrator to set limits on the amount of disk space a user can consume on a shared drive or directory. As Figure 1.5 shows, the limit is set in kilobytes (KB) and integrates with the Event Viewer administrative tool. KB is the smallest unit that you can use to set limits. By clicking the dropdown list, you can select other units such as megabytes, gigabytes, and even higher. When quota management is enabled, logging can optionally be turned on, as well, for both the warning levels and the limit levels. By setting a warning level, you ensure that users know when they are approaching their disk space limit (and you'll know, as well, if you enable logging for it). That way, users can be proactive about cleaning up their files, rather than waiting until they hit their limits and call you because they can't save a document that they have made a bunch of changes to.

Disk Quotas are available only on volumes that have been formatted with the NTFS file system or converted to NTFS under Windows 2000. They are a feature of the Windows 2000 version of NTFS, often referred to as *NTFS5*, which was not available in Windows NT 4.0's version of NTFS. Disk quotas are covered more extensively later in the book.

File System Changes

Administrators familiar with Windows NT 4.0 already know about the FAT (also known as *FAT16*) and NTFS file systems. Windows 2000 supports these files systems, as well as adding direct support for the Windows 9x (Windows 95 OSR2 and above) FAT32 file system. Neither FAT file system supports the features of NTFS, such as file level security, on-the-fly file compression, and Disk Quotas. As a rule of thumb, you should use the FAT file system only when you need to maintain backward compatibility with non-Windows NT or Windows 2000 operating systems running on the same computer (dual boot configurations).

In addition to the security benefits provided by NTFS, there are also features in NTFS 5 that were not available in NTFS 4. The list below summarizes some of the main features.

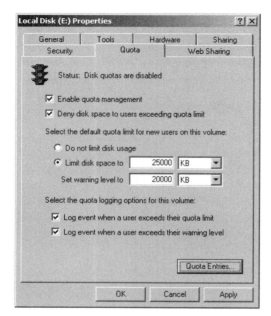

Figure 1–5

Disk quotas are a new feature of Windows 2000 that lets adminis-trators limit the amount of disk space that a user can consume.

- *Encryption*—NTFS now supports on-the-fly encryption/decryption of data as it is written to and read from a hard disk.
- *Disk Quotas*—As mentioned previously, administrators can control the amount of disk space used by users on NTFS volumes
- *Mount Points*—NTFS now supports the UNIX concept of drive mount points, overriding the previously existing limitation of being able to create only as many volumes as you had drive letters.

NTFS also supports a wealth of fault tolerance- and performance-boosting features over the FAT file systems. NTFS is covered more extensively later in the book.

Group Policies

Group Policy is another Windows 2000 feature that carries over from Windows NT. An administrator can use Group Policy to control the configuration and appearance of workstations, creating a consistent look and feel for user desktops. Group Policy is configured from the Group Policy MMC console, where you can specify policy settings for the following:

- *Registry-based policies*—Group Policy for the Windows 2000 operating system, its components, and applications.

- Security options—Local computer, domain, and network security settings.
- *Software installation and maintenance options*—Used to allow the central management of application installation, updates, and removal.
- *Scripts options*—Allows the administrator to specify scripts for computer startup and shutdown, and user logon and logoff.
- *Folder redirection options*—Allows administrators to redirect users' special folders to the network.

Group Policy can be a touchy area when administering a network. Too much policy can be bad for employee morale, whereas too little policy can increase the administrative burden. The key to group policy is consistency and managing users' expectations. Group Policy is covered extensively later in the book. Figure 1.6 shows an example of the Group Policy MMC snap-in.

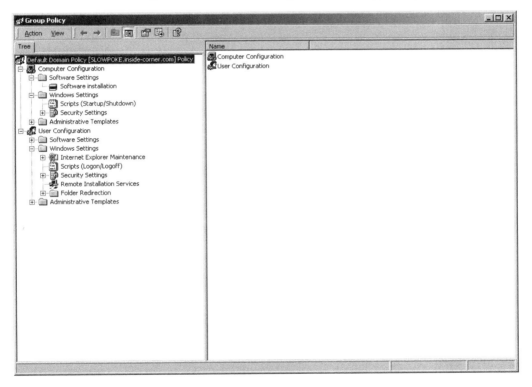

Figure 1–6   *The MMC snap-in for Group Policy.*

Security (Kerberos)

In previous versions of Windows NT, security was handled by Microsoft's LAN Manager technology. This security was considered weak, and in Windows 2000, Microsoft has implemented the Kerberos security protocol as a replacement. Kerberos, currently at version 5, is a security protocol used for authentication and access control of network resources. Kerberos is a more efficient protocol than is NTLM; when a user logs into the network they are given credentials to use to access resources based on who a user logs in as. When a user attempts to access network resources, the client presents the credentials to the server for authentication. With NTLM, the resource being requested had to go back to a domain controller to verify the authentication of the client. Kerberos eliminates that step, reducing network traffic and speeding up the authentication process.

One potential disadvantage of NTLM was that it was a one-sided authentication scheme, meaning that the server validated the client but not vice versa. Servers were always assumed to be authentic. This could give someone the opportunity to put up a rogue server masquerading as a valid server on a network.

The aspect of Kerberos that most people are talking about with Windows 2000 comes with respect to Active Directory and domain trees. The Kerberos security protocol is used to allow two-way transitive trust relationships between domains in a domain tree and between domain trees in a forest. Trust relationships had to be explicitly defined and managed in Windows NT between every domain that needed to trust another domain, so the ability to use transitive trusts greatly simplifies the administration of trust relationships.

Kerberos is discussed in more detail in the security chapters.

Distributed File System

The Distributed File System (DFS) originally was made available on the Windows NT 4.0 platform and has been improved for Windows 2000. The goal of DFS is to greatly enhance the end-user experience of using shared network files and folders. Without DFS, when users want to access a file or shared folder, they must know the name of the server where it resides. They can use Universal Naming Convention (UNC) names to access the shared folder, such as *\\server\share*. Often, a user will map a drive letter to a UNC name, where *X:* on their system will point to something like *\\myserver\data*. Even if drive letters are mapped, the folder they are mapping to might have subdirectories that must be navigated through, as well. If users need to access multiple folders on multiple servers, they can become confused as to where a particular resource is supposed to be.

Enter DFS. Rather than having a user navigate different servers and folders for resources, DFS allows administrators to create a common network location for folders and files. To the user, it appears that all of the resources are in

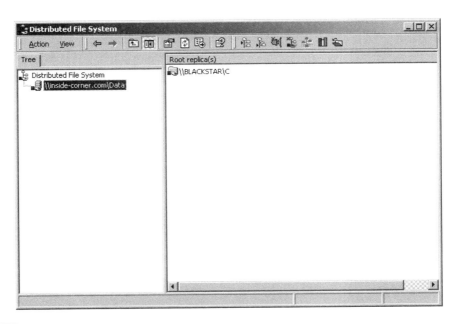

Figure 1-7   *The DFS Administrator Utility.*

one location, when in reality they can be on different servers. DFS unites the shared resources into a logical structure that makes more sense for the user, creating a transparent user experience. The great thing about DFS is that views can be customized to fit any network environment, and users can even create their own DFS volumes that can be linked, if given appropriate permissions. The Windows 2000 DFS Administrator, shown in Figure 1.7, is where you configure DFS volumes.

Chapter Summary

Windows 2000 is an exciting new family of operating systems from Microsoft, consisting of Windows 2000 Professional, Server, Advanced Server, and Data-center Server. Some aspects have changed dramatically since Windows NT 4.0, whereas many have remained similar. A plethora of new features exists, some of which we briefly touched on in this chapter. As you progress throughout the book, you will see these topics again, in more depth, as well as other features that we did not go into here. With an understanding of what Windows 2000 is, let's grab our CDs and get ready to install!

Installing
Windows 2000

••••••••••••••••••••••••••••••••••••

*W*indows 2000 represents a significant change in the abilities and complexity of the operating system. As with every significant M
icrosoft OS change, the minimum hardware requirements have increased. For many administrators, this will not be a factor, but some older server installations will require hardware upgrades before installing Windows 2000. Windows 2000 also offers several new installation options, including installing via a network.

Preparing for Installation

Hardware Requirements

The installation requirements for Windows 2000 have increased throughout the development process. The latest hardware requirements are listed on Microsoft's website at http://www.microsoft.com/windows2000/upgrade/upgradereqs/default.asp. The production release of Windows 2000 requires at least the following hardware:

Table 2.1	Windows 2000 Hardware Requirements		
Component	**2000 Professional**	**2000 Server**	**2000 Advanced Server**
CPU	133 MHz or higher Pentium-compatible CPU	133 MHz or higher Pentium-compatible CPU	133 MHz or higher Pentium-compatible CPU
Max CPUs	Windows 2000 Professional supports single and dual CPU systems.	Windows 2000 Server supports up to four CPUs on one machine.	Windows 2000 Advanced Server supports up to eight CPUs on one machine.
Hard Drive Space	2-GB hard disk with a minimum of 1 GB of free space.	2-GB hard disk with a minimum of 1 GB of free space.	2-GB hard disk with a minimum of 1 GB of free space.
RAM	64 MB of RAM recommended minimum; 4 GB RAM maximum.	256 MB of RAM recommended minimum (128 MB minimum supported; 4 GB maximum).	256 MB of RAM recommended minimum (128 MB minimum supported; 8 GB maximum).
Display	Video display card with VGA capability or better	Video display card with VGA capability or better	Video display card with VGA capability or better
CD-ROM	12X or better recommended.	12X or better recommended.	12X or better recommended.
Network	Network adapter card	One or more network adapter cards	One or more network adapter cards
Other	Mouse and keyboard	Mouse and keyboard	Mouse and keyboard

The Hardware Compatibility List

Windows 2000 supports a wide variety of hardware, including much legacy hardware. This helps protect the investments that companies have made in the past. Just as with past versions of Windows NT, there is a list of hardware that has been tested and approved for use with Windows 2000. This list is known as the Hardware Compatibility List (HCL). The HCL is available in the support directory on the Windows 2000 CD-ROM as hcl.txt. In addition, a searchable HCL list is available at the Microsoft website at http://www.microsoft.com/hcl/ or http://www.microsoft.com/windows2000/upgrade/compat/search/default.asp.

Not every device that will work with Windows 2000 is listed in the HCL. Manufacturer-written device drivers support many devices. Microsoft's official stance regarding manufacturer-supplied device drivers is included below:

The following computers and peripherals have passed compatibility testing with Microsoft Windows 2000. Some computers may be sold with peripherals that are not yet supported by the Windows 2000 operating system, or that require a device driver supplied by the manufacturer. Also, computers and devices on this list have not been tested in all possible configurations. This list is neither complete nor comprehensive; there are many devices that use compatible device identifiers, or emulate other devices that may work fine on Windows 2000. For a continuously updated list of devices supported by Windows 2000, see the Microsoft Windows 2000 Hardware Compatibility List at http://www.microsoft.com/hcl/.

Disk Partition Limitations

Windows 2000 can be installed on an existing partition or can create a partition during an installation. In most cases, upgrades will be performed on existing partitions and new installs on new partitions. Windows 2000 Setup examines the hard drives and shows the current configuration.

SELECTING A PARTITION

Depending on the current configuration of a system, there are several options available during the setup. Common Windows 2000 configurations will result in the following choices:

- If there are no partitions on the hard drive, the setup program will create a Windows 2000 partition.
- If the disk has an existing partition and has enough space, Windows 2000 can be installed on that partition. This can result in either a dual boot system or an upgraded system. An upgrade will replace the current operating system.
- If the disk has existing partitions and nonpartitioned free space, a Windows 2000 partition can be created in the free space.

• If the disk does not have sufficient unpartitioned space and has an existing partition, the setup program can delete the existing partition. All information on this partition will be deleted.

SIZE OF THE INSTALLATION PARTITION

Windows 2000 requires much more disk space than previous versions of Windows NT. Although it is possible to fit a Windows 2000 installation into a 1-GB partition, Microsoft's recommendation is a 2 GB minimum system partition. This additional space is recommended to allow for system updates, additional tools, and server-based application installs.

ADDITIONAL PARTITIONS

The Windows 2000 setup program can be used to create additional partitions, if desired. However, it is recommended that additional partitions be created after Windows 2000 is installed. The Windows 2000 Disk Management tool can be used to create partitions, create RAID arrays, and format drive space.

Choosing a File System

Windows 2000 supports three file systems for the installation partition. After the installation partition is created, the setup program will prompt for the type of file system. Windows 2000 supports FAT, FAT32, and NTFS.

Table 2.2	Features of File Systems	
NTFS	**FAT32**	**FAT**
File- and folder-level security	No file- or folder-level security	No file- or folder-level security
Supports disk compression	Supports dual-boot environment	Supports dual-boot environment
Supports Disk Quotas	Supports drives larger than 2 GB	
Supports file encryption		

NTFS FILE SYSTEM

NTFS is the default file system for Windows 2000 system and is the recommended choice for servers. NTFS supports the following features:

- **File and folder level security:** NTFS allows an administrator to control access to data on both a folder (directory) level and on a per-file basis. This level of control is not possible on FAT or FAT32 partitions.
- **Disk Quotas:** New in Windows 2000, NTFS partitions can restrict disk usage on a per-user basis.
- **Disk encryption:** New in Windows 2000, NTFS partitions can encrypt data stored on the hard drive to protect valuable information.
- **Disk compression:** NTFS partitions can be compressed to allow for more data storage.

FAT FILE SYSTEM

FAT is an earlier file system developed for use in MS-DOS system and later used in the Windows 3.x and 9x operating systems. FAT does not provide for file- or directory-level security, disk compression, encryption, or quotas. The normal use of a FAT partition in a Windows NT or 2000 system is providing compatibility with earlier operating systems. Many administrators used to use a FAT partition as the system partition to be able to access and repair the operating system via an MS-DOS boot disk, but this is no longer necessary under Windows 2000. The Recovery Console can now be used to access the system partition in the event of boot problems

The sole advantage of the FAT file system is the ability to dual boot with MS-DOS based operating systems, such as Windows 3.x, Windows 9x, or MS-DOS. Microsoft does not recommend that a server be built in a dual-boot configuration.

The Windows 2000 Recovery Console provides access to the system partition in the event of boot problems.

FAT32 FILE SYSTEM

FAT32 is functionally identical to FAT, with one exception. FAT32 supports partitions larger than 2 GB, whereas FAT supports only partitions smaller than 2 GB. If the FAT system is chosen during setup, Windows 2000 will automatically format the partition with FAT32 if the installation partition is larger than 2 GB and with FAT if the partition is less than 2 GB. The limitations of FAT also apply to FAT32.

Licensing Models

Windows 2000 has a fairly complex licensing structure. First, one must have a license for the installation of the Windows 2000 software on the server hardware. Second, client computers with a Microsoft OS must have a license for the client OS installed on that hardware. Third, any authenticated access to a Windows 2000 server requires a Client Access License (CAL).

AUTHENTICATED USE

According to Microsoft, an authenticated user is "one who directly or indirectly uses the Windows 2000 Server Integrated Sign-On Service or receives credentials from the Windows 2000 Active Directory service."

In the past, CALs have been required for file and print services and authentication within a domain. Changes in Windows 2000 will require a CAL for any authenticated access to a Windows 2000 web server and those using Windows 2000 as application servers (Table 2.3). The most controversial element of the updated licensing is requiring a CAL for authenticated access to an Internet web server. However, the new Internet Connector license allows for unlimited Internet CALs on a single server. Fortunately, anonymous access to an Internet site hosted on a Windows 2000 server does not require a CAL.

Table 2.3	Licensing Requirements for Windows 2000
Service	**Use**
File services	Accessing or managing files or disk storage
Terminal services	Using the terminal services feature of the server to enable client devices to use applications or data residing on the server
Remote access service	Accessing the server from a remote location through a communications link, including a virtual private network
Printing services	Printing to a printer managed by the product
Authenticated use by applications	Using applications that use Windows 2000 authentication or directory credentials

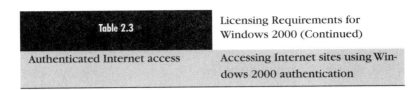

Table 2.3	Licensing Requirements for Windows 2000 (Continued)
Authenticated Internet access	Accessing Internet sites using Windows 2000 authentication

LICENSING METHODS

There are two license models for Windows 2000 Servers for CALs: Per Seat or Per Server. The style of licensing is chosen when the server is first installed. A company may select either style, depending on the needs of the organization, as long as sufficient CALs are purchased. If there is doubt as to the type of licensing needed, select Per Sever. The licensing can be changed one time only from Per Server to Per Seat at no additional cost. The licensing cannot be changed from Per Seat to Per Server.

It is not necessary to notify Microsoft of the licensing option selected.

Per Seat Licensing Per seat licensing requires a CAL for each workstation or other device that connects to any licensed server. CALs are required for computers running Windows for Workgroups, Windows 95, Windows 98, Windows NT 4.0 Workstation, or Windows 2000 Professional. A Windows 2000 Server CAL is required whether client connection software are supplied by Microsoft or by a third-party vendor.

A Windows 2000 Server CAL is tied to a particular computer or client. Client computers with a CAL are allowed access to any server within a Windows 2000 Server-based network.

Per licensing is most economical within an organization that has multiple Windows 2000 servers that provide services, such as file and print services, Intranet services, and RAS services.

Per Server Licensing Per Server licensing allows for a fixed number of connections to a particular Windows 2000 server. Only a set number of devices can be connected to a licensed server at a given time. The number of CALs set on the particular server determines the limit on the number of concurrent connections. An organization needs to have sufficient CALs on a server to cover the maximum number of concurrent connections to the server. With Per Server licensing, the server assigns a license temporarily to each connected computer; there is no association between a particular client and a CAL.

A Per Server license is best suited to single-server or specialty solutions, such as application servers, RAS servers, CD servers, or other similar uses. In an environments with widespread Windows 2000 file and print services, Per Seat licensing would be more economical.

Domains and Workgroups

During installation, a server must be joined to either a domain or a workgroup. With the exception of a domain controller, this choice can be changed after installation. Joining a domain requires different network resources than joining a workgroup. Table 2.4 illustrates the differences:

JOINING A DOMAIN

A Windows 2000 server can be added to an existing Windows 2000 domain during the installation of the OS. This is referred to as *joining a domain.* When a server joins a domain during installation, it joins as a *member server*. It can later be promoted to a domain controller, if desired, or removed from the

Table 2.4	Windows 2000 requirements
Domain	**Workgroup**
Functioning Domain Controller	Name of new or existing workgroup
Windows 2000 DNS server	
Domain name	
Computer account in domain	

domain completely. A server that functions within a domain but is not a domain controller is referred to as a member server.

Requirements to join a domain during Windows 2000 installation:

• A Windows 2000 domain controller. Without a domain controller, no changes to the domain can be made, including adding an additional server.

• A Windows 2000 DNS server. This is required to ensure proper registration of the new server.

• A domain name. The DNS name of the desired domain is required to locate and join the domain.

• A computer account. An administrator must authorize any server that joins a domain. This requires a computer account within the domain. This account can be created in advance or during installation. If it is created during installation, Setup will prompt for a user account and password that has the rights to add a computer to the domain.

JOINING A WORKGROUP

A Windows 2000 does not necessarily have to join a domain. A Windows 2000 server that is not part of a domain is referred to as a *stand-alone server*. If a server is not added to a domain, it must be added to a new or existing workgroup at the time of installation.

To join a server to a workgroup, simply enter the name of the new or existing workgroup during installation. There are no security or network prerequisites for joining a workgroup. Workgroups are not used for security, but rather are used to organize resources on a network. Servers that are joined to workgroups during installation can later be joined to a domain, if required.

Installing Windows 2000 from a CD-ROM

The most common method of installing Windows 2000 Server will be from the bootable CD-ROM. The bootable CD-ROM allows for a server without an existing operating system to boot directly to the setup program for Windows 2000. When a system is booted off the CD-ROM, several preinstallation files are copied to memory; and the installation begins.

Licensing the Server

In addition to the client access licensing discussed earlier, each Windows 2000 Server installation must also be licensed. The license for the Windows 2000 server appears early in the installation procedure. To accept the terms associated with the Windows 2000 licensing, press the <F8> key. If the license is not acceptable, press <Esc>. If the license is not accepted, the installation will halt.

Preparing the Partition

Once the license is accepted, the setup program scans the physical drives for the current partitioning scheme. Depending upon the current partitioning, Windows 2000 can be installed in an existing partition, can replace an existing partition, or can be installed in a new partition. In the case of a new server, there will likely be either no partitions or a single, small partition designated for manufacturer-specific utilities. Select either the unpartitioned space or the partition on which to install the OS (Figure 2.2). To create a new partition in free space, select C and follow the prompts. To delete a partition, select D and follow the prompts. To install Windows 2000 in an existing partition, highlight the partition and press <Enter>.

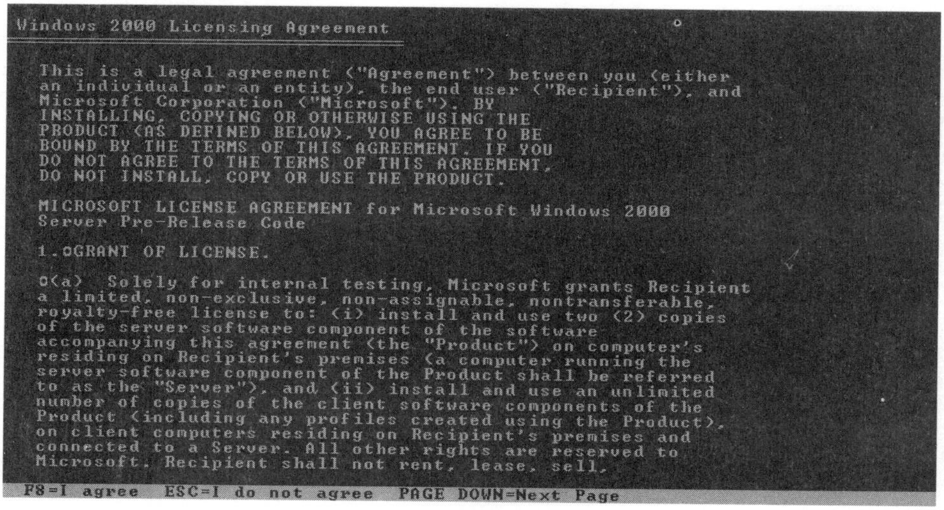

```
Windows 2000 Licensing Agreement                              o

This is a legal agreement ("Agreement") between you (either
an individual or an entity), the end user ("Recipient"), and
Microsoft Corporation ("Microsoft"). BY
INSTALLING, COPYING OR OTHERWISE USING THE
PRODUCT (AS DEFINED BELOW), YOU AGREE TO BE
BOUND BY THE TERMS OF THIS AGREEMENT. IF YOU
DO NOT AGREE TO THE TERMS OF THIS AGREEMENT,
DO NOT INSTALL, COPY OR USE THE PRODUCT.

MICROSOFT LICENSE AGREEMENT for Microsoft Windows 2000
Server Pre-Release Code

1. OGRANT OF LICENSE.

O(a)   Solely for internal testing, Microsoft grants Recipient
a limited, non-exclusive, non-assignable, nontransferable,
royalty-free license to: (i) install and use two (2) copies
of the server software component of the software
accompanying this agreement (the "Product") on computer's
residing on Recipient's premises (a computer running the
server software component of the Product shall be referred
to as the "Server"), and (ii) install and use an unlimited
number of copies of the client software components of the
Product (including any profiles created using the Product),
on client computers residing on Recipient's premises and
connected to a Server. All other rights are reserved to
Microsoft. Recipient shall not rent, lease, sell.

F8=I agree   ESC=I do not agree   PAGE DOWN=Next Page
```

Figure 2–1   *License agreement for Windows 2000 Server.*

Formatting the Installation Partition

If a new partition is created for the Windows 2000 installation, it will have to be formatted before the operating system can be loaded. As discussed earlier, the partition can be formatted in either FAT or NTFS file systems (Figure 2.3). Unless the system is required to dual boot with an earlier operating system, format the partition with the NTFS file system.

Text Mode Install

After the partition is prepared and formatted, the text mode install copies the installation files to the hard drive (Figure 2.4). In addition, the text mode phase installs the Windows 2000 operating system kernel and prepares the computer for the graphical user interface (GUI) mode phase of Setup.

Windows 2000 is installed into the system partition, and the root directory now contains *Ntldr*, *Ntdetect.com*, *TxtSetup.sif,* and *Pagefile.sys*. The Boot.ini will start the Windows 2000 GUI installation automatically. The timeout is set to 0 seconds to avoid starting other operating systems. If the timeout were not set to 0, the setup may not be completed, and the system may be unstable. After this phase, the computer is rebooted and the GUI stage of the install begins.

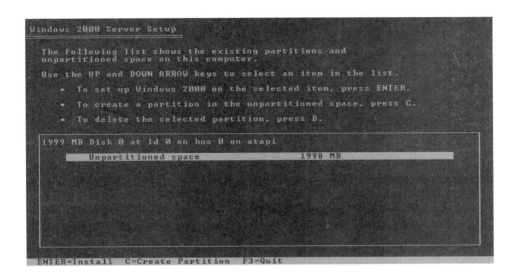

Figure 2-2   *Preparing the installation partition.*

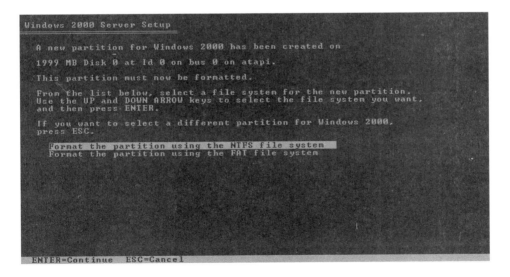

Figure 2-3   *Formatting the installation partition.*

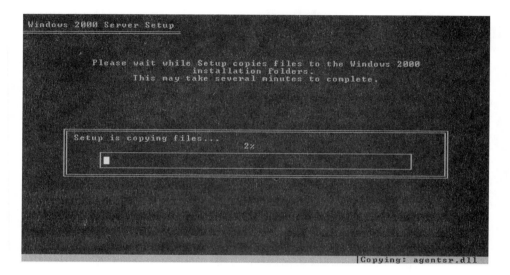

Figure 2–4   *Text mode install.*

Installing Devices

After the text mode installation, Windows 2000 Setup restarts the computer. Upon restarting, Setup is now in a graphical, or GUI, mode. Windows 2000 first scans the system to detect the hardware that is installed (Figure 2.5). If certain hardware is missed or does not have native Windows 2000 drivers, it can be added after installation through the control panel.

Regional Settings

A Windows 2000 install can be configured for almost any region of the globe. By default, the English language version of Windows 2000 will begin with a United States-centric setting of English (US) for the language and US English keyboard mappings (Figure 2.6). These settings can be adjusted to match the local environment via the Regional Settings setup options.

Name and Organization

Windows 2000 will prompt for the name and organization of the person to whom this copy of the OS is licensed (Figure 2.7). Although this is potentially useful on a Windows 2000 Professional installation, most server installations will receive a generic entry that represents the organization, but not an individual. Enter the information as defined by your organizational requirements.

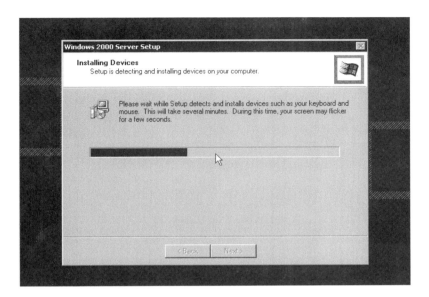

Figure 2–5   *Regional settings customization.*

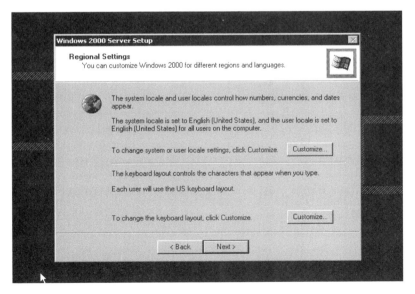

Figure 2–6   *Detecting system hardware.*

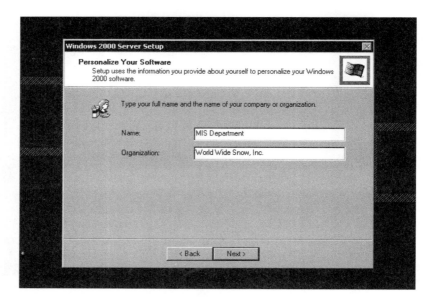

Figure 2–7   *Name and organization for the server license.*

Client Licensing

As discussed earlier, Windows 2000 supports client access licensing on Per Server or Per Seat basis. Select the proper licensing for your organization (Figure 2.8). If per server licensing is selected, enter the number of concurrent connections licensed on the server. All connections to a Windows 2000 server require a CAL, whether the connection is based on Microsoft software or a third-party client. If in doubt on the licensing, select Per Server. Per Server licensing can be changed once to Per Seat with no additional fee. The reverse is not true.

Computer Name and Administrator Password

Windows 2000 Setup will prompt for the server name and the local administrator's password (Figure 2.9). The setup program will suggest a server name based on the organization entered earlier. Although this suggestion can be used, most environments should have some form of naming standard to help guide in the naming of new servers. If your environment does not have a naming convention, it may make sense to devise one as part of the Windows 2000 migration planning process. The computer name can have up to 15 characters and must be unique to the network. The name cannot duplicate one used by another server, a domain, or a workgroup.

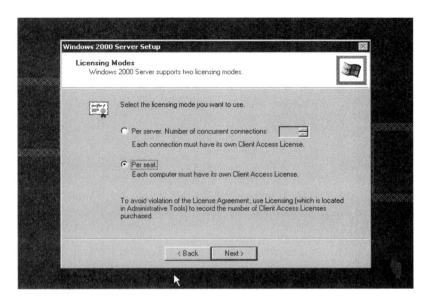

Figure 2–8   *Selecting a licensing mode.*

The local administrator's password will be used if the server is a stand-alone server, if the server is not yet configured as a domain member, or if local administrative access is needed on the server. The administrator's password is very important and should be chosen with security in mind. Some standard practices to improve the security of a password are listed below:

• Do not use words that can be found in a dictionary, including technical or literary dictionaries.

• Use a mixture of upper- and lowercase characters.

• Include at least one number.

• Include at least one special character, such as the question mark or an exclamation mark.

• Do not use common names or the names of family members.

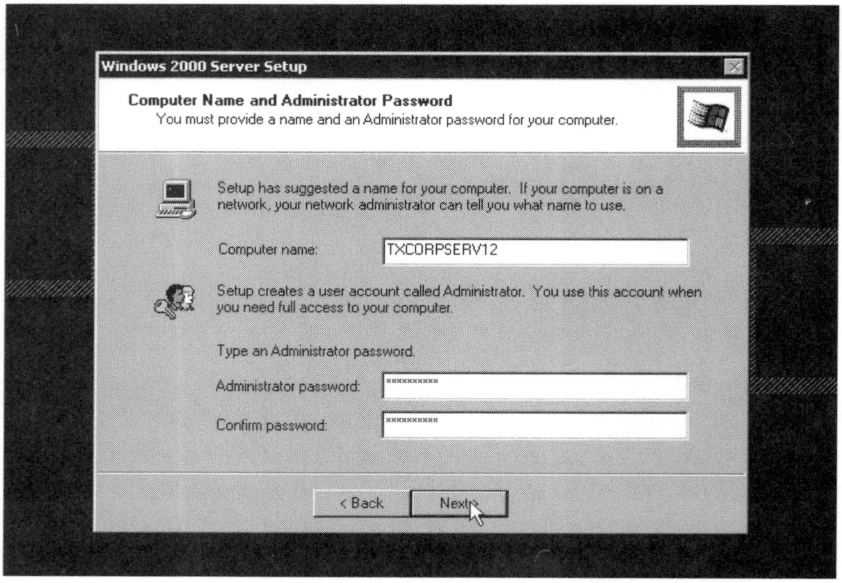

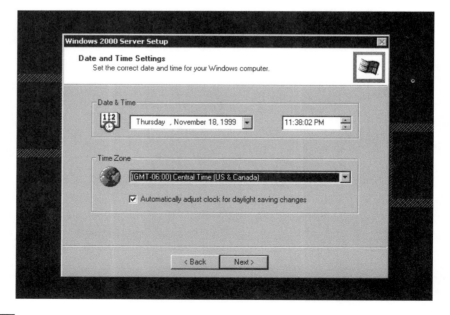

Figure 2–9   *Computer name and local administrator password.*

Figure 2–10   *Configuring the system time and date.*

Configure Local Time and Date

Windows 2000, like all other OSs, can be set to any desired date and time zone (Figure 2.10). Many organizations set their servers to GMT (Greenwich Mean Time), but the server can alternatively be configured for the local time zone.

Installing Network Components

Windows 2000 offers an improved wizard for installing the normal networking components on a server. In addition, all networking components can be manually installed and configured. The typical sequence for the networking wizard is the following:

1. Windows 2000 scans for the existence of any network cards and configures the hardware settings for any cards that are found. If a network card is not detected, one can be manually installed by selecting the card (if there are native Windows 2000 drivers) or by installing manufacturer-supplied device drivers.
2. The network components to be installed on the system are selected. The Typical Settings selection installs the Client for Microsoft Networks, File and Printer Sharing for Microsoft Networks, and TCP/IP(Figure 2.11). Each of these has a role in allowing a Windows 2000 server to communicate with other computers on a network.

   • **Client for Microsoft Networks:** Allows the server to gain access as a client to Microsoft network resources.

   • **File and Printer Sharing for Microsoft Networks:** Allows other Microsoft client computers on the network to access resources shared by the server.

   • **TCP/IP:** The default networking protocol for Windows 2000, this allows a computer to communicate over a LAN, WAN, and the Internet.
3. The server is joined to a workgroup or domain. As mentioned earlier, there are several prerequisites to join a domain, including a functioning domain controller, DNS server, and computer account. Most installations of Windows 2000 will be within a domain environment.
4. The selected network components are installed on the system, and the network drivers and services are initialized.

Final Configuration

After installing the network components, the setup program has several other tasks to complete. These tasks are performed automatically, with no intervention from the keyboard. The remaining tasks for the installation are the following:

1. Copy files to the local hard drive. Setup copies any needed files to the local machine, so that the OS can function after installation.

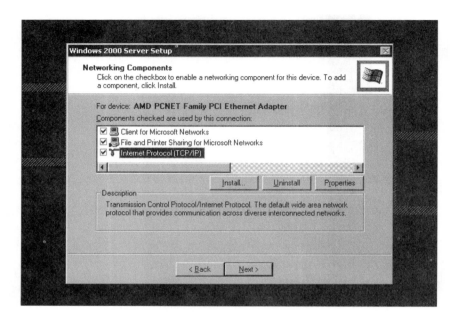

Figure 2-11 *Installing typical network components.*

2. Configure the system. Setup configures the operating system and applies any specified settings to the system. This step may take some time.

3. Save the configuration to the system. Setup saves the current configuration to the system and makes it the default configuration for the server.

4. Remove temporary installation files. Many files are needed only for the setup program. Windows removes these files from the local hard drive to save hard drive space.

5. Restart the computer. After these tasks are completed, setup restarts the computer (Figure 2.12). The system will reboot and begin functioning as either a member server or a stand-alone server, depending on the configuration.

Upgrading to Windows 2000 via CD-ROM

Windows 2000 can be installed as an upgrade to many current Microsoft operating systems. Windows 2000 Server can be installed as an upgrade from previous Microsoft server operating systems. As with a new installation, care should be taken with minimum hardware requirements.

Figure 2–12   *The final setup stage.*

Table 2.5	Supported Upgrade Paths for Windows 2000	
2000 Server	**2000 Professional**	**Cannot upgrade**
Windows 2000 Server Prerelease versions	Windows 2000 Professional Prerelease versions	Windows 3.x
NT Server 4.0	NT Workstation 4.0	Windows NT prior to 3.51
NT 4.0 Terminal Server	NT Workstation 3.51	Small Business Server
NT Server 3.51	Windows 98	Non-Microsoft operating systems
	Windows 95	

Table 2.5 discusses upgrade paths with Windows 2000. For the latest in upgrade information, visit Microsoft's website at http://www.microsoft.com/windows2000.

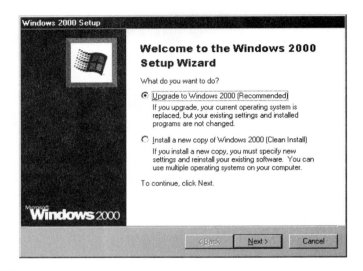

Figure 2–13   *Windows 2000 upgrade wizard.*

Beginning Setup

The Windows 2000 setup is essentially the same for new installations and upgrades, with the exception of the beginning of the process. To upgrade a Windows NT system to Windows 2000, insert the Windows 2000 CD-ROM. If autoplay is enabled on the system, the Windows 2000 upgrade wizard will begin. Setup will prompt whether an upgrade is desired. If so, select the upgrade option and click Next to begin the upgrade (Figure 2.13).

Setup Command Line Parameters

There may be times when a normal clean install or upgrade is not appropriate for a situation. In this case, there are several command line parameters that can be added to the base install command to modify its behavior. The base command to launch a Windows 2000 installation is *winnt32.exe*, located in the *I386* directory on the Windows 2000 CD-ROM. The optional parameters are given in Table 2.6.

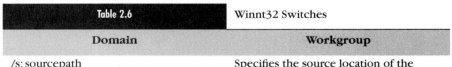

Table 2.6	Winnt32 Switches	
Domain		**Workgroup**
/s: sourcepath		Specifies the source location of the Windows 2000 files.

Table 2.6	Winnt32 Switches (Continued)
/tempdrive:drive_letter	Directs Setup to place temporary files on the specified partition and to install Windows 2000 on that partition.
/unattend	Upgrades the previous version of Windows 2000 in unattended setup mode. All user settings are taken from the previous installation.
/unattend[num]:[answer_file]	Performs a fresh installation in unattended setup mode. The answer file provides Setup with any custom specifications. num is the number of seconds between the time that Setup finishes copying the files and when it restarts the computer. answer_file is the name of the answer file.
/copydir:folder_name	Creates an additional folder within the folder in which the Windows 2000 files are installed.
/copysource:folder_name	Creates a temporary additional folder within the folder in which the Windows 2000 files are installed. Unlike the folders /copydir creates, /copysource folders are deleted after Setup completes.
/cmd:command_line	Instructs Setup to carry out a specific command before the final phase of setup.
/debug[level]:[filename]	Creates a debug log at the level specified, with the filename specified.
[/udf:id[,UDF_file]	Indicates an identifier (id) that Setup uses to specify how a uniqueness database (UDB) file modifies an answer file (see the /unattend entry). The UDB overrides values in the answer file, and the identifier determines which values in the UDB file are used.

Table 2.6	Winnt32 Switches (Continued)
/syspart:drive_letter	Specifies that Setup can copy startup files to a hard disk and mark the disk as active. When the disk is installed into another computer, it automatically starts with the next phase of the Setup. The /tempdrive parameter must always be used with the /syspart parameter.
/checkupgradeonly	Checks the system for upgrade compatibility with Windows 2000. Windows 98 and 95 create a file called upgrade.txt. For Windows NT, the file is named winnt32.log
/cmdcons	Installs the Recovery Console on a Windows 2000 computer. This is used after Setup is completed.
/m:folder_name	Specifies that Setup copies replacement files from an alternate location. If files exist in the alternate location, they are used instead of the normal installation files.
/makelocalsource	Instructs Setup to copy all installation source files to the local hard disk—very useful if the CD is not going to be available after setup.
/noreboot	Instructs Setup to not restart the computer after the file copy phase of winnt32 is completed—useful if additional commands or programs must be run before Setup continues.

Creating Windows 2000 Setup Disks

There may be a time when it is necessary to install or upgrade a Windows 2000 installation on a server that cannot boot from a CD-ROM. In this situation, Windows 2000 Setup can be started from the Windows 2000 Server Setup disks.

To create these disks, first gather four blank, formatted 1.44-MB floppy disks. If the disks are not blank, any information on the disks will be overwritten. The Windows 2000 Setup disks must be created on a computer running Windows 2000 or NT.

1. Label four blank formatted 1.44-MB floppies with Windows 2000 Server Setup Boot Disk, Windows 2000 Server Setup Disk 2, Windows 2000 Server Setup Disk 3, and Windows 2000 Server Setup Disk 4.
2. Insert the Windows 2000 CD-ROM into the system. Select NO when prompted for an upgrade.
3. Open a command prompt.
4. Change to the *bootdisk* directory on the CD-ROM.
5. Type *makeboot a:*
6. Windows 2000 will prompt for the first of the four diskettes. Insert the Windows 2000 Server Boot Disk and press <Enter>.
7. The disk image for the boot disk will be downloaded to the floppy. After the disk image is created, the system will prompt for the disk labeled *Windows 2000 Server Setup Disk 2.*
8. The process will repeat for the next three disks.
9. After the disks are created, exit the command prompt and remove the Windows 2000 CD-ROM.

Remote Installation Services

For years, configuring multiple identical workstations has been a thorn in the side of network administrators and anyone else involved in supporting a large organization. Various techniques have been developed, ranging from xcopy batch files in the DOS/Windows 3.x days to drive-mirroring programs, more recently. Unfortunately, Windows NT- and 2000-based machines suffer issues when drive-mirroring software is used to create identical systems.

Each Windows NT/2000 system has a security identifier known as a *SID*. A SID is a long series of numbers that is specific to a particular machine. Among other things, the SID is used for controlling access within a Windows NT/2000 network. Drive mirroring programs copy a Windows installation bit by bit, and, because of that accuracy, each mirrored image has the exact same SID. This can result in some odd behavior, including the ability to access files and information that should be secure. Most drive-mirroring programs now come with an add-on program that generates a random SID for each mirrored machine, but Microsoft has claimed that these solutions do not resolve all the issues with drive mirroring.

With Windows 2000, Microsoft has introduced the Remote Installation Service (RIS). This service allows the installation of a single image on many workstations, without the SID issues related to the drive-mirroring software. Because RIS supports only Windows 2000 Professional installations and not Windows 2000 Server installations, we will not spend much space on it here. It is important, however, to know that the service exists and how it can be used.

Prerequisites for RIS

Remote Installation Service requires a certain amount of support infrastructure before it can be installed and functional. First, RIS requires a Windows 2000-based domain with Active Directory functioning. This indicates that at least one domain controller is required. In addition, a DNS server that supports Windows 2000 functionality is required, and because the RIS clients use DHCP, at least one DHCP server is required.

Functions of RIS

Remote Installation Service can be used to install Windows 2000 Professional in multiple ways. The simplest way is through sharing an *I386* directory and running the install from the desktop. Unfortunately, this requires entering the configuration information manually on each client. The only advantage that RIS gives in this case is a simplified boot floppy.

The second method is essentially the same as the first, with the addition of */unattend* scripting files. In this method, the client PC is booted off the RIS floppy, and the installation takes care of itself.

The third and best use of RIS is to build an image that contains the complete operating system and all the required applications for a system. This still requires some hands-on setup, such as changing the computer name from the standard image.

Limitations of RIS

Remote Installation Service has some serious limitations that may affect its usefulness within your particular environment. The most important limitation is that RIS can image only desktop client PCs with particular PCI-based network interface cards. This limitation means that a laptop PC is not a candidate for a RIS installation. In today's increasingly mobile work environment, this can be a major issue.

The second limitation is the inability of RIS to deliver images other than with Windows 2000 Professional. While most environments may not have the need to configure several hundred or thousand identical Windows 2000 servers, the capability to do so would be attractive. Unfortunately, the capability is available only for the workstation operating system.

Third, RIS can image only the first partition on the first physical drive; in other words, the C: drive. This can be a significant limitation if your environment typically separates the operating system and application partitions.

Chapter Summary

In this chapter we discussed the hardware requirements for Windows 2000 and the importance of the Hardware Compatibility List. The current HCL is located within the *hal.txt* files in the support subdirectory on the Windows 2000 Server CD-ROM. In addition, an updated and searchable HCL is available on Microsoft's website at http://www.microsoft.com/hcl/. If Windows 2000 native drivers do not support a particular piece of hardware, the hardware manufacturer may have updated drivers that will ensure compatibility. Using hardware that is not on the Microsoft HCL is not recommended, because it can lead to instability of the system.

Windows 2000 Server can be installed in several ways. The two most common methods are a clean install from a bootable CD-ROM and an upgrade from a previous Microsoft Server operating system. After the initial boot process, the install process is very similar on both a clean install and an upgrade. A system partition must first be defined and formatted on a clean install, whereas an upgrade will use the current system partition.

During the Windows 2000 installation, the setup process will need to know the name of the computer, IP address, the type of licensing, whether to join a domain or workgroup, and more. Much of this information can be automated, using a combination of answer files and UDB files.

If a particular machine cannot boot off a CD-ROM, Windows 2000 Setup Disks can launch the setup program. These diskettes are created via the make-boot program, located in the *bootdisk* subdirectory on the Windows 2000 CD-ROM. The makeboot program requires 4 blank, formatted 1.44-MB floppies.

The Remote Installation Service was briefly mentioned. This is a service introduced with Windows 2000 that allows for remote installation of disk images of Windows 2000 Professional to certain desktop PCs. RIS does not support Windows 2000 Server, nor does it support non-PCI network cards. RIS is likely to be a useful tool in the rollout of Windows 2000 Professional within a corporate desktop environment.

Using the Microsoft Management Console and Task Scheduler

*O*ne of the most difficult tasks for new system administrators has been getting accustomed to the various tools they use to perform their jobs. In an ideal world, what you have learned in one administrative application would be transferable to the next. For instance, if you know that clicking on a particular mouse button brings up a property sheet in one tool, wouldn't it be easier if it performed the same task in every tool?

For Windows 2000, Microsoft has addressed this issue by bringing their administrative applications under the umbrella of the Microsoft Management Console (MMC). The goal of the MMC is to standardize the user interface to the many tools that are required to perform everyday tasks.

In previous versions of Microsoft Windows NT, it has been accepted that the application that is used for let's say, user administration, may not bear any resemblance to the tool used to apply permissions on files. Although this allowed the applications to be customized for specific tasks, it also made them more difficult to learn. Skills learned in one tool did not necessarily transfer to any other tool. This unnecessarily burdened the network administrator with having to learn many different ways of working.

In this chapter, we will be talking about the MMC and what it offers to the Windows 2000 Administrator. At first glance, using it is very simple. What you might miss by not looking beneath the surface, however, is the ultimate flexibility of the tool. In fact, any Windows 2000 administration application you use is simply an adaptation of this underlying tool. You will see that the MMC is easy to customize and that it will aid you in delegating tasks to individuals, departments, or others in your organization.

An Introduction to the Microsoft Management Console

The MMC has, in fact, been around for a number of years. It made its first appearance with Internet Information Server 4.0. Although the underlying idea of the MMC has not changed since this time, its flexibility has not been fully realized because Microsoft and others had yet to provide other tools that took advantage of what it offered.

With the release of Windows 2000 Server, this has changed. Not only has the MMC been adopted as the tool of choice for almost all of the server administration tools, but also you will see it increasingly adopted for all Microsoft products. It is already the primary administrative tool for Microsoft SQL Server 7.0 and Systems Management Server 2.0, for instance.

The interface for the MMC is very simple. As you can see in Figure 3.1, the basic interface presents you with two panes. The left pane is known as the *console tree,* and it provides you with the ability to navigate through the folders and containers that a particular administrative tool has available. The right pane is called the *details pane,* and it allows you to see the details and functions relating to the selection you have made in the console tree.

Apart from these two items, you will find that the look and feel of the MMC can change a little from console to console. This is because it is possible for consoles to be designed that add menu options, use ActiveX controls, and display charts and web pages. As you go through the examples in this book, you will see illustrations of this.

Terminology, Definitions, and Switches

Before we go any further with a discussion of the MMC we need to define some terminology. This will help you to understand that the MMC console actually does nothing more than provide you with an interface. The two major components of the MMC are:

- Console trees
- Snap-ins

Once you have gained an understanding of these two terms, you will better realize why the MMC offers an advantage over what preceded it.

Consoles Trees

The MMC plays host to console trees. Consoles trees look very similar to file listings that you have seen in previous versions of Microsoft operating systems. These can contain folders or containers that provide properties or access to configuration settings. This is analogous to folders and files you will have seen

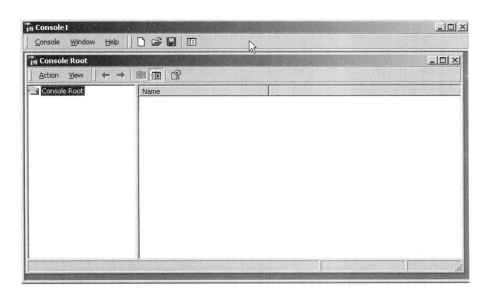

Figure 3–1   *The Microsoft Management Console.*

in Windows Explorer. Containers (in Explorer terms, similar to folders) can exist in the root of the console tree or off the root. This provides you with a hierarchy. You can see an example of the MMC with a console tree in Figure 3.1. By adapting tools to take advantage of the consoles and the functionality they offer, you will see how Microsoft has been able to simplify administration of Windows 2000 Server.

Snap-Ins

The term *snap-in* is used to describe a customized console tree that can be opened within the MMC. These are designed for specific purposes. For instance, Windows 2000 includes snap-ins for adding users and stopping services. There are two types of snap-ins that you will see as you work with Windows 2000 Server.

- Standalone
- Extensions

Although these are very similar, they are used in slightly different ways.

STANDALONE

A standalone snap-in is a self-contained unit that can be loaded by itself into the MMC. We will be looking at how you can load snap-ins later in this chapter. Standalone snap-ins are used to make the MMC useful. They contain the functionality and features you need to perform a given task. Without them, you won't find that the MMC does much at all! You should note that more than one can be loaded simultaneously. Think of snap-ins as documents that you load into your word processor.

EXTENSIONS

An extension is a snap-in that can be loaded only as part of another snap-in. In this sense, they add functionality to another snap-in. This is used to offer specialized tasks or simply to extend the available options. You will see examples of this as you work through the book.

In a sense, you do not really "use" the MMC for any tasks. What we mean by this is that the MMC is a shell into which you can load functionality. It is this functionality —in the form of snap-ins—that gives the MMC its real usefulness. When you use the MMC, you are interacting with consoles that have been customized to allow you to perform tasks such as viewing details of the disk drives in your server or viewing the properties of the networks users or files on the system.

One of the main advantages of the MMC is that you can load as many snap-ins as you want. This allows you to customize the look of your MMC and prevents you from having to open more than one MMC at a time. You will find that loading multiple snap-ins allows you to group administrative functions in ways that best suit you, rather than the vendor deciding which functions you should see at any given time. So, if you often have to assign directory permissions when adding users, you can load both of the applicable snap-ins into a single console tree.

Once you have created the console you need, you can then save that view and distribute it to others. You will recognize MMC consoles by their *MSC* file extension. This file can then be distributed to others, in much the same way that you can send a word processer document to others and have them open it on their own computers.

This is a very powerful feature of the MMC. As you adapt the MMC to suit your own way of working you will find that administration is simpler. This is because you do not have to remember which tool performs which function—you can just add it to your own console tree!

Of course, the ability to customize the administration tools by adding snap-ins is controlled. You probably do not want everyone being able to load snap-ins whenever they feel like it. Also, if you create a console tree for others to use, you might want to prevent them from altering it. Worse, there may be times when you want to add a snap-in to your console and tree and can't—the reason? You have not opened the MMC in the correct "mode." Now that you know the basic elements of the MMC we will discuss the different modes in which the MMC can run in. There are several modes, and each of them has specific uses. There are four different modes. These modes are:

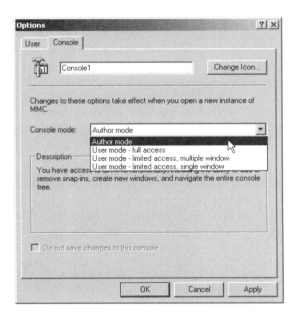

Figure 3-2   *Setting MMC modes.*

1. Author Mode
2. User Mode—Full Access
3. User Mode—Limited Access, Multiple Windows
4. User Mode—Limited Access, Single Window

Each of these modes offers different levels of access to the MMC. You can set the level of access that an individual will get through Group Policies. Group Policies are a method of controlling system access, among other things. They will be discussed in more detail in Chapter 14, "Group Policy." You can see these options in Figure 3.2.

Author Mode

Author mode is equivalent to the administrator login on a Windows 2000 Server. When the console is opened in Author mode, you can do whatever you want. This includes adding snap-ins, removing snap-ins, and viewing the entire console tree. You will use the MMC in this mode to create your custom consoles.

User Mode—Full Access

In this mode, the user has full access to the console tree. This means that if you have used the "Add" function to add a snap-in, the users who receive the MSC file will have access to the full range of functionality of that snap-in. They will be able to access every folder and container. However, they cannot add additional snap-ins, nor can they remove them. Since by default, any changes they do make to the view of the console are saved when the MMC is closed, the "Save" option from the MMC menu will be missing in this mode.

User Mode—Limited Access, Multiple Windows

This mode is more restrictive. When you save a customized MMC in this mode, the users will be able to view only the pieces of the console that were visible when the console was saved. In effect, when you create a custom console and save it in this mode, the MSC that you created will show only the folders and containers that were viewable at the time you saved it.

USER MODE—LIMITED ACCESS, SINGLE WINDOW

As the name suggests, this is an extension of the previous option. The only difference is that, in this mode, the user will not be able to open multiple windows. Otherwise, the same restrictions apply.

Opening the MMC from the Command Line

You might be wondering how you can open with MMC without an associated snap-in (an empty console.) To do this, you run the MMC from the command line or, more commonly, on Windows 2000 Server environments, from the Start, Run line.

To open the MMC do the following:

1. Click on the Start menu and select Run.
2. Type *MMC* on the open line and press <Enter>.
3. The MMC should start.

There are three options that you can use when opening the MMC. These options allow you to open the MMC in specific modes or to speed up the startup, if need be. You can also open the MMC with a path option. This allows you to open consoles you have saved. These options are as follows:

- /a
- /s
- <path>*.MSC

Each of these options provides you with additional flexibility.

/a

This option will start the MMC in author mode. As you will recall, this is the administrative option for the MMC. In this mode, you can create custom MMCs, or make changes to the MSC files. It is important to remember that this does not mean that any MSC file that a user has access to can be opened in author mode. When a custom MSC is saved, you effectively "imbed" its security in the file. This means that an MSC file saved with user mode—Single Window cannot be opened in an MMC with this option and altered.

/s

This option suppresses the splash screen. The splash screen shows the version of the MMC that you are opening. The administrative tools that have been shipped with Windows 2000 Server all incorporate this switch. That is why you do not see the splash screen every time you open a tool.

<path>*.MSC

If you append a full relative path to the end of the MMC command line, the MSC file will be opened automatically. If you check the properties of some of the tools in the Administrative Tools folder, you will see that this is how Microsoft has implemented its own custom consoles.

Creating A Custom Console

As you can see, the MMC allows you great flexibility. With it, you can create administrative tools that best suit your own way of working. Next, we will walk through an example of creating a custom MMC. In this example, you will combine three of the administrative tools that are available in the Administrative Tools folder, then save to your desktop. Then, whenever you want to use the console, you can simply double-click the icon on your desktop without navigating the Start menu.

It is assumed that you have access to a Windows 2000 Server and are logged on with administrative authority. This gives you full access to the server and available MMC snap-ins.

1. First, we must open the MMC. To do this, click on the Start menu and select Run.
2. Type *MMC /a /s* and press <Enter>. The MMC will open with an empty console.

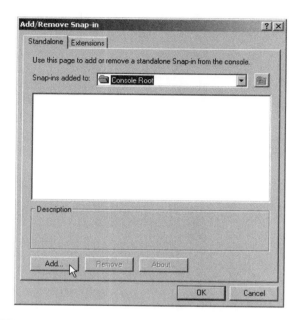

Figure 3–3   *The Add/Remove Snap-In dialog box.*

3. Now we will add a snap-in to the console. Click on the Console menu and select Add/Remove Snap-In. This opens the Add/Remove Snap-In dialog box. This dialog box is shown in Figure 3.3.

4. Next we will add a Snap-in to our console. To do this, click on the Add button. This is also shown in Figure 3.3. This will display the Add Standalone Snap-In dialog box. This dialog box displays all of the available snap-ins that have been registered on the system.

5. To add a snap-in, first select the snap-in name from the list, then click on the Add button. You will see the snap-in appear in the Add/Remove Snap-In dialog box. For the purposes of this example, select Component Services, Disk Defragmenter, and Performance Logs and Alerts. When you have added each of these click the CLOSE button.

6. You should now be at the Add/Remove Snap-In dialog box. The three snap-ins that you selected should be listed. One of these snap-ins has an extension snap-in associated with it. To see this, click on the Extensions tab. You will now be able to see that the Component Services snap-in has an associated extension. By default, the Add all extensions check box is checked; therefore, this extension is automatically loaded. If you uncheck the box, you will be able to prevent the extension from loading. When you are ready, click the OK button. You will now see the MMC console with the three snap-ins you selected open.

7. For the purposes of this example, we are going to save this MSC file in two modes. First, we will save it in author mode. Next, we will save it in user mode— limited access, single window. Finally we will open each of these files to see the differences. Because we opened the MMC with the */a* switch, the console has set itself to author mode by default. So let's save this file first. Click on Console, then select Save As. Navigate to the Desktop directory. Type *AUTHORMODE.MSC* and click Save. The default folder should be DESKTOP. When this is done an icon for this custom MMC should appear on the server desktop.

8. Now we will save the same console in user mode—limited access, single window. To do this, click on Console, then Options. This displays the Options dialog box. This dialog box is shown in Figure 3.2. Next, click on the Console Mode dropdown box and select User Mode—Limited Access, Single Window. When this is done, click on OK.

9. Now we must save the file using similar steps to 7, above. However, this time we will name the file *USERMODE.MSC*. When this is done, an icon for this custom MMC should appear on the Server desktop. Close the MMC by clicking the Console menu, then Exit.

10. Finally, we will double-click each of these icons and take a look at some of the differences. The most notable difference will be on the menu options. The file we saved as *AUTHORMODE.MSC* will allow you to have access to all of the menu options that you saw when we first opened the MMC. The *USERMODE* file will not display these menus. Clearly, this limits the functions that this version of our custom console can perform. USERMODE.MSC is shown in Figure 3.4.

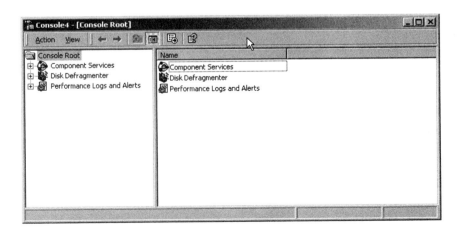

Figure 3–4   *The USERMODE.MSC MMC.*

Customizing Views

The default view of the information in the MMC can vary a lot, depending on the snap-in. That's due in large part to the flexibility that has been built into the tool. Most of the customized presentation of data will be displayed in the detail pane. This pane can display data as web pages, ActiveX controls and even in Java. Sometimes, as shown in Figure 3.5, the view presented bears a strong resemblance to the equivalent Windows NT 4.0 tool.

Earlier in this chapter, we spoke about customizing the content of the MMC. This limits (or increases) the amount of information that is presented. It is also possible to take this information once it is presented and reformat it to suit your needs. This can be done at each level of the console tree.

There are two methods by which you can customize the presented data. These are:

- Taskpads
- The View menu

To use the Taskpad option, you will need to start the MMC in author mode, as discussed earlier in this chapter. The View menu is part of the snap-in that you are using. We will take a look at an example of both to show you how these options can be useful.

Taskpads

There are four methods that you can use to interact with an MMC snap-in: clicking on an item to open it, right-clicking on an item to bring up the context-sensitive menu, using the menu system and finally, configuring a Taskpad. Taskpads are a way to customize a view in the MMC and to combine tasks (such as options from the context-sensitive menu) into that view. This can be useful for beginners—because all available options can be combined into a simple interface. Common functions can be presented as simple buttons within the MMC.

Taskpads are actually HTML files that are created through the Taskpad creation wizard. Once the Taskpad is complete, you are given the option to add tasks. Tasks are options that can be performed on the items in the new MMC view. The best way to understand Taskpads and their usefulness is through an example. In Figure 3.5, we took a look at the Disk Management snap-in. During the following steps, we are going to create a Taskpad of this snap-in and will add some common features of tasks (or buttons) to ease administration and minimize the amount of clicking you have to do to achieve a task.

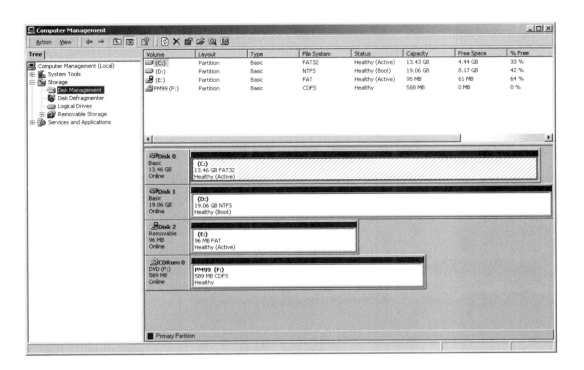

Figure 3–5   *Disk Management Snap-in looks a lot like the old Disk Administrator.*

1. First we must open the MMC in author mode. This mode allows you to add snap-ins and customize them. To do this, click on Start, Run and type *MMC /a /s* (Do you remember what each of these switches does? If not, refer to the relevant sections at the beginning of this chapter.)

2. You should now be presented with an empty MMC. The next step is to add the snap-in that we want to manipulate. To do this, click on the Console menu and select Add/Remove Snap-In. This displays the Add/Remove Snap-In dialog box.

3. Now we will add the snap-in for Disk Management. You have two choices on how to do this. The Disk Administrator Snap-in is a standalone snap-in that can viewed on its own or can be loaded as part of the Computer Management snap-in. For the purposes of this example we will load it on its own. Click the Add button to be presented with the Add Standalone Snap-In dialog box.

4. Scroll down the list until you find the Disk Management snap-in. Once you have found it, select it and click the Add button. You will then be presented with the dialog box shown in Figure 3.6. This allows you to create a snap-in that manages the disk storage on the local machine or on a

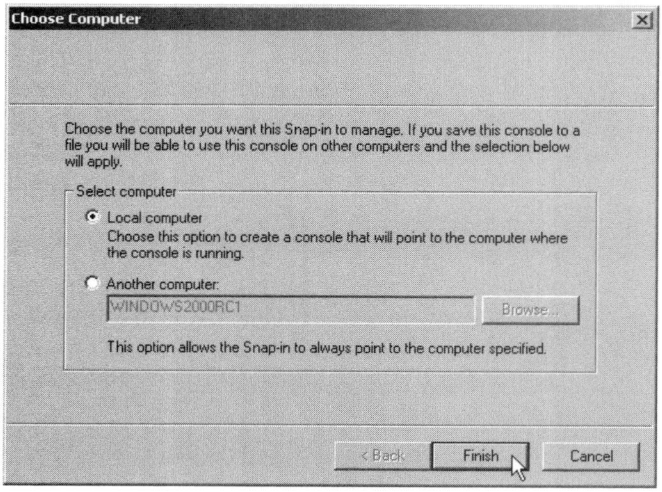

Figure 3–6   *Adding the Disk Management standalone snap-in.*

remote machine (such as a server on your network.) For the purposes of this example we are going to use the local computer. Accept this default by clicking the Finish button.

5. Finally, click Close, and then OK to be returned to your new MMC console.

6. Next, we will create a Taskpad that will include the following common tasks performed within Disk Administrator: Getting properties of a selection, exploring a disk, opening a Windows Explorer view on the disk, and formatting a disk. NOTE: Be careful which options you add as a task. If the newly created snap-in is intended for inexperienced staff, it might not make sense to allow them to have easy access to the options such as formatting a partition.

7. Now that we have the snap-in in place, let's make sure that it is working for us. Click on Disk Management (Local) and make sure that the details pane displays information on the disks in your machine. Once you have confirmed that this works, you are ready to create a Taskpad. To create a Taskpad, right-click on Disk Management in the console tree and select New Taskpad View. This will start the New Taskpad View wizard. This wizard will step you through the process of creating a Taskpad. Optionally, it will also aid you in the creation of tasks. For the purposes of this example, we will use the wizard to create the Taskpad and a single task. Then we will use the Edit Taskpad functions to go back in and create the additional three tasks that were mentioned earlier. Once the wizard has started, click Next.

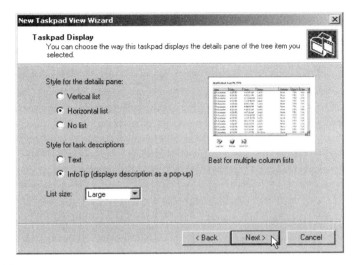

Figure 3-7   *The Taskpad display dialog box.*

8. The next choice you have to make is presented in the Taskpad Display dialog box. This dialog box is shown in Figure 3.7. You have several choices in this dialog box, and they relate to both Taskpads and tasks. The first choice is, Do you want to have the Disk Management information presented vertically or horizontally? A third option would be to choose the No list option. You would use the latter option to create an MMC Taskpad that contained only tasks. The choice you make here can be changed after the fact, so you might want to experiment a little. Although there are no arbitrary rules to be applied, remember that the purpose of a Taskpad is to make you job easier. Some data (such as that displayed in the Disk Management snap-in) does not work very well when displayed vertically. This is because the data is presented in rows. For the purposes of this example, we will leave the default option of Horizontal list selected. However, we will change the Style for task descriptions to Text. Notice that there is a preview panel in the top right-hand side of the wizard. This gives you an idea of what your Taskpad will look like once you have finished. When you have made the necessary changes, click the Next button.

9. You should now be at the Taskpad Target screen. Here you are given choices regarding the default view of the console item. We are going to set this as the default and will, therefore, accept the defaults. Don't worry, once the Taskpad is complete, you will see that it is easy for you to switch back to the default view if you don't like your new creation! Click Next.

10. You now get to name the new Taskpad you have created. The default name is the name given in the standard Disk Management MMC. You can change this so that it makes more sense. In the Name field, type *Disks in this sys-*

tem, and in the Description type *Created for test purposes only.* Once this is done, click Next.

11. Congratulations! You have now completed the Taskpad creation wizard. The final screen of the wizard contains a check box (which is checked by default). This check box will automatically start an additional wizard that will walk you through the process of creating tasks for this Taskpad. If you did not want to create any tasks, you would have to make sure that this box was not checked. However, for the purposes of this example, we are going to run the wizard to create one of our tasks. We will then use a different method to add our other choices. Click Finish to complete the Taskpad wizard and start the New Task Wizard.

12. You are first presented with three choices. Tasks can be very flexible. You can create buttons that are shortcuts to menu items or that start scripts or batch files that you have created. For this example, we are going to add a task that is a shortcut to a menu item. So we will accept the defaults. Click Next.

13. You are now at the Shortcut Menu Command dialog box. You now just specify the Command Source. That is, Where are the menu options that you want to create tasks for? The default selection is the List in details pane. However, this option does not have any menu options for us to choose from. First, we must change the Command source to Tree Item task. Once you have done this, you will see that you are now presented with all of the menu options that are available. Let's add the Properties option first. Scroll down the list of commands until you find the All Tasks->Properties option. When you have found it, select it by single-clicking, then click Next.

14. You will then be presented with the opportunity to label the new task and to provide a description. We will accept the defaults and click Next.

15. You can now select the icon that you want to be displayed. Although there is a wide choice of icons, try to select one that makes sense, given the context of the option you have just configured. For instance, selecting a Stop sign might be intimidating to new users who might think they can cause damage to the system by using that option. Once you have selected your icon of choice, click Next.

16. You have now completed the New Task wizard. Although we want to create additional tasks, we are not going to use the wizard to do this. However, note at the bottom of the Completing the New Task Wizard dialog box that there is a check box entitled *Run this wizard again.* If this were selected, the wizard would start from the beginning, and you could add all of the tasks you want. For our purposes, we will simply click Finish.

17. One final task that you might need to perform is the resizing of the various elements in the Taskpad view. If you can no longer see a clear view of the various storage devices on your system, expand the size of the window.

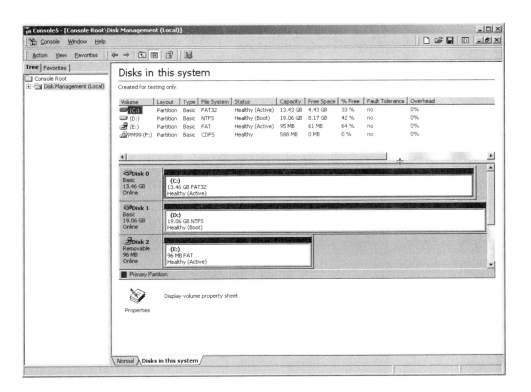

Figure 3–8   *Completed Taskpad with resizing icon.*

The newly created Taskpad—with the window resized—is shown in Figure 3.8.

You have now created your first Taskpad. Note the tabs at the bottom of the MMC console. These tabs allow you to switch between the custom view that you just created and the original view. You should also note that there is a description at the top of the screen that explains which tool you are looking at, and there is an icon at the bottom of the screen called *Properties*. This icon is a shortcut to the Properties menu item.

Of course, the purpose of the Taskpad is more than simple cosmetic changes. With a Taskpad view, you can customize the presentation of data and simplify your access to common tasks. This means that you can more easily start an MMC console, perform the tasks you have to complete, and get out of the tool. Hence, you will save time and be more efficient.

The following steps walk you through adding the additional tasks that were mentioned earlier. It is a good idea to put all the most commonly used tasks into a Taskpad. However, don't take the "kitchen sink" approach of adding everything just because you can. Taskpads will be more beneficial if you consider which menu options would be most useful the majority of the time. Oth-

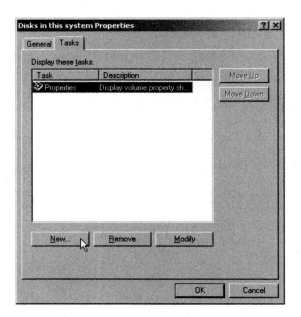

Figure 3–9   *The Tasks tab of the Disks in this system Properties dialog box.*

erwise, you will just find yourself hunting and pecking through all of the tasks you have added. Let's add some more tasks!

1. Right-click on Disk Management in the console tree and select Edit Task-pad View. This will bring up the Disks in this system Properties dialog box. If you did not follow each step of the preceding exercise, the name of this dialog box might be different. Notice that it took its name from the name I gave to the Taskpad. This dialog box presents you with the most important information from the wizard. You can make changes to the Taskpad from this menu option. This way, you can experiment with Taskpads. For the purposes of this example, we are going to switch to the Tasks tab so that we can add more options. Click on the Tasks tab, and you should see the dialog box shown in Figure 3.9.

2. As you can see, the task we added earlier is shown in this dialog box. It is possible to delete or edit the options for this task from this dialog box. We are going to add additional tasks. To do this, click the New button. This will start the New Task wizard that we used earlier. We are going to use the wizard to add three additional tasks to the Taskpad. If you do not remember how to do that, refer back to the previous exercises. The three tasks that we are going to add are: All Tasks-> Explore, Open, and All Tasks-> Format. Don't forget to select the Run this Wizard again option on the Completing the New Task wizard dialog box. If you forget to do this, you will

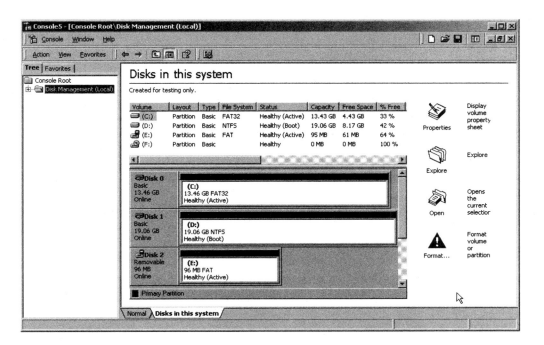

Figure 3–10   *A Taskpad showing all of the elements presented in the examples.*

have to start again from step 1. An example of what your Taskpad might look like is shown in Figure 3.10.

Taskpads take time to configure but, once they are done, they can reduce the amount of time it takes you to perform tasks. The examples given in this chapter have illustrated how menu items can be presented as tasks. However, don't forget that you can also create tasks that kick off scripts and batch files. With this option you can add even more customized options to a Taskpad. Once the Taskpad is complete, it is easy to save the MMC console and distribute it to other administrators or users of the network.

Navigating the MMC with Keyboard Shortcuts

As you might have imagined, there is a host of keyboard shortcuts that you can use while working with the MMC. These shortcuts will minimize the amount of mouse clicking you have to perform to navigate the MMC and its associated snap-ins.

Some of the shortcuts perform actions that help you move around the console tree; others affect the entire console or are specific to the snap-in that you have loaded. Tables 3.1, 3.2, and 3.3 list the keyboard options that are available, along with a description of what action each shortcut performs. Learning these shortcuts will help you to use the MMC more efficiently.

Table 3.1	Keyboard Shortcuts for Moving within or Between Console Windows
Key Combination	**Action**
TAB or F6	Moves forward between panes in the active console window.
SHIFT+TAB or Shift+F6	Moves backward between panes in the active console window.
CTRL+TAB or CTRL+F6	Moves forward between console windows.
CTRL+SHIFT+TAB or CTRL+SHIFT+F6	Moves backward between console windows.
+ on numeric keypad	Expands the selected item.
- on numerical keypad	Collapses the selected item.
* on numeric keypad	Expands the entire console tree below the root item in the active console window.
Up arrow	Moves the selection up one item in the pane.
Down arrow	Moves the selection down one item in the pane.
Page Up	Moves the selection to the top item visible in a pane.
Page Down	Moves the selection to the bottom item visible in a pane.
Home	Moves the selection to the first item in a pane.
End	Moves the selection to the last item in a pane.
Right arrow	Expands the selected item. If the selected item doesn't contain hidden items, behaves like the Down arrow.
LEFT arrow	Collapses the selected item. If the selected item doesn't contain exposed items, behaves like the Up arrow.

Table 3.2	Keyboard Shortcuts for Menu Commands that Act on the Entire Console
Keyboard Combination	**Action**
CTRL+O	Opens a saved console.
CTRL+N	Opens a new console.
CTRL+S	Saves the open console.
CTRL+M	Adds or removes a console item.
CTRL+W	Opens a new window.
F5	Refreshes the content of all console windows.
ALT+SPACEBAR	Displays the MMC window menu.
ALT+F4	Closes the active console window.

Table 3.3	Keyboard Shortcuts for the Contents of an Active Window within the MMC
Action	**Result**
CTRL+P	Prints the current page or active pane.
ALT+ MINUS SIGN	Displays the window menu for the active console window.
SHIFT+F10	Displays the Action shortcut menu for the selected item.
ALT+A	Displays the Action menu for the active console window.
ALT+V	Displays the View menu for the active console window.
F1	Opens the Help topic, if any, for the selected item.
F5	Refreshes the content of all console windows.
CTRL+F10	Maximizes the active console window.
CTRL+F5	Restores the active console window.
ALT+ENTER	Displays the Properties dialog box, if any, for the selected item.
F2	Renames the selected item.

Table 3.3	Keyboard Shortcuts for the Contents of an Active Window within the MMC (Continued)
CTRL+F4	Closes the active console window. When a console has only one console window, this closes the console.

Task Scheduler

One of the prime functions of computers is their ability to automate repetitive tasks. In applications such as Microsoft Word, this is achieved through macros. At the operating system level, we have Windows Scripting Host, application files, and commands. All that is missing is a feature that allows you to schedule when these scripts or applications run. This is the job of the Task Scheduler. Using this feature, it is possible to generate a series of functions and/or commands that run when no one is logged on to the system or after hours.

Previous versions of Microsoft Windows NT provided a command line utility, AT, that was very similar to Task Scheduler. However, its syntax was cryptic, and many people found it difficult to use. This was addressed, to a degree, by the Microsoft NT Server Resource Kit utility, WinAT, but, ultimately, the tool left a lot to be desired.

Although Task Scheduler offers extended functionality, the idea behind it remains the same. Task Scheduler is designed to allow administrators and others to have routine tasks performed either once, or on a regular schedule. The cryptic command line issues of previous versions have been addressed by implementing a wizard that steps you through the available options. If you are familiar with previous versions or similar programs, you will also be happy to see that Microsoft has extended functionality in significant ways.

Using Task Scheduler

Before you can schedule a program or script to run on a regular schedule, you must first create a task. A task is simply an item that contains all of the instructions and configuration options that this process will use. Before you create a task, you must first make some decisions. You will need this information before you create the task through the Scheduled Task wizard. This information includes:

- The name and/or location of the script that you wish to schedule
- The schedule on which the task will run. This can be run either once, daily, weekly, monthly, when the computer starts, or only when you log on to the system.
- The time and date that the schedule should start
- The user account under which the process will run under

In addition, you also have some advanced options that allow you to delete tasks that have been run or to tell the system what to do if a scheduled task fails or the host computer suddenly switches to battery power.

Once you are armed with this information, you can run through the wizard. The following example is a step-by-step guide. Although it may not be the most practical use of the tool, it will serve to illustrate the information that the wizard requires. We will also take a look at the Advanced options and how they can be used to ensure that the task does not interfere with someone who is trying to do work when a task is scheduled to run.

1. First we must navigate to the Scheduled Tasks folder. You will find it by clicking on Start, Programs, Accessories, System Tools, and Scheduled Tasks. This will open the Scheduled Tasks folder. This actually is the following directory on your local hard disk: *<System root>*\Tasks.

2. If this is the first time you have used the utility, the only option that will be showing is Add Scheduled Task. This is the wizard that is used to create tasks. To start the wizard, double-click this option. This will start the Scheduled Task wizard. The initial screen is shown in Figure 3.11. Once you have read the text, click Next.

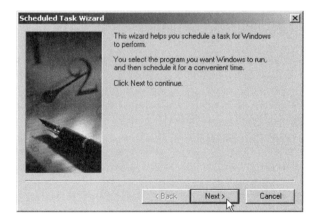

Figure 3–11   *The Scheduled Task wizard.*

3. You must now select the application or script that you want to run when the scheduled time arrives. Notice that all applications that have been registered by the system are already listed. If the script that you wish to run is not listed, use the Browse button and navigate to the directory that contains the necessary files. For the purposes of this example, we are going to schedule Calculator to run ten minutes after the wizard is complete. Select Calculator from the list of programs and click Next.

4. The following screen allows you to give the task a name (defaults to the name of application or script that you have chosen to run) and the frequency at which you want the task to run. For the purposes of this example, we are going to have Calculator run a single time. When you are using the tool for your own purposes, make sure that you give these options some thought. Although it might seem to be a good idea to have an certain application or script run every time someone logs on, you might find that others find it annoying—or worse, that the script places an unnecessary burden on the system. For now, let's select One time only and click Next.

5. You must now choose the time and date for the task to be performed. Check the system time and set the option for ten minutes from then. For example, if the system time reads 1:00 pm, schedule the Start time for 1:10 pm. This will give you time to finish the wizard and view some options before the task begins. Make sure that the Start date is set to the current date. When this is done, click Next

6. Now you have to enter the user account and password of a valid user account. This will set the security context for the task. Be careful which account you use. Although it might be tempting to use the Administrator account for all tasks, it is not good security practice to use it when it is not necessary. If necessary, create an account that has sufficient permissions to run the script of application in question. The baseline is to use an account with the *minimum* amount of permissions. By default, it will attempt to use the account that you are currently logged in under. Because this is a simple test, go ahead and enter the necessary password and click Next.

7. That completes the wizard. Although it is possible to select the Open advanced properties for this task when I click finish check box, do not do so right now. We will take a look at the advanced properties dialog box in a moment. Click Finish to end the wizard and have the task created.

If you wait until the specified time arrives, you should see Calculator start on your system. Although this might not be the most useful example of using scheduled tasks, it does serve to give an example of the types of information you will need to know before you can complete the wizard.

There are some Advanced options that can be set either after the initial wizard is complete or at any time. These options are configured from the Properties dialog box of each task. You can access these options by right-clicking on the newly created task and selecting Properties from the context menu. Take some time to explore the tabs in this dialog box. Many of the options allow you to make changes to the parameters you entered when completing the wizard. However, one of the tabs has some options that were not available through the wizard. This tab, Settings, is shown in Figure 3.12.

This tab allows you to decide what should happen if a task is never going to be used again, and to set a maximum amount of time that a task should run. You can even configure the task to run only during idle periods. *Idle periods*

Figure 3–12   *The Settings tab of the Task Properties dialog box.*

are defined as times when there is no mouse or keyboard movement on the system.

As you can see, the Scheduled Tasks wizard provides you with far more options than have previously been available in Microsoft's operating systems. With it, you can realize one of the key advantages of computers—the automation of tasks. By utilizing scripts, you should be able to perform a whole host of functions that would otherwise eat into your day!

Chapter Summary

Microsoft has recognized that performing administrative tasks on its networks was unnecessarily difficult and time-consuming. This was largely due to the disparate administrative tools that existed. The tools for performing user administration and viewing security logs on a server were completely different in both look and operation, for instance. To address this issue, it has designed and implemented the Microsoft Management Console (MMC).

The purpose of the MMC was to bring each administration tool under the same interface. At the same time, it is extensible and can be used by third-party vendors for their own tools. The tools in the MMC are known as *snap-ins*. These snap-ins provide a consistent interface and are highly customizable. Once customized, these snap-ins can be saved and then distributed in the same way you would send your word processer documents. Each customized console can have security elements assigned to it. This prevents recipients from performing additional customizations or from accessing functions that they are not authorized to perform.

The MMC is the default framework for all administration tools in the Windows 2000 operating system. It is also the new tool for the full range of BackOffice applications.

The Task Scheduler is a full-featured system that allows you to create tasks that run once or on a schedule. Unlike previous versions of the same tool, there is now a wizard that steps you though the process of creating a task. You can also easily set the security context that the task should run under and how the task should perform if the system is busy when the scheduled time arrives. Advanced options allow you to take into account advanced computer options, such as power management and Wake-up-on-LAN.

F O U R

The Windows 2000 Registry

*T*he Windows 2000 registry is a centralized repository for system configuration data. The registry was designed as a replacement for the various system and application initialization files that were used in the past and first made its debut in the Windows NT 3.x series of network operating systems. The registry includes application configuration data, hardware configuration data, device driver configuration data, network protocols and settings, and user preferences. The registry was designed to ease administration of Windows 2000 systems by providing a consistent format for application, hardware, and system data. Additionally, one can view and modify the registries of remote computers, assuming that one has the proper rights.

Most of the system and application configuration settings can be accessed through the Control Panel or application-specific menus. In almost every case, system configuration changes should be made through the Control Panel, rather than directly through the registry.

warning

Incorrect use of the registry tools may result in a system that is unstable or even unbootable!

Viewing the Windows 2000 Registry

The Windows 2000 registry can be viewed directly using two built-in tools. However, it is recommended that the registry not be modified directly if the same results can be generated via the system configuration tools available in the Control Panel.

The two tools that ship with Windows 2000 are *Regedt32.exe* and *Regedit.exe*. *Regedit.exe* is located in the *%systemroot%* directory, whereas *Regedt32.exe* is located in the *%systemroot%/system32* directory. By default, there are no shortcuts for these programs installed in the Start menu. To run either, double-click on it from Explorer or invoke it with the Start, Run,   Program Name command.

Regedt32.exe

This is the original registry-editing tool that made its debut in the NT 3.x product. Visually based upon the older Program Manager style of organization, this tool provides comprehensive security and permissions control, and allows opening the registry in a read-only mode to provide an additional amount of protection against accidental modification.

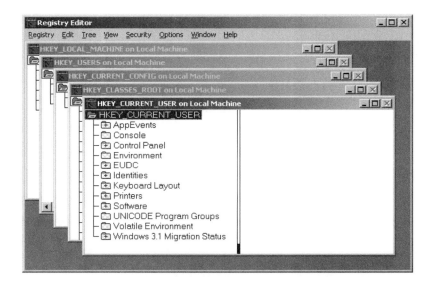

Figure 4–1   *Viewing the registry using* regedt32.exe.

Regedit.exe

Regedit.exe is loosely based upon the *regedit.exe* that debuted in Windows 95. It was first available in Windows NT 4.0. It is modeled after the Explorer model of file display, and shows the registry in a single hierarchical tree rather than the separate key windows of *Regedt32.exe*. This version of the registry tools does have a more advanced Find function that can check for value entries, as

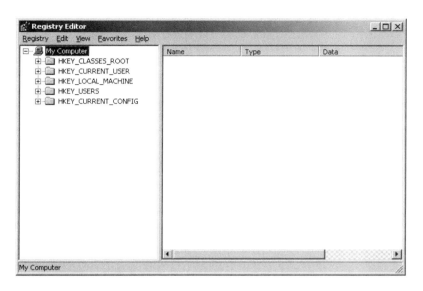

Figure 4–2   *Viewing the registry with* Regedit.exe.

well as key and subkey names, but does not provide the security and permission options that are available in *Regedt32.exe*, nor does it provide a read-only mode, which means that one has to be more aware of the consequences of accidental changes. A new feature in Windows 2000 is the Favorites function, with which one can jump directly to a particular key in the registry. This function is very similar to an Internet bookmark in a web browser.

Choosing a Registry Editor

Each of the registry editors has its own strengths and weaknesses, so one has to make a decision as to which to use. *Regedt32.exe* has the advantages of security and permission control, and a read-only mode. *Regedit.exe* offers the advanced Find functions and the Favorites options. However, *Regedit.exe* does not support editing or creating the REG_EXPAND_SZ or REG_MULTI_SZ value types. This author finds that a combination of the two tools provides the best functionality: *Regedit.exe* for finding the proper keys and values, and *Regedt32.exe* for making the actual modifications and for broader investigations of system configurations.

Structure of the Registry

The registry has a hierarchical structure that consists of subtrees, keys, sub-keys, and value entries. One can view a key as being similar to a directory, with values being similar to files and the subkeys being similar to subdirectories. There are five root subkeys that comprise the registry: HKEY_LOCAL_MACHINE, HKEY_CLASSES_ROOT, HKEY_CURRENT_USER, HKEY_USERS, and HKEY_CURRENT_CONFIG. These root subkeys are also referred to as *subtrees*. The five subkeys of the registry each begin with HKEY_ to indicate that these are the root subkeys. This HKEY_ tag is known as a *handle*, and is designed to assist software developers programming for Windows 2000.

Table 4.1	Root Registry Keys
Root Subkey	**Purpose**
HKEY_CLASSES_ROOT	These entries include application associations, filename extensions, and OLE information. This is the same as HKEY_LOCAL_MACHINE\Software\Classes.
HKEY_CURRENT_USER	These entries contain the profile of the current logged-in user, such as desktop settings, printers, network connections, and application preferences. This is the same as HKEY_USERS\userSID.
HKEY_LOCAL_MACHINE	These entries define the computer system, such as hardware configuration, device drivers, and installed software.
HKEY_USERS	These entries define users who have logged in locally, including the default profile and the current user.
HKEY_CURRENT_CONFIG	These entries define the current hardware profile of the local computer. Multiple hardware profiles are possible on Windows 2000 systems. This is the same as HKEY_LOCAL_MACHINE. \CurrentControlSet\HardwareProfiles\Current.

Each subtree is composed of keys, and within those keys, both value entries and subkeys are allowed. In both registry viewers, the left pane contains the keys and subkeys, and the right pane contains the value entries. A value entry consists of three parts: the data type of the value, the name of the value, and the value itself. These parts appear in different order, depending on the registry editor in use. *Regedt32.exe* displays the value in a Value-

Table 4.2	Registry Value Types
Value Type	**Purpose**
REG_BINARY	Raw binary data.
REG_DWORD	4 byte words, displayable in hexadecimal, binary, or decimal format.
REG_SZ	Human-readable text string.
REG_MULTI_SZ	Multiple line strings, with each entry separated by a null string.
REG_EXPAND_SZ	Expandable text string containing a variable that is replaced when the key is invoked. An example of this type is *%systemroot%*.

Name:REG_Valuetype:Value format, whereas *Regedit.exe* shows a graphical representation of the value type, the name, the value type itself, and, lastly, the value. These are arranged in columns, rather than the single-line entry of *Regedt32.exe*.

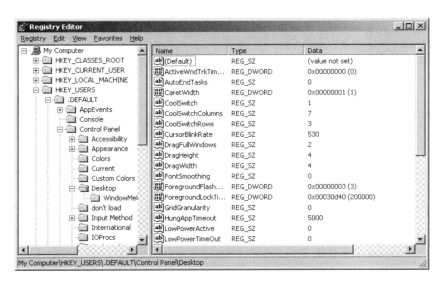

Figure 4-3   *Viewing key structures with* regedit.exe.

Value Data Types

There are five types of data types within the Windows 2000 registry. These are REG_BINARY, REG_DWORD, REG_SZ, REG_MULTI_SZ, and REG_EXPAND_SZ. *Regedit.exe* does not support the latter two values. If *Regedit.exe* is used to edit these entries, it will change the value type, with unpredictable results.

HKEY_USERS

This key is a repository of user profiles for each user logged in locally on the Windows 2000 computer. This key will always include at least two entries: the SID of the current logged-in user and the default user entry. In addition, the profiles of any other user who has logged in locally to the computer will be stored here. If a profile needs to be removed, it should be removed through the User Profile tab in the System applet in the Control Panel. Removing a profile via a registry editor can result in unpredictable behavior.

HKEY_CURRENT_USER

This key is a link to HKEY_USERS\UserSID and contains the same entries. This includes environmental factors, such as desktop wallpaper, colors, printer connections, persistent network connections, and similar information. Subkeys within this root key also contain information about user-specific software configurations, sound schemes, etc.

HKEY_CLASSES_ROOT

This key is linked to HKEY_LOCAL_MACHINE\Software\Classes and contains the exact same data and keys. This key contains the associations between file extensions and the various applications installed on the local computer, and provides compatibility with the Windows 3.1 registration database. **This key should not be edited directly.** Changes in the application associations can be made through the View,   Options,   File Types selection in Explorer.

HKEY_CURRENT_CONFIG

Introduced in Windows NT 4.0, this subtree was designed to increase compatibility with the Windows 9x series of operating systems and to allow software developers to write applications that would run on both operating systems. This key contains information about the current hardware profile in use on the local computer and is actually a link to HKEY_LOCAL_MACHINE\CurrentControlSet\HardwareProfiles\Current. As with HKEY_CLASSES_ROOT, this key should not be edited directly. Hardware profiles can be modified, created, and removed through the System applet in the Control Panel.

Editing the Registry

As mentioned earlier, two tools can be used to view the registry: *Regedit.exe* and *Regedt32.exe*. As the names imply, these tools can be used to edit the registry, as well. By default, both registry editors open with the local registry and with the windows in the same locations as when the program was last closed.

Finding a Key or Value in the Registry

In many cases, the actual location of an entry in the registry may be in doubt. Fortunately, a find function is built into both *Regedt32.exe* and *Regedit.exe* to help locate keys and subkeys. In addition, *Regedit.exe* has an advanced Find function that will search for value entries and value data.

FINDING A KEY IN REGEDT32.EXE

To find a key in *Regedt32.exe*, first select the root subkey in which to search. Then select View, Find Key and enter the desired key or subkey name. To maximize search capabilities, uncheck the Match Whole Word Only and Match Case options. Press the Find Next button to view the first match. To continue and view other matches to the search, press the Find Next button until the Registry Editor cannot find the desired key dialog box appears.

FINDING A KEY OR VALUE IN REGEDIT.EXE

To find a key or value in *Regedit.exe*, select either the desired root subkey or the entire computer from the right-hand pane. Unlike *Regedt32.exe*, one can search the entire registry with a single search, although it may take quite some time. Choose Edit, Find and enter the desired value. To modify the search parameters, select or unselect the Keys, Values, and Data check boxes. To maximize search capabilities, select each of those three boxes and unselect the Match Whole String Only option. A new option in Windows 2000 is the Favorites function. If you wish to jump directly to a key at a later time, simply highlight the key and select Favorites, Add to Favorites. Later, simply select Favorites and choose that location from the list.

Modifying, Deleting, and Adding Keys and Values

Whereas usually there is no need to edit the registry directly, in some cases, one might need to add keys and values or modify the properties of a particular entry. If this occurs, keys or values can be renamed, created, and deleted via the Edit menu in either *Regedit.exe* or *Regedt32.exe*. Root subkeys cannot be renamed or deleted.

CREATE A NEW KEY

To create a new key, select Edit, New, Key, and then type in the desired name. This key will always be generated as a subkey to the current location; so, therefore, new root subkeys cannot be created.

RENAME A KEY

To rename a key, highlight the desired key, Edit, Rename, then type the desired name of the key. Neither registry editor will prompt for a confirmation or check the syntax of the entry, so proceed with caution.

DELETE A KEY

To delete a key, highlight the desired key, Edit, Delete, then press yes on the confirmation dialog. *Regedit.exe* always has the confirmation dialog enabled, and *Regedt32.exe* has it enabled by default. This confirmation can be turned off in *Regedt32.exe* by choosing the Options menu and removing the checkmark from the Confirm On Delete option.

MODIFY A VALUE ENTRY

To modify a value entry with *Regedit.exe*, highlight the desired value entry, Edit, Modify, then enter the new data. In *Regedt32.exe*, highlight the desired value entry, Edit, <Value Type>, and enter the new data. **Neither registry editor will prompt for a confirmation or check the syntax of the entry, so proceed with caution.**

ADD A VALUE ENTRY

To add a value entry, highlight the key in which the value entry will reside, then choose the Edit menu. In *Regedit.exe*, select New,<value type>. The available options are String value, Binary value, and DWORD value. After selecting the type, a new value entry will appear within the key. Name it as desired, then modify the data as explained earlier. In *Regedt32.exe*, select the Add Value entry, and an Add Value dialog box will appear. Enter the desired value entry name and choose the value entry type from the dropdown menu. After pressing OK, enter the data for the value entry and select OK again. The complete value entry will then appear in the registry, with no further modification required.

DELETE A VALUE ENTRY

To delete a value entry, highlight the desired entry, select Edit, Delete, and select YES on the confirmation dialog. *Regedit.exe* always has the confirmation dialog enabled, and *Regedt32.exe* has it enabled by default. This confirmation can be turned off in *Regedt32.exe* by choosing the Options menu and removing the checkmark from the Confirm On Delete option.

Connecting to a Remote Computer

Both *Regedit.exe* and *Regedt32.exe* have the capability to connect to and modify remote computer registries, assuming that the currently logged-on user has correct rights on the remote computer. To connect to a remote computer in *Regedit.exe*, select the Registry, Connect Network Registry, then either enter the remote computer name in the dialog box or browse to the remote computer via the Browse button. In *Regedt32.exe*, select Registry, Select Computer, then either enter the remote computer name or browse to it using the tree structure in the Select Computer window. *Regedt32.exe* will not refresh automatically when connected to a remote computer; it must be refreshed by selecting View,   Refresh or by pressing the <F6> key.

Security and Permissions

Registry keys have similar properties as directories within the Windows 2000 NTFS file system: they have owners, have permissions associated with them, and can be audited to check for security issues. *Regedit.exe* cannot view or modify these properties, therefore use of *Regedt32.exe* will be assumed for the rest of this section.

VIEW THE OWNER OF A REGISTRY KEY

To view the owner of a registry key, select Security, Owner. A dialog box will appear with the registry key name and the owner of the key. Administrators and others with the proper rights can take ownership of the key from this dialog box by pressing Take Ownership. As usual, there is no confirmation dialog, so proceed with care.

VIEW AND MODIFY PERMISSIONS

To view and modify permissions, highlight the desired key and select Security,   Permissions. A dialog box will appear that is visually and functionally the same as the permissions dialog box on the NTFS file system. Permissions can be granted to and removed from specific users and groups.

ENABLE AUDITING REGISTRY KEYS

To enable auditing for a registry key, highlight the desired key and select Security, Auditing. A Registry Key Auditing dialog box will appear. To enable auditing, one must first select a user or group to audit by pressing the Add button on the right-hand side of the dialog. After selecting the users or groups to be audited, one can choose the events to audit and whether to audit failure, success, or both by selecting the appropriate boxes listed in the Events to Audit portion of the dialog box. If auditing is desired on all the subkeys beneath the selected registry key, check the Audit Permission on Existing Subkeys at the top of the dialog box.

Backing up and Restoring the Registry

The registry is the core of the Windows 2000 operating system environment and, as such, it is important to keep a current copy of the registry on backup media. This is essential in repairing a damaged Windows 2000 computer and should be a part of every Windows 2000 administrator's schedule.

Backing up the Registry

Without using third-party products, there are several methods of backing up the registry. First is to create an Emergency Repair Disk by running the NT Backup command and selecting Emergency Repair Disk. By default, this command creates a compressed copy of the System and Software hives. The Windows NT Rdisk command is no longer available in Windows 2000.

A second option is to start the computer with an alternate operating system and copy the files in the *%systemroot%\system32\config* directory to another location, preferably on another computer. Individual keys can also be saved with the *Regedt32.exe* program by selecting the Registry, Save Key command.

The third and most commonly used option is to back up the registry data to backup tape. The *NTBackup.exe* program has changed significantly since the NT 4.0 version of the software. One can back up and restore the following system components using Backup:

- The registry
- COM+ Class Registration database
- System boot files
- Certificate Services database
- Active Directory directory service
- SYSVOL directory

These system components are referred to as the *System State data*. For Windows 2000 Professional, the System State data consists of the registry, COM+ Class Registration database, and boot files. For Windows 2000 Server operating systems, the System State data consists of the previous components and the Certificate Services database, if the server is a certificate server. If the server is a domain controller, Active Directory and the SYSVOL directory are also contained in the System State data.

When you choose to back up or restore the System State data, all of the System State data that is relevant to your computer is backed up or restored;

individual components of the System State data cannot be backed up or restored, due to dependencies among the System State components. However, if one chooses to restore the System State data to an alternate location, only the registry files, SYSVOL directory files, and system boot files are restored to the alternate location. Restores to an alternate location do not include the Active Directory directory services database, Certificate Services database and COM+ Class Registration database

If there is more than one domain controller in an organization and the Active Directory directory service is replicated to any of these other servers, any Active Directory data will have to be authoritatively restored. To accomplish this authoritative restore, run the *Ntdsutil* utility after Backup has restored the System State data but before the server is restarted. The *Ntdsutil* utility allows one to mark Active Directory objects for authoritative restore. This will ensure that any replicated or distributed data is properly replicated or distributed throughout the organization. The *ntdsutil* utility and accompanying documentation is located in the *support\reskit\netmgmt* folder on the Windows 2000 installation CD.

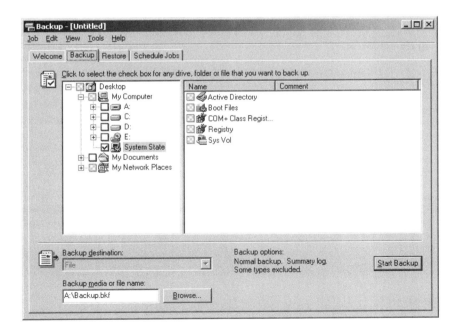

Figure 4–4   *Using Backup to save the System State.*

NOTES

- One must have the correct permissions to back up files and folders.

- In order to restore the System State data on a domain controller, start the server in directory services restore mode. This will allow Backup to restore the SYSVOL directory and the Active Directory.
- System State data can be backed up and restored only on a local computer.

Restoring the Registry

The registry can be restored in several different ways, depending on the amount of damage that has to be repaired and the method used to back up the registry. One option is to run a repair installation of the operating system, using the most current emergency repair disk. The repair installation will reload the saved registry to the existing Windows 2000 installation and can be used to rescue a corrupted install.

If the system can be booted with an alternative operating system, it is possible to copy registry files to the *%systemroot%\system32\config* directory from an alternate location.

Another method of restoration is to reload the registry from a tape backup. To restore System State data from a tape backup, begin by opening the Backup program by selecting Start, Programs, Accessories, System Tools, Backup.

Choose the Restore tab, and then select the box next to System State. This will restore the System State data along with any other data selected for the current restore operation.

NOTES

- One must have the correct permissions to back up files and folders.
- To restore the System State data on a domain controller, start the server in directory services restore mode. This will allow Backup to restore the SYSVOL directory and the Active Directory.
- System State data can be backed up and restored only on a local computer.
- If the System State data is restored and an alternate location for the restored data is not designated, Backup will erase the System State data that is currently on the server and replace it with the System State data from the restore.

If the System State data is restored to an alternate location, only the registry files, SYSVOL directory files, and system boot files are restored. The Active Directory directory services database, Certificate Services database, and COM+ Class Registration database are not restored to an alternate location.

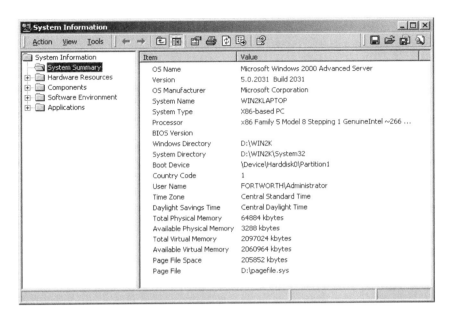

Figure 4–5   *Viewing registry data via* winmsd.exe.

Viewing Registry Data Indirectly

In addition to *Regedit.exe* and *Regedt32.exe*, there are several ways to view data in the registry without directly accessing the registry. One tool for viewing the registry is *winmsd.exe*. An expansion of the older Microsoft Diagnostics program, it is accessed by using the Start, Run, *winmsd.exe* command. This program is located in the *%systemroot%/system32* directory.

The System Information program will show information relating to the operating system, the hardware detected by Windows 2000, installed drivers, application settings, OLE registrations, print jobs, and much more. The information within this program is read-only but can be an extremely useful source of information and is much easier to navigate than the registry itself.

Perhaps the best way is through the setting applets in the Control Panel. These applets, which will be described in detail in the next chapter, allow manipulation of system settings without directly editing the registry. Some of the settings that can be manipulated via the control panel include hardware settings, accessibility options, system services, regional settings, and software installation/removal.

Chapter Summary

In this chapter, we have discussed the purpose of the registry in a Windows 2000 system. The registry is the core database of system, user and application data, and may be considered the root of the Windows 2000 operating system. The registry consists of keys, subkeys, and values. The root subkeys of the registry are HKEY_CLASSES_ROOT, HKEY_CURRENT_USER, HKEY_LOCAL_MACHINE, HKEY_USERS, and HKEY_CURRENT_CONFIG.

The registry should be backed up on a regular basis. Windows 2000 includes a backup program that can back up the registry and other important system data. This system data is known as the System State information. If the registry is damaged, it is possible to restore it from the archived data.

The registry may be viewed and modified with multiple tools included with Windows 2000. There are two registry editors, *Regedit.exe* and *Regedt32.exe*. *Regedit.exe* provides more extensive search capabilities, whereas *Regedt32.exe* offers greater control over security permissions within the registry and provides additional key value types. The values in the registry may be changed, deleted, or added via these tools. However, directly editing the registry can be dangerous and may result in an inoperative system if it is edited incorrectly. The values in the registry can be modified or viewed indirectly through other tools available in Windows 2000. *Winmsd.exe* offers a snapshot of system settings, and the applets in the Control Panel provide a way to modify the system settings if desired.

F I V E

Using the Windows Control Panel

As with previous versions of Windows, the Windows 2000 Control Panel is the central hub for making any variety of system changes. Control Panel is a collection of programs called *applets* that form the graphical user interface (GUI) through which most changes to the registry are made. As mentioned in Chapter 4, using the Control Panel applets is the preferred method for making Registry changes. This is due to the ease with which a mistake can be made using the Registry Editor.

Collectively, the Control Panel applets are the most powerful function of Windows 2000, next to the Registry Editor. The reason is that whereas Explorer provides the interface for file and folder manipulation, the Control Panel provides the ability to manipulate any of the hardware in your system, as well as to control the administrative functions of the operating system. In this chapter, we will take a look at the following topics:

- Defining the main applets in Control Panel
- Working with hardware settings
- Working with operating system settings
- Installing hardware

Defining the Main Applets in Control Panel

With Windows 2000, Microsoft has captured the best of both worlds with respect to the Windows NT 4.0 and Windows 9x (95 and 98) Control Panel applets. For example, Windows 9x users have long enjoyed the Device Manager (located under the System applet) for managing hardware, a feature that Win-

dows NT users did not have. Windows NT users have long been able to configure their environment variables and startup options through Control Panel
whereas Windows 9x users had to edit *config.sys*, *autoexec.bat*, and *msdos.sys*
files manually to obtain equivalent functionality. In many ways, Windows 2000
tries to converge the user friendliness of Windows 9x with the power and stability of Windows NT.

Many of the applets are similar to what Windows 9x and NT users have
seen in the past. The Display applet is practically unchanged from Windows 98
and eliminates the requirement to click Test in NT 4.0 before applying a new
display resolution. Other applets such as Printers, Fonts, Keyboard, Mouse,
Date/Time, Power, and Accessibility Options are very similar to what they have
been in the past, although in many cases are more wizard-driven than in previous versions of Windows. We'll focus on a few of the most highly used applets
as well as a couple of new additions.

Add/Remove Hardware

Add/Remove Hardware is an updated version of the Add New Hardware applet
from Windows 9x and NT 4.0. Add New Hardware, as the name implies, gave
users the ability to install and configure new hardware devices. The Windows
NT version of Add New Hardware did not include any Plug and Play (PnP) functionality, but rather allowed the user to install manually a device driver
included with NT or from a user-provided location ("have disk") after selecting
the appropriate category of device that was to be installed such as SCSI controllers or network adapters. Windows 9x gave the user the option of letting Windows search for a PnP device in addition to installing a device driver manually.

The Windows 2000 Add/Remove Hardware wizard includes all of the
functionality of the Windows 9x Add New Hardware wizard and more. When
you first open the Add/Remove Hardware wizard, you are given a choice of
hardware tasks, as shown in Figure 5.1.

The Add/Troubleshoot a device task is similar in function to the original
Add New Hardware wizard. First, Windows 2000 attempts to detect a device
through PnP, and if it doesn't detect a new device, it presents the option to
install a driver manually. Additionally, there is the option to troubleshoot a
device, which will be discussed later in this chapter, as will uninstalling and
unplugging devices.

Add/Remove Programs

The Add/Remove Programs applet has a fresh new look to it in Windows 2000,
as shown in Figure 5.2, but works the same as it did in NT 4.0.

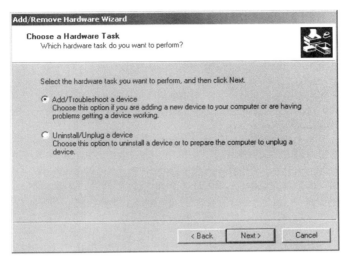

Figure 5–1

The Add/Remove Hardware Wizard allows the user to perform a variety of hardware-related tasks.

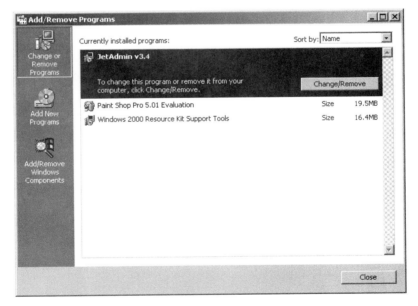

Figure 5–2

The Add/Remove Programs applet gives a new look to an old standby.

CHANGE OR REMOVE PROGRAMS

Change or Remove Programs lets you either uninstall complete applications or add or remove individual components of applications that support that feature. Multifaceted applications, such as office suites, typically allow you to change components of programs without having to remove and reinstall the entire application completely.

ADD NEW PROGRAMS

Add New Programs is another example of an applet that has converged Windows NT and Windows 9x. You can still install new floppy-based or CD-ROM-based applications through this applet, but Windows 2000 has also incorporated the Windows 98 Windows Update utility into Add New Programs. Windows Update is a utility through which you can add new Windows features, device drivers, and system updates over the Internet. This enables you to keep your Windows 2000 operating system up to date as bugs and security holes are found and patched and as Microsoft adds new functionality.

ADD/REMOVE WINDOWS COMPONENTS

Add/Remove Windows Components is where you can customize your installation of Windows 2000. As in NT 4.0, you can add components that were not installed during the initial operating system setup or remove components that you no longer want installed. A difference in Windows 2000 is that Microsoft has moved Networking Services from the Network Control Panel applet in NT 4.0 to the Windows Components wizard of Add/Remove Programs.

 You can still configure additional network services through the Network and Dial-up Connections Control Panel applet by clicking the Advanced menu and selecting Optional Networking Components. This brings up the Windows Components wizard without having to go through Add/Remove Programs first.

Administrative Tools

An important difference between NT 4.0 and Windows 2000 is that Microsoft has moved the Administrative Tools from the Start menu to the Control Panel. This move is in keeping with the strategy that the Control Panel is the central hub for configuring the operating system. A common complaint with earlier versions of NT was the lack of cohesiveness when it came to administering the system. Tools were scattered here and there and every tool had a different interface. Windows 2000 attempts to address those complaints by providing both a centralized location (Control Panel) and a unified look and feel (Microsoft Management Console [MMC]) to system administration. The Administrative Tools are implemented as a series of MMC Snap-Ins and will be covered in more detail throughout the book.

 For NT 4.0 users who preferred Administrative Tools on the Start menu, it can be added back through Taskbar Properties by checking the Display Administrative Tools check box on the Start Menu Options tab.

Users and Passwords

Users and Passwords replaces the older User Manager (NT Workstation) and User Manager for Domains (NT Server) applets from NT 4.0. In this applet, you can configure user and group settings, and configure whether or not users have to enter a username and password to login or press <CTRL>+<ALT>+<DELETE>. If your network uses a certification authority for authentication, you can manage certificates in this applet, as well.

System

The System applet is host to a wide variety of functions that enables you to configure your computer's settings. System is possibly the most important of the Control Panel applets, so we will look at each of the property sheets that make up the applet. It is divided into five property sheets, as follows:
- General
- Network Identification
- Hardware
- User Profiles
- Advanced

GENERAL

The General property sheet is the same as in NT 4.0. It provides information such as the version of the operating system, who the operating system is registered to, the license key, and information regarding the processor and amount of RAM installed in the computer.

NETWORK IDENTIFICATION

The Network Identification property sheet is new to Windows 2000 and is what used to be the General tab of the Network Control Panel applet in NT 4.0.

On this property sheet you can change the name of the computer and configure workgroup or domain membership for your workstation or server.

HARDWARE

The Hardware property sheet is the location for configuring your system's hardware. It includes a button that links to the Add/Remove Hardware applet and, like NT 4.0, gives you the ability to setup and configure multiple hardware profiles (discussed in the next section).

 Another exciting new feature of Windows 2000 is driver signing, which attempts to maintain the integrity of the operating system files by allowing you to configure whether or not to overwrite digitally signed files when you install applications. By default file signatures are ignored, meaning that all files will be installed, regardless (the same as NT 4.0). There are also options to warn you before installing an unsigned file or to block unsigned files from installing at all.

Device Manager is the applet that Windows 9x users have had available to them while NT 4.0 users had to rely on the archaic Windows NT Diagnostics that provided much less functionality. Using Device Manager, you can view and change device properties, update device drivers, configure device settings, and uninstall devices.

USER PROFILES

The User Profiles property sheet is where you configure local versus roaming profiles. Profiles are discussed in depth in Chapter 13.

ADVANCED

The Advanced property sheet contains options to configure performance options, environment variables, and startup and recovery options. Each of these is discussed later in this chapter.

Working with Hardware Profiles

Hardware profiles are a feature of Windows 2000 that enables the operating system to have multiple hardware configurations. By default, when Windows 2000 boots, every device driver that is currently installed is loaded into memory. A default profile called *Profile 1* is created during the Windows 2000 installation, and every device installed is enabled during the boot process. For desktop computers, that is usually desirable, but where hardware profiles are especially useful is with notebook computers. Many people have docking stations for using their notebook computer in an office but do not take it with them when they take their notebook home or when traveling. You might have a hardware

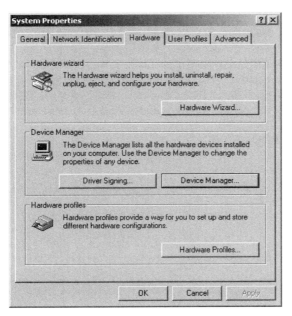

Figure 5-3

Configuring hardware profiles in Windows 2000 through the Control Panel System applet.

profile named *Docked* that loads device drivers for a network card and laser printer that are part of your docking station. You could also have a second profile called *Undocked* for use in a hotel room or at home that loads a modem rather than the network card. Although you could just load everything in one profile, regardless of your location, you would end up with error messages logged in the System Log (Event Viewer and logs are discussed in Chapter 26).

Creating and Modifying Hardware Profiles

As previously mentioned configuring hardware profiles is done through the System applet in Control Panel. After clicking the Hardware tab click the Hardware Profiles button at the bottom. That will bring up the dialog shown in Figure 5.3.

Creating a new profile is accomplished by selecting the generic New Hardware Profile and clicking Copy. Assign a name to your new profile and click OK. The new profile will default to enabling every installed device, so you will likely want to modify the profile to your specific needs. This is done through the Device Manager rather than the Hardware Profiles property sheet. The Device Manager, shown in Figure 5.4, is accessed from the Hardware property sheet of the System applet, just like Hardware Profiles.

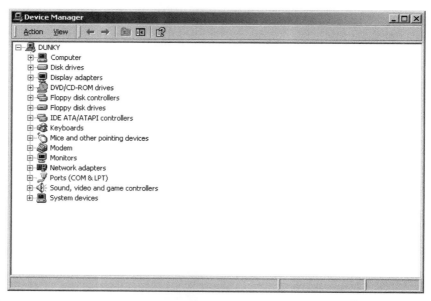

Figure 5–4

The Windows 2000 Device Manager console enables you to configure settings for hardware devices, including in what hardware profiles the devices should be enabled.

In Device Manager, a device can be enabled or disabled in a particular profile through the General properties of an individual device. For example, double-clicking on an installed modem will bring up the properties. At the bottom of the General property sheet is the Device Usage option. You can select your desired options from the dropdown list.

Using a Hardware Profile

If you have only one hardware profile Windows 2000 will, of course, use it every time you boot the computer. However, if you have more than one profile, you have a couple of options as to how Windows behaves during the boot process. As shown at the bottom of Figure 5.3, there are choices for hardware profile selection when Windows starts. By default, Windows will count down from 30 seconds before loading the first profile listed if you do not intervene. You can also have Windows wait indefinitely for you to make a profile selection.

VIEWING THE PROPERTIES OF A HARDWARE PROFILE

However, for this to work, first you have to make the profile available as an option when Windows starts. This is done by highlighting the profile and clicking Properties, which brings up the window shown in Figure 5.5.

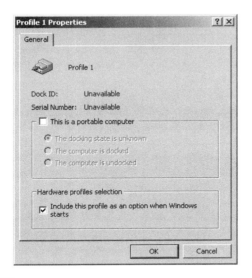

Figure 5–5   *Properties of a hardware profile.*

By clicking the Include this profile as an option when Windows starts check box, you can control whether a profile is available for use. This is handy if you no longer need a particular profile but you do not want to delete it right away or if you will be using one particular configuration for an extended period of time and do not wish to have other profiles available during that time. That scenario might take place if you went on an extended business trip where you were not going to be using the docking station back in your office any time soon.

Working with Operating System Settings

Windows 2000, like NT 4.0, gives you the option to configure settings that affect the behavior of the operating system through the System applet in Control Panel. After opening System Properties, click the Advanced tab to find the operating system settings. Configurable options include:

- Performance Options
- Environment Variables
- Startup and Recovery

Performance Options

Performance options give you the ability to control how applications use memory. When you click on the Performance Options button, you are presented with the window shown in Figure 5.6.

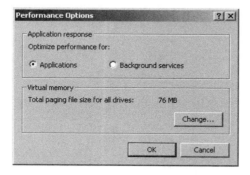

Figure 5–6   *Configuring Windows 2000 Performance Options.*

The first option on this property sheet is for application response. By default, Windows 2000 will optimize performance for applications, rather than background services. Windows 2000 manages system processing, which includes allocating processor time to processes that are running. The operating system can allocate tasks between multiple processors or multiple processes on a single processor. Choosing the Application Response preference, however, allows you to decide whether Windows should give more processor time to the programs you are working in or to background tasks, such as printing. Setting the response to favor applications will result in a faster response time from the application you are actively working in, which is generally the desired option. A print server, though, would be set up to favor background tasks, rather than active applications because the majority of the server's work would be processing background tasks. Windows 2000, like Windows NT, uses a thread priority process to determine which application to give CPU time and in which order to do it. Windows 2000 does this on a scale of 1–31, with 31 being the highest priority and 1 being the lowest. Table 5.1 shows a list of the thread priorities.

Table 5.1	Thread Priorities in Windows 2000	
Base	**Priority Class**	**Thread Priority**
31	Real-time	Time critical
26	Real-time	Highest
25	Real-time	Above normal

Table 5.1	Thread Priorities in Windows 2000 (Continued)	
24	Real-time	Normal
23	Real-time	Below normal
22	Real-time	Lowest
16	Real-time	Idle
15	Idle, Normal, or High	Time critical
15	High	Highest
14	High	Above normal
13	High	Normal
12	High	Below normal
11	High	Normal
10	Normal	Highest
9	Normal	Above normal
8	Normal	Normal
7	Normal	Below normal
6	Normal	Lowest
6	Idle	Highest
5	Idle	Above normal
4	Idle	Normal
3	Idle	Below normal
2	Idle	Lowest
1	Idle, Normal, or High	Idle

An obvious question would be, If Windows 2000 gives CPU time to the highest priority app, how are lower-priority apps ever executed? Good question! Windows 2000 dynamically adjusts the priorities, boosting lower priority applications so that, eventually, as the CPU continues to multitask, the application gets to use some CPU time. This process works very quickly, so even lower-priority apps will respond within a reasonable amount of time.

VIRTUAL MEMORY

The second configurable performance option is virtual memory, shown in Figure 5.7.

When Windows runs low on available RAM and needs more memory to complete a task, it uses the hard drive to simulate system RAM. This is called *virtual memory* and is much slower than system RAM because hard drive

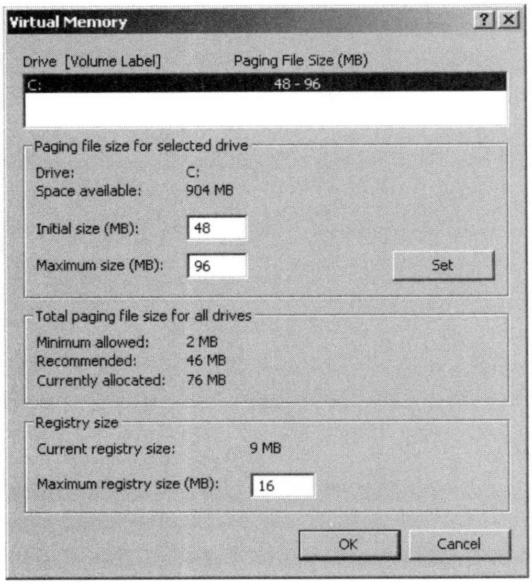

Virtual Memory

Drive [Volume Label]   Paging File Size (MB)

C: 48 - 96

Paging file size for selected drive

Drive: C:
Space available: 904 MB

Initial size (MB):   48

Maximum size (MB):   96   Set

Total paging file size for all drives

Minimum allowed: 2 MB
Recommended: 46 MB
Currently allocated: 76 MB

Registry size

Current registry size: 9 MB

Maximum registry size (MB):   16

OK   Cancel

Figure 5–7   *The Virtual Memory property sheet.*

speeds are measured in milliseconds, whereas RAM is measured in nanoseconds. Another name for virtual memory in Windows 2000 is the *pagefile* and, in fact, Windows creates and uses a special file called *pagefile.sys* for virtual memory.

The default size for the pagefile in Windows 2000 is the amount of system RAM plus 12 MB. So a system with 128 MB of RAM would initially have a *pagefile* of 140 MB. For a basic workstation or server, this number might be appropriate, but servers running other Microsoft BackOffice applications, such as Exchange Server or SQL Server, usually need to increase the default virtual memory size. Refer to the product-specific documentation for recommended virtual memory settings. You set the size of the pagefile by selecting the drive you want the file to be located on, typing a number into the Initial Size box (shown in Figure 5.7) and the Maximum Size box and clicking Set. You will be prompted to reboot after clicking OK. The initial size is just that, the size of *pagefile.sys* when Windows 2000 starts up. The maximum size is how large *pagefile.sys* is allowed to grow during the processing of tasks as the system works.

It might seem advantageous at this point simply to set a pagefile much higher than you need so you will not have to worry about running out of memory. However, Windows 2000 will not efficiently use a pagefile that is too large, resulting in potentially worse system performance than if the virtual memory size had been left at the default settings.

The default virtual memory settings are often not the most efficient, but there are some guidelines that you can use when configuring virtual memory settings.

Windows 2000 sets up the pagefile to be on the boot partition where the operating system was installed. This is inefficient because Windows will, by nature, perform a lot of disk I/O on the system files. Having to read and write to the pagefile simultaneously while doing the same with system files slows Windows down. Therefore, it is recommended that the pagefile be moved to a different physical disk, preferably onto a partition that has no other data or programs that will be frequently accessed. Windows 2000, like Windows NT before it, supports advanced disk configuration options on NTFS partitions, such as disk mirroring and disk striping. These features provide fault tolerance and performance benefits, and are discussed later in this book in a chapter on managing disks.

The downside to moving the entire pagefile, though, is that if Windows crashes, it will be unable to write debugging information to a dump file (discussed later in this chapter). To address that, a pagefile using the default settings should be left on the system partition, and another pagefile should be created on a different physical disk, as outlined above. The Windows 2000 operating system has algorithms that allow it to use multiple pagefiles in the most efficient manner, and, in this case, it will opt to use the pagefile on the less frequently used drive, rather than the one on the system partition. Should Windows crash, though, it would be able to create a dump file for troubleshooting purposes.

In addition to configuring the size of the pagefile you can also configure the maximum size of the registry from the Virtual Memory property sheet. As with the pagefile, you can specify the largest size to which the registry is allowed to grow, and nothing is gained by setting the maximum size artificially high.

Using Environment Variables

Most current systems administrators can remember the dark days of DOS, where manually editing system files such as *config.sys* and *autoexec.bat* was a way of life. Windows 2000, though, like NT 4.0 before it, provides a convenient GUI for configuring the environment variables that is shown in Figure 5.8.

Environment variables are divided into User variables and System variables. As the name suggests, User variables are specific to the user and, other than TEMP settings, are usually required only for specific applications. System variables are common to the operating system no matter who is logged in. Typically, the settings an administrator might edit under System variables would be the TEMP files folder and the PATH statement. In DOS and Windows 9x, these particular settings were located in the *autoexec.bat* file.

Figure 5-8   *Configuring environment variables in Windows 2000.*

By clicking New, you can create a new User or System variable, and Edit allows you to modify an existing variable, such as to add an additional folder to the PATH statement. Deleting a System variable should be done with great care and only if you are sure of the potential consequences of that setting being removed.

Understanding Startup and Recovery Options

The Startup and Recovery Options allow you to control the behavior of the system during startup and during a crash. If you have only Windows 2000 installed on your system, it will be the default operating system. It will be the default operating system as well in a dual-boot scenario if it was the last operating system installed. If, for example, you had a Windows 98 system and you installed Windows 2000 as a new installation, you would have the option when the Boot Menu appeared of choosing either OS. The menu by default counts down from 30 seconds before loading the default operating system if there is no intervention. On the Startup and Recovery property sheet, you can tell Windows which operating system should be the default and for how long the menu should be displayed before loading the default.

Although Windows 2000 is generally a stable operating system, there will be times when you experience the infamous "Blue Screen of Death" fatal error. The Recovery options let you determine what actions Windows takes when a fatal error occurs. By default, it will write an event to the system log, but you can also have Windows send an administrative alert to a remote user or computer if the alerter service is configured. This is especially helpful to notify system administrators immediately when a server goes down to ensure the quickest response time possible.

Windows can also write debugging information to a dump file, *memory.dmp*. This is enabled by default on Windows 2000 Server but must be manually enabled on Windows 2000 Professional. The contents of the dump file means nothing to most administrators but can be used by Microsoft to help troubleshoot the cause of the crash.

If debugging information is written to a dump file, it is beneficial also to check the box to automatically reboot. If an application caused the fatal error, typically, Windows will start back up without problem. This will enable users to get back to work while you work to determine the specific cause of the crash through the dump file. If the server does not automatically reboot, it will stay at the fatal error screen until someone manually resets the system.

Installing Hardware

Windows 2000 has made great strides over NT 4.0 in the process of installing hardware, mainly due to the more robust PnP support. NT 4.0 had very limited PnP capabilities through the pnpisa service, but pnpisa supported only a small variety of hardware. Windows 2000 has full-blown PnP support, similar to Windows 98, and supports a much larger variety of hardware than does NT 4.0.

You must be logged into the computer using an account that is a member of the administrators' group to install hardware.

Plug and Play Hardware

A PnP system is one that has a PnP-compatible BIOS, operating system, PnP devices, and PnP-aware applications. If you have a PnP-compatible system, installing PnP hardware is generally pretty simple. Follow the manufacturer's instructions to install the device physically and power up the computer. Windows 2000 should detect your new hardware and start the Found New Hardware wizard. Follow the on-screen prompts to install the appropriate device driver if Windows does not automatically install a driver for you. Windows 2000 comes with a substantial library of device drivers, so in many cases, it will already have a driver that will work with the device you are installing. If Windows does not have a driver, you will be prompted for the location of the driver.

Non-Plug and Play Hardware

If the hardware you are installing is not PnP compatible, also known as a *legacy* device, Windows will not detect it automatically and launch the Found New Hardware wizard. In most cases, legacy devices have physical jumpers on the device or proprietary software utilities that come with the device and are used to configure the hardware settings. Jumpers must be set at the time that the device is physically installed in order for the device to work properly. Installing a device driver for non-PnP hardware is done through the Add/Remove Hardware wizard.

Using the Add/Remove Hardware Applet

As previously mentioned, the Add/Remove Hardware applet builds on the functionality of Add New Hardware in NT 4.0. When you launch the Add/Remove Hardware wizard, it will first attempt to detect PnP devices that might not have been configured. If it does not detect a device, you will be presented with the window shown in Figure 5.9 and given the opportunity to "Add a new device" or troubleshoot a device that already has a driver loaded for it.

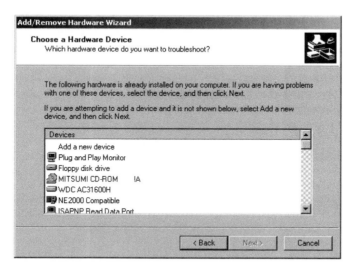

Figure 5–9

Installing a non-Plug and Play device or troubleshooting an existing device is done through the Add/Remove Hardware wizard.

In a bit of redundancy due to reusing exiting NT 4.0 code from its Add New Hardware wizard, Windows 2000 will give you the default choice of searching for PnP devices again when you select Add a new device. Alternatively, you can choose to select your hardware from a list. First, you select the

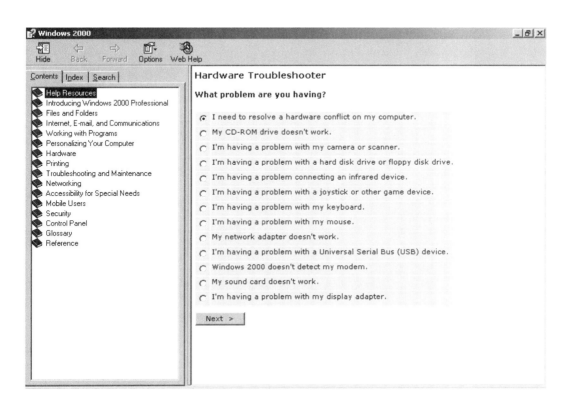

Figure 5–10   *The Hardware Troubleshooter helps you resolve problems with installed hardware.*

category of the device you wish to install, such as Display Adapters, then the specific make and model of the device you are installing. If Windows 2000 does not have a driver for your device you can select Have Disk to point the operating system to updated driver files. Follow the prompts and reboot if necessary to enable your hardware.

DEVICE TROUBLESHOOTING

If you are having trouble getting an installed device to work you can use the Add/Remove Hardware applet to launch the Hardware Troubleshooter, shown in Figure 5.10.

Using the Hardware Troubleshooter is a matter of selecting the general type of problem you are having and stepping through a series of questions and suggestions to get your device working. These are the basic troubleshooting steps that a repair tech would take in troubleshooting the problem and, in most cases, will enable you to get your hardware working without having to call the manufacturer's tech support.

UNINSTALL/UNPLUG A DEVICE

If you want to uninstall a hardware device from your system or unplug a device (most typically associated with notebook computers), you would also use the Add/Remove Hardware wizard. When you select this option, you are given two choices, one to remove a device and the other to unplug/eject a device. When you choose to uninstall a device, you are shown a list of installed devices that can be removed. By default, hidden devices, which are system level drivers usually essential to the operation of Windows 2000, are not shown. Checking the box to Show Hidden Devices makes them appear in the list, but great care should be taken before removing one of these devices. Remove only one if you are sure that the result will be desirable.

Unplugging or ejecting a device is usually related to notebooks and PCM-CIA (also known as PC card) devices. Windows 2000 does not directly support *hot swappable* devices, that is, devices that can be added or removed on the fly, where Windows will automatically detect their presence or lack thereof. Going through the unplug/eject option lets you tell Windows that you are about to unplug a device such as a PCMCIA modem from your system. The operating system will then tell you it is safe to eject the device.

If you frequently unplug/eject devices while Windows 2000 is running, you can select the check box to Show Unplug/Eject icon on the taskbar on the Completing the Add/Remove Hardware Wizard page. This will keep you from having to run the Add/Remove Hardware wizard every time.

Viewing Available Hardware Resources

Figure 5.4 previously showed the Device Manager console, which is the primary interface for viewing and modifying hardware resources. The Device Manager is organized in a tree format, with the top branches representing device categories. Expanding a branch shows devices of that type that are installed on the system. This view is called *Devices by type*. To view available hardware resources in Device Manager, click the View menu and select, Resources by connection. This will divide the console into groups for DMA, I/O, IRQ, and Memory. Expanding the IRQ branch, for example will show you a list of IRQs in use and what devices are using them. This information is also available through the Computer Management administrative tool (Device Manager can also be accessed through Computer Management), but you need Device Manager if you want to do more than just view the resources in use.

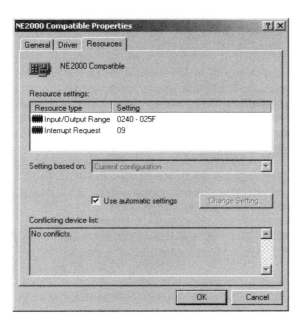

Figure 5-11

Windows 2000 allows you to configure resource settings for individual devices, useful for setting up non-Plug and Play hardware.

Altering Hardware Resource Assignments

The default view in Device Manager is Devices by type, which is the easiest view for modifying hardware resources. To change a resource setting for a device, first expand the branch for the device category, such as network adapters. Then double-click the device you want to modify to bring up the properties. Click the Resources tab to view the current resources for the device. If the Use automatic settings check box is checked, Windows has assigned resources to this device and is managing those resources. This is the preferred method because it allows Windows to juggle any PnP devices to accommodate special resource requirements. If it is a legacy device that requires manually setting the resources, though, you can uncheck the box and adjust the settings to match the hardware. Windows will dynamically update the conflicting device list at the bottom of the window to show you whether a resource you have selected is already in use by another device. Resource configuration is shown in Figure 5.11.

Chapter Summary

The Control Panel is the central location for managing operating system settings, hardware, and software. It is organized into a collection of programs called *applets* that contain the options for configuring your system. Microsoft has moved the Administrative Tools from their old location in NT 4.0 to the Control Panel in Windows 2000, further centralizing system management. Whereas many of the applets have similar functionality as in previous versions of Windows, many are updated to reflect the Windows 2000 interface look and feel, and many have added more features. Examples of an applet with new features include Add/Remove Hardware, which now, in addition to the basic add hardware functionality of NT 4.0, also lets you remove hardware easily (a feature borrowed from Windows 9x) as well as unplug or eject devices.

With Windows 2000, Microsoft has married some of the best features of Windows 9x, while building on the foundation of NT 4.0. Functionality such as true Plug and Play and the Device Manager for managing hardware goes a log way toward making Windows 2000 more user-friendly than previous versions of NT.

Windows 2000 Boot Process

· ·

*T*his chapter introduces you to the Windows 2000 boot process. It is divided into five sections: Overview of the Boot Process, Control Sets, Advanced Boot Options, the Purpose of the *boot.ini*, and the Windows 2000 Boot disk. The boot process overview takes you step by step through the boot process of an X86-based and Alpha-based Windows 2000 computer. The Control Sets section explains the mystery behind control sets—exclusively, the Last Known Good control set. In the advanced boot option section, each boot option is explained in detail. It also includes an advanced boot option quick reference table. The *boot.ini* section includes the purpose of the *boot.ini,* as well as full descriptions of all related switches. The chapter ends with the Windows 2000 boot disk section, which elaborates on the purpose of a boot disk, how to create one, and its usage.

This chapter will give you the foundation needed to troubleshoot problems with the Windows 2000 boot process. In addition, this chapter can be read in one reading session or can be used as a reference.

Overview of the Boot Process

This section explains the Windows 2000 boot process on an x86-based computer, the only platform now supported because Compaq dropped support for the Alpha platform. This section will walk you through the entire Windows 2000 boot process. The x86-based boot process also includes descriptions of the files used during the boot process and how they are used. With a better understanding of these processes, you will be able to troubleshoot the Windows 2000 boot process that much quicker and more effectively.

x86-Based Boot Process

The beginning of the Windows 2000 x86-based boot process starts with Windows 2000 Setup. Windows 2000 Setup creates the environment required to run Windows 2000. In the process, several files are copied to the boot partition of the hard disk on the system.

When Windows 2000 is installed, it copies the computer's boot sector and saves it as *bootsect.dos*. This is later used to load the operating system that was previously installed on the computer. The Windows 2000 installation then edits the boot sector to load *ntldr* after the preboot sequence has finished. This fundamental change is how Windows 2000 starts its first boot on your computer. As you read, you'll find that *ntldr* is the basic starting point in the x86-based Windows 2000 boot process.

Before we venture into the actual x86-based Windows 2000 boot process itself, look at Table 6.1. Table 6.1 lists the files and locations used in the x86 Windows 2000 boot process. A x86-based Windows 2000 boot process uses five required core files and two optional files.

Table 6.1	x86-Based Boot Process Files and Locations
File	**Location**
boot.ini	Root of the system partition
bootsect.dos	Root of the system partition
hal.dll	%systemroot%\system32
ntbootdd.sys	Root of the system partition
ntdetect.com	Root of the system partition
ntldr	Root of the system partition
Ntoskrnl.exe	%systemroot%\system32

The reason that two of these files are optional is because the *bootsect.dos* is present only if an operating system exists on the computer before Windows 2000 setup begins, and *ntbootdd.sys* is used only when a Small Computer System Interface (SCSI) controller with the SCSI BIOS disabled is present.

BASIC COMPUTER BOOT SEQUENCE

Now that we know what files the x86-based Windows 2000 boot process uses, let's discuss what role these files play in the boot process. When you turn on your computer, it runs a power-on self-test (POST). This is standard for all x86-based computers. At this point, the computer determines the amount of physical memory installed and what other hardware devices are attached to the system. This can include COM ports, hard disk controllers, video accelerator cards, etc. If the computer has a Plug and Play basic input/output system (BIOS) it will register those compatible devices and configure them at that time. The BIOS then loads the master boot record (MBR) from the configured boot device. The boot device can be configured as the floppy, CD, hard disk, or other external boot device, such as a JAZZ drive or Zip drive. The boot device can be configured manually by the user in the BIOS. The remainder of this discussion will assume that your computer is configured to boot from a hard disk. Once the MBR loads, it will scan the hard disk for the partition that is flagged as the active partition. Located somewhere on the active partition is the boot sector. The boot sector is found and loaded by the MBR into memory and executed. Remember that the boot sector was changed at the time of the Windows 2000 setup. Now the new Windows 2000 boot sector loads *ntldr* file. The *ntldr* file plays the pivotal role as the Windows 2000 operating system loader.

OPERATING SYSTEM BOOT PHASE

The operating system boot phase will start with the description of the *ntldr* file and it role in the x66-based Windows 2000 boot process, to the point that the *ntoskrnl.exe* passes control to the *winlogon.exe*. The process will also mention the use of control sets. These are further explained in detail in the control sets section.

As the *ntldr* file loads, it detects what kind of file system is loaded on the boot partition. It has the ability to do this because the *ntldr* file contains a set of minifile system drivers that enables it to detect and communicate with partitions formatted with either the File Allocation Table (FAT) (required on the boot partition to dual boot with non-NT operating systems) or Windows NT File System (NTFS). *ntldr* will then start the suitable minifile system driver for the boot partition. At this point, *ntldr* can read the *boot.ini* file from the boot partition into memory. With the *boot.ini* file loaded into memory, the *ntldr* file can read the information stored there and display the Operating System Selection menu as a result. Figure 6.1 shows an example the Operating System Selection menu. The contents of display of the menu can and will differ from system to system, depending on how the system is configured and what operating systems were on the system before Windows 2000 was installed.

The Operating System Selection menu lists the operating systems loaded on the computer. It lets you specify which operating system you want to load. If you do not select an operating system by using the arrow keys and pressing <Enter>, the operating system specified in the *boot.ini* as the default operating system will load automatically. The value for the default operating system entry

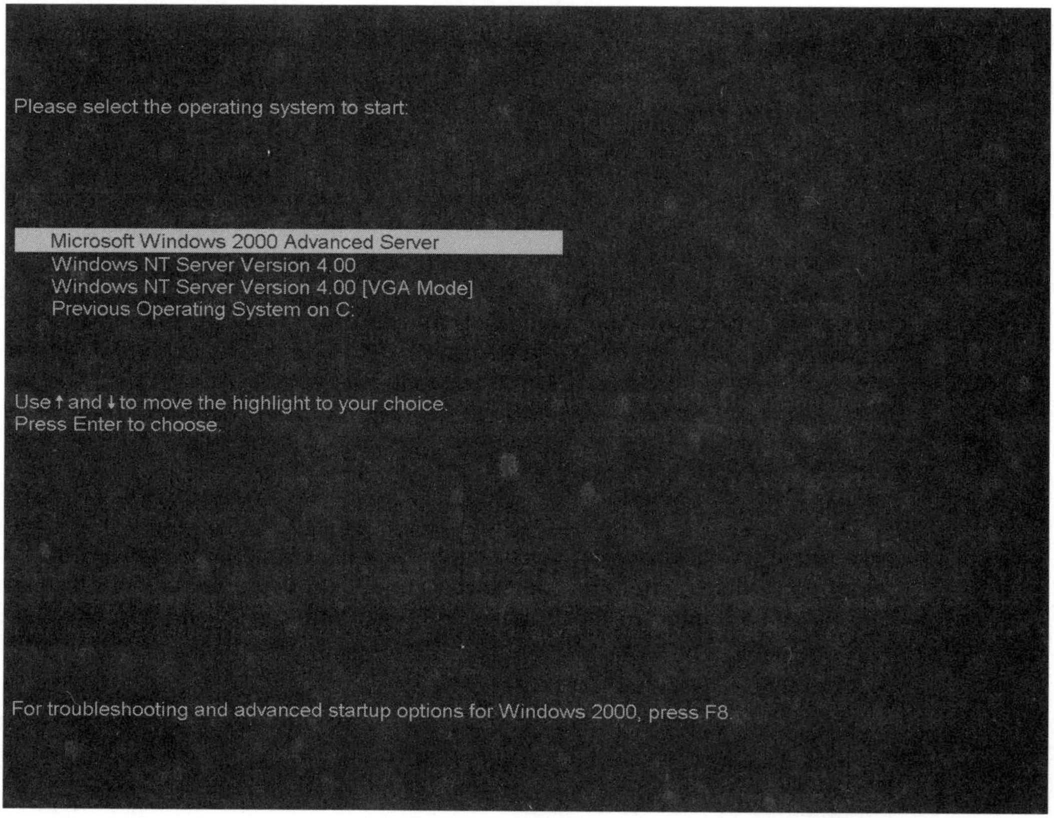

Please select the operating system to start:

    Microsoft Windows 2000 Advanced Server
    Windows NT Server Version 4.00
    Windows NT Server Version 4.00 [VGA Mode]
    Previous Operating System on C:

Use ↑ and ↓ to move the highlight to your choice.
Press Enter to choose.

For troubleshooting and advanced startup options for Windows 2000, press F8.

Figure 6–1   *Operating System Selection menu.*

is set by the Windows 2000 setup. The last Windows 2000 installation will be the default value for that entry.

Selecting an operating system other than Windows 2000 will load the *bootsect.dos* file. Remember that this is a copy of the computer's boot sector before the Windows 2000 installation. *ntldr* will load and execute the *bootsect.dos*, which will load the operating system previously configured as the default operating system. This might be an installation of Windows 95, Windows 98, or an earlier version of Windows NT.

If Windows 2000 is selected on the operating system selection menu, *ntdetect.com* is immediately loaded and executed. *ntdetect.com* does just what it sounds like it might do. It detects hardware installed on the system or, to be technical, *ntdetect.com* will enumerate a list of currently installed and config-ured hardware components. *ntdetect.com* then passes this list back to *ntldr*, which, in turn, gets written to the HKEY_LOCAL_MACHINE\HARDWARE regis-

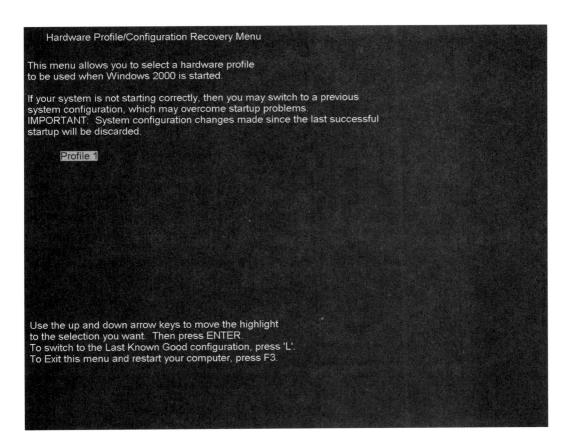

Hardware Profile/Configuration Recovery Menu

This menu allows you to select a hardware profile
to be used when Windows 2000 is started.

If your system is not starting correctly, then you may switch to a previous
system configuration, which may overcome startup problems.
IMPORTANT: System configuration changes made since the last successful
startup will be discarded.

Profile 1

Use the up and down arrow keys to move the highlight
to the selection you want. Then press ENTER.
To switch to the Last Known Good configuration, press 'L'.
To Exit this menu and restart your computer, press F3.

Figure 6–2   *Hardware Profile/Configuration Recovery menu.*

try key. Some examples of the hardware components that Ntdetect.com will
detect are floppy disks, a keyboard, a mouse, communication ports, parallel
ports, SCSI adapters or other hard disk controllers, and video adapters.

While *ntldr* is enumerating the hardware configuration list on the computer, you have the option to press the spacebar and start the Hardware Pro-
file/Configuration Recovery menu. The spacebar must be pressed when the
load sequence starts and the progress periods are displayed. The progress periods are displayed on the upper left-hand corner of the screen. Even though the
operating system is busy checking hardware and loading device drivers, you
have the ability to stop the entire thing by just pressing the spacebar. Figure 6.2
is typically what the Hardware Profile/Configuration menu looks like. Other
systems might have more than one or even several hardware profiles configured.

One example use of hardware profiles is to have separate hardware pro-files configured for a laptop in the docking station and not in the docking sta-tion. By default, the Hardware Profile/Configuration Recovery menu will display all configured hardware profiles for the computer. If you have not cre-ated a hardware configuration profile, only the default is listed. In addition to the hardware configuration profiles listed, you can pres <L> and select the Last Known Good Configuration. As discussed later in this chapter, Last Known Good Configuration can also be selected from the Advanced Startup Options menu.

LOADING AND INITIALIZATION OF THE KERNEL

There are two ways that the Windows 2000 kernel (*ntoskrnl.exe*) can be started. Either a hardware configuration profile was selected from the Hard-ware Profile/Configuration Recovery menu or you opted not to press the space-bar and interrupt the boot process but to let the Windows 2000 operating system continue to load without interruption. While the *ntoskrnl.exe* is load-ing, the screen will clear and display the progress periods in the upper left-hand corner of the screen.

The *ntoskrnl.exe* loads but does not initialize until *ntldr* completes the following steps:

1. *ntldr* will load the *hal.dll* (Hardware Abstraction Layer).
2. *ntldr* loads the HKEY_LOCAL_MACHINE\SYSTEM registry key from the *%systemroot%\System32\Config\System* registry hive. *ntldr* then selects the current control set to use while the operating system loads. This is a list of the services and device drivers that will be loaded to start the system. This is also defined by the hardware configuration profile and will discussed in further detail later in this chapter.
3. *ntldr* then loads the hardware device drivers that have a Start Entry value of *0x0*. The order in which these device drivers are loaded is specified in the registry under the List entry in the HKEY_LOCAL_MACHINE\ SYS-TEM\CurrentControlSet\Control\ServiceGroupOrder subkey. The data is formatted as a list in the registry as the REG_MULTI_SZ registry type. Usu-ally, the device drivers that are loaded first are for the hard disk controller cards and the hard disks themselves.

Once these steps have been completed, the *ntoskrnl.exe* is initialized and the *ntldr* passes control to it. After control has been passed to the Windows 2000 kernel, it loads the first graphical screen that displays the load status of Windows 2000. This screen taunts the new Windows 2000 logo and shows the Windows 2000 operating system load status via a graphical progress bar labeled *Starting Up*:

Four more tasks are completed during this stage of the Windows 2000 boot process:

1. After the Windows 2000 kernel has been successfully initialized, it writes the data collected by the *ntldr* during the hardware detection phase of the boot process to the HKEY_LOCAL_MACHINE\HARDWARE registry key. This subkey contains information about system board in the computer and all the interrupts used by other hardware devices, such as SCSI controller cards and vides accelerator cards.

2. In the HKEY_LOCAL_MACHINE\SYSTEM\Select subkey in the registry is a list of the control sets used by the operating system. At this point, the Clone control set is created by copying the control set referenced by the current entry in the this subkey. For example, if the value for this entry is 0x1, then the *CurrentControlSet001* will be copied to the Clone controls set.

3. Once the Clone control set has been created, the Windows 200 kernel initializes the device drivers that were loaded previously by *ntldr*. Now the Start entry is scanned in all of the keys under the HKEY_LOCAL_MACHINE\SYSTEM\CurrnetControlSet\Services subkey of the registry. Any device drivers with a Start value of 0x1 are loaded and initialized. The value of the Group entry in the device drivers' specific subkey specifies the order in which the device drivers load. One additional entry worth noting is the *ErrorControl* entry. It specifies what action the boot process should take in the event that one of the device drivers fails to load and initialize successfully. Table 6.2 is a list of the possible *ErrorControl* values and a description of the actions taken by the boot process. It is important to note that some drivers are dependent on others loading previously. In other words, a driver may fail to load if a different driver whose presence is required failed to load. As a troubleshooting procedure, you would want not only to examine the error that a particular driver failed, but to see whether it failed merely because a different driver failed first.

Table 6.2	Device Driver *ErrorControl* Values and Resulting Action
Value	**Result**
0x0	The Windows 2000 boot process ignores the error and continues without displaying an error message.
0x1	The Windows 2000 boot process continues by ignoring the error but displays an error message.

Table 6.2	Device Driver *ErrorControl* Values and Resulting Action (Continued)
0x2	The Windows 2000 boot process stops and restarts using the Last Known Good Configuration. If the Last Known Good Configuration is currently being used, the value is treated as if it were 0x0.
0x3	The Windows 2000 boot process stops and restarts using the Last Known Good Configuration. If the Last Known Good Configuration is currently being used, the boot process is stopped and an error message is displayed.

4. Once the device drivers with *0x1* for the value of the Start entry have been loaded and initialized, *smss.exe* (Session Manager) initializes the services and subsystems for the Windows 2000 operating system. The purpose of the Session Manager is to initialize and execute the instructions in the BootExec data item, the Memory Management Key, the DOS Devices Key, and the Subsystems Key.

The Session Manager executes the BootExec data item first before any services are loaded and initialized. The Sessions Manager then creates information about the paging file for the Virtual Memory Manager. Third, the information in the DOS Devices Key is executed, resulting in the creation of symbolic links that direct classes of commands to the congruent component in the file system. Last, the Session Manager executes the Subsystems Key, which starts the Win32 subsystem. The Win32 subsystem starts the Windows logon process (*winlogon.exe*) and controls all I/O access to the operating system, including the display.

The Windows 2000 kernel loading and initialization process is now complete as *winlogon.exe* is executed and Windows Logon begins.

WINDOWS LOGON

Now that the Session Manager has started *winlogon.exe*, *winlogon.exe* starts the Local Security Authority (*lass.exe*). The Local Security Authority loads and displays the Windows Logon dialog box. Once the Windows dialog box is displayed, it is possible to press <CTRL><ALT><Delete> at this time and login, but the Windows 2000 operating system is still completing the boot process.

After the Windows Logon dialog box is displayed, the Service Controller is executed. The Service Controller scans the HKEY_LOCAL_MACHINE\SYSTEM\ CurrentControlSet\Services subkey in the registry. Services with *0x2* as the value for the Start entry are loaded and initialized. Two of these services are the Workstation service and the Server service.

Some of the services loaded during this phase have dependent services. In the HKEY_LOCAL_MACHINE\SYSTEM\CurrentControlSet\Services subkey in the registry, two entries specify in which order these services will start. These two entries are the DependOnGroup entry and the DependOnService entry.

Last, but not least, the x86-based Windows 2000 boot process is not complete until a user or administrator successfully logs onto the system. Once a user or administrator completes a successful logon by having a username and password authenticated, the system copies the Clone control set to the Last Known Good control set.

Windows 2000 Control Sets

The previous section of this chapter discussed the x86-based Windows 2000 boot process and mentioned control sets and mentioned how the boot process uses them. This section will discuss control sets and explain them in further detail.

Control Sets

A control set is a collection of configuration data used to control the system. Typically, this data contains a list of device drivers and services to load and initialize as the system boots. The control set used when the system that is running is the CurrentControlSet. The CurrentControlSet is just a pointer to one of the actual control set subkeys.

Notice in Figure 6.3 that the HKEY_LOCAL_MACHINE\SYSTEM subkey in the registry has three control set subkeys. The CurrentControlSet points either to ControlSet001 or ControlSet002. To identify which control set is the Current-ControlSet, look at the Current entry in the HKEY_LOCAL_MACHINE\SYSTEM\Select subkey. The data type for the values of the Select entries will always be REG_DWORD. The value for the Current entry in Figure 6.3 is *0x1*. This shows that the CurrentControlSet points to ControlSet001. Also notice that the value for the Last Known Good entry is *0x2*. This shows that ControlSet002 will be used if the Last Known Good hardware configuration profile is used the next time the system restarts and is booted. All of the entries in the HKEY_LOCAL_MACHINE\SYSTEM\Select subkey are pointers to other control sets. Table 6.3 is a list of these entries and includes a description of them.

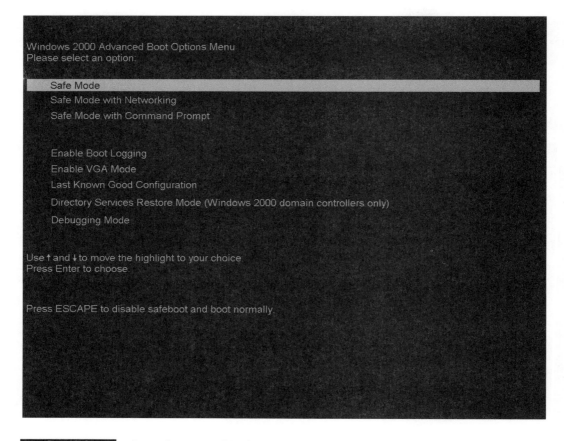

Windows 2000 Advanced Boot Options Menu
Please select an option:

   Safe Mode
   Safe Mode with Networking
   Safe Mode with Command Prompt

   Enable Boot Logging
   Enable VGA Mode
   Last Known Good Configuration
   Directory Services Restore Mode (Windows 2000 domain controllers only)
   Debugging Mode

Use ↑ and ↓ to move the highlight to your choice.
Press Enter to choose.

Press ESCAPE to disable safeboot and boot normally.

Figure 6–3   *Control sets stored in the registry.*

Table 6.3	Entries in HKEY_LOCAL-MACHINE\SYSTEM\Select
Entry	**Description**
Current	Specifies which control set is the current control set. Any changes made while the system is running are made to the CurrentControlSet.
Default	The Default entry specifies which control set will be used the next time Windows 2000 is restarted and the boot process begins.
Failed	The Failed entry specifies which control set failed the last time the system was booted using the Last Known Good control set.
Last Known Good	A copy of the control set used after the last successful Windows 2000 boot.

It is possible to have more control sets than Clone, CurrentControlSet, ControlSet001, and ControlSet002. This happens when many changes and/or problems occur to the operating system.

The Last Known Good Control Set

The Last Known Good control set is used to recover a Windows 2000 system that has problems booting. This is a very helpful way to get the system up and running before you decide to reinstall Windows 2000. For instance, if you load a new device driver on the system, reboot, and the system fails to load the Windows 2000 operating system successfully, you would restart using the Last Known Good control set. There are two ways to boot the Windows 2000 operating system using the Last Known Good control set.

1. Press <F8> on the Operating System Selection menu to display the Advanced Options Startup menu and select Last Known Good Configuration.
2. Press the spacebar when *ntoskrnl.exe* displays the progress periods in the upper left-hand corner of the screen to enter the Hardware Profile/Configuration Recovery menu and press <L>.

If Windows 2000 is recovering from a severe or critical error when loading a device driver, it will also use the Last Known Good control set.

When Windows 2000 starts, one of two control sets can be used—the Default control set or the Last Known Good control set. The Default control set is created when the Windows 2000 operating system is shut down. This is also the control set used by default when Windows 2000 is selected from the Operating System Selection menu. The Last Known Good control set is created when a user or administrator successfully logs onto the system and the Clone control set is copied to the Last Known Good control set. If a problem occurs when booting the system, **DO NOT** logon. If you logon, the previous Last Known Good control set will be overwritten by the Clone control set.

The Last Known Good control set is not failproof. If the problem is not related to Windows 2000 configuration changes, such as bad or missing files, incorrectly configured user profiles, a hardware failure, or incorrect files permissions, the Last Known Good control set cannot be used to restart the system successfully.

Advanced Boot Options

Windows 2000 has an integrated Safe Mode feature that enables you to get your computer up and running again quickly. The advanced boot options provide assistance when troubleshooting an operating system that will not boot. These options are available when pressing **<F8>** during the operating system selection screen. When **<F8>** has been pressed, the Windows 2000 Advanced Boot Options menu is displayed, and you can select from the list of options available. You select the option you want by using the arrow keys, highlighting the option you want, and pressing <Enter>. The startup screen is then displayed again, with the Advanced Boot Option you selected in red on the bottom left-hand corner of the screen. Figure 6.4 shows the Advanced Boot Options Menu on a Windows 2000 Server. You can see that Safe Mode has been selected. Now the %SAFEBOOT_OPTION% environment variable has been set and will designate what mode will be used when the operating system boots.

VGA Mode

Windows 2000 VGA (Video Graphics Array) Mode can be selected on the Advanced Startup Options menu. When Windows 2000 is started in VGA Mode, only the basic VGA driver is loaded for video. This is the same driver that was used during the Windows 2000 installation. This option is usually used after a new video card and/or drivers have been loaded. If Windows 2000 boots up and you have no visual display, restart your Windows 2000 operating system in VGA Mode. This will give you the ability to make changes to the display settings and correct your problem.

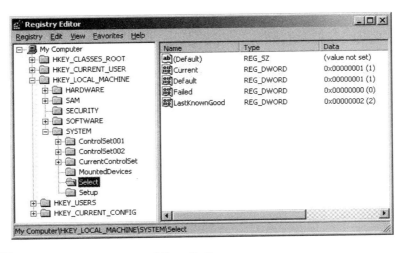

Figure 6–4   *Windows 2000 Advanced Boot Options menu.*

To start your Windows 2000 operating system in VGA Mode, follow the instructions below:

1. Click Start, then click Shutdown. Use the dropdown combo box and select Restart. Press Enter.
2. After the operating system reboots, press <F8>. The Windows 2000 Operating System Startup menu is displayed.
3. Now, by using the arrow keys on the Windows 2000 Advanced Startup Option menu, highlight VGA Mode and press <Enter>.

 Notice on the bottom left-hand corner of the screen that *VGA Mode* is printed in red. This identifies to you that when the Windows 2000 operating system has been selected, it will start in VGA Mode. To cancel VGA Mode and/or clear any advanced startup option that has been selected, press <Esc>.

Last Known Good Configuration Mode

The Last Known Good Configuration starts Windows 2000 using the registry information that Windows 2000 saved at the last successful logon. This advanced startup option should be used only in cases where the operating system has been incorrectly configured. Using Last Known Good Configuration does not solve problems caused by corrupted or missing drivers or files because it loads only the registry information from the last shutdown.

> **note**   Any changes made to the registry since the last successful startup will be lost when Last Known Good Configuration is used, including all changes made in the Control Panel.

To start your Windows 2000 operating system using the Last Known Good Configuration, follow the instructions below:

1. Click Start, then click Shutdown. Use the dropdown combo box and select Restart. Press <Enter>.
2. After the operating system reboots, press <F8> once the Windows 2000 Operating System Startup menu is displayed.
3. Now, by using the arrow keys on the Windows 2000 Advanced Startup Option Menu, highlight Last Known Good Configuration and press <Enter>.
4. Notice on the bottom left-hand corner of the screen that *Last Known Good Configuration* is printed in red. This identifies to you that when the Windows 2000 operating system has been selected, it will start in VGA Mode.

Directory Services Restore Mode

The Directory Service Restore Mode advanced boot option allows the restoration of Active Directory Services on domain controllers. This option is not available on Windows 2000 Professional. This topic is discussed in further detail in Chapter 21, "Installing and Configuring Network Protocols."

Debugging Mode

The Windows 2000 Debugging Mode advanced boot option enables the sending of debug information through a serial cable to another computer. This advanced boot option is not available on Windows 2000 Professional.

To start your Windows 2000 operating system in Debugging Mode, follow the instructions below:

1. Click Start, then click Shutdown. Use the dropdown combo box and select Restart. Press <Enter>.
2. After the operating system reboots, press <F8> once the Windows 2000 operating System Startup menu is displayed.
3. Now, by using the arrow keys on the Windows 2000 Advanced Startup Option menu, highlight Debugging Mode and press <Enter>.

Safe Mode

Safe Mode is useful when your Windows 2000 machine will not boot properly. It starts Windows 2000 using only the basic files and drivers necessary to boot the operating system, such as the mouse, monitor, keyboard, storage, base video, and default system services. No networking components or services are loaded during Safe Mode. When the operating system starts and you login, the background is black, with *Safe Mode* written in white in all four corners of the screen. This reminds you that you are in a troubleshooting mode.

There are three different Safe Modes to choose from, including Safe Mode, Safe Mode with Networking, and Safe Mode with Command Prompt. The Safe Mode with Networking advanced boot option starts Safe Mode with the services and drivers necessary to load networking. Safe Mode with Networking is useful when you need to run an update located on a network to fix a corrupt driver or service on your Windows 2000 machine. The Safe Mode with Command Prompt advanced boot option is the same as Safe Mode, except for the fact that when the machine restarts, it displays a command prompt.

To start your Windows 2000 operating system in one of the Safe Modes follow the instructions below:

1. Click Start, then click Shutdown. Use the dropdown combo box and select Restart. Press <Enter>.
2. After the operating system reboots, press <F8> once the Windows 2000 Operating System Selection menu is displayed.
3. Now, by using the arrow keys on the Windows 2000 Advanced Startup Option Menu, highlight either Safe Mode, Safe Mode with Networking, or Safe Mode with Command Prompt, and press <Enter>.

Boot Logging Mode

Designating the Boot Logging advanced boot option enables the logging of all services and drivers. Whether the services and drivers are loaded and initialed or fail to load and initialize, they are logged. The Boot Logging advance boot option writes the log to *ntbtlog.txt* in the *%WINDIR%* directory on your boot partition. This directory is typically C:\WINNT.

Table 6.4 is a quick reference table listing all of the advanced boot options and a brief description.

Table 6.4	Advanced Boot Options
Boot Option	**Description**
VGA Mode	Starts Windows 2000 with a basic VGA driver.

Table 6.4	Advanced Boot Options (Continued)
Last Known Good Configuration Mode	Start Windows 2000 with the registry information that was saved during the last successful shutdown of the operating system.
Directory Services Restore Mode*	Enables an Active Directory Services restore to a Windows 2000 domain controller.
Debugging Mode*	Enables the sending of debug information through a serial cable to another computer.
Safe Mode	Starts Windows 2000 with only the basic drivers and services to boot the operating system.
Safe Mode with Networking	Starts Windows 2000 with the basic drivers and services to boot the operating system and networking drivers and services.
Safe Mode with Command Prompt	Starts Windows 2000 with only the basic drivers and services to boot the operating system, but only a command prompt is displayed.
Boot Logging Mode	Writes log file of all drivers and services loaded in *ntbtlog.txt* in the *%WINDIR%* directory.

*These advanced boot options are not available on Windows 2000 Professional.

The Purpose of the *boot.ini*

The section discusses the Windows 2000 *boot.ini* file. The *boot.ini* file is stored on the active boot partition of the computer running the Windows 2000 operating system and is created by the Windows 2000 setup. The *ntldr* boot file reads the *boot.ini* to display the Operating System Selection menu. Once an operating system has been selected, *ntldr* uses the information in the *boot.ini* to load the selected operating system. The topics in this section include understanding the contents and Advanced RISC Computing (ARC) paths of the *boot.ini*, and modifying the *boot.ini*.

Understanding the Contents of the Boot.ini

This topic will explain the different sections of the *boot.ini* file and the items there. Figure 6.5 displays an example *boot.ini* file on a Windows 2000 system. Notice in Figure 6.5 that the *boot.ini* has two sections, the [boot loader] section and the [operating systems] section. The first entry in the [boot loader] section is timeout. The value of the timeout entry sets the amount of time, in seconds, that the Operating System Selection menu will allow a user to select an operating system before it starts the boot process specified by the default entry. The value of the default entry specifies the location of the default operating system. This is typically the last operating system installed.

The [operating systems] section of the *boot.ini* lists the name and location of all the operating systems loaded on the computer. The next topic, understanding *boot.ini* ARC paths, explains the information in the [operating systems] section of the *boot.ini* in further detail.

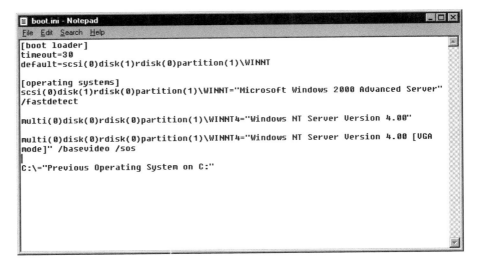

```
[boot loader]
timeout=30
default=scsi(0)disk(1)rdisk(0)partition(1)\WINNT

[operating systems]
scsi(0)disk(1)rdisk(0)partition(1)\WINNT="Microsoft Windows 2000 Advanced Server"
/fastdetect

multi(0)disk(0)rdisk(0)partition(1)\WINNT4="Windows NT Server Version 4.00"

multi(0)disk(0)rdisk(0)partition(1)\WINNT4="Windows NT Server Version 4.00 [VGA
mode]" /basevideo /sos

C:\="Previous Operating System on C:"
```

Figure 6–5   *Example contents of a Windows 2000* boot.ini.

Understanding boot.ini *ARC Paths*

Advanced RISC Computing ARC paths are used in the *boot.ini* to specify the location of the operating system's boot partition. RISC is an acronym for Reduced Instruction Set Computing, which is a microprocessor design that uses a small set of instructions for fast execution. An example of an ARC path can be found in Figure 6.5 as the value of the default entry in the example *boot.ini* file. Table 6.6 explains the four sections of an ARC path.

Table 6.5	ARC Path Section Descriptions
Section	**Description**
SCSI(*c*) or MULTI(*c*)	Specifies the hard disk adapter or controller. (*c*) Specifies the start order of the adapter or controller when more than one is present in a system.
Disk(*d*)	(*d*) Specifies the SCSI ID when SCSI is used, which identifies which disk to use. Otherwise, this value is always *0* for MULTI.
Rdisk(*r*)	(r) Identifies the disk on the controller when using MULTI. This section is not used for SCSI.
Partition(*p*)	(*p*) Identifies the partition on the disk for both MULTI and SCSI.

When specifying MULTI or SCSI, note that SCSI can be used only when configuring a SCSI controller with SCSI BIOS not enabled. For all other controller configurations, including SCSI controllers with SCSI BIOS enabled, use MULTI. When assigning numbers to partitions start with (*1*). All of the other numbers in the ARC path sections should start with (*0*). When mapping out your system, note that nonextended partitions are assigned before logical drives.

Using Switches in the boot.ini

A few switches can be added to the *boot.ini* file. They can be used in either the [boot loader] section or the [operating systems] section after the description of the operating system. Below is an example of a two *boot.ini* switches being used:

```
multi(0)disk(0)rdisk(0)partition(1)\WINNT="Windows 2000" /basev-
ideo /sos
```

The switches can be used in any order, and no switch is dependent on another one. A list and descriptions of the *boot.ini* file switches is shown here:

/basevideo Starts the computer with the basic VGA video driver. This is often helpful when a new driver has been loaded but is not functioning properly.

/fastdetect= This switch disables serial mouse port detection. You can specify which port to disable by appending *comx* at the end of the switch, where *x* is the port number.

/maxmem:*n* Specifies to Windows 2000 how much memory can be used where *n* is the amount of memory.

/noguiboot Specifies that when Windows 2000 boots, the fancy graphical startup status screen is not displayed.

/sos Specifies that the names of all the devices drivers be displayed on the screen as the system boots. This can be used when the boot process fails while loading the device drivers to identify which device driver is failing.

Editing the boot.ini

At some point in time it may be necessary to modify or edit the *boot.ini* file. To change the timeout entry in the *boot.ini* file, you can use the Control Panel. You can use the following steps below to change the timeout entry:

1. Click Start, then Settings, then Control Panel.
2. Double-click the System icon in the Control Panel.
3. Click on the Advanced tab at the top, then on the Startup and Recovery command button.
4. At the top of the startup section, you can select the default operating system to load and set the operating system selection timeout.

If you want to change the order in which the items are displayed in the Operating System Selection menu or the descriptions of the operating systems themselves, you will have to edit the file manually. Before you can edit the file, you have to be able to see it. By default when Windows 2000 is installed, hidden files are not displayed. So the first step is to change this in Folder Options. To do this, use the following steps:

1. Right-click My Computer on the desktop, then click Explorer.
2. In Explorer, click the icon for the hard disk where your active partition is located. This is usually your C drive.
3. Now click Tools on the menu, then Folder Options.
4. Click on the View tab in the Folder Options dialog box. Under Hidden files and folders, click Show hidden files and folders, and click OK.

Now that you can see the *boot.ini*, right-click on it and select properties to remove the read-only attribute. You can also change the *boot.ini* file attributes at the command prompt. If you were to do so, it would look something like this:

```
attrib boot.ini -s -r
```

When using the attrib command, -r removes the read-only attribute and -s removes the system file attribute. Once the attributes have been set for the *boot.ini* file, you can open and modify it with a text editor.

Windows 200 Boot Disks

This section discusses the importance of the Windows 2000 boot disk, as well as how to create and use one.

Importance of the Windows 2000 Boot Disks

The Windows 2000 boot disk can be used to boot a Windows 2000 computer that has missing or corrupt files. If there are missing or corrupt boot files on your computer, you can use the boot disk to boot the operating system and replace or fix the missing or corrupt files. A Windows 2000 boot disk should be created as soon as the Windows 2000 setup has been completed. This way, if any boot files on the system are deleted, the disk can be used and the files easily restored. Note that some boot files need to be loaded directly from the hard disk itself. In this case, the boot disk would not be of any help.

Creating the Boot Disk

To create a Windows 2000 boot disk use the following steps:

1. Verify that you are logged on as an administrator.
2. Verify that Show hidden files and folders has been selected in Folder Options. If this has already been done, proceed to step seven; otherwise continue with step three.
3. Right-click My Computer on the desktop, then click Explorer.
4. In Explorer, click the icon for the hard disk where your active partition is located. This is usually your C drive.
5. Now click Tools on the menu, then Folder Options.
6. Click on the View tab in the Folder Options dialog box. Under Hidden files and folders, click Show hidden files and folders, and click OK.
7. Open a command prompt, change directories to the root of the system partition, and type the following, then press <Enter>:

```
attrib boot.ini -s -r
```

8. Insert a 3.5-inch, 1.44-MB disk into the floppy disk drive.
9. At the command prompt type the following and press <Enter> to format the floppy disk with Windows 2000:

```
format a:
```

10. Now you can use either Windows Explorer or the command prompt to copy the *boot.ini, ntdetect.com, ntldr, bootsect.dos,* and *ntbootdd.sys* files from the root of the system partition to the boot disk. Remember that the last two files (*bootsect.dos* and *ntbootdd.sys*) might not be on your sys-

tem. If they are in the root of your system partition, they need to be copied, because they are being used.

Chapter Summary

In this chapter, we learned about the Windows 2000 boot process, how it functions, how to modify it, and, most importantly, how to troubleshoot it when problems occur. In most cases, once the system is initially setup and configured, you won't need to make many modifications (if any) to the boot process. In other words, most of your experience with the boot process will probably take place on the troubleshooting side. At this point, you should have a basic understanding of how Windows 2000 functions and its basic administrative functions. Now we will move into more advanced topics to build on your current knowledge.

Introduction to
Active Directory

·······································

*I*f you took a poll of IT professionals and asked them which new feature of
Windows 2000 they thought was the biggest evolutionary step, it is a safe bet
to assume that Active Directory would top the list. Although Windows 2000 is
full of new features and updates to old tools, it is the Active Directory component that will likely present the most opportunity and the most challenges
when implementing, or planning to implement Windows 2000 on a corporate
network. Many of the new features rely on Active Directory being in place and
working before they can be used—and its design will significantly impact the
granularity of the security model you can use and the efficiency of your network.

Many Microsoft Windows NT networks have grown from small begin-
nings into complex Internetworks of servers and workstations. As technology
has changed and new features have been added, new servers have been added
in a haphazard and random way. The previous domain model employed by Windows NT allowed machines to be installed without regard to the effect it might
have on the network. A domain was a large conglomeration of systems that
worked together, controlled by groups, logon permissions, NTFS permissions,
and trust relationships. On small networks, this worked very well, but once
Windows NT began to break into large enterprises, the domain model began to
strain under the weight of all the baggage trying to maintain accounts across
different continents and multiple trust relationships.

Step up, Active Directory! Active Directory is a "directory service." In lay-
man's terms, a directory is a list of resources. A service is a set of functionality
that allows you to administer and search the directory.

As you will see, many of the problems being experienced by medium to large enterprises are addressed in Active Directory. That is not to say that it doesn't also offer significant advantages to smaller organizations. Active Directory is going to allow you to redefine how your network has been put together and relieve you of some of the stress of trying to remember which domain trusts which other domain, and which users have permissions to access a particular shared or network device.

This chapter is going to serve as your introduction to Active Directory. We are going to discuss the reasons why Microsoft felt this was an important step to take with its enterprise-level network operating systems. We will take a close look at the elements that make up an Active Directory design, giving you the terminology and definitions for each one. We will even discuss the key differences between Active Directory and the older domain model that many people have grown familiar with.

As discussions regarding Active Directory have increased, a standard method of representing its various components has materialized. We have used these standard shapes in this book. This will make it easier for you to understand representations of other Active Directory designs as you go through the book and to expand your reading with Microsoft white paper and other guides. Do not be worried if the name of some of these components are not familiar to you yet, we will be discussing each of them as we go through this and later chapters. The basic components are represented as follows:

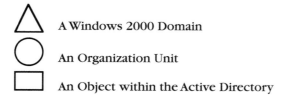

A Windows 2000 Domain

An Organization Unit

An Object within the Active Directory

Once you understand the information in this chapter, you will be ready to continue reading subsequent chapters on design decisions and how you can use the various elements shown here to build an Active Directory schema that suits your enterprise. This design is one of the key initial projects that should be undertaken when you are considering a move to Windows 2000. With the help of the information in this chapter and the chapters that follow, you should be armed with enough information to make good decisions the first time around and to identify and eliminate problems before they exist.

What Is Active Directory?

Let's be honest—a lot of mystique has grown up around Active Directory and what it is. So let's cut through that mystique right away. Active Directory is a database. This database is distributed to Active Directory servers so that access to the data is more efficient (and you have some level of fault tolerance). Of course, it is somewhat more complex than this, but sometimes it helps to have a handle on what the grass roots functionality truly is.

Like most databases, the types and amount of data that gets stored in Active Directory can vary. All of the necessary protocols and application interfaces that are required to allow updates to the data, deletion of information, and customization of data are supplied. Active Directory essentially ends the need for some of the proprietary name resolution methods that Microsoft has used in the past. So expect to see Windows Internet Naming System (WINS) used less and less in the future.

Active Directory is also known as a directory service. That is, it is a set of Windows 2000 services and processes that maintain and operate a directory on your network. The directory stores information about network resources. Each identified resource is stored as an *object* in Active Directory. Figure 7.1 gives you some examples of the types of information that you need to have stored in Active Directory. Along with each object name you will see some typical information that you might want to be stored along with the object.

Each object has a set of attributes (also referred to as *properties*). For instance, a user object will have attributes such as first name, last name, and telephone number. Different types of objects have a distinct set of attributes. An example would be a printer that does not have a requirement for a first name, last name attribute. However, it might have a unique set of attributes, such as whether it supports color printing.

We will be taking a closer look at the specific elements that make up the Active Directory later in this chapter. However, for the moment, keep in mind that it is simply a distributed database of information regarding the resources on your network.

If you are already familiar with a previous version of Microsoft Windows NT, then you can think of Active Directory as an extension of the SAM. However, the SAM in previous versions was not extensible, and its replication model was crude. You will soon see that Active Directory offers a far greater level of granularity, and you can even add custom objects to it.

There are two distinct pieces to an Active Directory design. The first is a logical design. This design will take into account the specific needs of your organization. It will most likely follow a similar pattern to the organizational chart in your enterprise, although this is not necessarily the case. The second

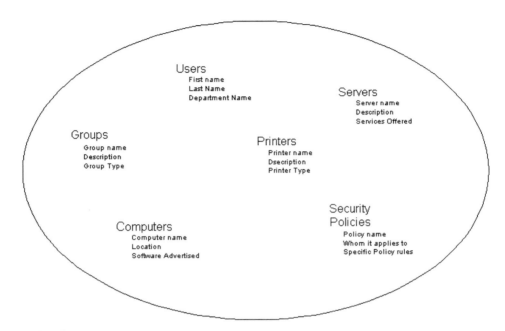

Users
First name
Last Name
Department Name

Servers
Server name
Description
Services Offered

Groups
Group name
Description
Group Type

Printers
Printer name
Dsecription
Printer Type

Security
Policies
Policy name
Whom it applies to
Specific Policy rules

Computers
Computer name
Location
Software Advertised

Figure 7–1   *Typical objects in Active Directory.*

element is the physical design. This design takes into account the realities of the underlying network. More specifically, if you have two buildings, each with its own LAN, and you have only a dialup connection between them—this would need to be taken into account. All of this and more will be discussed in this and later chapters.

Where Did Active Directory Come From?

Because the purpose of this chapter is to take a look at Active Directory, I won't spend a lot of time discussing its history and origins. Having said that, having an understanding of the origins of Active Directory will give you a glimpse into why it is so important and why other software vendors have either already implemented a directory service or are about to adapt to using one.

If you take a moment to think about the typical Microsoft network, you will soon realize that it contains a lot of duplicated effort. Let's take the example of user accounts. Every user of a Windows NT network (and, for that matter, of a Windows 2000 network) requires a user account. This account is used so that the individual can logon and be assigned any permissions to which they are entitled. This user account is quite separate from their email account. If you have Microsoft Exchange on your network, a completely different account will have to be created so that the messaging system can validate you. The same goes for Microsoft SQL Server. Add into that any custom applications you have—such as accounting systems, expense systems and the like—and you probably end up with four or five user accounts that you have to remember.

Even if your network personnel or software vendors have done a good job of hiding all of this from you (through pass-through authentication or cookies), the fact remains that someone, somewhere, has to look after all of these user accounts. What's more, the security policies for all of these accounts are probably different. That's why your network logon account expires every 90 days, yet your email password changes every 30 days. That's a lot of work!

Why is it this way? Because the methods that each of these systems uses to record and store data about users are completely different, and no one has yet come up with a way to make them compatible with each other. That was until the idea of directory services gained prominence. If there existed a single place where passwords and security policies could be set—think of all the administrative overhead that could be eliminated. That means money savings for organizations, and when you're talking about saving money, you can believe that something will change!

The most common analogy for a directory service is a telephone book. If we need a telephone number for someone, we pick up a book of data (telephone numbers) and we search through the alphabetical list of names until we find the one we want. That telephone book is also known as a telephone *directory*. It's a simple idea, but very effective.

A computer directory service is basically the same thing. However, it offers the additional piece that makes it really interesting—it also defines a method that can be used to do the searching for you—automatically. What's more, unlike a telephone directory, you are also given the functions that allow you to add to it or to delete entries on the fly—actually, just about everything that you would expect a computer to be able to do.

Now imagine being able to have an enormous database of all the resources on your network that can be distributed to the places where they are needed most. Think of a database that updates itself and replicates changes in the background, and you have a pretty good idea of what Active Directory is bringing to the table. However, we're getting a little bit ahead of ourselves.

If you look back at the history of PC computing, you can see that we have taken some steps toward achieving this goal in the past. In the early days of PC networking every server would have a database of user names. If a user needed to access data on more than one server, you would have to create an account for them on each one. Microsoft Windows NT improved upon this model by allowing users to have a single account and for that account to be granted permissions to access resources on all servers on the network. This is illustrated in Figure 7.2. However, the central account database (known as the SAM) could not be used by other application vendors and, to be quite frank, didn't scale to large enterprises very well. Active Directory is a worthy successor to these early efforts.

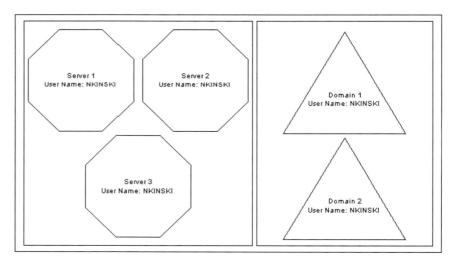

Figure 7–2   *Older directory models.*

Microsoft is not the first to implement a directory service. In fact, we have to go back to 1988 to read about the first attempts to define a standard for them. You see, designing a system that allows a directory service to work is important, but having all directory services from different vendors adhering to the same standard will have a more far-reaching effect on all of us.

The standard in question is known as *X.500.* This standard was defined and approved by the International Telecommunication Union (ITU) and the International Organization for Standardization (ISO) in 1988. This was followed several years later by a revision to the standard. This revision added some standards for additional functionality, such as replication of data and access control.

X.500 has, to this point, been used primarily for messaging systems. What exactly does it define? From the point of view of Active Directory, the X.500 standard defines a hierarchical structure for the data. It also includes standards for searching that data, creating namespaces that can scale to sizes required in enterprise networking, along with the data structure that the information should be stored in. Of course, this is not an exhaustive list of what is defined—that is beyond the scope of this book—but it is important to note that Active Directory is based on this long-defined standard.

The model defined by X.500 is hierarchical. You will see this time and again in the chapters of this book that relate to Active Directory. Let's be more specific about what we mean by *hierarchical.* The analogy that most people use to describe what an X.500 (and therefore an Active Directory) hierarchy looks like is that of an inverted tree. An inverted tree is a tree with the root at the top and the branches reaching down below it. Those branches that have other branches are known as *container objects,* and while branches that do not

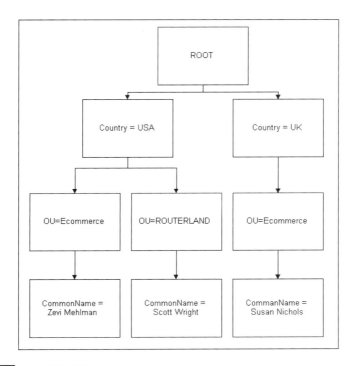

Figure 7-3   *An X.500 directory.*

have anything growing from them are known a *noncontainer objects.* Just to
keep the analogy true, noncontainer objects are also known as *leaf nodes*.

It might be a good idea to take a look at Figure 7.3 to see what this all
means. In this figure, you are presented with a simple but fairly typical view of
an X.500 directory. You should note that there is a root at the top (and only one
root) and that everything else is a branch off that root.

The hierarchy shown in Figure 7.3, looks a lot like a DNS hierarchy. By
stating an object's name, along with a list of all objects to which it is attached—
up to the root—you can uniquely identify objects. Naming conventions will be
covered later in this chapter.

X.500 standards go a lot deeper than simply defining a hierarchy. They
also define some standard container objects. These standard objects include
Organization, Organization Unit, and Country. They also define some standard
noncontainer objects. These objects cannot contain other objects. As mentioned previously, these are also known as *leaf objects*.

Although directories can have containers in addition to these types, it is
important to recognize that international standardization can be achieved by
their adoption. Standardization is what X.500 really brings to the table. We can-

not overemphasize the importance of the difference between objects that can contain other objects, and objects that cannot. As you will see later in this chapter, a process known as *inheritance* allows properties that are set for objects higher in a hierarchy to pass down through the tree. This allows for uniform administration. (Just to make things really interesting in Active Directory, it is also possible to block inheritance.)

So is it safe to assume that Active Directory is fully X.500 compliant? Actually, no! The reasons for this are many-fold. Not least among them is that the X.500 standard, although in theory is a great idea, in practice is somewhat rooted in the time and technology that was current while it was being defined. An example of this would be the emergence of TCP/IP as the world's preferred protocol. When X.500 was in its design phase, other protocols were being used. Today's X.500-compatible directories have taken the basic architecture but used different protocols to achieve functionality, such as directory searches.

Active Directory and Open Standard Support

Microsoft has done a lot of work to make Active Directory integrate into Windows 2000. Fortunately, some of the underlying protocols and specifications have been with us for some time. By building Active Directory around these open standards, Microsoft has ensured a broad range of support from day one. Not only are the technologies already well understood, but third-party vendors will quickly be able to adapt their tools and utilities to work with it.

Three key technologies utilized by Active Directory are:

• Domain Name System (DNS)
• Lightweight Directory Access Protocol (LDAP)
• Hypertext Transfer Protocol (HTTP)
• Naming schemes

In case you are not aware of the significance of each of these technologies, here is brief discussion of each. Even if you know about them, give the following descriptions a glance because Microsoft has adopted some critical new functionality to complement what you might already know.

DNS

If you are going to be an IT professional, you must know what DNS is used for. The answer is name resolution. Previous versions of Microsoft's network operating systems have used various methods of providing name resolution, but Windows 2000 is the first to be built around DNS specifically.

The primary reason DNS exists is to resolve names, such as *www.prenhall.com*, to the IP address that is needed in order to route to the website. Without this resolution, you would never be able to find websites or, in Win-

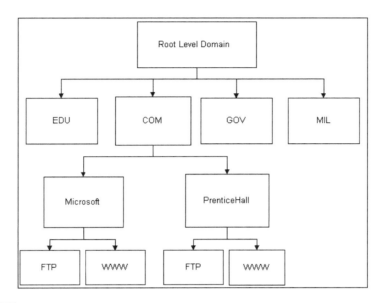

Figure 7–4   *The DNS hierarchy.*

dows 2000, any server on the network. DNS is important, so much so that we gave it its own chapter later in this book.

Windows 2000 domain names are DNS names. DNS is used to provide a naming scheme and for name resolution. Because DNS is a system that is widely employed on the Internet, the syntax of names is already familiar to many people.

In fact, the hierarchical nature of DNS echoes many of the concepts you will see in Active Directory. Figure 7.4 shows the DNS hierarchy. Although DNS is designed to store a smaller amount of information, the concept is the same.

However, Microsoft has gone a step further by utilizing an important extension to DNS, Dynamic DNS (DDNS). If you are familiar with WINS, you will appreciate what this new feature brings to the table. DDNS allows clients to register with a DNS server when they are started. When they register, the DNS tables are automatically updated. This feature, although not essential for the functioning of Active Directory, will nonetheless reduce the amount of administration you will have to do. So much so, in fact, that we're going to go as far as to say that if your DNS server does not support DDNS, don't use it! Fortunately, the version of DNS that ships with Windows 2000 is ready to go.

Eventually, DDNS will eliminate the need for WINS servers (in fact, WINS is being kept around in Windows 2000 only for the purposes of backward compatibility—in a full Windows 2000 network, there is no need for WINS). It is important that you note that Active Directory cannot work without DNS. If you attempt to install Active Directory without it, the installation will pause and you will be asked to install DNS before you can proceed.

Finally, a DNS server must include support for SRV records. These records are entries in the DNS tables that help clients locate a specific service on the network. In this case, that service is likely to be a domain controller. Again, those familiar with WINS will have seen this functionality before. Its addition to DNS is a huge step toward reducing the number of name resolution processes you need to maintain on your network. DNS is such an important topic that we have dedicated an entire chapter to it later in this book.

LDAP

As we have already explained, Active Directory is a directory service that stores information on network resources. However, this is only half of the story. What is also needed is a quick and easy way to search through the data for the objects you want. This is the job of LDAP. LDAP is an Internet standard. Clients use LDAP to communicate with Active Directory.

LDAP itself comes with a set of standards that are published on the Internet. One of the requirements of LDAP is that the underlying directory adhere to a particular naming scheme. The naming scheme is loosely based on X.500. In LDAP naming, a domain (and we're talking about a domain as in an Internet domain, not a Windows 2000 domain) is referred to as a *DC* (domain component.) So, in LDAP terms, *ph.books.printer* can also be referred to as *DC=ph, DC=books, DC=printer.*

Although LDAP is a good standard, those of you who love to code and want to access Active Directory data for your own use might find it worth investigating Active Directory Services Interface (ADSI). This is a proprietary API that Microsoft has come up with to access Active Directory. On the other hand, give LDAP a look. If you learn the intricacies of the LDAP API, you will be able to use that skill to access an entire range of directory services.

HTTP

HTTP is a protocol that most people are familiar with from using web browsers. HTTP is the commonly used protocol for displaying web pages. In the case of Active Directory, HTTP is used to display objects as HTML data in any web browser. This is convenient for users because they are already familiar with browsing information in their web browsers. This is achieved through Active Server Pages and ADSI. Unfortunately, an in-depth discussion of these is beyond the scope of this book.

Naming Schemes

Active Directory supports several different naming schemes. Support of these schemes ensures that both users and developers can continue to use standards and syntax with which they are already familiar. The standards supported under Windows 2000 include:

HTTP URL: This naming is in the form http://*domain/site*.

LDAP URL: This naming is in the form LDAP://whatever/PH.COM/CN=phone, *OU*=admin, DC=IT. In this case, *CN* stands for *Container*, *OU* for *Organizational Unit,* and *DC* for *Domain container*.

RFC 822: This naming scheme is most commonly seen in email systems. An example would be fbloggs@domain.

UNC: This naming scheme has long been supported in Microsoft operating systems. An example would be \\servername\sharename.

What Are the Real Benefits?

Well you might be thinking that this is all well and good—but why should you even care? Isn't life complicated enough without adding all this complexity? Well, as you will see, the benefits of Active Directory are very real and very important.

First, a full directory service such as Active Directory can be a repository for all kinds of information, not simply of relating to user names and passwords. As we talked about earlier, the fact that there exists on your network many different types of directories that store different yet related information is very inefficient. Active Directory will allow vendors to bring this data under a single, uniform umbrella. Expect this to be a major push for all Microsoft products in the future. Integration with Active Directory—where appropriate—will undoubtedly take place.

You will find that administration has been much simplified. This is especially true in networks that have multiple domains and trust relationships. With previous versions of Microsoft's Windows NT operating systems, the number of trust relationships required quickly got out of hand. This is shown in Figure 7.5. In this case, there are four domains with a complete trust relationship between them. You will notice that this meant that twelve trusts had to be created. Many large corporations have far more than four domains!

In Active Directory, this domain model changes radically. Domains remain as part of the model, but when additional domains are added to Active Directory, an automatic two-way trust is created between them. Trusts are also transitive, meaning that you can build paths between domains without explicitly having to create trusts between every one of them. Domains serve as basic units for administration and security.

More importantly, each domain essentially exists under one umbrella and can be centrally managed. Given sufficient security rights, it is an easy matter to administer multiple domains from a single point in the network. Without the overhead of managing trust relationships, you will be able to enjoy far greater flexibility and ease of management.

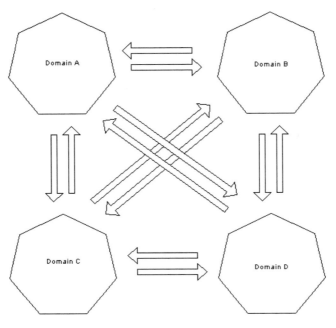

Figure 7-5

A complete trust relationship in Microsoft Windows NT 4.0 with four domains.

We also spoke earlier about inheritance. It is possible to assign policies to objects higher in the Active Directory hierarchy and have those policies filter down to all objects below that point. With careful planning it is possible to use this technique to simplify your enterprise administration further.

In current Microsoft networks, the mere act of an employee moving from one part of an organization to another can cause a lot of work for the already overburdened administrator. If a new office has its own domain, then, at the very least, the administrator would have to create a new account for the user. Along with this, necessary group membership has to be defined. Old account details in the previous domain have to be deleted. This is no longer true in Active Directory. It is entirely possible to drag and drop users from one domain to another. You can even perform this feat with user groups.

Imagine being able to take the next step and have applications assigned to users! It is likely that an employee in the Finance Department requires access to one particular set of applications, whereas members of the Personnel Department have their own unique set of requirements. When a user is moved from one department to another, it is very difficult to make sure that necessary programs are installed and that unnecessary ones are removed—not so with Active Directory. Through the use of Group Policy Objects (discussed later in this book), it is possible to have user's computers automatically configured to take such moves into account. That includes the installation and de-installation of the software. If you have spent any time at all working as a system administrator in a large (or even not so large) enterprise, you can begin to see the true potential already.

For those already familiar with the nuts and bolts of previous versions of Microsoft server products, here are some more specific items that you will find interesting. Domain Controllers (DCs) were also common network resources in previous versions of Microsoft Windows NT. However, although their function remains similar in Windows 2000, their method of accomplishing their task has changed. This is because all domain controllers in Windows 2000 are peers—or, in the verbiage of previous versions, they each act like as though they are a Primary Domain Controller (PDC).

This means that each domain controller maintains a complete replica of the Active Directory. When a change needs to be made in the Active Directory—such as a password change—the change can take place at the nearest domain controller. The domain controller will then see to it that the changes are replicated to all of the other domain controllers.

Because the Active Directory allows you to log in at one point on your network and be assigned permissions over all domains, you will quickly realize the benefits of its distributed nature.

Another area to which Active Directory brings much improvement is scalability. The method used to store Active Directory data means that it work efficiently for small organizations with a few hundred objects, as well as for large organizations with millions of objects. You will see more on this as you read through the following chapters.

The Structure of the Active Directory

Hopefully you are already becoming convinced that Active Directory is going to be an extremely useful and significant tool for your network. Until this point, we have spoken in generalities about its form and function. It's time to get into the specifics of what makes Active Directory work. In the following sections, we will introduce all of the major components that make up the Active Directory. Along with each component, we will give you a description and briefly discuss how the component fits into the schema of Active Directory. More detail will be added in subsequent chapters. This information is going to be essential if you are going to take the next step to both designing and implementing Active Directory on your own network. Take the time to read the rest of this chapter; it will pay big dividends later, we promise!

The Basics of Active Directory

Before we get into the details of the components of Active Directory, we should first make sure that we have some basic definitions in place. These definitions answer questions such as, What is an object? and What is a container? We have already used these terms generically but, once you start to get down to the specifics of Active Directory, a clear definition will make sure that you fully understand what we are talking about.

WHAT IS AN OBJECT?

An object is a unit that describes a set of attributes. An object represents something solid, such as a user, group, or printer. Different objects will have different sets of attributes. As discussed earlier, some objects have been defined as part of the X.500 specification. It is, however, quite possible to add custom objects to Active Directory.

WHAT ARE ATTRIBUTES?

Attributes are a set of data that describes an object. Typical attributes of a user would be last name, first name. The number of attributes can have an effect on the amount data that has to be replicated to all domain controllers. All objects will have at least one attribute. You might also see the term *properties* to describe the same thing.

CONTAINERS

A container is an object that can contain other objects. In this way, you can build a hierarchy of containers that make up the Active Directory. Inheritance takes advantage of this characteristic. The most common analogy is that of folders and files. Folders contain files; therefore, a folder is a container. A file cannot contain other objects and, therefore, is known as a *noncontainer* or *leaf* object.

The previous three terms can easily be defined by way of a figure. Figure 7.6 shows each of these terms and how they relate to each other.

OBJECT NAMES

Every object within the directory must have a name. Because Active Directory is hierarchical in nature, names can be expressed as *object name/relative path to the root*. Unlike previous versions of Microsoft Windows NT, you can have objects with duplicate names within Active Directory. However, in this case, the relative name *must* be different. This is illustrated in Figure 7.7. In this figure, you can see that there are three user objects with the same name. However, their relative names to the root are different and, therefore, valid.

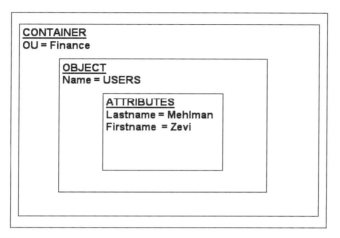

Figure 7–6 *How Objects, Attributes and Containers relate to each other.*

There are two different kinds of names. One name identifies the object and its relative path through the containers of the Active Directory. The other name is stored as an attribute of the object and simply specifies the name without the relative path. The former is known as the *Distinguished Name*. In the context of Figure 7.7, the Distinguished Name of user NKINSKI in the West Domain is /O=ACME/DC=WEST/CN=Users/CN=NKINSKI. Because the Domain of each user is different, their paths back to the organization will always be unique.

The latter type of name is known as the *Relative Distinguished Name*. In the example given in Figure 7.7, the Relative Distinguished Name of NKINSKI in the West Domain is simply CN=NKINSKI.

These definitions are usually for reference. However, you'll be more likely to remember them once you see how they operate in context. As we go through the rest of this chapter, you will be presented with figures and examples that show these terms being used in Active Directory designs. Over time, their use will become second nature.

Physical versus the Logical Structure

If we were to list simply the various elements that are used in the Active Directory and leave it at that, we would be doing a disservice. It is important that you realize that there are two considerations you will need to think about before completing your Active Directory design. First, Active Directory will have to provide you with a logical view of your organization. Its form and function must adhere to your needs. There are several models you can follow, one of which is simply to take a look at the organizational chart for your enterprise. Usually, an organizational chart will quickly suggest ways to group users

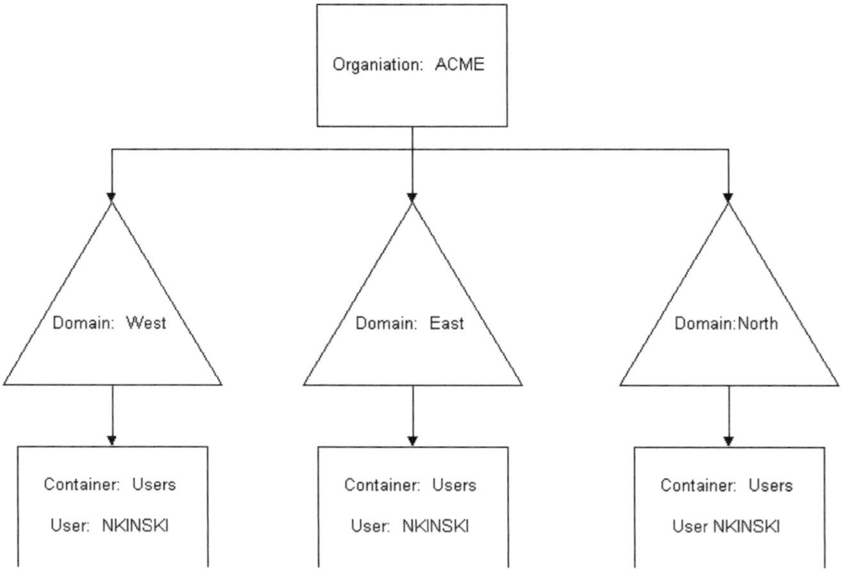

Figure 7–7 *Duplicate User Object names.*

together. You can use Active Directory to group computer accounts and assign administrative permissions in the same way.

On the other hand, you cannot simply ignore the real world. The real world does not adhere itself to this nice logical view. Although it might be a good idea to group your Finance Department in one group, the reality might be that half of the Finance staff is 3,000 miles away from the rest of the team.

So, Active Directory works at two levels: the physical level, which very much takes the real-world consideration of servers, routers, and link speeds into account, and the logical view, which is a representation of how you want to manage objects within your Active Directory. By the way, notice how I slipped the word *object* into that last sentence. I could just as easily have said *users* or *groups*, but to stick with Active Directory terminology, you can describe everything and anything in the Active Directory by referring to *objects*.

The Physical

The physical aspects of your network are not a limiting factor in your Active Directory design. However, they have to be taken into account. If you recall our brief discussion earlier, you will have noted that, unlike in previous versions of Microsoft's Windows NT product, each DC in Active Directory is a peer. Changes can be made to any one of them. It is then the responsibility of that DC to make sure the changes that it just received are distributed to every other DC. To optimize and understand the ramifications of this process, you need an accurate read on the underlying network.

DOMAIN CONTROLLERS

A DC is a computer on a Windows 2000 network that keeps an updatable copy of the Active Directory. This can then be used to authenticate users when they log in to the network or to accept changes to the Active Directory and make sure that all other DCs record any such changes. You probably are somewhat familiar with the concept of DCs from previous versions of Microsoft Windows NT. However, in the case of previous versions, there was a master DC called a *Primary Domain Controller* (PDC). It was the job of the PDC to keep the master copy of the SAM and to ensure that other Backup Domain Controllers (BDCs) had an up-to-date copy. This is not the case in Active Directory—all DCs are peers. They keep a full copy of the Active Directory, which can be changed at each DC. These changes are then propagated around the network. This will be discussed in more detail later in the chapter.

SITE

A *site* can be defined as a piece of your network that has fast connectivity. In more specific terms, a site is defined by IP subnets. It can even be a group of more than one IP subnet. (Don't forget, TCP/IP is a requirement of Active Directory; you cannot run Active Directory without first installing TCP/IP.)

You might be familiar with the concept of sites through other BackOffice applications, such as Microsoft Exchange 5.5 and Microsoft Systems Management Server 2.0 (SMS 2.0.) Exchange actually uses a different site model. These two concepts will be aligned in future releases. The site concept in SMS 2.0 is, in fact, very similar, so if you have used it, you have a head start here.

Sites are a necessity because no matter how good a job you do in designing your Active Directory security and administrative models, you have to adhere to the considerations and limitations of your network. By getting a good grasp of sites, you will be primed to understand not only *what* Active Directory does, but *how* it does it.

Why do we need sites? Because we need some control over how Active Directory moves data around. Let's think for a moment about the impact of having all DCs acting as peers. In a large enterprise with a distributed administrative staff, hundreds of administrative tasks could be going on at the same time. Users are being added to the system, passwords are changing, groups are being created and users are being added to them, new servers are being installed, and old ones are being decommissioned. Active Directory has to keep track of all of this data, and each DC has to make sure that any new information it has is sent to every other DC in the enterprise. That's a pretty daunting task—but Active Directory is up to it.

All of this data moving around is referred to as *replication*. As you might imagine, replication takes place much faster within a site. Once the new data has to traverse slow links (the very definition of a site being a piece of the network with fast links), it will take more managing.

But wait, there's more! Sites actually have another very important use—they help in ensuring that the DC that validates a user logging in to the network is actually closest to them. This is important, because being validated by a DC across a slow link is inefficient. When an IP address is assigned via a Dynamic Host Configuration Protocol (DHCP) server, the DC locator uses this IP information to find a DC in the same site. Of course, this also works for those clients that have statically assigned IP addresses.

These two tasks—replication of Active Directory data and validation of user logins—are the primary reason Microsoft has implemented the concept of a site. We will be looking at the replication process in a later chapter. Figure 7.8 shows two Windows 2000 domains that due to physical necessity, are broken into three sites.

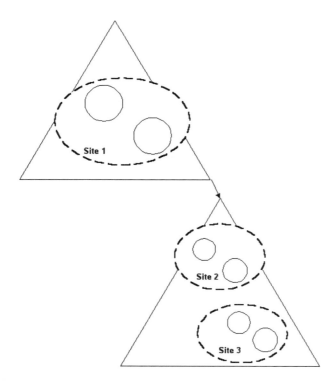

Figure 7–8   *Two Windows 2000 domains with three sites.*

The Logical

The logical elements of Active Directory are the pieces that you can more easily meld into whatever shape you want. Although it is important not to dismiss the physical aspects of Active Directory design, it will be the area of logical design that you will make your most important decisions.

This section does not attempt to provide you with extensive information on planning your Active Directory structure. It will, however, introduce the various elements that you have to work with. As you move through this and subsequent chapters on Active Directory, the terms defined here will begin to fall into place. We realize that it can be difficult to memorize long lists of names and definitions, but we hope the following pages will act as both an introduction and a reference point, should you need to refresh your memory in the future.

The following sections will cover these Active Directory terms:

- Domains
- Trees
- Forests
- Organizational Units (OU)
- Schema
- Global Catalog (GC)
- Namespace
- Replication

Once you have read and understood this terminology, you will be ready for the next step—taking a look at how to design an Active Directory hierarchy.

DOMAINS IN ACTIVE DIRECTORY

Contrary to what you might have imagined, domains still play a central role in Windows 2000. In fact, they constitute the basic building blocks of the logical structure of Active Directory. You might be used to the concept of domains in Microsoft Windows NT 4.0. In previous versions, a domain could be described as a unit of administration. Logins to the network were controlled by domains, user accounts were tied to domains, and security was set at the domain level. Some of these things are very similar in Windows 2000, whereas others have a new twist.

In Windows 2000—and, more specifically, in Active Directory—a *domain* can be defined as a piece of the namespace that can be used to set security boundaries. Much as you have seen in previous versions, domains are an independent parcel of the Active Directory. To illustrate this, let's look at the concept of DCs. DCs are specific to a domain. Each DC within a domain keeps a complete copy of the directory for that domain. They replicate changes to other DCs—but never to DCs outside of their domain. This is shown in Figure

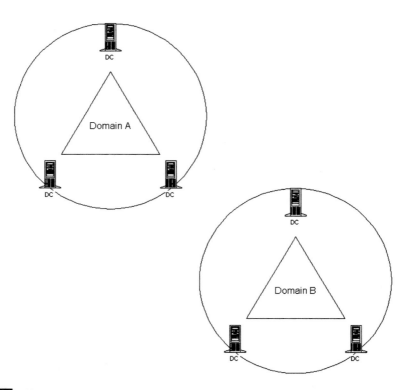

Figure 7-9   *Two domains with their own DCs.*

7.9. In this figure, you see two domains with their own DCs. Data is not transferred between these two sets of DCs

Therefore, you can think of a domain as an island within your Active Directory. They operate somewhat independently, they can be administered independently of other domains, and you can set security policies at this level.

As you will see in a moment, it doesn't end there. Domains can be further sub-divided into OUs. Using OUs gives you the ability to set a much finer degree of control over your Active Directory objects.

If you have more than one domain in your Active Directory, they will each have trust relationships (which are created automatically). These trusts are two-way trusts and are *transitive*. This trust relationship is shown in Figure 7.10. In this figure, there is a trust between domain A and domain B. There is also a trust between domain B and domain C. In previous versions of Microsoft's network operating systems, a trust between A and C was not implied. If you wanted such a trust, you would have had to create it as a separate entity. However, transitive trusts in Windows 2000 means that this trust is implied.

Because domains store only data about their own objects, you can use them to partition your objects to facilitate scalability. By partitioning your

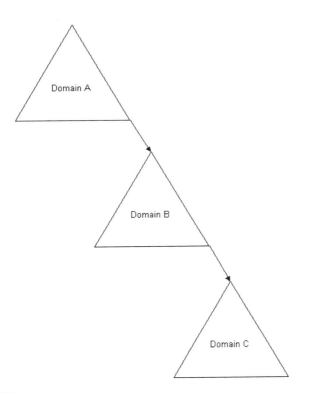

Figure 7–10   *Three domains with transitive trusts.*

objects in this manner, you can create an Active Directory hierarchy that contains as many objects as you want.

Security policies and administrative permissions can still be set at the domain level. This is an important issue if you have many domains within your Active Directory hierarchy. It will allow you a logical way to view your security model. Although domains have transitive trusts, these security policies and administrative permissions are not carried over from one domain to another.

Don't forget that the physical layout of your network need not be the boundaries for your Windows 2000 domains. Physical boundary issues are resolved through sites, which we discussed earlier.

Domains in a tree, when viewed in a hierarchy are said to share the same namespace. The first domain installed in Active Directory is known as the *root domain*. This is shown in Figure 7.11.

One thing to remember —because there are two-way transitive trusts between all domains, you can logon from anywhere on you network and get authenticated. In previous versions of Microsoft's network operating systems, this was only if the administrators c network designers had created all the necessary trusts themselves. This is a huge benefit to Windows 2000 and guarantees ease c administration.

In an ideal Active Directory design, there would be only one domain. A single domain in Active Directory can contain some 10 million objects. However, if this is not enough or if there are other considerations, you can create multiple domains and join them into a tree.

TREE

A tree is a hierarchy of domains. For domains to be part of a tree, there are some conditions that are implied. Domains in a tree share the same schema and configuration. They also exist in the same namespace.

A tree will show how different domains interrelate. You can easily see the relationship between objects when they are shown in a tree. It is also possible to figure out the path between two objects or a set of objects. Essentially, a tree enables people to understand Active Directory, even when the concept or structure is new to them or different from their everyday understanding of their network or organization. An example of a tree is shown in Figure 7.11. In this figure, we show three domains that form a tree. Notice the names of each of the three domains. Each domain in the hierarchy is given a name. This name is shown along with a path back to the root domain. This resembles a DNS hierarchy.

If a group of domains shares the same naming hierarchy—as we have shown in Figure 7.11, they are considered to share the same namespace. Each Active Directory you create will have a root domain (the first domain installed). Domains that exist beneath this root domain are considered to be *child domains*. Domains that are above other domains in a hierarchy are called, not surprisingly, *parent domains*.

On the smallest scale, a tree can exist when there is only one domain. However, it is easier to illustrate a tree when there are multiple domains. As you migrate your older network operating systems over to Windows 2000, you will need to determine how many domains you need. In an ideal world, we would all have a single domain. However, this is not always practical.

FOREST

So what happens if you have a company with a registered DNS name, for example, WIDGETS.COM, which you have used as your domain name in Active Directory, and you suddenly purchase a company with an Active Directory called GROWNUP.COM? This poses something of a problem, because

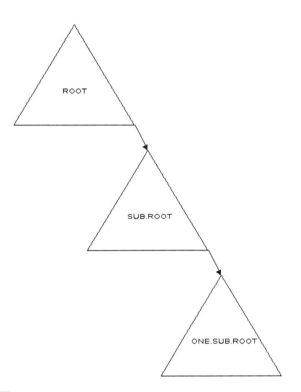

Figure 7-11   *An example of a tree.*

GROWNUP.COM already has its own Active Directory tree. Well, never fear, you could always create a forest.

A forest is created when you combine trees. The same rules for domains within a tree apply to trees within a forest. Each tree that will participate in a forest must share the same schema and configuration. When you join two trees into a forest, you end up with two root domains. These two root domains are connected via a two-way transitive trust. The forest is known by the name of the first tree created. Once a forest is created, users can access resources in their own tree and in other trees in the forest.

Forests are to be discouraged. Searching for data within a forest can be problematic and can take a long time. Users performing LDAP searches can search only for objects within their own tree. To search for objects within a forest, you must query GC servers. Global Catalog servers are defined later in this chapter.

ORGANIZATIONAL UNITS

An OU is a container object that exists within a domain. Objects that are created within an OU include users, groups, and printers (among other things). OUs really are one of the key areas where you will have to focus a lot of attention when designing your Active Directory. It is OUs that truly extend the functionality of Windows 2000 domains beyond their previous capabilities.

You can use OUs for many things. An example of a good use for an OU would be a department of twenty-five people who want to have their own system administrator. The administrator will have permissions to administer the people within the department, but nowhere else in the company. In this case, it would be a simple matter to create an OU for the department and to assign administrator permissions to that OU—and only that OU within Active Directory.

OUs can be used to partition different groups of objects together. Once they are grouped, you can apply policies to that OU. OUs form a hierarchy within a domain. Then, through a process called *inheritance,* access rights given at the topmost level of the hierarchy can be allowed to flow down throughout the entire hierarchy.

You might decide to recreate your organizational structure within a domain through the use of OUs. This would allow you to have a good logical view of your network. Alternatively, it might be more beneficial for you to base your design solely on the network administrative model you are going to use.

Windows 2000 makes it very easy to move or copy objects from one OU to another. You will see examples of this later in this book. With this flexibility, along with the ability to assign permissions at the OU level and have it inherited, you will find that you will be able to design an infrastructure that will save you time and reduce the total cost of ownership (TCO).

To realize these benefits you will need to create an OU plan and use it across all domains. All domains within a tree do not have to adhere to the same OU structure, but if they do, you will find administration easier, and future changes to your plans will be easier to accommodate.

SCHEMA

The schema defines which objects can exist within the directory and which attributes those objects can have. You might also see the term *class* in this regard. A class is a list of attributes that an object of a specific type either must contain or can optionally contain. For instance, the user object (which also can be referred to as the *user class*) can contain a first name attribute.

It is also possible within the schema to define what types of data an attribute can hold (for instance, a telephone number attribute must contain only numeric data). Keep in mind that the schema can be extended. That is, attributes can be added to the basic schema.

THE GLOBAL CATALOG

We have spoken a lot about Active Directory and all the data that it can contain. However, that is only half of the story. To really get down to it, how does Active Directory manage to scale when hundreds, and possibly tens of thousands, of users are trying to query all that data at the same time? The answer is the GC.

The GC is a storage for a subset of Active Directory data for domains in a tree and/or forest. DCs that were discussed earlier are concerned with only data within their respective domains; GCs reach out across all domains. A GC will answer user requests for searches against the Active Directory data.

GCs facilitate the scalability of Active Directory. Imagine for a moment the situation that would exist without them. Let's say that you have a tree with three domains in it, Domain A, Domain B, and Domain C. A user in Domain C wants to query for data in Domain A. Without GCs that user would have to send a query to Domain A directly. That domain could be a long way away, across one or more slow links. Once you multiply this by many users, you can see that the amount of traffic that would be generated would soon become prohibitive. GCs solve this problem by having a server local to the users that can answer these queries without the client having to traverse the network to resolve the query. Think of the GC as DCs for an entire tree or forest. In Windows NT 4.0 parlance, think of a GC as a type of BDC.

Now, given the amount of data that could be contained within Active Directory (especially if you have a forest), it should be clear that the GC does not contain all the data in Active Directory. Instead, it contains a subset of data. This data is read-only, which ensures that GCs do not get bogged down when changes are made within Active Directory. Although an entry for every object is contained within the GC, not every attribute of the object is stored there. In fact, the only attributes that are stored are those that are most likely to be searched for.

Earlier, we spoke about the difference between LDAP searches and queries to the GC. Remember that if a query is made to the GC and the search for data fails, the query will be made via LDAP. The LDAP query will search only the local tree—not the entire forest. The only way to absolutely prevent this from happening is to make sure that you have only a single domain tree.

At first you might get confused about the difference between a GC and a DC. The difference is that DCs contain an updatable copy of the Active Directory data for the domain to which they belong. GCs contain a read-only subset of Active Directory for the entire tree or forest.

NAMESPACE

A namespace, in the context of Active Directory, is any space that can be resolved to a name. Using the analogy given earlier of a telephone directory, a telephone directory is a namespace in which the names and telephone numbers of telephone subscribers can be resolved.

In Active Directory, every object can be resolved to a name. Therefore, Active Directory is said to be a namespace for these objects. Namespace becomes doubly important in Active Directory terms, because it is also used in the process of defining the scope of replication.

REPLICATION

Earlier in this chapter, a DC was defined as "a computer on a Windows 2000 network that keeps an updatable copy of the Active Directory." All DCs are peers, which means that, in terms of Microsoft Windows NT 4.0, each DC acts as though it is the PDC. This type of replication is known as *multimaster replication;* this is because each DC is acting as though it is the master for the Active Directory data.

Well, that's easy to say, but how does Windows 2000 deal with managing the process of keeping each DC up to date? If any DC can make a change to Active Directory, it means that there must be a mechanism in place to make sure that the change gets propagated through the network to all other DCs—not to mention GCs.

Windows 2000 has built-in, automatic replication of this information to all DCs and GCs. There is more than one process in place to make this happen, because sometimes there might be special circumstances that mean a change cannot be made. For instance, what if a user changes their password twice in a short period of time? And what if each of those changes is made on different DCs? How does Windows 2000 decide which is the most recent change?

One way this could have been achieved would have been to follow a model used by previous versions of directory services. These versions used timestamps to make sure that the most recent change was written to the Directory. However, in today's dispersed environments, where DCs might be over relatively slow links and in different time zones, the task of making sure that all computers have their time synchronized proves to be quite difficult. Instead, Microsoft has employed two methods to ensure accuracy of information in Active Directory.

UPDATED SEQUENCE NUMBER

The Updated Sequence Number (USN) is a 64-bit number that is maintained by each DC. Whenever a change is made to the Active Directory the USN is incremented and written, along with the property that is being changed. The process of incrementing the USN and storing it along with the property being changed is guaranteed. This means that if any of the three processes—the incrementing of the USN, the storing of the changed property, or the storing of the USN along with that property change, fails, then they are all considered to have failed.

Each DC stores a table that records the USNs from other DCs. Every time an update is received from another DC, a USN accompanies the update. This table records the highest-valued USN from the DC sending the change.

When a replication partner informs a DC that replication is required (changes need to be propagated), the replication partner will return only those changes with a higher USN than that stored in the USN table. This is a very effective way of making sure that unnecessary data is not transferred over your network. This entire process is discussed in more detail in the next chapter.

PROPERTY VERSION NUMBERS

Our discussion thus far has dealt with simple updates to the Active Directory and the method used to propagate those changes to all DCs in the domain. But what if a user's password is changed on two DCs at the same time?

This issue is dealt with by the use of Property Version Numbers (PVN). A PVN can be thought of as a partner of the USN. The main difference is that USNs are stored and managed by each DC in the domain and are server-specific (each DC has its own set of USNs). PVNs, on the other hand, are stored as part of the property in Active Directory.

Replication is an important topic, and its intricacies can be quite complex. In fact, it is so important that we have dedicated an entire chapter to discuss it. The introduction here gives you some idea of how the system works. For more detailed information, refer to the later chapter.

Chapter Summary

Active Directory is perhaps the most anticipated new feature of Windows 2000. It offers functionality that goes beyond anything Microsoft has offered in prior versions. This chapter defined Active Directory and explained why it is such an important new development.

The bases for Active Directory are the X.500 standards. X.500 standards can be thought of as the parent of the Active Directory concept. Active Directory is simply a distributed database of objects on your network. The fact that it is distributed means that it is scalable and fault-tolerant. Its functionality goes beyond simply storing data; it also allows its users to add data, delete data, and add definitions to its schema.

Active Directory offers Open Standard Support. This means that the means and methods by which you can access Active Directory data is an industry-defined and agreed-upon standard. These standards include use of the LDAP protocol, DNS, HTTP, and many commonly agreed-upon naming standards.

Active Directory stores information about resources on your network as objects. Objects have attributes or properties associated with them. Objects are stored in containers. Containers can also contain other containers, which forms a hierarchy. Containers higher in the hierarchy are known as *parent containers*. Containers below parent containers are known as *child containers*. Security policies can be assigned to a high-level container in the hierarchy, and they can be allowed to flow down to child containers. This is known as *inheritance*.

There are two considerations when designing an Active Directory infrastructure. There are physical considerations—link speeds, number of servers, location of clients—and logical considerations. Both of these work hand in hand to provide an efficient and fault tolerant directory.

Active Directory comes with its own set of acronyms, terms, and definitions. These terms include *tree*, *forest*, *Organization Units*, and *schema*. These terms were defined. It is important that you become familiar with these terms. If you do not understand what each of them mean, you will not be able to take the next step and design your own Active Directory.

Finally, we took a brief look at replication. *Replication* is the term used to describe the Active Directory processes that facilitate the maintenance of data on Domain Controllers and Global Catalog servers. Replication is a complex process that will be dealt with in more detail in the next chapter.

Active Directory Replication

*I*n the previous chapter, we briefly touched on the replication of Active Directory data. In this chapter, we are going to drill down into the detail of how this works. Replication is a task that is automatic, but that is not to say that you do not need to be familiar with its inner workings. There are two very good reasons for this: 1)By gaining a deeper understanding of *how* something works, you will be better equipped to design more efficient infrastructures and troubleshoot problems; 2) By digging beneath the surface of the processes involved you will further pull back the curtains of Active Directory and demystify it.

So what is replication all about? *Replication* is the term used to describe the process of making sure that every component that stores Active Directory data is kept up to date as things change. That means that it makes sure that clients can logon with the current credentials and that clients are able to find a network resource, such as a printer, no matter where it happens to be on the network. This includes searches in the local domain and across the entire tree or even forest.

Now, on a large enterprise network, the amount of data that constantly has to be updated is tremendous. It is going to be up to you to make sure that your clients have local access to an Active Directory storage mechanism, whether that be a domain controller (DC) or a Global Catalog (GC.) However, you are not on your own. There are some things that only the process can deal with. For instance, what happens in the instance when a user changes his or her password at precisely the same time that an administrator on the other side of a WAN link does the very same thing? How does Active Directory decide which entry should be valid? How does Active Directory decide what pieces of data should be replicated to all DCs and which should not? How does it prevent duplicate data from being replicated? How does it prevent broadcast storms as constant changes are made?

All of these questions will be answered as you read through this chapter. Replication is a key function of Active Directory—so let's go in and see what we find.

An Introduction to Active Directory Replication

As you have already read, Windows 2000 still makes extensive use of domains. In some ways, these domains are very similar to what you might already be familiar with in previous versions of Microsoft Windows NT. In other ways, they are subtly different. These differences were mentioned in the previous chapter, but you will see some repetition here. That is because grasping the differences is key to your understanding of how Active Directory works.

When we talk about replication in Active Directory we are actually talking about the replicas of the Active Directory data on each DC. It is the job of the CD to participate in the authentication of user logons and assignment of permissions. Therefore, it is essential that each DC has an accurate replica—that is, a replica that is as up to date as possible.

Domain controllers in a Windows 2000 domain are peers. That is, any DC in the domain can accept changes to the Active Directory data. This is in contrast to previous versions of Microsoft Windows NT. In previous versions, all changes were made at the Primary Domain Controller (PDC) and were then copied out to the Backup Domain Controllers (BDC). This method caused some problems. In a sense, you had all your eggs in one basket. If the PDC for the domain failed, then you were unable to make any changes to the users' passwords or group memberships. In this case, you had to promote a BDC, which was a manual process that may or not have made your network less efficient.

By having each DC in Windows 2000 act as a peer, Microsoft has, in effect, introduced better scalability and fault tolerance. Scalability is increased because by placing your DC in strategic locations throughout your network (usually ensuring that users and administrators have local access to it), you have ensured that access is fast and distributed. Fault tolerance is achieved because even if one DC goes down, users would still be able to logon to the network, and administrators and users alike are still able to make changes to Active Directory data. The only problem is that there is now additional complexity because each DC has to let every other DC in its domain know when a change has taken place—that is the task of replication. Because no one DC is the primary DC or master domain controller, Active Directory's method of replication is known as *multimaster replication*.

Directory Synchronization

As you read white papers or other books on Active Directory, you might see the term *directory synchronization.* You should not confuse the term directory synchronization with the term *directory replication.* When you read about directory synchronization you are most likely reading about the synchronization between two different directory systems. As you saw in Chapter 8, Active Directory, is a directory service built upon industry-defined standards. Other vendors have already implemented directory services, or will be in the near future. As these services become available, you might come across the need to transfer information from one directory service to another. That is known as directory synchronization. This is usually achieved through an agent. However, this task is outside the scope of this book. Just make sure you know the difference between the two. We have illustrated this in Figure 8.1

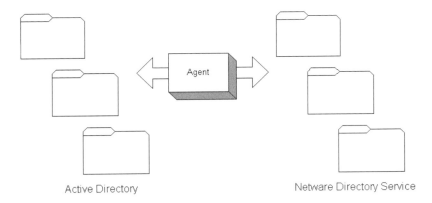

Active Directory   Netware Directory Service

Figure 8–1   *Directory synchronization.*

How Does Replication Work?

Finally, we get down to the details of how replication actually works. There are several different methods and processes that are involved with replication. That is because there are many eventualities that have to be taken into account, and you cannot always rely on network connections to be available. This will be explained as you go through the rest of this chapter.

We are going to look at the process in some detail. In the process we will be introducing you to many new terms. Sorry about that, but we have tried to make sure that we adhere to Microsoft's terminology when discussing this topic. By doing so we can ensure that you can fully appreciate any additional documents that you might find in the future.

Originating and Replicated Updates

There are two distinct types of updates that must be made at each DC. The first of these two types is known as an *originating update*. An originating update is an update that takes place at a DC. That is, if an administrator makes a change in one of the graphical user interface (GUI) tools, that change will first be recorded by a single DC before being replicated to all the others. This first recording is known as an *originating update*.

The second type of update is known as a *replicated update*. Once an originating update has taken place, it is then passed on to all the other DCs in the domain as a replicated update. A replicated update is an update that was sent from another DC.

Active Directory accepts several different types of originating update. These updates are as follows:

- Adding a new object to the directory
- Changing the name or parent of an object
- Moving an object from one domain to another domain
- Deleting an object from the directory
- Changing the attributes of an object

Although this might sound like a very simple process, don't forget that these changes could be taking place at many different DCs—all at the same time. You have no control over which DC is recording changes that you make to the directory from the Windows 2000 GUI. Therefore, the number of changes that are made can become quite large. Let's take a look at one of the methods that Active Directory uses to make sure that unnecessary data is not replicated.

Update Sequence Numbers

An Update Sequence Number (USN) is a 64-bit number stored at each DC. When a change is made at a DC this value is incremented. It will be incremented for *both* originating updates and replicated updates.

The USN value is written along with the changed attribute. This is said to be *atomic*. This term basically means that if both the USN value and the new attribute cannot be written to the directory, don't write either. Either they are both successful, or they both fail. This is necessary because the USN is an important part of replication.

Along with the DC's own USN, each DC also keeps a table that contains a list of USN numbers belonging to other DCs on the network. This "Server—USN" table maps a server name along with the highest received USN. When a DC is informed that data needs to be replicated, only the changes to a USN that are higher than that recorded in the table will be sent.

This is illustrated in Figure 8.2. In this example, there are two changes at DC Peacock. This DC wants to send these updates to DC Bley. These updates

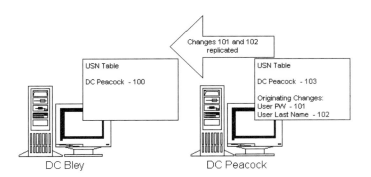

USN Table

DC Peacock - 100

Changes 101 and 102
replicated

USN Table

DC Peacock - 103

Originating Changes:
User PW - 101
User Last Name - 102

DC Bley   DC Peacock

Figure 8–2   *Replication and USN.*

have an assigned USN number that is higher than the value in DC Peacock's USN table. Therefore, they are sent.

Don't worry too much about the precise contents of the USN table. The example given in Figure 8.2 is not completely accurate because, as was mentioned earlier, the USN number is actually a 64-bit number. However, for the purposes of this example, we hope you get the idea. Note that the USN number is used in two vectors. These are discussed in the next section.

USNs are a good, simple idea. It is worth noting that previous directories have attempted to use timestamps as a method for achieving the same thing. The problem with timestamps is that every DC on the network would have to be time-synced with every other DC. Although this is a noble enough task (and obviously a good idea), it is easier said than done. To have it as the fundamental method by which replication is driven does not make sense in today's highly distributed networks. That's not to say Active Directory will never use timestamps. As you will see later, they do come in useful should there ever be a tie break required.

One key point that you should commit to memory is that the USN is server specific. That is, each server has its own USN. This will become relevant later as we talk about additional methods of ensuring that the correct data is replicated. Note that all changes (originating and replicated) cause the USN to increment. This change can cause a DC to begin the replication process again. This process is discussed in the next section.

Before we leave the topic of USNs behind, let me give an example of when they come in useful to Active Directory. Let's assume that you have a Windows 2000 network with three DCs. You perform a backup of each DC once a week (not good practice, but you haven't gotten to that part of the book yet!).

One day, one of your DCs suffers a hard disk crash. All data is lost, and you will have to rebuild it and restore from a tape that is a week old. You perform the work in record time (hey, you have this book, so you're a good administrator!). The new DC comes online—but its Active Directory data is now a week out of date. In this case, the DC can restart replication by asking all other DCs for all changes that are greater than the last USN number held in the week old USN table. As you can see, this is a fast and simple way for a restored DC to get up to date.

Replication Loops

The problem with trying to discuss a new topic and what is, to most people, a new technology, is that you have to be careful not to get ahead of yourself. It is sometimes difficult to explain the basic processes without introducing some more advanced concepts—before their time. As is the case at this point. Stay with it and I promise we'll get around to explaining precisely how Active Directory manages the feat of calculating multiple routes from one domain controller to another on the network. Just take my word for it, it can and does.

Let's give some thought to the process as we know it so far. In Figure 8.2, we had two DCs. A set of changes were made at DC Peacock, and they were replicated to DC Bley. We now know that, through a simple system of USNs, Active Directory can make sure that unnecessary data is not replicated.

Things get a bit more complicated when you introduce a third DC. An example of this is shown in Figure 8.3. In Figure 8.3, you can see that DC Peacock has a change that it needs to replicate. It successfully manages to do this. Therefore, both DC Peacock and DC Bley have up-to-date information. The problem is—what is going to prevent DC Bley from noticing this change and replicating it around the network a second time?

The answer is something called *propagation dampening*. To ensure that directory replication can take place even if a particular route between DCs is unavailable, Active Directory has multiple paths by which they can communicate (precisely how this works is discussed later). It is this very feature that can introduce the kinds of problems that were illustrated in Figure 8.3.

Obviously, what is required in our scenario is for DC Motian and DC Bley to detect that they have both received the update from DC Peacock. This would ensure that neither of them would replicate it again.

This is achieved by two vectors. The first is called the *up-to-date vector*. Each server has an up-to-date vector. This vector is a server–USN pair that records the *last originating update* received from each DC. We spoke about originating updates earlier in this chapter.

The second vector is known as the *high-watermark vector*. Each object has an attribute called the *usnChanged* attribute. When a change is made at a DC, the USN is advanced, and that new USN is stored in the usnChanged attribute of the object. Don't forget, each DC maintains a table containing server and USN mappings.

By now you are probably scratching your head a bit, wondering what all this means. It just happens that this concept is one that is better described in

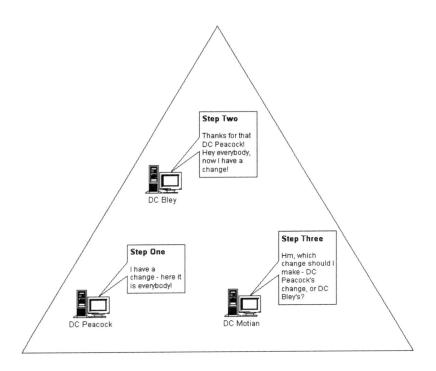

Figure 8–3   *A replication loop.*

an example, rather than by the straight laying out of facts. So let's take a look at how these things come into play.

Let's take a look at how two DCs might communicate. Take a look at Table 8.1 to see what entries are in the USN tables on each machine.

Table 8.1	USN Table Entries at DC B	
Server Name	**High Watermark**	**Up-to-Date Vector**
DC Peacock	5	2
DC Bley	12	6

DC Peacock signals that it has just recorded an originating update. It would like to replicate that change to DC Bley. DC Bley will first look in its USN table and see what the high-watermark value for DC Peacock is. It will then use this number to request all attributes that have a higher value. In this case, DC Bley will request that DC Peacock sends all data that has a high watermark greater than 5.

DC Peacock will send the data if two conditions are met: first, it will scan all attributes to gather all those that have a high watermark of greater than 5. It will send this data if the high-watermark USN is higher and if the target DCs up-to-date vector is greater.

Now, here is where things can get tricky. Let's introduce another DC, let's call it DC Motian. DC Motian also gets those changes from DC Peacock. Once it receives them, it will start a cycle on that DC. In other words, DC C is going to say, "Hey, just got some changes, let me replicate those to DC Bley." In this case, DC Motian will contact DC Bley and inform it that it has changes. DC Bley will reply with, "Okay, here is my USN entry for you—and oh, by the way, I have updated by up-to-date vector from DC Peacock—here's my current value."

On receiving this information, DC C will be able to compare the up-to-date vector from DC A that it now holds against that which DC B holds. It will see that they are the same. In this case, no replication will take place. This is because DC C is able to see that DC B has already received all necessary changes. This prevents endless replication on the network—or rather, replication loops.

This process is somewhat difficult to follow. This author certainly had to spend some time thinking through this example. If you are confused, go back and read this section again. Soon you'll be thinking, "Oh, I get it!"

What About Change Conflicts?

Now let's consider a situation that will undoubtedly occur. What happens when a change is made to the same attribute on one Active Directory replica by two people on two different DCs, at the same time? How does Active Directory determine which change is the most current?

At first glance, you might be thinking that this will happen all too often. In fact, you might be surprised to find out that, although it will certainly occur, it will probably happen less than you would imagine. This is because Active Directory data is replicated at the attribute level. If replication took place at the object level, it would be far more likely to be an issue. Because it is at the attribute level, one administrator could make a change to a user's password while another changed group membership, and this would not cause a conflict. If Active Directory replicated at the object level, this would have been a problem.

The first thing that might come to your mind is the use of USN. We talked about USNs in the last section. However, USNs do not provide us with the mechanism we will need to sort out this predicament. Why? Because the USN is a server-based attribute. It can be used to find out what the last update from a DC was, but there really isn't any way we can use this information to figure out which DC should have priority over any other DC, should a conflict take place. We need something more specific to the attribute itself, rather than at the server level.

So what Active Directory mechanism is in place to resolve these circumstances? The answer is something called a *Property Version Number* (PVN). When an attribute is first created, a PVN is also written along with it. This number will stay with the attribute for its entire life. Again, this is unlike USNs. In the case of USNs, the USN is specific to a server—it really does not have any underlying uniqueness to the Active Directory data.

Only originating updates increment the PVN. So, whenever a DC makes an originating update, this number is incremented, and it will then be sent, along with the changed metadata, as it is replicated throughout the network.

So how does this help us when there is a collision? Well, in the first instance, if a DC receives replicated data, it will compare the PVN for the metadata to see whether the received update has a higher PVN value than that stored locally. The version that has the highest PVN can be considered to "win." That is, the highest PVN always wins.

What if the PVNs are the same, but the metadata in question is different? In this case, we have the only instance in which Active Directory will use timestamps. We spoke earlier about timestamps and why their use was impractical. This is the exception that breaks the rule. If the PVNs are the same and the metadata is different, then timestamps for each piece of data are compared. The one with the latest timestamp wins.

Finally, we have the last tiebreaker. Although it might seem unlikely that the PVN and the timestamp would be exactly the same, it is possible. So in this case, Microsoft has used the Global Unique Identifier (GUID) of the DCs to resolve the conflict. The one with the highest GUID will win.

When each of the tiebreakers has been applied, you can see that there cannot be a conflict. By adding what is essentially a version number to each attribute in the directory, Microsoft has ensured that conflicts cannot confuse Active Directory to the point where it won't know what to do.

Directory Partitions

So far, we have looked at replication in the context of a single domain. We have also worked on the assumption that everything gets replicated to every DC. For the purposes of addressing basic replication issues, this has been a good approach. However, now it is time to dig down just a little deeper to gain better understanding of precisely what is being replicated and to where.

In the previous chapter, we defined a lot of new terms and briefly discussed their purpose in Active Directory. One of those terms was *Global Catalog Server* (GC). These servers operate in a domain, tree, or forest to answer queries against the Active Directory data. A simple DC cannot perform this function alone, because a DC knows about only the objects that exist within its domain; it has no knowledge of other domains in a tree or forest. Enter the GC. What is the relationship between a DC and a GC, as far as data is concerned? How does the GC gets its information, and when a change is made at a DC, how does a GC know about it? This section is going to discuss these points and clear up any confusion you might have been feeling.

Active Directory contains a lot of data. We tend to think of that data as information on network resources, such as users, groups, and printers. However, the truth is somewhat more complicated. In fact, Active Directory also contains additional data, such as data that defines which objects can exist in the directory and information on the number and names of domains in a tree or forest.

Some of this data is relevant to a domain. A user account in a particular domain is a case in point. Other pieces of data are more important on a global basis. To this end, the Active Directory data has been broken out into three partitions. That's just a fancy way of saying that you have a big pot of data and that it has been broken out into three different pieces.

Let's take a look at the three different partitions and what they contain.

SCHEMA PARTITION

The schema partition is a set of data that defines which objects can be created in Active Directory. Along with the object definitions, it also contains a list of attributes that each object can contain. This is extensible, but there are defaults, such as much of the user information, that are defined right out of the box. This partition also contains a set of rules for both creating and manipulating these objects.

Now, don't forget that all DCs work as peers. That is, objects can be added, deleted, or changed on any one of them. Therefore, this type of data is relevant to all domain controllers in a forest and will have to be replicated and stored on every DC.

CONFIGURATION PARTITION

This partition contains information regarding the structure of Active Directory. By *structure* we mean information such as the number of sites and domains in the directory. It also stores information on the number of DCs in a domain and what services are being offered. Again, because changes can be made at any DC, this information must exist on every DC.

DOMAIN PARTITION

You might have been wondering where the actual object data is—that is, where the user account and group data is stored. The answer is in the domain partition. This information will vary from domain to domain. Users in one domain will gain access to data and resources in other domains by way of two-way transitive trust relationships. Therefore, this data is relevant only to the specific domain. There is no need for the data to be replicated to all DCs in a tree or forest.

PARTIAL DOMAIN DIRECTORY PARTITION

Wait a minute! If the user data is part of the domain partition and is stored only on the DCs in a particular domain, how does Active Directory manage to find everyone? Also, how can you search for a user in the forest if the DCs in your local domain know about only those accounts created in that domain?

The answer is twofold. The most important thing to remember is that this is the job of the GC. We discussed this in the last chapter. We hope that now the importance of these servers is beginning to sink in.

So how does a GC get its information? They get it from the partial domain directory partition. This partition is a read-only subset of information in a domain. The subset must contain a list of all objects (otherwise, you wouldn't be able to search for them) but does not contain all attributes. This is partly due to a need to minimize the amount of data stored at a GC. If everything was replicated, we would be talking about possibly a huge amount of data going across the wire.

Note that a GC will store a partial domain directory partition for every domain in a forest. That is how it can ensure being able to answer queries from any client about any other object, no matter where it is.

We will soon be talking about the replication process in more detail. The thing to remember here is that the schema and configuration partitions have the same scope. Therefore, they share a replication topology. A partial domain directory partition shares a scope (on a domain-by-domain basis) with the domain partition. So, partial domain directory partition takes place when domain partition replication happens. They share the same topology. We'll take a look at these topologies in a moment.

What about the Real World?

Okay, so it's time to admit that although replication is pretty impressive, in the real world it cannot happen in real time. That is, there are simply going to be times when a replica on a DC is going to be out of sync with other DCs. This is because, in the real world, things take time to happen. Network congestion can cause this problem, or the speed of a link might delay the propagation of data.

The term used for this problem is *replication latency*. To be honest, there isn't anything you can do about it. It is going to be your job as a Windows 2000 system administrator designing an Active Directory infrastructure to place your DCs in such a way that it is minimized.

Further, there are some things that just don't quite fit the Active Directory model we have outlined. Let me give you an example. All DCs are peers, so a change can be made at any one of them. Earlier, we discussed the schema partition. The schema partition is the partition of AD data that stores descriptions of which objects can be created in Active Directory and what attributes those objects can have. Changes to this partition are pretty important. If any DC were allowed to make changes to the schema partition, you could end up with a situation where a new object type was added to a DC, and no other DC in the domain has any idea that it exists. Given replication latency, it could mean that half of your DCs know, and the other half don't.

Clearly this is not a good situation to be in. Also, it is not the only situation where the peer nature of DCs causes potential problems. Let me go through another example. User A changes his password on DC B. He then reboots his machine. When User A tries to logon after the reboot, DC A tries to validate him. However, DC B has not yet had time to replicate its changes to all other DCs.

In this case, User A might be denied access to the network. This is because User A is trying to logon with a new password that has yet to be replicated. So DC A sees this as an invalid password. Clearly, this is unacceptable. The solution to this problem is to dedicate certain machines to certain tasks.

Operations Masters

Because certain tasks (or, in Active Directory terminology, operations) are so important, a dedicated resource is assigned to it. These servers are known as *operation masters*. There are five in all. Each one plays a critical role in ensuring that Active Directory functions correctly.

SCHEMA OPERATIONS MASTER

The operation master is the only DC allowed to make changes to the directory schema. The schema operations master then replicates the changes to all other DCs. Schema changes would include adding new object definitions to Active Directory. There is one schema operations master per forest.

DOMAIN OPERATIONS MASTER

It is the purpose of the domain operations master to add new domains to Active Directory and to record the removal of a domain. It also has responsibility to record information regarding the synchronization of Active Directory with other directory systems. There is one domain operations master per forest.

PRIMARY DOMAIN CONTROLLER EMULATOR

It is the job of the PDC emulator to ensure downward compatibility to BDCs in Windows NT 4.0 domains. However, even if Active Directory is running in native mode (no Windows 4.0 on the network), it still has a very important role to fulfill. Let's say a user changes her password on a DC. That DC has yet to replicate this change to all other DCs. So when she logs on, if she hits a different DC, her logon will be rejected (incorrect password). In this case, the DC that is about to reject the logon will first check with the PDC emulator to see whether it knows about a new password. The PDC emulator gets preferential replication of password changes within the domain. If it knows about the change, it will authenticate the user.

RELATIVE IDENTIFIER OPERATIONS MASTER

Every user, group, or computer has a security identifier (SID). The SID is partly made up of something called a resource identifier (RID). RIDs are assigned, 512 at a time, to DCs from a pool. Once those 512 are used up, another 512 are assigned. They are assigned from the relative identifier operations master. This DC manages the pool. It also is needed when objects are moved from one domain to another. There is one per domain.

INFRASTRUCTURE OPERATIONS MASTER

The infrastructure operations master updates SIDs and domains for objects as they moved from one domain to another. In this sense, it works with the relative identifier operations master. There is one per domain.

The five operations masters perform a key role in Active Directory. Without them, chaos would ensue as changes were made to the Active Directory.

Site and Replication

In the last chapter we spoke about sites and their purpose. A site is a single or a collection of subnets that have fast connectivity. These sites allow you control over replication. They also have some effect on the DC that is used to authenticate you.

Do not forget, sites do not have to match your domain structure—or the logical design of Active Directory. Sites should be based entirely on connectivity. If you have fast connectivity between two sets of resources, put them in the same site. If not, create separate sites.

Replication is handled differently within a site than it is between two different sites. The reasons for this are obvious—within a site, connectivity can be guaranteed, and it's fast. When data needs to be moved from one site to another, neither of these two things can be assumed. What follows is a brief discussion of the difference between replications in these two scenarios.

REPLICATION WITHIN A SITE

Domain controllers within a site need to replicate information. Within a site, bandwidth is considered to be fast and plentiful. In this case, replication is tuned such that it makes sure that things happen quickly—that is, to reduce latency. It also takes into account CPU load, because bogging a machine down isn't a good idea. The topology for replication within a site is calculated automatically. We'll take a look at that process in a moment. You might see the term *intrasite replication* to describe replication within a site.

Figure 8–4   *A direct partner relationship.*

REPLICATION BETWEEN SITES

The major difference here is that the tuning for replication is geared toward reducing the amount of network traffic. To this end, data is compressed as it moves between sites. You can also manually schedule when replication takes place between two sites. You might see the term *intersite replication* to describe replication between sites.

Replication Topology

The final topic in this chapter is replication topology. When we talk about topology, we are referring to the path data takes as it moves from one DC to another—or when data moves between sites. Earlier, we spoke about the different partitions of Active Directory, a DC might have a different replication topology for each of these partitions.

The topology within a site can be calculated automatically. We will take a look at that. However, you can also manually configure the topology. Manual configuration tends to complement automatic calculation.

When a connection is created between two DCs, an object is created to represent that link. Not surprisingly, this is called a *connection object*. Automatic topology is created with the Knowledge Consistency Checker (KCC). Connections between two sites must be created manually.

What Is a Connection Object?

Replication is performed by one DC pulling data from another DC. That is, a DC informs a partner that it has changes to replicate. The partner then says, "Okay, send me what you have." The relationship between the two DCs is said to be that of "direct partners." A direct partner relationship is shown in Figure 8.4.

As with trusts between domains in Windows 2000, replication can also be achieved through transitive replication partners. That is, a DC can obtain replication data indirectly. The best way to view these types of relationships is by using the Active Directory Replication Monitor.

A connection object is created in one of two ways. First, you can create them manually. Of course, this method gives you the most control over the replication topology. However, it introduces administrative overhead. Also, there is no "self-repairing" function for manually created connection objects. So if a connection fails, you will have to reconfigure the connections manually.

The best option is automatic configuration. This is achieved through KCC. This service will automatically generate connection objects, but the connection operates in only one direction. So if you want communication to go both ways, there will be two connection objects.

For the KCC to do its work, it first needs some data. This data includes the sites you have on your network, the subnets, the protocols you are going to use for replication and a "cost" for sending data between different sites. KCC then will calculate the best topology based on this data. The default configuration is a two-way ring topology. KCC tries to make sure that there is a maximum hop count for the data (three hops by default).

A connection object can be used to replicate any partition within Active Directory. So there may be times when a single connection object is sufficient. Keep in mind, however, the scope of each partition—some are domainwide; others are forestwide. You should never have to create more than one connection object between two DCs. If there is a connection between two DCs, it will be used for all replication activity.

When Should I Create Manual Connections?

Manual connection objects might be necessary if the KCC does not create the connections you deem necessary. For instance, the KCC creates a two-way ring for topology purposes. This works because of transitive replication. You might decide, however, that this is insufficient and want to manually create a connection object between two DCs.

Your main concern when adding additional connection objects is that replication has a cost involved with it. The cost can be measured in terms of network traffic generated, CPU utilization as data is processed, and the reading and writing of data to disk. Make sure that you monitor these attributes on your DCs both before and after you create connection objects.

There are also some rules you might want to consider. For instance, the KCC is dynamic. That is, if something changes on your network that prevents the replication topology that the KCC has created from working, it will automatically kick in and generate new connections between DCs. This process can save you a lot of administrative overhead.

The KCC can both create and delete connection objects. However, it will never delete a manually created connection object. Also, because a single connection object is capable of performing replication for each partition of the Active Directory, if the KCC detects that a manually created connection object exists between two DCs, it will not create an additional connection. In these cases, creating manual connections can be seen to undermine the KCC's operation. Because your goal should be to automate processes as much as possible, this clearly is not a good idea. Although there may be circumstances where you will have to manually create a connection between DCs, it is good practice to rely on the KCC as much as possible.

How Do I Know What's Going On?

So, all theory aside, what tools do you use to keep tabs on replication? Given the complexity of replication, it should not surprise you to learn that Microsoft has added a new tool to the administrator's arsenal. This tool is known as *Replication Monitor.*

Replication Monitor offers a wealth of information on the replication topology in your enterprise. This information includes:

- Display replication partners for each DC;
- Display USN for each DC;
- Write data on monitor failed replication attempts to the event log;
- Allow you to view which objects have yet to be replicated from a DC;
- Allow you to kick off replication manually between two replication partners; and
- Allow you to start the KCC manually to regenerate a replication topology.

Replication Monitor will be one of the primary tools you will use to administer replication. However, it is not the only tool. When dealing with a new topic such as replication, make sure that you don't forget the basics of network administration. Specifically, one of the main tools you will have at your disposal is good old Performance Monitor. Earlier, I mentioned the costs involved with creating a manual connection object. These costs should be tracked with Performance Monitor.

Also, do not overlook Network Monitor. Network Monitor can be used to view data as it crosses the wire. You also can use it to generate protocol statistics and to calculate bandwidth requirements. Note, however, that replication can use one of two protocols: RPC and SMTP. It is far easier to track SMTP traffic because it uses a well-known port number (Port 25). For security purposes, RPC uses dynamic port assignment, so it will be more difficult to assess which traffic is, in fact, related to replication and which traffic actually belongs to another process using the same protocol.

Finally, do not forget Event Viewer. Data will show up in the logs, and you should monitor them for information. By using tools such as Replication Monitor, it is possible to post events to the event log, based on a set of defined criteria.

By using each of these tools, you should be well on your way to designing replication topologies that work in your environment. Monitoring replication is an ongoing task. Your network will change over time, and you will need to keep a close watch on the effect of adding or removing DCs from your network, or increasing bandwidth between sites.

Chapter Summary

This chapter has mostly talked about the theory behind replication and how it works. Although this might seem a little out of place in an administrator's handbook, it is necessary because you cannot troubleshoot situations if you do not have a fundamental knowledge of the tasks at hand. Replication is a complex function within Active Directory, and an in-depth discussion of it is beyond the scope of this book. If you have read and understood the information in this chapter, however, you should be well placed to take your understanding to the next level.

One of the primary goals of this chapter was to remove some of the mystery from Active Directory replication. Replication can be automatically or manually configured. Without a good understanding of how it works, however, and of the types and amounts of data being replicated, it is difficult—if not impossible—for an administrator to know how effective his or her replication topology is.

We started the chapter by defining what replication is. *Replication* is a term used to describe the process of moving updated Active Directory data between domain controllers within a domain, tree, or forest. We talked about originating writes and replicated updates. An *originating write* is the term used to describe a new change being made to a replica of Active Directory. This change then needs to be copied to all other domain controllers. As this change is written to other domain controllers, this is known as a *replicating update*.

The amount of data that needs to be replicated is calculated by use of the Update Sequence Numbers. These numbers, unique to each domain controller, are used to prevent replication loops from occurring. A replication loop would be a change to an Active Directory replica that is propagated endlessly on your network. Clearly, this is undesirable because it would eat up bandwidth and cause unnecessary processing at each domain controller.

Active Directory has three partitions: the schema, configuration, and domain partitions. The schema partition defines which objects can be created within Active Directory. The configuration partition stores information on sites and domains that exists within the Active Directory. Finally, the domain partition contains data specific to a domain, such as user accounts and groups. Each of these partitions has a "Scope." The scope of the schema and configuration partitions is relevant at the forest level. The data in the domain partition is important only at the domain level and, therefore, does not have to be replicated throughout a forest.

Of course, for most queries, the same set of data is being searched within Active Directory. For instance, you might search for a user name fairly often, but never search for someone's room number. To facilitate these searches and to minimize the amount of data needing replication within the forest, we have something called Global Catalog Servers. These servers answer user requests. Because they contain a limited number of attributes on an object, they are more lightweight than, say, a domain controller.

Although all domain controllers (DCs) within Active Directory are peers, this introduces a level of complexity that has to be overcome, For instance, if all DCs were allowed to accept changes to the schema—perhaps the adding of another object type—what mechanism would be in place to make sure that all replicas get this new data in a timely fashion? To deal with these types of issues, we also talked about operation masters. Operation masters are computers in the tree or forest that take on special roles. There are five operation masters: Schema, Domain, Primary Domain Controller Emulator, Relative Identifier, and Infrastructure. Each of these operation masters is tasked with performing a specific role within Active Directory and are the only computers allowed to perform these roles. It is their responsibility both to accept changes and to propagate those changes to all other domain controllers.

Replication occurs within a site. A site can be defined as a subnet or group of subnets that have fast connectivity. Replication needs to occur within a site (between DCs of that site) and between sites. The process is somewhat different, depending on whether you are replicating within a site or between different sites. Data being replicated between sites is compressed before being sent. This minimizes the bandwidth requirements. Because connectivity within a site is assumed to be fast, there is no need to compress data as it is replicated within a site.

We then discussed connection objects and the Knowledge Consistency Checker (KCC). Connection objects are objects within Active Directory that represent connections between two domain controllers. This connection is used to transfer data between DCs. The KCC is a service that automatically generates these connection objects. Although it is possible to create connection objects manually, it is a good idea to let the KCC take care of most of your replication needs.

Finally, we mentioned some tools that you can use both to administer and troubleshoot replication. These tools include Replication Monitor, Performance Monitor, Event Viewer, and Network Monitor. You should periodically use these tools to make sure that replication is occurring efficiently within your enterprise.

Planning and Installing Active Directory

*I*f this is your first exposure to the concept of directory services, all of the theory and terms from the last chapter can be rather confusing. However, beyond the theory is the actual hands-on implementation of Active Directory. Before diving into an installation, however, it is wise to plan your network setup carefully. There are many considerations to take into account with Active Directory. These considerations will affect not only how Active Directory is implemented, but also how well it functions in your environment and how easy it will be to expand in the future. In this chapter, we will discuss:

- Planning Active Directory Implementations
- Installing Active Directory
- Working in a Multiple-Domain Environment

Planning Active Directory Implementations

Although it is typically considered to be one of the more boring aspects of any project, planning is critically important when it comes to implementing Active Directory on your network. The choices you make before you start will either haunt you or make you look like a genius down the road, as your organizational needs change or grow.

Some of the general aspects of an Active Directory that you will need to take into account are:

- Active Directory Namespace
- Site Planning
- Organization Unit Planning

Active Directory Namespace

As we learned in the previous chapter, the Domain Name System (DNS) service is a requirement for implementing Active Directory. DNS is covered in depth later in this book, so this chapter will not go into much detail explaining DNS concepts. Feel free to refer to the DNS chapter if you run into concepts and terminology you aren't familiar with as you work through this chapter. This chapter will also assume that you already have a viable DNS server installed and configured that you can access on your network, if not on the Windows 2000 Server system on which you are performing your lab work.

When planning your DNS namespace for Active Directory you really have two options, creating a new namespace and extending an existing namespace. Namespace is simply a definable context in which a specific name can be resolved. A telephone directory, for example, is a namespace that allows telephone subscriber names to be resolved to telephone numbers. Active Directory forms a namespace in which the name of an object in the Directory can be resolved to a specific object.

CREATING A NEW NAMESPACE

Creating a new namespace is often done when you have not been using DNS internally in the organization (such as in an environment that has exclusively been using WINS for internal name resolution). Another reason might be that there is currently a DNS server that handles name resolution for external resources (e.g., Internet names) but you don't want to use the same namespace for both internal and external resources. If you use a different namespace for internal and external resources, you will be able to make a clear distinction between the two, both administratively and physically.

Having multiple namespaces will require registering the second namespace with an Internet domain name registering authority, even if the second name will be used only for internal resources. Network Solutions is currently the most popular name registration authority. Registering the name will ensure that you will be able to use the namespace for external resources on the Internet, should you ever decide you want to do that. In addition, it prevents someone else from using that name on the Internet. In this case, users on the internal network would not be able to access that namespace on the Internet because there would be no way to differentiate between the internal and external namespaces.

Typically, if you are going to use separate namespaces for internal and external resources, the external namespace will be the common name of the company. External namespace is that which is accessed most often by the public, such as a website presence on the Internet or a public FTP site. The internal namespace could be a variation of the company name. For instance, Acme Corporation could use acme.com as its external namespace and acmecorp.com as

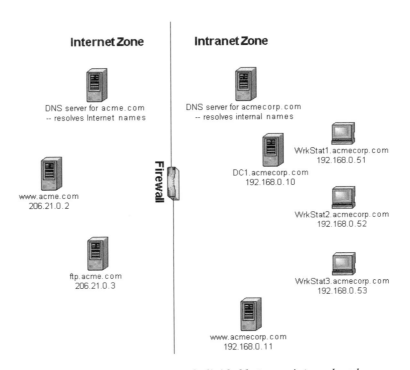

Figure 9-1 *The Acme Corporation network divided between internal and external namespaces.*

its internal namespace. Figure 9.1 shows an example of what a network with that namespace would look like.

DNS configuration is straightforward with this type of configuration. A DNS server is set up outside of the corporate firewall to resolve the public acme.com namespace while another DNS server is set up inside of the firewall to resolve the internal acmecorp.com namespace. There are advantages and disadvantages, however, to having two namespaces to manage. Advantages include:

• Easy to differentiate between internal and external resources when they use separate namespaces.

• Administration is simplified because it can easily be divided between the internal and external namespace.

• Client configuration of web browsers and proxy settings is simplified because the entire internal namespace can be marked as internal, rather than having to specify explicitly what is an internal resource and what is external to the LAN.

Disadvantages include:

• Multiple DNS names must be registered with an Internet domain naming authority—only a problem if one of the names you want to register is already in use.

• If your company has Internet email, a user's address will be different from his or her logon name. For example, the user account Bubba@Acmecorp.com would have an Internet email address of Bubba@Acme.com. This could be potentially confusing to corporate users, because they have to make the distinction between internal and external addresses.

• Not as convenient to administer either. An administrator who is responsible for both namespaces has to make updates and manage them separately.

EXTENDING AN EXISTING NAMESPACE

If you do not wish to create a new namespace for your internal network and you already have an Internet presence, you can choose to extend the existing namespace for internal use. When you use the same namespace for both internal and external resources, you create separate DNS zones that enable you to keep track of internal versus external resources. One zone file is set up on a DNS server outside of the firewall, which resolves publicly accessible resources such as a website or FTP site. Another zone file is set up on a DNS inside of the firewall to resolve all resources that are to be accessed only internally. Having two zone files configured prevents public Internet users outside of the firewall from being able to resolve DNS names for internal corporate servers and potentially launch an attack against one or more of them. Figure 9.2 shows an example configuration for Acme Corporation, based around one contiguous namespace, acme.com.

The following are advantages of using the same namespace for both internal and external resources:

• The structure of the Active Directory tree is contiguous for resources on both the private intranet and the public Internet.

• Logon names and email names can be the same, a benefit to both administrators and users.

• The end user experience is enhanced, because access to internal and external resources is seamless.

The disadvantages are:

• Complex client proxy configurations are required since the client computer must be able to determine what resources are internal vs. external.

• Administrators must be careful not to publish internal content on publicly accessible resources. The potential for confusion exists.

Site Planning

Once you have planned the DNS naming scheme, you will need to look at site planning. A site is a network location connected at speeds that make LAN com-

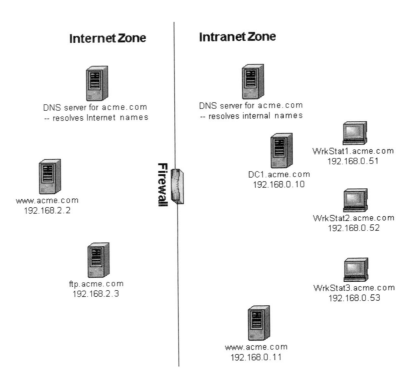

Internet Zone

DNS server for acme.com
-- resolves Internet names

www.acme.com
192.168.2.2

ftp.acme.com
192.168.2.3

Firewall

Intranet Zone

DNS server for acme.com
-- resolves internal names

DC1.acme.com
192.168.0.10

WrkStat1.acme.com
192.168.0.51

WrkStat2.acme.com
192.168.0.52

WrkStat3.acme.com
192.168.0.53

www.acme.com
192.168.0.11

Figure 9–2 *Acme Corporation DNS configuration using one namespace, both internally and externally.*

munication possible. Simply put, a site is usually a physical organization of resources in Active Directory. A site can contain one or more domains, and a domain can span multiple sites.

Consider our Acme Corporation, acme.com, from earlier. Let's say that they have one office building in each of the following cities: Dallas, Houston, Sioux Falls, Omaha, and St. Louis. Each location is connected by Frame Relay links to corporate headquarters in Dallas, as shown in Figure 9.3. All traffic funnels through Dallas, so if Houston sends data to St. Louis, it passes through Dallas to get there.

The designer of the Acme network created one big domain, with domain controllers at each location. So when you are setting up your Active Directory site structure, how many sites should you create? The potential answers are one, four, and five.

ONE SITE

Setting up acme.com as one big site sounds like a simple enough plan to keep everything nice and simple from an administrative standpoint; however, setting

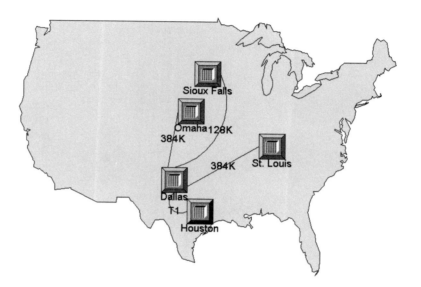

The Acme Corporation network structure.

up this Windows 2000 WAN as a single site would probably be a bad idea. The reason is that sites are used primarily to control authentication and replication. Because you have a domain controller at each location, authentication will not generate much traffic across the slow WAN links. However, domain controllers replicate information between themselves quite often, generating a lot of network traffic. Replication within a site takes place almost immediately, so replication data is sent between domain controllers as a change is made. This can lead to the low-bandwidth Frame Relay connections becoming saturated as they pass replication data as well as other network data, between sites. Microsoft recommends there to be, at minimum, a 512 K connection between two locations before combining them into a single site. However, that is an ideal minimum; 128 K is realistically the absolute minimum bandwidth that must exist between locations to form a site. Replication is covered in much more detail in the next chapter.

FOUR SITES

Given that there must be a 512 K connection between locations realistically to combine them into a single site, we see that our acme.com network should have at least four sites. Because there is a T1 connection between Dallas and Houston (1,544 K), those two locations could potentially be combined into a single site. However, a T1 connection is still a WAN link that could become saturated if a lot of data is moved back and forth between the two locations. Ideally, they would be broken up into separate sites unless there is a compelling reason not to.

FIVE SITES

Although there is no "right" answer between four or five sites, five is definitely the preferred answer. This configuration maintains consistency for one, because each physical location is its own site. Second, potential unreliability of a WAN link between locations in a site is avoided.

The advantage to having multiple sites again relates to replication. Unlike replication within a site, replication between sites can be scheduled for off-peak hours, when the resources are not in as high demand by network users and possibly cheaper in the case of dialup connections. In addition, a nice feature of Active Directory is the services it can provide. Configurations can be set up that are site aware, such as the Distributed File System (DFS). DFS is covered extensively in the chapter on Shared Folders later in the book. Site-aware services adjust their behavior based on what site a user logs in from, so if you have a user who travels between sites, he or she will be able to access network resources in the most efficient manner without any intervention on their part.

 A general "best practice" is to create a separate site for each physical TCP/IP subnet. Using a one-to-one mapping of sites to subnets provides a convenient organizational structure that is easy to manage.

Organizational Unit Planning

As we learned in Chapter 8, Organizational Units (OUs) are containers that can be used to group objects within a domain into a logical structure to suit an administrative or business organizational need. OUs are contained entirely within a single domain, so they cannot contain objects from multiple domains. OUs are not required in an organization, because you can still use security groups to manage your domain. However, groups are not as flexible as OUs.

OUs can be set up according to several different models, so you will need to analyze your organization and decide which model works best for you. Some of the more popular OU models are:

- Geographic OU model
- Administrative OU model
- Object OU model
- Departmental OU model
- Business Unit OU model

GEOGRAPHIC OU MODEL

The geographic model is as simple as it sounds, with resources grouped by their physical location. For this example, we will assume that Acme has gone global since earlier in this chapter, now having offices in London, Mexico City, Toronto, and Ottawa. Figure 9.4 shows Acme Corporation's OU structure based on the geographic model. Because OUs can contain other OUs, we have created a first level of OU that is the country name, with the second level OU being the city where the office is located. Even larger global companies might go so far as to create a first-level OU that reflects the continent, such as North America or Europe, with the second level OU being the country. The less specific your OUs are, the more likely it will be that the structure will survive organizational changes. That gives a slight advantage to the higher-level OU structure of continent/country over country/city, although, for most organizations, the latter provides enough stability.

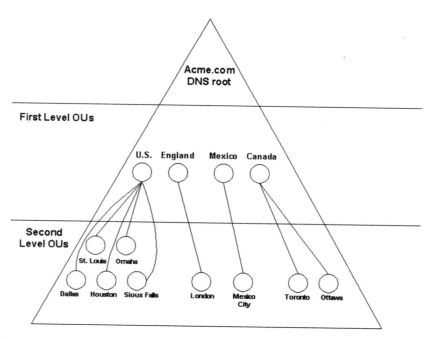

Figure 9-4   *Acme Corporation, based on a geographic OU model.*

ADMINISTRATIVE OU MODEL

Another option for setting up OUs is to use an administrative model. With this model, you are having the OUs reflect the way the organization is administered and the way administrative control is delegated throughout. Acme might set up

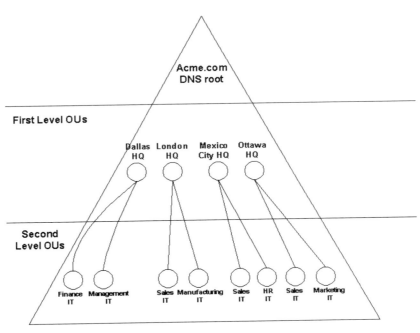

Figure 9-5   *Acme Corporation based on an administrative OU model.*

this model as shown in Figure 9.5, with each country's headquarters being the first-level OU and the second level OUs being IT management units within each country. The downside to this model is that if the business undergoes a significant restructuring, there will be a need to redesign the OU model. Luckily, unlike domains, managing OUs is very easy. Objects can be moved between OUs, and OUs can be renamed, moved, or deleted.

OBJECT OU MODEL

The object OU model organizes OUs based on the type of objects they contain. Acme might create first-level OUs for various objects, such as users, computers, printers, groups, and security policies. Second-level OUs would divide these first-level OUs down to a more granular level, with the OU under users being domain admins and domain users. Computers could be broken down into desktops, servers, and notebooks. This logical model is very extensible upon future growth.

DEPARTMENTAL OU MODEL

This model creates an OU structure that organizes objects by department. In a small company, there might be a need only for first-level OUs that describe

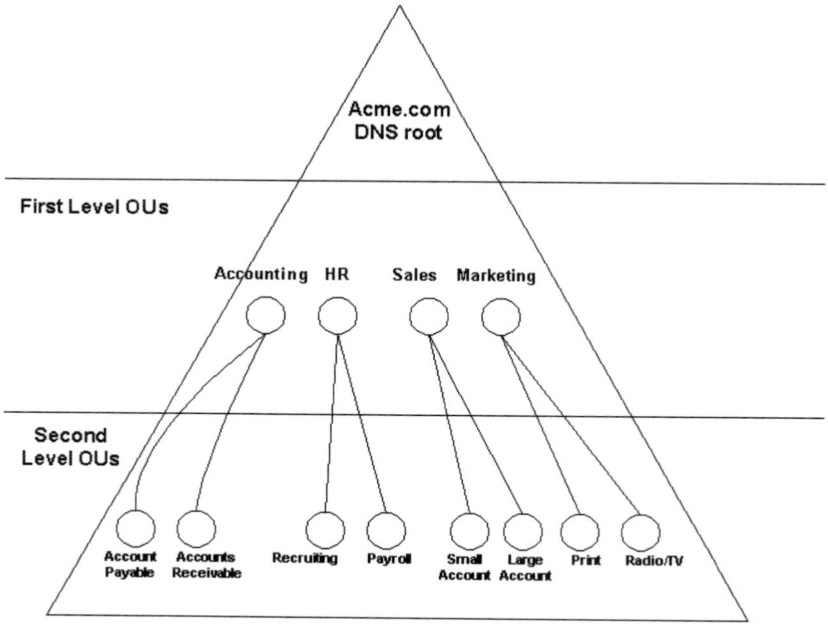

Figure 9–6   *Acme Corporation based on a departmental OU model.*

departments, such as sales, marketing, and human resources. In larger companies, such as Acme Corporation, these business departments might be broken down further into second-level OUs, as shown in Figure 9.6.

BUSINESS UNIT OU MODEL

The business unit OU model is similar to the departmental model, in that the OUs are structured according to business function. First-level OUs are typically divisions within the corporation that represent individual cost centers. Divisions are often created based around financial considerations, with each division having its own budget. The second-level OUs would be the departments that make up a division. In Acme, there might be a division called *Financial Services* that would be a first-level OU that could be broken into second level OUs such as accounts payable, accounts receivable, and payroll. This model takes a higher-level view of a corporate organization than does the departmental model.

PLANNING CONSIDERATIONS

As was stated previously, creating OUs is not a requirement for managing an Active Directory environment. For many smaller companies, using standard groups will often be sufficient. However, you should consider the use of OUs if the following conditions exist:

• You have a need to reflect your organization's structure within an Active Directory domain. If you do not use OUs, Windows 2000 stores all of your users and groups into a single large list that can become unmanageable if it grows too large. Creating OUs enables you to have a logical grouping of these objects that simplifies management.

• You have a dynamic organization that experiences frequent structural changes. User accounts can be moved easily between OUs, whereas moving them between domains is often difficult.

• You need to delegate systems administration roles within the domain. Administrative permissions can be granted at the OU level, making them ideal for companies that have department-level IT personnel responsible for managing departmental resources. Using OUs enables you to eliminate the NT 4.0 concept of resource domains, again simplifying administration.

• You want to restrict what resources users can see in the Active Directory. Users are able to view only objects to which they have access.

Planning the OU structure usually revolves around the organizational needs of your company. During the planning stages, it is valuable to establish a planning team that includes not only members of the IT department, but also other business unit managers that can add additional insight into business processes and needs. Creating a viable design from the beginning will save you many headaches after the implementation has long been completed.

Installing Active Directory

Here is where all of the theory from the last couple of chapters comes together. You have learned about the different Active Directory terminology and have planned your namespace, site structure, and organizational units. At this point, we are ready to get hands-on and finally install Active Directory on our Windows 2000 Server.

Installing Active Directory is done through the Active Directory Installation wizard, which is started by running *DCPROMO.EXE* (think Domain Controller [DC] Promotion, or promoting a standalone or member server to a DC). When you run the Active Directory Installation wizard, you have the following options:

• Creating a DC for a New Domain
• Adding a DC to an Existing Domain

Creating a Domain Controller for a New Domain

When creating a DC for a new domain, you have to decide between a couple of choices. First, you can make your DC the first DC in a new forest or create a new domain tree in an existing forest. Second, you can create a child domain within an existing domain.

NEW DOMAIN TREE

When you opt to create a new domain tree, you are setting up an entirely new security structure. You can make the new tree be part of an existing forest or create an entirely new forest. You will choose this option if this is the first DC being installed and configured.

CHILD DOMAIN

If you already have an existing domain, you may decide to add an additional child domain for administrative reasons. A company without a centralized IT department might want to create separate domains for each major department, such as marketing.acme.com and sales.marketing.com. A child domain is administratively separate from its parent domain; however, unlike creating a new domain tree, the child domain shares the namespace of the parent domain.

THE ACTIVE DIRECTORY INSTALLATION WIZARD

Figure 9.7 shows the welcome screen of the Active Directory Installation wizard. This screen appears when you run *DCPROMO.EXE*.

Once you click next, you are given the choices described above, creating a DC for a new domain or adding a DC to an existing domain. For this exercise, we will choose the first option, as shown in Figure 9.8, and click Next.

As we also mentioned above, once you decide to create a new DC, you are given the choice of creating a new domain tree or creating a child domain within an existing domain tree. This is shown in Figure 9.9. For this exercise, we will assume that this is the first DC in our entire Enterprise. Choose to create a new domain tree and click Next.

When you choose to create a new domain tree, the choice is given as to how to handle forest membership. You can join an existing forest or create a new forest of domain trees. Because this is our first DC, we will create a new forest, as shown in Figure 9.10.

Now we have reached the point where we will have to start supplying the Active Directory Installation wizard with specific information. In Figure 9.11, we are asked to enter the full DNS name for our new domain. If you have a registered domain name, you can use it for your domain name. If not, go ahead and create a name of your choice, knowing that you will not be able to

Figure 9-7   *The welcome screen for the Active Directory Installation Wizard.*

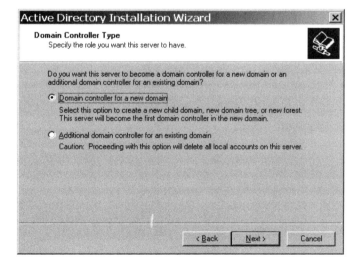

Figure 9-8   *Choosing the domain controller type.*

make resources from this domain available on the public Internet without first registering your name and DNS server.

The next step in setting up your DC is to supply a NetBIOS domain name for your domain, as shown in Figure 9.12. "What?" you might ask, "NetBIOS? I thought Windows 2000 eliminated NetBIOS." Well, under the right circum-

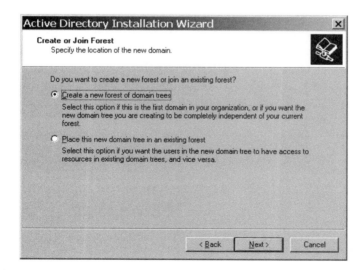

Figure 9–9

Choosing between creating a new domain tree and creating a
child domain within an existing domain tree controls how the
Active Directory tree structure is set up.

Figure 9–10

You must choose whether to create a new forest of domain trees
or place this new domain in an existing forest.

stances, it does. One of those circumstances is that you are operating in a pure
Windows 2000 environment. For backward compatibility with down-level cli-

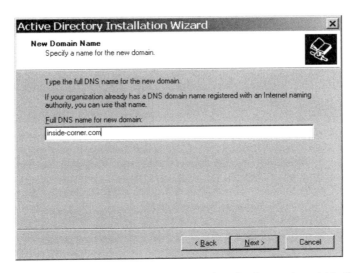

Figure 9–11

The Active Directory Installation wizard asks you to supply the full DNS name for your new Active Directory domain.

ents (Microsoft's term for NT and Windows 9x systems) a NetBIOS name is assigned to the domain. Typically it is the domain name minus the *.com*, which the Installation wizard will offer. Click Next to continue.

After creating the NetBIOS name, you must determine which drives and directories to configure the Active Directory database and log files to use. The database and log files are discussed later in this chapter but, for now, know that they must be set up on an NTFS partition. For performance and fault tolerance, it is recommended to put the database and logs on separate NTFS partitions, if possible. The Installation wizard will offer suggestions for the drives and directories to use, as shown in Figure 9.13. You can accept the recommendations in most cases and click Next.

Once you have specified the installation directories for the database and log files, you have to decide on what drive and directory to install the Shared System Volume. The Shared System Volume is also discussed later in this chapter but, like the Active Directory database and log files, it must be installed on an NTFS partition. The Shared System Volume is a repository for the domain's public files. The Active Directory Installation wizard gives a recommended destination for the directory, as shown in Figure 9.14. The reason the Shared System Volume, also known as *SYSVOL*, must be installed on an NTFS partition is that its contents are replicated to all DCs in a domain. This replication relies on the Change Journal (formerly known as the *USN Journal*), a feature of the NTFS 5 file system.

The Windows 2000 Active Directory Installation wizard will next check your DNS settings for configuration. If it cannot find the proper DNS settings,

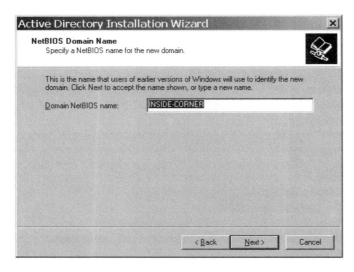

Figure 9-12
You must supply a NetBIOS domain name to preserve compati-
bility with non-Windows 2000 clients.

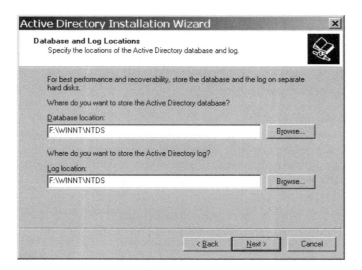

Figure 9-13
Determining on what drives and directories to install the Active
Directory database and log files.

you will be given the option to install and configure DNS during this wizard or
to skip it and manually configure DNS later. This is shown in Figure 9.15.

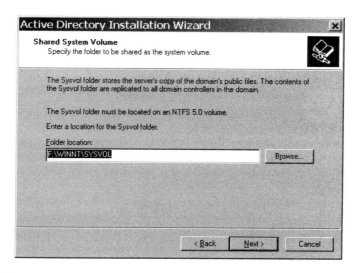

Figure 9-14   *Configuring the directory for the Shared System Volume.*

The next option in the Installation wizard is to determine how you want to set up your access permissions, as shown in Figure 9.16. By default, Windows 2000 chooses the backward compatibility mode with pre-Windows 2000 servers. If you know that you will have only Windows 2000 servers on your network, you can select the option to have permissions compatible only with Windows 2000 and click Next.

The last option in setting up a new DC is to define an administrator password to be used when the computer is started in Directory Services Restore Mode, shown in Figure 9.17. This password prevents unauthorized users from restoring parts or all of the Active Directory during a repair installation, a measure of security.

The very last step is to review your settings, as shown in Figure 9.18, and to confirm that everything is how you want it to be before the installation actually starts. If you are satisfied with the choices, click Next, and Active Directory will be installed. After your computer finishes copying files and reboots, you will have your first DC up and running.

Adding a Domain Controller to an Existing Domain

Once you have your first DC up and running in your Active Directory, you can start exploring the different Active Directory management utilities. However, in many cases, you will want to have more than one DC. One reason could be fault tolerance: if one DC goes down, your network can still service logon requests and maintain Active Directory information. In addition, having multiple DCs provides load balancing in larger environments. So, before we

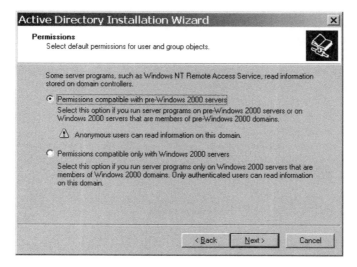

Figure 9–15 *You have the option to configure DNS automatically or manually if the Installation wizard cannot find the proper DNS settings.*

Figure 9–16 *Defining the permissions settings for your new Windows 2000 domain.*

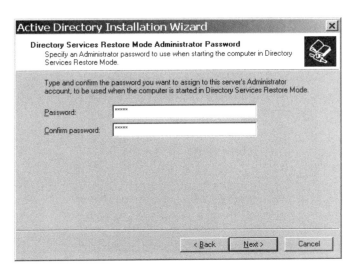

Figure 9–17 *The Installation wizard allows you to specify a password to protect against unauthorized restoring of the Active Directory.*

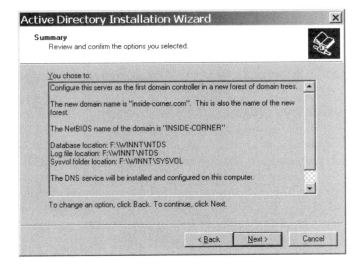

Figure 9–18 *Confirming your settings before starting the actual Active Directory installation. You can go back and make any necessary changes at this point or simply accept what you have already chosen.*

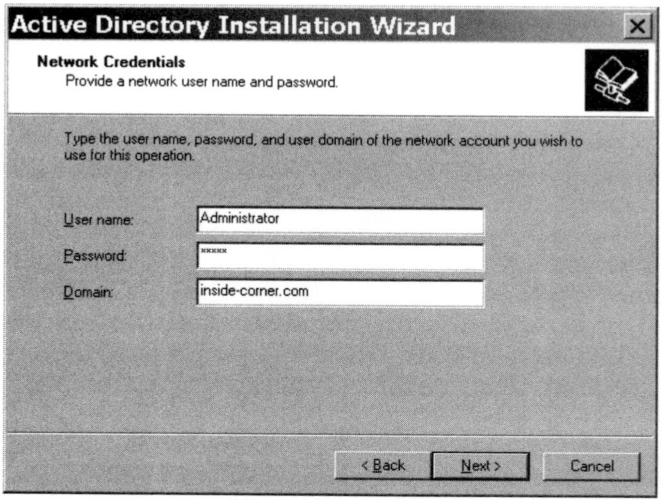

Figure 9–19 *You must supply proper network credentials in which to add a DC to an existing domain.*

start administering our Active Directory, let's set up a second server as a DC. Like with creating a DC for a new domain, *DCPROMO.EXE* promotes an existing server.

THE ACTIVE DIRECTORY INSTALLATION WIZARD (REVISITED)

As we showed previously in Figure 9.8, running *DCPROMO.EXE* launches the Active Directory Installation wizard and presents you with the option of creating a DC for a new domain (the default) or creating an additional DC for an existing domain. Because we already have an existing domain after the previous section's exercises, we will now choose the additional DC option and click Next.

At this point Windows 2000 wants to see some credentials—network credentials, that is. For obvious security reasons, not just anyone can promote a server to a DC, so you will need to supply the name and password of an administrative account for the domain you are joining, as shown in Figure 9.19.

The next step is to specify the name of the domain in which you want to make this server a DC, as shown in Figure 9.20.

Once you have told Windows 2000 in what domain you want your server to be a DC, you are asked a few of the same questions that you had to answer when you set up the initial DC. The first is the NTFS partition on which you want to store the Active Directory database and log files. You might ask, why do you need to have an Active Directory database on this new DC when it already exists on the first DC? All DCs have a copy of the Active Directory database for

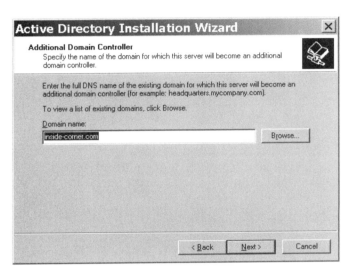

Figure 9–20
Specifying the Fully Qualified Domain Name (FQDN) for the domain in which you want your server to be a DC.

fault tolerance and load balancing. As before, this data must be stored on an NTFS partition. Figure 9.13 illustrates this step in the installation process.

The next question is where to store the Shared System Volume, just like when creating the first DC. Figure 9.14 showed this installation step and, like the Active Directory database and log files, the Shared System Volume must be contained on an NTFS partition.

The next step is the same as in Figure 9.17, specifying the administrative password to use when starting the computer in Directory Services Restore Mode. After that, you confirm your choices and start the promotion process. When it finishes, the system will prompt you to reboot and, upon startup, will be a DC and start replicating data from the existing DC.

Uninstalling Active Directory

The process is very simple, should you ever decide you want to uninstall Active Directory and return the DC to a standalone or member server. Simply run *DCPROMO.EXE* on your DC. The Active Directory Installation wizard will know that the machine is a DC and start the demotion process. You have the option of specifying whether the DC you are demoting is the last DC in the domain. If it is, the domain will no longer exist once the demotion process is complete. Existing computers will no longer be able to login to the domain, so they should be removed first before the DC is demoted. If the domain will still exist, the DC being demoted will be turned into a member server. When the last DC is removed, it becomes a standalone server. The Installation wizard will require the username and password of an administrative account that can perform the demotion, and, in the case of removing the last DC, you will be asked to give a password for the new administrator account on the standalone server. This is because when Active Directory is uninstalled, the Security Accounts Manager (SAM) is removed with it. Once the wizard is complete, the system will need to be rebooted and will come up as a standalone or member server.

The Active Directory Database

Administrators of Microsoft Exchange Server will find the topics in the section to be very familiar, because Active Directory borrows heavily from the Exchange Server concept of a transaction-based database. With a transaction-based database, there is a combination of the database itself, called *NTDS.DIT*, and log files (*edb.log, res1.log, res2.log*). In Windows 2000, the default location for the database and log files is in the *systemroot*/NTDS folder, where *systemroot* is the directory that Windows 2000 was installed into, such as *E:/WINNT*. Exchange administrators know that the log files are always 5 MB in size, and files that are not that size are usually corrupt. In Windows 2000, the log files are 10 MB in size.

LOG FILES VERSUS DATABASE

So, what is the point of the log files? Well, to understand the point of log files is to understand how the transactional database works. Whenever a change or update is made to the database, the change is first written to the log file (not directly to the database). Once the change is logged, it is then written to memory. The transaction is then confirmed, and finally written directly to the database.

Still, why not write changes directly to the database in the first place? The answer lies in performance. Since log files are all the same size, they already take up specified room on the hard disk. However, because a log file is 10 MB in size does not mean it is full, it just means it has allocated 10 MB of disk space. Knowing this, transactions are written sequentially to the log file, eliminating any sort of seek time on the hard drive. This would not be the case with the database itself, which grows as more data is added, and can become fragmented. This elegant use of log files dramatically reduces the time perceived on the client end for the update to take place, and allows Win2K to commit the change to the database on its own afterward.

PERFORMANCE AND RECOVERY

When Active Directory services shut down gracefully (such in the case of a server reboot), all transactions are committed to the database. When the server is not shut down gracefully, the transactions cannot be committed from memory to the database, leaving the database out of date. Log files can then be

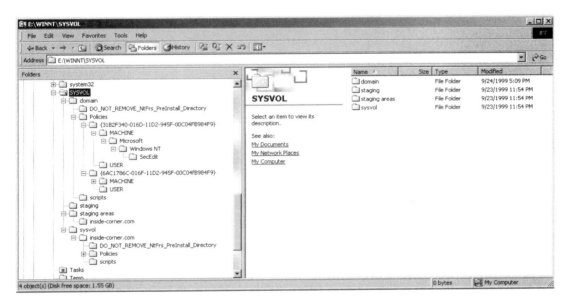

Figure 9–21   *The structure of the SYSVOL folder, which lies under the system-root folder.*

"played back" in the event of recovery, which brings the database back up to the current state. For this reason alone, it is recommended that the log files be stored on a separate physical disk than the database (not just a separate partition, but a physical separate disk). The chances of recovery from disaster become much greater when they are separated, and performance is better because Windows 2000 is not having to queue disk write requests while the database and log files are trying to update simultaneously (previous changes being committed to the database while new changes are written to the logs). Taking advantage of Windows 2000's dynamic storage options using the NTFS, such as disk striping with parity, increases the fault tolerance and performance, as well. These options are discussed later in the book.

The Shared System Volume

If you remember from the Active Directory Installation wizard, you were asked to assign a directory for the Shared System Volume. Unless you changed the default setting, the path is *systemroot/SYSVOL*. Figure 9.21 shows the directory structure of the *SYSVOL* folder on a newly created DC in the inside-corner.com domain.

As you can see with everything expanded, there are a few different items here. This *SYSVOL* folder replicates to all DCs within a domain, so the information will be the same on each machine, pending current updates that have not been replicated.

The policies folder contains group policies for Windows 2000 clients and system policies for down-level Windows 9x and Windows NT4 clients. The scripts folder is identical to the *systemroot/system32/REPL/Export/Scripts* directory found on NT4 servers. This scripts folder, shared as *NETLOGON* in NT4, contains logon scripts for down-level clients. The replication process manages inbound and outbound file transfers with other DCs through staging folders.

Active Directory Domain Modes

Active Directory supports two different domain modes, depending on the circumstances under which you plan to use Active Directory. They are:

- Mixed Mode
- Native Mode

MIXED MODE

When you install an Active Directory domain, by default, it operates in mixed mode. Mixed mode allows both Windows 2000 and down-level Windows NT Server DCs to coexist in the domain. There is a tradeoff in running mixed mode, in that some Windows 2000-only features, such as universal groups, are not available.

NATIVE MODE

When all of your domain controllers are running Windows 2000, you can change the domain mode to native. **Be warned, once you change to native mode, you cannot change back to mixed mode.** When you switch to native mode, any down-level replication stops, and you cannot add any down-level DCs to your domain from that point on.

Changing the domain mode is done by opening an Active Directory Microsoft Management Console (MMC, either Domains and Trusts or Users and Computers is fine) and opening the domain property sheet. Right click on the domain and select Properties to accomplish this. You will see the dialog shown in Figure 9.22.

Working in a Multiple-Domain Environment

Although a single domain is the preferred domain structure for a Windows 2000 network, there are times when you will find a need for multiple domains. A domain tree is created by adding child domains underneath existing parent domains. All domains within a single domain tree share the same Active Direc-

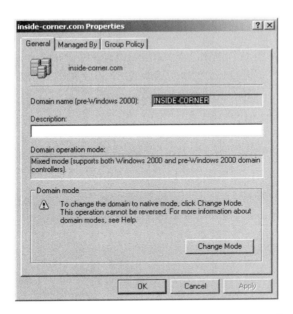

Figure 9-22

The domain properties, where you can change from Mixed to Native mode.

tory and, as we learned earlier, share a contiguous namespace. The other option is to have domains that are not part of the same domain tree, which creates a disjointed namespace. The domains that are not part of an existing domain tree can belong to the same forest or a separate forest. When working in a multiple-domain environment, there are additional considerations to take into account that are not present in single-domain environments. Some of them are:

- Trust Relationships
- Domain Security in the Active Directory
- Multiple Domains in a Tree

Understanding Trust Relationships

A trust relationship is simply a security link between two domains that allows the users of the domain being trusted to access resources in the domain that is doing the trusting, without having a user account defined in the trusting domain. There are two types of trust relationships in Windows 2000, one-way trusts and transitive trusts.

ONE-WAY TRUSTS

Windows NT Server administrators working in multiple-domain environments are familiar with the concept of trust relationships, where one domain trusts another domain to use its resources. One-way trusts are set up when an administrator from one domain explicitly allows users from another domain to use its resources. This capability in Windows 2000 is provided to link Windows 2000 domains to Windows NT domains and to allow domains in different domain trees to be linked. Again, these links are explicitly set up so that the trusting domain (the domain with the resources to be accessed) allows the trusted domain access.

TRANSITIVE TRUSTS

Transitive trust relationships are a new concept to Windows 2000 and apply to domains within the same tree and to top-level domains within the same forest. The transitive trust, a feature of the Kerberos authentication protocol employed in Windows 2000, is two-way and is created automatically by Windows 2000. By *transitive*, we mean that the trust relationship passes through to other domains. If you have three domains where Domain1 trusts Domain2, and Domain2 trusts Domain3, then through transitive trust, Domain1 automatically trusts Domain3. In Windows NT Server domains, each trust relationship would have to be explicitly defined. In the above scenario, Domain1 would not trust Domain3 automatically, a trust relationship between the two would have to be manually defined. Transitive trusts ease the often tedious administration of trust relationships that NT4 administrators faced in complex environments.

Domain Security in the Active Directory

Although transitive trusts ease network administration, they do make it possible in large environments for users to be able to access resources they shouldn't if administrators are not careful about the domains being added to the tree. Care should be taken to ensure that the ability to add a domain to a tree can be done only by authorized administrators. To the end user, however, the domain tree functions as a single domain. The Kerberos authentication process is transparent to them when they attempt to access resources in another domain. A user can login from one domain and access resources in another if given permission to use that resource.

The concept of the domain remains a security boundary, however, so domain admins can administer only the domain they belong to unless given appropriate permissions in another domain. Administrator privileges are not transitive, meaning that they do not flow down the domain tree. Therefore, an administrator in inside-corner.com does not have administrator privileges in dugout.inside-corner.com by default.

Administrative permissions can be granted to admins in other domains, however. One way is the same as in Windows NT Server, by adding the administrator account from another domain to the local administrators group. The other way is to grant permissions to specific objects and OUs within the Active Directory.

Multiple Domains in a Tree

Although having a single domain network is preferable, there are times when you will want to have multiple domains. The following are some circumstances when you might want to consider having multiple domains in a tree:

• Your company does not have a centralized IT department and relies on departmental administrators to manage departmental resources. Creating a separate domain for each allows you to restrict administrator access of each domain to only the department admin.

• Your company spans multiple sites connected by WAN links (slower than 512 K). Having multiple domains eliminates much of the replication traffic that takes place within a domain. Replication will occur for only certain key attributes of objects, rather than all Active Directory changes.

• Your company is global and works in multiple languages. You can have localized Windows 2000 domains with administrators who work in the local languages.

Chapter Summary

In this chapter, we concluded the planning stages of our Active Directory implementations and moved into the installation process. We learned the importance of planning a namespace, site planning, and Organizational Unit (OU) planning in determining how to install Active Directory. We then installed a domain controller (DC) into a new forest and domain tree, and then added a second DC to the domain. We discussed uninstalling Active Directory, as well, for situations where it is necessary or desirable to return a DC to a member or standalone server. Concluding the installation section was a discussion of the Active Directory database and database log files, and the Shared System Volume. From there, we learned about issues involved in working in a multiple-domain environment, such as trust relationships and domain security. Now that we have set up our Active Directory network, we are ready to move into administering it in the next chapter.

Administering the Active Directory

Other than actually installing Active Directory, what we have discussed so far are largely planning and organizational issues. Although not as exciting as actually getting your hands dirty with Active Directory, the theory helps you to design and develop an infrastructure that is going to be best suited to your environment. A well-designed infrastructure will also make this section, Active Directory administration, easier and more efficient.

However, now that we have installed and configured Active Directory on one or two domain controllers (DCs), we're ready to delve into working with the Active Directory itself and not just talking about it. Therefore, in this chapter, we will look at:

- Creating Active Directory Objects
- Finding Active Directory Objects
- Understanding and Controlling Access to Active Directory Objects
- Assigning Administrative Control of Active Directory Objects

By the end of this chapter, you should have a firm grasp of the basic administration functions within the Active Directory.

Creating Active Directory Objects

As we learned previously, Active Directory is the Windows 2000 directory service. It identifies all network resources and makes them available in an organized fashion to users and administrators. A key aspect of administering Active Directory is customizing and making networking resources available, which involves creating objects. However, to create active directory objects effectively, you will need to understand the following topics:

- Common Active Directory Objects
- Adding Resources to the Active Directory
- Creating Organizational Units

Common Active Directory Objects

Before you can add resources into the Active Directory, it is helpful to have an understanding of the different types of objects that can be included. There are many different types of objects that can be created. This section summarizes them.

USER ACCOUNTS

The most obvious directory object is the user account. Without user accounts, there is not much of a network. Windows 2000 user accounts have all of the same information as their Windows NT predecessors do, such as logon name, password, group membership, profiles, and account options, such as "must change password" and "account disabled." Windows 2000 also borrows heavily from the information fields available in Exchange Server mailboxes, such as address, display name, email address, phone number, and organization. User accounts are discussed extensively in the next chapter.

GROUPS

Groups are a fundamental security concept that has been carried over from Windows NT with little change. The standard groups, such as Domain Users and Domain Admins, are still around, and Windows 2000 adds many new groups on its own, depending on what services you have installed on your network. Figure 10.1 shows an example of a Windows 2000 network that is running DNS, DHCP, and DNS services that were setting up during our previous installing chapter.

Groups exist to simplify systems administration. By adding users to groups, applying security permissions is a much simpler process. If an entire department needs to access a network printer, for example, it is much more efficient to give one group the access permission, rather than having to grant access to each individual user account. Groups are discussed in more detail later in the book.

SHARED FOLDER

A shared folder in the Active Directory exists as a published pointer to an existing network share. Although you can still connect to a shared folder through My Network Places and navigate to the domain and computer that contains the shared folder, creating a shared folder in the Active Directory provides a conve-

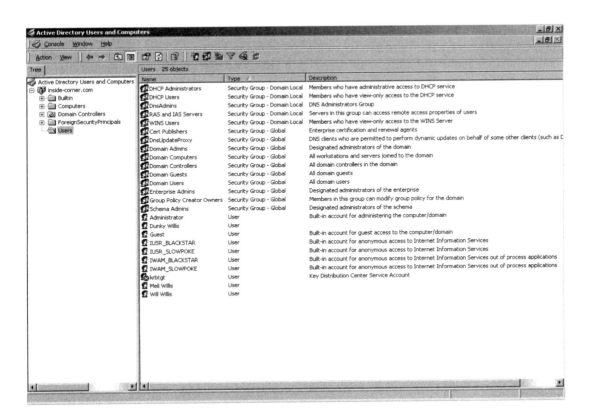

Windows 2000 includes a number of new groups that are added automatically, depending on the network services that have been installed.

nient object that users can search for and access in the directory. Publishing a shared folder into the Active Directory is essential if you want to disable the NetBIOS protocol in Windows 2000. If you disable NetBIOS without publishing the shared folders into the directory, users will be unable to locate those network resources. NetBIOS is the basis for previous Microsoft network operating systems and still exists for backward-compatibility reasons. By publishing shared folders into the Active Directory, a Windows 2000 network no longer has to rely on the cumbersome and security-weak NetBIOS protocol. Resources that are not published, however, won't be available through the Directory and, therefore, will not be available at all if NetBIOS is disabled.

PRINTER

Like a shared folder, a shared printer is merely a registry setting on a local computer that tells Windows to make the resource available to other users who meet the security criteria that has been configured. A printer attached to a computer that is not in the Active Directory has to share a printer manually for network use, whereas printers attached to DCs are automatically added to the directory at the time they are created. As with shared folders, printers must be published into the Active Directory to turn off the NetBIOS protocol support in Windows 2000.

COMPUTER

The computer object is more or less the same as in Windows NT. In an NT domain, all Windows NT computers were required to be added to the domain because they participated in domain security. Windows 9x computers were not required to be added; a user just needed a valid username and password to logon to the network from a Windows 9x computer. When you create a computer in Windows 2000, you have to supply not only a Windows 2000 computer name, but also a name that is compatible with pre-Windows 2000 operating systems. The computer group contains Windows 2000 Professional workstations and member servers.

DOMAIN CONTROLLERS

The DC object is similar in concept to the computer object, except that, rather than being a container that holds Windows 2000 Professional workstations and member servers, it holds DCs. For DCs, additional information is supplied that isn't contained in a computer object, such as operating system and service pack levels, and who manages the server. Additional DC information that is stored includes a pre-Windows 2000-compatible computer name, the DNS name of the server, and whether or not the DC is trusted for delegation.

ORGANIZATIONAL UNIT

An organizational unit (OU) is similar to a group. It is used to organize Active Directory objects, and OUs can contain other OUs or any of the objects previously listed. Although useful for administration in the sense of organizing objects, OUs can also have group policies applied directly to them, making them useful in a security context, as well. An OU is the smallest unit to which you can assign Group Policy or delegate administrative authority. Group Policy is discussed extensively later in the book.

CONTACT

A contact object is an informational object only. It can be used to define a contact person who is responsible for administering a particular OU. The only information that a contact contains is the name (first, initials, last), full name, and display name. Contacts are most useful in multiple-site organizations with non-centralized IT departments, where it may not always be easy to determine who is responsible for a particular OU.

Adding Resources to the Active Directory

When you add resources to your network, you create Active Directory objects that represent those resources. By default, only administrators have permissions to add resources, and they can create objects anywhere in the Active Directory. Administration can be delegated as well, which is discussed later in this chapter.

When you create objects, you will often find that only a small number of attributes is available for configuration while you are actually doing the object creation. This is normal, and by going into the properties of the object after you create it, you usually have many more attributes that can be configured.

Object attributes and object properties are usually used interchangeably to mean the same thing. Although many different types of objects have the same types of attributes, the values of the attributes are what make an object unique. Some attributes are required to be unique, such as display name (you cannot have two objects with the same display name). Other attributes are not required to be unique, such as first name (you can have multiple objects with a first name of Joe).

So you are ready to add resources, right? Well, how do we do it? First, we need to look at the tools of the trade. If you have looked at the Administrative Tools folder on the Start menu since we installed Active Directory, you will have noticed that we now have some additional utilities, which are described next.

ACTIVE DIRECTORY USERS AND COMPUTERS

Active Directory Users and Computers is the primary administrative utility that we will use for managing and publishing information into the Active Directory. With this utility, you can add, edit, delete, or otherwise configure any of the objects listed in the previous section, with the exception of a DC. However, you can view and edit the properties of DCs within Active Directory Users and Computers, because the DC's OU is present. Figure 10.1 showed the Active Directory Users and Computers console window.

ACTIVE DIRECTORY DOMAINS AND TRUSTS

Active Directory Domains and Trusts is a utility to manage Active Directory in a multiple-domain environment. In a single-domain environment, this tool does not have any use, because there are no trust relationships to consider. In an Enterprise environment, however, you can manage other domains participating in a forest, configure the domain modes (mixed or native) for other domains, and manage trust relationships between domains.

ACTIVE DIRECTORY SITES AND SERVICES

Active Directory Sites and Services is another tool that will have little use in a single-site environment. As Figure 10.2 shows, there is not much information available to configure in a single domain.

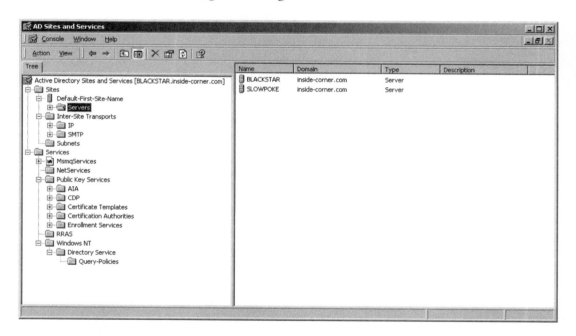

Figure 10–2   *In a single-domain environment, Active Directory Sites and Services does not provide many configuration options.*

In a multiple-site environment, however, Active Directory Sites and Services allows you to administer site information, such as replication schedules, authentication across sites, and Active Directory-enabled services. Some network service-related information can be published into the Directory, such as service bindings and configurations. These can be managed through this utility, simplifying administration of network resources. By default, however, the Ser-

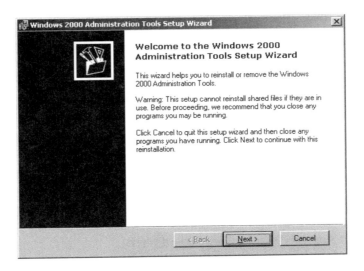

Figure 10-3   *The Windows 2000 Administration Tools Setup wizard.*

vice branch is not shown in the Active Directory Sites and Services window. It can be turned on, however, by clicking the View menu in the console window and selecting Show Services Node. Figure 10.2 had already enabled the viewing of the Services Node.

ACTIVE DIRECTORY SCHEMA MANAGER

The Active Directory Schema snap-in is not installed by default when you set up Active Directory. You install it manually from the Windows 2000 Server CD-ROM, by double-clicking the *I386\Adminpak.msi* file and following the Installation wizard. Figure 10.3 shows the welcome screen to the Setup wizard.

After clicking next to the welcome message, you will be presented the options shown in Figure 10.4, to uninstall or install the Administration Tools. Choose to install and click Next.

Once you have made your selection, the wizard begins installing and configuring your system for the Administration Tools, as illustrated in Figure 10.5.

After installation completes and you click Finish, you still must add the new snap-ins to a console to use them. Click Start->Run->*mmc/a* and press OK. You will be presented with a blank console window. Click the Console menu then Add/Remove Snap-In, then Add. You will see a window similar to that shown in Figure 10.6; select Active Directory Schema and click Add, then click OK.

Active Directory Schema is primarily a developer's tool, although experienced systems administrators can also use it. Feel free to browse through the objects and their attributes. However, be careful not to make any changes

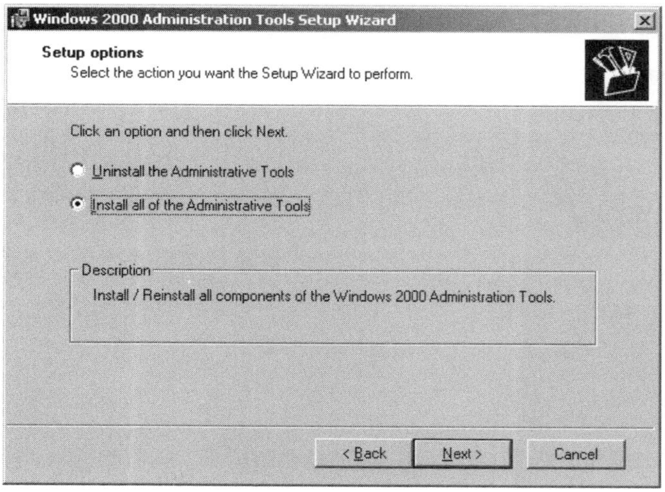

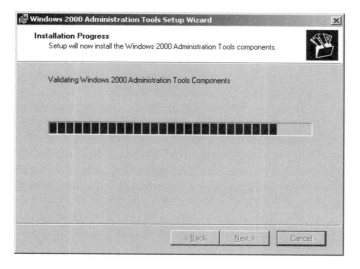

Figure 10–4   *Choosing to install or uninstall the Administration Tools.*

Figure 10–5   *The Windows 2000 Administration Tools Setup wizard installs and configures the components on your server.*

unless you are sure of the ramifications. Figure 10.7 shows the Active Directory Schema console.

In Active Directory, classes are the possible directory objects that can be created. Each class is a collection of attributes. When you create an object, the

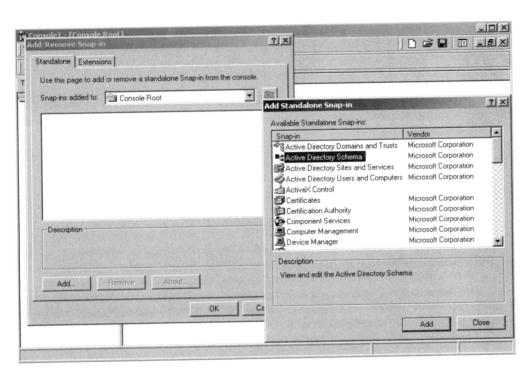

Figure 10–6   *Adding the Active Directory Schema to a new console.*

attributes store the information that describes the object. The user class, for example, is composed of many attributes, including network address, home directory, and so on. Every object in Active Directory is an instance of an object class.

COMPUTER MANAGEMENT

Although not specifically an Active Directory administration tool, Computer Management is one of the more used utilities in Windows 2000. As you can see from Figure 10.8, you use Computer Management to view and configure information from hardware to storage, to shared folders, to event logging, and more. Computer Management consolidates several of the administrative tools into a single, easy-to-use console.

One aspect of Computer Management is very important to point out. Notice that there is a red circle with an *X* through Local Users and Groups. The reason is that, once a computer is promoted to an Active Directory DC, it loses its local Security Accounts Manager (SAM) and draws from the domain SAM. If you attempt to use Local Users and Groups, you will receive an error message to this effect. A DC no longer has local users or local groups.

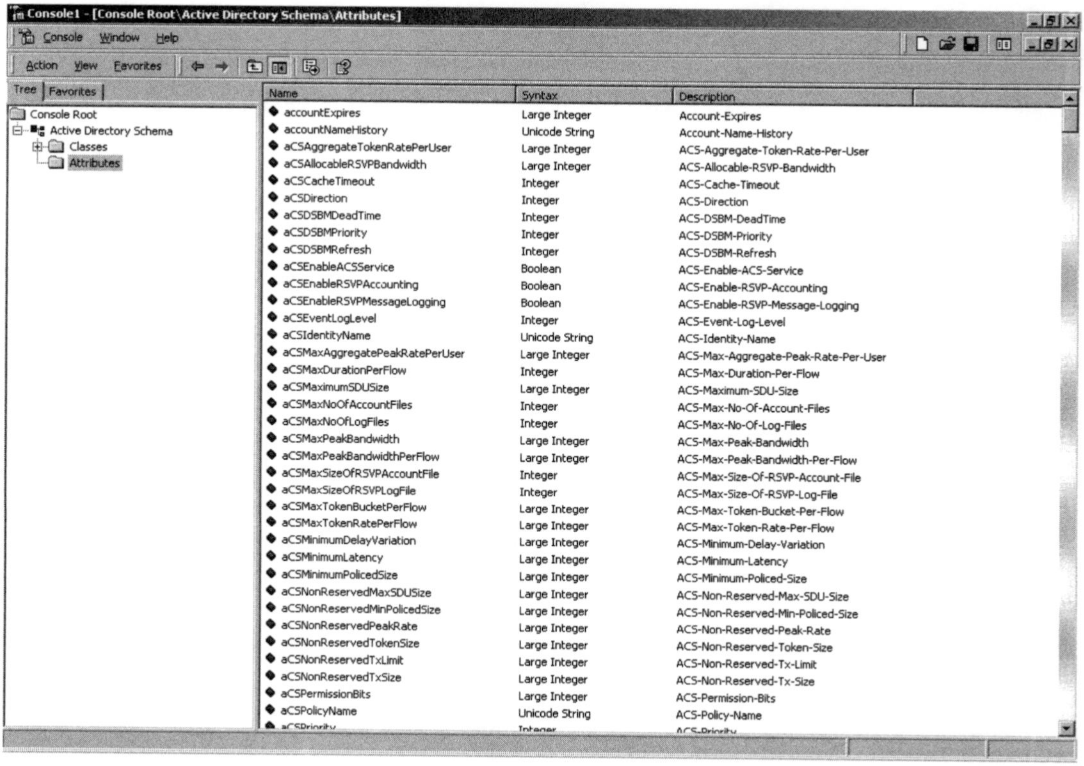

Figure 10-7

The Active Directory Schema is a tool for programmers and experienced systems administrators.

Creating Organizational Units

When you first create your Active Directory domain, two OUs are created automatically. They are:

- Users OU—default location for new user accounts
- Computers OU—default location for computer objects

These two OUs cannot be moved in or deleted from the Active Directory. However, you can create additional OUs that you can administer. Creating an OU is done by right-clicking on the OU container that you want to hold the new object and clicking New->. Your choices after New are Computer, Contacts, Group, Printer, User, and Shared Folder. As an example, next we will step through the process of creating a new user OU.

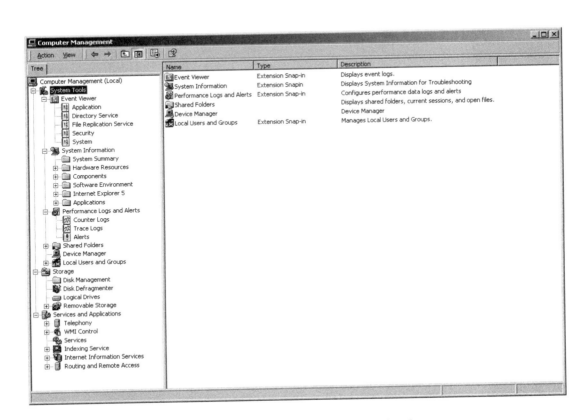

Figure 10–8

Computer Management provides a consolidated tool to manage your server.

CREATING A USER OU

We will put our new user into the existing Users OU, so let's right-click on the Users OU and click New->User. You will see a window in which you need to supply the information for the user account, as shown in Figure 10.9.

User accounts are discussed in the next chapter, so if you have any questions regarding what the individual fields mean, feel free to skip ahead and find out what they mean. Once you have filled out the fields and clicked Next, you have to supply a password and some basic password requirements, as seen in figure 10.10. Supply the required information and click Next to continue, then Finish to create the new user account.

After you have finished creating the new user, notice that they appear in the Users OU in the Active Directory. Right-click on the new account that you just created and click Properties. As you can see in Figure 10.11, mentioned previously, there are now many more attributes that you can configure for this

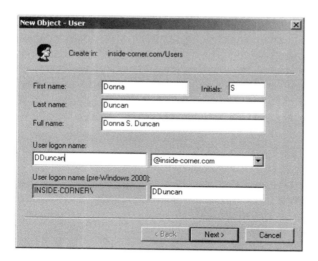

Figure 10–9   *Configuring a new User object.*

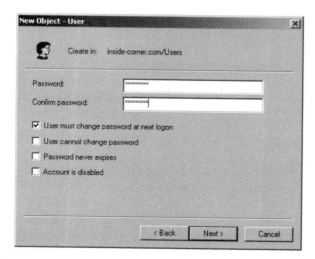

Figure 10–10   *While creating a new user account, you must supply basic password information.*

user account. The different property sheets are discussed in the next chapter, with user accounts.

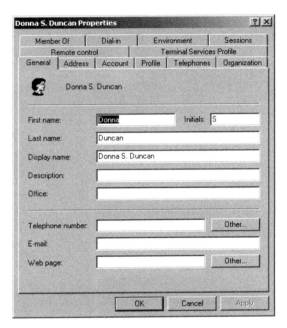

Figure 10–11

There are many more properties available for configuration than what was presented when initially creating the user account.

Finding Active Directory Objects

As domains and sites grow and more and more objects are added, it becomes somewhat unwieldy to browse through the Directory every time you want to locate a network resource. Luckily, Windows 2000 includes a powerful search utility, modestly named *Find*. This feature is similar to the Find feature in Windows 9x and Windows NT, in that you can search for resources and specify criteria for your search; however, the Windows 2000 Find allows you to search across the entire Active Directory. Figure 10.12 shows the basic Find window, while Figure 10.13 shows the dropdown list illustrating the different types of OUs that can be searched on. Figure 10.14 shows the Advanced Find window, where search criteria can be configured, with the dropdown list selected for Find type. You access the Find utility through the Active Directory Users and Computers administrative tool. You can narrow your search by right-clicking on an individual OU and selecting Find, which will automatically limit the search to that particular OU. You can also search the entire domain by right-clicking on the domain name before clicking Find, or you can search entire domain tree or forest.

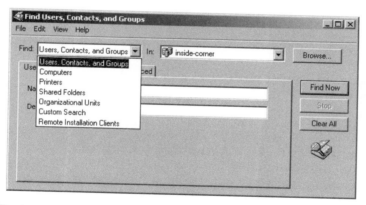

Figure 10–12

The Windows 2000 Find utility lets you search for network resources.

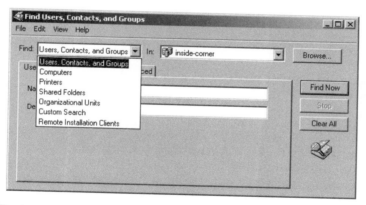

Figure 10–13

Any type of OU can be searched on, and Windows 2000 will even let you perform customized searches, based on criteria you provide.

When you use the Find utility, you are searching the Global Catalog for published network resources. The Global Catalog, as we previously discussed, contains a partial replica of the entire Active Directory. The Global Catalog is what allows the user to search for any resources, regardless of in what domain the resources are located.

Let's step through the following exercise, using the Find utility.

1. Open the Find utility by right-clicking on your domain in Active Directory Users and Computers and clicking Find.
2. From the Find dropdown list, select Computer.

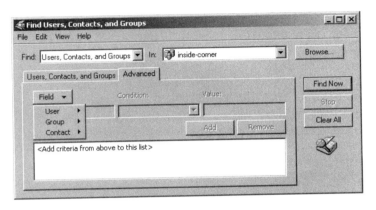

Figure 10–14

The Advanced tab of the Find utility allows you to specify additional criteria for your search.

3. Type in the name of a computer of a DC on your network in Computer Name and click Find Now.
4. The results box should show the computer. Notice that the default Role was selected as Any. Click the dropdown list, choose Domain Controllers, and do the search again. You should get the same results. Now, select Workstations and Servers and conduct the search. What happens?
5. Now let's try a new search using the Advanced options. Clear the Computer Name field so that it is blank, and set the Role to Domain Controllers.
6. Click the Advanced tab. Click the Field dropdown list and select Operating System.
7. Select Starts With as the condition. If you use the Is condition, the value you specify must exactly match; otherwise, you won't get any results.
8. Under Value, type in *Windows 2000* and click Add.
9. Click Find Now. All of your Windows 2000 DCs should appear in the Results Field, as in Figure 10.15.

Understanding and Controlling Access to Active Directory Objects

One of the basic tenets of systems administration is security and controlling access to resources. Windows 2000 uses an object-based security model, where permissions are applied to Active Directory objects. Every Active Directory object has a security context that describes who has access to it and what level of access they have. When a request is made to access a network resource, Windows 2000 checks the security properties to see whether the object making

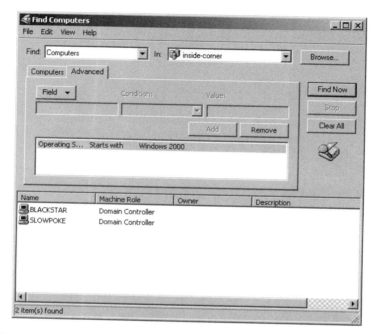

Figure 10–15   *Search results from the inside-corner.com domain for all DCs with an operating system of Windows 2000.*

the request (such as a user account) has the appropriate permissions. In this section, we will look at the following security-related issues:

- Active Directory Permission Types
- Using Active Directory Permissions
- Permission Inheritance
- Moving Objects

Active Directory Permission Types

Because object permissions determine who can access an object and what type of access is allowed, the owner of an object must assign permissions before that object can be accessed by other users. Windows 2000 carries over the NT concept of Access Control Lists (ACLs). Every object has an ACL that lists the permissions for that object. Permissions can be granted not only for user access, but for administrative access as well. Assigning administrator rights for a user to an object gives them access only to that object. It does not give them access to other objects. The exception is that giving administrator rights to an OU gives the person with those rights administrator privileges to the entire OU.

There are different permission types, depending on what it is you are trying to accomplish. We will look at object permissions and standard versus special permissions.

OBJECT PERMISSIONS

The permissions that are available to assign are completely dependent on the type of object you are working with. Permissions that are relevant to one type of object may not be relevant to another type of object. An example of this would be the change password permission that applies to user accounts and computer accounts but not to shared folders in the Directory.

Objects, such as users, can belong to multiple groups or OUs. When this happens, the permission-assigning process can become confusing. As an example, let us look at a user account, DuncanW. DuncanW belongs to two groups, one that has write permissions to a shared folder and one that has only read permission to the same resource. In this case, the rights are cumulative, meaning that the user account would have read and write access to this shared folder.

What happens, however, in the case where a user has been denied access to a folder as a member of one group while being granted full control as a member of another group? Windows 2000, like NT before it, treats a deny case specially. **Having a "deny" attribute set in an ACL will always take place over any sort of "allow" attributes.** Therefore, in our example above, the user would have no access to the shared folder. Because of this, be careful with denying permissions. A user or group should be denied only when specifically required because of membership in a group that has been granted permissions. It is best to just not assign any permissions whatsoever to a user if they should not have access. Also, ensure that at least one user has full control over an object. Otherwise, you could find yourself in a situation where an object could become inaccessible to an admin through the Active Directory Users and Computers console.

STANDARD PERMISSIONS VERSUS SPECIAL PERMISSIONS

When you are configuring the permissions on an object, you have both standard and special permissions that you can set. By far, the most used options are the standard permissions, because they provide an appropriate level of security in most cases. Standard properties for most objects include Read, Write, and Delete, among others (as above, some permissions are available on some objects and not others). Special permissions provide a more granular level of control over the security of an object. For example, the standard permission of Write consists of the standard Read permission plus special permissions Write All Properties and All Validated Writes.

Using Active Directory Permissions

With an understanding of the types of permissions in hand, let's turn our attention toward actually doing something with our theory. Typically, the utility you will use to manage object permissions is Active Directory Users and Computers. With that in mind, fire it up and we'll go to work.

Before we get too far along, you'll need to click on the View menu and ensure that Advanced Features is checked. Doing this enables the Security tab on the object property sheets. If you looked around in Active Directory Users and Computers during the last section and could not find where to set permissions, this is probably why.

ASSIGNING STANDARD PERMISSIONS

In this exercise, we will assign standard permissions to the Computers OU in Active Directory Users and Computers.

1. Click the View menu and ensure that Advanced Properties is selected.
2. Right-click on the Computers container and click Properties.
3. Click the Security tab. You will see a window similar to that shown in Figure 10.16.
4. You can either modify existing permissions or add new permissions.

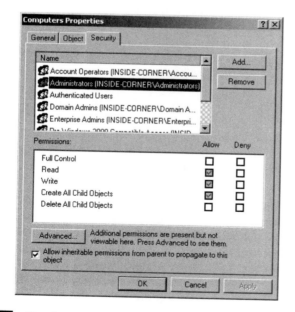

Figure 10-16   The Computers Properties property sheet.

- To modify existing permissions, simply click the user account or group whose permissions you wish to modify and make the appropriate changes. For example, upgrade the permissions for Authenticated Users from Read to Write and click OK.
- To Add new permissions, click the Add button and select the user or group that you want to assign permissions to for this object. Click Add, then click OK to return to the main Security Properties window.

5. With the user or group selected under Name, look under the Permissions section and check or uncheck the boxes to allow or deny the different types of access to this resource.

ASSIGNING SPECIAL PERMISSIONS

To view and assign special permissions to the Computers OU, do the following:

1. On the security tab in Computers Properties from Figure 10.16, click on the Advanced button. Figure 10.17 shows the Access Control Settings for Computers.

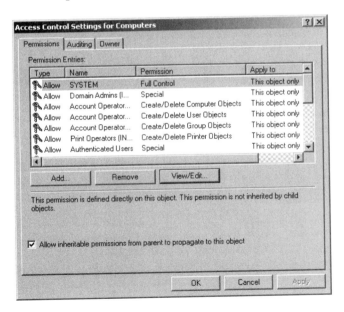

Figure 10–17   *Access Control Settings for the Computers OU.*

2. Click on the View/Edit button. This brings up the special properties for this object, the Permission Entry for Computers. Figure 10.18 illustrates this window.

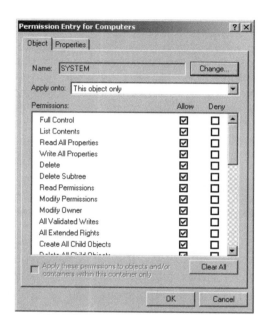

Figure 10-18   *Viewing/Editing the special properties of the Computers OU.*

Once you have completed your changes, click OK until you are back out to the main Active Directory Users and Computers window. It is important to note that, whenever possible, standard permissions should be used. Although special permissions offer a much finer level of control over an object, they increase the administrative burden and can be difficult to troubleshoot, should there be permissions-related problems after they have been set. In most instances, the standard permissions provide a sufficient level of security.

Permission Inheritance

The concept of permission inheritance is fairly simple but nicely streamlines the administration process of objects. It does this by reducing the number of times that an administrator has to apply object permissions. In Figures 10.16 and 10.17, you'll notice a check box at the bottom for "Allow inheritable permissions from parent to propagate this object." This option allows you to have the permissions assigned to this object carry down to all objects and OUs beneath it. So, from our previous example, if you assigned special permissions to the Computers OU, then created an object in that container, by default, the special permissions you set would carry down and exist in the child object.

When you use inherited permissions, the check boxes on the security tab are unavailable for the permissions that have been inherited from a parent

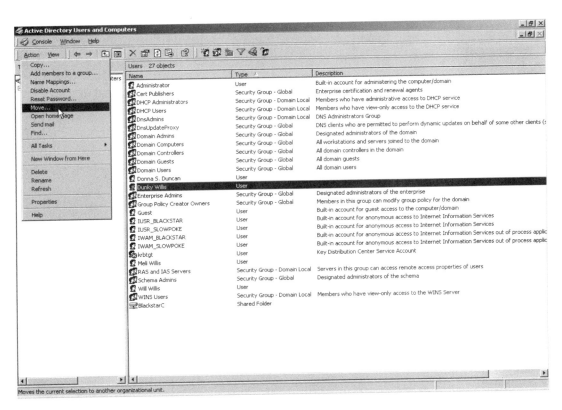

Figure 10–19

Moving an object between two OUs is a two-step process, the first step being to select the object you wish to move and selecting Move from the Action menu.

object. These grayed-out check boxes are your indicator of what permissions have been inherited versus those that exist specifically in the child object.

The child object can choose not to use inherited permissions by unchecking the box that allows permissions to be propagated from a parent. Doing so will remove all permissions from an object and require that the administrator explicitly define all permissions for that object.

Moving Objects

One of the nice features of the hierarchical Windows 2000 Active Directory structure is that objects can be moved around between OUs. There could be any number of reasons why you would want to move an object from one OU to another, such as a corporate reorganization or simply a user getting transferred from one division to another. Moving an object from one OU is easy; just select

Figure 10–20   *Step two of moving an object is selecting the desired destination OU for the move.*

the object you want to move and either right-click it and select Move or click the Action menu and select Move. A list of available OUs to move the object to appears. Select the desired OU and click OK. Figures 10.19 and 10.20 illustrate this procedure.

Assigning Administrative Control of Active Directory Objects

Only in small corporate environments can a single person administer the entire network and all of the resources on it. In medium to large networks, there are usually multiple administrators and, often, many people responsible for select network resources. Windows 2000 and Active Directory make an administrator's life easier by allowing the ability to delegate control over individual objects and OUs to other people, so that they can perform administrative functions as needed.

Planning for Delegation

Delegation of objects is done by assigning permissions to an object, allowing users or groups to administer that object. An administrator can assign permissions to a user so that he or she can create or modify objects within an OU. They can also grant the user permissions to modify attributes of an object, such as the ability to change or reset passwords.

Assigning permissions is best done at the OU level, for ease of administration. If you get into the habit of assigning permissions to individual objects, you might find your network resources difficult to manage as your network grows. Typically, you group objects in OUs in such a way that the chances of a situation occurring where a user should have permissions to administer one object in an OU but not another are minimal.

Even on a network that is administered by one person, it is often handy to delegate control of departmental OUs. Having someone in a particular department who can administer objects in that department reduces burden on the main systems administrator and increases the response time for tasks being done. In many cases, a departmental OU administrator need only make slight changes, and having permissions allows him or her to do that without having to get the primary administrator to perform the function.

Assigning Administrative Control with the Delegation of Control Wizard

There are different ways to delegate control of Active Directory objects. In this section, we will primarily deal with the Delegation of Control wizard, which is activated by selecting the object you want to delegate control of (such as the Users OU), clicking the Action menu, and selecting Delegate Control. When you do, a welcome screen is presented. After clicking Next, you have the win-

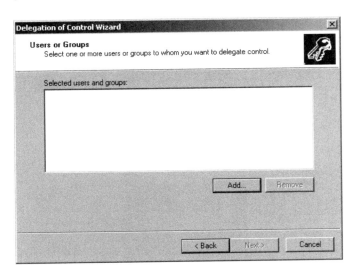

Figure 10–21   *The Delegation of Control wizard.*

dow shown in Figure 10.21.

Once you click Add on this window, you will see the window in Figure 10.22, where you can choose the users or groups to whom you want to delegate control.

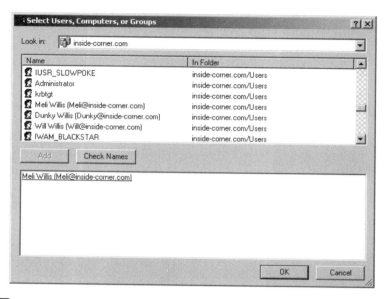

Figure 10–22   *Adding users or groups to delegate control of an object.*

Next, you are asked to select the scope of the delegation task, as in Figure 10.23.

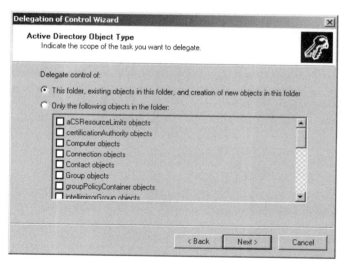

Figure 10–23   *Selecting the Active Directory Object Type in the Delegation of Control wizard.*

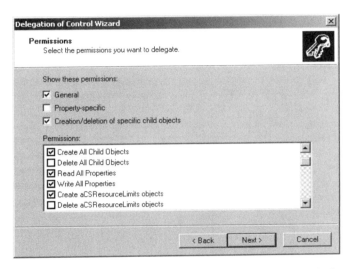

Figure 10–24   *Configuring specific permissions to be delegated through the Delegation of Control wizard.*

Once you have determined the scope of the task delegation you want to have, it is time to configure the specific permissions to be delegated. By default, only General permissions are checked in Figure 10.24, but you can drill down to a more granular level of control by enabling the Property-specific and Creation/deletion of specific child objects options and selecting or deselecting the check boxes below.

The last step is to confirm your choices, as in Figure 10.25. You can go back at this point and make any last-minute changes you need to before clicking Finish. Once you do click Finish, the permissions are applied as you have configured them.

Guidelines for Active Directory Administration

The following are some general guidelines (or best practices, if you will) for administering Active Directory.

• Plan, plan, plan! You might consider it boring, but you will save yourself many future headaches if you plan your Active Directory structure right from the start, without having to move too many objects around later.

• Take the time to fill out all of the relevant information when creating an Active Directory object. Although it may seem easier at the time to supply only the bare minimum amount of information, the old programmer's cliché, "garbage in, garbage out" applies. You make the Active Directory Find utility that much more powerful if it has more attributes that are available.

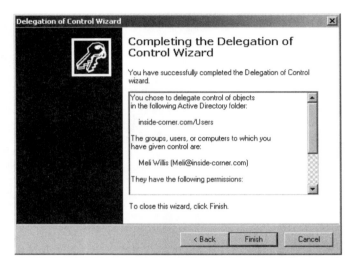

Figure 10–25   *Windows 2000 lets you review and confirm your choices before finishing the wizard and applying the permissions.*

• Don't explicitly deny permissions unless it is absolutely necessary. Deny permissions take precedence over any allow permissions, so you can run into problems where users who belong to multiple groups cannot gain access to resources that they need if one group has been denied. Leaving a group or user completely off a permissions list allows no access to a resource, which is a better approach than specifically denying permission.

• At least one administrator or user should always have Full Control of an object. If not, an administrator may not be able to administer an object in Active Directory Users and Computers.

• Be careful to whom you delegate administrative control, and ensure that they are aware of the responsibility that they have. A delegate should be accountable for his or her actions, and you should be able to track what a delegate is doing in an OU. An administrator is ultimately responsible for "cleanup" if a delegate messes up.

Chapter Summary

In this chapter, we continued our progression beyond the theory of design and planning of Active Directory into its hands-on administration. We took the Active Directory domain that we set up in the previous chapter and customized it by creating objects and Organizational Units (OUs), and we learned about adding resources to the Active Directory.

We discussed the different types of Active Directory objects: user accounts, groups, shared folders, printers, computers, domain controllers, and OUs. In addition to creating objects, we used the Find utility to locate Active Directory resources. With the Find utility, we leaned about filters to narrow our search to specific types of objects in specific OUs.

The last part of the chapter dealt with controlling access to objects and delegating control of objects to other users and/or groups. Delegation provides efficient administration, whereas controlling access lets the administrator control the security of his or her network.

Now that we have covered the basics of Active Directory administration, we will look more in depth at user accounts and groups over the next few chapters.

User Accounts
and Their Role

··◄

*U*ser accounts have grown more complex under Windows 2000 than they were in NT 4.0. As previous chapters have shown, Active Directory and Microsoft Management Console (MMC) change many of the old "rules" of administering a Windows 2000 network, when compared with an NT 4.0 network. User accounts and groups are no exception to the change. In this chapter, we will discuss these broad subjects:

- Understanding the different types of user accounts
- Using new user accounts
- Creating domain user accounts

Understanding the Different Types of User Accounts

Windows 2000 has the following types of user accounts, depending on the role of the particular machine. This can be a workstation (Windows 2000 Professional), a standalone server, or a domain controller (DC) participating in an Active Directory. The types of user accounts you will encounter are:

- Built-in user accounts
- Local user accounts
- Domain user accounts

Built-In User Accounts

Administrators of NT 4.0 and earlier networks already understand the concept of built-in user accounts. These are accounts that are set up by default during the installation of the operating system. In fact, those with NT 4.0 experience will find that the built-in user accounts are basically the same in Windows 2000. Figure 11.1 shows the user account list for a Windows 2000 system without Active Directory installed. Administering these accounts is done through the Computer Management MMC snap-in. On this system, I have also created a standard user account for my everyday use. Figure 11.2 shows the built-in accounts on a DC that has both Active Directory and Internet Information Server (IIS) installed. IIS adds the *IWAM_computername* and *IUSR_computername* accounts.

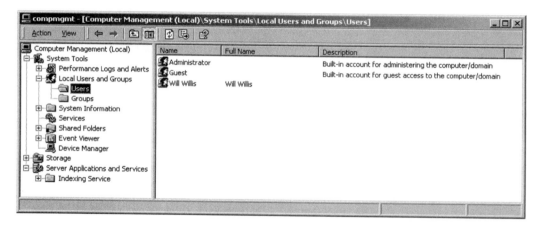

Figure 11–1   *The Administrator and Guest built-in user accounts on a Windows 2000 non-domain controller.*

Notice in the window of Figure 11.2 that, above the contents pane (the right side of the window), reads [Filter Activated]. The reason for this is that we applied a filter to our users container to show only the built-in user accounts, rather than every user account on the system. Depending on the services you have installed on your server, you will have a varying number of service accounts added to your Active Directory Users and Computers list.

Adding a view filter is often very helpful when administering a large number of user accounts. Under the View menu on the console, select Filter Options, then click Custom under Filtering Options, and click Edit Filter. Just don't forget later that you have applied a filter if you cannot find a particular user!

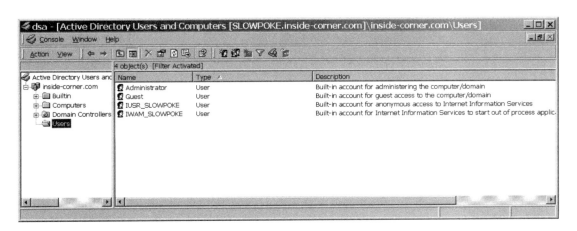

| Figure 11–2 | *The built-in user accounts on an Active Directory domain controller with IIS installed.* |

These built-in user accounts are designed primarily for initial logon and configuration of a local computer. Each account has a different combination of rights and permissions. The Administrator account has the most omnipotent rights and permissions, whereas the Guest account has limited rights and permissions.

THE ADMINISTRATOR ACCOUNT

As with NT 4.0, Windows 2000 creates Administrator and Guest accounts by default. The Administrator account is obvious because you were prompted to provide a password for it during the installation of the operating system. It makes sense that this account is included by default because, without an administrative account, there would be no way to set up additional users or perform any kind of function that requires administrative access, such as installing most software packages (software typically makes changes to the registry, which requires administrative permission).

The type of account used should always fit the purpose. Administrators should have separate accounts for administrative activity and general user activity. To avoid accidental changes to protected resources, the account with the least privilege that can do the task should be used. For example, viruses have the potential to do much more damage if activated from an account with administrator privileges. In Figure 11.1, I noted the account that I had created for my day-to-day use. Even though I am the administrator and only user of my computer, not everything I do requires administrative permission. This is an idea that is held very strongly in UNIX circles. No UNIX systems administrator worth his salt would be caught dead using the root (administrator equivalent) account for normal computer use. This all relates to security. A standard user account that is inappropriately used can do far less damage than can an administrator account.

It is also a good idea to change the name of the built-in Administrator account to something less obvious. This is the one account that can never be locked out due to repeated failed logon attempts and, consequently, is attractive to hackers who try to break in by repeatedly guessing passwords. By renaming the account, you force hackers to guess the account name, as well as the password.

If the built-in account rights and permissions are not modified or disabled by a network administrator, they could be used by any user or service to logon to a network, using the Administrator or Guest identity. To obtain the security of user authentication and authorization, create an individual user account for each user that will participate on your network by using Active Directory Users and Computers. Each user account (including the Administrator and Guest account) can then be added to Windows 2000 groups to control the rights and permissions assigned to the account. Using accounts and groups that are appropriate for your network ensures that users logging onto a network can be identified and can access only the permitted resources. Groups and Group Policy are covered in subsequent chapters.

THE GUEST ACCOUNT

The Guest account is an account that allows nonauthenticated users to access resources on the system. Often, the Guest account is used in workgroup environments, where there are no domain global accounts. Consider the network shown in Figure 11.3.

In this example workgroup, there are five workstations, with one of the Windows 2000 Professional workstations functioning as a print server. Each workstation is a standalone system, even though there is a network connection between all of them. The Guest account allows users of the other workstations to access the shared printer on the Windows 2000 workstation that is sharing it without having to have a local user account and password for that Windows 2000 system. This would also apply to the other Windows 2000-Professional workstation, as well as to the NT 4.0 workstation. Without the Guest account enabled, users on the other workstations would not be able to login and access shared resources on a Windows 2000-based system without having a local user account on that system.

The Guest account is disabled by default for security purposes. In the next chapter, we will discuss account options that include enabling and disabling user accounts.

Local User Accounts

Figure 11.1 showed a management console displaying user accounts. These were Local Users and Groups, which are user accounts specific to an individual

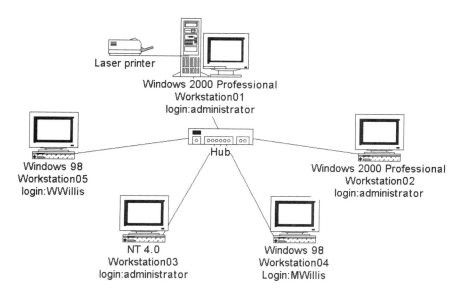

Laser printer

Windows 2000 Professional
Workstation01
login:administrator

Hub

Windows 98
Workstation05
login:WWillis

Windows 2000 Professional
Workstation02
login:administrator

NT 4.0
Workstation03
login:administrator

Windows 98
Workstation04
Login:MWillis

Figure 11-3   *A basic networked workgroup.*

machine. Each Windows 2000 Professional system and Windows 2000 Server system acting as a standalone server has its own Security Accounts Manager (SAM). The SAM keeps track of all of the user accounts and their properties on the local machine.

Local user accounts are specific to a machine. Let's revisit our workgroup from Figure 11.3. The Administrator account on one Windows 2000 workstation is not the same as the Administrator account on the other Windows 2000 workstation. The Administrator of the first workstation with the printer, which we'll call *Workstation01*, has no security context on the second workstation, or *Workstation02*, and, therefore, no access unless the Administrator of Workstation02 has enabled the Guest account or created a user account on Workstation02 for its counterpart. Compare that to an Active Directory domain that contains two DCs, *Server01* and *Server01*. In this case, the Administrator accounts on each machine would be the same. These are domain user accounts, which are discussed in the next section.

If a local computer is a member of a domain, global domain accounts can be added to local groups to give remote users access to the computer. Using groups is discussed in Chapter 14. Management of local user accounts, such as changing passwords, however, cannot be done remotely. For example, you cannot change the password of a user accessing the local computer over the network because the user account does not reside in the local SAM.

Domain User Accounts

Whereas local accounts are specific to a particular computer, domain user accounts apply across a domain or even multiple domains, if trust relationships have been established. A DC is a computer running Windows 2000 Server that has been configured using the Active Directory Installation wizard, which installs and configures components that provide Active Directory directory services to network users and computers. Domain controllers store directory data and manage user-domain interactions, including user logon processes, authentication, and directory searches. Figure 11.4 illustrates a network of two pure Windows 2000 domains connected by a router.

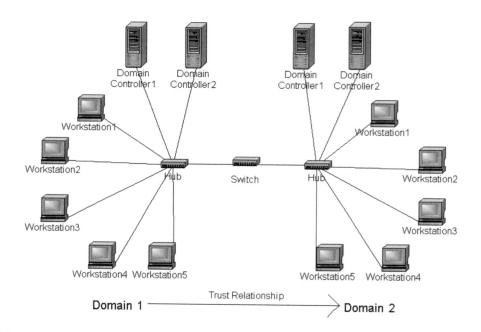

Figure 11–4   *Two Windows 2000 domains where Domain1 trusts Domain2.*

DOMAIN CONTROLLERS

The DCs in each domain share directory information with each other, including domain user and computer accounts. Windows 2000 Server DCs provide an extension of the capabilities and features provided by Windows NT Server 4.0 DCs. For example, DCs in Windows 2000 Server support multimaster replication, which synchronizes data on each DC and ensures consistency of information over time. Multimaster replication, as discussed previously with Active Directory, is an evolution of the primary and backup DC of Windows NT

Server 4.0, in which only one server, the primary DC, had a read and write copy of the directory.

DOMAIN ACCOUNT VALIDATION

In our example network, a user in Domain1 could sit down at any workstation in the domain and login with a single user account. This, as we saw in Section 11.1.2, is a contrast to the workgroup model, where each individual workstation would require a separate login account and password. Also, because Domain1 trusts Domain2 in our diagram, users from Domain2 would be able to login and access resources on computers in Domain1 with the same network account they use to login to Domain2. This is because the DCs share the same accounts database, stored in the Active Directory. Each workstation is a member of the domain, and when a user sits down at any workstation and logs in using his or her domain account, the login request is passed on to a DC for authentication, rather than to the local accounts database. A user could login to the computer, using a local account by selecting the local computer name from the drop-down list next to Logon To. This would cause Windows 2000 to validate the user against the local accounts database and not the domain. If the user then attempted to access domain resources while logged in locally to the workstation, that user would be validated with the Guest account if it is enabled or prompted with a Connect As dialog box to enter a valid domain user name and password that would be authenticated by a DC.

SERVICE ACCOUNTS

Earlier in this chapter, we showed a figure of an Active Directory Users and Computers management console with a filter applied to show only built-in user accounts in Figure 11.1. Without the filter applied, we have the console shown in Figure 11.5.

In our Active Directory, we currently have three service accounts, the two created by IIS 5.0 that we discussed previously and one for Exchange Server 5.5. Service accounts are domain user accounts created by some server applications that require the ability to login to a domain and make changes or manipulate data behind the scenes. BackOffice applications, such as IIS, Exchange Server, and SQL Server, use service accounts to process information without manual intervention by an administrator. IIS, for example, uses the *IUSR_computername* account in the following way:

1. The *IUSR_computername* account is added to the Guests group on the computer.
2. When a request is received, IIS will impersonate the *IUSR_computername* account before executing any code or accessing any files. IIS is able to impersonate the *IUSR_computername* account because the user name and password for this account are known by IIS.

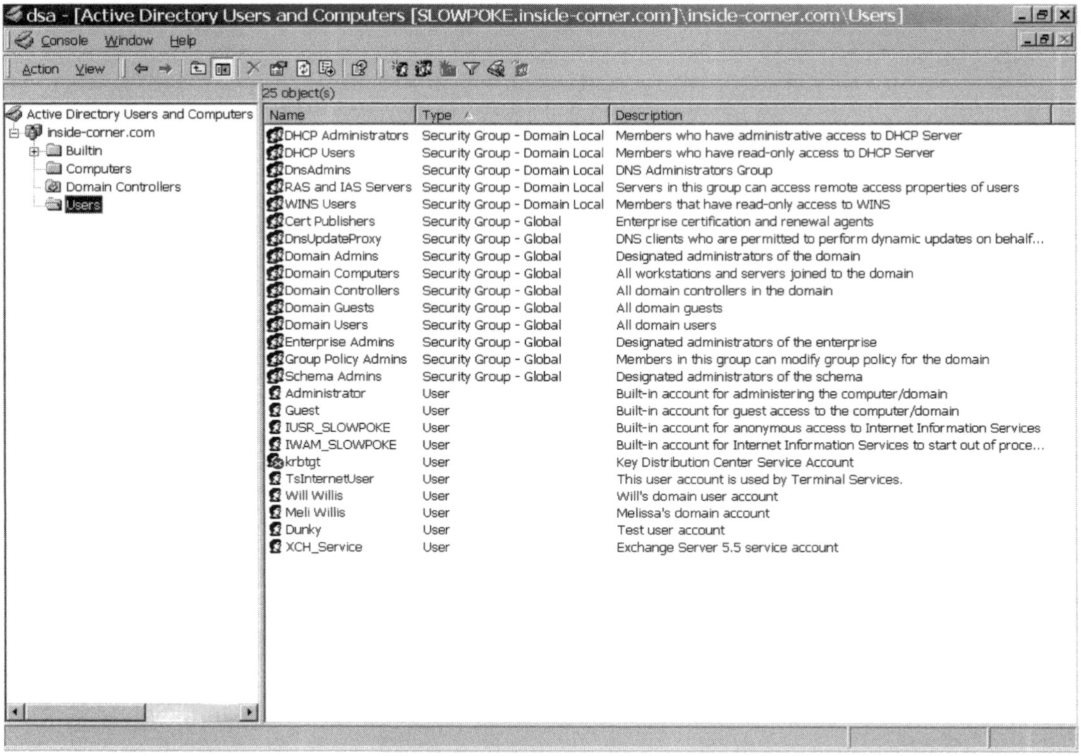

Figure 11-5   *An Active Directory Users and Computers console without a view filter applied.*

3. Before returning a page to the client, IIS checks the NTFS file and directory permissions to see whether the *IUSR_computername* account is allowed access to the file.

4. If access is allowed, authentication completes, and the resources are available to the user.

5. If access is not allowed, IIS will attempt to use another authentication method. If none is selected, IIS returns an "HTTP 403 Access Denied" error message to the browser.

This illustrates that user accounts are actively used not only by actual people (network users), as typically expected, but also by server applications running in the background. Service accounts often require a higher level of access than even an administrator account, such as being able to act as part of the operating system, logging in as a service, or logging in as a batch job. Most

BackOffice products will set the security level of the service account during the product installation, although they can always be modified manually later.

Using New User Accounts

Typically, when a new employee joins a company, a network administrator goes through the process of creating a network user name and password for that person. Whereas creating a new user account may seem rather obvious, an initial planning stage should be gone through—ideally, before any user accounts are created. Changing an established user name and password strategy is much more difficult politically (not to mention the amount of actual labor it will take to create all new user accounts and deactivate old ones) than getting it right the first time. With that in mind, we will look at the following:

- Suggested naming conventions
- Defining password requirements
- Other account options

Suggested Naming Conventions

Creating a naming convention is an important planning step in setting up a network. The number of users you will have on your network will play a role in your naming convention, because you will want to devise a standard that minimizes the chance for duplicates that would cause you to have to make exceptions for some user accounts. There is also a need to plan for future growth, because a network that has 250 users today may have a good deal more or less than that in a year, or it may not see any significant change. There is a balance to be maintained between higher levels of security, such as not having easily guessed usernames and passwords and reducing administrative overhead. In that respect, a naming convention can be considered a weakening of security, although the benefits outweigh the risk and can be combated with an effective password policy.

Whenever you are involved with any sort of long-term IT strategic planning, it is always a good idea to include business managers from other divisions in your discussions. Often, they will be able to provide insight into business requirements and potential change that might affect the processes you put into place later.

FIRST NAME

The most basic naming convention is to use the person's first name as the user name. Unfortunately, this works on only the smallest of networks—typically, 25 users or less. When a second employee is hired who has the same first name as an existing employee, the naming convention is broken. At that point, the new employee either has to go by a nickname to maintain the convention or an exception has to be made, such as adding a last initial or some other designation that will differentiate the two user accounts.

You might be asking yourself why you should care; anyone could keep up with 25 or fewer user accounts, so why does it matter that you have an account or two outside the normal convention? Well, for a very small network such as this, you might be right. It may not matter because there are few enough users that you can keep track mentally of who is different. However, it is still good practice to get into the habit of maintaining a naming convention; that way, it will be second nature when you take a new job where you are responsible for 2,500 user accounts, rather than 25.

FIRST NAME, LAST INITIAL

A naming convention that works for many small and medium-sized networks is a first name, last initial format, for example, *WillW.* This provides a little more flexibility; that way, if there are two employees with the same first name, chances are that their last names don't start with the same initial. As the number of employees goes up, however, the chances also go up that this convention will be broken. If you already have a Michael Jones working for your company and Michael Johnson and Michael Jordan get hired, you are put in a position to have to make an exception to your naming convention to accommodate the new employees. The other thing to note about this convention is that you have to take it a step further and decide whether you will use the person's given first name, such as William (preferred) or a nickname, such as Will. The reason that the given name is preferred is that, whereas someone may be named Joe, a colleague who works in another city and doesn't know him or her personally but needs to send an email won't know whether he is Joe, Joey, or Joseph. Sticking with only given names, even if her mother never calls Beth by her given name, Elizabeth (except when she is mad at her), this naming convention lends itself to consistency and ease of use.

FIRST INITIAL, LAST NAME

Probably the best naming convention in terms of most flexibility to use is the first initial, last name format (WWillis, for example). Although it is still possible to have this convention broken, especially with popular last names, such as Smith and Jones in the United States, it is generally not as easy to break as a first name, last initial format. This format is also easier on the administrator and users because, unlike first names, where we often go by a nickname or some variation of a given name, last names don't vary. You may occasionally have to change a user account if someone gets married and the last name changes but, other than that, it is stable.

Some companies add another twist to this naming convention by limiting the length of the user name. This is usually because some applications support only a maximum number of characters, such as eight. With many people having long last names, fitting into that eight-character limit would be impossible. To get around this, the naming convention merely truncates the person's name at eight characters, so Ludwig Von Beethoven would be LBeethov. User names of eight characters or less are left alone. The convention can be set to six, seven, or however many characters you want, as long as you are consistent.

You may still be asking yourself what the point of a naming convention is. After all, why *can't* user accounts be named just anything? Why do you need to keep track of them? The reason is twofold. First, most companies these days have email—definitely internal email and probably Internet email, as well. In most cases, a person's email address mirrors his or her network login, so if I login to the network as WillW, chances are that my email address would be WillW@mycompany.com. At the very least, on the internal email system, people would be able to look me up as WillW on the address list to send me email.

This is relevant, primarily from a productivity standpoint. How much time would your users waste if they needed to send an email to a colleague but didn't know the address and had to look it up? Someone may have to spend a minute or two looking my name up if they didn't know whether my email address was Will, William, WillW, WilliamW, WWillis, Willis, or maybe even something completely different. Compound that frustration if they have to go through that routine every time they need to email someone. Users will quickly grow tired of having to look up names and addresses constantly, and productivity will be lost. Ultimately, IT serves to make business processes more efficient and productive, which is not the case if the systems are not easy to use.

A naming convention makes life easier on users because they know what the recipient's address is without having to look up a user name in an address list. If a user knows to simply type *WWillis* when addressing an email, he or she will have a less frustrating experience and, more importantly, won't waste a lot of time that could be better spent elsewhere.

Defining Password Requirements

Although naming conventions serve to ease administration time and user frustration, they do give potential hackers one piece of the puzzle in breaking into a network. As long as they know any employee names and can figure out the naming convention (not hard if they have an email address), they have a basis to start trying to hack into a network. As an administrator, ultimately, your network is only as strong as the weakest link, which is often the user account password. The following are some "best-practice" guidelines for password policies.

MINIMUM PASSWORD LENGTH

A minimum password length forces a user to create a password that is at least as long as the policy requires. This should be set to a number above zero, because there is no reason a user account should ever have a blank password. Hackers often use password-cracking programs that rely on *brute force* methods of discovering passwords. Simply put, the program uses either a very large database of words (such as a dictionary) that it tries one at a time or it uses an algorithm that tries every possible sequence of numbers, letters, and special characters (!, @, #, $,%, ^, &, *, (,), -, _, +, =, etc.) until it uncovers the correct password. The shorter the password, the faster a hacker will be able to crack it and gain access to your network. Microsoft documentation for Windows 2000 incorrectly claims that the maximum password length is 14 characters (the same as in NT 4.0) but, in fact, you can create a password up to 128 characters in length. Of course there's no word that is that long, but you could write a sentence for your password, such as, How long would it take for some hacker to crack this password? I bet it would take 10 years! Still, that's only 104 characters. Realistically a minimum password length of six to eight characters is reasonable for most environments.

PASSWORD AGING/MAXIMUM PASSWORD AGE

Setting password aging options is another key step in protecting your network. You should set the maximum password age options so that users will be forced periodically to change their passwords. This is usually very unpopular with users who can keep up with PIN numbers for eight different ATM and credit cards and voice mail systems but find remembering one network password to be too much of a challenge. However, forcing users to change their passwords helps keep ex-employees who might know someone else's password from being able to try to hack in six months down the road. It also discourages people from keeping track of colleague's passwords because they will be changed later, anyway.

You don't want to force passwords to expire too frequently, however. Otherwise, users will have too difficult a time keeping up with their current password and will often resort to writing them on sticky notes and leaving them under their keyboards on their monitors, defeating the security you are trying to maintain. As a general guideline, having passwords expire every 60–90 days is appropriate for most networks.

PASSWORD UNIQUENESS

Having passwords expire does not serve much of a purpose if users can simply reuse their existing passwords. All that does is inconvenience them. Password uniqueness enables you as the administrator to create a policy whereby Windows 2000 will remember the previous number of passwords you decide, up to a maximum of 24 passwords. The number of passwords you choose to have Windows 2000 remember will depend on your environment but, in a typical environment, keeping track of a year's worth of passwords would be prudent. Depending on how often you force passwords to expire, that could be anywhere from 2–12 passwords, most likely 4–6.

MINIMUM PASSWORD AGE

Another trick that users like to play to foil your password scheme is to change their passwords over and over until they reach the limit of your password uniqueness setting; then they can go back to their original password. Setting a minimum password age lets you defend against that tactic. A minimum password age requires a user to have a password for a specified number of days before it can be changed again. This number must be less than or equal to the maximum password age, because a password cannot expire before it has reached its minimum age. A reasonable setting for minimum password age would be about seven days, which would allow users to change their passwords when they wanted for the most part, yet not allow them to change it constantly to get around your password uniqueness configuration (not without a lot of persistence, anyway!).

Typically, if you don't want users to change their passwords, you can either prevent it by setting the account option (discussed later in this chapter) or force them to change passwords only when you want them to by setting the minimum and maximum password age settings to the same number of days.

CONTROL ISSUES

When setting up a new user account, you have the option of assigning an initial password to the user account. You should always assign an initial password to a user account (and you will have to if you followed 11.2.2.1, above, and set a minimum password length). Depending on your environment, you will decide on exactly how you want to implement this. For a typical environment, it is often easiest to create a generic initial password, such as the first name of the user, and check the "User must change password at next logon" box (discussed later in this chapter). This gives control to the user in creating a password that they want to use that meets the requirements you have set forth on the Group Policy configuration.

Another option on higher-security networks is to create a random initial password that you supply to the user, rather than relying on an easy-to-figure-out scheme. The reason for this is that, if someone wanted to break into your network and they knew that you used a generic initial password-naming scheme, such as the local football team mascot, they could login as that user and gain unauthorized access to the network before the intended user initially logged in.

The last option is to create and assign passwords to users manually, which puts you in control of the password and forces the user to remember something that may have no meaning. This is useful in high-security environments, where it is an unacceptable risk to rely on merely educating users on secure passwords and hoping for the best. There will always be somebody who, no matter how much you stress the importance of creating a "good" password, will end up using the name of his or her dog, kid, or spouse as a password. Most networks do not require the level of security that would make administrator-created user passwords worth the headache in keeping up with them, but it is a viable option in networks requiring passwords that can't be easily cracked or guessed.

CONFIGURING PASSWORD OPTIONS WITH GROUP POLICY

Although we have talked about general guidelines for setting up password policies, we have yet to discuss how to actually do it. As shown in Figure 11.6, configuring password options is done through the Group Policy MMC.

There are several ways to start the Group Policy snap-in. You can start an empty MMC and add the Group Policy snap-in to the console. However, for our purposes, we will start Group Policy as follows:

1. Click Start→Programs→Administrative Tools→Active Directory Users and Computers.
2. An Active Directory Users and Computers console similar to that back in Figure 11.5 will appear. When it does expand your Active Directory domain, right click on the Domain Controllers container and click Properties. Figure 11.7 illustrates this.
3. Click on the Group Policy tab, where you will see the Default Domain Controllers Policy link. This is the only option by default, although you could add additional group policy links or create new ones. With Default Domain Controllers Policy highlighted, click Edit, as shown in Figure 11.8.
4. You are now in the Group Policy MMC, shown previously in Figure 11.6. Password options are located under Computer Configuration→Windows Settings→Security Settings→Account Policies→Password Policies. Here, you find the options previously discussed. When you double-click a security attribute, you are presented with a security configuration window. Figures 11.9 and 11.10 show the configuration options for Enforce Password Uniqueness and Minimum Password Length, respectively.

By default, these options are not configured, so when you open the security attributes there will be a check box in "Exclude this setting from configuration." This is not very conducive to a secure network, so you will want to uncheck the box and configure an appropriate setting for each item. The

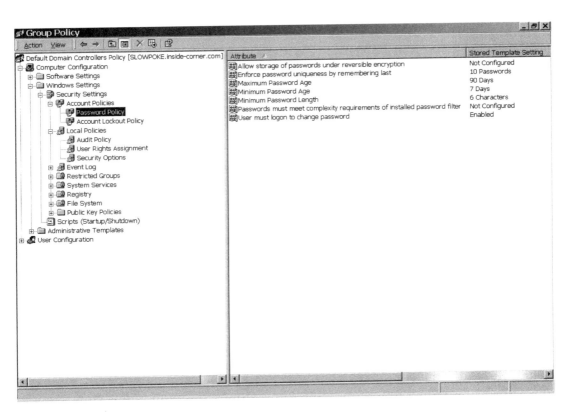

Figure 11–6

The Group Policy console allows you to configure your password options for all user accounts in the Active Directory.

changes you make here will affect all user accounts in the Active Directory domain.

Other Account Options

Although an important piece of the puzzle, passwords are not your only line of defense in securing user accounts. Other account options can be set on a per-user basis, giving you a granular level of control over user account security. Administrators of Windows NT 4.0 networks will be familiar with these settings:

- Logon Time Restrictions
- Workstation Logon Restrictions
- Change Password at Next Logon
- User Cannot Change Password
- Password Never Expires
- Membership in Groups

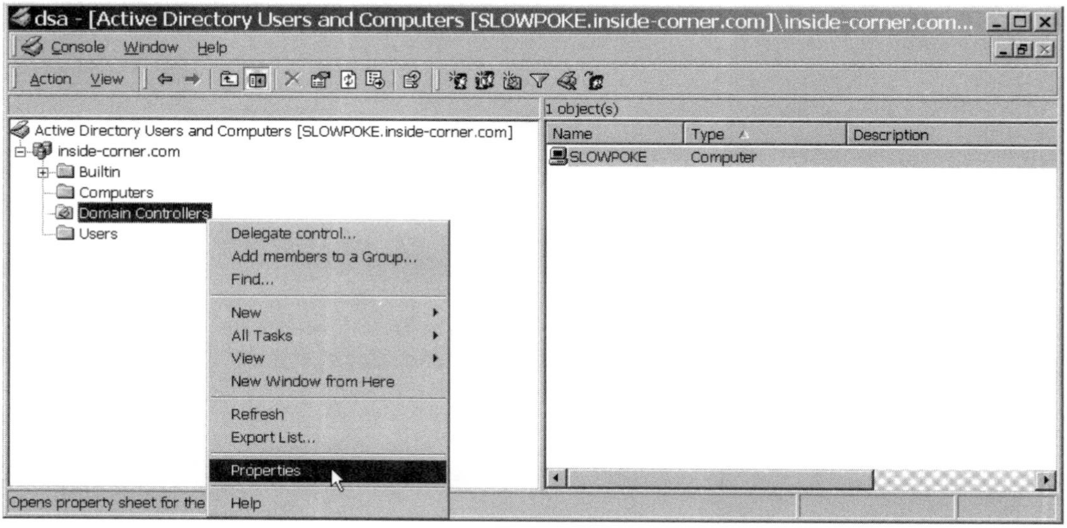

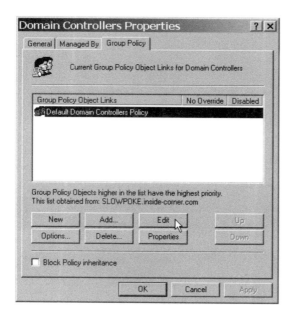

Figure 11–7   *Opening the Domain Controller property sheet.*

Figure 11–8   *Editing the Default Domain Controllers Policy within Domain Controller properties.*

Figure 11-9   *The Password Uniqueness security attribute configuration.*

Figure 11-10   *The Minimum Password Length security attribute configuration.*

- Profiles
- Dial-in Settings

Navigating to the Users container in Active Directory Users and Computers, right-clicking the desired user account to configure and clicking Properties accesses the user account property sheet, similar to that in Figure 11.11. Click on the Account tab to view these configuration options.

LOGON TIME RESTRICTIONS

Networks are often hacked into during the middle of the night or otherwise off-peak hours, typically when the IT staff is not at full strength and most likely to let unauthorized network activity go unnoticed. There might also be a situation where employees are inappropriately using network resources after work hours. In either case, you can reduce the chance of this happening by using logon time restrictions to control when the user account can be logged into the network.

To configure the time that a user is allowed to logon to the network, click the Logon Hours button in User Properties on the Account tab. This will bring up a window similar to that in Figure 11.12.

By default, a user can logon and use the network 24 x 7. In most cases, that is fine, but if your company is not a 24 x 7 organization, you might want to limit when a user account can be used, for security purposes. In our example,

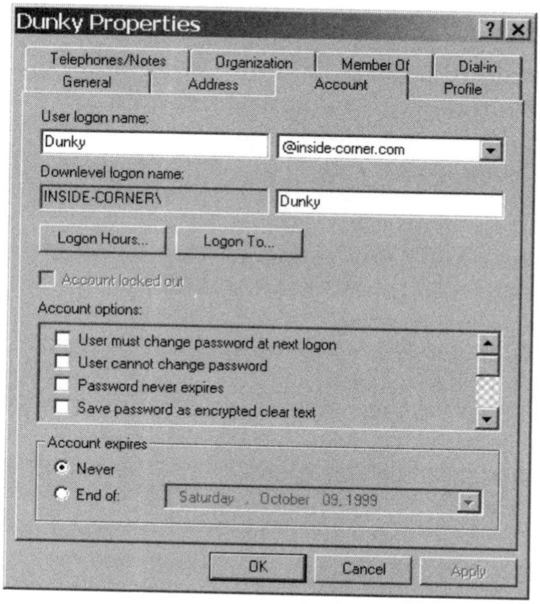

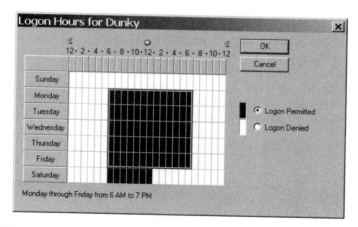

Figure 11–11   *A user account property sheet showing Account options.*

Logon Hours configuration allows the administrator to specify when a user is allowed to gain access to the network.

Figure 11–12

we have a user named Dunky, who works for a company that is open 7:00 AM to 6:00 PM Monday through Friday, and 7:00 AM until noon on Saturday. We have configured the user account Dunky to be able to logon only between 6:00

AM and 7:00 PM Monday through Friday, and 6:00 AM until 1:00 PM Saturday. We give him an hour cushion on each side, in case he needs to come in early or work late, but we make his logon hours closely reflect the hours of the day that the business is open.

There is one small catch to our grand plan, however. By default, users are not logged off when their logon hours expire and, actually, as long as they don't ever log their computers off the network, they can bypass the logon hours setting. So how do we keep someone from doing that? We look to our Group Policy friend again.

If you will refer back to Figure 11.6, you will see that there are many other configuration options in the Group Policy MMC. Right below the Account Policies we configured earlier is Local Policies. Below Local Policies is the Security Options container, which is what we are looking for. One of the security attributes on the right-hand side of the MMC is "Forcibly logoff when logon hours expire." Enabling this setting will ensure that the user account is in use only during the desired time frame that you have configured.

WORKSTATION LOGON RESTRICTIONS

Another security option that is not often used, except in high-security environments, is restricting users to particular workstations. From the Account options of the user properties sheet, click the Logon To button; you will see a window similar to that shown in Figure 11.13.

Figure 11–13 *Logon Workstations configuration.*

By default, a user can logon to any workstation in a domain, which is usually desirable. However, in some environments, where employees are working with highly confidential or classified information, restricting what workstations they can access is necessary. If you need to restrict access, click the User may logon to these workstations radio button and type in the NetBIOS names on the workstations, clicking Add after each one.

One of the big selling points of Windows 2000 and Active Directory to many people is the death of the archaic NetBIOS naming scheme. Unfortunately for some, the rumors of its demise have been premature. Even in a pure Windows 2000 environment, if you restrict workstation logons, you will have to use NetBIOS to identify the computers that the user is allowed to logon to. This is an inconvenience for organizations wanting to rid themselves of NetBIOS and use pure DNS for name resolution.

CHANGE PASSWORD AT NEXT LOGON

Setting the "User must change password at next logon" account option will force the password to expire instantly the next time the user logs onto the network and to prompt them for a new password. As previously mentioned, this option is most useful when initially setting up a new user account. Assign an initial password and force the user to change it to something of his or her choosing. This option can also be used if a user calls you, having forgotten a password. You can reset the password to something generic, then let the user logon and change it immediately to something else.

USER CANNOT CHANGE PASSWORD

Another account option that can be set is User cannot Change Password. As the name implies, this setting prevents the password from being changed, except by the administrator. This option is most commonly used for service accounts, where it is undesirable to have the password changed. If someone figures out a service account password and uses it to logon as a user on the network, that person wouldn't be able to change the password and prevent the network service from working properly.

PASSWORD NEVER EXPIRES

Often used in conjunction with User Cannot Change Password is the Password Never Expires option. Again, this is used frequently with service accounts that are required to make BackOffice applications such as Exchange Server or Internet Information Server work. Service account passwords are not often changed, so setting the password not to expire allows the account to not be affected by the maximum password age group policy setting.

MEMBERSHIP IN GROUPS

As with NT 4.0, in Windows 2000, network access permissions are generally assigned to groups, rather than to individual user accounts. Groups are discussed extensively in Chapters 14 and 15. To view and configure group mem-

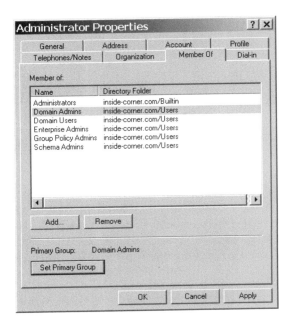

Figure 11-14   *Configuring group memberships in Windows 2000.*

bership, click the Member Of tab in the user account's property sheet. Figure 11.14 shows a sample of the configuration window.

You should use groups, rather than individual user accounts, to assign access rights, in order to reduce the administrative burden. User accounts can change frequently, whereas groups tend to stay fairly stable over the course of time. In addition, if you have a large network and add a new printer that 500 people in three departments need access to, it is much easier to assign permissions to three departmental groups than to 500 user accounts.

PROFILES

Profiles give the administrator the ability to specify certain configuration options, such as wallpaper, as well as to restrict users' access to utilities that allow them to make changes to their systems (install drivers, etc.). Figure 11.15 shows the Profiles tab of the user properties sheet.

Other options on the Profiles tab include login script and home directory, that were common to NT 4.0, as well, and Shared Documents Folder, which is new to Windows 2000. This option allows the administrator to set up a network folder for a user to store data files in, rather than using the often-default c:\My Documents. Configuring a network folder is useful for backup and recovery purposes. Profiles are discussed in more depth in the next chapter.

Setting profile options for a user account.

DIAL-IN SETTINGS

The default settings in Windows 2000, like NT 4.0, do not give users permission to dial into the network from a remote location. This permission must be explicitly granted to the user before he or she can dial in. Figure 11.16 shows the property sheet for dial-in settings.

Once you have granted access to a user, you have options that control how a call into the remote-access server (RAS) is handled. The default is the least secure option—No Callback. The server authenticates the user immediately, based on username and password.

The second option is for the server to disconnect and dial the user back at a number that the user specifies in the initial call. In this case, when the server calls the user back, a connection is made, and the user is authenticated. Although a user can be called back anywhere, limiting this security option's effectiveness, the number is logged. That gives the administrator a record of the call having taken place if there is an incident of a network breaking through the modem pool.

The last option, which is the most secure, is for the server to call the user back at a predetermined number that is stored in a database on the RAS server. When the user dials into the server and attempts to authenticate, the callback number is looked up, and the server disconnects and initiates the callback to

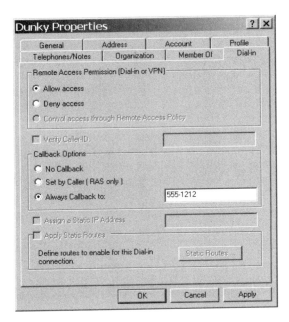

Configuring dial-in permissions and settings for a user account.

the user. At that time, authentication takes place, and the user is granted access to the network.

Creating Domain User Accounts

We have discussed a lot of the theory and guidelines for using user accounts in this chapter, and now it is time to put that knowledge into practice by going through the process of creating a new domain user account. Because this is a domain account, we will be using the Active Directory Users and Computers MMC snap-in.

Using the Directory Management Snap-in

Creating a new domain user account into the Active Directory is done through the Active Directory Users and Computers console, which was discussed extensively in the previous chapter. Follow these steps:

1. Expand the domain, navigate to the Users container, and click the Action menu and New→User.
2. Figure 11.17 shows the Create New Object (User) window. The Down-Level logon name is used for backward compatibility with NetBIOS and

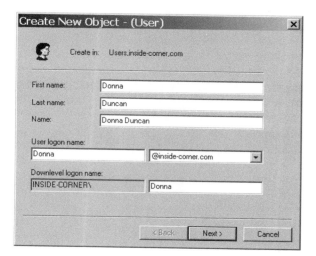

Figure 11–17   *The Create New Object (User) window is where you configure the identification of a new user account.*

NT 4.0 domains. Fill in the fields to create a new user account and click Next.

3. Create a generic password for the user account, select the option for User must change password at next logon, as shown in Figure 11.18, and click next.

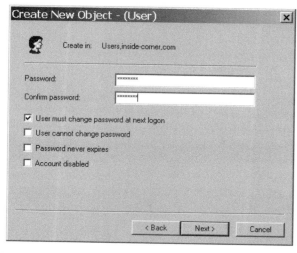

Figure 11–18   *Assigning a password and initial account options for the new user.*

4. You are presented with a window that summarizes the options you have selected and confirms your configuration. At this point, you can go back and make any necessary changes or click Finish to complete the new user setup. Click Finish and notice how your new user account appears in the Active Directory. Open the New Account properties and explore the other options we have discussed previously in this chapter.

Chapter Summary

User accounts are the foundation of Windows 2000 because, after all, without users, there is not much use for a network. In this chapter, we examined the role of the different types of accounts, which were built in, local, and domain user accounts. We also discussed general administrative practices for user account naming conventions and the requirements of a good password.

We explored other account options that can be used to control access to network resources and improve security, such as setting logon time restrictions and restricting what workstations a user can use to logon. Last, we put our learned knowledge into practice by creating a user account and configuring the account options that we learned about previously. At this point, you should be ready to move on to more advanced user management involving profiles, home directories, and setting account policies.

Administering
User Accounts

In this chapter, we are going to discuss some basic administration tasks that you will perform when dealing with user accounts. In the previous chapter, we talked about creating user accounts and adding them to groups. In this chapter, we are going to concentrate on some key areas, such as locating user accounts and user account properties within Active Directory, configuring profiles and home folders, and a brief introduction to Group Policy. The latter topic is a significant one and will be dealt with in greater detail in Chapter 14.

User accounts are obviously one of the key tasks for a system administrator. Much of your work is going to revolve around their administration. There are many aspects to this. User account passwords will need to be periodically changed, user data will need to be saved to a network share—or home folder—to ensure that it is backed up to tape each night. It is also going to be important that the user experience on your network is consistent.

The user experience on a network is a good measuring stick for your success as an administrator. In a sense, you are working for each of the users. Whereas the technical side of our brain can easily become embroiled in considerations of bandwidth, load balancing, and resource sharing, from a users perspective, things can be much simpler. Many users simply want to be able to turn on their computers, access their data, and have an environment that is both familiar and productive. This is the goal you should strive for. The more invisible you are to your users, the better. Often, an administrator who appears to be doing nothing is the best there is. They are efficient, on top of problems before they become huge issues, and have everything under control.

User accounts are the basic unit of control that you have. You use user accounts for security, administration, and resource sharing. Having a firm grip on the basic administrative requirements will free you to deal with larger issues on the network. Also, having an understanding of the issues at hand also gives you a firm foundation to understand how you might improve upon the infra-structure you currently have in place.

Introduction to Administration of User Accounts

We are going to discuss some key tasks regarding the administration of user accounts. In a pure Windows 2000 environment, user account information is stored within Active Directory. One of the first questions you are going to have is, How do I find a user account? We will be showing you how you can initiate user account searches. You will see that you can search for a user name or any of the user properties. This will greatly aid the efficiency of your administration tasks.

Once you have located a user account, you might want to make some changes to the account properties. Account properties include password changes, renaming an account, or deleting it from Active Directory. These can be considered to be basic user account management tasks.

You also might want to exert some control over the user environment. This control might extend to which icons exist on the desktop, and which applications users have access to. This type of information is stored in a *profile*. There are three different types of profiles that we will be discussing. Once you understand what each of them are, you will be able to determine which works best for your own environment.

User profiles can be thought of as functions that affect user accounts. Another aspect of this within Windows 2000 is Group Policy. This feature has far-reaching effects on both the user environment and possibly the entire net-work. In fact, it is so important that, after a brief introduction here, we will later dedicate an entire chapter to show you how it works and how it can help you on your own network.

The users on your network expect things to work the same way every day. Even a minor outage or a small loss of data can set them back days or weeks. To ensure that their data is backed up, secure, and available to them, no matter where they go within the organization, you are going to want to store critical user data on a network disk drive. The creation of home folders is a key aspect of this function.

User accounts are so key to the network that the number of people who can perform the tasks that have been outlined is limited. To create user accounts, you must be an administrator. Alternatively, you can have an administrator assign you sufficient permissions to perform some or all of the tasks that are going to be discussed. One way or the other, your privileges on the network will have to be elevated from those of a "normal" user. This ensures accountability.

Locating User Accounts

Before you can administer user accounts, you need to be able to locate them. In a native Windows 2000 environment, user accounts are stored within Active Directory. The details of Active Directory were covered earlier in this book.

As an all-too-brief recap, remember that Active Directory is no more than a database that stores data about network objects. These network objects include, but are not limited to, user groups, computers, files, printers, and—you guessed it—user accounts. To perform an administrative task, you are going to have to locate the user account (or accounts) to which you wish to make changes.

Fortunately Active Directory has some sophisticated searching mechanisms in place that can help you. Actually, it is quite easy to search for user names or a number of user properties. The process is much the same as the search engines found within older versions of Microsoft operating systems. For instance, you might already be familiar with searching for files on a hard disk within Microsoft Windows 98. The engine used by Windows 2000 to find user accounts looks very similar.

In the following example, we are going to locate a user account within Active Directory. Because your network is unlikely to resemble our network precisely, you can substitute some of the information for your own purposes. For the purpose of illustrating the finding of user accounts, I am going to search my network for UserA.

1. To find users within Active Directory, you will have to access the Find option. First, we must start the Active Directory Users and Computers administration tool. To start this tool, click on Start, Programs, Administrative Tools, Active Directory Users and Computers. This will start the administrative tool.
2. This tool is used to administer user accounts. You can do everything from creating a new account to deleting old ones from this tool. However, for the purposes of this example, we are going to assume that we already have our user accounts in place. We are simply going to search Active Directory for UserA. To search Active Directory, we must use the Find feature. To access this, locate the domain name in the left-hand panel and right-click on it to bring up the context-sensitive menu. Then click on Find. You should now see the Find Users, Contacts, and Groups dialog box. This is shown in Figure 12.1.
3. This dialog box packs a lot of functionality into a small space. Before we go ahead and search for our user, let's take time to navigate around the box a little bit. Doing so will help you to understand ways in which you search for any type of object within Active Directory. First, let's click on the dropdown box next to Find: You will see a list of objects you can search for. The categories include computers, printers, shared folders, and

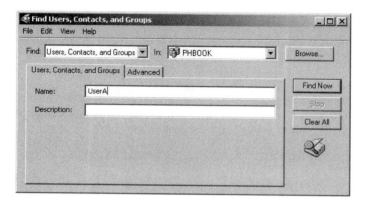

Figure 12–1   *The Find Users, Contacts, and Groups dialog box.*

even a Custom Search. A Custom Search allows you to select individual properties of an object. This is a far more granular search. However, until you become more familiar with the properties, it is likely to be less efficient to use a Custom Search. If you have changed the default choice, then change the Find option to read Users, Contacts, and Groups. Next, click on the In dropdown box. This allows you to choose the domain in which to search. If you are working in a large enterprise with many domains, this allows you to narrow down your search. If you are not sure of the domain, you can also select Entire Directory. This causes the search to look through the entire Active Directory database. Obviously, this will take longer and will require more system resources to perform.

4. For this example, we are going to search for the user named *UserA*. Type *UserA* into the Name option. Click on the Find Now button. After a moment, you should see a screen that resembles Figure 12.2. Of course, if this user does not exist in your environment, the Find function will not be able to find it. In this case, substitute the user name for a user account name that you know exists. If need be, use your own account name.

5. If you want to execute a search for a user account down to the user account property level (or if you are just curious to know which properties are available within Active Directory), click on the Advanced tab. This takes you to a screen with some additional options. To see a list of properties that are available, click on the Field button. Then select User to see a list of the fields. As you will see, the list is quite extensive. At times when you have many accounts (and possibly accounts with the same user name), it can help to use more than one field. Of course, your organization might not be using all of these fields. It is also possible that Active Directory has been extended since it was installed. Only an intimate knowledge of your network will inform you which fields are useful and which are not. However, because you cannot damage anything by running

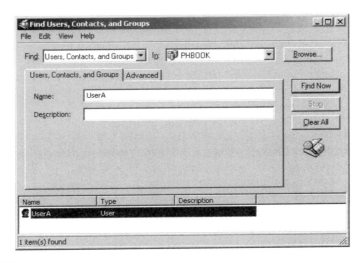

Figure 12–2   *Locating a User account.*

searches, you might want to practice using different fields to see which ones your organization is using.

6. Finally, once you have found the user you were looking for, double-click on the user name. This will take you to the Properties window for the user. From here, you can make changes to the user account. Examples of this will follow later in this chapter.

Performing Administrative Tasks

Now that you know how to find user accounts, it is time to show you how you can make changes to user account properties. There are many different options that can be configured for a single user. In fact, there are far too many for us to cover all of them in this book. However, there are some common tasks that you will find yourself performing fairly regularly; it is these that we will concentrate on for the moment.

So what constitutes a "common task"? Well, life as a system administrator will have a certain amount of repetitiveness about it. Users will have to change their passwords, they will have to be added to security groups, or someone might leave or a new user might join. These are common everyday events that trigger a lot of work for the administrator.

You can simplify these tasks by making sure you have a process in place to deal with it. For instance, if you have used groups efficiently, you should easily be able to determine which groups a new user account needs to be a member of. Having a documented process that a new user account must go through—or even a password change request—will help you deal with day-to-day tasks quickly and efficiently.

Password changes should occur on a regular basis. Although it is convenient to have passwords set and never expire (you'll never be prompted to change the password, and you won't have to remember new passwords), it is a security hole that ought to be plugged. Passwords are not for convenience; they are in the front line of protecting the data on your network. If a password is breached, your network can quickly become compromised.

Password problems can also occur when users simply forget their password. Although this might seem a little strange, believe us, it happens. In these cases, it is going to be up to you to change the password. There is no built-in function that allows you to see someone's password. So you cannot go into the admin tool and simply tell the user the old password.

You might also decide to rename a user account. Renaming a user account allows you to change the logon name but preserve all group memberships and permissions. An example of this would be a member of the Finance group who has just left your organization. A replacement has been hired, and the replacement requires network access identical to that of the person they are replacing. It is far easier to rename the user account than to recreate it from scratch. The only thing to remember is that you should reset the password. If you don't do this, you have a possible security breach.

In the following example, we are going to walk you through resetting a password. You would use this function if you had a user who had forgotten his or her password. As you will see, this is a common but simple task. To reset a password, you must be a member of the Administrators group or have been added to the Account Operators group. Make sure this is the case before you attempt the following example.

1. In this example, we are going to reset the password of a user account. To do this we are going to need to access our user account administration tool. To start this tool, click on Start, Programs, Administrative Tools, Active Directory Users and Computers. This will start the administrative tool. In the previous example, we performed a search of Active Directory. In this example, we are simply going to drill down to find the user we want. In this case, we are looking for UserB. It is likely that you will not have a UserB defined on your own network. Don't worry, you can use any user account for this example. **However, if you are using a network that belongs to someone else, do not change users' passwords without telling them!** This will cause them to be unable to log on next time. Instead, change the password of your own user account.

2. Instead of searching for the user name in question, we are going to navigate through the admin tool. To do this, click on the plus (+) sign next to the domain name. This displays the various object types that are stored in Active Directory. Because we are looking for a user, you will need to click on the Users object. This displays a list of users in the right-hand panel. Scroll down until you find the user you are looking for.

Figure 12-3   *The Reset Password dialog box.*

3. In our case, we are looking for UserB. Once you have located the user, right-click on the user name and select Reset Password. This displays the Reset Password dialog box shown in Figure 12.3.

4. The Reset Password dialog box has three important options. First, you should enter the new password in the New password text box. Once this is done, tab down to the Confirm password text box and reenter the password. This ensures that you have typed the correct password. If you mistyped the password the first time, the user would still be unable to log on. By making you confirm the operation, you can be sure that the new password is correct. Perhaps the most important option is the check box called *User must change password at next logon*. Because the password on the user account has been breached (at least two people know it—the administrator who is changing the password, and the user whose account you are changing) it is strongly suggested that you check this box. If you do this, the user will be prompted to make a second password change. However, this time they can choose one themselves—and it will be known only to that person.

5. Once you have made the change click on OK. You will be see a dialog box that says, "The password for UserB has been changed." This is simply confirming the change you have made. Of course, if you were changing another user account, a different user name would appear.

As you can see, changing a user's password is fairly simple. Combine the example we have just completed with the first example in this chapter, and you have a method to both locate and change the password of any user account in the enterprise. Now, that's pretty powerful!

So what will be the first sign that a user needs to have a password changed? Well, one of the most common times that this occurs is when a user types an incorrect password at the logon screen. In Windows 2000, you can configure the behavior that will occur when a user mistypes or forgets a password. This is known as *Account Lockout*. You will want to configure these options through Group Policy. Group Policy gets a whole chapter to itself later in this book. For the moment, let me say that within Group Policy, you can configure the number of times a user can attempt to logon with an incorrect password. If this limit is exceeded, the user account is locked out. This means that regardless of whether the user now enters the correct password, he or she will not be logged onto the system and given access to the network.

This behavior is a reaction to brute force password-cracking programs. A brute force password-cracking program will try thousands of different passwords for a user account until it finally gains access to a network. By limiting the number of times a user can attempt to logon before having to request assistance, you can prevent these types of attacks on your network.

However, most of the time account, lockout occurs when a user simply mistypes a password. You will be surprised at how often this happens. When it does, there are two things you can do. Within Group Policy, you can set an option that will unlock the user account after a period of time. So, if you set this option to 30 minutes, a user will not be able to log on—even if they now know the password—for a period of 30 minutes.

Alternatively, you can, as an administrator, unlock the user account yourself. Remember that security is a balancing act; your goal should be to attain as secure an environment as possible while minimizing the amount of administrative overhead. The following example walks you through unlocking an account manually. It also serves to show you how to access the User Property dialog box where most user configuration takes place.

1. Once again, you use the user account administration tool. If you do not already have it, click on Start, Programs, Administrative Tools, Active Directory Users and Computers.

2. You now have to locate a user. In our case, we have disabled an account. This account is UserA. In order for you to follow the steps precisely as written, you will need a user account that is locked out. One of the easiest ways of doing this is to create a new user account, then attempt to logon with an incorrect password. Because we have our account lockout set to three failed attempts, after three incorrect passwords, the account gets locked out. We need to locate UserA. We will use the same method we used in the previous example. Click on the plus (+) sign next to the domain name. This displays the various object types that are stored in Active Directory. Because we are looking for a user, you will need to click on the Users object. This displays a list of users in the right-hand panel. Scroll down until you find the user you are looking for. When you find UserA (or the user you are going to unlock on your own system), right-click on the user name and select Properties. You should see the dialog box shown in Figure 12.4.

3. As you can see, there are a lot of options that can be set on a per-user basis. Clearly, we will be unable to detail every single option. Also, be aware that the options can also be affected by group policies. In this

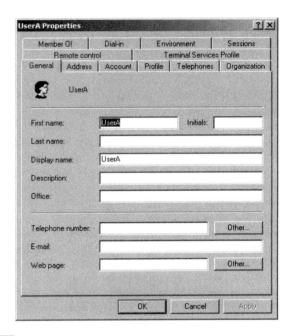

Figure 12–4   *The UserA Properties dialog box.*

example, we are going to check to see whether this account is locked out. To do this, click on the Account tab. In our case, UserA is locked out. You can see this, in Figure 12.5.

4. As you can see, the Account is locked out check box is checked. This means that the user is unable to login to the network. To unlock the account, simply uncheck this box. When you have done this, click OK. The user will now be able to logon.

Some of the other more common administrative tasks are accessed from a context-sensitive menu. This is useful, because it prevents you from having to hunt around the user interface to find the option you are looking for. You can use this menu to delete a user account that is no longer needed or to disable an account. To access the menu, simply right-click on a user name in the Active Directory Users and Computers Administration Tool. This menu is shown in Figure 12.6. If the menu you have looks different, it is probably because you right-clicked on a group. You get different options for groups.

The following table lists some of the common tasks that can be accessed from this menu and examples of when you might use them. As a system administrator, you can be assured that you will be using this tool a lot!

Obviously, this is not an exhaustive list of all the functions that are available to you. It is a good idea to spend some time looking at all of the options

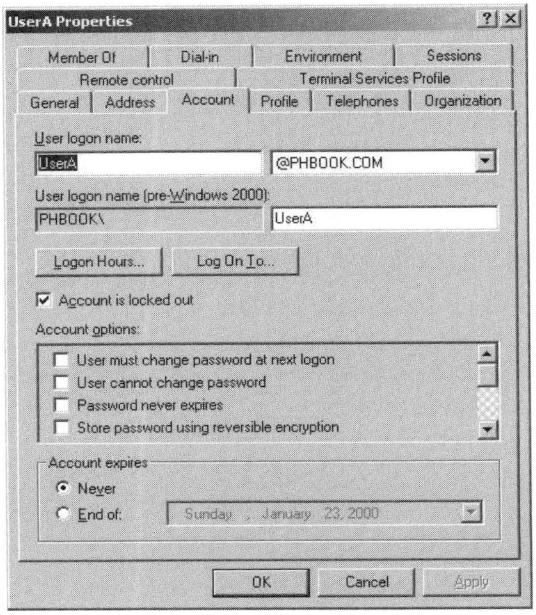

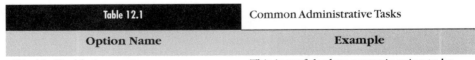

UserA Properties

Member Of | Dial-in | Environment | Sessions
Remote control | Terminal Services Profile
General | Address | Account | Profile | Telephones | Organization

User logon name:
UserA   @PHBOOK.COM

User logon name (pre-Windows 2000):
PHBOOK\   UserA

Logon Hours...   Log On To...

☑ Account is locked out

Account options:
☐ User must change password at next logon
☐ User cannot change password
☐ Password never expires
☐ Store password using reversible encryption

Account expires
◉ Never
○ End of: Sunday , January 23, 2000

OK   Cancel   Apply

Figure 12–5   *An account that is locked out.*

Table 12.1	Common Administrative Tasks
Option Name	**Example**
Disable/Enable Account	This is useful when a user is going to be away for an extended period of time. It prevents you from having to delete and then recreate an account with a lot of permissions. It is good security practice to do this. If you know an account is not going to be required for awhile, you should disable it. If an account is already disabled, this option will read *enabled*. Use this to reenable an account. A red *X* through a user account name means that the account is disabled.

Introduction to Administration of User Accounts

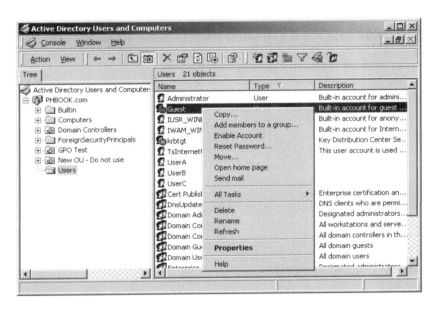

Figure 12–6   *Active Directory users and computers context-sensitive menu.*

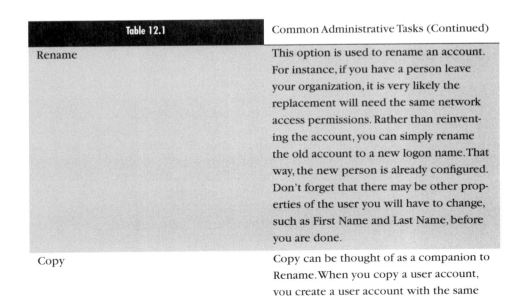

Table 12.1	Common Administrative Tasks (Continued)
Rename	This option is used to rename an account. For instance, if you have a person leave your organization, it is very likely the replacement will need the same network access permissions. Rather than reinventing the account, you can simply rename the old account to a new logon name. That way, the new person is already configured. Don't forget that there may be other properties of the user you will have to change, such as First Name and Last Name, before you are done.
Copy	Copy can be thought of as a companion to Rename. When you copy a user account, you create a user account with the same permissions and privileges, but the original account still exists.

Table 12.1	Common Administrative Tasks (Continued)
Delete	You should always delete user accounts if they are no longer needed. This ensures security for your network.
Add members to a group	Use this option to add a user to a group. This can be useful when you want to add several people to a group. Simply highlight each user by holding down the <CTRL> key and clicking on their names, then right-clicking. This brings up the Select Group dialog box. You can choose the group names from here.

so you know where they are. If you are under a deadline to get something done, you will not want to be hunting and pecking for options!

User Profiles

One of the most important things you will need to keep in mind is that your user community isn't like you at all. As a system administrator, you likely enjoy new hardware and software and experimenting with new ways of doing things. Most non-IT people tend to be focused on getting their jobs done.

In fact, what is far more important to users is that they can get to tools they need to use—be that word processors and email programs or programming tools. They simply don't share your excitement regarding the technology of the network.

That's okay, because at the end of the day, the network exists to support a business, and the user community is at the heart of the business. Anything you can do to help them do their work will be appreciated, both by the users and by management.

What might seem like a minor change to you—perhaps a new screensaver or wallpaper—can, in fact, cause all kinds of interruptions for everyday users who are used to seeing things a certain way. One of the features that Microsoft Windows has brought to users is the ability to customize their computers to suit their needs. If users can add their own wallpapers or move icons around, they feel more comfortable with their computers. However, once these changes have been made, it can be confusing when the settings change.

On the other hand, there may be times when you want to dictate a "look and feel" for a group of computers, preventing anyone from making a permanent change. For instance, if you have a computer in a lobby, and the logon is a guest account, you would not want someone logging onto that computer and changing the way it looks or works.

These might appear to be contradictory ideas—flexibility with a locked-down desktop—but, in fact, they are one and the same thing. It is one of the jobs of a system administrator to exert as much control as necessary to prevent users from breaking their systems and protecting the organization's assets and data from intruders while, at the same time, allowing users to make changes they feel would help them.

These kinds of issues can be dealt with through user profiles. A user profile is essentially a group of settings that defines the look and feel of a user's environment. In basic terms, a user profile is a group of files and folders that store information about a user's desktop—such as which icons appear on the desktop. When a user logs onto a system, this profile is read, and the look and feel is restored to where the user left off.

When you first log onto a Microsoft Windows computer, you are assigned a default user profile. The profile is stored on the local machine. As you make changes, you customize this default. As a user logs off a computer, changes are written to the profile so that the computer can "remember" it the next time he or she logs on.

This type of profile is local to the machine on which you are logged in. Although this is very useful, you should know that because the information is stored locally on the machine, the user will have to "lose" this profile and start with the default profile again if he or she goes to another machine. To prevent this from happening and to ensure a common interface for a user who moves from computer to computer in your enterprise, you can implement what are known as *roaming user profiles*.

Roaming user profiles work in the same way as before, with the exception that the folders and files associated with the profile are stored on a network server. Because the profile is stored on a server, the user can access it every time when logging onto the network. This gives the impression that the profile is following the user from machine to machine.

There is also another type of profile, one that would be good for our public computers. These are known as *Mandatory* profiles. A Mandatory profile offers similar features to other profiles types, a common look and feel, and the ability for the user to make changes to the way things look. However, once the user logs off, the changes are not saved. Instead, they are simply lost. When the user logs on again, the default profile will return.

In fact, profiles can be about as flexible as you would like. You can create a custom profile and assign it to numbers of users. You can even make a custom profile, assign it to several users, and make it a Mandatory profile. Profiles should be used with care, but they can have enormous productivity benefits for users. Have you ever seen a user move from one computer to another, then struggle for thirty minutes, trying to find applications? This can all be avoided with profiles.

What Does a Profile Contain?

Earlier in this chapter, we said that a user profile retains the look and feel for a computer. That's a nice general statement, but it doesn't say much about precisely what gets saved. So let's take some time to find out the kinds of settings that get saved in a profile.

A user profile can contain both settings and connections for a user. That means that it can contain customizations that users make to the operating system, and it will also maintain a record of all the shared drives to which the user connects. These settings are reestablished when the user logs onto the system.

More specifically, a user profile contains things such as entries on the Start button. If an application is added to the Start menu of a user, a record is kept in the profile. This will cause the icon to appear every time the user logs on. It allows the user to rearrange icons based on preference. Since profiles will store network connections, it means that a user can map a drive and have it mapped at every logon. This maintains drive letters, so users do not have to remember where something is mapped to, they have to remember only the drive letter itself.

You might be wondering where all this data is stored. Well, when users log on to a Windows 2000 machine for the first time, they are assigned the default profile. A folder is created in the root of the system drive (the drive where Windows 2000 is installed) called *Documents and Settings*. A new folder for each user that logs on at the machine is created inside that folder. Figure 12.7 shows you this folder on our current system.

If you take a close look at Figure 12.7, you will see a *My Documents* folder within the user profile. This is the default location for users' documents. If you perform a Save function or a File, Open, this is the first place that Windows 2000 will look. An icon is also created on the user's desktop that points to the same location. This consistency helps users find their data, especially if you are using roaming profiles.

Whereas this behavior of *My Documents* is, in most cases, satisfactory—even preferred—there might be cases where it can cause problems. For instance, if you are using roaming profiles and a user has large files, his or her logoff time might become extended. This is because of having to save data across the network to a server.

You also should not confuse *My Documents* with the users' home folders. We will be talking about home folders a little later. Home folders are always kept on the network, whereas *My Document* folders are only optionally kept there.

We have said that if a profile does not already exist for a user, a default profile is used. However, as in most things, it is not quite as simple as that. In fact, there are *two* default profiles. When users log onto the network, they are assigned a default profile, but before they get the default profile specified on a

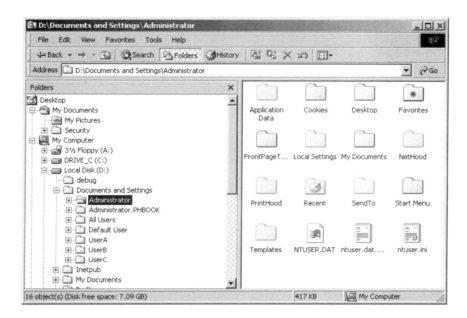

Figure 12-7   *A user profile folder.*

particular computer, Windows 2000 first checks the domain controller that authenticates the user, looking for a default user profile in the Netlogon share. This profile is known as the *network default profile*. If this exists, the local default profile is ignored. The network default profile is used, instead.

By editing the network default profile, you can, in effect, make the default settings for your entire network. This is obviously far more efficient than trying to edit the default profiles on each machine. Simply place all of the shortcuts and customizations in the network default profile, and you're done!

Roaming User Profiles

User profiles are intended to offer a method of saving a "standard" look and feel for a user. When users log into the computer, they do not have to hunt down an icon or set of documents, because these are maintained within the profile. However, what happens in the real world when a user gets up and logs on at a totally different computer? If you are using standard profiles, the user would be assigned the default profile for the local machine again. This is because there is no folder for the user in the local *Documents and Settings* folder.

This can be disorienting and counter-productive. If you are likely to have users moving from computer to computer in your organization, you should consider using roaming user profiles.

With roaming user profiles, the configuration data is stored on a network drive. When a user logs on, the profile is accessed and the user appears to retain desktop settings. To use roaming profiles, the administrator needs to modify a user's account. This causes the profile to be stored on the network. Don't forget, this is a powerful feature that can affect performance on your network.

It might be interesting to go quickly through the steps in which a roaming user profile is stored and maintained. When a user logs on, Windows 2000 finds the roaming user profile on the server and copies it to the local computer. It then applies these settings to the desktop. Also note that the contents of the *My Documents* folder is also copied from the network to the desktop.

Because the amount of data in the *My Documents* folder can be quite large, Windows 2000 has some intelligence built in. After the folder is copied the first time, subsequently, only changes are sent up to the server (and vice versa). This makes the logon process much shorter.

When a user logs off, all changes the user made to the local profile are copied back to the server. That way, the user can go to another computer and retain all new settings. Roaming user profiles are a useful tool within the enterprise. Users appreciate the consistent look, and help desk personnel appreciate the reduced number of calls they receive, asking where icons are placed or how to change settings.

You might also be wondering where these settings are actually saved. The answer is in a file called *Ntuser.dat*. You can see this file in Figure 12.7. This file stores the environment settings and desktop appearance for the user. If you look on your own computer and cannot find it, make sure you are displaying hidden and system files.

You might be wondering how you can set up roaming user profiles. Well, that's a good question, so let's go through an example of setting it up. In the following steps we will show you how to set up a roaming user profile for UserC. Because you probably do not have a user named *UserC* on your own network, feel free to substitute another user in its place.

1. In the following steps, we will walk through the process of creating a roaming user profile. Before you configure the user account, you must first create a share. This share will store the user profile settings. You can name this share anything you like, but it is good practice to name it in a logical fashion. That way, others will be able to work out what it is just by glancing at it. Let's create a share. To do this, we will open Windows Explorer. To open it, click on Start, Programs, Accessories, Windows Explorer. This starts Windows Explorer. In the right-hand pane, select the disk drive where you want to store the roaming user profiles. Then, in the right-hand pane, right-click and select New, Folder. Enter the name of the folder you want to use. For the purpose of this example, I created a folder called *Profiles*.

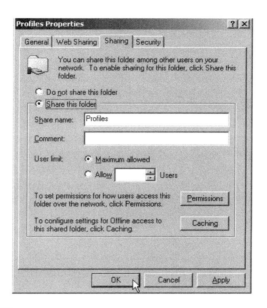

Figure 12–8   *Sharing a folder for profiles.*

2. Now that you have created the folder, it has to be shared. This allows your users to connect to it. To share the folder, click on the folder name in the right-hand panel of Windows Explorer and right-click. This brings up the context-sensitive menu. Select Sharing. This brings up the Profile Properties dialog box. This is shown in Figure 12.8. We need to share this folder, so click on the Share this folder option and accept the default options. When you have done this, click on OK. The folder should now be displayed in Windows Explorer with a hand on the icon. This shows that the folder is now shared.

3. It is now time to edit the user properties. Don't forget, we have chosen a user account named *UserC*. Feel free to substitute anything you want. However, do not use a user account without the administrator's permission, because this will cause a user profile to be stored on the network. First, we must open the user account administration tool. If you do not already have it open, click on Start, Programs, Administrative Tools, Active Directory Users and Computers. We will need to access user properties. You should now be an expert at locating them. Because we do not have many user accounts, we are simply going to click on the domain name in the left panel. Next, we click on Users to see a list of the user objects in the right-hand panel. Then we will select UserC from the list, right-click on the name, and select Properties. This displays the user properties. We first showed you these properties in Figure 12.4. We are interested in the Profile tab. This is shown in Figure 12.9.

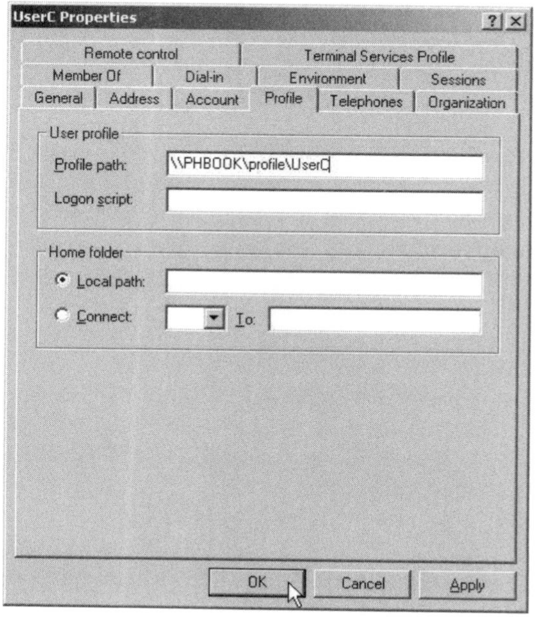

Figure 12–9   *The Profile tab.*

4. As you can see in Figure 12.9, we have entered some information onto the Profile path line. This is the path to the share we just created. The //PHBOOK is the server name. This is followed by the share name, and finally by the name of the folder that will contain this user's settings. This should be the user's logon name. To make life a little easier, you can use the variable *%username%*, rather than typing each user's name in here. This is a system variable that takes the currently logged on user's name and uses that.

5. The next time the user logs on his or her profile information will now be copied from the computer to the server.

Using the above example, you will be able to redirect profile information to a network server. In lab environments, it might be acceptable to use a domain controller (DC) to store user profiles. However, on your enterprise network, we suggest that you use a member server especially for this purpose. This is because the copying of profiles can take up a lot of system resources, including CPU and bandwidth. It is a good idea to leave the DC performing its role for authentication unhindered.

Customizing Roaming User Profiles

So we have now taken two big steps. We started with a profile that was stored on the local computer. This served a useful purpose but, unfortunately, when a user logged on at a different computer on the network, the profile failed to follow them. So then we showed you how to move that information to a network share. We then implemented a roaming user profile. This improved our situation because it allowed the profile settings to follow the user.

However, let's go a step further. Wouldn't it be a good idea if you standardized the default profile? Although the default profile that comes with a Windows 2000 installation might be good for some, you might want to create a custom profile for your organization. Then, when new users join your network, you can train them on what to expect. This is known as a *custom roaming profile*.

As it turns out, creating a custom roaming profile is very easy. In simple terms, all you have to do is to logon to a computer as a user account. Make all of the changes to the user environment that you want—such as moving icons, hiding applications, etc. When you do this, that profile information is stored locally on the computer. Because you know the folder where this information is stored (*Documents and Settings*), all you have to do is copy these files into the default user profile on the server!

If you do this from the beginning, the user will logon for the first time and receive the new default profile. This is in contrast to the behavior we have seen up to this point. Earlier, we explained that the roaming profile is a copy of the local profile. However, in this case, because the files already exist on the server, they are used instead.

Customizing roaming profiles is a useful tool because it helps to set a standard for your organization. Although you could implement the same type of operation using local profiles, it is obviously far more difficult to do so. Customizing is a good idea because it allows you, as system administrator, to define the initial look and feel for the user. You can also use it for more than one user, so it allows you to customize the look for groups of people who share the same job function. Finally, your help desk will find it easier to troubleshoot problems, because they will be aware of the standard look and feel and can make assumptions about how the computer is operating.

Mandatory Roaming User Profiles

We are gradually working our way toward a more controlled environment. In the previous section, we moved profiles to a server. We then talked about customizing the server profiles to aid troubleshooting and administration. You are about to take the final and, some might say, ultimate step in using profiles. The mandatory roaming user profile.

The truth is, users are always going to make mistakes. That is, they will change a setting on a machine, log off, and simply hope to get things back to normal by logging on again. Unfortunately, with the methods we have discussed so far, this might not be the case. The act of logging off will not reset the computer. Instead, it does the opposite—it saves the new profile information to either the local profile folder or the profile directory on the network. Next time the user logs on, the changes—however disastrous—are going to stick!

This is more likely to be the case when you have computers in public areas. In this case, users are tempted to come and play on a computer, changing things as they go. If they log off, profile information can be updated, rendering the computer inoperable or, at the very least, unsuitable for the task at hand.

So what's the answer? Easy, make the profile a Mandatory Profile! Unfortunately, the name of a Mandatory Profile does not clearly explain what it is. After all, all profiles are somewhat "mandatory" by dictionary definition. In this case, *mandatory* means that users cannot save their new settings when they log off. It does not stop them from making changes as they work, but if they make a mistake and want to return to the default settings, all they have to do is log off and log back on again. The profile information is recopied from the server, and everything on the machine will "reset."

Again, there is no magic to Mandatory Profiles. In fact, making a profile mandatory is as simple as renaming a single file. Remember *Ntuser.dat*? Earlier, we said this file stores information regarding local settings and network connections. Well, if you rename this file to *Ntuser.man*, the profile becomes mandatory! It's as simple as that.

Profiles are implemented automatically on every Microsoft Windows computer. Our discussion of profiles has attempted to explain how you can use this feature to take better control of your network and ease the daily routine of your users. You can do this by moving profiles to a server and assigning users a roaming profile; this makes users' custom settings "follow" them around as they logon to different workstations. We also explained how you can prevent users from making changes to profiles. This allows you to set a standard desktop. It also prevents users from making changes to the computers that might render them inoperable. This helps you when troubleshooting problems.

Home Folders

One of the primary tasks of a system administrator is to ensure that users' data is available 24 hours a day, 7 days a week. In this day and age, this is not as easy as it seems. For one thing, hardware prices have decreased to such an extent that it is not unreasonable to allow your users to have massive amounts of local storage, usually in the tens of gigabyte (GB) range. Although this has been useful for the installation of new, larger applications, it has also made the job of administrators a little more difficult.

On the one hand, allowing users to have a large amount of local storage on their computers means that they can have a lot of flexibility. If the network is suddenly not available, the world does not come crashing down. Usually, users can continue to work relatively unhindered—perhaps they cannot print, but at least they can access their applications and data.

On the other hand, hardware inevitably fails at some point. Although the life of a hard disk has increased over time, there is bound to come a time when it simply crashes. When this occurs, user data is in danger.

We know what the answer to this dilemma is—backup and restoring of data. However, how do you do this if all data is stored locally on hard disks? How do you do it for computers that are laptops? Whereas there are solutions to this—such as backup agents that allow you to connect to a remote machine and back up data, the most efficient solution all around is to encourage users to store their data on a server. If data is stored centrally on a server, you can take advantage of the extra disaster recovery options, such as RAID 5 and network backups.

Another advantage of storing users' data on a network server is that the data can be accessed from any location. If users wander from computer to computer on your network, they will still be able to access their files. If files are stored locally on a hard disk, this would not be the case. This concept is not unlike what we discussed with user profiles. Storing data on a network server allows the administrator to take responsibility and guarantee that data will be available at all times, no matter what disaster occurs. It also means that an administrator can take advantage of other Windows 2000 features, such as Disk Quotas. Disk Quotas are discussed in some detail in Chapter 18 of this book.

Microsoft Windows operating systems have for a long time had a *My Documents* folder. This folder has become a default location for user files. The problem with the *My Documents* folder is twofold. First, by default, it is stored on the local machine. This makes it vulnerable to hard disk crashes and means that the user data does not follow the user from location to location in your enterprise.

This issue can be addressed somewhat with user profiles. However, over time, you will soon come to realize that this function of profiles can quickly become a problem on your network. Don't forget, if you store profile information on the network, this is called a *roaming user profile*. When a user logs on, the data is copied from the network share onto the local machine. When a user logs off, data is copied back to the server. Data in the *My Documents* folder can quickly become quite large, and that data has to be moved across the network. This can consume a lot of bandwidth. It will also slow down the user logon and logoff process.

When you have a large enterprise, with possibly tens of thousands of users, it is easy to see that this problem could become quite unmanageable. There has to be a better solution, and there is—home folders.

Home folders have the advantage of being stored on a server. Therefore, they are available to users, no matter where they logon in your enterprise. Because they are not part of a user's profile, you eliminate the network traffic as the user logs on and logs off. At the same time, you can schedule backups whenever you want and protect the data with standard techniques such as hot-swappable disk drives and RAID.

The home folder will exist in addition to the *My Documents* folder. This means that there will be some user education involved with using them. On the plus side, not all applications are able to use the *My Documents* folder, and a home folder will give you greater application compatibility.

In a moment, we will go through the steps of creating home directories. Before we do that, let's suggest that you always create home directories on NTFS partitions. NTFS allows you to assign permissions in a far more granular level than if you decide to use FAT.

Okay, let's walk through the steps of creating a home folders for our users. As you will see, many of these steps will already be familiar. One of the best learning tools is repetition, so let's go ahead and see what we can do.

1. First, we need to create a share. Each user folder will be created within this share. You can expect that the size of the user folders will grow quite large over time, so it is a good idea to create this share on a disk that has a lot of space. It should be on a computer that does not have a lot of other tasks, such as an SQL Server. If you attempt to create this share on a computer that is already busy, the server is likely to get bogged down with all the disk writes and reads. Because users will notice this in every application, it tends to generate a lot of help desk calls. Plan accordingly—choose a server that is underutilized, or better yet, install a server dedicated to the purpose. First, we must create a share. To do this, we need to open Windows Explorer. To open Windows Explorer, click on Start, Programs, Accessories, Windows Explorer. This starts Windows Explorer. In the left-hand pane, select the disk drive where you want to store the roaming user profiles. Then, in the right-hand pane, right-click and select New, Folder. Enter the name of the folder you want to use. For the purpose of this example, create a folder called *Hfolders*.

2. Next, we must share the folder. To share the folder, click on the folder, name in the right-hand panel of Windows Explorer, then right-click. This brings up the context-sensitive menu. Select Sharing. This brings up the Hfolders Properties dialog box. We need to share this folder, so click on the Share this folder.

3. Because this folder is going to be used for user data, we need to offer some level of security. Because this is the case, the default options for a share are insufficient. So, in this case, we are going to remove the default permissions and add some permissions of our own. Click on the Permissions button. This brings up the Permissions for HFolder dialog box. This is shown in Figure 12.10.

4. As you can see, the default option for a new share is that Full Control is assigned to the Everyone group. We want to be more specific than that

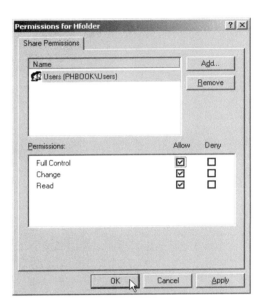

Figure 12-10   *The Permissions for Hfolder dialog box.*

(because this introduces a possible security problem.) Click on the Everyone group under Name to select it, then click on the Remove button, then click on the Add button. This brings up the Select Users, Computers and Groups dialog box. We are going to assign full control permission to the Users built-in group. This ensures that only users with domain accounts will have permission to the new home folder share. Once you are done, the Permissions for Hfolder dialog box should look like Figure 12.10.

5. Click on OK, then on OK again. You have now shared the folder. If you look in Windows Explorer, the folder should appear with a hand beneath it. This means that you have shared the folder correctly. Your work on the folder is complete—it is now time to configure a user account to have access. To do this, we need to access the User Properties. If you do not already have it open, click on Start, Programs, Administrative Tools, Active Directory Users and Computers. Because we do not have many user accounts we are simply going to click on the domain name in the left panel. Next, we click on Users to see a list of the user objects in the right hand panel. Then we will select UserA from the list, right-click on the name, and select Properties. This displays the User Properties. We now need to access the Profile tab. So click on Profile. This dialog box was first shown in Figure 12.9.

6. We need to enter a path statement into the Local Path text box. This will direct the user's account to the share we created. Enter the path

X:\HFOLDER\UserA. The first part of this path specifies the server, the second the shares we are going to use. Finally, we specified the user name. This will automatically create the user's directory. The drive letter assigns a letter to the user's home folder. In this case, to save data to the home folder, the user should save to the *X:* drive.

Creating home folders is going to make your life a little easier. They will be easier to implement—and will be accepted more readily—if they exist at the very outset of your network. So make home folders on a network server a high priority when designing your network.

The Purpose of Group Policies

We wanted to take a brief detour and take the unusual step of introducing a technology before we are really ready to discuss it in detail. The reason for this is that group policies have a key role to play in the administration of user accounts. On the other hand, the topic is so large that it warrants an entire chapter on its own. So that is what we did. This section will serve as a brief introduction and nothing more. For more detail, read the chapter on Group Policy.

At its simplest level, group policies are simply configuration settings that are used to enforce organizational and network settings. They are very flexible, so once a group of settings are defined, they can be applied to objects within Active Directory. This includes Users, Computers, and Organizational Units.

Group policies can be used to define a user's desktop. This includes customizing the Start menu, copying files to the *My Documents* folder, installing applications, and setting permissions. Basically, everything you could possibly want to do!

Because group policies can be set higher in the Active Directory hierarchy, you might find that you are affected by them, even if you did not create them yourself. So it is a good idea to become familiar with them, even if the task of creating and applying them belongs to someone else.

At the very least, you should be aware of the group policies that are being enforced on your network. It is likely that there is a Group Policy administrator. They should be able to inform you of the policies that are in effect on your network and precisely what each policy does.

Do not assume that every problem you have is related to Group Policy. For instance, while logon settings such as the number of failed logon attempts are set with group policies, the task of unlocking accounts, as you have seen, belongs to other administrators, not to the Group Policy administrator.

If nothing else, let this section serve to inform that there is another topic that affects everything we have said here. Make sure that you read the Group Policy chapter for further details.

Common Problems

There are many facets to user account management. So many, in fact, that it would take the rest of this book to document them. Despite that, let's talk about some possible problems you might come across in the context of this chapter's topics.

It is possible that a user can make changes to his or her computing environment that will render a computer inoperable. If this occurs, have the user log off, then log back on. It is possible that a refresh of the user profile will fix the issues. However, it is also possible that the changes that have been made have already been saved to the user profile, and simply restarting will not fix the problem.

In these cases, there is nothing to do but to delete and recreate the user profile. Don't forget, you will have to delete the profile from possibly two locations. First, it should be deleted from the local computer. If you are using roaming user profiles, it should also be deleted from the server. When this is done, have the user log in again. Because the user does not have a user profile, he or she will be assigned the default user profile again. Sure, customizations will have been lost, but at least the user will be back up and running.

If a user reports no access to the data in his or her home folder, there could be several reasons. One of the most common would be that the server storing the home folders is down. In this case, you must ensure that the server is brought back online as soon as possible. This is one of the only times when a central home folder is a potential risk.

If a user cannot log on to the network, check to make sure that the user has not been locked out. This occurs when a user attempts to log on with an invalid password a number of times. The number of times is set with group policies. If this is the case, simply unlock the user's account.

Chapter Summary

This chapter dealt with some of the many facets of user administration. User administration is likely to take up quite a bit of your time as a system administrator. One of the first areas we addressed was finding user accounts. Although this might seem like a simple task, Active Directory has made things a little more difficult. This is because Active Directory is enterprise-wide and stores a lot of data.

Although it is possible simply to scroll down a long list of users until you find the one you want, it is also tedious and time-consuming. If you work in an enterprise that contains tens of thousands of users, it is also very difficult and slow. As an alternative, we showed you how to search Active Directory by user name. We also showed you how you can access properties of the user object. This helps you to refine your search.

Once a user account was located, we showed you how you can reset a user password or delete an account from Active Directory. For each of these tasks, you need to access the Active Directory User and Computers administrative utility. This can be found in the Administrative Tools folder. This is a flexible tool, and you will likely find yourself using it on a daily basis.

In our discussion of user profiles, you learned that users' desktop settings are, in fact, stored in a folder. Any changes a user makes to the environment, such as customizing the Start button, is saved to these folders. By default, this folder is saved to the local computer. This, however, can cause problems when you have users using multiple computers—a likely event in an enterprise.

To alleviate this problem, we discussed roaming user profiles. These profiles are stored centrally on a server. Because they are stored on a network, a user can logon at any computer and gain access to personal settings. This makes the user experience of the network easier and will help to reduce the number of support calls.

Roaming profiles are very useful, but they do not prevent a user from making changes to the computer that render it inoperable. To help with this problem, we discussed mandatory profiles. These profiles operate in a similar fashion to roaming user profiles, with the exception that users are no longer able to make changes to their environment. Although this reduces the flexibility of Windows 2000 for the user community, it has the advantage of having the largest impact in reducing help desk calls. It also ensures that the user experience is consistent.

Another area of concern is user data. Large hard disks have encouraged users to store their data locally. However, local hard disks are not usually backed up, nor do they take advantage of fault tolerance technologies, such as RAID and clustering. Therefore, we showed you home folders. Home folders is a method of assigning a space on a network server for each user. All user data should be saved to the home folder so that it can be backed up. Because the home folder settings are not part of the user profile, they have no effect on logon performance.

Finally, we briefly spoke about group policies. Although not discussed in detail, it is important that you realize that Group Policy has a huge impact on the administration of user accounts and the user experience on your network. This will be discussed in more detail later in this book.

Windows 2000 Groups

*A*nything that makes administration easier is something worth learning about—and groups fall into that category. If you are familiar with groups from previous versions of Microsoft Windows NT, you might be tempted to skip this chapter. However, I want to ask you not to do that. There have been some changes to groups in Windows 2000. Some of these changes are subtle, others are not. Although some of the information might seem like old hat, I can assure you that there will be enough new information to keep you on your toes.

Groups have long been a fundamental building block for the simplification of administration. This chapter is going to start at the basics, by discussing the different group types and how and when they can be used. Some of these are new to Windows 2000. We will then talk about various strategies you can use on your own networks to maximize the benefits that groups bring to the table.

Why Do We Need Groups?

Your network is a collection of many things. These "things" are collectively known as *resources*. You'll see the term *resources* used quite often. This term can be broken out further by taking a closer look at what we mean by resources.

A resource on your network might include many things, but generally, they would be hardware, software, or data-related resources. *Hardware* refers to servers and workstations. It also includes printers. These three elements, alone, make up a fair chunk of your network investment. Because they are valuable and are, indeed, the lifeblood of your network, it is clearly important that you control who has access to these resources.

Then we have software. Software is another valuable asset for your organization. Software licensing has become an increasingly important topic. Wouldn't it be nice if you could dictate who could access an application?

Finally, we have our data-related resources. *Data-related*, in this sense, is a catch-all for everything else. Specifically, I want to mention documents that are saved on your network, shares on your network that allow you to access these documents or applications, and databases that contain important company data.

One of your jobs as a system administrator in Windows 2000 (or any network) is to formulate a strategy to both protect and regulate access to all of these resources (and any other resource you can identify). So who wants to access these resources? Well, obviously, we're talking about the users on your network. Users will want to run applications, save and retrieve data from shares on your network, and print out their documents.

If everyone's requirements were the same, this task would be easy. However, nothing is that simple. For instance, a system administrator needs access to all areas of the network—whereas a sales person might need access only to an order database and catalog application. You could just make everyone an administrator, but it would soon become impossible to track who was doing what on your network. You are going to need a more structured approach.

It is entirely possible for you to assign permissions to resources on a per-user basis. That is, Joe Green needs access to a share—so you give him change permissions to the share, and he can do his work. Although this would work, you now have an administrative storm brewing. In a large network (in this case, you get to determine personally what a large network really is, but I'm going to say it's anything more than 10!) you are soon going to grow tired of assigning permissions on a per-user basis.

Here's why. Let's say that you have 10 users, and each of them needs access to a share. So you assign change permissions to the share for each user individually. That's 10 units of work. Then one of your users leaves and goes to another company. You hire a replacement and assign him permissions to the share. While you are doing that, you have to remove the person who left—that's two more units of work.

The manager from Sales calls and says that he has a junior member of staff they want to restrict. They ask you to give him only enough permissions to read the data in the share. So you remove the change permission from that person. At the same time, the head of Finance calls about three people who post information to the share but never read data from it—so could you please remove the read write from them? That's four more units of work.

Then the company expands to 20 users—the Sales Department gets three new people, and they need read access but not write. Finance gets two new people, and one needs read access only and the other needs write access. The remaining five new employers need read and write.

Wow, things are starting to get complicated! What's more, this is all for a single share. Multiply this by 10 different shares and three different printers, and you can see that it can quickly get out of hand. There has to be a better way—and there is—it's called *Groups*!

Groups are going to allow you to define a set of permissions one time, then to apply those permissions to a number of people at a time. If those permissions change, you change them in one place, and all users who are members of the group will pick up the new permissions the next time they log in. Isn't that a lot simpler than having to change permissions on a per-user basis?

Once you stop thinking about small companies and start to think about the enterprise, you'll get a better idea of the scale of this issue. For instance, the other extreme of this is a large multinational organization. In these circumstances, you might have thousands of shares existing on a network. Many of the employees will be working regionally and will have no need to have access to data in other countries or even departments in the same building.

In these circumstances, you are going to need to get a better idea of what your network is doing for you. One of the challenges for a system administrator is thinking beyond technology. In the case of groups and security, you need to define what resources you have on your network (or which resources you have control over). Then decide who needs access to these resources. Along with the list of names, you should make a list of the level of access they need. This will determine the permissions that you assign.

When formulating your plans, you need to know where the users you wish to include are located. Are they in a single domain? Do you want to make the resource available to a single domain, or will you want to include users from other domains? In Windows 2000, you might also want to define a single set of permissions for users in a forest.

This chapter is going to talk about the specific technological issues and resolutions that Windows 2000 offers. However, this up-front work is really going to dictate the level of success that you achieve. Success, in this regard, should be considered as minimizing the administration of user permissions. If you are spending a significant part of your day setting and resetting permissions, you likely have not done enough work with groups.

Finally, it's always good to have a very basic definition. If you ever lose sight of what groups are for, simply remember this: Groups are collections of user accounts. You will use groups to assign permissions or create lists of users for distribution purposes. It's that simple.

Using Groups in Windows 2000

As we mentioned in our opening paragraph, experienced administrators might feel that they know all about groups and, therefore, can skip this chapter. We advised against doing that, and here is why. Windows 2000 offers extensions to the basic concepts introduced in previous versions of Microsoft Windows NT. The following discussion is going to cover some of these differences.

The three areas that we wish to clarify include some basic usage rules for groups, the different types of groups that exist, and the scope of each type of group. Do not worry if you do not understand this yet; we'll be covering each subject in a moment.

It is important that you realize some rules regarding groups in Windows 2000 because it is fairly common for new administrators to make incorrect assumptions. These assumptions might be, "I just added a user to a group and then assigned permissions to that group, but the user still can't do what she is supposed to be able to do. There must be something wrong with my network!" We'll answer why this problem might occur in a moment.

The different types of groups are important for several reasons. You might find that a group you have created cannot grant sufficient permissions to a group of users, and knowing about group types will prevent that. Finally, knowing the scope of a group will guide you in deciding which group types will fit your needs. Because Active Directory is an enterprise-wide directory service, you will soon see that a new group type has been added to Windows 2000.

The Rules of Group Usage

We have already spoken at length regarding reasons why groups are a good idea. Hopefully, you don't need too much more persuading. Using groups is going to simplify your security structure. However, incorrect usage could just as seriously compromise your security model. So you need to give some thought not only to the technological issues, such as the different group types and their scope, but also, from a practical standpoint, which group of users should be allowed to do what on your network.

In simple terms, it is easier to assign permissions singularly to a single object than it is to assign permissions to many different objects. That is the primary reason we use groups. This is shown in Figure 13.1. In this figure, we have a share. In one case, we have assigned permissions to five different users. In another instance, we have created a group and assigned permissions to that group. If requirements change, it is a simple matter to alter permissions for the group. These changes will be put into effect the next time the user logs on.

As you will see in a moment, there are two different group types available in Windows 2000. One of these is used for security purposes, the other is not. For the latter group type, you might want to group machines into a group. This

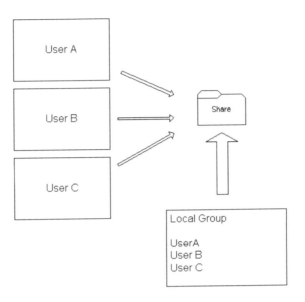

Figure 13–1   *Assigning permissions to groups.*

is entirely possible in Windows 2000—so don't feel as if you are restricted to only including user accounts in all group types.

Now for some simple rules regarding groups. First, when users are authenticated on a Windows 2000 network, they are assigned a Security Token. This token contains, among other things, a list of groups to which the user belongs. Note that this is *determined at the time the user logs on.* In other words, if you go back and change the permissions that a group has been assigned, the users will not know about the change until after they have logged off the network and logged back on.

This is a significant issue and one of the first areas that new administrators find confusing. Group permissions are not really dynamic. By that I mean that the user permissions are not altered dynamically as they are changed by an administrator. It is only when the user logs off and back on that the new permissions get assigned.

A group is simply a reference to a set of user accounts. This means that a user can belong to many different groups. This increases flexibility but can also lead to some confusion. Permissions and their use are covered in Chapter 16. However, keep in mind that if a user is having problems accessing a resource, it might very well be a problem with their group membership. If you have added a user to a group, yet the user is still unable to perform a particular function, it might very well be that another group membership is preventing access. Documenting your groups is a good idea. We will be talking about these issues later in this chapter.

Groups can also be members of other groups. This is known as *nesting*. Nesting groups can help you to reduce the amount of administration you perform even further. But it's a double-edged sword. Although nesting can, indeed, simplify the assignment of permissions on your network, it can also lead to some confusion. If you do not document your groups and how they are nested, it is easy to get lost. Perhaps a user is a member of multiple groups, perhaps you want to change the permissions for every group except one and find that, due to nesting, you are unable to assign the permissions without a lot of work.

Nesting is a nice feature, but try to keep it to a minimum. One level of nesting is recommended, as you will see later, but when you move beyond that and start to include multiple nested groups, things start to get difficult to manage. The tools built into Windows 2000 do not really help you track this very easily—so it is going to be up to you to follow the "best practices" in this chapter.

Windows 2000 Group Types

Windows 2000 introduces a new group type that you won't have seen in previous versions of Microsoft Windows NT. This new type was introduced to allow applications to utilize Active Directory. The first major application to take advantage of this new feature is Exchange 2000.

SECURITY GROUPS

As the name implies, security groups exist so you can group users together and assign them permissions. This is the common usage that groups have been put to in previous version of Microsoft Windows NT. You can also use security groups to send email messages. When you send an email message to a security group, each member of the group will receive the email. The basic rule to remember is that security groups are primarily designed to allow you to assign permissions.

DISTRIBUTION GROUPS

Distribution groups are designed to collect user accounts together so that the list of users can be used by another application. An example of an application that has this level of integration into Active Directory would be Microsoft Exchange 2000. Security groups share the same functionality as distribution groups—but the reverse is not true, That is, distribution groups are never used to assign permissions.

Distribution groups are available only to applications that have a level of integration into Active Directory. That means that their use during the initial implementation of Windows 2000 might be limited. However, as other applications on the network get upgraded and applications that are integrated into

Active Directory begin to reach the marketplace, expect to see distribution groups used more frequently.

Examining Group Scopes

Now that we know a little bit about the different types of groups that are available, we need to dig down a little deeper and find out how they might be used. Before we do that, however, we need to make sure that we understand some basic concepts.

Groups have, indeed, been around for a long time, but even those who have been using them might be under the impression that group types should have included definitions for things such as local groups and global groups. We will be talking about these things in a moment, but the point that needs to be made is that these different groups vary only in their scope. The basic principle of grouping users together for the purpose of assigning permissions still holds true. The only thing that needs to be considered is that you need to decide from which pool of users you want to pull members—and where you will want to use the groups you are creating.

For instance, if you are sitting at a Windows 2000 Professional machine, you might want to create a group—local to your machine—that includes members from the domain of which you are a member. This is one example of group scope. On the other hand, you might be administering a forest, and you might want to create a group with sufficient scope that you can include as members of that group user accounts from anywhere in that forest. That would require a group with an entirely different scope.

The point is, each of these are different scopes; they are not types of groups. This may seem like a subtle difference, but having clarification will help you to clarify the nature of groups in relation to their scope. Our definition of a group always holds true, no matter what the scope.

So what is the purpose of a scope, and what do they bring to the table? Well, a scope is going to determine several things. First, the scope of a group is going to determine which users you can include in your group. Some scopes allow you to include users from multiple domains; others restrict you to users who belong to the local domain.

The scope will also dictate the domains in which the group can be assigned permissions. If you create a group with scope that is restricted to the local domain, you will not be able to use this group in other domains in the tree or forest. This works both ways; it is sometimes a good idea to create groups with a scope of the local domain. That way, you make sure that you don't give people permissions in your domain inadvertently.

Finally, the scope of a group is going to determine into which groups you can nest. That is, groups can also be members of other groups, but the groups of which you can be a member will be limited by the scope of the group you are creating. Again, this works to both your advantage and disadvantage. If you create a group with a scope that is too limited, you will not be able to use the group in its intended way. However, by creating groups with limited scope, you can ensure that your group is used only in a particular context.

There are three different group scopes available within Active Directory. A fourth type, known as *local groups*, will be discussed separately because they cannot exist within Active Directory. The three scopes are:

- Global
- Domain Local
- Universal

We will discuss each of these scopes in a moment. Before we do that, remember that there are two issues here. Although it might seem logical simply to determine the scope of the permissions you want to assign and choose a scope based on this, it would, in fact, run contrary to our recommendations, or best practices. This topic will be covered later in this chapter. For now, let's get familiar with each of these scopes, so that we can better understand their place in Windows 2000.

GLOBAL GROUPS

Global groups are going to provide the foundation for your group management. Global groups are used to group users together for the purposes of assigning permissions to access resources. Whenever a group of users needs similar access to a network resource, you should create a global group and add user names to it. Once this is complete, you can go ahead and add the necessary permissions to the group.

Global groups work in the following way. You can add users from only the domain in which the global group is being created. This is illustrated in Figure 13.2. In this example, we have two domains in a tree. If you create a global group in domain Europe, only users from that domain can be added as members of that group. Users from the US domain cannot be added.

However, once a global group has been created, you can assign permissions to resources outside the domain in which it was created. This is also shown in Figure 13.2. The global group that has been created in Europe contains users from the Europe domain, but it has been assigned permission to a resource in the US domain.

Global groups can also contain other global groups—don't forget, this is known as *nesting*. Once again, however, because we are talking about membership within the group, the global groups you can nest within a global group are going to be limited to global groups within the same domain. In other words, a global group created within the Europe domain can be nested with our new global group—but global groups from the US domain cannot.

As you will see later in this chapter, global groups can also be nested within universal groups and, more commonly, within domain local groups. This is an example of a best practice. Once you see the scope of these other group

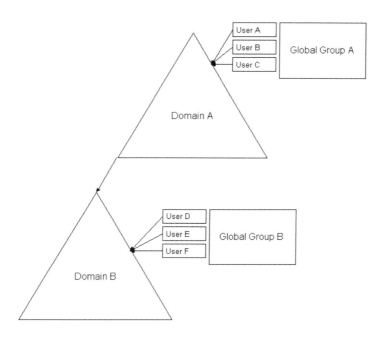

Figure 13–2   *Using global groups.*

scopes, you'll understand why we suggest that you work this way. For now, remember that the most common use of global groups is to group a number of user accounts together. We do not suggest that you take the next step and assign permissions directly to the global group. For that, we suggest you use domain local groups.

DOMAIN LOCAL GROUPS

Domain local groups will be used to assign permissions. Most commonly, you will not add users as direct members of a domain local group. Instead, you will create a global group, add members to it, then nest the global group within a domain local group.

Domain local groups are specific to the domain in which they are created. They cannot, under any circumstances, be used outside the domain in which they were created. So a domain local group created in Europe can be used to assign permissions within that domain, but it could not be used to assign permissions to resources in another domain.

You can nest both universal groups and global groups with a domain local group. Because these groups have different scopes, you can use domain local groups to assign permissions that will affect users in another domain, contrary to the hard and fast rule outlined above. This is shown in Figure 13.3.

```
                  Domain: Europe


                    ┌──────────────┐
                    │ Global Group │
                    │    User A    │
                    │    User B    │
              ┌─────┴──────────────┴─────┐
              │                          │
              │  Domain Local Group      │
              └──────────────────────────┘

                         ⇓

                    ┌──────────┐
                    │  SHARE   │
                    └──────────┘
```

Domain local groups used with global groups.

In Figure 13.3, a domain local group has been created in the Europe domain. The only users that can be direct members in this group are users that exist within the Europe domain. However, in the example given, a share exists, where you would like users in the US domain to be able to both save and retrieve documents. So a global group is created in the US domain. Because global groups have a scope outside the domain in which they are created, this global group has been nested into the domain local group in Europe.

This would achieve the desired result of giving access to users in another domain in a structured and organized way. This is an example of a best practice.

Finally, it should be noted that domain local groups cannot be nested within other groups. It is not possible to see them outside the domain in which they are created, and domain local groups cannot contain other domain local groups.

UNIVERSAL GROUPS

Universal groups are new to Windows 2000. They were introduced because the Windows 2000 infrastructure can be much more far-reaching than ever before. This group type can be thought of as a logical extension of the other two scopes.

This group type can be used to assign permissions in any domain in a tree or forest. That is, membership to a universal group is not limited to any one domain. You can nest both global groups and other universal groups within a universal group. This is a good use of universal groups; it is strongly suggested that you do not assign permissions directly to a universal group.

Universal group membership is very open. What we mean by this is that anyone in a tree or forest can be a member of a universal group. This is illustrated in Figure 13.4. In this example, we have introduced a third domain, Africa. A Universal group has been created within the Active Directory that contains users from the Europe domain, the US domain, and the Africa domain. This gives you a lot of flexibility.

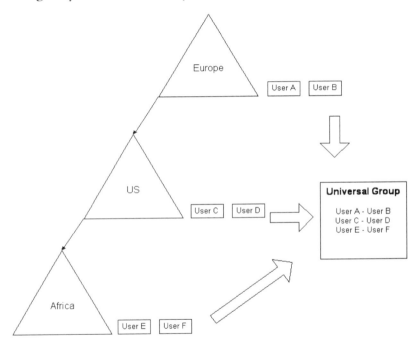

Figure 13–4   *Using universal groups.*

You can think of universal groups as "enterprise" groups. They allow you to view all users in your enterprise and to assign them to a group scope so that you can control access to resources. They are the only group type that allows you to do this.

There is one drawback to universal groups—they can be used only if Active Directory is working in Native Mode. Those organizations that are in the process of migrating from a Microsoft Windows NT 4.0 network and have their

Active Directory working in Mixed Mode will not be able to use universal groups.

The Effect of Groups on Your Network

There are two aspects to group planning. First, you need to make sure that the groups you are creating achieve the desired result. To make sure that this is the case, you need to create groups that have sufficient scope.

However, there is also another consideration—the effect that groups and group memberships can have on the performance of your network. This might seem like a strange consideration. Most administrators of earlier versions of Microsoft Windows NT networks never had to worry too much about it, but with the additional power of groups within Windows 2000 and the changes to the basic infrastructure, there are some things you need to be aware of.

Earlier in this chapter, we talked briefly about the security token that gets created for a user when logging into a Windows 2000 network. This token contains a list of the groups to which the user is a member. This will include a list of all global, domain local, and universal groups. It is likely, especially if you will be working in a large enterprise environment, that your users will be members of many different groups. You need to be aware that the size of the security token will increase as the user is added to additional groups.

The security token for a user is passed around the network as the user attempts to access shares and other resources. If a user is a member of hundreds of groups, this token can grow to being quite significant in size. This might impact the performance of your network.

It will also have an effect on the time it takes for your users to log on. The security token has to be generated on the fly, which means that group membership and permissions are determined at the time the logon takes place. If there are a lot of groups, this process will take an increased amount of time.

On the same topic, try not to use security groups as a substitute for distribution groups. Although this is certainly a capability of security groups, you can increase logon performance by using distribution groups. This is because distribution groups are not evaluated at logon and stored in the security token.

Finally, we need to talk about Global Catalog servers. The concept of a Global Catalog was introduced in Chapter 7. The Global Catalog is used for searching for data in Active Directory. The amount of information stored in the global catalog is limited. In fact, although it will contain a list of all objects within Active Directory, it usually stores only a subset of the attributes of these objects. This is not quite the case for groups.

Global groups and domain local groups are stored within the Global Catalog. However, membership for these group scopes is not. This reduces the amount of data that needs to be replicated to your servers. However, in the case of universal groups, both the name and membership list are stored.

This can have a far-reaching effect on your network. It means that whenever a change is made to the membership of a universal group, every Global Catalog server on your network will need to replicate that change. Because Global Catalog servers serve an entire forest, it can create a significant impact on network performance if you misuse universal groups. The basic rule you should follow is that universal groups should contain members that do not change very often. It is suggested that you use them in much the same way that you use domain local groups. If you have to use universal groups, create global groups and add global groups to universal groups. This way, you change membership in the global group and you do not cause replication of new membership rules to all Global Catalog servers.

That is not to say that they should never be used, but it is important for you to realize that groups can have an impact in three critical areas: user logon time, access to resources, and network bandwidth. If you keep these in mind when designing your group strategy, you will be ahead of the game later, as your Windows 2000 network develops into an enterprise.

Using Groups in Windows 2000

Now that you have a good understanding of the different group types and their scope, it is time to consider effective ways for you to use them on your network. You actually have several options, so we are going to lay them out for you, then suggest an optimal way to move forward and begin your implementation. It is far too easy to break the rules you decide upon for groups and group membership. Over time, groups get created on the fly, and you might forget why they were set up in the first place and precisely what each group does.

It is important that you start out with a good understanding of groups and that you think through how you are going to use them. It will pay dividends later, when you are asked simple questions regarding user permissions and access to resources. Don't lose sight of the fact that groups exist to make administration easier. If they are not achieving that goal, something is wrong with your implementation. More often than not, the problem stems from a lack of a strong plan for their use.

Of course, if there were only one way of doing this, we wouldn't need to explain all of the various options. However, things are never that easy. One of the most obvious things that will control the group scopes you need to use is the size of your Windows 2000 infrastructure. If you have a single domain, you will have no need for universal groups. If you have multiple domains, you will likely have a need for all of the different group scopes.

In a single-domain environment, you will use domain local groups and global groups to assign permissions. This best practice also applied to previous versions of Microsoft Windows NT. Let's take a closer look at how this works.

CREATING A SIMPLE GROUP STRATEGY

There are many different ways of using groups to achieve the ultimate goal of simplifying system administration. Although it is going to be up to you which one you choose, you should ensure that you are consistent. There are best practices for applying permissions, but it will be consistency that returns the greatest rewards.

The suggested method of using groups is to utilize a combination of global groups and domain local groups. This is shown in Figure 13.3. In this figure, you saw that you should try to avoid making users direct members of a domain local group. Instead, decide on the list of users to whom you want to assign permissions. Then create a global group, create a domain local group, add users to the global group, and nest the global group in the local group. Finally, assign permissions to the domain local group.

Let's take a look at this one step at a time. The list of users can be based on many things; perhaps you want to provide access based on a job function or use a model that more closely fits the organizational structure of your enterprise. It is unlikely that you will come up with a hard and fast rule about drawing up a list of users. The resource that you are either assigning permissions to, or removing permissions from, will dictate this list.

Your next step is to create the global group. We will be creating a global group in a moment. Because we have a best practice here, the scope issue does not become an issue (don't forget, we suggest that you create a global group, then nest it within a domain local group). However, make sure that you have a standard naming scheme for your groups. For example, if you have a temporary employee, Siobhan Chamberlin, and you need to create a user account, name that account *T-Chamberlin*. The *T* helps you to see at a glance that this employee is temporary. If you simply use the first name that comes into your head, you are going to run into problems later, when you are trying to remember why a particular group was created. If you work in an enterprise, the naming convention becomes even more important. This is because you can search Active Directory for groups, and other administrators in your enterprise will not have the intimate knowledge of your domain. Confusing naming conventions will just confuse them. More tips are included in Chapter 29.

The next step is to identify the resource to which you are assigning permissions and to create a domain local group to use for this function. Once again, the naming convention you employ will be key to success. Make sure that your fellow administrators are able to determine quickly why the group was created.

The third thing we must do is to nest the global group into the domain local group. Because you have not granted the domain local group permissions to the resource yet, this will not have a dramatic effect, but it is an important step. You are systematically creating your security structure as you follow these steps. If you don't do this, you might assign permissions too early. Also remember that you might want to nest several global groups into the domain local group. For instance, if the resource you are assigning permissions to is a new printer called *Printer General Use*, you might want several of the departments in your organization to have the ability to use it. In this case, you might decide to use departmental global groups (this makes sense because global groups are reusable) and simply nest all of them within the domain local group.

The final step is to assign the specific permissions. You can now quickly see the benefits of nesting global groups within domain local groups and why this is a best practice.

If you had created global groups (e.g., for the Finance, Sales and Marketing departments) and used them to assign permissions to the new printer, it would have been three sets of permissions—one for each group. By creating a domain local group and nesting the three global groups within it, you have reduced the amount of administrative overhead. You have to assign permissions only once. Should a fourth global group need to be created and assigned permissions, you only have to create the group and nest that within the domain local group to achieve the result. As you can see, this is very efficient!

Other Group Strategies

Having gone into some detail regarding the best practice, it is only fair that we acknowledge that there are other ways of using groups. We are going to discuss these other strategies now briefly, but keep in mind that we have already covered the preferred method.

An alternative method would be to use domain local groups exclusively. In this scenario, you would create a domain local group, assign permissions to it, then add the users that require access. On the face of it, this seems like a pretty good idea and one that is not too far removed from our best practice.

The main problem you will run into with this method is one of scope. Domain local groups are local to the domain in which they are created. You cannot use domain local groups to assign permissions to resources outside the local domain. This severely diminishes the power of your groups and, in a large enterprise, is probably a death knell for this strategy. To make this system work in an enterprise, you are going to find yourself creating many groups in each domain over which you have administrative control. This is time-consuming and difficult to manage.

So how about taking the other route? Don't use domain local groups at all, just use global groups. That way, you get the same benefits of domain local groups but you can also assign permissions to resources outside the domain in which it is created.

Well, this almost works. Unfortunately, you run into an issue if you have multiple domains. If you have a resource and wish to allow users from several domains to access it, you are going to have to assign permissions to several global groups. This is unnecessary overhead.

So what does that leave us with? The answer is it leaves us with our best practice. Create global groups, add users to global groups, nest the global group in a domain local group, then assign the permissions to the domain local group.

The best practice is a tried and true method of organizing groups and reducing the amount of administrative time you spend organizing your users and resources. I think you will agree, when you consider the alternatives, that it makes good sense. To make this easier to visualize, we illustrated this concept in Figure 13.3.

Creating Groups in Windows 2000

So enough with the theory, what about the practice? In the following pages, we are going to walk through the creation of groups and the various options you have. We will look at creating a group of a particular scope and converting it to a different scope. We will also show you how to delete groups and nest groups within other groups. Finally, our work would not be done if we didn't show you how to search for groups within Active Directory by using the Find function.

Before we go ahead and get some hands-on experience, we need to sit down and give some thought to our group strategies. This chapter has spoken at length about these strategies, but as we move into the hands-on portion, it is time to put them into practice.

The first thing that needs to be clear is the group scope that you are going to use. If you have a multiple-domain environment and Active Directory is running in Native Mode, you have the option to create universal groups, as well as global and domain local groups. If you want to group users from different domains into a group, this is your only choice. Otherwise, we are going to follow our best practice and create both a global group and a domain local group.

Next, you need to determine whether you have sufficient rights on your network to create groups. Given the importance of groups within the network, it should be obvious that the ability to create and manage groups is restricted.

To create groups, you will need to be either an administrator or a member of the Account Operators group. We have yet to talk about built-in groups, but we will be discussing them later in this chapter. For the moment, just make sure that you have enough rights to perform the task.

The final step is to come up with a name for the groups that you are about to create. This is important for several reasons; we discussed most of them earlier in the chapter. One final thought is that you might find yourself having to create global groups in multiple domains that have similar—if not identical—permissions. If this is the case, try to make sure that the same naming convention is used in each domain. This level of standardization is going to help you if you suddenly need to start administering in a different domain.

Okay, let's go ahead and create a global group. This hands-on exercise will get you familiar with the tools within Windows 2000.

1. In this exercise, we are going to create a local group. A local group is a group that can be used to assign permissions within a single domain. To do this, we must first open Active Directory Users and Computers. Click on Start, Programs, Administrative Tools and select it.
2. This tool is very flexible. It allows you to create many different types of objects. To create a group, right-click on the domain name. This is shown in Figure 13.5.

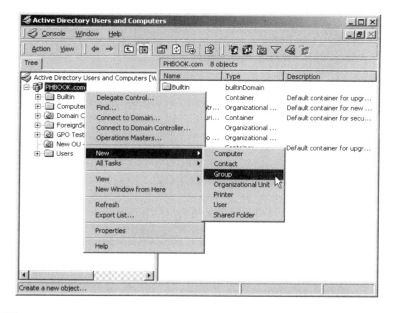

Figure 13–5   *Creating a group.*

3. You are now presented with the New Object–Group dialog box. There are several options in this dialog box. For this example, we are going to create a Domain local security group. In the Group name, type *New Local*. Then select Domain local in Group scope. When this is done, click OK. The group should now appear in the new right-hand panel. This is your first group!
4. Before we add users to a group, we should remember some best practices. Best practice tells us that we should create a global group, add users to the global group, then add the global group to a local group. So let's go ahead and create our global group.
5. Since we already have the Active Directory Users and Computers Microsoft Management Console (MMC) open, go ahead and right-click on

the domain name, as we did previously, and select Group. You will be presented with the same New Object–Group dialog box. This time, we will call the group *New Global.* When this is done, click OK. You should now see the new group in the right-hand pane.

6. We will now add a user to this global group. In this example, we are going to add a single user, but don't forget that there is no limit to the number of users you can add to a group. Right-click the New Global group and select Properties. This brings up the New Global Properties dialog box. To add a user to the group, select the Members tab. This is shown in Figure 13.6.

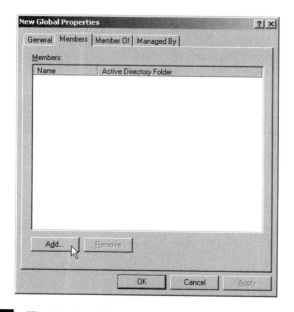

Figure 13–6   *The Members Tab.*

7. We will now add a user as a member of the group. Click on the Add button. This brings up the Select Users, Contacts, or Computers dialog box. For the purposes of this example, we are going to add the Guest account to this group membership. Select this account and click Add. Then click OK to exit. You should now be returned to the Members tab of the New Global Properties dialog box. However, now the name of the user account you selected—in this case, Guest—should appear. Click OK.

8. There, you have now added a member to your group. Now we will add this group as a member of the New Local group we created earlier. Don't forget, this is a best practice when using Windows 2000. To add the global group as a member of the local group, we will follow similar steps as before. First, right-click on the New Local group and select Properties.

Then click on the Members tab. Click on the Add button. This brings up the Select Users, Contacts, or Computers dialog box. Scroll down the list of names until you find the New Global group. When you find it, click on it to select, then click Add. Click OK to exit. You should now be returned to the Members tab of the New Local Properties dialog box. However, now the name *New Global* should appear. Click OK.

If you are using a test system to perform this example, it is not very difficult to find groups within the Active Directory Users and Computers MMC. However, if you are working in a large organization, it can become quite difficult to navigate through the interface, trying to find a specific group. Fortunately, Microsoft included a simple Find utility that can help you. In the following example, we will perform a search of Active Directory for the new groups that we have created.

1. If you still have the Active Directory Users and Computers MMC open from the last example, we will use that. If not, you can start it by clicking on Start, Programs, Administrative Tools, Active Directory Users and Computers. Select the domain name and right-click. Select Find. This will bring up the Find Users, Contacts, and Groups dialog box. This is shown in Fig-

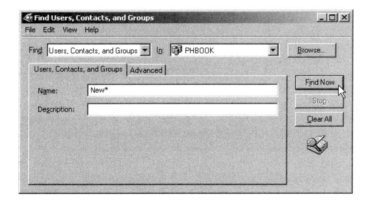

Figure 13–7   *The Find Users, Contacts and Groups dialog box.*

ure 13.7.

2. Your cursor should appear in the Name option. Type New* (the asterisk acts as a standard wildcard and will match any groups it finds that start with *New*). When this is done, click Find Now to find the groups. The two groups you just created should appear beneath this dialog box. By right-clicking on the names in this list, you can access Properties and perform the steps in the previous exercise.

3. Now let's take a brief look around this dialog box. Click on the down arrow next to Find. Now you can select which type of object you want to

find. Notice that you can search for Organizational Units, Computers, Printers, or more. Now click on Browse. This brings up the Browse for Container dialog box. Notice that you can search any type of container. The Find feature is a very powerful tool, yet it is easy to use. In complex Active Directory implementations, this will prove to be a valuable tool.

4. Finally, we will undo all of this good work and delete the New Local group we created in the previous example. To do this, click Cancel and exit the Find tool. This should return you to the Active Directory Users and Computers MMC. Select the New Local group in the right-hand panel, then right-click. Select Delete from this menu. You will be prompted to make sure that you mean to delete it. Click Yes. The group is deleted.

The Purpose of Local Groups

In the section on group scopes, we defined three different scopes and how they can be used. However, the information we gave at that time was related to groups being created within a Windows 2000 domain. In fact, there is another group scope that we need to mention.

The reason that this additional scope was not discussed earlier is that it cannot be used to assign permissions within a domain. The scope of a local group is on the computer on which it is created. Read those words carefully, I said on the *computer* on which it was created. More specifically, local groups can be created only on member servers, standalone servers, or systems running Windows 2000 Professional.

Local groups are used to assign permissions to resources that exist on the local machine. For instance, let's say that you have a folder on your Windows 2000 Professional computer and want to create a share and give access to a small group of users. To do this, you would create the share, then create a local group on the local machine. You would then add either global groups from the domain or specific users into the local group.

Local groups work because member servers and Windows 2000 Professional workstations have their own security database. Domain controllers (DCs) that operate as part of Active Directory share a security database (after all, that's the whole point of Active Directory). Because these two types of hosts have their own security database, it is possible to create groups that exist only on that host. In other words, it is not possible to create local groups on a DC, because all security information stored in them is shared.

Using local groups within your enterprise is not a very good idea. One reason for this is that the creation of groups specifically on a workstation or server will remove your ability to manage the group process centrally. Because local groups are not seen by the domain, they will not appear in Active Directory, and you will not be able to search them.

The scope of a local group is the machine on which they are created, which severely limits their usefulness. If there is an important set of documents to which users need access, it is probably time to move that data to a network share and create groups within the domain to control access.

Local groups can contain users from the host on which it is created, and it can also nest both global and universal groups from the domain. Although this might appear to be an advantage, it might very well cause problems later. It is unlikely that the person creating the local group has any control over the membership of the global and universal groups. Therefore, a domain administrator might add a user to a global group, not realizing that they are giving the user access to a local resource. This is one of the issues that can arise when you use local groups and take away the ability for a set of administrators to manage the process centrally.

Finally, a local group cannot be nested within any other type of group. There is no way to use this grouping within the domain. If you are spending time designing a group strategy, it is a good idea to implement your plan in the place where it will have most reusability—in the domain or within Active Directory.

However, if you have a use for local groups, make sure that you follow the best practices outlined earlier in this chapter. In the case of local groups, create a global group first. Add the users to the global group, then nest the global group within the local group. Finally, assign the local permissions to the local group.

Using Built-In Groups

When Windows 2000 is installed, a set of predefined groups is created. These groups are designed to group together users for common networking tasks. There are four scopes of built-in groups. These scopes are:

- Built-in Global Groups
- Built-in Domain Local Groups
- Built-in Local Groups
- Built-in System Groups

All but one of these scopes has been discussed in general terms earlier in this chapter. The fourth type, built-in system groups, is new. These groups are precreated because there are some basic tasks that are performed on all networks. Because groups are used to simplify administration, it makes sense that Microsoft would supply us with a basic set.

Rather than discuss the scopes any further, we are simply going to note the various groups that exist and their intended use. It is good practice to use built-in groups whenever practicable. Although you could duplicate their functionality, why bother? These groups are going to be common to every installation of Windows 2000, so getting to know what they are and how they work is a good idea.

Built–In Global Groups

You should be familiar with the scope of a global group. It should also come as no surprise that Microsoft follows the good practice rules and does not assign permissions directly to any of the built-in global groups.

There are four built-in global groups and, by default, three of them are added to local groups. That means that some users on your network will automatically gain permissions without you creating any groups of your own. For example, if you need to grant permissions to all administrators in your domain, you will see that a global group has already been created for this purpose. Think of these groups as a good starting point. Here are the four groups that are created.

DOMAIN USERS

Each domain user that you create automatically becomes a member of the built-in Domain Users global group. This group is automatically made a member of the Users Domain local group. This is how your users gain access to the network. As you create new users, you do not have to worry about this group. New users are added to the global group and, therefore, the Users Domain local group, automatically.

DOMAIN ADMINS

Administrators need access to all systems on the network. This is achieved through the built-in Domain Admin group. This group is automatically made a member of the Administrators domain local group. The Administrator account (created during installation of Windows 2000) is made a member of this group without your intervention. It is the method used to ensure that administrators have access in a domain.

DOMAIN GUESTS

The Guest account is, by default, a very restricted account. However, it exists so that you do not have to create user accounts for casual users of your network. The Guest account is automatically made a member of this built-in group. The group is then nested within the Guest domain local group. This allows the Guest account to have guest permissions in the domain.

ENTERPRISE ADMINS

Enterprise Admins is a group designed to be used in large enterprises. If you are administering a single domain, there is no need to worry about this group. The intention is that you add user accounts that need to have Administrator access to multiple domains into this group. This group is then added into the Administrators domain local group in each domain.

Built-In Domain Local Groups

These built-in groups are created so that the administrator can assign users permissions to perform tasks in Active Directory and on DCs within a domain. Because these are domain local groups, permissions have been assigned to them directly. This is in keeping with our best practice.

What follows is a brief discussion of what each of these groups are able to do. You should use these groups, rather than trying to create your own set of groups to perform similar tasks. These groups will exist in all installations of Windows 2000 so that, once you have learned what they are, the knowledge is freely transferable.

ACCOUNT OPERATORS

Account Operators is a subset of the Administrator account. As suggested by the name, an Account Operator can add accounts into a domain. It can also delete and modify accounts that already exist. The only restriction on this type of account is that an account operator cannot modify the Administrators group or any of the other operator groups. These restrictions prevent Account Operators from granting themselves additional permissions on the network.

SERVER OPERATORS

Members of this group can control access to disk resources and backup and restore files on a DC. This includes creating shares. Once a share is created, a group would have to be created to assign permissions to users. The server operator cannot create groups, so these would have to be created by an administrator.

PRINT OPERATORS

The purpose of the Print Operators group is to assign the ability to create and maintain network printers on DCs. Creating a printer would include sharing the printer so that groups can be assigned permissions.

ADMINISTRATORS

The Admin domain local group grants administrative access within a domain and on all DCs. A member of this group can perform all tasks. In effect, this group is the sum total of all other groups. Membership to this group should be restricted. By default, the Administrator and Domain Admin global groups are members of this group. This makes it somewhat more difficult to manage. You need to make sure that any restrictions you have in place regarding administrators is enforced at the domain level. If a user is added to the Domain Admin global group, they will also gain administrator permission through this local group.

GUESTS

The Guests group has very limited permissions. In fact, you should review your usage of Guest accounts and decide whether additional permissions should be added. However, the permissions should never be elevated to match those of regular users in the domain. If you really need that level of access, go ahead and create an account for the user or users in question. Guests are even prevented from making permanent changes to their desktops. Therefore, any changes to the wallpaper or screen settings will not be saved when the user logs on and logs off. By default, the Guest user account and the Domain Guests global group are members of this local group.

BACKUP OPERATORS

Backup Operators are given permissions that enable them to perform a backup and restore on a DC with the built-in Windows 2000 backup application.

USERS

This group is used to assign permissions to the users in your domain. You can think of this group as a template for all users. If there is a permission that you want every user in your domain to receive, apply that permission to this group. By default, the Domain Users group is a member of this local group.

Built-In Local Groups

If you recall our definition of a local group from earlier in this chapter, you will remember that local groups can be created only on member servers, standalone servers, and Windows 2000 Professional workstations. So it should not come as any surprise to find out that the following built-in local groups exist only on these limited sets of clients. These groups will not be found on a DC operating within a domain.

You will notice some cross-functionality between these groups and those we have just mentioned. This is because some of the basic tasks that are required within a domain are just as applicable to a standalone server or a Windows 2000 Professional computer.

USERS

User accounts that are created locally on the host are added to this group. As we discussed previously, you can think of this group as being a template for all users that will have access to the system. This concept is extended once the standalone server or Windows 2000 professional host is added to a domain. When this happens, the domain Users group from the domain is added to this local group. This means that domain users will inherit any permissions that have been assigned to this group.

ADMINISTRATORS

Members of this built-in group have full control over the local machine. By default the built-in Administrator account is made a member of this group. Also note that when a standalone server of a Windows 2000 Professional host joins a domain, the Domain Admins group is made a member of this group. This means that administrators in the domain become administrators on the local machine, as well.

GUESTS

Once again, this group has limited access to resources. You will have to go in and grant permissions to this group as you see fit. Be careful with overextending use of this group. If you find yourself adding many rights to the group, you should probably be taking a different path to achieve your desired result. When a standalone server of a Windows 2000 Professional host joins a domain, the Domain Guests group is made a member of this group.

BACKUP OPERATORS

As we saw earlier, members of this group have the ability to perform both backup and restore of data on the local machine using the built-in Windows 2000 backup application.

POWER USERS

This group is a combination of some of the built-in groups we saw on DCs. A member of the Power Users group has a large amount of control over the local machine, but not complete control. Some people are confused by this group and think it is a user account. It is not; it is simply another local group. It combines the functions of both the Account Operator and the Server Operator that we spoke of earlier. A Power User can create users and share resources on the local machine.

Built-In System Accounts

The final set of built-in accounts might, at first glance, seem rather strange. For instance, you cannot add members to these groups. Instead, users are added to these accounts on the fly, based on their activity on the network. The mere act of logging on to a machine locally is enough to cause you to be added to the interactive group. In another case, accessing a resource stored on a system causes you to be added to another group.

While you will not see these groups when you are administering your system you can add permissions to them if you want to alter the default behavior. However, because these groups are often seen as something of an art, rather than a science, you might find that you are better off creating your own groups to model behavior. However, don't forget that group membership, in this case, is based around a user's activity. It is impossible to create a group in the standard fashion and emulate this feature.

EVERYONE

The Everyone group has all currently logged on network users as members. This includes both guests and users from other domains. Whenever users log on, they are added to the group.

AUTHENTICATED USERS

This group works in much the same way as the Everyone group. The main difference is that *Everyone* really is a catch-all. It does not differentiate between those users that have logged on and been authenticated within the domain and those users that have logged on anonymously. So you can think of this group as being a subset of the Everyone group. Users in this group have been authenticated by the domain and Active Directory or by the local machine.

CREATOR OWNER

The user account that creates a resource or that owns a resource is a member of this group. You will most often see the Administrators group nested within this group. This is because administrators tend to create most resources.

NETWORK

The Network group includes users that are accessing a resource across the network (as opposed to logging in directly to a host and accessing the resource). The members of this group will change fairly regularly as users connect and disconnect to a resource.

INTERACTIVE

This group works in a similar fashion to the Network group. However, members are added to this group when they log on locally to a machine and access a resource. Members of the Network group access the resource across the network and, therefore, would not be assigned to a group if they logged on locally. This group plugs that hole.

Tips on Using Groups

We have certainly made a big deal of our best practice for creating groups. As you have read about the built-in groups, you will have seen that Microsoft takes this practice to heart and has implemented it extensively. We are not going to repeat ourselves here. Just take this as a reminder that you create global groups, add users to them, add the global group to a local group, then assign permissions to the local group. Following these simple steps will provide you with flexibility as you move forward.

Rather than repeat all the details of the best practice, let's consider a few more things regarding groups. First, try not to create groups unnecessarily. We have spoken about the effect this can have on network performance and the like, and this certainly should be a consideration. Beyond that, realize that every group has to be managed at one time or another, and the more that exist in your domain, the more work it will be to keep them all up to date.

Also, try not to oversubscribe users. What we mean here is that the permissions given to users should always be the most restrictive that it is possible to give. If users need only read permissions, it might be convenient to add them to a currently created group with both read and write permissions. However, this might compromise your network. This is especially true when you begin to nest groups. Adding a user to one group may cascade into far broader permissions through nesting. So make sure that you understand what each group does and how nesting has been implemented.

Take advantage of the built-in groups as much as possible. These groups usually give a good set of default permissions, and making a change to one of them is an easy way of affecting a large group of users. Also, if you have a user who is going to be allowed to, let's say, create and delete user accounts, consider using a built-in group for this purpose, such as the account operators group. This is predefined and easily understood by other administrators on the network, and it also cuts down on the number of groups that exist on your network.

Finally, be careful when using the built-in system groups. The Everyone group might seem like a tempting place to add permissions, because all users that are logged on are members of this group. Don't forget that even users who are logged on anonymously become members of this group. To be safe, use the authenticated users group instead.

Once you have gained a deep understanding of groups and the impact they can have, some of these tips might seem like stating the obvious, but all to often, we get rushed in our day-to-day jobs, and we make rash decisions that we later come to regret. By taking the time up front to define our group policies and naming conventions, we can drastically reduce the number of errors that we make.

Chapter Summary

In this chapter, we spoke about the different types and scopes of groups that are available within Windows 2000. There are two different group types; security groups are used for security purposes and distribution groups are designed to be used by applications. The first application to use distribution groups is Exchange 2000.

There are four different scopes for groups. Three of these scopes are applicable to domains, whereas the fourth is applicable only to standalone, member, and Windows 2000 Professional clients. The scope of a group determines which users can be added to the group and how the group can be nested within other groups. The three domain scopes are global, domain local, and universal. Global groups have a scope outside the domain in which they are created. This means that you can use global groups to assign permissions to resources that exist in another domain.

Local groups cannot be used outside the domain in which they are created. It is best practice to assign permissions to domain local groups, then add users to global groups. Finally, nest global groups within domain local groups.

Universal groups are available only if Active Directory is being used in Native Mode. Universal groups are groups that can be used in any domain in a tree or forest. It is best practice to assign permissions to universal groups and to nest global groups within them.

You should be careful with universal groups because they can impact the performance of the network. This is because universal groups and their member lists are replicated to all Global Catalog servers on the network. Try to keep the membership of universal groups static. The suggested best practice will help you do this.

We also discussed local groups, which can be created only on standalone and member servers and Windows 2000 Professional workstations. The use of local groups on your network should be reduced as much as possible. This is because they make it difficult to maintain central management of groups.

We spoke about group practices, which should include applying a naming strategy to any groups you create. This is especially useful when you are going to be nesting groups or creating groups with the same permissions in multiple domains.

Along with any groups that you create for yourself, there is also a number of built-in groups. Membership to these groups is usually assigned by the automatic nesting of global groups into the defined domain local groups. As with groups that you create yourself, the built-in groups have a scope. The four built-in group types are global groups, domain local groups, local groups, and system groups.

The built-in system groups differ from other groups, in that the group members are based on the activity the user is performing on the network. Members are not explicitly made members of the built-in system groups. The two main examples of this are the Everyone group and the authenticated Users group. Anyone who is logged onto the network, whether he or she has a user name or is using an anonymous account, is automatically made a member of Everyone. Authenticated users can provide you with a list of all network users who have a valid account in Active Directory.

The primary reason for the existence of groups is to simplify administration. By drawing up a set of standard practices and following them rigidly, you should be able to minimize the amount of time you spend on routine tasks, such as assigning permissions to the various network resources.

Group Policy

*T*imes are definitely changing. Information technologies have clearly seen a surge as networks have been installed in corporations around the globe. With promises of a paperless office, virtual commuting networks were adopted as a way of streamlining business processes and, ultimately, as a way to stay competitive and save money.

The rabid rush into networking technologies has brought us many benefits indeed. However, the relentless pursuit of connectivity has left a void for management and business types. Finally, they are beginning to take a look at what all this technology is really costing. Maintenance costs for our networks will become an increasingly important topic over the next few years, and it will become increasingly rare to hear the mantra, "We have a problem, let's apply a new technology."

Not that new technologies won't be adopted and developed. Of course they will. However, before technology gets thrown at a problem, you are going to be asked to justify projects in increasingly nontechnological terms. What will the project really cost? What are the real benefits of implementing a technology?

The term most commonly used in this regard is *total cost of ownership* (TCO). A discussion of TCO is beyond the scope of this book. Researchers such as Gartner Group, Inc. can supply you with a lot of data on the topic. However, we can talk about the ways in which Windows 2000 has addressed some of the typical TCO issues of operating a network.

When we talk about operating a network, we are encompassing all elements of the network. TCO must take servers, cable, and routers into account. It should include costs of backup strategies, hard disk space, and support staff.

Most importantly, it must include the costs of supporting all of the computers on workers' desks. Supporting your user community is likely to be one of the biggest costs in your organization.

As operating systems have evolved, good intentions have become a hindrance for IT professionals. On the one hand, software vendors have striven to give users complete freedom to do whatever they want. If they want to install software on their machines, fine. If they want to change a video driver to a higher resolution, fine. If they want to go into Control Panel and change a performance setting for their machines, fine.

This was seen as a benefit in the early days. Users were able to configure their operating systems to work the way they wanted them to work. Everyone was happy except the support desk and system administrators, who found their time getting eaten up by errors, unpredictable results, and computers performing poorly because of changes to their configurations. It became difficult to plan for software upgrades because you could never be quite sure what you were going to find on users' machines.

There have been many ways of dealing with this issue. Some organizations have attempted to set a "standard build" for computers on their networks. Others have been even more stringent and have used tools supplied for Microsoft operating systems, such as Policy Editor and the Zero Administration Kit technologies. Finally, vendors such as Novadigm came up with entirely new technologies to address the problem.

However, the entire time, there has been a vital part missing—good clean integration of these configurations into the server environment. We trust our server infrastructure with many complex tasks relating to security, network bandwidth control, and load balancing. So why not have it take care of controlling the user desktop as well?

That brings us to the topic at hand—Windows 2000 Group Policy. Wouldn't it be nice if you could put together a collection of settings, much in the same way that you create user groups, then apply them to sets of users? If they worked in a fashion similar to Windows 2000 groups, they would be easy to understand and could be applied right down to the user level without difficulty. This is precisely what group policies allow you to do.

The scope of group policies is very large. We will be talking about the various options open to you, but we will not be able to cover every aspect of group policies in the space available here. One of the reasons for this is that group policies will be used in different ways in different organizations. Although the idea of preventing user error is appealing, it often hits a political brick wall as users realize that they have less control over their own environments.

Of course, from a managerial and administrative point of view, these issues are small, when compared with the spiraling costs of supporting environments in which this is no control. We mention political issues only because they are inevitable and common. These concerns cannot be covered in detail in this book; rather, we are going to concentrate on the technological considerations. This is one area where you are going to have to include many different groups to arrive at a consensus of what must be done to solve the problem of escalating support costs.

So let's move onward and take a look at the features that Windows 2000 provides for us. There is quite a lot to group policies, but I think you will quickly see that they have an important role to play in taking control of your desktops.

Group Policy in Windows 2000

Put simply, group policies are sets of configuration options applied automatically to users, computers, or members of a site, domain, or Organizational Unit (OU). By setting these configuration options at a high level (the administrative level) and applying them automatically, you can ensure that the computers and user accounts that are participating in your network have a standard list of options applied.

Because of their power, group policies should generally be defined by your system architects. The definition of what policy you want to apply should not change on a regular basis. However, it is the job of the administrators to apply these policies to objects within Active Directory. Therefore, Group Policy is, at minimum, a two-step process.

In the past, the process of defining a user environment has been known as a *locked-down desktop*. You can think of Group Policy in the same way. Although you might be familiar with the goals of Group Policy, keep in mind that the new implementation is far more flexible.

As you will see as you work your way through this chapter, group policies can be applied at several levels of your Active Directory. Once applied to an object, the policies are *inherited* by all child objects. This default behavior can be altered, but it is going to be important that you understand the scope of any changes you make. We will talk about testing and applying policies later in this chapter.

As technical professionals, we often do not pay enough attention to business needs and processes. Group Policy is an area where a business process will need to be in place to ensure that you are achieving the goals of your network. If you are going to work with a multinational implementation of Windows 2000, it is unlikely that you will be able to control all of the group policies for the entire enterprise. It is more likely that there will be an individual—or a group of individuals—who have been nominated "group policy administrators." It will be the task of these people to configure group policies.

This is necessary because group policies set at, for example, the domain level, may not be appropriate for all levels of the local organization. In this case, the local administrator will have to contact the Group Policy administra tors and work with them to resolve any issues. Furthermore, it is important that duplicate policies are not applied at the local level. This work is completely unnecessary and increases TCO.

Despite the obvious complexity, do not lose sight of the value of Group Policy. Group Policy can help you secure your users' desktops by preventing users from making changes on their systems that disable them or make them perform inefficiently. It also enhances the user's experience by automatically installing applications to the user's computer, installing shortcuts and files on systems, and running applications or scripts when the users log on and off a system. These can be used for cleanup tasks or security settings.

It might be usual to detail what types of information a Group Policy can affect. So let's now take a look at the different types of policy that are available. You can set policy options in the following categories:

- Software Settings
- Windows Settings
- Administrative Templates

Each of these categories contain different options. You navigate within the Group Policy Microsoft Management Console (MMC) to configure them. The group policy MMC is shown in Figure 14.1.

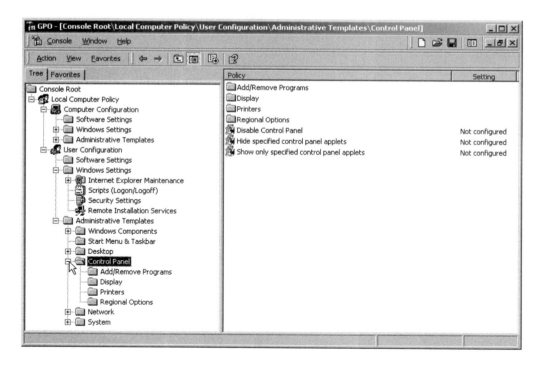

Figure 14–1 *The Group Policy MMC.*

As you can see, there are many options available. It is not possible for us to detail all of them, but we will take a look at some of the most common uses.

Group Policy User and Computer Settings

Group policy affects either a user or a computer. By allowing you to target one or another of these, you will find that you have great flexibility. Some of the options are unique to each type. For instance, a computer never "logs on" to a network and, therefore, settings that are triggered by this event are not available under the Computers options.

When we talk about managing users and computers with Group Policy, we are actually talking about registry-based policies. That is, policies configured here then modify the registry which, in turn, causes changes or options to be enforced at the computer.

DESKTOP POLICY SETTINGS

The first set of policies we will look at is listed under User configuration, Desktop options. These options allow you to change the appearance of the user's computer interface. It also allows you to prevent users from performing certain tasks on their computers. By controlling user access to certain options, you can prevent them from making changes that might stop a computer from working.

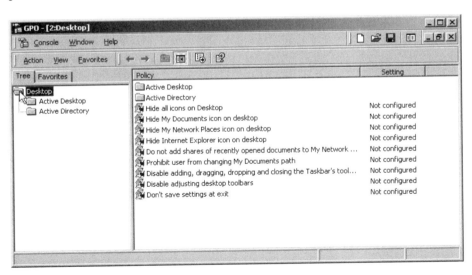

Figure 14—2   *The User Configuration, Desktop Policy settings.*

Some of the desktop options are shown in Figure 14.2.

Within the hierarchy shown in Figure 14.2, you will find many useful options. Some of the most commonly used options are shown in Table 14.1.

Take some time to familiarize yourself with all of the options by using the group policy snap-in in the MMC.

Table 14.1	Group Policy Options
Group Policy	**Setting Function**
Hide all items on desktop	This is used to simplify the user's interface. If enabled, this will cause all menus, folders, and shortcuts to be removed from the user's desktop.
Prohibit user from changing My Documents path	This option allows you to enforce a location for the user's documents.
Don't save settings on exit	If enabled, this option allows the user to make changes to the desktop. However, when the user exits Windows 2000, none of these changes are saved and carried over to the next session. This causes each session to be a "clean start."
Disable adding, dragging, dropping, and closing the Taskbar's toolbars	This will prevent the user from losing a taskbar. Without this policy enabled, it is easy for an inexperienced user inadvertently to drag the taskbar to a different location on the screen. This option will prevent users from doing this and, therefore, enable a consistent user interface.
Disable changing wallpaper	This will prevent users from making changes to the wallpaper on the system. You might do this if you have a wallpaper that incorporates your corporate logo or for computers that are used in public areas, when you want to make sure that inappropriate wallpapers are not applied.
Disable Task Manager	Task Manager is a very powerful utility. This option will prevent users from being able to run Task Manager on their computers.

START MENU AND TASKBAR

The Start menu and Taskbar are interfaces with which your users are going to be very familiar. The appearance of these two options should remain consistent. It is possible for the Start menu to become crowded over time, with items in locations that are difficult to find. The Start Menu also contains several key functions, such as Run and Shutdown commands. All of these options and more can be controlled within the Start menu and Taskbar options of the Group Policy MMC. We have listed some of these options in Table 6.2.

There are many different options available. Tables 14.1 and 14.2 show a small subset. By setting combinations of these settings, you can address many different issues on your network. For instance, if you are primarily interested in securing your network, you might remove items from the Start menu, remove options to map drives, and disable Task Manager. If, on the other hand, you simply want to ensure that users get a consistent interface that is familiar to them, you might decide to dictate or disable wallpaper settings and access to the items in Control Panel, such as Display, that allow people to alter the way a computer looks.

It's going to be up to the Group Policy administrator to determine how far you want to go with group policies. Keep in mind that, many times, this is a very politically sensitive issue. Many users do not like it when you remove an option that allows them to make their computers operate in the way they prefer. Many people personalize their machines, for instance, by scanning family photographs and using them as custom wallpapers. Only by careful discussion can you determine which features you should truly disable.

Table 14.2 — Start Menu and Taskbar Options

Group Policy	Setting Function
Remove Search menu from Start menu	Performing searches across the network can consume network bandwidth. By limiting access to this option, you can ensure that users do not do this.
Disable personalized menus	By default, Windows 2000 "hides" menu options that are not used. This means that only commonly used items show up on the Start menu. This option can be enabled or disabled with this policy option. With this option enabled, Windows 2000 default behavior is disabled, and all menu options will appear.

Table 14.2	Start Menu and Taskbar Options (Continued)
Disable and remove the shut down command	A Shutdown command appears in two places within the Windows 2000 interface. It appears by default in the Start menu and in Task Manager <CTRL><ALT><DEL>. By enabling this option, both of these options will be hidden in the interface.
Disable Logoff on the Start menu	This option enables you to remove the Log Off option from the Start menu. The option will still appear in Task Manager.
Remove Run menu from Start menu	The Run menu allows you to execute applications when you specify the path and program name. This can be the cause of virus infection or allow your users to install unauthorized applications. By disabling this option, you can protect your systems.
Remove common program groups from Start menu	By default, the items that appear on a user's Start menu are a combination of the All Users' profile and the individual user's profile. This menu option prevents shortcuts from the All Users profile from appearing.
Disable and remove links to Windows Update	Microsoft has provided an automated update system to its operating systems. However, sometimes it is not a good idea to leave this update process to the discretion of individual users. By enabling this option, you can prevent users from seeing the shortcut.

How are Group Policies Stored in Active Directory?

You will hear two terms that are used interchangeably but, in the strictest sense, mean two very different things. The two terms are *group policies* and *group policy objects* (GPOs). When we talk about GPOs, we are actually talking about the objects created in Active Directory.

The settings that you configure through the Group Policy MMC are stored within Active Directory as GPOs. It is the GPOs that are applied within Active Directory. GPOs can be applied at the site level, the domain level, or the OU level. This allows you a lot of flexibility. Also, any site, domain, or OU level can have one or many GPOs assigned to it, and a GPO can be reused and applied at different levels at the same time. Of course, this can cause some confusion, not to mention Group Policy conflicts. We will be talking about these issues later in the chapter.

First, let's take a look at how Active Directory actually stores this information. There are two elements that you will need to understand. One is an Active Directory object, whereas the other defines a directory structure under which group policies are stored.

GROUP POLICY CONTAINERS

A Group Policy Container (GPC) is an Active Directory object that is used to store a small amount of data regarding a policy. The larger pieces of data are stored in a Group Policy Template (GPT), which we will talk about in a moment. The reason for this is that, because a GPC is part of Active Directory, it is replicated in the same way as all Active Directory data. Given the amount of data required to implement all of the options of Group Policy, storing the entire option set within Active Directory is inefficient.

Also, the data stored in the GPC is data that rarely changes. Once again, this is to make sure that Group Policy does not cause a lot of Active Directory replication traffic. Data that changes frequently is stored in the GPT.

The types of information stored in a GPC include:

- Version Information
- Status Information

The version information is used to match a GPC with corresponding data in a GPT. The status information indicates whether a particular group policy is enabled or disabled.

GROUP POLICY TEMPLATES

GPTs are actually folder structures where the group policy data is stored. These are replicated to all domain controllers (DCs). This folder structure—often referred to as a *container* in Microsoft documentation—stores information on all settings you have made.

The folder structure is created automatically. However, the naming structure is very cryptic. When a GPO is created, it is assigned a globally unique identifier (GUID). Windows 2000 uses this GUID to create the folder structure. Let's assume that we have created a GPO in a domain called *PHBOOK.COM.* The GPT folder structure might be:

<systemroot>\Sysvol\sysvol\phbook.com\policies\{31B2F340-016D-11D2-945F-00C04FB984F9}.

Of course, you will not be expected to edit files directly within the GPT, so the difficult task of figuring out which folder applies to which policy should not really happen. Within each GPT folder, you will find a *GPT.INI* file. This is a small file that stores information, such as the version of the GPT. This folder and associated folders are shown in Figure 14.3.

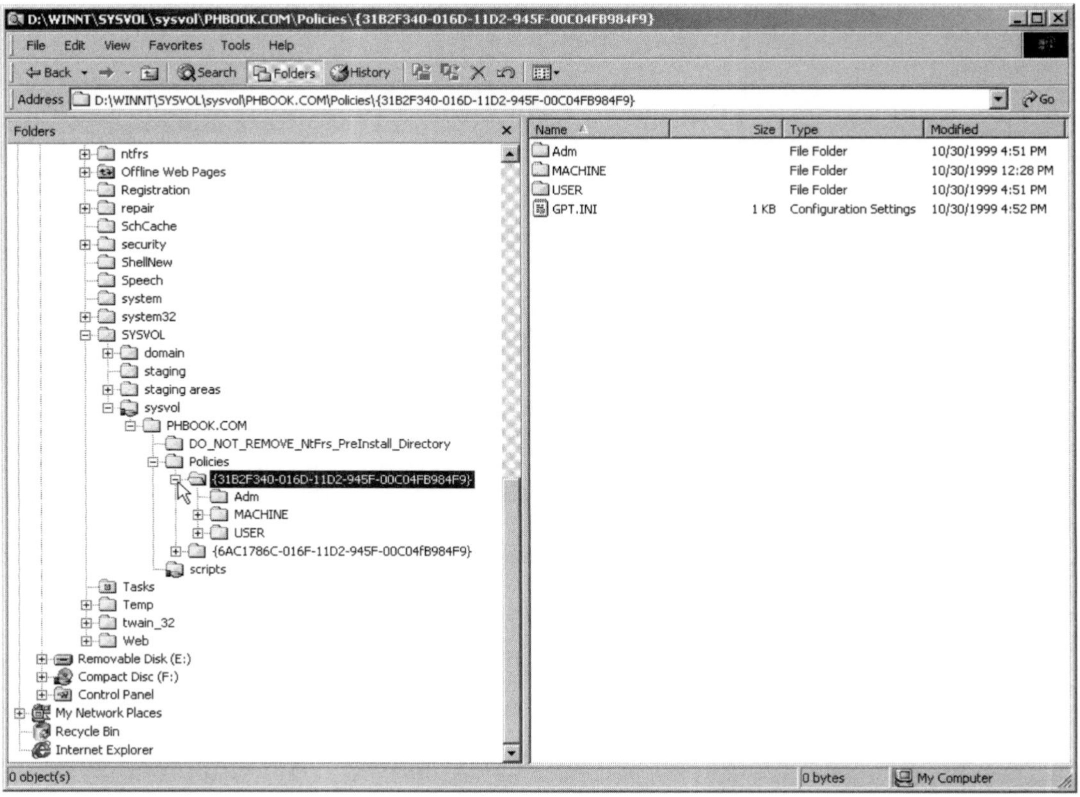

Figure 14-3 *The folder structure of a GPT.*

As you can see in Figure 14.3, there are three folders contained at this level of the GPT. These folders are used to store the settings that were changed when the GPO was created. These changes are then applied to computers and users, as indicated within Active Directory. Table 14.3 contains information about each of these folders.

All settings that affect a computer or user are, in fact, registry settings. The key file in any of these folders is *registry.pol.* You will find a *registry.pol* file in both the *MACHINE* and the *USER* files (if you have configured settings for both). The *MACHINE registry.pol* file is read during the boot process and is, therefore, applied before any users have logged on. The *USER registry.pol* file is applied only when a user logs on.

One final, yet very important, thing to understand is that GPTs have to be replicated to every DC. Because you don't know which DC is going to authenticate a user, Windows 2000 requires these files to exist on every DC. This is

Table 14.3	Folders in a GPT
Folder	**Contents**
ADM	This is where the Administrative templates (ADM files) are stored. All Administrative templates associated with this GPT will be stored in this folder.
MACHINE	Depending on which options are being set within the GPO, there can be several folders or no subfolders beneath MACHINE. However, if many options were set, you would likely see subfolders, including APPLICATIONS, SCRIPTS, and STARTUP. These subfolders would contain settings that are to be applied to a computer
USER	This folder is populated if you have set policies that affect user settings. Subfolders you might see under this folder would include APPLICATIONS, DOCUMENT and SETTINGS, and SCRIPTS. Any setting you have configured for users will be stored in here.

achieved by having the Group Policy snap-in connect directly to the PDC Operations Master when it is opened. Any GPO you create is, therefore, first created there. It is then the job of the PDC Operations Master to replicate this data.

It is possible that the PDC Operations Master is not available when you want to create a new GPO. In that case, an error message will appear and you will be able to point the MMC to a different DC. However, this is not recommended. If an error occurs because the PDC Operations Master is not available, it is strongly suggested that you wait until it is available before creating the new GPO. This is because data can be lost if administrators edit a GPO on different GPOs. When this data is then replicated, you might get unexpected results. By ensuring that all Group Policy administrators take the default action and edit or create GPOs only on the PDC Operations Master, you are ensuring data integrity.

How Settings are Applied

Now that you understand what some of your options are and how they are stored within both Active Directory and on the server, it is time to find out how these policies are applied to users and computers.

As we have already said, group policies can be applied to either sites, domains, or OUs. This brings up some interesting questions. What happens if an OU has been nested within another OU? Does the policy get applied to all child OUs? What happens when a conflicting policy is applied at the domain and the OU levels? Can you prevent a setting in one GPO from affecting certain users in another GPO?

We are going to supply the answers to these questions as we work our way through this section. Understanding not only how group policies are applied, but also how they interact when applied is essential in ensuring that you do not create more problems, instead of solving them.

Group Policy Inheritance

In fact, as you might have guessed, group policies are inherited. That means that if you have an OU with six child OUs, a policy applied at the topmost level will automatically be inherited by all of its children. This is an important topic because this might not be the way you want things to work on your own networks.

Further, there is an order of inheritance, depending on where the policies are applied. Because policies can be applied to sites, domains, and OUs, what happens if a policy that affects a user is set at all of these places?

The general concept to understand is that Windows 2000 gives precedence to the policy applied closest to the user. In Windows 2000, sites contain domains, and domains contain OUs. Therefore, if you have conflicting policies set at the site and the OU levels, the policy at the OU level will win. This is because the OU is considered to be closest to the user.

It is also worth noting that it is possible to enter conflicting computer and user policies. If this is the case, the user policy will always win. Although this might sound like an ideal solution, remember that you should strive to minimize any policy conflicts from happening. Policies have to be processed before they can be overwritten, and unnecessary policies simply take up time with no benefit.

Overriding and Blocking Inheritance

The explanation we have given so far explains the default inheritance process on a Windows 2000 computer. It is also possible to change this default behavior. You do this by either overriding or blocking inheritance.

These two options are useful because they allow those people who are applying group policies to change the way they affect users in a particular OU.

• No Override—If this option is set, all child containers are prevented from overriding a policy set at a parent. You set this option at the GPO (not at the OU). If this is set, there is no way to prevent the GPO from being applied at the parent and all children.

• Block Inheritance—If a container requires unique settings that override those set above it (and the No Override option has not been set on the GPO), you can use this option to block inheritance. In this case, policies set in parents will not flow through to the child.

As you can see, both of these options have their place. The Block Inheritance option is useful for special circumstances, whereas No Override ensures that parents to a container will always have the ultimate authority over whether a GPO is applied.

Processing Order

We have already explained that when a conflict within GPOs occurs, the GPO from the object closest to the user takes precedence. However, that does not take into account conflicts that might occur in GPOs applied to the same object. For instance, it is possible to apply two policies to a single OU and for those two policies to have contradictory attributes. This has to be resolved.

Unlike the circumstance of a conflicting GPO applied to a different object, you can actually determine which GPOs have precedence if applied to the same object. This is achieved by changing the order in which GPOs appear in the Group Policy tab of the object. In Figure 14.4, you can see that we have an OU called *GPO Test*. There are three GPOs being applied to this OU.

GPOs are processed from this list. The order of processing is bottom to top. So, in this case, the Computer GPO will be processed first, then the User GPO and, finally, the Default Domain Policy will be processed. Given that the default domain policy will be processed last, it should be clear that it is this policy that has the final say in what is and what is not applied.

Preventing GPOs from Executing

It is also possible to prevent a specific group of users from executing the commands in a GPO by using security groups. It is possible to create a security group within Windows 2000, then to remove the necessary permissions to execute a GPO. To execute a GPO, a user needs at least Read permission.

To change the permissions on a GPO, click on the Properties button of the GPO. You can see this button in Figure 14.4. When you click on the properties of a GPO, you are presented with a dialog box showing a security tab. This is shown in Figure 14.5.

Figure 14–4   *The GPO Test OU with three GPOs assigned.*

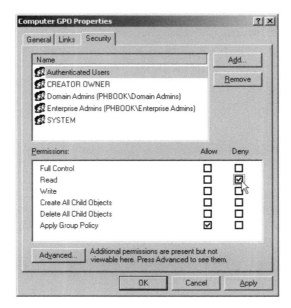

Figure 14–5   *The security tab of a GPO.*

In Figure 14.5, you can see that the built-in group Authenticated Users is having its Read permissions removed. Therefore, members of this group will be denied access to the GPO. Although this is a useful feature, don't forget that there is always a price to pay for this complexity. Managing a large environment at this level of detail is going to be very difficult. Although it might sometimes be necessary, try to keep your GPO structure as simple as possible. Apply GPOs to sites, domains, or OUs only. If you need to apply a GPO to a small subset of users, consider creating a new OU, rather than filtering at this level.

Creating a GPO

Now would probably be a good time to create a GPO from scratch. Before we do that, we need to make sure that we are not going to create any havoc on your system. So the first thing we will do is create an OU that we can use for testing. We will then go ahead and create a GPO, then apply it to our new OU.

1. First, we will create an OU that we can use to apply our new GPO. It is important that you do not miss this step, because you do not want to inadvertently apply a GPO to a group of users on your network. This step should be followed whenever you create a GPO—either as an example or in the real world. Always test your GPOs before you apply them within Active Directory. If you do not do this step, you might find that you experience unexpected results. First, open Active Directory Computers and Users by clicking on Start, Programs, Administrative Tools, Active Directory Users and Computers.

2. Next, we will create a test OU. To do this, right-click on the domain in which you wish to create the new GPO, click on New, then Organizational Unit. This is shown in Figure 14.6.

3. You will be then be prompted to give the new OU a name. Type *New OU—Do not use* as the name. We chose this name so that no one would mistake it for an OU that is being used in your domain.

4. You now have an OU that you can use for testing. We must now create a new user as a member of this OU. We do not recommend adding real users to this OU because you have yet to test the effectiveness of the GPO we are about to create. Right-click on the New OU—Do not use container and select New, then User. This will bring up the New Object—User dialog box. Enter the following data: First Name: User1, User Logon Name: User1. Click Next. You will now have an opportunity to enter a password for this new user. Enter a password of *user1* and select User cannot change password and Password never expires from the checkbox list. You are then presented with a summary of the options you have entered. Click on Finish to complete the creation of the new user account.

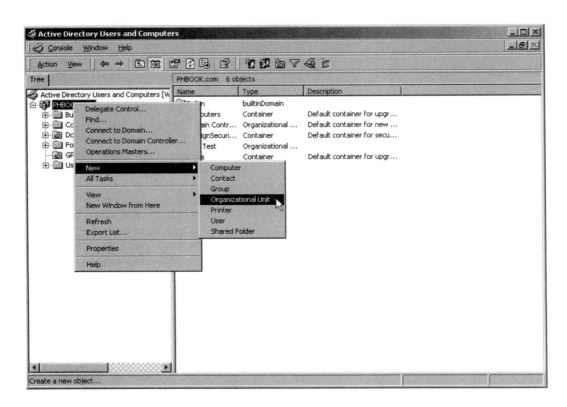

Figure 14–6 *Creating a test GPO.*

5. It is now time to create our GPO. To do this right-click on the New OU—Do not use container and select Properties. This displays the Properties dialog box for the new OU. Click on the Group Policy tab and you will be presented with the dialog box you first saw in Figure 14.4. Because this is a new OU, there will not be any entries in this tab. So let's go ahead and create our first GPO. Click on the New button. This will display a new GPO with the default name of *New Group Policy Object.* We'll change this to *Our Test GPO.* If you have inadvertently pressed the <Enter> key before following this step, you can no longer enter a new name. If you have done this, simply right-click on the new GPO and select Rename from the menu.

6. Congratulations! You have now created your first GPO. Of course, it doesn't do much yet. When a GPO is first created, it accepts the default settings, which is everything in the GPO disabled. We're going to go ahead and make some changes to this GPO. Select Our Test GPO, then click on Edit. This will open the Group Policy MMC. This is shown in Figure 14.7.

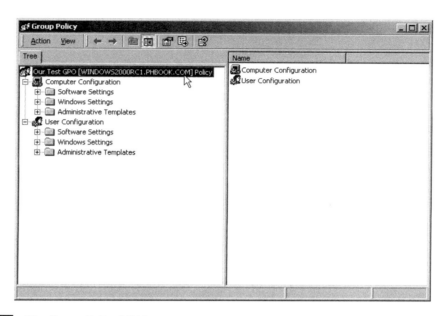

Figure 14–7   *The Group Policy MMC.*

7. There are many options that can be set within the GPO MMC. We are going to select a few of them to show you how this is done. Of course, you might want to familiarize yourself with all of the options for use in your real-world environment. We are going to remove Help from the Start menu, Disable the Display icon in Control Panel, and Disable Task Manager. We will also show you how to find out what each of these options does for the user environment. First, let's remove the Help option. To do this, expand the Administrative Templates tree and select Start Menu & Taskbar. The screen you should now see is shown in Figure 14.8.

8. As you can see, there are many options available to you. Notice the Setting column that has an entry, Not configured, for each item. This means that these entries have not been assigned a value yet. Let's go ahead and enable the Remove Help menu from the Start Menu option. You will find this option in the right-hand pane, as shown in Figure 14.8. Highlight this entry and right-click. Select Properties from the menu.

9. You are now presented with a dialog box with two tabs, a Policy tab and an Explain tab. Click on the Explain tab for a moment. You will see a detailed explanation of what this option will do. This is an important feature that lists all of the options that are available to you. Some options are dependent on other options. Make sure that you familiarize yourself with these explanations. Once you have read the explanation, go ahead and click on the Policy tab and select Enabled. Once this is done, click on OK.

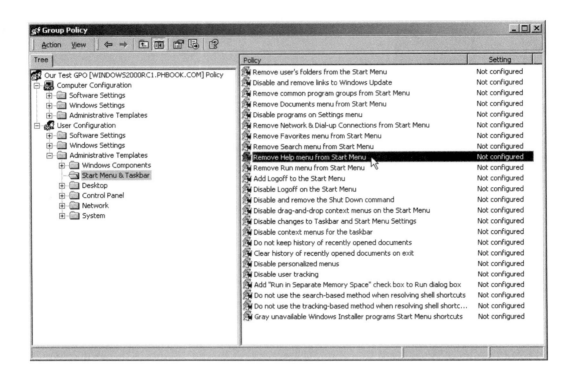

The Start Menu & Taskbar options.

You should see that the Setting column now has Enabled next to this option. This means that you have enabled this option in this GPO.

10. The previous step walked you through setting an option in a GPO. We are going to go ahead and set two more options. This time, we won't give as much detail. You already know how to navigate around. However, make sure that you always click on the Explain tab the first time you are using an option. Click on Control Panel, then Display. Set the option Disable Display in Control Panel to enable.

11. Click on System, then Logon/Logoff and enable the Disable Task Manager option. Once this is done, close the Group Policy MMC. Congratulations, you have now created your first GPO. Logoff your system and then logon as the user you just created. You should see a Start menu with the Help command missing. Make sure you also open Control Panel to confirm that the Display option is gone. Finally, press <CTRL><ALT><DELETE> and confirm that Task Manager has been disabled.

Delegating Control

You have now created a new GPO. You have read and write access to the GPO and can make any change that you want to it. However, in the real world, we suggest that you make sure you are not the only person who has access to edit a GPO. It is always a good idea to have at least two methods to access and modify an object in Active Directory. You never know when one method is going to be compromised. If you have only a single method, you could find yourself in trouble.

   Instead, you can also delegate control of an object. In this case, we are going to allow a group called *GPO Admin* to have write access to this new GPO. This means that they will be able to make changes to the GPO.

1. First we need to create the new group called *GPO Admin*. First, open Active Directory Computers and Users by clicking on Start, Programs, Administrative Tools, Active Directory Users and Computers. Next, click on the domain name to select it.
2. Right-click on the domain name and select New, then Group. This brings up the New Object–Group dialog box. We are going to create a group called *GPO Admin*. Enter this value into the Group Name dialog box and click OK.
3. You should now see the GPO Admin group in the MMC. Now we will add this group to permissions for our new GPO. Click on New OU—Do not use to select it. Then right-click and select Properties. Finally, select the Group Policy tab.
4. Select the GPO we created in the earlier exercise and click the Properties button. This brings up the Group Policy properties dialog box. Select the Security tab. You should now see the dialog box shown in Figure 14.5. Notice that our new group is not listed.
5. We will now add the GPO Admin group to this GPO and assign the necessary permissions so they can edit the GPO. Click Add. Click on the Name column heading to sort the list by this column and press <G>. This should take you to the GPO Admin group we just created. Note: If you are using a system that has had several groups added to it, you might need to scroll down the list to find the GPO Admin group.
6. Click the Add button, then OK. You should be returned to the Security Tab. Notice that the GPO Admin group now appears in this dialog box. All that is left is for you to give sufficient permissions for the members of this group to have to edit this GPO. Notice that there is already an entry for both Domain Admins and Enterprise Admins. By default, these two groups have permissions to edit a GPO. Click on Domain Admins in this list. Make a note of the permissions a Domain Admin has. We are going to give the GPO Admin group the same permissions.

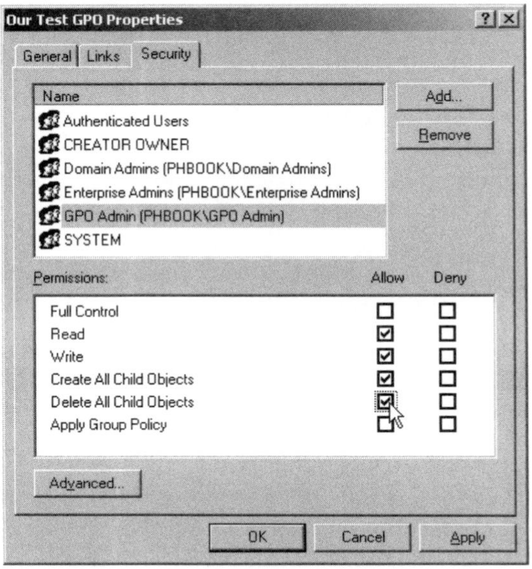

Figure 14–9   *The Security Dialog box with GPO Admin.*

7. Click on GPO Admins and assign them the same permissions. If you have done this, the security dialog box should look like the one shown in Figure 14.9.

8. You have now delegated control of this new GPO to the group we created.

   Make sure that you spend some time defining how GPOs will be administered in your organization. It is suggested that you create a group and make users who should have access to GPOs members of that group. Then assign permissions to the group shown in the previous exercise. Although it is possible to assign permissions on a user basis, this is to be discouraged; it will become far too difficult to track permissions this way.

Security Settings

Group Policy introduces a host of new features to choose from. Some features that administrators of previous versions of Microsoft Windows NT have been used to seeing can easily get lost in the new user interface. Many of these settings, such as Account Lockout policies and Settings for Event Logs, are now found within GPOs.

   By creating a GPO with all the necessary default settings, then applying it at the domain level, you can configure default settings. If you need to make a

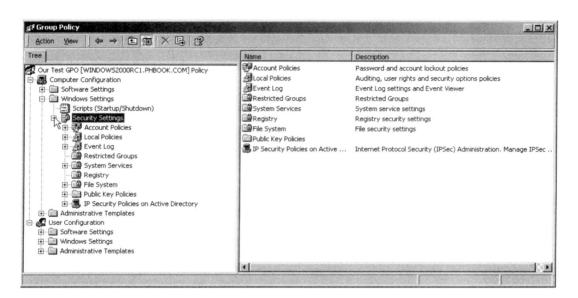

Figure 14-10   *The Security Settings in the Group Policy MMC.*

change for a particular group of users, you can then create another GPO at the OU level to override the settings.

You will find the security options in the Group Policy MMC. This is shown in Figure 14.10. As you can see, there are many different categories you have to choose from. These categories contain some essential security settings that should be configured.

The following defines what each of these categories contains. Once you are familiar with this, we will list some of the most common options that you will want to define.

• Account Policies—These options affect user accounts in your domain. These include such options as enforcing password histories, minimum password ages, and password length.

• Local Policies—These policy options affect the local machine only. This includes all local user rights and auditing options and permissions.

• Event Log—Windows 2000 maintains three key event logs: Application, System, and Security logs. These are viewed with Event Viewer. These options allow you to configure the amount of data that is stored in an event log and who has access to the logs.

• Restricted Group—These options allow you to track the built-in groups on your system. Every Windows 2000 machine has built-in groups with predefined permissions. You can use these options to track and manage these groups.

• Public Key Policies—You are able to configure policies for several public key technologies in this area. These include encrypted data recovery agents and Enterprise Trusts.

• IP Security Policies on Active Directory—Windows 2000 allows you to configure security on your network Internet Protocol (IP) These options allow you to customize these options.

We are going to take a look at some of the options that are available to you. Once again, there are far too many for us to list them all. Also, since we have already been through an exercise where you selected options and enabled them, we won't duplicate that effort. Instead refer to Table 6.4 for some of the most common settings, and the path within the Group Policy MMC to find them.

Table 14.4	Common Security Settings.
Group Policy SettingFunction	
Minimum Password Length	Enforces a minimum password length. The longer the password is the harder it is for someone to guess. Note that making this option too large will make passwords difficult for your users to remember. You will find this option under Computer Configuration\Security Settings\Account Policies\Password Policy.
Account Lockout Duration	An account is locked out when a user enters an incorrect password more than three times. This setting enforces a duration for this lockout. Once this time has expired, the account is unlocked. You will find this option under Computer Configuration\Security Settings\Account Policies\Account Lockout Policy.

Table 14.4	Common Security Settings. (Continued)
Maximum Application Log Size	The Application log is shown in Event Viewer on a Windows 2000 system. If you set this option too low, it might not be as useful, because entries might get overwritten before you have had time to analyze them. If you set it too large, you might be using unnecessary disk storage. You will find this option under Computer Configuration\Security Settings\Event Log\Settings for Event logs.
Prompt User to Change Password before Expiration	This option is useful so that you can let your users know they must change their password because it is about to be expired. You can set this to alert them days in advance. You will find this option under Computer Configuration\Security Settings\Local Policies\Security options.
Logon Locally	By default, users cannot logon to a domain controller locally—that is, at the DC console. To allow a user to do this, you must be granted the Logon Locally right. You will find this option under Computer Configuration\Security Settings\Local Policies\User Rights Assignment.

Take some time to investigate this interface. You will find all the familiar Microsoft Windows NT security settings, as well as a host of new options in the aforementioned areas of the Group Policy MMC.

Folder Redirection

One of the issues that a network administrator has to deal with is disaster recovery. Your users' data is the lifeblood of your organization, and it goes without saying that a backup strategy is a vital element to be considered.

Although it is easy for an administrator to accept this, your user community may feel very differently. It is easy to save files to their local hard disks or to accept the default paths in applications such as Microsoft Office. However, this leaves users open to loss of data. If a local hard disk crashes, it is unlikely that a backup has been performed. So the data is lost.

One of the most common ways of preventing this type of data loss is to direct your users to save their files on the network. That way, the standard procedures for backing up data can take care of making sure that data is never lost. All that is left is making it easy for your users to save their data in the right location. In Windows 2000, you can achieve this by using the folder redirection capabilities of group policies.

Folder redirection allows you to make the saving of data to the network transparent to your users. You can redirect the following folders:

- *Application data*
- *Desktop*
- *My Documents*
- *My Pictures*
- *Start Menu*

Note that some of these folders, such as *My Documents*, are also part of a user's roaming profile. This means that when a user logs off Windows 2000, the contents are copied to the network. When the user logs onto a different computer, the contents are copied down so that they are available locally. This can take time and creates network traffic. By redirecting *My Documents* to the network, you can considerably cut down on this time.

These options are configured within the Group Policy MMC under User Configuration\Windows Settings\Folder Redirection. Setting these options enables you to standardize the user's desktop and ensure that disaster recovery is possible for users' data. It is a good idea to use this option. However, keep in mind that storing user data on the network will require additional hard disk space on your servers.

Guidelines for Group Policy

As you have seen, there are many options available to you in Group Policy. Before you implement them, you will need to give a lot of thought to which options you really need to implement and at which level in Active Directory they should be applied. Do not be tempted to use settings just because they are there—it takes time to process group policies when a user logs on, and if you have too many of them, you might find that user performance becomes unacceptable.

What follows are some guidelines for using and implementing group policies. Careful thought should go into this process.

Implementing Registry-Based Settings

GPOs are not something you should jump into without careful thought. They affect your users' experiences, as well as having an impact on your network performance. Defining some basic parameters before you set out is a good idea.

When it comes to registry-based settings, there are several things you should keep in mind. First, you will need to decide where in Active Directory you intend to apply the policy. Don't forget that you can apply group policies at the site, domain, and OU levels. This is commonly written as SDOU. You have been given this flexibility so that you can make sure that the policy you are about to apply affects only the users for which it was intended.

The policy that is closest to the user will have precedence. So, given the acronym SDOU, it is the OU that has the final say, then domain, then site (read from right to left). If multiple policies are set at a single level (for example, three policies at the OU level), you can set the precedence level yourself, as described earlier in this chapter. There is more on this topic in the next section.

You will also need to decide whether you intend to create one big GPO with many settings or a number of smaller GPOs. By choosing one big GPO, you can quickly apply a lot of settings to your users and computers. However, it makes it more difficult to apply selectively specific policies, because everything is being applied at the same time.

It is possible to set a Background refresh rate to your registry policy settings. This setting dictates at what intervals registry-based policies are applied to client computers. The consideration here is network traffic. If you set this interval to be too frequent, you will generate unnecessary network traffic. Have the policies applied only when you absolutely need them.

Finally, don't forget that you can delegate control of GPOs. This will help offload some of the administrative work. In large organizations, it is likely that those people configuring group policies will not be the same people as those applying them. Therefore, delegate control as necessary.

Options for Applying Group Policy

Your Active Directory structure is going to dictate how you can apply Group Policy. A single GPO can be applied at three different levels within Active Directory, and it can also be applied multiple times. So a single GPO can be applied to three or four distinct OUs separately. This is known as *Linking group policies*.

Unless you also designed the Active Directory structure, you will have no control over how it has been laid out. Some of the most common structures and how group policies can be applied in those environments are covered in the following paragraphs. We have taken it from the simplest structure to the most complex.

SINGLE DOMAIN WITHOUT OUS OR SINGLE SITES

This is the simplest Active Directory structure but perhaps one of the most difficult environments in which to apply group policies. In this environment, you are limited to applying policies at the site and domain levels. Although these are useful, they are also somewhat large. To get a level of granularity in this environment, you are going to have to set permissions for security groups within the OU. This was discussed earlier in this chapter.

In these circumstances, it is advantageous to apply group policies to one or another of the levels; we suggest the domain level. If you do this, you are far less likely to have conflicts, and precedence can be set within a single dialog box.

SINGLE DOMAIN WITH OUS

With OUs, you are able to define subsets of users far more easily. Simply create an OU, add users to it, then apply the GPO to the OU itself. Don't forget, it is possible to nest OUs. Using this feature, it is possible for group policies to filter down the levels. If you have a lot of levels, it is possible to fine-tune which settings get applied to sets of users.

In this model, it is possible that conflicts in settings could occur. This happens when a policy is set at multiple levels. Because you now have OUs, it is possible that group policies at the domain or site levels can conflict with those at the OU level. Try to avoid this by having a structured approach to group policy design and implementation.

Finally, don't forget that it is possible to delegate authority at the OU level. You can give users at each OU administrative access to alter OUs and have the policies inherited in child OUs.

MULTIPLE DOMAINS

In this circumstance, you have several options. On one level, it might be easier simply to create group policies within each domain. Using this method, you are duplicating effort, but it is fairly simple. Because GPOs cannot be copied, you will have to create the GPOs manually in each domain.

As an alternative, you can create a GPO in one domain, then "link" it to another domain. GPOs are not inherited from domain to domain, so only those GPOs applied within a domain can affect a user or group of computers. You will also have to take into consideration GPO administration in this model. Unless specifically specified, members of the linked domain would not have access to administer the GPO unless you assign the permission to do so.

MULTIPLE SITES

It is possible to apply GPOs to multiple sites. However, applying GPOs to sites can be somewhat problematic and might not always give you the desired results. Don't forget, within Active Directory, a site is a single or group of IP subnets. If you apply a GPO to a site, all users and computers within that site will be affected.

However, if a user then logs on in a different site, the GPO will not be applied to that user. This could be a double-edged sword. It is unlikely that you will want to set critical options at the site level only. Try to use the domain level for critical options. If you try to use sites for these options, you are probably going to find yourself creating multiple GPOs unnecessarily.

Different Scope Options

The scope of your GPOs should be organized around the administrative model that you intend to use. For instance, if you have a set of administrators that is going to be responsible for user settings but not computer settings, you can create GPOs with only the relevant settings and assign administrative permissions to them.

Your goal is going to be to minimize the number of GPOs that you have in your organization. There are several reasons for this. First, it is easier to keep on top of the administration of a smaller number of GPOs. Second, a single GPO will almost always complete before multiple GPOs have been applied.

There are still many options that need to be considered. What follows are several scenarios that you might want to consider when working with GPOs.

CREATE A DIFFERENT GPO FOR EACH TYPE OF SETTING

In this scenario, it is assumed that you have many administrators who are each responsible for a different type of policy. In this case, you would create your GPOs based around these different types and assign administrative permissions to each user (or group of users).

CREATE SEPARATE GPOS FOR USERS AND COMPUTERS

This is similar to the option explained above, except that there are only two different types of settings. In this case, you would create two GPOs—one with the user settings, the other with the computer settings. You would then assign administrative permissions to each type.

Strategies for Delegating Control of GPOs

Although it is easy to delegate control, this should not be taken lightly. If you assign permissions on a random basis or simply as requested, you will end up with an environment that is difficult to manage. Instead, give some thought to how you anticipate administrative authority being applied. What follows are several scenarios that detail some of the options available to you.

GIVE THE RIGHT TO MODIFY AN EXISTING GPO

You would use this strategy when you want to assign the right to modify a single GPO. In this case, you are using a very granular level of control. However, don't be fooled into thinking this is too limited. Because GPOs can be linked to other domains, it is possible for someone with administrative rights in a single

GPO to affect computers and users in several domains, even if they would not ordinarily have access to those domains.

To assign this to a user, you must give them both read and write permissions to the GPO.

CREATE NEW GPOS

You will want to consider this strategy when the people who administer Active Directory and your network are not the same as those that will administer your GPOs. Once created, you would have another set of administrators who will link the GPOs to the respective containers.

This permission is assigned to Group Policy administrators. These administrators also have the right to delete a GPO.

DELEGATE CONTROL TO LINK GPOS

You might also want to assign permissions allowing a user or security group to link the GPOs to sites, domains, or OUs. This will be part of the strategy where you have a separate group creating GPOs. To do this, you must run the Delegate Control wizard. You do this by right-clicking on an OU and selecting Delegate Control. You must assign the users or group Manage Group Policy links permission.

What to do Before Applying Group Policy

Having gone through the formalities of what Group Policy offers, it is time to talk about the steps you should take before applying Group Policy. You should now have a good idea of the vast range of things you can achieve and how they can be applied. One thing should be clear: You can create a huge problem if you apply group policy incorrectly!

It is possible to render every machine inoperable with a group policy, and if that policy is applied at the domain level, you might have a real problem on your hands. So the first order of the day is testing. You should test any policy that you plan to use on your network.

There is no magic GUI to help you perform tests of GPOs. In simple terms, you should first decide what you are hoping to achieve with your GPO. You should also make an early decision about the level at which you are going to apply the GPO. Are you going to apply it at the site, domain, or OU level?

When these decisions are made you should go ahead and create a test user account at the level you wish to apply the GPO. This user account will act as a dummy account for your GPO testing. When your GPO has been created, you should go ahead and apply the policy to the test user account. Logon to Windows 2000 using the test account, then test out the various options that you are trying to apply.

Without a positive result from this test, you obviously should not apply the policy on a wider basis. Instead, fix any problems you find and try the test again. Only when the results are consistent and completely successful should you apply it to a wider audience.

Again, Microsoft has not provided you with a test environment beyond what has been described here. It is going to be up to you to make sure your policies work as advertised.

Keep in mind that it can be quite a challenge to keep track of all your GPOs. The more you have and the more granular you get with implementing and administering them, the more difficult it is going to be for you to keep track of what each one does. Make sure that you document your GPOs. This should include the options you have implemented, the level at which the GPO is going to be applied, the administrative model you have applied, and the users or groups that the GPO is supposed to affect. You can keep this information in a book or database.

You should have a plan in place in the event that there is a conflict between GPOs. This should be decided before you ever run into a problem. This will minimize the effect of a mistake being made and give you a clear line at a solution. Making decisions at the spur of the moment is hardly ever a good idea.

Don't forget that you can turn on event logging for GPOs. If you do, you will easily be able to view whether a policy was applied. This is a good idea, especially when you have an isolated incident where a policy is not having the desired effect. Events are logged to the Winlogon event log. The only problem with this solution is that the logs are machine-specific—not user-specific. However, it should still act as a guide.

Resolving Problems

Finally, here are some tips you can use to troubleshoot conflicts you might be having. A conflict would be a situation where several GPOs are being applied but you are not sure why a client is behaving in a certain way.

First, if you are having problems, you should start your search for a solution at the highest level in Active Directory. Don't forget, GPOs are applied at the site, domain, and OU levels. These are listed in a very specific order (as they have been throughout this chapter). You should start your search at the site level first, then go down to the domain level and, if necessary, to the OU level.

Check to make sure that the priority level of the GPOs is correct. Don't forget that the order in which GPOs are listed at a level is significant (the topmost GPOs take precedence).

If you have a GPO set but it is being overridden, check for the No Override and the Block inheritance options. Either of these options could be changing the default behavior and causing strange results. You should check for these options at every level and in every GPO. If you have documented your GPOs, it should not be difficult for you to find out where this option has been set and the effect the setting is having.

Finally, you should check to make sure that the users or computers you intended to be affected by the GPO have, indeed, been assigned the necessary permissions. Without these, you will not achieve your desired goal of centrally managing your enterprise.

Chapter Summary

In this chapter, we took a look at Group Policy. Group Policy is a system that allows you to configure computer and user settings centrally. The aim of group policy is to reduce Total Cost of Ownership (TCO).

You can set policies in three categories. These are Software settings, Windows settings, and Administrative templates. With these settings, you can define behavior for the registry on a machine or for the Start menu and Taskbar for an individual user (or vice-versa). Options include disabling options in Control Panel or preventing the user from shutting a system down.

Group policies are stored within Active Directory as objects. These objects are known as Group policy Objects (GPOs). Along with GPOs, there are also Group Policy Containers (GPCs) and Group Policy Templates (GPTs). The GPT is actually a folder structure on the *SYSVOL* of the domain controllers. Because it is a folder structure, replication for this data is dealt with separately from replication of Active Directory objects.

Group policies are applied to users, groups, or machines at any one of three levels with Active Directory. These levels are the site level, the domain level, or at the Organizational Unit (OU) level. Because you can apply policies at each of these levels, you can be as granular about their implementation as suits you.

Group Policy is inherited. That is, if a policy is applied to an OU and that OU has child OUs below it, those child OUs will also have the policies applied to them. This can be prevented through use of the Block Inheritance option. Further, this option can be prevented from having an effect with use of the No Override option. The latter has precedence.

Control of policies is delegated. This means that you are able to decide who will be able to change the policies or who has permission to apply the policies to users. By using care in this phase of GPO deployment, you can minimize the amount of work you have to do with GPOs.

GPOs take over much of the functionality that people were most used to seeing in User Manager for Domains. For instance, you can use policies to define password length and expiration. Once you have configured these settings, they can be applied at whatever level makes the most sense in your environment.

Group Policy also contains options that allow you to define folder redirection. This feature allows you to have your users save documents to the network, rather than locally. To the user, it appears that the files are local. In this sense, Group Policy hides the network from the user.

We discussed how you might decide to implement GPOs. However, there is no "right" way of doing this. A lot is going to depend on the environment in which you are going to be working, and, more importantly, the administrative model you have employed.

You should always document Group Policy. Microsoft has yet to supply any tools that do a good job of this. It is going to be up to you to document each GPO you create and the options that are set within the GPO. Finally, make sure that you test GPOs before using them. An incorrectly configured GPO can cause a lot of problems in your enterprise.

Managing Disks

One of the most common tasks of a network or LAN administrator is managing the data on his or her company's network. To properly manage the data, you must be able to manage the hard disks themselves. Windows 2000 has added some new features to the hard disk management arena. These features and the Disk Management snap-in for the Microsoft Management Console (MMC) are discussed.

This chapter is also an introduction to disk management. It includes a brief discussion on the basics of a physical hard disk, setting up a hard disk, differing storage types, partition types, volume types, Redundant Arrays of Inexpensive Disks (RAID) sets, adding and removing hard disks, and administration of disks via the MMC. The objective of this chapter is to provide a solid understanding of the functionality of hard disks as they relate to Windows 2000.

Windows 2000 Hard Disk Basics

This section includes a discussion on hard disk components, which delves into the actual components of the physical disk, Windows 2000 storage types, partition types, volume types, and file systems.

Hard Disk Components

This discussion briefly covers the components of a physical hard disk. For most of you, this is common knowledge, but I felt that including it in a guide such as this might prove useful; at least as reference material. For the rest of you who haven't heard the latest dissertation on hard disks and how they work, listen up.

THE PHYSICAL DISK

The physical hard disk is made of aluminum and is coated with a magnetic recording material. It is illustrated in Figure 15.1. Each individual disk is called a *platter*. Most disks are made of five platters, each with two sides. The platters are stacked inside a vacuum-sealed container to keep out dust and other contaminant particles. The read/write head is also sealed inside a vacuum and reads the data as it travels from the outside to the inside of the disk.

The platters revolve clockwise at 3,600 revolutions per minute (rpm) to more than 10,000 rpm for most new hard disk brands. The higher the number of revolutions per minute, the faster the drive. A small motor called a *spindle motor* rotates the platters. The read/write heads are held by a head carriage that floats on a cushion of air above the platters. It is important to note that the read/write heads never actually touch the platter. When a user requests a data file, the stepper motor actuator moves the heads to the correct position on the disk. This is made possible by the three remaining components of the disk:

1. Tracks
2. Sectors
3. Cylinders

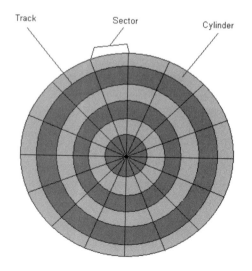

| Figure 15–1 | *The layout of a hard disk platter.* |

The process of segmenting each platter is called *formatting*. Formatting entails logically dividing the disk into concentric circles called *tracks*. These tracks encircle the disk. The platter is then further divided into pie slices called *sectors*. Each location on the disks is represented as a cross-section between a track and a sector. Cylinders are cross-sections that span parallel platters. Cylinders provide a three-dimensional capability of reading data from multiple platters as well as multiple sectors and tracks.

Each cross-section on the disk is called a *block*. Each block has a location defined by its track, sector, and cylinder. This is how the read/write head locates a file on the disk. Once the read/write head finds the correct file, it reads the magnetic composition of the disk surface and translates that information into a stream of bytes. The disk controller interface is responsible for this translation and for shuttling the bytes off to the processor.

Before the hard disk can be used to store files, is must be partitioned and formatted. Hard disk partitioning divides the disk into separate units of storage and prepares the platters for formatting. Formatting is the process in which the hard disk is divided into blocks and the file system is installed.

Any discussion concerning the physical components of the hard disk beyond this point is out of the scope of this book. Furthermore, there are plenty of other fine materials that go into further detail about the components of the physical disk and how they relate to one another.

Windows 2000 Storage Standards

There are two different storage standards supported by Windows 2000. These are basic storage and dynamic storage. The storage standards being discussed define the fundamental structure of the physical hard disk and how the partitions (or lack of partitions) and volumes on those disks are related and configured. A physical hard disk configured to use the Windows 2000 operating system is either one of these two storage standards. Both the basic storage type and the dynamic storage standard can be used in the same system but, conversely, they cannot be implemented on the same hard disk itself. Certain points will be noted so that you will be able to distinguish more easily the differences between the two storage standards.

BASIC STORAGE

Network administrators who have worked with Microsoft Windows NT 4.0 disk management and disk organization will be familiar with the basic storage concept. Basic storage is the concept of dividing the hard disk into partitions. All disks defined within the basic storage standard are called basic disks. Windows 2000 initializes all new disks as basic disks to provide backward compatibility with Microsoft Windows NT 4.0. Windows 2000 will automatically recognize any primary or extended partitions previously configured on these disks as well.

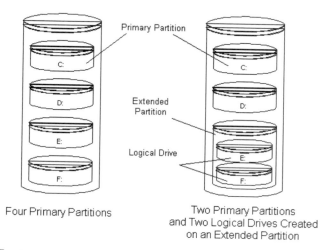

Primary Partition

C:

D:

E:

F:

Extended
Partition

C:

D:

Logical Drive

E:

F:

Four Primary Partitions

Two Primary Partitions
and Two Logical Drives Created
on an Extended Partition

Figure 15-2 *Primary and Extended Partitions.*

All Microsoft platforms, including Microsoft Disk Operating System (MS-DOS) Microsoft Windows, Microsoft Windows NT, and Windows 2000 support basic storage. You will find that this is not the fact concerning dynamic storage when it is discussed in the next topic. In addition, basic disks can also contain spanned volumes (volume sets), mirrored volumes (mirror sets), stripe volumes (stripe sets), and RAID-5 volumes (stripe sets with parity) created using Windows NT 4.0 or earlier. You can access basic disks using MS-DOS.

 Basic storage is supported by all Microsoft operating system platforms and can be accessed via MS-DOS.

DYNAMIC STORAGE

The dynamic storage standard cannot contain multiple partitions. Instead, the dynamic storage standard can be defined as having one or more disks containing a single partition. Each disk initialized within the dynamic storage standard is called a *dynamic disk*. Because dynamic disks cannot be partitioned, they are instead divided into volumes. A dynamic disk within the dynamic storage standard can contain simple volumes, spanned volumes, mirrored volumes, striped volumes, and RAID-5 volumes.

Upgrading basic disks creates dynamic disks within the dynamic storage standard. Windows 2000 takes the use of dynamic storage to the next level. One of the grand pitfalls of Microsoft Windows NT 4.0 was having to reboot the operating system every time a change was made to the disk organization within Disk Administrator. This is a fact link to basic storage. Dynamic storage does not use the same principles. When a volume is created on a dynamic disk and sized and resized, Windows 2000 does not have to be rebooted. That's absolutely wonderful. Every time something was changed in Microsoft Windows NT 4.0, the operating system had to be rebooted. I'm glad that Microsoft has come up with and developed the dynamic storage standard and integrated it into Windows 2000.

 Dynamic storage is supported only by the Windows 2000 operating system and cannot be accessed via MS-DOS.

Windows 2000 Partition Types (Basic Disks)

Partitions are used to separate data storage physically on basic disks. This way, you can separate user data, applications, and application data on the same disk. If you are limited on the number of disks that you can purchase or have another business reason to separate data on a single disk, partitioning is the way to go. Basic disks can be separated into two different kinds of partitions.

1. Primary partitions
2. Extended partitions

There are limitations on the number of partitions that can be created on a basic disk. Only four primary partitions can exist, and only one extended partition can exist on a single basic disk. A basic disk is also limited to four partitions all together—primary and extended partitions combined. In this case, a basic disk can contain three primary partitions and one extended partition for a total of four partitions. Look at Figure 15.2 for an example of a basic disk that has been partitioned.

PRIMARY PARTITIONS

Primary partitions are used by Windows 2000 to start the operating system. Primary partitions can be marked as active. Only one primary partition on a single disk can be marked as active at a time. Windows 2000 looks at this active partition for the boot file necessary for the Windows 2000 boot process.

Primary partitions can also be used to separate multiple operating systems on a single disk. For instance, you can have Microsoft Windows 95, Microsoft Windows 98, and Windows 2000 all running from the same disk. The primary partition that has been marked as active will have a *boot.ini* file on it that will designate where each operating system is located on the disk. For more detailed information on the *boot.ini* and how the rest of the Windows 2000 boot process works, look at Chapter 6 of this book.

If you wanted to dual boot (to have two operating systems load on the same computer) Microsoft Windows 98 and Windows NT 4.0, the active partition must be formatted as FAT (File Allocation Table). Microsoft Windows NT 4.0 cannot recognize or read data from an active partition formatted as FAT32, nor can Windows 98 recognize or read data from an NTFS (NT File System) partition without the aid of a third-party utility. In addition, to dual boot Microsoft Windows 98 and Windows 2000, the active partition could be formatted as FAT or FAT32, but not NTFS. Microsoft Windows 98 also has the same ability to read a partition formatted with either FAT or FAT32. Microsoft Windows NT and Windows 2000 are the only operating systems that can recognize and read data from an active partition formatted as NTFS.

Primary partitions must be formatted to be used and can have drive letters such as *C:* or *D:* assigned to them.

EXTENDED PARTITIONS

An extended partition is usually the last partition created on a basic disk. This is because an extended partition is created from all the free space available on a disk. It is important to remember that only one extended partition can exist on a single basic disk, so that all available free space on a basic hard disk can be placed in the extended partition. The available or remaining free space on a basic hard disk excludes the primary partitions that might have been created on the disk.

Extended partitions differ from primary partitions in that they cannot be formatted. How can you use an extended drive? Extended partitions are separated or segmented into segments called *logical drives*. These logical drives can then be formatted with one of the many file systems. Logical drives can also be assigned drive letters such as *E:* or *F:*. The reason that I use *E* or *F* as examples is because I assume that you already have one or more primary partitions created with drive letters assigned.

Windows 2000 Volume Types (Dynamic Disks)

Within Windows 2000, basic disks can be changed or converted into dynamic disks. These dynamic disks can then be separated into volumes. These volumes can be separated by disks or can span many disks. The next few topics will discuss the many volume configurations available to a Windows 2000 administrator using dynamic disks. After reading these topics, you have a better understanding of the volume types available in Windows 2000 and will know which one will best suit your needs.

When judging which volume type is suited for you and your organization, think about the following:

- Efficient use of space
- Overall performance
- Fault tolerance

These three criteria should be considered whenever a new Windows 2000 system is installed—especially on a server. A server should be fault tolerant, meaning that, should any catastrophic event occur, the data on the disk is preserved and overall loss of data is minimized. A catastrophic event could be anything from a disk failure to an earthquake or fire. The most common fault-tolerant configuration is RAID-5. In the following topics, I will convey which of the volume types are fault tolerant and which ones are not. Chapter 22, "Disaster Recovery Planning," also goes into more detail concerning RAID and fault-tolerant Windows 2000 volume types.

Do you remember that all new disks in Windows 2000 are initialized as basic disks? Table 15.1 shows how basic disks and partitions relate to dynamic disks and volumes, once they are converted via the disk upgrade wizard.

Table 15.1	Basic to Dynamic Disk Conversion Table
Basic Disks	**Dynamic Disk**
Partition	Volume
System and boot partitions	System and boot volumes
Active partition	Active volume
Extended partition	Volumes and unallocated space
Logical drive	Simple volume
Volume set	Spanned volume
Stripe set	Striped volume
Mirror set	Mirrored volume

SIMPLE VOLUME

A simple volume is a volume made up from disk space on a single dynamic disk. This volume can be a single region on a dynamic disk or multiple regions linked together on a single dynamic disk.

A simple volume cannot be created on a basic disk and can span across only a single dynamic disk.

SPANNED VOLUME

A spanned volume is a simple volume spanned across more than one disk. For example, if you have three simple volumes on three separate dynamic disks and you link them together, you create a spanned volume. Spanned volumes have the limitation of combining up to 32 disks. Some might see this as a limitation, but I think that this is a great improvement over Microsoft Windows NT 4.0.

Figure 15–3 *Dynamic Disks in a Spanned Volume.*

To give you a better idea of how spanned volumes work with dynamic disks in Windows 2000, look at Figure 15.3. Notice how each dynamic disk is written to and filled with data before the next disk is used in a set. Windows 2000 starts with the first dynamic disk and moves to the second and so on, until every dynamic disk in the spanned volume set is filled with data. Because of this methodology, spanned volume sets are not fault tolerant. If any physical disk within the spanned volume set fails, all data on the spanned volume set is lost.

A spanned volume is not fault tolerant and is created by combining multiple simple volumes. Also, simple and spanned volumes have the most efficient disk space usage of all Windows 2000 volume types. All free space on the dynamic disks can be used for data.

STRIPED VOLUME

A striped volume is created by combining free space or regions on two or more dynamic disks (up to 32 physical disks). Unlike spanned volumes, in all dynamic disks within a striped volume, data is written to and read from by Windows 2000 at the same time. This increases overall physical disk performance and Windows 2000 server performance. Striped volumes also efficiently use the disk space allocated to them on each dynamic disk. This is true only when each physical dynamic disk within the striped volume set is of equal size.

One last note on striped sets—they are not fault tolerant. Even though striped volumes are categorized as RAID Level 0, if a dynamic disk fails within the striped volume set, all data is lost.

A striped volume is not fault tolerant and is created by combining two or more dynamic disks. Striped volumes are also known as *RAID-0*. When striped volumes are created using dynamic disks of equal size, disk space usage is efficient.

MIRRORED VOLUME

Linking two separate, identical dynamic disks creates a mirrored volume. Mirrored volumes are most commonly known as *RAID-1* in the technology industry. A mirrored volume is also the first Windows 2000 volume type that is fault tolerant. They are fault tolerant because the exact same data is written to both drives, virtually simultaneously. If either of the dynamic disks fails, the other one holds all of the data and no business down time occurs.

Mirrored volumes contain two identical dynamic disks and are fault tolerant. Mirrored volume sets are also described as *RAID-1*.

RAID-5 VOLUME

RAID-5 is also a fault-tolerant Windows 2000 volume type and is created using three or more disks (up to 32 physical disks). RAID-5 is disk striping with parity. What does that mean? Look at Figure 15.4 before you finish reading the rest of this paragraph and refer to it as you read. Basically, Windows 2000 writes a stripe of data to each disk within the RAID-5 volume. As each stripe of data is written to disk, a block of parity information is written to one of the dynamic disks, as well. If a dynamic disk fails within the RAID-5 volume, the data can be reconstructed. The data is reconstructed using the data and parity information on the other dynamic disks in the RAID-5 volume.

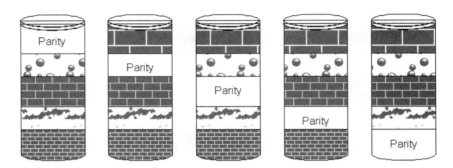

Figure 15–4   *RAID-5 data striping with parity information.*

Managing Disks within Windows 2000

This section of the chapter will discuss the basics of managing hard disks within the Disk Management window. The topics covered include using the Disk Management window, viewing and updating information using the Disk Management window, managing basic disks, and managing dynamic disks. More in-depth and advanced disk management practices, such as managing and optimizing data storage on local and remote computers, can be found in Chapter 19.

Using the Disk Management Window

Before we discuss the specifics of managing disks with the MMC Disk Management window, let's briefly discuss how to use the Disk Management window itself. The topics covered will be how to display disks and volumes in graphical or list view, how to change the colors and patterns for volume and disk regions, how to change how disk sizes are displayed, and how to change how regions are displayed.

The following discussions will give you a knowledge and understanding of the Disk Management window that will enable you to personalize the Disk Management window to suit your needs.

DISPLAY DISKS AND VOLUMES IN GRAPHICAL OR LIST VIEW

Use the following steps to change how the disks and volumes are displayed in the Disk Management window:

1. Click on Start, then point to Settings, and click on Control Panel.
2. Double-click Administrative Tools, then double-click Computer Management.

3. Once the MMC has completed loading, click on the plus sign to the left of storage.
4. Now click on Disk Management. This opens the Disk Management window on the right-hand side of the console.
5. In the Disk Management window, click View.
6. Under the menu separator bar, Top and Bottom are listed. For now, ignore the other entries in the list. The console has two windows on the right, separated by a divider. To change the disk or volume display characteristics in the top window, point to Top, or to change the disk or volume display characteristics in the bottom window, point to Bottom.
7. If you used your mouse to point to Top, you have the option of clicking Disk List, Volume List, and Graphical View. If you used your mouse to point to Bottom, you have the option of clicking Disk List, Volume List, Graphical View, and Hidden. If you click Hidden, the bottom window is hidden. Disk List displays a list of the physical hard disks installed and configured on the system in a list. Volume List displays the current volumes configured on the system in a list. Graphical View displays a graphical representation of how the physical disks and volumes are configured on the system and how they relate to one another.

You can configure the views on the top and the bottom windows to display more than one view at the same time. This is completely customizable. In addition, once an item has been selected in the View menu, notice that it puts a check to the left of that list item until another list item is chosen.

CHANGE THE COLORS AND PATTERNS FOR DISK REGIONS

Use the following steps to change the colors and display patterns for disk regions:

1. Click on Start, then point to Settings, and click on Control Panel.
2. Double-click Administrative Tools, then double-click Computer Management.
3. Once the MMC has completed loading, click on the plus sign to the left of Storage.
4. Now click on Disk Management. This opens the Disk Management window on the right-hand side of the console.
5. In the Disk Management window, click View, then click Settings.
6. On the Legend tab in the Items list box, click the item that you would like to change.
7. Now use the Color and Pattern dropdown list box to change the color and pattern displayed for the selected item.

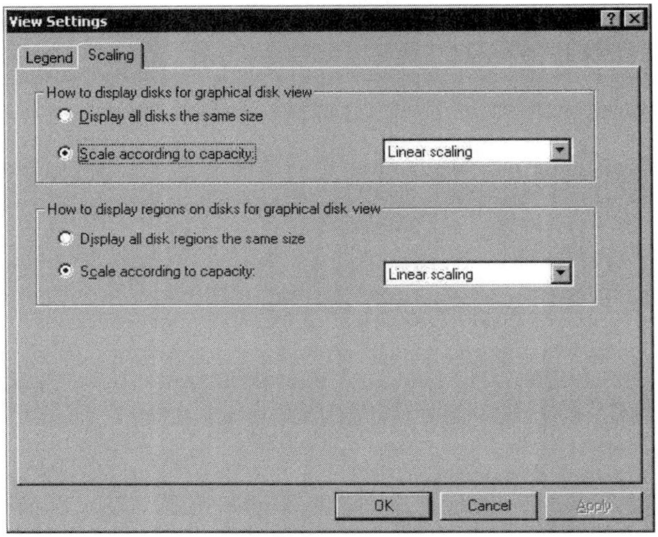

View Settings

Legend | Scaling

How to display disks for graphical disk view
- ○ Display all disks the same size
- ● Scale according to capacity: | Linear scaling ▼ |

How to display regions on disks for graphical disk view
- ○ Display all disk regions the same size
- ● Scale according to capacity: | Linear scaling ▼ |

| OK | Cancel | Apply |

Figure 15–5   *Scaling tab in the View Settings window.*

8. Click Apply to make the changes effective immediately and see the change in the Graphical View display in the background, or click OK to finalize the settings.

> **note** A good use for these changes would be to change all unallocated space to red. This would alert another Windows 2000 administrator of available or unused space that could still be configured for use.

CHANGE HOW DISK SIZES AND REGIONS ARE DISPLAYED

Use the following steps to change how disk sizes are displayed in the Disk Management window:

1. Click on Start, then point to Settings, click on Control Panel.
2. Double-click Administrative Tools, then double-click Computer Management.
3. Once the MMC has completed loading, and click on the plus sign to the left of Storage.
4. Now click on Disk Management. This opens the Disk Management window on the right-hand side of the console.
5. In the Disk Management window, click View, then click Settings.
6. Click on the Scaling tab in the View Settings window or press <CTRL>+< TAB>.

7. There are three options when choosing how to display disks for graphical disk view. To display each disk size equally, regardless of the disk's capacity, click Display all disks the same size. Or to display each disk based on its size relative to the largest disk, click Scale according to capacity, then click Linear scaling. This is a useful option if you manage disks of similar sizes. Also, you have the option to display disks by using a logarithmic computation of each disk's capacity by clicking Scale according to capacity, then clicking Logarithmic scaling. This is useful when you are administering disks of varying sizes.

These same steps can also be used to change how regions are displayed in the Disk Management window. Just use the regions section shown in Figure 15.5 on the View Settings window. All of the same concepts apply.

Viewing and Updating Information

Now that I have discussed how to customize the Disk Management window, let's discuss some of the basic uses of the console concerning Windows 2000 disk management. The next topic discusses viewing and updating information on disks and volumes, and covers the refresh and rescan options in the Disk Management window.

DISK PROPERTIES

The properties page of a physical disk displays information about the physical disk, including Status, Capacity, Unallocated Space, etc. To display the properties page for a selected disk in the Disk Management window, right-click the disk and click Properties. Table 15.2 is a list and description of the information shown in the Disk Properties dialog box.

Table 15.2	Descriptions of the Properties in the Disk Properties dialog box
Property	**Description**
Disk	This is the number that identifies the disk on this system. The first disk always starts with 0, then continues 1, 2, etc.
Type	This identifies the type of storage— whether the disk is basic, dynamic, or a removable storage disk.
Status	This shows the status of the disk— Online, Offline, Foreign, or Unknown.
Capacity	This displays the total disk space on the disk.

Table 15.2	Descriptions of the Properties in the Disk Properties dialog box (Continued)
Unallocated Space	This displays the amount of free disk space not configured in a volume.
Device Type	This displays the hard disk controller type and basic properties of that controller. For example: SCSI (Port 1, Target ID: 6, LUN: 0)
Hardware Vendor	This property identifies the hardware vendor of the disk and displays the disk type.
Adapter Name	This shows the name and type of the controller to which the disk is connected.
Volume Contained on this Disk	This is a list box containing all configured volumes on the disk.

VOLUME PROPERTIES

To display the Properties dialog box of a configured volume on a disk, open up the disk's property page and select the volume you would like to see the properties on. Then click Properties in the bottom right-hand corner of the Disk Properties dialog box. In addition, if the volume has a drive letter assigned to it, you can also use Explorer to access the properties of that volume. In this case, you would right-click the drive in the folder window of Explorer, then click Properties. Figure 15.6 shows the General tab in the Volume Properties dialog box.

Table 15-3 lists brief descriptions of the properties on the General tab of the Volume Properties dialog box.

Table 15.3	Descriptions of the Properties in the Volume Properties Dialog Box
Property	**Description**
Label	This displays the volume label in an edit box, which can be changed here.
Type	This displays the volume type, such as Local or Remote disk.
File System	This displays the file system: FAT, FAT32, NTFS, or EFS.

Table 15.3	Descriptions of the Properties in the Volume Properties Dialog Box (Continued)
Used Space	This displays the total disk space used on the volume.
Free Space	This displays the amount of free disk space configured on the volume.
Capacity	This displays the total amount of space configured on the volume.
Compress drive to save disk space*	When checked, the files on the volume are compressed to save disk space.
Index drive for fast file searching*	When checked, the volume is indexed for fast file searching.

*These options are available only on drives configured with the NTFS file system.

REFRESH AND RESCAN

When you read *refresh and rescan*, what does that say to you? It is basically self-explanatory, but we will cover some of the specifics related to the Win-

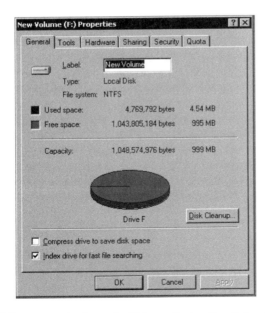

Figure 15–6   *General tab on the Volume Properties dialog box.*

dows 2000 Disk Management window. Refresh and rescan are two menu items that can be selected to update the information in the Disk Management window.

Refresh updates drive letter, file system, and removable media information. During the refresh process, Windows 2000 also checks to see whether volumes that were unreadable before are now readable. To select the Refresh menu item in the Disk Management window, use the following steps:

1. Click on Start, then point to Settings, and click on Control Panel.
2. Double-click Administrative Tools, then double-click Computer Management.
3. Once the MMC has completed loading, click on the plus sign to the left of Storage.
4. Now click on Disk Management. This opens the Disk Management window on the right-hand side of the console.
5. In the Disk Management Window, click Action, then click Refresh.

The Rescan Disks menu item updates the hardware information in the Disk Management window. Rescan Disks collects all of the same information that the Refresh does, in addition to scanning all attached disks and CD-ROMS. The Rescan Disks process can take up to several minutes because it is scanning for disk configuration changes. If you want only to update drive letters after you have reassigned them, use the Refresh menu option to save some time. To select the Rescan Disks menu item from the Disk Management window, use the following steps:

1. Click on Start, then point to Settings, and click on Control Panel.
2. Double-click Administrative Tools, then double-click Computer Management.
3. Once the MMC has completed loading, click on the plus sign to the left of Storage.
4. Now click on Disk Management. This opens the Disk Management window on the right-hand side of the console.
5. In the Disk Management window, click Action, then click Rescan Disks (see Figure 15.7).

Managing Basic Disks

The following topics explain in detail how to create and delete partitions and logical drives.

CREATE A PARTITION OR LOGICAL DRIVE

To create a partition or logical drive on a basic disk, use the following steps:

1. Click on Start, then point to Settings, and click on Control Panel.

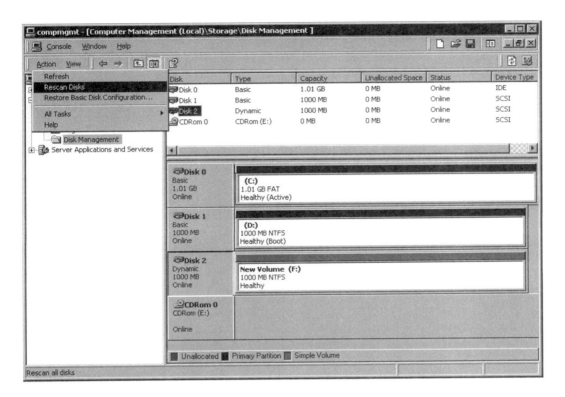

Figure 15-7   *Selecting Rescan Disks from the Disk Management window.*

2. Double-click Administrative Tools, then double-click Computer Management.
3. Once the MMC has completed loading, click on the plus sign to the left of storage.
4. Now click on Disk Management. This opens the Disk Management Window on the right-hand side of the console.
5. Right-click an unallocated region of a basic disk, then click Create Partition, or right-click Free Space and click Create Partition.
6. In the Create Partition wizard, click Next, click Primary Partition, Extended Partition, or Logical Drive, then follow the instructions on your screen.

DELETE A PARTITION OR LOGICAL DRIVE

To create a partition or logical drive on a basic disk, use the following steps:

1. Click on Start, then point to Settings, and click on Control Panel.

2. Double-click Administrative Tools, then double-click Computer Management.
3. Once the MMC has completed loading, click on the plus sign to the left of storage.
4. Now click on Disk Management. This opens the Disk Management Window on the right-hand side of the console.
5. Right-click the partition or logical drive that you want to delete.
6. Now click Delete Partition.

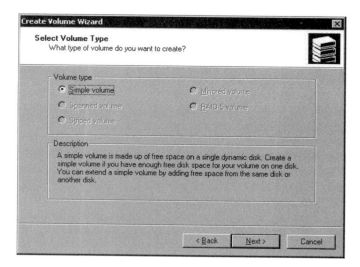

Figure 15–8   *The Create Volume wizard.*

 It is important to remember that all data on the deleted partitions or logical drives will be lost and cannot be recovered.

Managing Dynamic Disks

This discussion will include topics on creating simple volumes on dynamic disks, creating spanned volumes, creating striped volumes on dynamic disks, creating mirrored volumes, and creating fault-tolerant RAID-5 volumes.

CREATING SIMPLE VOLUMES

Simple volumes are created using the disk space on a single dynamic disk. Simple volumes can be mirrored but are not fault-tolerant themselves. The following steps detail how to create a simple volume on a dynamic disk.

1. Click on Start, then point to Settings, and click on Control Panel.
2. Double-click Administrative Tools, then double-click Computer Management.
3. Once the MMC has completed loading, click on the plus sign to the left of Storage.
4. Now click on Disk Management. This opens the Disk Management window on the right-hand side of the console.
5. Right-click the dynamic volume where you want to create the simple volume.
6. Click Create Volume.
7. When the Create Volume wizard is finished loading, click on Next (see Figure 15.8).
8. Now you can select the Volume type that you want to create. Click Simple volume, then click on Next.
9. Follow the rest of the instruction through to the end of the wizard to complete the creation of your simple volume.

Dynamic disks can be sized and resized on the fly with the Windows 2000 Disk Management window without rebooting the system. A dynamic disk must be formatted with NTFS before it can be dynamically resized. As always, it is best to make a full backup before making changes to disks that could result in data loss.

CREATING SPANNED VOLUMES

Spanned volumes consist of free space from multiple dynamic disks linked together to create a single large volume. The steps below show the steps necessary to create a spanned volume.

1. Click on Start, then point to Settings, and click on Control Panel.
2. Double-click Administrative Tools, then double-click Computer Management.
3. Once the MMC has completed loading, click on the plus sign to the left of Storage.
4. Now click on Disk Management. This opens the Disk Management window on the right-hand side of the console.
5. Right-click the dynamic volume where you want to create the spanned volume. This dynamic disk must contain unallocated space.
6. Click Create Volume.
7. When the Create Volume wizard is finished loading, click on Next.

8. Now you can select the Volume type that you want to create. Click Spanned volume, then click on Next.
9. Follow the rest of the instruction through to the end of the wizard to complete the creation of your spanned volume.

CREATING STRIPED VOLUMES

Striped volumes are similar to spanned volumes except for how the data is written to disk dynamic disks themselves. The data in striped volumes is written evenly across all disks in the volume. For this reason, striped volumes offer the best overall performance within Windows 2000. Use the following steps to create a striped volume.

1. Click on Start, then point to Settings, and click on Control Panel.
2. Double-click Administrative Tools, then double-click Computer Management.
3. Once the MMC has completed loading, click on the plus sign to the left of Storage.
4. Now click on Disk Management. This opens the Disk Management window on the right-hand side of the console.
5. Right-click the dynamic volume where you want to create the striped volume. This dynamic disk must contain unallocated space.
6. Click Create Volume.
7. When the Create Volume wizard is finished loading, click on Next.
8. Now you can select the Volume type that you want to create. Click Striped volume, then click Next.
9. Follow the rest of the instruction through to the end of the wizard to complete the creation of your striped volume.

CREATING MIRRORED VOLUMES

Mirrored volumes are created from two simple volumes. This is a fault-tolerant data solution. Windows 2000 writes all data to both disks. If one disk fails, the other still holds all of the data intact. Use the following steps to create a mirrored volume:

1. Click on Start, then point to Settings, and click on Control Panel.
2. Double-click Administrative Tools, then double-click Computer Management.
3. Once the MMC has completed loading, click on the plus sign to the left of Storage.
4. Now click on Disk Management. This opens the Disk Management window on the right-hand side of the console.
5. Right-click the dynamic volume where you want to create the mirrored volume.
6. Click Create Volume.

7. When the Create Volume wizard is finished loading, click on Next.
8. Now you can select the Volume type that you want to create. Click mirrored volume, then click on Next.
9. Follow the rest of the instruction through to the end of the wizard to complete the creation of your Mirrored volume.

CREATING RAID-5 VOLUMES

A RAID-5 volume is a fault-tolerant data solution that uses data striping with parity information. Use the following steps to create a RAID-5 volume:

1. Click on Start, then point to Settings, and click on Control Panel.
2. Double-click Administrative Tools, then double-click Computer Management.
3. Once the MMC has completed loading, click on the plus sign to the left of Storage.
4. Now click on Disk Management. This opens the Disk Management window on the right-hand side of the console.
5. Right-click the dynamic volume where you want to create the RAID-5 volume.
6. Click Create Volume.
7. When the Create Volume wizard is finished loading, click on Next.
8. Now you can select the Volume type that you want to create. Click RAID-5 volume, then click on Next.
9. Follow the rest of the instruction through to the end of the wizard to complete the creation of your RAID-5 volume.

Chapter Summary

A physical disk is made up of platters. Platters are sectioned and separated into regions called *tracks*, *sectors* and *cylinders*. Hard disks must be partitioned and formatted before data can be written to them.

Windows 2000 has two storage standards: basic storage and dynamic storage. Basic storage is a common storage standard used on all earlier Microsoft operating system platforms. All hard disks within the basic storage standard are called *basic disks*. Basic disks can be divided into primary and extended partitions. Only four total partitions can exist on a single basic disk.

Dynamic storage is a new storage standard introduced with Windows 2000. Hard disks defined within the dynamic storage standard are called *dynamic disks*. To use the free space on dynamic disks, they must have volumes created on them. Windows 2000 supports simple volumes, spanned volumes, striped volumes, mirrored volumes, and RAID-5 volumes. Only mirrored and RAID-5 volumes are fault-tolerant data storage solutions. In addition, all dynamic volumes can consist of up to 32 disks, except for simple and mirrored volumes.

NTFS Permissions

*T*his chapter discusses resource security using NTFS permissions. It specifically discusses security on files and folders within the NT File System (NFTS). The chapter covers NTFS file and folder permissions, access control lists, using NTFS permissions, planning NTFS permission, using special access permission, copying and moving data with NTFS permissions assigned, and troubleshooting NTFS permission problems.

This chapter also introduces you to the next generation of NTFS, NTFS 5.0, which Windows 2000 touts as its standard file system. In addition, this chapter outlines all of the components of using NTFS permissions on an NTFS 5.0 file system effectively on a Windows 2000 network. Once you have read and digested this chapter, you should be able to secure your Windows 2000 network with NTFS permissions with ease.

Understanding NTFS Permissions

This discussion covers the basics of file and folder permissions. It walks you through the kinds of permissions you can assign to files and folders and how to use them. The new and improved Access Control List is discussed, as well as the effects of multiple applied permissions and inherited permissions. First, let's answer a couple of common questions about NTFS permissions:

- *What is a permission?* A permission is a rule associated with an object to regulate which users can gain access to that object and in what manner.

• *When can I use a permission?* Permissions can be used only on NTFS formatted partitions or volumes, and that is why they are commonly referred to as NTFS permissions.

• *Who can set or apply permissions?* Administrators, the user that owns the files or folders, and all other users or groups that have the Full Control permission to those file and folders.

NTFS Permissions and Files

NTFS file permissions are used to control the access that a user, group, or application has to files. This includes everything from reading a file to modifying and executing the file. There are five NTFS file permissions:

1. Read
2. Write
3. Read & Execute
4. Modify
5. Full Control

The five NTFS file permissions are also listed in Table 16.1 with a description of the access that is allowed to the user or group when each permission is assigned. As you can see, the permissions are listed in a specific order. They all build upon each other.

If a user needs all access to a file except to take ownership and change its permissions, the Modify permission can be granted. The access allowed by Read, Write, and Read & Execute are automatically granted within the Modify permission. This saves you from assigning multiple permissions to a file or group of files. In later discussions in this chapter you will see what happens when multiple NTFS file permissions are assigned and applied and how you can determine the net access the user or group has to that file or folder.

Table 16.1	NTFS File Permissions
NTFS File Permission	**Allowed Access**
Read	This allows the user or group to read the file and view its attributes, ownership, and permissions set.
Write	This allows the user or group to over-write the file, change its attributes, view its ownership, and view the permissions set.

Table 16.1	NTFS File Permissions (Continued)
Read & Execute	This allows the user or group to run and execute the application. In addition, the user can perform all duties allowed by the Read permission.
Modify	This allows the user or group to modify and delete a file including perform all of the actions permitted by the Read, Write, and Read & Execute NTFS file permissions.
Full Control	This allows the user or group to change the permission set on a file, take ownership of the file, and perform actions permitted by all of the other NTFS file permissions.

A file's attributes are properties of the file such as Read-Only, Hidden, Archive, and System. The System attribute is usually applie only to operating system boot files.

NTFS Permissions and Folders

NTFS Folder permissions allow what access is granted to a folder and the files and subfolders within that folder. These permissions can be assigned to a user or group. This topic defines each NTFS folder permission and its effect on a folder. Table 16.2 displays a list of the NTFS file permissions and the access that is granted to a user or group when each permission is applied.

Notice that the only major difference between NTFS file and folder permissions is the List Folder Contents NTFS folder permission. By using this NTFS folder permission you can limit the user's ability to browse through a tree of folders and files. This is useful when trying to secure a specific directory such as an application directory. A user must know the name and location of a file to read or execute it when this permission is applied to its parent folder.

Table 16.2	NTFS Folder Permissions
NTFS File Permission	**Allowed Access**
Read	This allows the user or group to view the files, folders, and subfolders of the parent folder. It also allows the viewing of folder ownership, permissions, and attributes of that folder.
Write	This allows the user or group to create new files and folders within the parent folder as well as view folder ownership and permissions and change the folder attributes.
List Folder Contents	This allows the user or group to view the files and subfolders contained within the folder.
Read & Execute	This allows the user or group to navigate through all files and subfolders including perform all actions allowed by the Read and List Folder Contents permissions.
Modify	This allows the user to delete the folder and perform all activities included in the Write and Read & Execute NTFS folder permissions.
Full Control	This allows the user or group to change permissions on the folder, take ownership of it, and perform all activities included in all other permissions.

Understanding the Access Control List (ACL)

Everyone who is familiar with Microsoft Windows NT 4.0 will find here a big change for the better. The ACLs or Access Control Lists of the past were written and assigned to a user once a successful Windows NT domain login had been established. The operating system would summarize the user's allowed access in an ACL. When a user in Microsoft Windows NT 4.0 tried to access a file or folder, the operating system would look at the user's ACL and determine whether the user was allowed access. One aspect of this feature turned out to be a huge drawback for everyday user access. If a user called the helpdesk or any other support person to gain access to a file or folder and that person made the appropriate change to the permissions, the user would have to log off and log back on. This is because the ACL in Microsoft Windows NT 4.0 was created only after a successful logon. As you will find out, Windows 2000 has made a change in how ACLs work and how users use them.

NTFS 5.0 in Windows 2000 stores an ACL with every file and folder on the NTFS partition or volume. The ACL includes all the users and groups that have access to the file or folder. In addition, it indicates what access or specifically what permissions each user or group is allowed to that file or folder. Then, whenever a user makes an attempt to access a file or folder on an NTFS partition or volume, the ACL checks for an ACE (Access Control Entry) for that user account. The ACE will indicate what permissions are allowed for that user account. The user is granted access to that file or folder, provided that the access requested is defined within the ACE. In other words, when user wants to read a file, the Access Control Entry is checked in that file's Access Control List. If the Access Control Entry for that user contains the Read permission, the user is granted access to read that file.

If a user does not have an ACE in the ACL of the file that he or she wants to access is denied.

Consider the same user/helpdesk situation discussed earlier. When the support person makes the change to the permissions on the file the user needs access to, the change is immediately saved in that file's ACL. The user can then access the file without having to log out and back in.

This is only the case when assigning permissions to users for file or folder resources. When a user is added to a group to gain access to additional resources or otherwise, the user must log out and back in to access those resources. That is because NTFS permissions granted to groups are read in a different manner. For a more in-depth look at groups and group policies see Chapter 14, "Group Policy" and Chapter 15, "Managing Disks."

Applying Multiple NTFS Permissions

Multiple permissions can be assigned to a single user account. They can be assigned to the user account directly or to a group the user account is a member of. When multiple permissions are assigned to a user account, unexpected things can happen. To prevent any heartache we are going to discuss the rules and regulations for assigning multiple NTFS permissions to a single user or group. This will include how file and folder permissions work together, and how denying a specific permission can affect a user's allowed access.

First of all, NTFS permissions are cumulative. This means that a user's effective permissions are the result of combining the user's assigned permissions and the permissions assigned to any groups that the user is a member of. For instance, if a user is assigned Read access to a specific file, and a group that the user account is a member of has the Write permissions assigned, the user is allowed the Read and Write NTFS permission to that file.

FILE PERMISSIONS OVERRIDE FOLDER PERMISSIONS

NTFS file permissions override or take priority over NTFS folder permissions. A user account having access to a file can access that file even though it does not have access to the parent folder of that file. However, a user would not be able to do so via the folder, because that requires the "List Folders Contents" permission. When the user makes the attempt to access the file, he or she must supply the full path to it. The full path can either be the logical file path (F:\MyFolder\MyFile.txt) or use the Universal Naming Convention (UNC). To access the file via UNC the user must supply the server name, share, directory, and file, for example:

\\MYSERVER\Win2kShare\MyFolder\MyFile.txt

If the user has access to the file but does not have an NTFS folder permission to browse for that file, the file will be invisible to the user and he or she must supply the full path to access it.

DENY OVERRIDES ALL OTHER PERMISSIONS

The concept of permission denial has not changed through the evolution of the Microsoft Windows operating systems and NTFS. **If a user is denied an NTFS permission for a file, any other instance where that permission has been allowed will be negated**. Microsoft does not, nor do I, recommend using permission denial to control access to a resource—for one main reason. For instance, if a user has access to a file or folder as being a member of a group, denying permission to that user stops all other permissions that the user might have to the file or folder. This can be very hard to troubleshoot on a large network with thousands of users and groups.

This is another example of how multiple NTFS file and folder permissions are cumulative and what happens to the user's effective permissions. For an example of Deny overriding all other NTFS permissions look at Figure 16.1.

In Figure 16.1, User A is a member of Group 1 and Group 2, where he is granted access to Folder A. Group 1 allows access to Folder A and both of the files within that folder. Group 2, on the other hand, denies access to a specific file, File 1. When a user account is denied access to a file or folder, all other permissions granting that user access to that file or folder are negated. Figure 16.1 shows that User A's combined access to File 1 is no access at all.

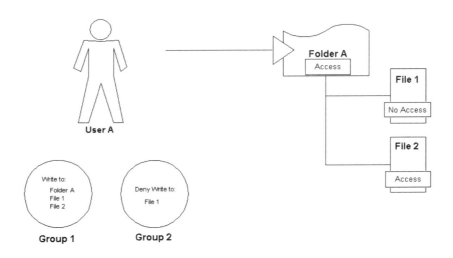

Figure 16–1 *Deny permission overrides all other permissions.*

Understanding Inherited NTFS Permission

By default, when NTFS permissions are assigned to a parent folder, all of the same permissions are applied or propagated to the subfolders and files of that parent folder. Alternatively, the automatic propagation of these permissions can be stopped. An example of NTFS permission inheritance is shown in Figure 16.2.

Subfolders and files inherit NTFS permissions from their parent folder. As the Windows 2000 administrator you assign NTFS permissions to a folder. All current subfolders and files with that folder inherit those same permissions. In addition, any new files or subfolders created within that parent folder assume the same NTFS permission of that parent folder.

You can prevent NTFS permission inheritance, so that any file and subfolders in a parent folder will not assume the same NTFS permissions of their parent folder. Now here is the tricky part. The directory or folder level in which you decide to prevent the default NTFS permission inheritance becomes the new parent folder for NTFS permission inheritance.

Using NTFS Permissions

This discussion is about using NTFS permissions. The topics include planning and working with NTFS permissions. The discussion will give guidelines to use when planning NTFS permission on a Windows 2000 network and will explain the step-by-step process for assigning such permission.

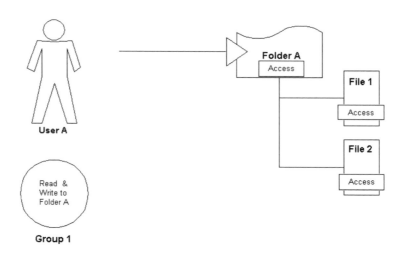

Figure 16-2   *NTFS permission inheritance.*

Planning NTFS Permissions

A Windows 2000 network should be well thought out and planned for. The first thing that comes to mind is the Active Directory and Windows 2000 domain infrastructure. This is very important, but a plan for NTFS permissions should also be thought out way in advance before a Windows 2000 network is implemented.

Having a plan for NTFS permissions on your Windows 2000 network will save time and money for your organization. You will also find that a network with well-planned NTFS permissions is that much easier to manage. Use the following guidelines to help you plan NTFS permissions on your Windows 2000 network. Notice that some steps are not directly related to NTFS permissions themselves, but they help organize the data on your network. This makes it easier for you to manage the resources on your Windows 2000 network and make sure those resources are secure.

1. The data on your Windows 2000 network needs to be organized into manageable units. Separate the users' home directories from applications and public data. Try to keep data in centralized units. For instance, group all of the home directories into one folder and place them on an NTFS volume away from other data. By doing this you gain benefits such as not having to assign NTFS permissions to files, but only to the grouped folders. In addition, backup strategies become less complex. Now application files are grouped separately and do not have to be backed up with the home directories. Organizing your data can make many things easier to manage, including assigning NTFS permissions.

2. Assign a user only the level of access that is required. If a user needs only to read a file, grant only the Read permission to the resource that they require access to. This precludes the possibility of a user damaging a file, such as modifying an important document or even deleting it.

3. When a group of users require the same access to a resource, create a group for those users and make each a member of that new group. Assign the NTFS permissions required to that resource to the newly created group. If at all possible avoid assigning NTFS permissions to users and only assign them to groups.

4. When assigning permissions to folders with working data, use the Read & Execute NTFS folder permission. This should be assigned to a group containing the users that need to access this folder and to the Administrators group. This will allow the users to work with the data, but will also prevent them from deleting any important files in the folder.

5. When assigning NTFS permissions to a public data folder, use the following criteria as a guideline. Assign the Read & Execute and Write NTFS permissions to the group containing the users that need access to the public data folder. The Creator Owner of the folder should be assigned the Full Control NTFS permission. Any user on the network that creates a file, including one in a public data folder, is by default the Creator Owner of that file. After that file has been created, the Windows 2000 administrator can grant NTFS permissions to other users for file ownership. If the Read & Execute and the Write NTFS permissions are assigned to a group of users that needs access to the public data folder, they have Full Control to all files that they create in the public data folder and can modify and execute files created by other users.

6. If at all possible do not deny NTFS permission to a group or user. This is not a recommended way to manage resources on a Windows 2000 network, because only NTFS permissions assigned for that resource elsewhere for the user or group are automatically stopped. This can cause a great deal of time and frustration in troubleshooting permission problems.

7. User education is always a good idea. If users have a basic understanding of the NTFS permissions and how to secure resources on a network, they can assign and manage their own files. Unfortunately, user education does take a bit of time and money, but if done successfully it will pay off in the end.

This is it for the NTFS permission guidelines. When planning how to organize your data on a Windows 2000 network, remember to consider NTFS permissions and how they will be affected. Every business and organization is different, but if most of these simple guidelines can be followed, managing your resources in a secure environment will be that much easier. And remember that Total Cost of Ownership is the name of the game.

Working with NTFS Permissions

After a newly created volume is formatted with the NTFS 5.0 file system in Windows 2000, by default the Full Control NTFS permission is granted to the Everyone group. This, of course, should be changed as soon as possible. The reason is that allowing Everyone full control means just that, *everyone*. That includes guests, if the Guest account is enabled, and even anonymous Internet users, if security settings on the firewall are such that they can access files on that server. By default, even though you are running NTFS, no security at all is applied. The approved NTFS permission plan should be implemented immediately. If an NTFS permission plan does not exist yet, at lease change the access for the Everyone group from Full Control to Read. Then you can assign the appropriate NTFS permissions to users as they are needed.

Now let's look into working with NTFS permissions and how to assign them. Let's start by looking at Figure 16.3.

Figure 16.3 displays the Security tab in the folder Properties dialog box.

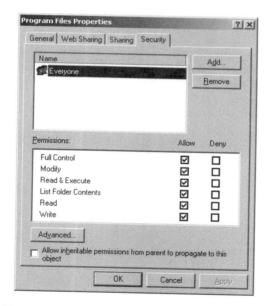

This is the Security tab on the Properties dialog box for a folder.

To get to this tab take the following steps:

1. On your Windows 2000 desktop, right-click My Computer.
2. Click Explore. This will start the Windows Explorer.
3. Click the plus sign to the left of an NTFS volume that you would like to view.

4. Find a folder and right-click on that folder.
5. Click the Properties option on the list.
6. Now use Alt-Tab to switch to the Securities tab, or select it by clicking on it.

When viewing the Securities tab from the Properties dialog box of a file, the List Folder Contents NTFS permission is not listed in th Permissions list box.

Now that we are all on the same page, let's look at the options available to us on the security tab. Table 16.3 lists the options available on the Securities tab and describes briefly what they are used for.

Table 16.3	Securities Tab Options
Options	**Descriptions**
Name	The name list box displays a list of the users that currently have access to the selected resource. You can highlight an object in the list and either change that object's current NTFS permission or select Remove to remove it from the list.
Permissions	In the Permissions list box is a list of all the NTFS permissions. To allow or deny a NTFS permission to the object selected in the Name list box click the appropriate check box.
Add	By clicking the Add command button, the Select Users, Computers, or Groups dialog box opens. This is where you can select what objects to add to the Names list box.
Remove	You can remove objects in the Names list box by selecting an object and then clicking Remove.

For the purposes of this discussion we are going to skip the Advanced command button and what it does. That will be covered when we discuss the next topic, Using Special Access Permissions. The only other option on the Securities tab check box to allow inheritable permissions from parent to propagate to this object. By default when a folder is created on a NTFS volume this option is set. To turn it off, open the Securities tab and clear the check box. Figure 16.4 displays the message box that is displayed.

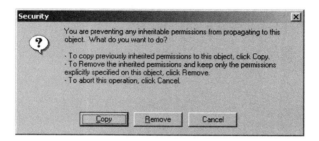

Figure 16–4   *Security warning message box.*

Using Special Access Permissions

NTFS file and folder permissions for the most part are a sufficient way to secure your resources on a Windows 2000 network. Where they do not provide the level of granularity required, you can use Special Access Permissions.

Defining Special Access Permissions

There are fourteen Special Access Permissions, and they provide the finite level of security to resources on a Windows 2000 network that some administrators require. I will use three tables to explain the Special Access Permissions and how they relate to NTFS file and folder permissions. Table 16.4 lists the Special Access Permissions and provides a description of the kind of access they allow or deny

Some of the Special Access Permissions have two parts, as shown in Table 16.4. The first applies to folders and the second only to files. Remember this when referring to these tables.

Now let's look at how these new special access permissions are related to the standard NTFS file permissions. Table 16.5 displays a cross-reference chart of NTFS file permissions and special access permissions. You will see that each

Table 16.4	Special Access Permissions
Permission	**Description**
Traverse Folder/Execute File	This allows or denies a user to browse through a folder's subfolders and files where he would otherwise not have access. In addition, it allows or denies the user the ability to run programs within that folder.
List Folder/Read Data	This allows or denies the user to view subfolders and fill names in the parent folder. In addition, it allows or denies the user to view the data within the files in the parent folder or subfolders of that parent.
Read Attributes	This allows or denies a user to view the standard NTFS attributes of a file or folder.
Read Extended Attributes	This allows or denies the user to view the extended attributes of a file or folder, which can vary due to the fact that they are defined by the programs themselves.
Create Files/Write Data	This allows or denies the user the right to create new files in the parent folder. In addition, it allows or denies the user to modify or overwrite existing data in a file.
Create Folders/Append Data	This allows or denies the user to create new folders in the parent folder. In addition, it allows or denies the user the right to add data to the end of files. This does not include making changes to any existing data within a file.
Write Attributes	This allows or denies the ability to change the attributes of a file or folder, such as Read-Only and Hidden.

Table 16.4	Special Access Permissions (Continued)
Write Extended Attributes	This allows or denies a user the ability to change the extended attributes of a file or folder. These attributes are defined by programs and may vary.
Delete Subfolders and Files	This allows or denies the deleting of files and subfolder within the parent folder. It also is true that if this permission is assigned, files and subfolders can be deleted even if the Delete special access permission has not been granted.
Delete	This allows or denies the deleting of files and folders. If the user does not have this permission assigned but does have the Delete Subfolders and Files permission, she can still delete.
Read Permissions	This allows or denies the user the ability to read the standard NTFS permissions of a file or folder.
Change Permissions	This allows or denies the user the ability to change the standard NTFS permissions of a file or folder.
Take Ownership	This allows or denies a user the ability to take ownership of a file or folder. The owner of a file or folder can change the permissions on the files and folders she owns, regardless of any other permission that might be in place.
Synchronize	This allows or denies different threads to wait on the handle for the file or folder and synchronize with another thread that may signal it. This permission applies to only multithreaded, multiprocessing programs.

of the standard NTFS file permissions is actually a group made up of special access permissions. Notice also how the Write NTFS permission is made up of six special access permissions. The Write NTFS permission is actually made up of the Create Files/Write Data, Create Folders/Append Data, Write Attributes,

Write Extended Attributes, Read Permissions, and Synchronize special access permissions.

You will find that having these reference tables will be very helpful when deciding which special access permissions to use in your organization.

Table 16.5	Special Access Permissions and NTFS File Permissions				
Special Permission	**Full Control**	**Modify**	**Read & Execute**	**Read**	**Write**
Traverse Folder/ Execute File	X	X	X		
List Folder/Read Data	X	X	X	X	
Read Attributes	X	X	X	X	
Read Extended Attributes	X	X	X	X	
Create Files/Write Data	X	X			X
Create Folders/Append Data	X	X			X
Write Attributes	X	X			X
Write Extended Attributes	X	X			X
Delete Subfolders and Files	X				
Delete	X	X			
Read Permissions	X	X	X	X	X
Change Permissions	X				
Take Ownership	X				
Synchronize	X	X	X	X	X

Table 16.6 displays the same list of special access permissions but shows how they interrelate to the NTFS folder permissions.

Table 16.6			Special Access Permissions and NTFS Folder Permissions			
Special Permission	**Full Control**	**Modify**	**Read & Execute**	**List Folder Contents**	**Read**	**Write**
Traverse Folder/ Execute File	X	X	X	X		
List Folder/Read Data	X	X	X	X	X	
Read Attributes	X	X	X	X	X	
Read Extended Attributes	X	X	X	X	X	
Create Files/Write Data	X	X				X
Create Folders/Append Data	X	X				X
Write Attributes	X	X				X
Write Extended Attributes	X	X				X
Delete Subfolders and Files	X					
Delete	X	X				
Read Permissions	X	X	X	X	X	X
Change Permissions	X					
Take Ownership	X					
Synchronize	X	X	X	X	X	X

CHANGE PERMISSIONS

Two of the special access permissions are particularly useful in application. We discuss here the first one, the Change Permissions special access permission.

When using special access permissions it is no longer necessary to assign a user or Windows 2000 administrator the Full Control NTFS permission so that they have the allowed right to change permissions. Using the Change Permissions special access permission, a user or Windows 2000 administrator can change permissions to a file or folder. However, they do not have access to delete any files or subfolders. That way the user or Windows 2000 administrator can control the access to the data but not delete any of the data itself.

TAKE OWNERSHIP

The second particularly useful special access permission is Take Ownership.

All files and folders on a nNTFS volume have an owner. By default, the owner is the person installing the volume and formatting it with the NTFS file system. This is usually a Windows 2000 Administrator. File and folder ownership can be transferred to another user or group. You can grant a user account or a user group the ability to take ownership of a file or folder. As an administrator, you have the ability to take control of any files or folders on the NTFS volume.

Two hard-and-fast rules apply here. Remember these when thinking about granting someone the ability to take ownership of a file or folder.

1. The owner of a file or folder or any user with the Full Control NTFS permission to a file or folder can assign the Full Control standard NTFS permission or the Take Ownership special access permission, which allows taking control of that file or folder. For instance, if User A has the Full Control standard NTFS permission to *D:\Apps* and assigns the Take Ownership special access permission to User A, User A can now take ownership of any files or folders in *D:\Apps*.

2. A Windows 2000 administrator can take ownership of a file or folder at any time. This is one of the inherited rights that administrators have. Administrators can then assign the Take Ownership special access permission to another user or group, so that they can take control of the files and folders in a parent folder. For instance, if User A leaves the organization for another position, a Windows 2000 administrator can assign the Take Ownership special access permission to the former employee's manager for the former employee's files and folders. The manager can then take ownership of those files and folders.

 The Take Ownership special access permission can be assigned to a user account or group. The receiving user account or group can then take ownership of the respected resources. You cannot, however, give ownership of a file or folder to a user account or group.

Using Special Access Permissions

Special access permissions provide a more finite level of security than the standard NTFS permissions. We suggest learning how to use them in your own environment. This subtopic will give you a quick glance at how to assign special access permissions to an NTFS volume.

To set special access permissions to a folder take the following steps:

1. On your Windows 2000 desktop, right-click My Computer.
2. Click Explore. This will start the Windows Explorer.
3. Click the plus sign to the left of an NTFS volume that you would like to view.
4. Find a folder and right-click on that folder.
5. Click the Properties option on the list.
6. Use Alt-Tab to switch to the Securities tab, or select it by clicking on it.

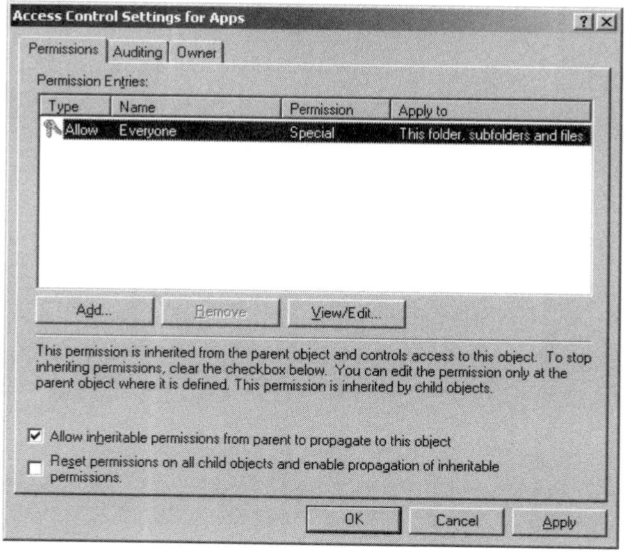

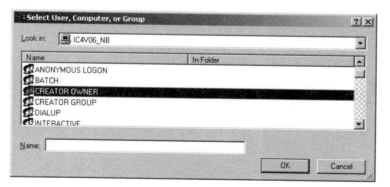

Figure 16–5   *Access Control properties dialog box.*

7. Now click Advanced to view the Access Control properties dialog box, as shown in Figure 16.5.
8. Now click on Add.
9. This opens up the Select User, Compute, or Group dialog box, as shown in Figure 16.6.

Figure 16–6   *Select User, Computer, or Group dialog box.*

10. After you select the object that you would like to add the special access permissions to, click OK.
11. This displays the Permission Entry dialog box, as shown in Figure 16.7.

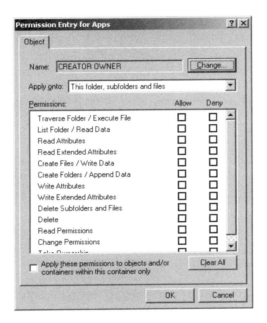

Figure 16-7   *Permission Entry dialog box.*

Now we see that all of the special access permissions are listed in the permissions list box. This is where all special access permission are assigned and denied. Let's discuss the options for a moment. Table 16.7 lists the options and their descriptions.

Table 16.7	Option in the Permissions Entry Dialog Box
Permission	**Description**
Name	This is the user account or group name that will be affected by the special access permissions. Clicking on the Change command button can change the user account or group affected.
Apply onto	This dropdown list box lists the level of the folder hierarchy at which the special access permissions being assigned will be applied.
Permissions	This is a list of all the special access permissions. To allow a special access permission click the check box in the Allow column to the right of the permission. In addition, to deny a special access permission click the check box in the Deny column to the right of the special access permission.
Apply these permissions to objects and/or containers within this container only	This allows or denies permission inheritance for the parent folder. To allow permission inheritance for the special access permissions being assigned select this check box, otherwise clear the check box.
Clear All	This clears all of the check boxes in the Allow and Deny columns in the permissions list box.

Taking Ownership of Secure Resources

A Windows 2000 administrator working with NTFS file and folder permissions should know how to take ownership of a resource. This doesn't mean walking down to the local parts shop and picking up a new hard disk. I am talking about using the Take Ownership special access permission.

To take control of a file or folder the user or group member must have the Take Ownership permission assigned to them for that file or folder. Then they must explicitly take ownership of that file or folder. The following is a list of the steps that you would take:

1. On your Windows 2000 desktop, right-click My Computer.
2. Click Explore. This will start the Windows Explorer.

3. Click the plus sign to the left of an NTFS volume that you would like to view.
4. Find a folder and right-click on that folder.
5. Click the Properties option on the list.
6. Use <Alt><Tab> to switch to the Securities tab, or select it by clicking on it.
7. Click Advanced to view the Access Control Settings dialog box.
8. In the Access Control Settings dialog box use <Alt><Tab> to switch to the Owner tab, or select it by clicking on it.
9. Select your name in the Change owner to list box. This specifies that you are going to take ownership of the resource.
10. Check the Replace owners on subcontainers and objects check box, and click OK.

That is all for special access permissions and how they relate to the standard NTFS permissions. Now you can assign NTFS permissions with ease on your Windows 2000 network, confident that you have the knowledge to do so.

Copying and Moving Data

Copying and moving data is something that every administrator does, usually on a pretty frequent basis. When copying files and folders with NTFS permissions assigned to them you need to follow certain guidelines. The NTFS permissions sometimes change as the file and folders are moved or copied. It is important to know these guidelines before you start shuffling data around your Windows 2000 network. This discussion outlines these rules and explains what happens to the NTFS permissions when files and folders are moved or copied.

Copying Files and Folders

When files and folders on a NTFS volume are copied to another volume, the permissions change. For instance, if you copy a file from one NTFS volume to another NTFS volume, the following things happen if the right criteria are met.

• The receiving NTFS volume treats the file as a new file. Like any new file, it gains the permissions of the folder it is created in.
• The user account used to copy the file must have the Write NTFS permission in the destination folder on the receiving volume.
• The user account used to copy the file becomes the Creator Owner of that file.

This means that any permissions assigned to that file before it is copied are lost during the copy itself. If you want to keep those same permissions, they will have to be reassigned at the destination folder.

When files and folders are copied from an NTFS volume to a FAT partition, the permissions are lost. This happens because FAT partitions do not support NTFS permissions.

Moving Files and Folders

When files or folders are copied from an NTFS volume, the permissions change. Now when files or folders are moved from an NTFS volume, the permissions might or might not change. This depends entirely on where the destination folder lies. We can safely assume that when files or folders are moved to a FAT partition, the permissions are lost. That is correct, and for the same reason that NTFS permissions are lost when copying files and folders from a NTFS volume to a FAT partition. There are in fact two other cases worth pointing out when moving files and folders from an NTFS volume: moving files and folders within a NTFS volume and moving files and folders to another separate NTFS volume.

When moving files and folders within a single NTFS volume, these rules are followed:

1. The files and folders keep the original permissions assigned to them.
2. The user account moving the files and folders must have the Write NTFS permission to the destination folder.
3. The user account moving the file must have either the Modify standard NTFS permission or the Delete special access permission assigned. This is because during a file or folder move, the files and folders are deleted from the source directory after they have been copied to the destination folder.
4. The user account used to move the files and folders becomes the Creator Owner of those files and folders.

When moving files and folders from one NTFS volume to a separate NTFS volume, these are the rules followed:

1. The files and folders being moved inherit the permissions of the destination folder. For example, if you move a file from a folder that has Everyone with Read permission into a folder on another partition that has permissions only allowing Domain Admins Read access, the file will now carry the latter security settings.
2. The user account moving the files and folders must have the Write NTFS permission to the destination folder, since a move is really a combination copy/delete.
3. The user account moving the file must have either the Modify standard NTFS permission or the Delete special access permission assigned. This is because during a file or folder move, the files and folders are deleted from the source directory after they have been copied to the destination folder.
4. The user account used to move the files and folders becomes the Creator Owner of those files and folders.

Troubleshooting Permissions Problems

The number one goal of a Windows 2000 administrator should be making sure that resources are always available to the users. This includes many things, but we're talking here about the secure data on the network. If users cannot access the data they need to do their jobs, production slows. Now your boss is breathing down your neck, asking why the users can't get to their data, and how long will it take for you to fix the NTFS permission problem. This discussion will lay down some rules on NTFS permission problems. The topics include avoiding NTFS permission problems and troubleshooting NTFS permission problems.

Avoiding NTFS Permission Problems

Avoiding permission problems involves following some basic guidelines. Below is a list of do's and don'ts when assigning NTFS permissions on a NTFS 5.0 file system. Use this list as a reference when assigning NTFS permissions on your Windows 2000 network.

- When assigning NTFS permissions, try to assign only enough access for a user or group of users to perform their job.
- Try not to assign any NTFS permissions at the file level. This increases the complexity of managing the permissions. Assign the NTFS permissions at the folder level only. If several files require the same access, move them to a common folder and assign the permissions to that folder.
- Application executables should have Read & Execute and Change assigned to the Administrators group. The Users group, on the other hand, should have only Read & Execute. This will prevent users or a virus from modifying the files. When an administrator wants to update the application executables, he or she can temporarily assign himself or herself Full Control to perform the task.
- Assign Full Control to the Creator Owner of public folders and the Read and Write NTFS permissions to the Everyone group. This way users have full access to the files that they create, but the members of the Everyone group can only read and create files in the folder.
- Try not to deny any NTFS permissions. If you have to do this to a user or group, document it well and state that this is a special case. Instead of denying access to a resource by denying NTFS permissions, don't assign the permissions to gain access.

Troubleshooting NTFS Permissions

This topic is designed to help you troubleshoot the most common NTFS permission problems. Table 16.8 lists the most common ones and their solutions.

Table 16.8	Common NTFS Permission Problems and Solutions
Problem	**Solution**
A user or group cannot access a file or folder.	Check the permissions assigned to the user or group. Permissions may not be assigned for the selected resource, or permission could be denied. In addition, the permissions could have been changed if the file or folder has been copied or moved.
The administrator assigns access to a group for a selected file or folder, but the users of that group still cannot access the file or folder.	Ask the user to log off and then log back on. When the user logs back on, his NTFS permission are updated to include the new group that they were added to. Another way to update a user's permissions is to ask them to disconnect the network drive on which the file or folder resides and then reconnect it. This forces the permissions to update on the reconnect of the network drive.
A user with Full Control to a file has deleted some files in a folder, and you want to prevent them from doing it again.	Open the Permission Entry box for that folder and remove the Delete Subfolders and Files special access permission for that user.

With a little perseverance any NTFS permission problem can be solved, and I hope that this table provides a starting point for the resolution.

Chapter Summary

We have discussed the many faces of NT File System (NTFS) permissions being utilized on a Windows 2000 network. Now we know that the standard file system for Windows 2000 is NTFS 5.0, and that NTFS permissions can be assigned only on an NTFS formatted volume.

We learned the effects of assigning multiple permissions to a single resource and how to use permission inheritance effectively. For administrators in need of a more granular level of security on file and folder resources, we now know that special access permissions are available. When possible, permissions should be applied at the folder level rather than the file level for ease of administration. Also, it is important to remember that a permission of No Access will always override any other permissions assigned. Use this setting sparingly; it is usually better to simply omit a user account from the Access Control Lists (ACL) than to explicitly list the account with No Access specified.

The tables in this chapter can be used for reference while assigning NTFS permission.

Shared Folders

*T*here can be two conflicting goals for the data on your network. First, users want the data to be freely available. It should be as easy to retrieve and save data as if all the data existed on their local computers. On the other hand, from a system administrator's perspective, data needs to secure. This means it is far better if data exists on network servers, rather than local hard disks. This server could be in the same building as the users, or on the other side of the globe. The actual location will depend upon many things, such as capacity, security, and load balancing requirements.

If data is going to exist on a network, then it needs to be secure. This can also introduce some conflict for system administrators. How do you make data freely available, yet lock it down to protect it against unauthorized users? Part of the answer this problem was discussed in the preceding chapter. By using NTFS permissions it is possible to secure data. But we are left with the problem of making this data available, in a generic way, to our user community.

The answer to this problem is "shared folders." Otherwise, the only way to access data stored in a folder is to physically sit at the computer where the data is stored. Obviously this is not practical. Essentially, by sharing a folder you are publishing the availability of the data to your network. However, that does not mean anyone can access the share. By setting share permissions you can prevent unauthorized users from accessing the data in a shared folder. What's more, you can break your user community into different groups, allowing some people to perform a specific task while denying that task to others. For instance, perhaps one set of users can read the data in a shared folder, while a separate group can write data into the folder.

In this chapter, we will talk about shared folders at various levels from the most basic—sharing a folder for everyone's use—to one more complex, when you want data to be available but only in a restricted fashion. We will also discuss what constitutes "data" in this context. There are many different types of data; the NTFS permissions you will want to apply to each type will vary.

Even if you are familiar with shared folders, it is a good idea to read through this chapter. There are some new features of Windows 2000 that help you design and implement shared folders in your enterprise. Let's take a closer look.

Introduction to Shared Folders

Shared folders are the only way to make files and folders that exist on your network available to your users. When a folder is shared, your users can connect to the share and access the files and folders that exist there. The default behavior is to allow everyone to have access to the new share. However, it is possible to further restrict access through NTFS permissions.

A shared folder contains data that users need access to. But what constitutes "data" in this context? Folders can contain user files, such as word processing documents; they can also contain application files, or database data. There are other types of folders that are shared, known as home folders. Home folders are used to store users' personal data. These were discussed in Chapter 13.

The system administrator (you) will have to create the shared folders and then secure them with NTFS permissions. Here are some things you will need to consider when performing this task:

• There are two types of permissions, shared folder permissions and file permissions. We are concerned here with the former. Shared folder permissions are applied to a folder and affect all files and subfolders beneath the folder; they offer fewer options and are therefore less secure than file-level permissions. File permissions allow you a far greater degree of granularity. With this granularity comes additional complexity. It can be time consuming to apply permissions at the file level, and troubleshooting can be difficult. Intelligent design decisions when creating shared folders should minimize the number of file permissions that exist within a shared folder.

• The default permission for a share is Full Control to the Everyone group. In effect this allows just about anyone to access the share and save data to the share. Because of this, it is probably not a good idea to leave the default permissions in place in your enterprise. At the very least you will want to review them before you create a share.

• The file system you have installed has an effect on your security model. If you are creating a share on a File Access Table (FAT) partition, then you will not be able to use file permissions, even if you want to. For FAT partitions, folder permissions are the only way to secure the folder and its underlying data.

This is an important design decision and should be considered before the folder is shared.

• Shared folder permissions only affect users that are accessing the share across a network. They do nothing to secure the physical folder at the server. That is to say, while a user may be denied access to a shared folder through folder permissions, it is possible that they could log on to the server that stores the folder and access it locally. The folder permissions are not applied, and therefore the user will not be restricted. If this is going to be an issue, consider file-level permissions.

Keeping this set of rules in mind, you can begin to think about how shared folders should be implemented on your network. Let's take a look at different types of permission that can be assigned at the shared folder level. Don't be surprised when you find there are far fewer permissions available at this level than at the file level. The requirement for shared folders is far smaller.

Shared Folder Permissions

Before you can begin to fully consider your security requirements, you have to know which permissions are available to you. Three sets of permissions can be set at the shared folder level. We will define these in a moment. After we have done that, we need to explain how these permissions interact with file permissions, and how users are affected when permissions have been set at the group level and there are conflicting permissions.

The three sets of permissions that can be set at the shared folder level are defined in Table 17.1. These permissions can be either "Allowed" or "Denied"; this gives you flexibility to specifically deny a set of users a permission within a share. Don't forget, by default the Everyone group has full control. If you have not taken this permission away, you will likely want to deny users certain permissions.

As you can see, working from the top to bottom, you have a range from the most restrictive access to the least restrictive. You are going to want to make permissions as simple to implement and maintain as possible. To this end, we suggest that you limit the number of permissions you assign.

For example, if you have a shared folder that will be accessed by a thousand users, it is far more difficult to assign permissions at the user level. This will require a complex set of steps, and maintaining the list over time will be difficult. Instead, apply permissions to groups. In our example you would create a group within Active Directory and assign the users as members of this group. Then set folder permissions at the group level.

It might seem strange, but it is far better to allow permissions than to deny permissions. Often it is easier to restrict access to a shared folder through intelligent use of groups rather than to create a long list of users who are

Table 17.1	Shared Folder Permissions
Permission	**Allows**
Read	This allows the user to read information in this shared folder. With this permission the user will be able to display subfolder names, to change those subfolders, and to view file names and attributes.
Change	With the change permission a user (or group of users) will be able to write data into the shared folder. This includes creating new files and folders, appending data to data folders stored within the folder, and changing file attributes. It also encompasses all of the permissions assigned by the Read permission.
Full Control	This can be thought of as administrative access. Full Control allows the user (or group of users) to change file permissions. They will also be able to take ownership of a file. In addition, it also bestows all permissions assigned through the Change permission. By default the Everyone group is given Full Control to a new share.

denied access to a shared folder. The deny option (you will see this in a hands-on example in a moment) should only be applied if you are having difficulty excluding a user or group of users. An example would be the Everyone group. If everyone on your network, except five users, were to be allowed access to a shared folder, it would probably be wise to assign sufficient permissions to the Everyone group, and then deny access to the users in question. We will discuss the interaction of permissions in a moment.

There are two times when a user is denied access to a shared folder. First, if they are not personally assigned permissions, and if they are not members of a group that has been assigned permissions, then they are denied access. Second, if they have been specifically denied, either individually or as part of a group, they are also denied access.

Permission Interactions

It's all very well knowing the types and levels of permissions that can be assigned to a shared folder, but what happens when there is a conflict? For instance, what happens when a user is a member of two groups, and one group have been assigned permissions and the other has been denied? At the most basic level, a denied permission will override an allowed permission. So, in our example here, the user would be denied access.

The term most commonly used to explain this concept is *effective permissions*. The effective permissions for a user is the sum of their permissions, allowing for the set of rules as explained a moment ago.

The calculation of effective permissions can occur when a user has been assigned individual permissions (user level) and at the same time is a member of a group that has also been assigned permissions. This is almost certain to occur in a large enterprise. To minimize this you need to make sure that you add groups and users to shares only when they absolutely require access and that you keep on top of the groups that exist.

As you have seen, if a user has been allowed access to a share and also denied access, the end result is that the user will *not* be able to access the share. This is "most restrictive" practice. It helps to make sure that the overriding need to protect data through a denial is always applied. So what happens if a user has been assigned both Read permission through one group and Change permission through another? In this case the user would enjoy Change permission. This is because Change permission is the cumulative of all permissions granted (don't forget, change permission allows a set of permissions with the addition of Read permission—refer to Table 17.1 for details).

This behavior assumes that where the user is supposed to have access to the share, the permission that grants the most access will take precedence. If you have a user that is a member of two groups, and those groups have been assigned Read and Change permissions, respectively, but you want a single member of the group to be restricted to Read only, then you have to deny the user Change permission. While this might be necessary, it is not a recommended practice. Things can soon become complex, and maintenance over time can become overwhelming.

Don't forget, the most powerful weapon you have is the Deny permission. No matter what happens, the Deny permission will always override an Allow. Even if a user has been assigned Full Control through membership in a group, a single entry denying such a permission will override it.

Now that we have a good understanding of shared folder permissions, it is time to add an additional level of complexity. Windows 2000 supports several different file system types. The two most prevalent are NTFS and FAT. FAT was introduced many years ago and was supported under DOS systems and early versions of Microsoft Windows. One of FAT's failings was its security model—or lack thereof. As we mentioned earlier, the only way to secure a shared folder on a FAT volume is through Shared folder permissions. You are pretty well versed in how that works now. NTFS, on the other hand, is more complex.

NTFS permissions are in effect no matter what you do with the file system. Put another way, assigning shared folder permissions without applying underlying NTFS permissions will not get you the desired result. It is important to remember this as you create shared folders. When a user logs on locally to a server that stores the contents of a shared folder, shared folder permissions will no longer apply—however, NTFS file permissions will! We will be taking a closer look at strategies you can use to manage this process in the next section.

Before we discuss some best practices when working with shared folder permissions, we should talk about copying and moving shared folders. When a shared folder is copied from one location to another, the copy will not be shared. This is partly because you cannot have duplicate share names on a single server; it is also a good security feature. When a share is moved, then it will no longer be shared. Once again, this is a good security default.

Recommendations for Using Shared Folder Permissions

What follows is a set of guidelines you can use to design your shared folder permission strategy. It is always easier to write about such things in the abstract, so it might be that you are unable to achieve all the goals listed here. However, having a set of goals toward which you can aim will keep you on track.

The first thing you should do is document everything. As a system administrator you should know what each group on your network is for, and how it can be used. If groups are no longer required, they should be deleted. Document the groups on your network, and document all shared folders, along with the permissions you have set. This will make troubleshooting far easier. It will also help others who are new to your network understand how everything works. A truly great administrator has everything documented!

Try not to assign permissions at the user level. In large enterprises this can become very cumbersome, and it is very difficult to understand over time. Even in relatively small environments, it takes far more time to assign permissions to a hundred users individually than it does to assign the same permissions to a group. This will also aid your documentation process. It is easier to track a group than individual users. Always try to assign permissions to groups.

Never be tempted to give your users Full Control to a shared folder simply because it is "easiest." While this will work for many tasks, it is not a good idea to introduce the possibility for error. It is not necessarily a malicious user who deletes files or creates folders. Sometimes it is an uneducated user simply making a mistake. You can avoid this by assigning the most restrictive permissions only. For instance, if a group of users require Read permission only, don't be tempted to assign Full Control. While the latter includes the Read permission, it also opens up the opportunity for a security breach or user error.

Try to minimize the number of shares you create. While shared folders are relatively easy to use and understand, having a great number of them can be confusing for users and administrators alike. Try to group files and folders that require the same permissions together. For instance, if you have a set of applications that need to be read by sets of users, create a single share and then copy all the application files to it. Then you will be able to create a single share that gives access to all application folders. This is obviously easier than sharing each application folder and assigning permissions to each. We will discuss this topic in more detail in the next section.

Finally, use shared folder names that are intuitive for the user community (not to mention for administrators). In an ideal world you would be able to understand what a shared folder contains simply by the share name. Try to avoid generic share names such as "Files," "User stuff," or "Executables." Instead use descriptive names such as "Finance Data," "Home Folders," and "Applications."

However, keep in mind that there are some restrictions upon shared folder names. This is largely due to the need to support many operating systems. Some older operating systems (systems we hope you will soon be replacing with Windows 2000) cannot read long file names. Keep in mind that DOS, Windows 3.x, and Windows for Workgroups systems cannot read long file names. If you have to support these operating systems, then restrict your shared folder names to 8.3 notation. For all other Microsoft operating systems, including Windows 9x, Windows NT 4.0, and Windows 2000, a shared folder name can be a maximum of 12 characters long.

Shared Folder Strategies

We have been hinting about proper shared folder usage, and it's time that we became more specific. Shared folders should be planned on your network. This means that it is not a good idea to simply create them whenever a need arises. It is essential to put a process in place so all aspects of shared folder design can be considered.

There are two primary reasons for using shared folders. The first is ease of use for your user community. The more shared folders you create, the easier it is for something to get lost. Users are going to have a hard time keeping track of all the different folders and what they contain. Second, shared folders should aid in the centralization of administrative tasks. As you will see in a moment, intelligent planning can help you minimize the amount of time you spend administering shared data.

One of the first things you should ask yourself is—what data needs to be shared? Are there groups of data that have objectives in common? Is there a group of data that requires users to have the same permissions? For instance, it is a good idea to have a shared folder on your network so members of different departments can share data. You could create a share for each department, or you could create a single share and then store each department's folder beneath it. The latter option would, over time, require far less administrative maintenance, while the former could become quite complex and difficult to manage—not to mention the confusion a user might suffer if he moved from one department to another.

Centralizing data in shared folders also helps with disaster recovery. It is far easier to back up and restore data to a single location than it is to worry about many different locations spread across many different servers.

There are two primary types of information you will want to share, applications and data. The data portion could be users sharing files, or database files. Let's take a look at each of these and make some recommendations as to how they should be implemented.

Application Folders

If your organization is anything like the ones we have worked at, there are probably hundreds of different applications being installed on workstations. Organizations have gone from one extreme to the other as hardware prices and operating systems have evolved. Initially, applications were installed on a server and run from there. This was largely due to the extremely high cost of disk drives and the relatively slow performance of workstation hardware.

The advantage of this model was that administrators maintained complete control over the application. It was backed up, and enjoyed protection through RAID and other plans. The disadvantage was that performance could suffer (performance was governed somewhat by network bandwidth availability).

Then hardware became less expensive, and we started installing our applications locally on each computer. This gave us performance advantages, since we were no longer relying upon the network infrastructure to support our applications. However, it left us somewhat vulnerable to corrupt applications, and applications were rarely backed up.

Whatever model your business currently uses, it is a good idea to centralize applications on your network. Applications in this regard can be either the files your users execute to run an application, or the source files for the application that are used for installation purposes. The recommendations that follow will help you administer applications over time.

• Create a single shared folder, and store all applications beneath it. Since applications require the same shared permissions, this will save you time, and it is a perfect example of centralized management.

• Administrators require Full Control for administrative purposes. Usually, administrators are automatically granted sufficient permission to do this. However, this can be removed.

• Since you will only want the accounts that you created to have access to the applications share, the default share behavior is not ideal. Don't forget, the default behavior is for the Everyone group to have Full Control permissions.

The Everyone group contains all users who have access to the network, including accounts such as Guest. Instead, remove the Everyone group from the permission list and grant Read permission to the Users Built-in group.

• If you have assigned the administration of applications to someone other than an administrator, they will need to grant those users additional permissions. However, they are unlikely to require Full Control. Instead, grant the Change permission.

• Do not make any exceptions. If you have an application that does not fit into the model we have just described, simply create a second share and assign the necessary permissions to it. While it is our goal to minimize the number of shares we have to administer, it is not a good idea to compromise your security plan to accommodate a single application.

Data Folders

The second type of share that you will need is a data share. A data share is used for user data, which in this context could be data such as a user's word processing documents. Alternatively, you might be using a share simply to share data across geographic boundaries—in other words, as a depository. Depending on which of these you choose, you might want to try a slightly different approach. As always, it is a balance between being as tight as you can on security, while allowing your user community to have just the right amount of permissions to get their job done.

USER'S DATA FOLDERS

In the case of shared folders where your users are storing their own files, the following recommendations should be applied:

• You should strive to keep all user data within the same shared folder structure. This aids in backups and system management. However, in this case you will have a little more work to do. We suggest that you create a single folder to contain your users' data. Beneath the folder you will be creating your user folders. Generally you will want users within a single department to chart their data in the same place. So we suggest you create a shared folder called "Finance," "Accounting, or "Personnel," etc. Once you have done this, you need to assign permissions. Assign the Change permission to users within the folder they need access to. Do not assign permissions to the other share folders. Make sure you have removed all permissions from the Everyone group from all shares.

• Assign Full Control to anyone who will be administering the shared folders.

FOR DATA REPOSITORIES

A data repository is a location on your network where users from any department can store their data for sharing purposes. You might use such a location to post personnel announcements, employee handbooks, and the like. Here are some guidelines you might want to follow:

    • If you have this requirement, create a single share for the purpose. It does not make good administrative sense to have several different shares filling the same role.

    • Users should be granted Change permissions within this folder. This allows them to copy their files and to read all files. Remove the Everyone group from the permissions list. Assign Full Control to those personnel who are going to be administering it.

Spend some time considering how data is likely to be used on your network. Only by having a good understanding of what the data is being used for can you make a good decision about how best to create shared folders. If you are inheriting an older network, then it might take you some time to find all of the shares and to find out what they are being used for. However, it is time well spent. It is entirely possible that shares exist in inadequate locations on your network, or that permissions have not been set correctly.

For instance, if you have a shared folder on the other side of a slow network link, do you really want your users saving and retrieving large files from it? These types of considerations can cause you to create more shares than you would ordinarily like, but the goal is simplicity for the users and the easing of administrative tasks for yourself.

Creating Shared Folders

It is now time to look at the process by which you can share folders. Sharing a folder is an important task, though you might think it is fairly mundane. We want to discourage you from thinking that it is a simple task that does not require careful planning. When you create a shared folder, you are likely opening up an area of a server for users to both read and write data. This ought to increase productivity, but it is also important that you be aware of all the options that are available to you.

Until this point we have addressed the issues of permissions. However, other items need to be considered. For instance, when you create a share, you can further limit the number of simultaneous users who can access the share. You can also edit any of their share properties, such as the share name, and user and group permissions.

GROUPS THAT CAN SHARE FOLDERS

Since creating a shared folder is such an important task, not everyone can create one. This prevents unauthorized shared folders from being created on your servers. It is worth remembering that shares can be created on servers—the primary focus of this chapter—or they can be created on workstations running Windows 2000 Professional. Like all such options, you should carefully consider whether it is a good idea to have your users creating shares.

In principle it does not matter whether users create shares on their own. However, shares created on Windows 2000 professional are unlikely to be backed up. What's more, it is far more likely that insufficient permissions are assigned to these types of shares. In this case "insufficient" means permissions that are too lenient. If a department within your organization has come to rely on a shared folder created on a Windows 2000 Professional computer, then it is probably high time that it was moved to a server and brought under administrative control of the system administrators.

In Windows 2000 there are two types of possible configuration. Either the computers are linked together in a domain model, or they are joined as a workgroup. Obviously we discard standalone workstations that are not part of either of these, since they would not have any need to share resources!

In order to create a shared folder you must be a member of a security group. The scope of the power assigned to these groups varies, depending on whether your computers are operating as a domain or a workgroup. There are three groups that can create shares: Administrators, Server Operators, and the Power Users group.

If your computers are configured as a domain, then the Administrators and Server Operators have the widest scope and can create shares on any machine within the domain. Since the Power Users group is created locally on a computer, the scope for the Power User is to create shares only on the machine the account was created on.

If your computers are configured as a workgroup, then the Administrators and Power Users group can share folders on any Windows 2000 server and Windows 2000 Professional computer. In order to create a share, the user performing the task requires a Read access to the folder.

Creating Administrative Shares

When you install Windows 2000, a number of shares are already created for you. These shares are created for administrative purposes. However, if you browse the computer in the normal way, you will not see them. This is because they are "hidden" shares. A hidden share is a share that you can attach to, but that will not be displayed if a computer is browsed.

In order to create a share that is hidden, simply append the "$" character to the end of the share name. Using this technique, you can hide any share on your network. The hidden shares created on a server are shares to the root of each volume (*C$, D$,* etc.) a share to the systemroot (*Admin$*) and a share to printer drivers (*Print$*). Let's take a closer look at each of these and see what they can be used for.

• Root shares *C$, D$,* etc. These shares are created at the root of each volume on a server. This includes CD-ROM drives. You use this share to connect to the volume of a server. Since you are at the root of the volume, you can change any folder on the volume, giving you complete freedom. Of course, security on this share is very tight—you don't want just anyone being able to connect to the root of a volume. So, not only is the share name appended with a "$," which makes it hidden, but only Administrators are given Full Control to this share.

• Admin$. This is a share that points to the systemroot of a server. Usually this is the *C:\WINNT* folder, but not always. Rather than hunting around trying to find the folder into which Windows 2000 has been installed, you can simply connect to this share. It is used for administrative purposes. Only the Administrators group is assigned Full Control to this share.

• Print$. Whenever you share a printer, a copy of the driver is copied to the *\system32\spool\drivers* folder. This driver is used for installing on client computers. Therefore, this folder is also shared. Members of the Administrators, Server Operators, and Print Operators have Full Control permissions to this share. The Everyone group is assigned Read permissions, since they must be able to read the folder in order to install the drivers.

A hidden share is a useful tool when you want to create a share but not have everyone know it exists. Remember that its being hidden does not, in itself, prevent users from accessing the share. If a user knows the name of a share, he can attempt to connect. It is the permissions that a user has been assigned that will determine whether he can connect and what actions he can perform.

It is probably high time that we went ahead and created a share. In the following example we are going to create a share into which users can copy their word processing documents. While we are doing this, we will describe each of the options that are available.

1. In order to create a share we will use Windows Explorer. Click on Start, Programs, Accessories, Windows Explorer. Expand "My Computer" to expose the volumes that are available on your server. We want to create a share on an NTFS partition. In our case we are going to choose the "*D:*" volume. If you do not have a *D* volume, then simply substitute any NTFS volume to which you have access.

2. Once you have selected the volume onto which you are going to create your share, right-click in the right-hand panel to bring up the context-sensitive menu. Choose New, Folder. A folder named "New Folder" will be created. Rename this folder "UserData" and press ENTER. This will create the folder. In the unlikely event that a folder of this name already exists, then simply enter a unique name for this folder.

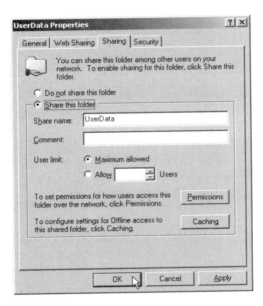

UserData Properties

General | Web Sharing | Sharing | Security |

You can share this folder among other users on your network. To enable sharing for this folder, click Share this folder.

○ Do <u>n</u>ot share this folder
◉ <u>S</u>hare this folder

S<u>h</u>are name: UserData

<u>C</u>omment:

User limit: ◉ <u>M</u>aximum allowed
              ○ Allo<u>w</u> [   ] Users

To set permissions for how users access this folder over the network, click Permissions.   [<u>P</u>ermissions]

To configure settings for Offline access to this shared folder, click Caching.   [<u>C</u>aching]

[OK]   [Cancel]   [<u>A</u>pply]

Figure 17–1   *The UserData Properties dialog box.*

3. Next we will share the folder. Right-click on the folder you have just created and choose "Sharing…" This brings up the "UserData Properties" dialog box. This is shown in Figure 17.1.

4. The first thing we must do is to gain access to all the options. We do this by clicking on the "Share this Folder" option. Notice that Windows 2000 creates a default share name for you, taking the name of the folder. For our purposes this is sufficient. One thing that we want to change is the permissions assigned to this share. Since we know that the Everyone group has Full Control, we are going to go ahead and remove that permission and assign Full Control to the User's Built-in group instead. Click on the Permissions button to bring up the "Permissions for UserData" dialog box.

5. This dialog box allows you to set permissions for users and groups, and also allows you to deny access. Don't forget, a Deny permission will always override an Allow. Click on the Everyone group in the "Name" panel and then click on the Remove button. This group no longer has permissions to this share. Next we must add the Users group. Click on the Add button to bring up the "Select Users, Computers or Groups" dialog box. Find the Users Built-in group and click the Add button. The Users group is added to the box at the bottom. This is shown in Figure 17.2.

6. When this is done, click on OK. You will be returned to the Permissions for UserData dialog box. Notice that the Users group has been added to the "Name" panel. Also notice that by default, this group has been granted the least amount of permissions—that is, Read. Since we want users to

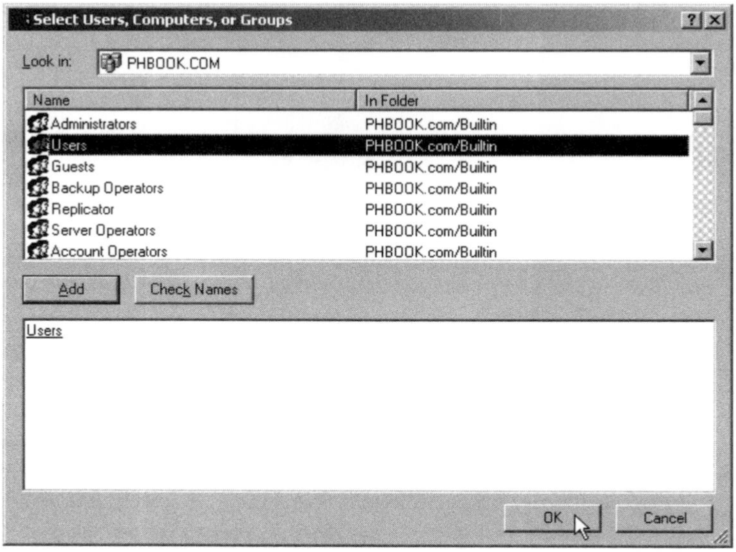

Figure 17-2 *The Select Users, Computers or Groups dialog box.*

both copy and read data from this share, we are going to go ahead and change this permission to Full Control. Click on Full Control in the Permissions panel. Make sure you click under the "Allow" column and not the "Deny." If you click on the wrong one, all users will be denied access, rather than allowed it. Notice that when you clicked on "Full Control," all of the other boxes became checked. This is by design. If you remember from our definitions earlier, Full Control bestows both Change and Read permissions. Finally, click on OK. This returns you to UserData Properties. Click on OK again to return to Windows Explorer. The UserData folder is now shared. You should see the icon in Windows Explorer change to a folder with a hand beneath it. The hand signifies that the folder was successfully shared.

As you can see, sharing a folder is not a very difficult task. However, it is the process that takes time; it is the planning. In the preceding example we accepted some of the defaults, but made changes to others—such as the list of groups and default permissions. Let's refer back to Figure 17.1 and define each of the options that are available.

Table 17.2	The Sharing Tab
Option	**Purpose**
Share Name	This is the name that users will use to connect to the resource. Don't forget the restrictions mentioned earlier in this chapter. If you have to support older operating systems, then try to keep share name to 8.3 notation. For Windows 2000 you are limited to 12 characters. Appending a $ to the end of the share name will cause the share to be hidden.
Comment	This is a description field. When users browse for shares on the network, this description will be displayed along with the share name. Use this to offer some guidance for users.
User Limit	This option allows you to limit the number of simultaneous connections to a share that can exist. In Windows 2000 Professional there is a maximum allowable number of ten simultaneous connections. In Windows 2000 Server there is no limit. However, a client access license is required for each connection. You might use this option on a server to limit the number of connections that are being made to a share across a slow link.
Permissions	Use this to add or remove permissions to users for this share. Do not forget, these permissions only apply to the share if it is accessed across a network. A user logging in locally to the server that stores the share data is not limited by these permissions. Instead, rely on NTFS permissions to deny access to local users.

Table 17.2	The Sharing Tab (Continued)
Caching	These settings allow you to configure the offline caching features of a share. For instance, you can have documents in the share copied to users computers when they access the share, so that users can access the data even if they are not logged into the network.
New Share	This allows you to share a folder multiple times, with different share names. You would do this when you wanted to share a folder with different permissions.

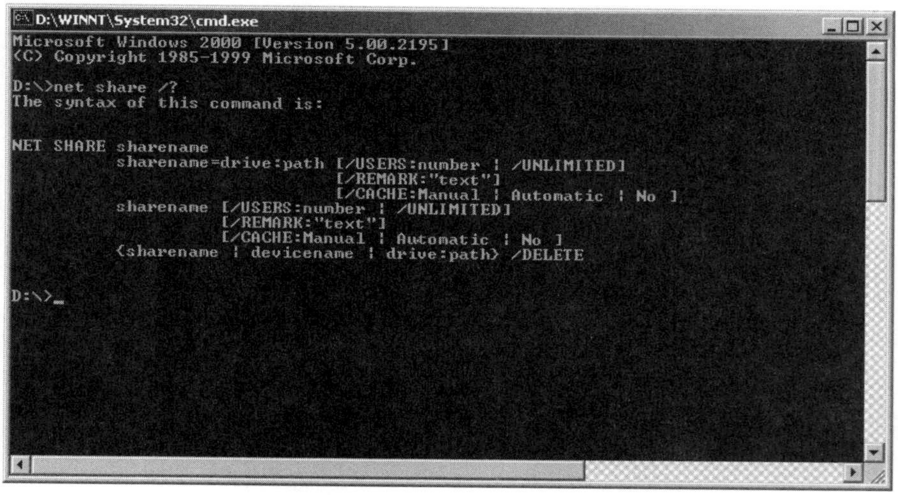

```
D:\WINNT\System32\cmd.exe                                              _ □ X
Microsoft Windows 2000 [Version 5.00.2195]
(C) Copyright 1985-1999 Microsoft Corp.

D:\>net share /?
The syntax of this command is:

NET SHARE sharename
         sharename=drive:path [/USERS:number | /UNLIMITED]
                              [/REMARK:"text"]
                              [/CACHE:Manual | Automatic | No ]
         sharename [/USERS:number | /UNLIMITED]
                   [/REMARK:"text"]
                   [/CACHE:Manual | Automatic | No ]
         (sharename | devicename | drive:path) /DELETE

D:\>_
```

Figure 17–3   *The Net Share help command.*

It's also possible to create a share using the command line. To do this you use the "Net Share" command. The options for this command can be displayed by typing *Net Share /?* at the command line. This is shown in Figure 17.3.

This command line can be useful for creating multiple shares within a script, perhaps during system setup. For everyday operations, it is far easier to use Windows Explorer.

Shared Folder and NTFS Permissions Combined

We alluded earlier to the complexities of permissions. Hopefully you are comfortable at this point with shared folder permissions. It is time now to show you how NTFS permissions and shared folder permissions work together.

As you will see, you can assign permissions within a shared folder both at the shared folder level and at the file and subfolder level with NTFS permissions. In keeping with our earlier statements, it is worth noting that Windows 2000 always leans toward the most restrictive access. If there is a conflict between shared folder permissions and NTFS permissions, the least amount of permissions will be applied.

One of the problems with shared folder permissions is that they are not granular enough. As a first line of defense they work very well, but once you set permissions at the shared folder level, those permissions apply to all files and subfolders within that share. So, if you have a share called "UserData" and you want users to have access to everything in that shared folder, with the exception of a subfolder for managers, you will find this is not possible with shared folder permissions. Once Change permission is assigned at the shared folder level, it will allow users access to everything in the folder. However, you can achieve this through use of NTFS permissions.

We also had the problem of denying a user access to a share and its contents. When the user logs on locally to the server that stores the share and its data, the shared folder permissions no longer apply. This breach is an obvious one and, once again, cannot be solved through shared folder permissions. Don't worry, NTFS permissions will come to the rescue and save the day!

Think of NTFS permissions and shared folder permissions as working in tandem to protect your data. These are the very issues that lead us to strongly suggest that you never create shares on FAT partitions. There are no NTFS permissions on FAT, and you must rely entirely upon shared folder permissions for protection—a shaky proposition, indeed.

Here are some rules that you will have to consider when using NTFS permissions. If we are repeating ourselves somewhat, there is good reason. Understanding these fundamental principles is going to be key to your implementing secure, but functional, shared folders.

• NTFS permissions can be applied at a much more granular level than shared folder permissions. However, they only work when you want to be more restrictive. For instance, if you have a shared folder with the Manager group assigned Change permissions, you can assign NTFS permissions to a single file within the shared folder and prevent them from accessing the file. However, it would not do you any good to change the permissions on a file so that the Everyone group had permission to read it. Due to the lack of permissions at the shared folder level, members of the Everyone group would be denied access to the underlying share.

- In the same vein, there is no point in applying shared folder permissions to a group of users if that group does not have NTFS permissions. Without NTFS permissions, the users will be denied access.

- When combined, the most restrictive permissions apply. This means that when users report problems, it will almost always be because they are denied access, rather than because they have too much. Careful management of user group will be required to ensure that users have sufficient access.

To learn more about NTFS permissions, and how they are applied, read Chapter 16, "NTFS Permissions."

Distributed File System

Windows 2000 has one other trick up its sleeve when it comes to Shared Folders. This trick has a fancy name, the Distributed File System (DFS). Sounds impressive, doesn't it? Actually, it won't disappoint; DFS brings ease of use to users, ease of administration, and even fault tolerance. These are all things we have been striving for, and DFS delivers.

Let's look at the goals of DFS and see if we can explain why it is going to be so useful to you. Earlier in this chapter we spoke about the importance of designing and implementing shared folders intelligently. Users are going to get confused if you have too many shares, and from an administrative point of view, it can be a lot more difficult to administer many different shares when they are scattered about your network on different servers.

However, no amount of careful planning is going to prevent you from having many different shared folders. If you work in a large environment, with possibly tens of thousands of users situated throughout the world, it is going to be hard work trying to minimize the number of shares users need to connect to.

DFS attempts to solve this problem for you by simplifying the method users employ to access shares. While it does not reduce the number of shares (in fact, technically it creates at least one additional one), it does aid the user in accessing the shares, and prevents the user from having to connect to many different shares individually.

So let's get right down to it. In DFS, you can create a logical tree. At the top of this tree is a root (this is what the users connect to). Beneath this root you can add shared folders. Now, by connecting to the root, the shared folders simply appear to be subfolders—much as you will have seen in Windows Explorer.

The most important term here is "logical." By logical we mean that it really does not exist. The shared folders that are added beneath the DFS root do not have to exist on the same computer. In fact, the whole point of DFS is that they do not. With DFS you can have a single point of entry to many shared folders across your network. To the user they all appear as though they were grouped in one place, when in fact, from an administrator's point of view, the shares can physically exist anywhere. That's a neat trick, and one that greatly simplifies your workload.

Here are the main features of DFS. Keep them in mind when you are trying to decide how best to implement shared folders on your network.

• A DFS share looks a lot like the folder structure in Windows Explorer. Off the root of a DFS share are what is known as child nodes. Each child node represents a shared folder on your network. This shared folder can exist on any server on your network. There are two types, a standalone DFS and a fault-tolerant DFS. These vary in the following ways. The DFS information (known as the DFS topology) has to be stored somewhere—in standalone DFS it is stored on a single server. If this server crashes, then the DFS topology will be lost, and users will not be able to connect to shares through DFS (users would still be able to connect directly to the shares if they knew the server on which they existed). A fault-tolerant DFS topology is one that is stored within Active Directory. Since Active Directory is fault tolerant, you have some protection. In this case, a child node can point to more than one location on the network. If child node disappears because a server crashes, or is rebooted, then a duplicate child node (shared folder) can be used. In other words, the users will not notice that the share location has changed. This function is supported through file replication.

• DFS simplifies network access for your user community. This is a key concern and is really one of the main advantages to using DFS. Since the user does not need to know each server that the shares are stored on, the level of complexity is reduced. All the user needs to know is how to connect to the logical root – DFS takes care of the rest.

• DFS simplifies network administration. For administrative purposes administrators benefit in much the same way that users do. You no longer have to keep track of where each share is stored. It also is very easy to move a share. To move a DFS child node from one server to another you simply have to move the folder, share it, and then make a change to the DFS child node. Users need never know that the share has been moved. Contrast this to the administrative headache of performing this task without DFS. Users would have to be told to connect to the share using a different server name. This can be quite difficult in an enterprise—and you do not always know precisely how many people are using a share.

• DFS supports the underlying security model. DFS does nothing to alter the way permissions are assigned or interpreted. You can still use shared folder permissions in tandem with NTFS permissions.

• Only clients with DFS client software installed can access DFS. Users running Windows 98, Windows NT 4.0, and Windows 2000 already have the client installed. You will have to download and install the client on Windows 95 clients.

It's time for us to show you how to create a DFS root. In the following example we show you how to consolidate a set of shares. We explain options to you as we go.

1. We won't get very far without opening up the Distributed File System administration tool. This tool is an MMC snap-in. To do this click on Start, Programs, Administrative Tools, Distributed File System. If you have never used DFS before, you should look at the screen that is displayed in Figure 17.4.

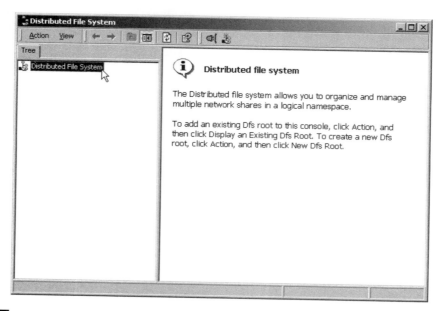

Figure 17-4 *The Distributed File System administration tool.*

2. There isn't much to see right now. That's because we do not have a DFS root yet. Let's go ahead and create one. Click on "Distributed File System" in the left-hand panel to select it, and then right-click. This brings up the context-sensitive menu. Select "New DFS Root." This brings up the "New DFS Wizard." This wizard walks you through the process of creating a DFS root. Click on Next.

3. In the next pane you are offered two choices. You have to decide whether you want to store the DFS topology within Active Directory (fault tolerant) or as a standalone. The default is to store it in Active Directory. Leave that option selected, and click Next.

4. Next you have to choose the host domain in which you want the DFS topology stored. It is a good idea to choose a domain that contains the greatest number of users that will be using DFS. Select the domain name and click Next.

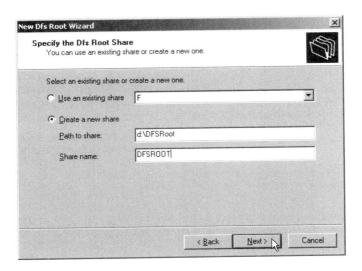

Figure 17–5   *Creating a share for the DFS root.*

5. Now you have to select the server that will store the DFS information. This is an important decision, because a single server can be responsible for only one DFS root. Since Active Directory is offering us fault tolerance, there is little chance that a system crash will prevent users from accessing shares through DFS, but this is still an important consideration. It is a good idea to choose a server close to the users who will be accessing this DFS root. You will notice there is a browse button. You can use this to browse the servers on your network. Once you have selected the server you want to use, click on Next.

6. In order to access DFS, you have to enter a share name. This can be an existing share, or you can create a new share. We are going to create a new share. This share is called *DFSRoot* and is going to be on an NTFS partition. This is shown in Figure 17.5. Once you have entered the drive letter and share name, click on Next. You will be prompted to confirm the creation of the share. Click on OK; the share will be created at this point.

7. Now you will be prompted to enter a share name and comment. These are similar to what we saw earlier with shared folders. Make sure that you give the DFSRoot a descriptive name, keeping all naming conventions in mind. We will name ours *DFSRoot* with a comment of "DFS Share Point." Enter this information and click on Next.

8. You are now shown a summary screen of the options you have chosen. Our summary is shown in Figure 17.6. Since everything is correct, click on Finish to complete the process. You will be returned to the Distributed File System administration tool. Do not close the tool; you will be using it in a moment to add child nodes.

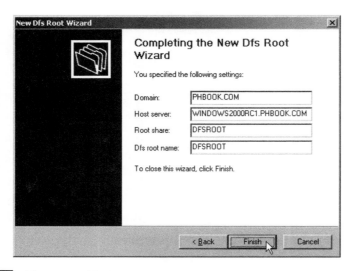

Figure 17-6   *The create Dfs Root summary screen.*

Congratulations, you have just created your first DFS root! However, the root is not much use to us without some child nodes. So before we can really say we are done, we will add three shares. Since you are unlikely to have the same shares on your own system, feel free to substitute share names for those used in this example.

1. Make sure you have completed the example above before proceeding; you will not be able to complete this example if you have not created a DFS root. Once you have created the root, click on the DFS root to select it, and then right-click. This brings up the context-sensitive menu. The first option on the menu is "New Dfs Link." Select this option to bring up the "Create a Dfs Link" dialog box. This is shown in Figure 17.7.
2. First you must enter a Link name. This is the name that will be displayed in the administrators console. In the "Send user to this shared folder" text box you must enter the UNC path to the physical share. This is the magic that is DFS. Once you have pointed DFS at this path, it will then disguise it from the user. Use the browse button to locate shares on your network. Notice that you can browse to all servers in your domain. In our case we have chosen a "Finance" share that exists on a Windows NT 4.0 server in the "BDC" domain. Once you have selected your share, you should enter a comment. This comment will be displayed along with the share name. The final piece of information in this dialog box is the "Clients cache this referral for" text box. This is the amount of time a client will cache this data for. In other words, if you decide to move the physical share to another server, it will take this amount of time, at the most, before your users will retrieve

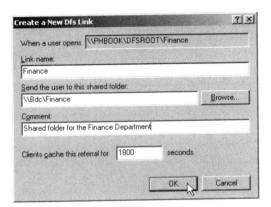

Figure 17–7   *The Create a Dfs Link dialog box.*

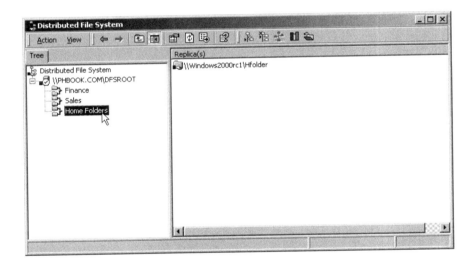

Figure 17–8   *Our complete DFS Administrators Console.*

the updated data. When you are done, click on OK. You will be returned to the Distributed File System administration tool. Now the new child node will appear.

3. To make this example useful, let's go ahead and add two additional child nodes. Since we are unlikely to have the same shares on our computers, go ahead and choose any two you want from your own network. The steps to do this will be the same as those listed in steps 1 and 2 above. When you are done, your Distributed File System Administrators Console should resemble Figure 17.8.

Once this is done, it is time to test and make sure that DFS is working for us. To do this, we're going to go out to the DOS prompt and map a network drive. This can also be performed from Windows Explorer, but we thought we'd throw in this little trick just for fun. To start a command Prompt click on Start, Run. This brings up the Run dialog box. Type *CMD* and press enter. The Command Prompt window opens. Now, earlier in this example we gave our DFS-Root a share name. In our case that was *DFSRoot*. If you used a different name then you will have to substitute it here. At the command prompt type *Net use* * *\\phbook\DFSRoot* and press Enter. Substitute your server name for "PHBOOK." The "*" means "assign the next available drive letter to the mapped drive." You should connect the share. Now, type *Dir* and press Enter. If everything worked, you should see all of those mapped drives as though they were a standard folder structure, even though some of the shared folders are in fact on different servers. This is shown in Figure 17.9.

DFS at work.

DFS is a wonderful addition to the Windows 2000 tool set. There are a few more things you would probably like to know before we move on. First, a domain-based DFS has its name stored in DNS. This allows anyone in the domain to resolve the name. You can also create "Root Replicas" which replicate this topology (right-click on DFS root name and select "New Root Replica") for fault tolerance. DNS will take care of making sure users can find the new root.

You can also easily make replicas of any shared folder. Simply right-click on the shared folder name and select "New Replica"; this allows for fault tolerance and load balancing between shared folders.

There is a limit within Windows 2000 of a maximum path length. This length is 260 characters. As long as the path remains within this limit, you can add more child nodes.

DFS is a good logical extension to your shared folder plans. Using it simplifies both your user and administrative experience. When your shared folders start to get out of hand and unmanageable, use DFS to clean things up.

Chapter Summary

In this chapter, we discussed shared folders and their purpose. Once that was defined, we began to talk about the difference between creating shared folders on File Access Table (FAT) partitions, and on NT File System (NTFS) partitions. You will be able to secure shared folders on NTFS partitions far better than on FAT. It is strongly recommended that you do not create shares on FAT.

We then discussed shared folder permissions. Three sets of permissions can be assigned at the shared folder level, and each of these can be either allowed or denied. These permissions, ranging from most to least restrictive, are Read, Change, and Full Control. If you are assigned Full Control, then you get a set of permissions, plus you get all the permissions granted to the other two options.

By default the Everyone group is assigned Full Control permissions to any new share that is created. The Everyone group contains users such as Guest, and it is good practice to remove this permission straight away. You want to make sure that you assign the most restrictive permission, while at the same time allowing the users to perform whatever task they need. Just keep in mind, if users need only to read data, then give them only Read permissions.

We strongly suggest that you assign permissions to groups rather than individual users. Administration will be easier when you are dealing with a smaller number of groups. However, this introduces the likelihood of a permission conflict. If there is a conflict, a Deny will always override an Allow. If a user has been assigned different levels of Allow, then the user will be assigned the *least* restrictive (a Read and a Full Control assigns Full Control).

The set of permissions a user enjoys, once all of the conflicts have been tallied up, is known as the user's "effective permissions." This will usually be an issue only when a Deny has been placed on an account.

We suggested that you minimize the number of shared folders you have. Do this by grouping folders that require the same level of user access into a single shared folder. For instance, we recommend that you group all applications under a single shared folder. Do the same for shared folders that store user data.

We then created a share using Windows Explorer. We showed you how to change permissions on the shared folder. You can also create shares from scripts using the "Net Share" command.

Several shares are created when Windows 2000 is installed. These are hidden shares. Hidden shares work the same way as normal shares, with the exception that they do not show up when you browse a computer. In order to connect to a hidden share, you must know the share name. To make a share hidden, simply append a "$" to the end of the share name. The shares created during installation are known as "Administrative shares."

If you create shares on an NTFS partition, then users will need to be assigned NTFS permissions as well as shared folder permissions. NTFS permissions allow you to be more granular with your security model.

Finally, we introduced you to the Distributed File System (DFS). This new feature allows you to combine many shares into a single logical hierarchy. This helps users by giving them a single point of access to many shares (regardless of where they are created) and helps administration in the same way.

DFS offers load balancing and fault tolerance for shared folders. If a DFS topology is stored within Active Directory, then it is possible to make replicas of both the topology and shared folders. This way users will not be affected if a server goes down; DNS will simply reroute them to the replica.

Managing Data Storage

*D*ata is the lifeblood of your network. While some new system administrators might imagine that their job is going to revolve entirely around working with servers and hardware, they will soon realize that another set of tasks are equally as important—the managing of the data on the network.

"Managing data" is a term which has many definitions. In this chapter we are going to take a look at some of the tools Microsoft has provided with Windows 2000. Few things will cause you as much trouble as the mismanagement of data. Microsoft Windows NT has lagged behind other network operating systems for quite some time in several key areas; Windows 2000 has addressed this with the inclusion of extensions to NTFS and the addition of utilities. To be more specific, when we talk about data management we are talking about storage management, security, and performance.

While it is true that hard disk space has become cheaper over time, the amount of data being generated has also increased. This has led to an increase in the amount of space available to us, and an increase in the rate at which we use it. Overall it is difficult to conclude we are better off—data management needs are still important (if not the most important) area for system administrators. Windows 2000 addresses this issue in many ways. One is by allowing you to compress files on your Windows 2000 servers. By compressing files you are maximizing the amount of data storage you have available. From a user's perspective this needs to be seamless—that is, the user should not have to be concerned with small details. We will take a look at file compression in some detail.

One of the most anticipated new features of Windows 2000 is the inclusion of Disk Quotas. Most people realize that it is a good idea to store user data on the network (meaning on a disk drive attached to a server). If you do this, then you can perform backups of data, and your users can take advantage of server performance enhancements such as RAID 5. However, in earlier versions of Windows NT, Microsoft failed to provide some essential tools. One of these was the ability to limit the amount of disk space a user took up on a particular volume. In this case, a user would be assigned his or her own "user directory" on the network, and all files would be stored there. However, there was nothing to stop a single user from copying her entire hard disk to the network! This could lead to server problems, or even performance issues, as large amounts of data traversed the network.

In Windows 2000 Microsoft has introduced disk quotas. This is a method whereby you can limit the amount of disk space a particular user has been assigned on a volume.

Security is also an issue for many people. While we like to think our network is secure (after all, you need to logon to access it), it is an unfortunate truth that we need to be ever vigilant. To further strengthen the security features of Windows 2000, Microsoft has now introduced an enhancement to NTFS—the Encrypted File System (EFS). EFS allows users to encrypt files on their local hard disks. This prevents unauthorized users from accessing files on the hard disk. While this is valuable on the server, you might find it is even more useful on laptop computers with Windows 2000 Professional installed. You can finally protect users when they are on the road and lose their laptops!

The final topic in this chapter will be performance related. In the early days of Windows NT, Microsoft went on record stating that NTFS volumes did not get fragmented, and therefore there was no need to have a defragmentation utility. This was proven incorrect by third-party vendors, who were quick to fill the gap. Finally, Microsoft now ships a defragmentor with Windows 2000. We will be taking a look at the features of this program, and why it is going to be an important tool for optimizing server performance.

Once you have read this chapter you will have a good idea of some of the new tools that are available to you. You should also have a better understanding of why data management is such an important part of the system administrator's job.

Data Compression

Many of you will be familiar with data compression. We come across this technique most often when downloading files from the Internet. Since new drivers or software patches are large, it is far more efficient to compress the files and then pull them across the network. One of the most popular desktop utilities to perform this function is Winzip. Without utilities such as Winzip, the Internet would be a much slower place!

The reason for data compression is simple: You can store more data on a disk if data is compressed. How is compression achieved? Well, that's beyond the scope of this book. But just to give some idea, assume we have a file on our network. Don't forget that at the end of the day, all data is represented in binary—that is, 1s and 0s. Let's say that the first six bits of this file are 100001. Now, we could have a nice algorithm that analyzed this stream of bits and said, "Hm, there are four zeros in a row, let's change that value and leave a marker that tells me how many zeros there were! So it replaces the four zeros with, say, a 1, and a pointer that indicates that the one really represents four zeros. That is two bits of data (the 1 and the pointer), but we have removed the four zeros, giving us a total "gain" of 2 bits. Our six bits are now represented by four bits, a nice bit of data compression.

Of course, expect the data compression algorithms used by Microsoft to be a tad more complex than our simple example! But hopefully you get the idea of how data compression can be achieved.

As you might have guessed, data compression requires some overhead at the server. So it is not a good idea to simply compress all files on a server. But if there is a folder or set of files that are rarely accessed, then it might be a good idea to compress them. Disk space represents one of the many investments you have in your network. Anything you can do to maximize its usage is a good idea!

There are other issues that we will need to cover as well. For instance, what happens when you copy a compressed file? Does it stay compressed, or does Windows 2000 decompress the file? All will be revealed as we go into the details of data compression.

Introduction to Data Compression

You can compress either folders or files that reside on an NTFS partition. The key point here is that the files must exist on an NTFS partition and not a FAT partition. Because you can compress at the folder level, or the file level, you can end up with some interesting combinations. For instance, the fact that a folder is compressed does not necessarily mean that all files within it are compressed. The opposite is also true; just because a single file is compressed, it does not follow that every file stored in the same folder is also compressed.

This can lead to a confusing state of affairs where a folder might be compressed but all files within it are not compressed. This will occur when a folder has been compressed but you have gone in and set the files to be uncompressed. The bottom line is, don't assume, just because a folder has been compressed, that all the contents are compressed also.

The data is compressed only on the disk. In order for the file to be used it must first be uncompressed. This is an important point. For instance, let's assume we have a file that is 100 KB in size. We set it to be compressed, and the file now takes up only 50 KB on the disk. This is a huge saving of 50%. However, if we want to copy that file from one disk to another, it must first be uncompressed (back to 100 KB in size) and copied. It arrives on the destination drive as 100 KB and then is compressed once again to 50 KB. This means that the destination drive must have enough disk space to accommodate the uncompressed version of the file. If the destination had only 50 KB of free disk space, the copy operation would fail due to insufficient space. Don't forget this. You might run into problems when copying entire compressed folders.

So how do applications deal with compressed files? The answer is pretty much the same as the example we just went through. Any application that is MS DOS or Windows compatible will be able to use a compressed file, but before it can be used it must be uncompressed. For instance, if you have a Microsoft Word document that has been compressed on a disk, you can retrieve the file using the usual methods. Before the file is retrieved it is uncompressed. It will exist in your computer's memory as an uncompressed file. Not until the file is saved is it compressed once again.

How do you know if a file is compressed or not? Well, it's simply a matter of displaying the compressed files and folders in a different color in Windows Explorer. To make sure that you have this option set, follow these steps.

1. First, start Windows Explorer. To do this, click on Start, Programs, and Accessories. Windows Explorer should appear on the menu. (This is the default location. You may have moved it, or put it on your desktop. If this is the case, simply start it from the new location.)
2. Once Windows Explorer has started, we need to look at the folder options that you have set. Click on the Tools menu and select Folder Options. This displays the Folder Options dialog box. This dialog box has several tabs. We are going to select the View tab.
3. Click on the view tab and you should see the view options as shown in Figure 18.1. The first option is "Display compressed files and folders with alternate colors." You must make sure this option has been checked.

Right now you do not have any compressed files or folders on your disk, so you will not notice anything different within Windows Explorer. But in a moment we will show you how to compress a file, and then an entire folder. You will then see the benefits of making sure this option has been selected.

Compressing Files and Folders

Compressing files and folders is a simple task that can be performed within Windows Explorer. Since you cannot set levels of compression, this is a simple on/off switch. The file or folder is then compressed.

As in all system administration, it is far better to formulate a plan on how you are going to use compression, rather than compressing on an ad-hoc basis. While there is nothing to prevent you from compressing on a random basis, you might find that administrative time increases if you have not approached compression from a logical standpoint. For instance, as we mentioned earlier, it

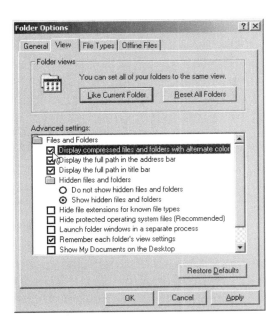

Turning on the necessary Windows Explorer options.

can cause issues when copying or moving files. If you have not approached compression systematically, you might find problems later on.

First let's compress a file and see how it works. In the following example we will compress clock.avi. You will soon see that compressing a file is very simple.

1. In this example we are going to compress a file in the WINNT folder on your hard disk. This is just an example. In an effort to compress a file that will exist on every installation of Windows 2000, we have chosen clock.avi. If you do not want to compress this file, you can choose any file you want. If you have a document, such as one created with Microsoft Word, then you can simply substitute it for clock.avi.

2. First we must open Windows Explorer. If you do not already have it open then click on Start, Programs, and Accessories. Windows Explorer should appear on the menu. Select it. Windows Explorer should open.

3. With Windows Explorer open we will now go down into the WINNT folder. On a standard Windows 2000 installation this folder will exist on the C:\ drive on your computer. However, if you are dual booting your system between different operating systems, or did not accept the default installation for some reason, the folder might be on another disk. We will assume defaults for this example. Click on "My Computer" to access the folders on your local machine. Then double-click on the disk that contains

the WINNT folder. Finally, double-click the WINNT folder to view the files and folders that are stored within it.

4. The file we are looking for is "clock.avi." This is a simple multimedia file that can be used to test the multimedia function (sound and video) on your system. The list in Windows Explorer defaults to alphabetical. So scroll down until you find it. When you do, you might want to test that it works. To do this, double-click the file. By default, "Windows Media Player" should start and clock.avi will open and play. As you can see, this is a simple count from 1 to 12.

5. Now that you have seen that the file works, it is time to see how large it is. (If you double-clicked on the file and received an error message, don't worry—it might be that you do not have multimedia capabilities on your computer, or that they are not yet configured. You can still perform the important parts of this example without multimedia.) To find the size of the file, right-click on the file within Windows Explorer and select "Properties." The Properties dialog box is shown in Figure 18.2.

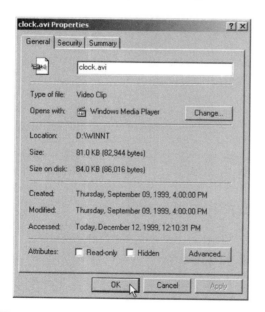

Figure 18-2   *Viewing the precompressed size of clock.avi.*

6. As you can see in Figure 18.2 (and hopefully on your own screen) the size of this file is 81 KB and "size on disk" is 84 KB. Why is the size on disk greater than the actual size of the file? That's because all data is stored on disks in blocks—and Windows 2000 uses 4-KB blocks. If files are saved in 4 KB "chunks," then it is easy to determine why an 84-KB file requires 84

KB of disk space. (If you don't believe we simply divide those two numbers by 4. Don't forget, you cannot use only part of a block. It's all or nothing!)

7. Now it is time to compress this file and see how much space we can save on our disk. Since we are still in the Properties dialog box, all we have to do now is click on the "Advanced" button under "Attributes" toward the bottom of the dialog box. This displays the "Advanced Attributes" dialog box. There are four options in this dialog box. One of the options is "Compress contents to save disk space." Make sure this is checked. Click OK to return to the Properties dialog box.

8. Now, let's see what we can save. Click on the "Apply" button to see how much space is saved with compression. When you have clicked on the button, take a look at the "Size on disk" figure. This is shown in Figure 18.3.

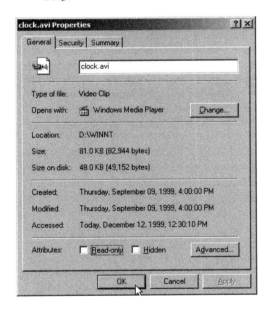

Figure 18-3   *Clock.avi as a compressed file.*

9. As you can see, this file now takes up 48 KB on disk. This is a savings of more than 25% over the original size of the file. Not bad indeed! Let's make sure that the file is still available to use. Click on OK to return to Windows Explorer. We are going to run this file again to illustrate that the file is usable. Double-click clock.avi to see the countdown.

10. Now let's make sure that the alternate color option we chose earlier has taken effect. In Windows Explorer choose another file or folder. That is, deselect clock.avi. Once it is no longer highlighted you should see that

clock.avi is now displayed in a different color. This illustrates that the file is compressed.

11. As a final step, let's go back and uncompress the file. To do this, simply click on the "Advanced" button a second time. This time you should deselect the "Compress contents to save disk space" option. When you have done that, click OK. This returns you to the Properties dialog box. Click on "Apply" and the file will be uncompressed.

The steps for compressing a folder are almost the same. Follow the steps above, but instead of selecting a file, select a folder name. Be careful — it would not be a good idea to select WINNT or one of its subfolders. This is for performance reasons. However, once you have selected a folder you can compress it using the same options. The only difference you will see is if the folder you are compressing contains subfolders. If this is the case you will see the "Confirm attribute changes" dialog box shown in Figure 18.4. This gives you the opportunity to select between compressing the contents of this folder only, or compressing this folder, and every subfolder and file within those folders. Make your selection and click OK.

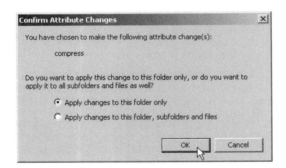

Figure 18–4   *Choosing folder compression options.*

Using Compressed Files

We have already said that using files that have been compressed within your applications is simply a matter of retrieving them. Windows 2000 takes care of uncompressing the file so that it can be used, and then compressing it once you have finished with it. But what are the rules for normal file management tasks such as moving files or copying them? What about floppy diskettes?

Using compressed files is akin to file permissions; there is a set of standard behaviors that need to be taken into consideration as these files are moved or copied. Let's take a look at copying a file first and see what these rules are.

There are two places to which you might copy a file. First, you might copy a file to another folder on the same disk partition. Alternatively, you might copy the file from one partition to another. In these cases Windows 2000 will operate in the same way—whenever you copy a compressed file or folder, it will inherit its new behavior from the destination.

An example would be moving a single uncompressed file from a folder on drive *C:* to another, compressed folder on the same partition. In this case, since the destination is compressed, the file will be copied and then compressed. It has inherited its behavior.

Things get a little tricky when you begin to move files. Moving a file is different than copying, because when you copy a file it exists in two places (the source and the destination). When you move a file, then the file exists in only one place – the destination. When moving files, you will find that there is a difference in behavior, depending upon whether you have moved the file to a folder on the same partition or on a different partition. If you move a compressed file to a folder on the same partition, and the destination folder is uncompressed, then the file will retain its compressed status, even if it is the only file in that folder that is compressed.

However, if you move a file from one partition to another, then the file will inherit its behavior from the destination, just as we saw with copying files. This is caused by the nature of moving files. As far as Windows 2000 is concerned, a file (or folder) "move" is in fact a copy-and-delete operation. NTFS takes care of copying the file to the destination, and then it goes back and deletes the original file from the source. This is in contrast to a move within a partition, when only a file pointer needs to be changed to note the file move.

So is this a good way to get some more life out of your floppy diskettes? Can you now get 2.8 MB of data on a single disk? Well, no, unfortunately not! Windows 2000 does not support compressed files and folders on floppy diskettes, or on any file system other than NTFS.

It is worth noting that copying compressed files and folders (especially large amounts of them) will consume more system resources than the same operation performed on uncompressed files and folders. This is because the files and folders have to be uncompressed before the move or copy operation can be performed. Then, if the files and folders are going to retain compression at the destination, they have to be compressed all over again.

Like all administrative tasks, it is best to think through how you intend to use file and folder compression before you go off compressing things left and right. There are a few points that you should consider when thinking about compression. First, it might not be a good idea to compress files that are used frequently. This is because the files have to be constantly uncompressed so they can be used, and compressed when the file is saved. This will consume system resources. If you are hasty and decide to compress the user folders on your Windows 2000 system, you might find that the system gets overburdened with all this compressing and uncompressing.

It might seem like an obvious thing to say, but don't try to compress files that have already been compressed. You won't gain any additional space, and the server will, once again, become burdened with unnecessary processing.

Keep in mind that the space that is saved through compressing a file will vary from file type to file type. Generally speaking, you will gain the best compression from text file (that is plain text, or ASCII files, and not your word processing files). You also gain a lot from compressing graphics files, such as bitmaps. However, files that have been compressed by a third-party utility such as Winzip probably won't compress at all (although Windows 2000 will make a valiant effort, eating up CPU cycles as it goes). You generally do not get a lot of compression from executables, either. Just keep in mind that the type of data you are trying to compress will make a difference. Before compressing a file type, you might want to perform the compression on one or two files to see the savings you are going to be able to achieve.

Finally we will mention one confusing situation. If you have a file that is 100 KB in size, you might compress it to, say, 50 KB. However, Windows Explorer will still show the file with its original file size. It does not display the new file size. This is an unfortunate oversight. However, you already know how to check the amount of disk space the file or folder is consuming.

That about sums up everything you need to know about compressing files and folders. As you can see, it is a simple operation, and if used properly, it can really save you some disk resources.

Disk Quotas

As a system administrator, there are some things you can control, and some things that you can't. Take the amount of disk space each of your users consumes. On the one hand you want to encourage your users to save their data to the network because you are monitoring the network for problems and are performing backups of data. On the other hand, disk space is a finite resource, and it is difficult to explain to a user that they should use disk space carefully.

This problem was further complicated by the lack of tools built into previous versions of Windows NT to monitor, and then limit the amount of disk space that a user could be assigned. Without native tools system administrators were basically at the mercy of their users. Of course you could purchase third-party tools that helped you with this problem, but wouldn't it be nice if there were a facility within Windows 2000 that let you set definite limits to the amount of disk space a user, or group of users, was able to consume?

Well, there is. This feature is called "disk quota." A disk quota is a feature that allows you to define a set of rules and then apply those rules to a single user or a group of users. Windows 2000 allows you to set these limits on a partition basis. This means you can set a small limit on partitions with little free space, and greater amounts on partitions with more space.

Along with these limits disk quotas also allow you to set warning levels based on disk space usage. This means users can be alerted to when they are running out of disk space. You can also more easily monitor how much disk space each user is consuming.

In this section we are going to take a closer look at disk quotas and what they mean to system administrators and users alike. This is a feature you are probably going to want to use, so let's move on and see what we have.

INTRODUCTION TO DISK QUOTAS

It is important to remember that Windows 2000 keeps track of disk quotas on a per user and a per-partition basis. So, on a single server, with three partitions, you can set three different limits on a per-user basis. Disk quotas cannot be specifically set at the folder level. That is, you cannot say, "Give UserA 10 MB of space in her user folder, and 5 MB of space in the Data folder on that same partition." Windows 2000 would interpret this as 15 MB on that single partition and would not alert UserA until the total space reached the limit. That means UserA could save 15 MB worth of data in the user folder and be denied access to the Data folder.

How does Windows 2000 know to whom a file belongs? Easy: file ownership! All files on a Windows 2000 system have a file owner—usually the person who created or installed the file. Windows 2000 uses this data to figure out how much space a user has remaining against their quota. If a user takes ownership of a file from someone else, then the amount of disk space the file consumes will count against the new owner's quota.

When it comes time to install software on a partition that has a disk quota assigned, Windows 2000 will report the amount of free disk space. However, this figure is based not on the amount of physical disk space that the server has, but rather on the remaining amount of space of the user's quota. This means that a server might have plenty of disk space, but you will be unable to install a simple 500-KB file. If your quota has been used, Windows 2000 will prevent you from installing anything.

In the previous section we talked about disk compression. Disk compression can achieve some pretty wonderful space-saving feats. But before you go off and think you can use that feature to circumvent disk quotas, think again. Disk quotas use the uncompressed file size to determine how much space a user has remaining. While it might have been convenient for Microsoft to have built in disk compression as an added benefit for disk quotas, it was not possible. If you recall the way disk compression works, before a file can be used it must be uncompressed, and that eats up disk space. Because the uncompression might push a user over the top of their quota, Windows 2000 simply takes the uncompressed as the true size of the file.

Finally, you can only use disk quotas on a NTFS partition. This means you cannot limit partitions that are formatted with FAT. This is not really a problem, since you should be using NTFS for all your enterprise needs.

IMPLEMENTING DISK QUOTAS

Disk quotas are a powerful new addition to the system administrator's arsenal, but their implementation takes careful planning. For instance, if you are migrating over from a previous installation of Windows NT, then you are likely inheriting a system that has been in place for quite some time. In that case it will take some planning before you implement an arbitrary limit. This will prevent you from instantly locking out a user, or group of users, because they already have an excessive amount of disk space in their name.

When Windows 2000 is installed, disk quotas are turned off—that is, they are not applied. This is a good choice, because it gives you time to plan. Some of the decisions you will need to make include how much total disk space you are going to assign to user files. Don't forget, this is on a partition basis, so you might have to make the analysis several times.

You also need to decide what you are going to do when a user exceeds her limit. You can either log the incident to the Windows 2000 log file, or you can enforce the limit you have set, and have the user denied. While the latter might seem like the most obvious option, keep in mind that preventing a user from performing her job might not be in the best interest of the organization you are working for. You might find that rather than being appreciative of all the hard work you have put in to managing the network, you have instead landed yourself in hot water for being too harsh!

When considering the partitions you want to apply limits to, pay particular attention to the system partition. This is the partition on which the Windows 2000 application files exist. If you set limits on this partition, it is possible that you won't be able to install applications because of quota limits.

There is always a back door if you find yourself in hot water with disk quotas. This back door is left open because you might find yourself unable to perform normal system administration tasks if your own account has quotas applied to it. The failsafe is that administrative accounts are not limited by disk quotas. As long as you have an administrative account, you will have unlimited access to server disk space. Only administrators have access to disk quota tools.

Alternatively, you might want to assign a much higher than normal disk quota for users who have to install software on a given partition. Remember, you can be flexible with disk quotas on a per-user basis—as long as you plan!

USING DISK QUOTAS

It's time to look at how to actually use disk quotas. Some of the options that have already been mentioned will be clearly evident as you configure your server. First we will simply turn on disk quotas; then we will take a closer look at limiting particular users.

In the following example you will be walked through configuring disk quotas on a Windows 2000 server.

1. By default disk quotas are disabled. So the first thing we have to do is to turn this feature on. To do this click on Start, Programs, Administrative Tools, and select "Computer Management."
2. Computer Management is a tool that allows you to configure disk resources on your server (among other things). This covers everything from formatting a disk to setting quotas. Our next step is to bring up the disk quotas dialog box. The "Storage" folder should be opened, if it is not, click on the "+" sign next to it. Once it is open, right-click on "Disk Management," select "All Tasks," and finally select "Properties."
3. You should now have displayed the "Local Disk Properties" dialog box. There are several configuration option tabs available to you. The one we are interested in is "Quota." Click on "Quota." As you can see, by default everything is grayed out. This is because it is disabled. To gain access to the many options, click in the check box next to "Enable quota management." This is illustrated in Figure 18.5.
4. You should now have access to all the options. It is important that you understand what each option provides you with before you continue.

There are two parts to disk quotas. The first option, shown in Figure 18.5, allows you to set default behavior for all users on a partition. However, there will likely be circumstances where you need to go down to a per-user basis to set limits. This might happen when a single person, or a small group of people,

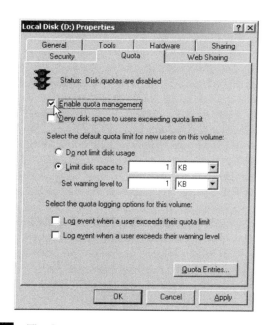

Figure 18–5   *The Quota dialog box.*

are working on a project that requires additional space. In this case you would use the "Quota Entries" options.

Before we go into the details of setting individual limits, let's define the options that are shown in the Quota dialog box. The first is "Enable quota management." You won't be doing much if this check box is not marked. You must check it in order to gain access to the other options.

The second option, "Deny disk space to users exceeding quota limit," is one of the key decisions you need to make. You have to decide how stringent you want to be. While disk space is certainly a commodity worth preserving, it might not be desirable to have users denied access to the network if they exceed the limits you are setting. If you check this box, then a user that is attempting to exceed his disk space limit will be denied access with an "insufficient disk space" message. This is the greatest level of control you can enact. It will have the benefit of truly limiting the amount of space a user can occupy. However it will also create the most work for the administrator, who will have to deal with calls from users asking for more disk space. Weigh your options before turning this on.

The next option allows you to take advantage of the reporting functions of disk quotas, without actually limiting the users on your network. As you will see later, you are going to be able to see how much space each user is taking up on a partition. If you only want this information, but do not want to impose a specific limit, then check this box.

The next two options work in tandem. They allow you to set the limit for all users on this partition, and to tell Windows 2000 at which point it should begin to log events, warning you that someone has exceeded her limit. Make sure you give yourself enough time to react to a log entry. You can set these limits to KB, MB, GB, TB, and PB. The expectation is that you will see the event that is logged and either increase the amount of space the user needs or contact her to delete some data as soon as possible.

There are two additional entries in this dialog box. They control the behavior of disk quota logging. Two events can be logged. First, you can decide to have an event logged when a user exceeds his limit. Don't forget, this works in tandem with the other options you have set in this dialog box. From a user perspective he could either be denied the ability to save a file or be allowed to continue. If you choose the latter approach, then it is going to be up to you to react to this event.

The options in this dialog box are the heart of disk quotas. Configured correctly they will form the basis for your disk quota system. By choosing combinations, either you can allow your users a lot of freedom, minimizing the amount of administrative time you have to put aside to monitor events, or you can lock down the environment pretty tightly. This might be desirable in situations where disk space is truly at a premium.

Either way there is one final piece to this puzzle—the quota entries window. We are going to take a closer look at it in a moment.

One final topic to discuss in this section is the traffic light that is displayed in the "Local Disk Properties" dialog box. This traffic light is giving you status on disk quotas for the partition. A red light means that disk quotas are disabled. No monitoring of disk space occurs when the light is red. A yellow light means that Windows 2000 is building disk quota information. You will see the light turn yellow when you have turned on disk quotas for the first time.

The last option is when the light is green. A green light signifies that disk quotas are enabled and Windows 2000 is monitoring disk usage. The traffic light gives you a quick view of the status of disk quotas.

MONITORING DISK QUOTAS

In the previous section we showed you how to configure disk quotas on a partition. The options we talked about are partitionwide options. This means that any options that you set in the Local disk properties dialog box are applied to all new users on the partition you are configuring.

As time passes, you are going to need to view the status of your disk quotas. You might decide that a single user, or a group of users, need additional space, or you might simply want to know who is using the most space on your server. You will perform these tasks from the quota entries window.

The amount of time you spend in this window will depend entirely upon the configuration options you set earlier. The less space you assign users, the more time you are going to have to spend making "exceptions." However, some adjustment is inevitable. Figure 18.6 shows a typical quota entries window.

In Figure 18.6 you can see we have three users (other than administrative accounts). Each user has consumed disk space on the partition. UserA has a green arrow to the right of her name. This indicates that this user is within her quota limit. UserB, on the other hand, has a yellow exclamation mark. This mark indicates that this user has exceeded his warning level and is about to exceed his quota. You should be thinking about this user at this point. You

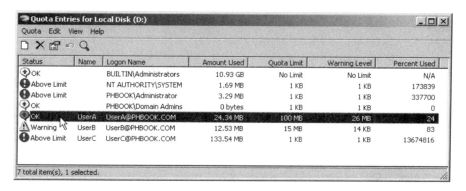

Status	Name	Logon Name	Amount Used	Quota Limit	Warning Level	Percent Used
OK		BUILTIN\Administrators	10.93 GB	No Limit	No Limit	N/A
Above Limit		NT AUTHORITY\SYSTEM	1.69 MB	1 KB	1 KB	173839
Above Limit		PHBOOK\Administrator	3.29 MB	1 KB	1 KB	337700
OK		PHBOOK\Domain Admins	0 bytes	1 KB	1 KB	0
OK	UserA	UserA@PHBOOK.COM	24.34 MB	100 MB	26 MB	24
Warning	UserB	UserB@PHBOOK.COM	12.53 MB	15 MB	14 KB	83
Above Limit	UserC	UserC@PHBOOK.COM	133.54 MB	1 KB	1 KB	13674816

7 total item(s), 1 selected.

Figure 18–6   *The quota entries window.*

should either raise his limit or let him know that he will soon have to erase some files.

Finally we have UserC. This user is probably already breathing down your neck. The red exclamation mark indicates that this user has exceeded his limit. If you have selected "Deny disk space to users who have exceeding quota limits," then this user can no longer save files to this partition. Note that administrators are not affected by these limits.

Table 18.1 defines each of the columns that are shown in the Disk Entries Window. This will help you understand the data that the screen is presenting you with.

In the following exercise, simply to give an example, we will increase the quota for UserC. In this example we will increase his limit to 150 MB. However, on your own network we suggest that you do not make any changes to disk quotas without a fully defined system in place. Quotas should be increased in a logical way. Managing quotas means having a process in place so you are not making decisions on the spur of the moment.

To complete this example you must have a user account in place, and that user must have consumed some disk space on the partition. If you do not have a user account for this example, then you can create one for testing purposes. Create a user account, and then log on as that user. Take ownership of a group of files on this partition. Once this is done, you can log on as an administrator and complete the following example:

1. First, make sure the quota entries window is open. If it is not, then click on Start, Programs, Administrative Tools, Computer Management. This starts the Computer Manager application. Right-click on the Disk Management option. Select All Tasks and then Properties. Click on the Quota tab. Finally, click on the Quota Entries button.

2. Your screen should now resemble that shown in Figure 18.6. In this example we are going to increase the disk quota for UserC. To do this, right-click on UserC (or the user for whom you wish to increase the disk quota) and select Properties. This brings up the "Quota Settings for UserC" dialog box, as shown in Figure 18.7.

3. You now have two choices. You can either turn off disk quotas for this user by selecting the "Do not limit disk usage" button, or you can increase the amount of space this user has been allocated. We are going to perform the latter task. First we must increase the unit of measurement. Currently this user is limited at the KB level. This is a very fine level of increment. We are going to change this to MB. Click on the dropdown arrow next to KB and select MB (megabytes) from the list. Also make this change in the drop-down box next to "Set warning level to."

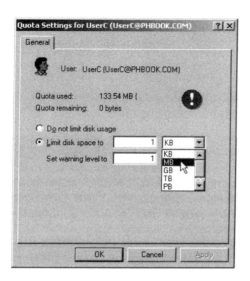

Figure 18–7   *The "Quota Settings for UserC" dialog box.*

Table 18.1	Quota Entries Window Definitions
Column Name	**Definition**
Status	There are three levels of status. Think of this as a traffic light; green is "good" (as indicated by a green arrow), yellow is "warning" (as indicated by a yellow exclamation mark), and red is "stop" (as indicated by a red exclamation mark).
Name	Displays the name of the user to whom the entry applies.
Logon Name	Displays the logon name of the user to whom the entry applies. This is different from the "name" column because this column includes the full logon name. While "name" can contain duplicates, "logon name" cannot.
Amount Used	This is the amount of disk space currently being consumed by this user.

Table 18.1	Quota Entries Window Definitions
Quota Limit	This is the limit that has been placed upon this user. The user should not exceed this limit.
Warning Level	This is the amount of space that a user must consume before a warning is recorded. This indicates that the user is nearing capacity on this partition. It causes the status to turn to a yellow exclamation mark.
Percent Used	This is the percentage of quota that this user has consumed.

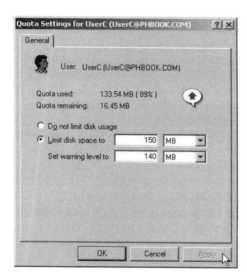

Figure 18–8 *The correctly configured "Quota Settings for UserC" dialog box.*

4. Change the value to 150 in the "Limit disk space to" box, and to 140 in the "Set warning level to" box. This is shown in Figure 18.8. Finally click on the Apply button. Notice that the red exclamation mark has now changed to a green arrow.

5. Finally, click on OK to be returned to the quota entries window. This user is now within his quota limit, as indicated by the green arrow.

IDEAS FOR USING DISK QUOTAS

Disk quotas are a significant—and much requested—new feature of Windows 2000. We give you some guidelines in this section. While you might be tempted to simply turn on the feature immediately, it is a good idea to think things through first, taking into account the issues here.

Keep in mind that disk quotas do not get applied to Administrative accounts. If you are an administrator, then you should have two accounts on the network—an administrative account and a user account. You should use the administrative account only when you really need to. For day-to-day operations, such as word processing and email, you should use the user account. This prevents any inadvertent errors and also helps you emulate the "user experience" as much as possible.

Your user account will be affected by disk quotas. Therefore, if you perform any administrative tasks while logged on as that user, you might find your quota being consumed more quickly than normal. An example would be if you installed an application while logged on with the user account.

To prevent this, make sure that all software installations are performed while logged on with the administrative account. If you don't do this, you will need to sharply increase the quota for your user account.

Disk quotas allow you to have partitions shared among many users in an organized and "fair" way. In the past, it has been possible for a single user to exhaust disk space and deny access to everyone else. Clearly this was not ideal.

However, do not be tempted to turn on disk quotas for all partitions. This is inefficient. Disk quotas cause overhead, and collecting data for data's sake is not a good idea. Only turn on this option for shared partitions—that is, on partitions where multiple users are expected to share disk resources.

Disk quotas also allow you to generate disk usage data. You saw this earlier in the quota entries window. If you only want to monitor how much disk space each user is consuming, without putting restrictions in place, then turn on disk quotas and do not check the "Deny disk space to users exceeding quota limit" check box. Windows 2000 will then record disk space used but will not prevent usage, no matter how much space has been consumed.

There will always be some users who require more disk space than others. The two choices you have are to offer everyone a large amount of space—therefore accommodating those that need a great amount—or to restrict everyone and make exceptions. We suggest the latter option: restrict your users and then allow selected users to have more space. This is a managed process and will benefit you over time.

The quotas entries window can become outdated over time, and it should be periodically cleaned up. For instance, if a user leaves an organization, then her name and files will still show up. These entries should be deleted. However, you cannot do that until you have deleted, or had someone else take ownership of, all the files and folders that belong to that user account. While this might sound like a lot of work, it is a good policy to clean up files after a user has left an organization. This will force you to deal with those issues.

Finally, we suggest that you turn on disk quotas on new partitions whenever possible. This is because it can cause a lot of processing for Windows 2000 to calculate disk usage on a partition that already has a lot of data stored on it—with many different users. If you use a new partition, this is not a consideration.

Encrypting Data

It goes without saying that networks offer many advantages over standalone PCs. One obvious advantage is in the area of security. Networks offer enhanced security over standalone PCs because of a collection of many features. For instance, to access a network you have to provide a user name and password. This user account can have a set of restrictions placed upon it, preventing it from accessing folders and files, or applications. Group Policy within Windows 2000 can also prevent a user from logging on at a particular PC.

Along with logon security, networks also provide permissions down to the file level. It is a common practice to protect data either by allowing restricted access to a file or folder or by denying a set of users access. This information keys off the user account entered during the logon process.

We could talk at length about additional security features, but you get the idea. Networks have helped businesses not only to share information, but to share it intelligently.

However, by far the most important security measure you can take is physical security. All the measures in the world won't help you if an unauthorized user has access to the physical server.

With this in mind Windows 2000 has gone a step further by adding support for encrypting data. This is not a substitute for any of the measures mentioned so far. It does, however, complement your set of tools.

File encryption is going to be most useful in situations where the other security options you have are insufficient. For instance, knowing that physical security is the most important step you can take doesn't help you when you have users on the road with their own laptop computers. There simply isn't a way for you to ensure that the computers do not fall into the wrong hands. Encrypting data can help you in these circumstances.

Of course there are restrictions in place to prevent unauthorized staff members from encrypting data. In order to encrypt data you must either be the file owner or have Full Control permissions over a file. Much as we saw with compression, the file is decrypted before it can be used, and then encrypted once it is saved. This process is invisible to the end user.

As you will see in the following pages, encryption is a powerful tool if used correctly. The qualifier in the proceeding sentence is very important.

Encryption can be affected if a file is copied or moved. It reacts to inheritance. Therefore, you need a clear understanding of what encryption brings to the table, and once again, careful planning will increase its effectiveness.

Introduction to File Encryption

Security on your network is a very important task for a system administrator. At the end of the day the ultimate value of your network isn't about computers and lengths of cable, it's about the data stored on your servers and workstations. If you don't believe me, lose your users' email in a system crash, and see how long it takes everyone to get very upset. Believe me, it won't be long!

Despite the best efforts of Network Operating System vendors, it is likely that there always will be an Achilles heel in all systems. Over the past few years we have seen an increasing number of security breaches documented in the press, and vendors scramble to plug holes in protocol suites, firewalls, and authentication algorithms.

It is important to understand that the entire burden of securing a network does not fall upon the shoulders of software vendors. It is much less likely that you will be affected by some obscure bug than simply by having insufficient enforcement within your own network.

To be more precise, Microsoft provides you with a host of functionality and features. But the key to success is going to be the way in which you implement these features. EFS is just one more tool you can use to secure data on your network, but it isn't the only one—it's not even the most important. The level of security will be defined by the combination of all these features.

Even with EFS, you will still need to have a clearly defined—and implemented—file and folder structure. These files and folders should be secured with NTFS permissions. Think of EFS as an addition to this type of security. If you need to go one step further, then EFS can help.

NTFS permissions can fail if you are unable to guarantee physical security on a server (or host machine). EFS, on the other hand, will prevent unauthorized users from accessing a file—even if the person has physical security.

Let's consider a couple of circumstances where normal NTFS file permissions are not sufficient. First, let's consider an obvious one. If someone had physical access to the server hardware, then there is nothing to stop him from booting the server from a floppy diskette. In this case it is possible to boot from another OS and thereby bypass NTFS permissions entirely. This gives him access to the files on the hard disk. NTFS permissions does not protect you from this—EFS does.

Second, there is another circumstance where security can be just as easy to circumvent. That is, it is possible to remove a Windows 2000 hard disk from one server and mount it on another server. If a user has administrative rights on the new server, then she will be able to take ownership of any files on the system, and therefore read them. Again, EFS would cure this. This is also an illustration of why you should keep your backup tapes in a secure location.

Since encryption and decryption is invisible to the user, there is little penalty for encrypting files. However, you will need to make some decisions regarding encryption before deciding to use it.

First, it is not easy to share files that have been encrypted. An encrypted file can be read only by the file owner and the Administrator. No one else has access to the file. You should not encrypt a file that needs to be shared among many people.

EFS can generate helpdesk calls if some files in a folder are encrypted and some are not. It is difficult for users to follow which files they are allowed to access if there is a mix on a single share. Don't forget, if a user suddenly quits, the only person who can access these files is the administrator, and the burden of supporting EFS falls to him or her.

Encrypting Files and Folders

There are two things you can encrypt—a folder or a file. If you are going to encrypt folders, then you need to make some decisions. For instance, are you going to encrypt just the folder, or are you are going to encrypt the folder and all files within it? You can also choose to encrypt subfolders within the folder.

Likewise with file encryption. If you encrypt a file then you need to decide whether you are going to encrypt a single file, or whether you also want to encrypt the folder in which the file resides.

These decisions should be made before you start encrypting files. You should also note that encryption does not work with file compression. This means that if you have a folder with a few compressed files in it, then you will not be able to compress the entire folder.

To help you understand these principles it is probably best that we go ahead and encrypt a file, and then a folder. For this example to work on your machine you will need a folder with one subfolder. You will need at least two documents in the parent folder, and at least two documents in the subfolder. We suggest that you do not use documents that are essential to your business in this example. Use dummy files; that way nothing will be lost if you make a mistake. The specific folder structure used in this example is shown in Figure 18.9.

1. In this example we have a "My Documents" folder on our computer. There are three documents in this folder. There is also a subfolder which contains three additional files. We have been asked to encrypt "baserc.doc" to make it secure. We will use Windows Explorer to encrypt the file. To start Windows Explorer click on Start, Programs, Accessories, Windows Explorer. Windows Explorer should open on your desktop.
2. The folder we are going to work with is stored on our D:\ drive. If you have chosen another partition, then you will need to navigate to it now. If your files are on the D:\ partition, then click on "My Computer" and then

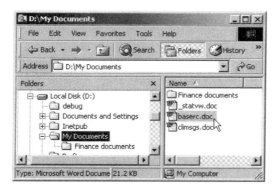

Figure 18–9 *Folder structure for example.*

Figure 18–10 *The "Advanced Attributes" dialog box.*

the partition that contains your files. Finally, double-click the partition and single click on the folder you are going to use for this example. In our case, that is the "My Documents" folder.

3. We are going to encrypt a file called "baserc.doc." There is nothing unique about this file, and for the purposes of this example, you can use almost any file you want. The two exceptions are files in your *<systemroot>* folder and files that have been compressed. Right-click on "baserc.doc" and select "Properties." This brings up the "Baserc.doc Properties" dialog box.

4. This dialog box gives you a lot of information regarding this file. Information includes file size, date, and location. At the bottom of the dialog box are "Attributes" options. This is where you can set the file to be read-only, or Hidden. To the right of Hidden is an "Advanced" button. Click on it. You are now in the "Advanced Attributes" dialog box, as shown in Figure 18.10.

5. We are going to choose the "Encrypt contents to secure data" option. This will cause the file to be encrypted. Click on this option, and then click on OK.

6. This returns you to the "Baserc.doc Properties" dialog box. Click on OK, and you will see the "Encryption Warning" dialog box. This is shown in Figure 18.11.

Figure 18-11   *The Encryption Warning dialog box.*

7. There are three important options you need to consider in this dialog box. The first two are whether you want to encrypt the file and the parent folder (which encrypts all files within the folder) or whether you simply want to encrypt the file only. Be careful which of these you select. Don't forget, once a file or folder is encrypted, the only people who gain access to it are file owners and administrators. In this example we are going to select the "Encrypt the file only" option. Click this option, and then click OK. The dialog box will disappear, and the file is encrypted.

8. Finally we will go ahead and encrypt a folder. The process is similar to what we have seen before. This time, however, we will see a "Confirm Attribute Changes" dialog box. This allows you to choose the options you want. First, right-click on the folder you want to encrypt—in our case this is the "Finance folder." Select Properties. This brings up the "Finance Documents Properties" dialog box.

9. As before, you must click on the "Advanced" button in the "Attributes" section. This brings up the "Advanced Attributes" dialog box, as shown in Figure 18.10. Select "Encrypt data to secure data" and click OK. This will return you to the "Finance Documents Properties" dialog box. Now click on the "Apply" button. You are now presented with the "Confirm Attribute Changes" dialog box, as shown in Figure 18.12. You have two options. The first (selected by default) is the "Apply changes to this folder only" option. The second causes the encryption to cascade. In the latter case, all sub-

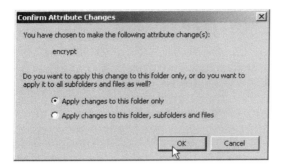

Figure 18–12 *The "Confirm Attribute Changes" dialog box.*

folders and files are encrypted also. Click on OK, and the folder will be encrypted.

COMMAND-LINE OPTIONS

In the preceding exercises you used the Graphical User Interface (GUI) to encrypt files and folders. Windows 2000 also provides a command-line utility that enables you to achieve the same results. For most tasks it is not going to matter which of these tools you use—it is entirely user preference. However, if you intend to script operations, the command-line options are obviously more flexible. You might initially use command-line options in setup scripts, or to rebuild systems that have been restored from backups.

The command-line option for encryption is "Cipher." You can use cipher with switches to achieve the results you require. Table 18.2 includes a list of switches that can be used. You can see these displayed on-screen by typing "cypher /?".

Table 18.2	Switch Definitions
Switch	**Definition**
No Switch	When executed without a switch, this command will tell you the status of a file or folder. You can use this to check whether a file or folder is encrypted.
/e	Use this switch to encrypt a folder. All files added to this folder will subsequently be encrypted.

Table 18.2	Switch Definitions (Continued)
/d	Decrypts a folder. All files added to this folder will subsequently be unencrypted.
/s:dir	Directs the command to a specific folder and subfolders.
/a	Performs the action on a specific file. If no file is found, is ignored.
/i	By default cipher will stop if an error is encountered. This command will change this behavior. If an error occurs with this switch, cipher ignores the error.
/f	Causes encryption of all objects. Objects already encrypted are ignored.
/q	Forces cipher to report concise information only.
/h	Displays files with the hidden and system attribute. By default these are ignored by cipher.
/k	Creates a new cipher key for a user. All other switches are ignored.

In the following steps we will use the cipher command. This example will illustrate two of the switches that are available. Once you have seen it work, it will not be difficult for you to use other switches. To perform these steps you will need to have a folder that contains files to work with. We are going to use the same structure you saw in previous exercises.

1. Cipher is a command-line utility. That means the commands are executed from the "command prompt." So the first thing we must do is to start the command prompt. To do this click on Start, Programs, Accessories, Command Prompt. This should open the prompt on your screen. This is also commonly known as the "DOS PROMPT" because of the resemblance to the older Disk Operating System.

2. First we need to change the folder we are going to use. For the purposes of this example we are going to use the folder structure from earlier examples. If you want to use a different folder, then simply change the path in the following statement. To change to the "My Documents" folder on the D: partition, type D: and press enter. Then type *CD My Documents* and press Enter.

3. You should now see a command prompt that looks something like this: *D:\My Documents.* We are going to encrypt a file with the cipher utility. First type *Dir* and press Enter. This will show you a list of all the files in this folder. We are going to encrypt the file called "climsgs.doc." You can substitute any file you want. The syntax to encrypt this file is *cipher /e /a climsgs.doc.* Type this and press Enter.
4. To confirm that the file is encrypted type *cipher* and press Enter. You should see a screen that resembles Figure 18.13.

Using an Encrypted File or Folder

Now that you have seen how to encrypt a file, it is time to introduce you to the nuances of using such a file. File or folder encryption is a feature that helps you safeguard against unauthorized use of your confidential material. However, there are some things you need to know before you can be sure you are having the desired effect. For instance, what happens when you copy a file, or move a file? To truly ensure that your data is secured, you need to have a good understanding of the various effects that each of these operations can have.

First, let us make sure that you are aware of the effect of encrypting a folder. If you choose to encrypt the folder and all files within the folder, then all files created beyond that point within the folder will also be encrypted. In effect the folder becomes a safe haven for your documents. If you want everything you do to be encrypted, then encrypt the folder. However, don't forget, you will not easily be able to share data with others if you choose this option.

There are two kinds of "copy," and they have different effects. Don't forget, a "move" is really a copy-and-then-delete operation. In other words, when a

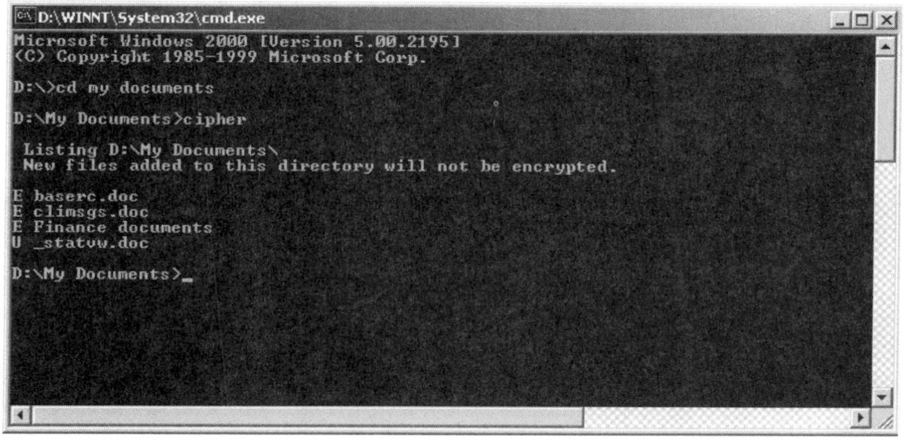

Figure 18–13 *Using the cipher command-line utility.*

file is moved, it is first copied from point A to point B. If the operation is successful, then the file is deleted from its original location.

If you copy or move a file within the same partition, then the file or folder will remain encrypted. This occurs even if the folder you are moving it to is unencrypted. Even renaming a file will not change the encryption attribute.

The only area of vulnerability is when you decide to copy or move the file to a non-NTFS or floppy diskette. In these cases there is no support for encryption. The file will be copied in plain text format. Of course, this is less secure and should be avoided if you are trying to protect your data.

Encryption is a powerful tool, and it should not be used without careful consideration. While it might seem like a good idea to be "better safe than sorry" and encrypt everything in sight, this is to be discouraged. Data sharing can become quite difficult if this practice takes hold. Support calls will undoubtedly increase, and this will have an impact on the efficiency of your organization.

Rather than leaving encryption in the hands of your users, it is suggested that you first draft a "best practices" document. This document should detail how encryption should be used, and when it is and is not appropriate. If you have a security group within your organization, then they would be a good starting point for this process.

Encryption will likely have the greatest effect on laptop users. If you have a salesman or executive who will be on the road, then you can use encryption (if they are running Windows 2000 Professional). These users need to be educated, and they need to be well versed in the pluses and minuses of encryption.

Some applications create temporary files when you are working on a file. For instance, many word processors will create a temporary file which is automatically deleted when the application is successfully closed. If you are editing an encrypted document, the temporary file is not encrypted. This means the data in the file is vulnerable until the application is closed. To prevent this from occurring, encrypt the temporary folder and all of its contents. If you do this at the folder level, then all new files created in the folder are also encrypted.

While it is possible to encrypt files on a remote machine, keep in mind that some network protocols, such as TCP/IP, do not encrypt data as it is moved across the network. Therefore, the data is encrypted on the disk, but once you read it across the network it is moved unencrypted. In this case you should choose a protocol that does allow you to encrypt data as it traverses the network, such as SSL or IPSEC.

Finally, don't forget that the encryption and decryption of files and folders takes some system processing time. If you encrypt a lot of files and folders, you might find that the overhead becomes too great. This will vary, depending on the hardware involved, but don't underestimate it when you have many files to encrypt.

Disk Defragmentor

System performance should always be a key concern for system administrators. There are many different methods you can use to fine-tune performance, and one of the easiest to implement is disk defragmentation. Earlier versions of Microsoft Windows NT did not provide you with tools for dealing with this issue—leaving it open to third-party vendors to fill the gap—but with the advent of Windows 2000, we finally have tools built into the operating system.

Fragmentation is a problem with many operating systems. It occurs without you knowing, and can have a significant effect on the efficiency of your server. To ensure that your servers are always running optimally, you will want to make sure that you stay on top of it. Fragmentation will show itself in poor disk performance.

The worst part of fragmentation is that it is never fatal to a system. The decrease in performance is subtle at first, and then gradually gets worse. The amount of time this takes depends on a lot of different issues, such as the number of files stored on a server and the frequency with which they are deleted and created. This subtle degradation can be easy to miss. Indeed, since earlier versions of Microsoft Windows NT did not include any method of dealing with it, it was easy to imagine that fragmentation simply was not a problem with Windows NT. This is a mistake. In Windows NT 4.0 environments you can realize a performance boost from purchasing a third-party defragmentation tool; in Windows 2000 you can use the free tools that shipped with the OS.

INTRODUCTION TO DISK FRAGMENTATION

Before we look at the built-in tools in detail, it would probably be a good idea to go through a brief overview of disk fragmentation. If you don't know what it is and why it occurs, then you will not be able to get a good understanding of why it is so important that you perform the tasks covered in this section of the book.

So let's start from the beginning. A hard disk stores data—be it databases, word processing documents, or other information. It stores that data in blocks. We tend to think of data on computers as streams of bits and bytes, but the truth is, disk drives have to store data in chunks, and in bit terms, they're pretty big chunks. These chunks are called "blocks."

These blocks vary in size from operating system to operating system. Or, to be more accurate, they vary depending on the type of file system you are using. Earlier file systems, such as those used in MS DOS, were fairly inefficient. This means that the block size was large. Then Microsoft introduced FAT32 and NTFS, which has smaller block sizes.

Windows 2000 uses NTFS as its preferred file system, and the block size of NTFS is 4 K. So what is the significance of this block size? Well, it might surprise you to know that Windows 2000 cannot save any file in increments of less than 4 K. So, if you have a 1 K file and save it to disk, it will take up 4 K of space. That extra 3 K simply gets lost. This explains why you can have a 20-GB hard disk but find yourself hurting for disk space even though you know you have much less data than the capacity of the drive.

This is problem enough—but there is another aspect to consider. What happens if you have a file that is 12 KB in size, and you want to save it? NTFS will save it in three blocks, since 3 multiplied by the 4 KB block size is 12 KB. However, NTFS will store this data in the first empty spaces it can find. If it is able to find three blocks that exist side-by-side, then it will neatly line up the data in a row. This is called "contiguous." However, if it finds a block sitting all alone at the front of the disk, it will fill that block first, before looking for the next free space. In this case, you have a simple 12 KB file physically stored across a disk. This is known as "incontiguous."

Now, from a user's perspective everything is working fine. The file is perfectly usable. But from the hard disk's perspective, things are beginning to become difficult. When a user wants to retrieve that piece of data, the head of the hard disk has to move first to the start of the file and read that 4 KB block. Then the head has to move to find the second block, and so on. This takes time, and it makes the hard disk less efficient.

Of course, we have been discussing a very small file. Imagine what happens when you start saving files of many megabytes! Files can soon become scattered all around the disk, and the disk drive itself has to work much harder to find the data when it is needed. This degrades performance. And this is the problem that disk defragmentors have been designed to take care of.

A disk defragmentation tool is designed to take a look at a disk, figure out how best to organize the data in those blocks so they are closer together on the physical disk, and then move the data around. If the disk head does not have to move so far to retrieve data, then disk performance will increase.

The tool built into Windows 2000 has several significant features. First, it can defragment NTFS and non-NTFS partitions (including FAT and FAT32). It also makes sure that all free space on your disk drive is in one place—that is, contiguous. In this way, future disk writes will be able to find free space. However, no matter how good a job the tool does, keep in mind that you will still have to run it periodically to maintain optimal performance. This is because as soon as a file is deleted from a disk drive, you no longer have optimal performance. No matter, that's the nature of the beast. There is no permanent fix for this issue, just due diligence from the administrator!

The only drawback worth mentioning is that the defragmentation process can take quite some time on a large disk drive that has a large number of fragmented files. If you are running it on a Windows NT 4.0 machine for the first time (or for the first time on a Windows 2000 machine, for that matter), you will very likely be surprised at the number of files you have that are fragmented. This problem is solved by continued use of the fragmentation tool.

Of course, you do not need to run the tool every day. We will talk about some usage issues later in this chapter, but before you start to defragment a

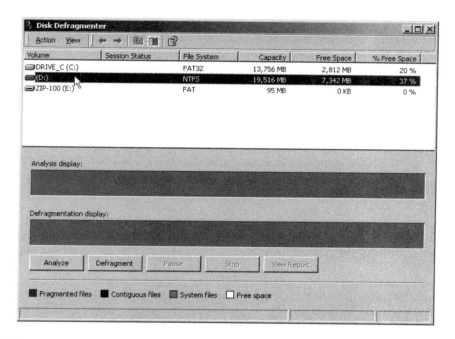

Figure 18-14   *The disk defragmentor.*

disk drive you should first use the tool to "Analyze" the disk. The analyze function will report the state of the hard disk. If you have a lot of fragmented files, then go ahead and run the tool. If you do not, then you might not realize a performance gain at all.

Using the Defragmenting Tool

The disk defragmentor utility has been designed for ease of use. It enables you to analyze a disk drive and view a report to ascertain whether the disk needs to be defragmented. Then it offers an easy pushbutton option to begin the process.

The disk defragmentor utility should be run periodically. Although there is no "schedule" option, you could use the Windows 2000 Task Scheduler to start the tool on a regular schedule. Alternatively you might want to consider purchasing a third-party utility which is more feature rich. Figure 18.14 is an illustration of the tool.

As you can see, the interface for this tool is fairly simple. There are, in fact, three panels. The first panel, at the top of the utility, lists the partitions that are available on your computer. The second panel shows you a graphical representation of the state of the files on your computer. The more red you see, the worse things are. Finally, a third panel shows the same information as the second panel, except as you begin the defragmentation process it will show you the progress as it is made.

In the following example we will walk you through an analysis of a partition and then the defragmenation process. Since it is unlikely that your computer will look exactly the same as our own, the steps we are about to outline may not match your own precisely. Feel free to substitute different drive letters in this example for letters that match your own.

1. First, we must start the disk defragmentor tool. As is often the case, there are several ways to do this. If you want to maintain a central management console—with most common tools at your fingertips, then click on Start, Programs, Administrative Tools, Computer Management. This starts the Computer Management console. Click on "Disk Management." This displays a list of all partitions on the right-hand side of the screen. Now, right-click on the partition you wish to defragment and select Properties. Click on the Tools tab and finally, click on the Defragment Now button. You can arrive at the same location by double-clicking "My Computer" on your desktop and then right-clicking on any of the partitions that are listed. If you want to run this tool from the command line then you need to know that this tool is simply an MMC snap-in. You can also start it from the command line with the following command: *MMC <System-Root>\System32\dfrg.msc.* In this case *<Systemroot>* is the folder into which you installed Windows 2000.

2. You should now be presented with a screen that resembles what you saw in Figure 18.14. Of course, if you have fewer—or more—partitions, then your disk defragmentor may look a little different. Before we defragment a disk drive, we need to know the extent of the fragmentation. So first we will run an "analyze" to see how we're doing. We are going to analyze the *D*: drive on our computer. To do this, click on the disk drive you want to analyze, and then click the "Analyze" button at the bottom of the screen. The "Analyze Display" box will change to "Analyzing." If you have never run the tool before, be advised that this process can take some time. Finally, you will be presented with the "Analysis Complete" dialog box.

3. The "Analysis Complete" dialog box will tell you whether you need to defragment the disk drive or not. This is based on the total number of fragmented files you currently have. Below this statement are three buttons. The first is "View Report"; this will display a list of the files that are fragmented on your disk drive. An example is shown in Figure 18.15. The other buttons are "Defragment" and "Close." The former button begins the defragment process, while the other simply closes the window and returns you to the disk defragmentor utility. When your analysis is complete, click the "View Report" button.

4. The report generated from the previous step gives you a lot of information. In the "Volume Information" window take the time to scroll down

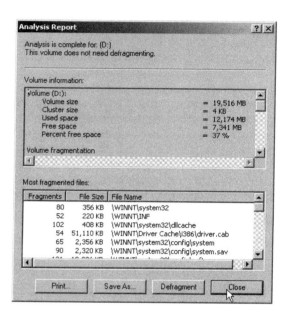

Figure 18–15   *The View Report option.*

and read all the information. You can find out the cluster (or block) size for your partition, the amount of free space available, and a host of other valuable data. In the lower portion of the windows you will see the "Most fragmented files" option. This lists the files that are most fragmented, and the number of different fragments that exist. However, this is not really enough information to judge the impact the fragmentation is having on your machine. For instance, if a file is accessed infrequently, then the fact that it is heavily fragmented is not a huge deal. You can also click on the Print button to print this report, or save this information to a text file. This is a good idea, since it allows you to maintain a history of the state of your hard disks. If you are ready, go ahead and click the Defragment button. This will begin the defragment process. Keep in mind that this might take some time on a large disk with a lot of fragmented files—anything from minutes to hours. Also, it is highly recommended that you do not use your computer while this process is taking place! In enterprise environments this should be done late at night, or during periods of little to no activity.

Recommendations

Disk fragmentation is the silent killer on your computer systems. It eats up processing time, makes your disk drives inefficient, and over time can have a severe impact on the overall performance of your system. The worst part is that the symptoms of fragmentation are often mistaken for something completely different. If a server is slow to retrieve a file, is it network congestion, a network card problem, or a client issue? Perhaps none of them!

However, some guidelines should be followed when you are defragmenting a disk. First, defragmenting takes a lot of processing power. It will have an impact on memory, CPU, and disk performance. Therefore, it is essential that you do not run the utility at the most busy time for your network. Preferably there is no activity taking place on the disk drive while it is being defragmented. The first time you run this utility you might find there is a lot of fragmentation. This means the impact of running it is going to be quite severe. Don't worry, once you have cleared up the problem, regular maintenance will prevent your having the same issues next time.

The disk defragmentor tool also ships with Windows 2000 Professional. It is a good idea to educate your users on its use and to encourage them to defragment their own hard disks periodically. Of course, the same rule applies: it is not a good idea for the users to run it while they are in the middle of their workday.

Always run an "analyze" before defragmenting. Don't assume that you will always have to defragment. Sometimes the performance gain will be minimal. It is also much slower to defragment if there is only a tiny amount of free space on a hard disk—so always make sure there is plenty of room free before you start the process.

Finally, come up with a schedule for defragmenting. Some hard disks will need to be defragmented more often than others. For instance, a disk drive that contains shares that have a lot of files added and deleted will need to be defragmented far more often than a disk drive with a relatively static amount of data that hardly ever changes. More than anything else, it is the addition and deletion of files that causes fragmentation. For instance, many applications create temporary files when you are using them. These files are saved on the disk drive and deleted when the application is closed. This can cause fragmentation.

Chapter Summary

In this chapter we focused on managing user data. There are many aspects to doing this, but we concentrated on four key areas: compression, disk quotas, encryption, and disk defragmentor.

These areas affect everything from cost savings and security to overall performance. Working in tandem, they can ensure that you have enough resources to allow your users to use the network, that the data they generate is secure, and that the servers and client computers operate with the utmost efficiency.

First we discussed file and folder compression. Compression is a method whereby an administrator can reduce the amount of disk drive space required on a given server or client computer. Disk compression works by shrinking the amount of disk space that is required to store data. Users will not notice any difference when using a compressed file, although it does take somewhat more system resources to use them. Since it is invisible to the user community, it is extremely efficient.

We learned that compression works only on files and folders stored on an NT File System (NTFS) partition, and that moving or copying files can cause the file to become uncompressed. Generally, moving or copying a file within the same partition causes the file to continue to be stored compressed; moving or copying the file to another partition causes the file to be uncompressed. Exceptions would be when the folder on the destination partition is also set for compression.

You can compress files and/or folders. If you compress a folder, then any files saved into that folder will also be compressed. This is the preferred method, since you only have to set compression once, and then all files are automatically compressed after that. You should not compress your "temp" directories, as this can decrease application performance. You also cannot compress the operating system files. This is largely because the operating system has to be fully loaded before NTFS can read compressed files.

Before NTFS can save a compressed file it needs to have an amount of disk space free equal to the *uncompressed* size of the file. If you attempt to save a file, and find you are unable to, check to make sure you have enough free space for the uncompressed size of the file.

The levels of compression vary from file type to file type. Files that are already compressed will not compress further, while some graphic files and plain text files compress to a greater degree. You should remember that compression does not have any effect on other disk management tools. For instance, if you are using disk quotas, you cannot get around your disk space limits by compressing files and folders.

We then discussed disk quotas. This has been one of the most requested new features. Disk quotas allow you to limit space on a per-user basis, on a partition. This is useful when disk resources are tight, or when you simply want to know who is using the most space on your servers.

You will likely use disk quotas on partitions that store users' home folders, but they are useful in any situation where you need to limit disk space. Disk quotas are set at a default level, but then you can use the Quota Entries window to limit space on an individual basis. This tool also allows you to see who is using the most disk space.

Administrator accounts are not affected by disk quotas. Make sure that all software installations on a server are performed using this account. If you install them under a regular account name, the disk space will count against their quota.

Make sure that you delete user names of people who have left your organization from the Quota Entries window. To do this you must first make sure that all files and folders owned by that user are either deleted or taken over by someone else. You will be unable to delete users if they still own files and folders. Administrators can take file or folder ownership, or they can grant someone else permission to do so.

Encryption is used to secure data. Most network security is achieved through file permissions. However, it is still possible for unauthorized users to gain access to secure folders and files if a Windows 2000 disk is mounted in another server. File permissions are ultimately only as good as the level of physical security you can achieve. If a server is not physically secure, then you cannot guarantee data.

Encryption can be set at the file or folder level. Once encrypted, a file can be read only by the file owner. Compressed files cannot be encrypted. There are two methods of encrypting files: you can use either Windows Explorer or the "Cipher" command-line utility.

Encrypted File System (EFS) is useful for laptop users who are taking their computers on the road. If the laptop is stolen or lost, you can be assured that no one will be able to read unauthorized data. You can implement EFS on either servers or desktop computers running Windows 2000 Professional. You cannot share EFS files and folders.

The use of encrypted files is invisible to the file owner. They can use the file as though it were unencrypted. If an unauthorized user tries to access the file, they receive an "Access Denied" message.

If you attempt to encrypt a file and find you are unable to, then the issue might be disk-space related. Because of the fallback techniques employed (in case an encryption operation fails) you need disk space equivalent to double the size of the file before you can perform file encryption. This is because a copy of the file is made before encryption takes place. This copy is deleted if the encryption is successful, but you still need the space initially.

Finally we spent some time discussing Disk Defragmentor. File and folder fragmentation is a performance-related issue. If the files and folders on your disk drives are fragmented, then you will not be able to realize peak performance.

The disk defragmentor tool allows you to move files into contiguous streams of blocks—or clusters—on a hard disk. This makes it easier for the computer to retrieve the files and improves access time. There is no way to prevent fragmentation from occurring over time, so you are going to have to come up with a schedule for running this utility.

You should not run this utility on computers that are being used. While it will not cause any damage, it will increase the amount of time the process will take and might also affect the quality of the job it can do.

Disk fragmentation is a "silent" threat to your computer. Regular defragmentation can increase overall performance of your system for little to no cost. Make sure you perform an "analyze" before running a defragmentation to make sure that it is necessary. Do not assume that running it will automatically increase performance—it won't. However, not performing it certainly will have a negative effect.

Backing Up and Restoring

*N*o matter how well you maintain your systems, eventually a hard drive will fail. It is not a question of *if* a drive will crash, but rather *when*. That is just the nature of magnetic media. Knowing that regardless of what you do for your systems, losing a drive at some point is inevitable, the importance of backing up and restoring data becomes clear. Fortunately, Windows 2000 provides at least a rudimentary backup program for backing up and restoring data. Keep in mind that there are much more robust third-party backup solutions on the market than Windows Backup, but they are beyond the scope of this book. You might research alternative solutions if you find Windows Backup does not offer the features and support you need for your environment.

In the next chapter, "Planning for Disaster Recovery," you will learn about ways to keep your data online even in the event of a hard drive crash. Even with disaster recovery methods in place, however, you might find yourself needing to restore files. You can only restore what you've backed up, which makes a solid backup strategy essential even for organizations with advanced disaster recovery configurations. In this chapter we will discuss:

- Understanding Backup and Restoring
- Performing Data Backup
- Performing Data Restores

Understanding Backup and Restoring

The concept of backup and restoring is easy enough to understand: you want to save your data to a safe location so that if data loss occurs (such as a hard drive crash), you can quickly recover by restoring lost files. Complications may arise, however, as systems administrators struggle to devise a backup strategy that affords them the opportunity to recover quickly when problems do arise. Recovery could be an entire hard drive or a single, critical file. You should be prepared for either case; that way you will be the hero to your users when you save the day, rather than having them angrily beating down your door while you sweat over your backups trying to find the right files to restore.

As previously alluded to, there are much more robust third-party backup solutions available, such as Cheyenne ARCserve and Veritas Backup Exec (Veritas recently bought the popular Backup Exec from Seagate). These third-party programs offer a wealth of features and, with the appropriate add-ons full support for backing up SQL Server, Exchange Server, Lotus Notes databases, and more without having to take the live databases offline first. They are beyond the scope of this book, which covers strictly the free Windows Backup that comes with Windows 2000. If, as you read this chapter, you find Windows Backup to be lacking, you might research alternative backup solutions.

Windows Backup

Windows 2000 provides a backup utility, aptly named Windows Backup, which provides many basic backup features. Windows Backup can be launched by going through the Accessories group on the Start menu or by executing ntbackup.exe from a run line. When launched, Windows Backup displays the window shown in Figure 19.1.

STORAGE OPTIONS

A severe restriction on the backup utility in Windows NT 4.0 and earlier was its ability to back up only to tape media. Furthermore, NTBackup only supported SCSI tape drives, which further limited the backup options. Windows 2000 corrects this shortcoming in a big way, allowing you to back up files practically anywhere you would want to, such as:

- Tape/magnetic media
- Optical/CD-recordable drives
- Removable storage drives such as Zip and Jaz drives from Iomega, or EZ-Flyer and SyJet drives from SyQuest
- Floppy diskettes and floppy replacements, such as the LS-120 drives
- Local hard drives
- Hard drives located on remote systems

BACKUP REQUIREMENTS

Like many tasks in Windows 2000, there's a certain level of user rights that you must obtain in order to perform a backup or restore. User rights and permissions may be summarized as follows:

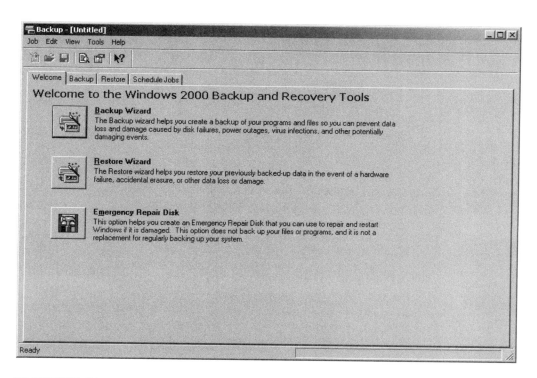

Figure 19–1
The Windows Backup welcome screen appears when you first launch the program.

- Users can always back up their own files and folders, as well as files and folders to which they have at least Read access.
- Users can restore files and folders to which they have at least Change access (Write and Modify).
- Users granted the "Backup Files and Directories" and/or "Restore Files and Directories" advanced user right can perform the appropriate function regardless of ownership of files and other assigned permissions.
- The Administrators, Server Operators, and Backup Operators groups by default have the above permissions and can back up and restore any file or folder on a system.

Remote Storage

Remote Storage is a separate utility from Windows Backup that makes it easy to extend disk space on your server without adding more hard disks. Remote Storage automatically copies infrequently used files on your local drives to a tape library, then monitors the amount of space available.

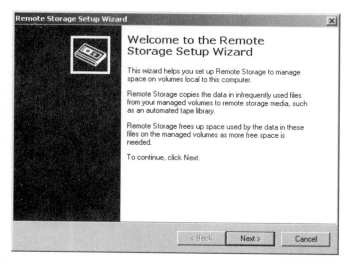

Figure 19-2 *The Remote Storage setup wizard allows you to quickly config-ure your desired drive and tape media settings.*

When you first launch the Remote Storage console, shown in Figure 19.3, Windows 2000 presents a setup wizard (Figure 19.2) that steps you through configuring your Remote Storage settings. You can define the local drives you want Remote Storage to manage, as well as the amount of free space you want maintained on the volumes, the file-selection criteria for copying files to remote storage, and the type of tape to use for remote storage.

The way Remote Storage works is this: File data is cached locally so that it can be accessed quickly when needed. When the amount of available space on a volume managed by Remote Storage drops below the level you specify, Remote Storage automatically removes the content from the cached files, pro-viding the disk space you need. When data is removed from a file, the disk space used by the file is reduced to zero. Data from cached files is not removed until more disk space is needed. When you need to open a file whose data has been removed, the data is automatically recalled from remote storage and restored from the tape media.

Since removable tapes in a library are less expensive per megabyte (MB) than hard disks, this can be an economical way to provide both maximum data storage and optimal local disk performance. Figure 19.3 shows the Remote Storage console, which must be installed manually through Add/Remove Pro-grams and Add/Remove Windows Components. Remote Storage is not installed by default in a typical installation of Windows 2000.

Remote Storage supports all SCSI class 4 mm, 8 mm, and DLT tape librar-ies. When you need to access a file on a volume managed by Remote Storage, you simply open the file as usual. If the data for the file is no longer cached on

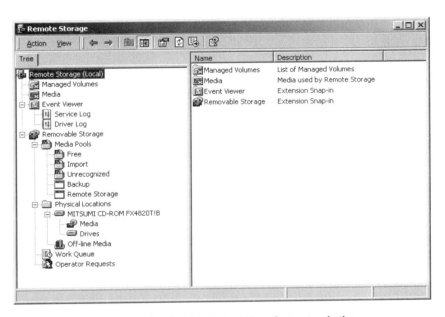

Figure 19–3

The Remote Storage utility is a backup option that extends the amount of available disk space on a server by moving infrequently used files to tape.

your local volume, Remote Storage recalls the data from a tape library. Because this can take more time than usual, Remote Storage removes the data only from those files on your local volumes that you are least likely to need, based on criteria that you set.

Remote Storage uses Removable Storage (discussed next) to access the applicable tapes contained in libraries. It is important to note that Remote Storage is not a backup program in the traditional sense, nor is it any kind of replacement for a backup strategy using Windows Backup or some other third-party backup program. However, it is a relevant tool to understand for backing up and restoring files. Performance can be an issue with Remote Storage files that are dynamically restored from tape will take significantly longer to open than if opened directly from the hard drive.

Removable Storage

Removable Storage, part of the Remote Storage console, is actually a separate program from Windows Backup that works in conjunction with Windows Backup and Remote Storage, which you use to manage the actual data stored on the media.

Removable Storage organizes all the media in your libraries into different media pools, which are collections of tapes or discs to which the same management properties apply. All media in a Removable Storage system belong to a media pool, and each media pool holds only one type of media. Data-management programs such as Windows Backup use media pools to gain access to specific tapes or discs within a library, which is comprised of media and the device used to read from and write to the media. The two common types of libraries are:

- *Robotic libraries*—automated units that hold multiple tapes or disks, and sometimes consisting of multiple drives. These libraries are sometimes called *changers* or *jukeboxes* and commonly use robotic subsystems, or drive bays, to move media stored in the library's storage slots. The drive bay locates the desired tape or disk, mounts it into an available drive, and then returns it to its assigned storage slot after a task is completed. Robotic libraries can also consist of other hardware components that are managed by Removable Storage, such as doors, inject/eject ports, cleaner cartridges, and bar-code readers.

- *Standalone drives*—single-drive, nonautomated units, such as tape or CD-ROM drives, that hold a single tape or disk. With these, you manually insert a tape or disc into the unit.

The group of libraries and associated media that are managed by a Removable Storage installation is called a *Removable Storage system*.

Removable Storage does not provide volume management or file management, as these services are done by data-management applications such as Backup or Remote Storage. In addition, Removable Storage does not support multiple data-management programs running on different computers that are connected to the same library.

Windows Backup Strategies

For the remainder of the chapter we will focus on the Windows Backup utility, not because Remote Storage and Removable Storage are not important topics, but because they do not take the place of a solid backup strategy. Remote Storage and Removable Storage are also utilities that provide functionality beyond what the typical systems administrator needs. It is important, however, to know they exist and to understand the previous overview given in case you do work in an environment that uses those technologies. Most systems administrators, though, will be content with a backup plan that provides data security and recovery in case of a hardware failure or other event that causes data loss.

Designing a backup strategy is like many other Windows 2000 designing tasks. It requires careful planning before you ever start installing or configuring hardware or software on your computer. A solid plan on paper is a lot easier to translate into a successful backup routine than a plan made up on the fly as you click through options in the Windows Backup software. It is essential to analyze the environment you are in when designing a backup strategy. Questions you should be prepared to answer include:

• What files do I need to back up? Whether you need to back up all or only certain files will affect the decisions you make in your planning. Even if you do not back up all files, you should always back up the Registry and Active Directory.

• Do I have more than one server or system that needs to be backed up to a single location? Windows Backup provides the ability to back up systems across the network, which can save time for you as the administrator. Rather than having to go to each system and do a local back up, you can back up multiple machines to a single location on the network.

• What type of media will I be backing up data to? Hard drive? Tape drive? Optical drive? The type and characteristics of the media you choose play an important role in the decision-making process. Tape media, while slow, still offers the most bang for the buck with the lowest cost per megabyte. Hard drives provide the advantage of speed in backing up and restoring files.

• Will the capacity of my media allow me to back up all of my data to one unit (disk, tape, CD, etc.)? This question is critical. If you only have a single drive library, you must either make backup jobs fit on a single medium or make plans to manually swap tapes or disks as needed during the backup process. This is not a pleasant thought if your backups run in the middle of the night. If your drive is too small you might have to purchase a larger standalone drive or consider purchasing a robotic library.

• How often do I need to back up? The answer will depend on how dynamic the data on your servers is. Some servers may change infrequently or slowly enough that weekly backups are sufficient. Other servers may require daily backups or, in the case of mission-critical servers, backups multiple times throughout the day.

• Do I need to back up just servers, or some workstations too? In many environments, only servers get backed up, and users that want their files backed up store them in home directories on a server. Looking at your environment, however, you may find that certain workstations should be backed up as part of your routine.

Answering the questions above will give you a good idea of what data needs to be backed up, how frequently, and to where. With that knowledge in place, we will look at the different types of backup jobs we can perform and design a system to back up our data.

Different Backup Types

Windows 2000 offers five different types of backups that you can perform. Following is an overview of the different types.

NORMAL BACKUPS

The most common backup type has a name that reflects just that, normal. A normal backup simply backs up all files and folders that have been selected for backup. In that sense, it is often called a full backup.

Many times I have heard questions from techs when it comes to file attributes. They always understand the read-only, system, and hidden attributes of a file, but initially many techs have no idea what the archive attribute is for. Well, the archive attribute plays a significant role in backups. When a file is modified, the system turns the archive bit on a file on. A normal backup, as we said, backs up all files and folders that have been selected for backup. When the backup runs, Windows Backup clears the archive bit on each file as it is backed up. By "clears" we mean it turns the archive attribute off for the file. The archive attribute being off indicates that a file has not been changed since the last backup. The normal backup doesn't care about that, since by nature it backs up everything, but as we'll soon see, the archive attribute is important to other types of backups.

INCREMENTAL BACKUPS

An incremental backup is used in conjunction with a normal backup. You perform a normal backup, maybe at the start of the week, then perform incremental backups throughout the remainder of the week. An incremental backup backs up only those files that have changed since the last backup of any kind. When you perform an incremental backup, Windows Backup clears the archive attribute for each file it backs up. That way, if you are performing a series of incremental backups, only files that had changed from one day to the next would be backed up.

For example, let's say you did a normal backup on Monday and an incremental backup on Tuesday. The Tuesday backup would back up only those files that had changed since Monday. Monday's normal backup cleared all of the archive bits, and when a file was modified on Tuesday, it would turn the archive bit back on. That's how the incremental backup would know what files to back up. Since the incremental backup also clears the archive bits as it backs up files, if you did another incremental backup on Wednesday it would only back up files changed since Tuesday, since the last incremental backup was done. If a file was backed up on Monday and didn't change on Tuesday, it wouldn't be backed up again. Same thing from Tuesday to Wednesday.

The key advantage to performing incremental backups is speed. Since not everything is being backed up every day, the backups run quicker and take up less space on a tape. The key disadvantage is that in case of a crash you have to restore the normal backup tape plus every incremental backup that has occurred since the last normal backup in order to recover all of your files to their most current versions. If a server crashes on Friday afternoon, you will have to restore the Monday full backup plus the Tuesday, Wednesday, and Thursday incremental backups.

DIFFERENTIAL BACKUPS

A differential backup is like an incremental backup in the sense that it does not back up every file, it looks at the archive attributes to see what files should be backed up. The key difference between an incremental backup and a differential backup, however, is that the differential backup does not clear the archive bit when it backs up a file. By not clearing the archive attribute, a differential backup always backs up every file that has changed since the *last normal backup* rather than just every file that has changed since the last backup of any kind. In effect, each day the backup will take a little longer and take more space, since it is backing up every file that has changed since the last normal backup.

Let's look at our above example again, this time using differential backups instead of incrementals. On Monday night you perform a normal backup. On Tuesday night a differential backup is run, which backs up every file that has changed since Monday as determined by looking at the archive attributes of the files. Files with archive bits that are turned on are backed up, since the normal backup cleared all of them the day before. On Wednesday night another differential backup is performed. Since the differential backup run on Tuesday did not reset the archive attributes on files, the Wednesday backup backs up all of the files that were changed both on Tuesday and on Wednesday. This continues throughout the week until another normal backup is run that clears all of the archive attributes again. Then the process starts over.

The key disadvantage to the differential backup is that as you get further and further away from your last normal backup, the backup times increase as more and more files that have been modified need to be backed up. The key advantage is that in the event of a system crash, you only need the last normal backup plus the last differential backup to restore the files to their most current version. If a system crashes on a Friday, you only need the Monday normal backup and the Thursday differential backup to recover, since the Thursday backup also includes everything backed up on Tuesday and Wednesday nights.

COPY BACKUPS

A copy backup is similar to a full backup in that it backs up all selected files. Where it differs, however, is that a copy backup pays no attention to the archive attribute. It neither resets the archive bit when it backs up a file nor uses the archive bit as any sort of criterion for choosing files. A copy backup is used when you need to make a backup and not have it interfere with your usual backup routine of normal backups with incremental or differential backups.

For example, say you had a backup routine where you did a normal backup on Monday and differential backups Tuesday through Sunday. On Thursday you need to install the latest service pack on the server and you want a full backup before you start replacing operating system files. If you simply did a normal backup, all of the archive bits would be reset, which would mess up the daily differential backups. When you ran the Thursday differential backup, only files that had changed since the impromptu Thursday normal backup would be backed up, not all files since the Monday normal backup. So you would instead use a copy backup that would accomplish the goal of getting a full backup on tape, without interfering with the differential backups.

DAILY BACKUPS

Daily backups are like copy backups in that they back up files without interfering with a backup routine. In other words, daily backups do not reset archive attributes when they back up files. A daily backup is a special kind of backup that backs up only those files that have been modified the day of the backup. This is useful for situations where you want to back up all files changed on a given day without affecting your usual backup routine, and you don't want to have to manually search and find the files to select for a copy backup.

Table 19.1 summarizes the backup types together with the advantages and disadvantages associated with each.

Table 19.1	Backup Types			
Backup Method	**What's Back Up**	**Archive Bit**	**Advantage**	**Disadvantage**
Normal	Every file	Cleared on all files	Restore only needs one tape	Time-consuming
Incremental	Files changed since last backup of any type	Cleared on files	Backed up fast	Restore requires full plus all previous incremental tapes
Differential	Files changed since last **full** backup	Unchanged	Faster than full, restore only requires full plus last differential tape	Backup time is slower, as days pass since last full backup
Copy	Every file	Unchanged	One off backup doesn't affect backup schedule	Time-consuming

Table 19.1	Backup Types (Continued)			
Daily	Files changed the day of backup	Unchanged	Quick backup of files changed that day without affecting backup schedule	Situation backup only

Backup Strategy Best Practices

While it is useful to understand the different types of backups available in Windows Backup, it is more important to understand how to use them to create an effective backup strategy. One such best practice is to use tape media for backups in most situations. Not only do they provide the best value in terms of cost per megabyte, they can come in capacities such that it is easy to back up multiple servers to a single tape. Our backup strategies below will be under the assumption of using tape media.

A severe limitation of Windows Backup, as you will quickly discover, is its job scheduling ability and media management. Actually, the Removable Storage utility previous mentioned handles media management, rather than Windows Backup. When we say that job scheduling is severely limited, it is because Windows Backup does not support tape rotation schemes the way some third-party backup programs do. A tape rotation scheme is an important aspect of a backup strategy.

TAPE ROTATION SCHEMES

What is a tape rotation scheme? It is a system where the tapes used to back up data are changed out (rotated) in order to provide the ability to recover data not only from recent backups, but from a history as well. The most commonly used tape rotation scheme is known as the Grandfather-Father-Son rotation scheme, or GFS for short.

The GFS strategy is a method of maintaining backups on a daily, weekly, and monthly schedule. GFS backup schemes are based on a five-day or seven-day weekly schedule. Which one you use will depend on your organization. The scheme begins any day of the week, though typically Friday or Monday. A full backup is performed at least once a week. On all other days, full, partial (incremental or differential), or no backups are performed. The daily incremental or differential backups are known as the Son. The Father is the last full backup in the week (the weekly backup). The Grandfather is the last full backup of the month (the monthly backup). Tables 19.2 and 19.3 show examples of weekly backup schedules using full and differential backups.

Table 19.2	An Example of a Weekly Backup on a Five-Day Schedule					
Sun	**Mon**	**Tues**	**Wed**	**Thur**	**Fri**	**Sat**
None	Diff	Diff	Diff	Diff	Full	None

Table 19.3	An Example of a Weekly Backup on a Seven-Day Schedule					
Sun	**Mon**	**Tues**	**Wed**	**Thur**	**Fri**	**Ssat**
Diff	Diff	Diff	Diff	Diff	Full	Diff

By default, you can reuse daily tapes after four days (five-day schedule) or six days (seven-day schedule). A weekly tape can be overwritten after five weeks have passed since it was last written to. Monthly media are saved throughout the year and should be taken off-site for storage. The primary purpose of the GFS scheme is to suggest a minimum standard and consistent interval at which to rotate and retire the tapes.

Table 19.4 shows an example GFS implementation over the course of two months. Starting out, we do a full backup on Sunday the first just to get a good full backup. The initial differential backups are actually going to be full backups. The reason is that since backups have not been occurring, the archive attributes are all turned on. Those archive bits won't be cleared until the first Friday weekly backup. While we use differential backups for the daily backups, the schedule would be the same using incremental backups instead.

Table 19.4	An Example of a Two-Month GFS Rotation Scheme on a Five-Day Schedule					
Month 1 (Full-W = Weekly, Full-M = Monthly Backup)						
Sun	Mon	Tues	Wed	Thur	Fri	Sat
1	2	3	4	5	6	7
None	Diff	Diff	Diff	Diff	Full-W	None
	Tape1	Tape2	Tape3	Tape4	Tape5	
Sun	Mon	Tues	Wed	Thur	Fri	Sat
8	9	10	11	12	13	14
None	Diff	Diff	Diff	Diff	Full-W	None
	Tape1	Tape2	Tape3	Tape4	Tape6	
Sun	Mon	Tues	Wed	Thur	Fri	Sat
15	16	17	18	19	20	21
None	Diff	Diff	Diff	Diff	Full-W	None

Table 19.4 An Example of a Two-Month GFS Rotation Scheme on a Five-Day Schedule (Continued)

	Tape1	Tape2	Tape3	Tape4	Tape7	
Sun	Mon	Tues	Wed	Thur	Fri	Sat
22	23	24	25	26	27	28
None	Diff	Diff	Diff	Diff	Full-M	None
	Tape1	Tape2	Tape3	Tape4	Tape8*	
Sun	Mon	Tues				
29	30	31				
None	Diff	Diff				
	Tape1	Tape2				

Month 2

Sun	Mon	Tues	Wed	Thur	Fri	Sat
			Wed	Thur	Fri	Sat
			1	2	3	4
			Diff	Diff	Full-W	None
			Tape4	Tape5	Tape9	
Sun	Mon	Tues	Wed	Thur	Fri	Sat
5	6	7	8	9	10	11
None	Diff	Diff	Diff	Diff	Full-W	None
	Tape1	Tape2	Tape3	Tape4	Tape10	
Sun	Mon	Tues	Wed	Thur	Fri	Sat
12	13	14	15	16	17	18
None	Diff	Diff	Diff	Diff	Full-W	None
	Tape1	Tape2	Tape3	Tape4	Tape5	
Sun	Mon	Tues	Wed	Thur	Fri	Sat
19	20	21	22	23	24	25
None	Diff	Diff	Diff	Diff	Full-M	None
	Tape1	Tape2	Tape3	Tape4	Tape11*	
Sun	Mon	Tues	Wed	Thur	Fri	Sat
26	27	28	29	30	1	2
None	Diff	Diff	Diff	Diff	Full-W	None
	Tape1	Tape2	Tape3	Tape4	Tape6	

From the above rotation, you can quickly calculate that it will take a total of 21 tapes to perform this GFS rotation for a year. There are four daily tapes (Sons) that are recycled (reused) weekly, five weekly tapes (Fathers) that are recycled after the fifth full weekly backup is complete, and 12 monthly tapes (Grandfathers) which are the last full backups of the month and are taken off-site. The grandfather tapes are noted with an asterisk in the above schedule. Tapes have on average about a year lifespan before they start becoming more susceptible to media errors, so after the first year you would want to replace the daily "Son" tapes and the weekly "Father" tapes.

As we previously said, a GFS tape rotation scheme is something that third-party backup programs often provide as part of their job management functions. Windows Backup does not offer this feature, so you will want to sit down with a calendar and plot out a schedule similar to that above in order to keep track of your tape rotation. You *can* schedule backups with Windows Backup, so using the above scheme you could create differential backup jobs to run Monday through Thursday and a normal job to run on Friday.

Performing Data Backup

You should now have planned a solid backup strategy for your organization. With the strategy in place, we move on to the specifics of Windows Backup itself and actually backing up data.

Preparing to Perform a Backup

Before actually backing up data there is some preparation to do. In many cases this will already be done, but if not you will need to ensure it is complete. The following preparations need to be made:

- Install and configure the tape drive or other storage device
- Ensure open files will be closed if their being backed up is required
- Decide if backups will be run unattended or manually, and plan a time schedule accordingly.

INSTALLING AND CONFIGURING YOUR BACKUP DESTINATION

Obviously, before you can back up your files you have to have a destination configured for it. Often this will be a tape drive, but Windows Backup also supports backing up to removable drives, to optical drives like CD-R, and even to hard disks. Whichever, medium you choose, you will need to have the device installed. Microsoft maintains a Hardware Compatibility List, or HCL, for Windows 2000 that lists every device that has been tested as compatible with the operating system. For best results, you should try to use hardware that is on the HCL.

CLOSE OPEN FILES

With Windows Backup, files in use by the operating system are not backed up. If you are performing a manual backup, you might use the console messaging feature of Windows 2000 (discussed in Chapter 27) to notify users that they need to save their work and exit so that you can back their files up. Otherwise you might schedule the job to run after business hours, when users are least likely to have files open. In the case of server services such as WINS or DHCP, you will have to schedule the temporary stopping of those services while the backup is running in order to back up their databases. Once the backup is complete, the services can be automatically restarted.

MANUAL VERSUS AUTOMATED BACKUPS

An important consideration is whether you are going to run backups manually (cumbersome, since you always have to sit down at the console and execute that backup job at the right time) or automatically through a scheduling mechanism. Automating backups is discussed later in this chapter.

How to Select Files and Folders to Back Up

With your preparation complete, you are ready to implement your backup strategy. The easiest way to accomplish this is by using the Windows Backup wizard. In this section we will walk through creating a backup job using the wizard.

1. Launch Windows Backup from the Start menu as described earlier and click the Backup Wizard button. This starts the wizard as shown in Figure 19.4.
2. After clicking Next, the wizard prompts you to specify what you want to back up. It defaults to backing up the everything in My Computer, though you can choose to back up only selected files and folders or just the System State data. Figure 19.5 shows these choices. Keep the default option for now and click next. Note, however, in Figure 19.6 that if you select the option to back up selected files and drives, you will see an extra dialog that prompts you to specify what specifically to back up. This is an extra step between step 2 and 3 below.

Backup Destination and Media Settings

3. Figure 19.7 shows the next step of the wizard, which asks you where you want to store your data. This is where you pick your backup destination. If you are using a tape drive, choose it; if a removable drive of some kind, pick it. In our example, we have decided to do a quick backup to our *C*:\ drive.

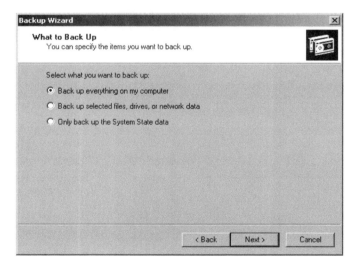

Figure 19–4   *The Windows Backup Wizard.*

Figure 19–5   *Windows Backup asks you to choose what to back up.*

4. At this point, you will see the dialog shown in Figure 19.8, which indicates
   to you that Windows Backup has enough information to perform the
   backup. You have the option of clicking Finish and running the backup or
   clicking the Advanced button to change the settings from default. For this
   example, we will click Advanced.

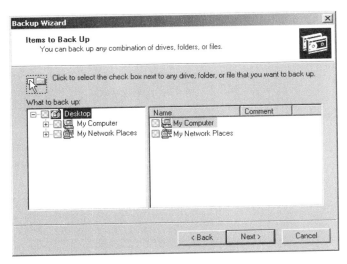

Figure 19–6

Choosing to back up only selected files adds an extra step to the backup wizard process, in which you manually select what you want to back up.

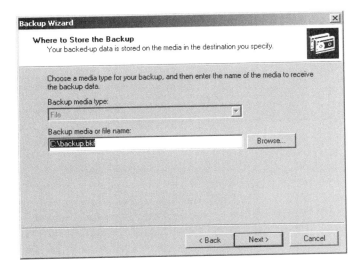

Figure 19–7

Defining the destination for your backup.

Figure 19–8

Windows Backup gives us the option to run the backup "as-is" or change the Advanced settings.

Using the Advanced Backup Settings

5. When you click the Advanced button, you see the dialog shown in Figure 19.9, which lets you choose what type of job you want to perform. You also have the option to back up files that have been moved into Remote Storage according to your settings. Figure 19.10 shows the same figure with the list of backup types exposed, so you can see the choices you have available.

6. Once you have selected the type of job, such as Normal, you can click Next. You then see a dialog that asks if you want to verify the files after they've been backed up to ensure data integrity. If you are backing up to a device such as a tape drive that supports hardware compression of files to save space on tape, you can select it here. Figure 19.11 shows this.

7. Windows Backup in Figure 19.12 now asks for your media options, specifically if you want to append to or overwrite the existing backup (if there is one). If you choose to replace existing data, you also have the security option to restrict access to the backup to Administrators.

8. When sorting through your tapes to see what is on them, it is helpful to have a software embedded label. Windows Backup allows you to create such a label, as shown in Figure 19.13.

Automating Backup Jobs

9. The last step in configuring your backup is to decide when to run it. Usually you choose the "now" option when it is a one-off backup, like a copy

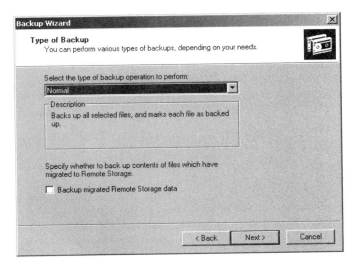

Figure 19–9

The Advanced settings allow you to choose the type of backup job and whether to include Remote Storage files in your backup.

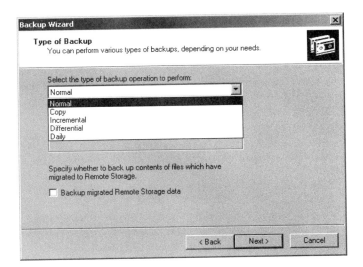

Figure 19–10

Dropping down the list shows you the type of jobs Windows Backup is capable of performing.

backup before upgrading the operating system with a new service pack. In most cases, you will schedule a job to run after business hours or when

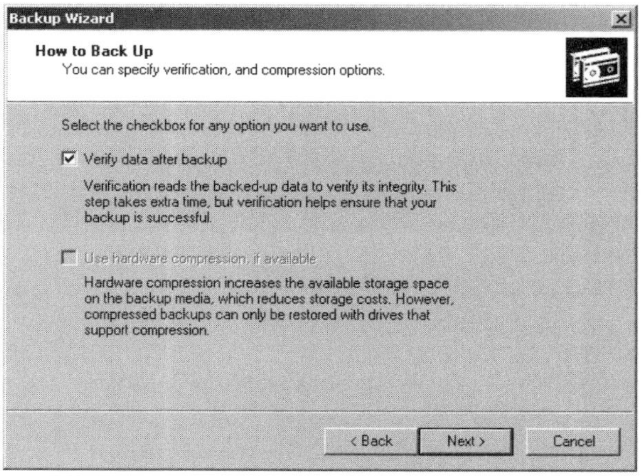

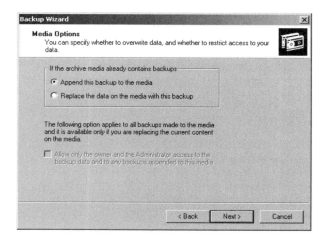

Figure 19–11

Windows Backup lets you decide whether to verify files after they've been backed up or to enable hardware compression if supported.

Figure 19–12

Windows Backup allows you to decide whether to append the backup to the media or to replace any existing data.

network activity is at its lowest in 24x7 organizations. Figure 19.14 shows the scheduler dialog. Click "Later" and click Next.

When you click Next, you will be prompted for security information, shown in Figure 19.15, for the backup job. Enter a username and password and click OK. Figure 19.16 shows that once the security information is checked, the Start Date of the job is filled in.

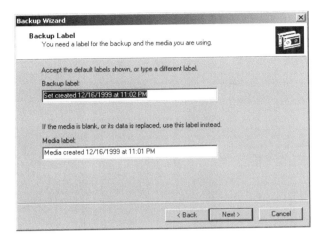

Figure 19-13   *Creating a label for the backup.*

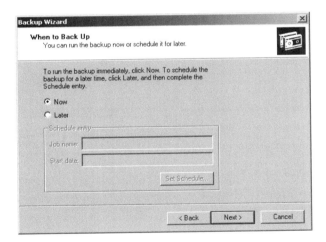

Figure 19-14   *Windows Backup supports scheduling backup jobs to run at a later time.*

Next you click Set Schedule to create the schedule for when you want this job to run. Figure 19.17 shows this window. As you can see, it is possible to set the job to run when you want it to, and to configure it to run daily, weekly, only once, or even on a custom schedule you create. Figure 19.18 shows the Settings tab, which allows you a finer level of control over the behavior of the job.

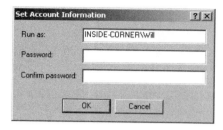

You are required to enter security information to schedule the backup job.

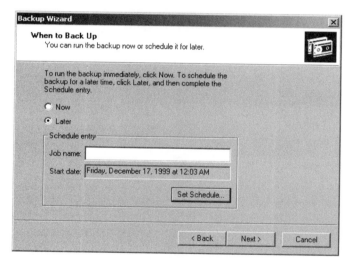

Once the security information is entered, Windows Backup fills in the job start date and time.

At this point, click OK to return to the backup schedule screen, and then Next to continue the wizard. You will see the last window, shown in Figure 19.19, that summarizes your choices and prompts you to click Finish to either start the job immediately or put the job into the Windows 2000 Task Scheduler, depending on the schedule options you selected. Windows Backup will now run according to how you configured it.

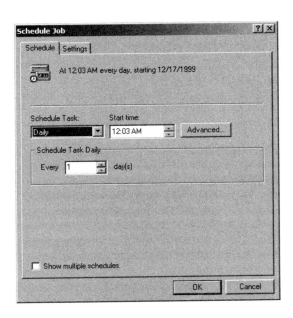

Figure 19–17

Windows Backup allows you to set the schedule for when you want the backup to run and how often you want it to repeat.

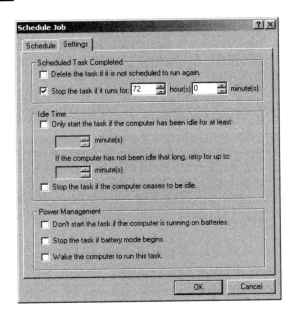

Figure 19–18

The Settings tab offers an increased degree of control of job execution behavior.

Figure 19-19   *The last step is to confirm your choices and click Finish.*

Performing Data Restore

We always hope that, although we are making backups, we never have to actually use them. Unfortunately, at times we do have to restore backups. In this section we will examine the Restore wizard and how to restore files from a backup.

Preparing to Restore Data

Preparing to restore data involves not only selecting the files you want to restore, but also making sure that you are ready to restore if the need ever arises. To this end, you should periodically perform test restores, even if you don't need to actually restore anything, just to make sure that your backup system is in good working order and saving viable data to your media of choice. That way, you won't be in for a rude surprise when you attempt to restore and find out the backups are unreadable by the system or contain otherwise corrupted information.

How to Select Which Backup Sets, Files, and Folders to Restore

1. After starting the Restore Wizard, you are given a list of backup sets that are on the system. You can also import a backup set file if you'd like. The

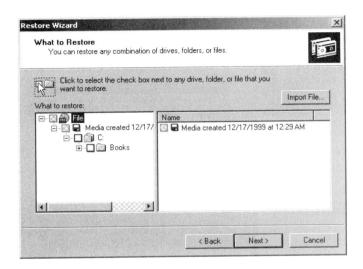

Figure 19–20   *Selecting the backup sets and files to restore.*

backup set shown in Figure 19.20 is the one we just created in the previous section by backing up some files from our *C:* drive.

2. Actually, step 1 is all you have to do unless you want to make changes from the default settings. By default, Windows Backup will attempt to restore the files to their original locations, and it won't overwrite any existing files in those locations. If you want to change those options, click the Advanced button shown in Figure 19.21.

Using the Advanced Restore Options

3. When you click Advanced, the first setting Windows Backup offers to have changed is the location to restore the files to. Figure 19.22 shows these options. Figure 19.23 shows the following option, which controls the behavior of the restoration process with regard to replacing existing files in the restore location. The option you choose will depend on your restore situation. If you are replacing a bunch of corrupted files, for instance, you will want the files replaced.

4. Windows Backup provides some special restore options, such as restoring the Removable Storage database if it is missing or corrupt. Remember, Windows Backup works in conjunction with Removable Storage for its media management functionality. Once you have selected your special restore options, as shown in Figure 19.24, click Next, and click Finish after reviewing the restore settings in a dialog similar to that in Figure 19.25.

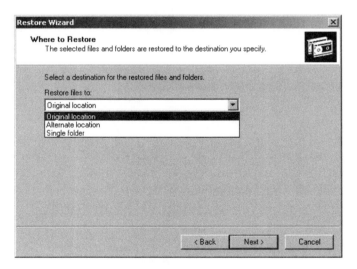

Clicking the Advanced button lets us change the default restore settings.

You can control the location to which Windows Backup restores files to through Advanced settings.

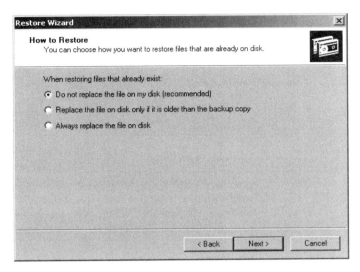

Figure 19–23

Windows Backup allows you to choose whether or not to over-write existing files in the restore directories.

Chapter Summary

In this chapter we examined the common systems administrator task of backing up and restoring data. We discussed backup planning issues such as backup strategies, the different backup types (normal, incremental, differential, copy, and daily), and the Grandfather-Father-Son tape rotation scheme. We also discussed the Remote Storage and Removable Storage utilities that work in conjunction with or in addition to Windows Backup. After planning our backup strategy, we learned how to use the Backup Wizard to save our data, and how to schedule backup jobs. We then discussed how to perform a restore with the Restore Wizard. Backing up data is a repetitious, daily chore …but one you will be very glad you took the time to do correctly, should you ever have to recover from a crash.

Figure 19–24

Windows Backup allows you to choose whether or not to over-write existing files in the restore directories.

Figure 19–25

After reviewing the restore settings, you can click Finish to begin the restore process.

Planning for Disaster Recovery

The primary focus of any Information Technology worker is to support the business needs of the company. New technology and cool toys are fun, but too often a technology focus blinds an administrator. Consider for a moment whether the company you own or are employed by could survive if the business-critical data stored on the servers simply disappeared. Would the business be able to pick up where it left off, or would missing billing records, trade secrets, correspondence, and legal documents cripple its ability to function in the marketplace?

Disaster recovery is the ability to minimize the impact and scope of problems related to the network and the servers on that network. Examples of disasters are hardware failures on servers, loss of power to a building, fire damage to the server, and accidental or malicious damage to the server operating system. The goal of disaster planning is to develop detailed documentation that will provide guidance in the case of a major problem. In addition, prudent preventative measures should be implemented.

Disaster Protection

During the daily operations of a network, the administrator can be lulled into a sense of comfort or even complacency by smooth operation. Too often, disaster planning is ignored until a mission-critical element of the network is no longer available At that point, the action could more properly be termed disaster reaction, rather than disaster recovery.

Preventative measures that provide a layer of protection against problems are known as fault-tolerant techniques. Many potential disasters can be averted through use of fault-tolerant techniques. Several major causes of server failure are listed below along with the fault tolerant technique that can prevent issues.

Power Issues

The most common problem facing servers is the loss of power. A sudden loss of local power to a server will result in a hard shutdown, possibly corrupting the operating system and data stored on the server. At a minimum, the system outage will be extended due to the need to test for data integrity after a hard crash. In addition, multiple power outages can result in a server that is unbootable due to damaged operating system files.

An *uninterruptible power supply* (UPS) is a device that uses rechargeable batteries to maintain power to a system after an outage. UPS devices are placed between the outside power-supply lines and the computer power inputs. If the power flow into a UPS fails, the UPS continues to power the server from its batteries. This prevents a hard crash of the system and allows time for an orderly shutdown. Some UPS software allows for email or network notification in the event of power failure, monitoring of remaining battery life, and automated system shutdown when the battery reaches a certain level.

The data center for most large companies is protected from power problems via a UPS that operates on a room or building level. In these cases, individual servers are usually not attached to separate UPS devices. If the power is disconnected to the data center, the room or building UPS takes over, and the systems never notice or know that they are on emergency power.

In either case, prompt notification that the systems are on emergency power is vital. Administrators should be aware of the situation, so that they can make the decision whether to shut down the systems. If the UPS is connected directly to a Windows 2000 system, notifications are configured in the Power Options applet in the control panel. Additionally, the system can be set to run a particular program before shutting down the system. A command-line email program invoked by a batch file can be an effective notification system. The batch file could send an email message to administrators, page someone, or, with proper communication packages, call a cell phone.

CONFIGURING THE UPS IN WINDOWS 2000

In earlier days, UPS devices functioned as dumb batteries, and the host systems were unaware that the UPS was active. Unfortunately, this lack of communication meant that an automated response to a power failure was not possible. Most modern UPS devices now communicate with the host system via serial cables. The UPS device connects to a COM port on the system and can send status information to the host system. This enables a Windows 2000 server to monitor the active status of a UPS, determine the remaining life of the UPS, and

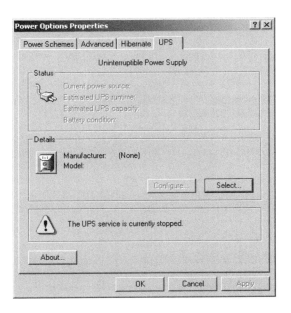

Figure 20-1   *UPS property sheet.*

automatically shut down the system if the batteries are fading on the UPS device.

Physically attaching a UPS device to a host system is quite simple. In most cases, a single serial cable must be attached to a COM port on the server. Additionally, the power cable of the server must be plugged into the UPS device.

To configure the UPS service within Windows 2000 Server, open the Power Options applet in the Control Panel. Select the UPS tab to bring up the UPS options (Figure 20.1).

Choose the *Select* button to choose the manufacturer and model of UPS attached to the Windows 2000 system, and also to select the COM port that the server should monitor (Figure 20.2). If the particular UPS device is not available in the predefined lists, a custom configuration is possible. Consult the UPS device's manual for proper settings.

After choosing the manufactures and model of the UPS device, configure the device options. Selecting the Configure button on the UPS tab brings up these options (Figure 20.3). Options include notifications, elapsed time before a critical alarm, whether to run a particular program or script on alarm, and shutdown options for both the server and the UPS device. Once these options are configured, select OK twice to enable the UPS service and begin monitoring the UPS device.

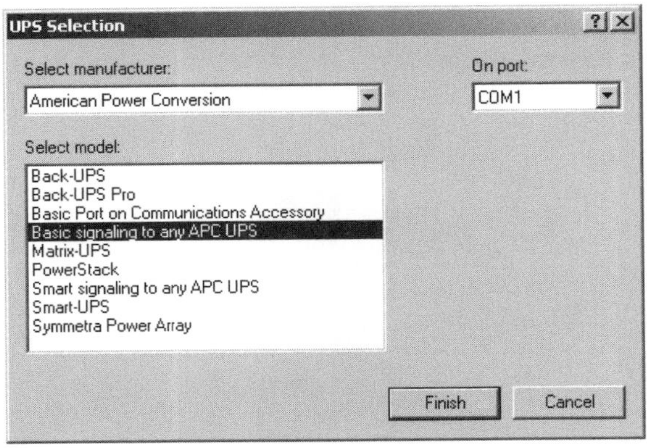

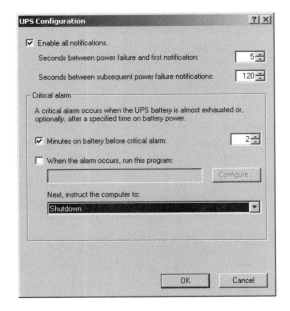

Figure 20-2   *Selecting the UPS device and communication parameters.*

Figure 20-3   *UPS configuration options.*

Hardware Failures

The second major cause of server outages is hardware failure. While manufacturers have greatly increased the mean time between failure on hardware over the years, hardware failures can still halt a server with little or no warning. Fortunately, most hardware failures involve moving parts. This means that fans, power supplies, and hard drives are the most likely candidates for hardware failure, while solid-state components tend to be reliable.

Given that moving parts will eventually fail, a server should have the capability to conpensate for that failure without suffering catastrophic problems. This ability is known as *fault tolerance*. A fault-tolerant server will have the capability to survive hard- drive and power-supply failures without losing data or affecting the applications running on the server. Modern computers that are designed as servers usually have redundant power supplies, fault-tolerant disk subsystems, and the ability to monitor various hardware subsystems for failure.

REDUNDANT POWER SUPPLIES

As mentioned earlier, power failure is a major cause of data loss, server downtime, and system corruption. While UPS devices can protect against loss of power to the server, a UPS cannot protect against a failure in the power supply located in the server. In the event of a power-supply failure, the system will suffer a hard crash.

Server manufactures have resolved this problem by installing redundant power supplies in many models. A server equipped with redundant power supplies will normally function on a single power supply, while a second one located in the server is also plugged in and running. In the event that the primary power supply quits functioning, the server will automatically switch to the redundant supply. This prevents computer downtime, while allowing support personnel to replace the damaged supply. In many server models, the power supplies are *hot swappable*, which means that a damaged unit can be replaced without downing the server.

FAULT-TOLERANT DISK SUBSYSTEMS

The most common hardware problem is a failed hard disk. Hard drives contain a large array of moving parts, and spin at speeds up to 10,000 rpm. While the capacity and lifespan of hard drives continues to improve, hard-drive failures continue to plague network administrators. In a system that is not fault tolerant, a hard-drive failure can result in system downtime, data loss, operating system failure, and monetary costs.

Fault-tolerant systems protect against hard-drive failures by writing and reading data across multiple drives. In the event that a single drive fails, the server can continue to function. These fault-tolerant systems are called RAID systems, which stands for Redundant Array of Inexpensive Disks. Within a fault-tolerant RAID system, data is written across multiple physical drives, while the RAID controller or the operating system tracks the location and value of the data. While the need to calculate the location of data and write the information to multiple drives does generate system overhead, the ability to survive a failure is worth the delay.

RAID arrays provide varying levels of fault tolerance, depending upon the configuration. RAID arrays are described in levels that represent the structure and fault-tolerance capability of the array. RAID levels range from 0 to 5, as described below:

RAID LEVEL 0: STRIPED DISK ARRAY WITHOUT FAULT TOLERANCE • This is not a fault-tolerant configuration. In this form of RAID, multiple physical drives are joined into a single logical drive. However, no parity is used in this configuration, so the overhead normally associated with RAID is not present. This results in a larger logical drive and faster I/O, especially if the physical drives are located on separate drive controllers. However, there is no fault tolerance, and the loss of any single physical drive results in the destruction of the entire logical drive. RAID 0 is not recommended for any mission-critical storage. RAID 0 requires at least two physical drives to implement.

RAID LEVEL 1: DISK MIRRORING AND DUPLEXING • Disk mirroring is the process of writing and reading the same information to two physical disks simultaneously. If the two drives are on separate drive controllers, then the drives are *duplexed*. The two disks together form a *mirrored volume* and are treated as a single logical drive. If one of the drives in a mirrored volume fails, the server continues to function using the second drive. RAID 1 is a fairly simple fault-tolerant system to design, but there is both a performance and a space penalty for the redundancy. Because the system requires writing to two separate disks, write speed is slightly slower than for a nontolerant system. The larger penalty is the space required to implement a RAID 1 solution. Due to the nature of mirroring, the system loses 50% of the available hard-drive space to the RAID array. As an example, a RAID 1 array with two 20 GB drives will only provide 20 GB of storage, despite the fact that there is actually 40 GB of physical space on the system. RAID level 1 requires at least two physical drives to implement. Windows 2000 can implement a RAID 1 array via software.

RAID LEVEL 2: HAMMING CODE ECC • Developed in the 1950s, this RAID system uses an array of disks for storage and a second array for storing error correction codes. In the event that there is a hard-drive error within the data drives, the ECC can be used to reconstruct the data. The typical RAID 2 system includes ten data drives and four ECC drives, and all drives must be synchronized. As a result, the data transfer rate of a RAID 2 array is not significantly higher than that of a single disk. A RAID 2 array is usually created and controlled via hardware, rather than an OS. RAID 2 arrays are essentially never used within a Windows 2000 environment.

RAID LEVEL 3: DISK STRIPING WITH PARITY DISK • Disk striping writes data across multiple disks and uses a separate disk to maintain an ECC table on the data. This system allows for very high read and write speeds. In the event that a data disk fails, the ECC code from the parity disk can be used to recreate the data. RAID 3 is a fairly efficient storage structure. The storage efficiency of a

RAID 3 array is calculated by dividing the number of data disks by the total number of disks. This can be written as $n/(n + 1)$, where n = number of data disks in the array. The higher the number of data disks, the better the storage efficiency. RAID 3 requires a minimum of three physical drives.

RAID LEVEL 4: INDEPENDENT DRIVES WITH PARITY DISK • This RAID configuration is similar to the RAID 3, except that the data is stored in fixed blocks called chunks. The chunks are striped across the data disks, and the parity is written to a corresponding chunk on the parity disk. Because of the design of a RAID 4 array, the parity disk quickly becomes a bottleneck. Each write to the array requires two accesses to the parity disk. As a result, write speed is the slowest of the RAID configurations. The storage efficiency of a RAID 4 array is calculated by dividing the number of data disks by the total number of disks. This can be written as $n/(n + 1)$, where n = number of data disks in the array. The higher the number of data disks, the better the storage efficiency. RAID 4 requires a minimum of three physical drives.

RAID LEVEL 5: DISK STRIPING WITH DISTRIBUTED PARITY • RAID 5 resolves the bottleneck associated with parity disks in RAID 3 and 4 by distributing the parity information across the data disks. Each hard drive within the system contains both data and a portion of the parity information. In the event of a hard-drive failure, a RAID 5 array uses the data and parity stripe from the remaining disks to recreate the missing data. RAID 5 arrays have high storage efficiency and good data integrity. A RAID 5 array must lose two drives before the system will fail. Windows 2000 can implement a RAID 5 array via software. RAID 5 requires a minimum of three physical drives.

Implementing Software RAID

A RAID system can be controlled either by a hardware RAID controller or via the operating system. Many environments use a hardware RAID solution, in which the disk controller handles the striping and parity among the physical disks. A hardware RAID solution is faster than a software solution, and in some cases allows for hot-swappable hard drives. However, using hardware RAID solutions is also more expensive than using a software version, and many hardware RAID solutions require proprietary controllers, drive bays, and disk drives.

Windows 2000 can implement two different RAID levels. Both mirrored or duplex drives (RAID 1) and striped volumes with parity (RAID 5) can be created by a Windows 2000 server. Software raid arrays can be created only on dynamic disks, though RAID arrays created under earlier Windows NT operating systems are still functional under Windows 2000.

System and Boot partitions cannot be located on a software RAID 5 array; they can be located on a RAID 1 (mirrored volume) software RAID array (Table 20.1).

Always have a recent backup of your information before creating or changing any RAID arrays.

Table 20.1	Software RAID Comparisons
RAID 1	**RAID 5**
System and Boot partitions allowed	Does not support System or Boot partitions
Requires 2 hard drives	Requires at least 3 hard drives. A volume can contain up to 32 drives
50% space loss for redundancy	Redundancy overhead of 1/3 to 1/32 of total space
Good write performance	Average write performance
Good read performance	Excellent read performance
Lower use of system resources	Requires more system resources

Windows 2000 Professional does not support software RAID.

Implementing RAID 1

RAID arrays are created through the Disk Management snap-in within the Management Console. Selecting the Disk Management snap-in will show existing partitions and volumes, as well as unallocated space. To create a volume, select an unallocated space or a dynamic disk. From the context or action menu, select *Create Volume* (Figure 20.4).

The Create Volume wizard will offer several options about the type of volume to create. For a RAID 1 volume, select Mirrored Volume (Figure 20.5).

After choosing the volume type, select the physical drives to be included in the array (Figure 20.6). A RAID 1 array will allow only two physical drives to be included. The storage space of a mirrored volume is limited by the smallest drive in the array. If a larger drive is mirrored with a smaller one, the unused space remains unallocated space.

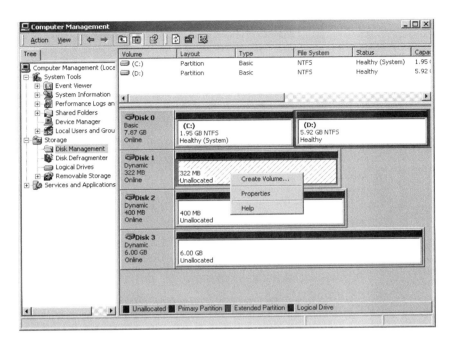

Figure 20–4   *Creating a RAID 1 volume.*

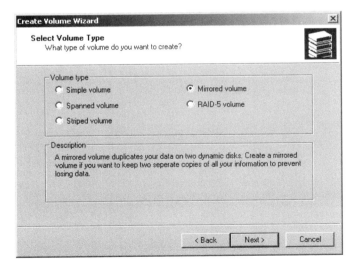

Figure 20–5   *Select Mirrored Volume to create a RAID 1 array.*

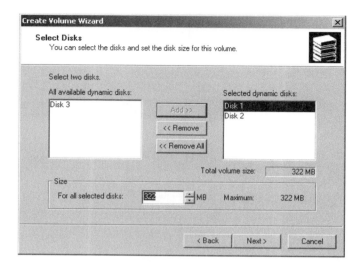

Figure 20-6   *Select the physical disks for the array.*

After selecting the drives, the system will prompt for the desired drive of the resulting volume (Figure 20.7). Additionally, the volume can be mounted at a drive path, as in UNIX systems. Assigning a drive path to a volume can be useful in situations where the drive letter limit may be reached. If desired, the volume can be left unassigned.

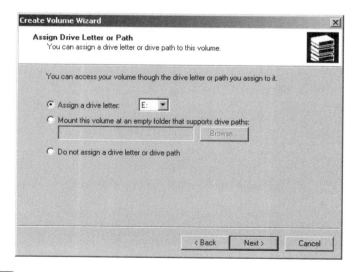

Figure 20-7   *Assigning a drive letter or path.*

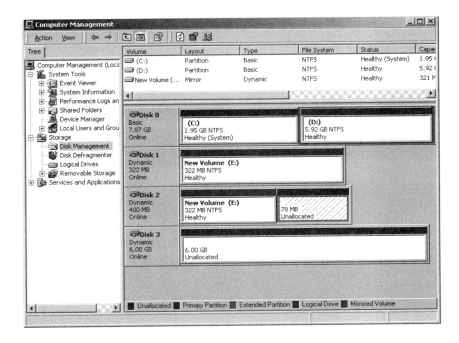

Figure 20-8   *Mirrored volume shown in the Disk Management console.*

After desired file system is chosen and the settings for the volume are verified, Windows 2000 will create the volume and format the resulting volume. When the volume is complete, the new drive will appear in the Disk Management snap-in (Figure 20.8). At this point, the drive is available for use.

Implementing RAID 5

RAID arrays are created through the Disk Management snap-in within the Management Console. Selecting the Disk Management snap-in will show existing partitions and volumes, as well as unallocated space. To create a volume, select an unallocated space or a dynamic disk. From the context or action menu, select *Create Volume* (Figure 20.9).

The Create Volume wizard will offer several options about the type of volume to create (Figure 20.10). For a RAID 5 volume, select RAID-5 volume from the available choices. After the RAID-5 volume option is selected, the system will prompt for the drives to include in the volume. A RAID 5 array requires a minimum of three drives and can include up to 32. The smallest disk in the array determines the size of the array on each physical disk. The total available space is calculated by the formula $(n - 1)*M$, where n is the number of physical disks in the array and M is the size of the smallest disk in megabytes.

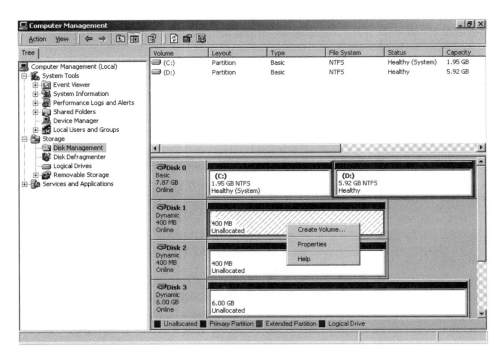

Figure 20–9 *Creating a RAID 5 volume.*

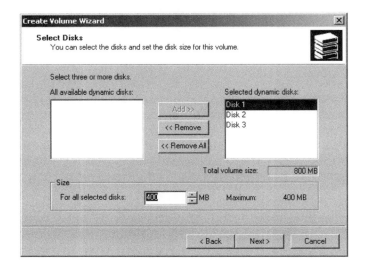

Figure 20–10 *Adding drives to a RAID 5 array.*

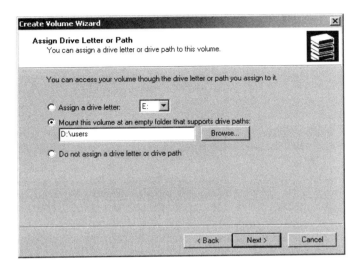

Figure 20–11   *Mounting a volume on a NTFS partition.*

The next steps involve selecting the file system type and volume path. Windows 2000 software RAID arrays can support both FAT and NTFS volumes. A drive letter can be assigned to the volume, or the volume can be mounted as a subdirectory on an NTFS drive. In this example, the new volume is mounted under *d:\users* (Figure 20.11).

After the desired file system is chosen and the settings for the volume are verified, Windows 2000 will create the volume and format the resulting volume. When the volume is complete, the new drive will appear in the Disk Management snap-in (Figure 20.12). At this point, the drive is available for use.

Disaster Recovery with Software RAID

Hard drives contain a myriad of moving parts and spin at a high rpm. As a result, hard drives are the most likely source of failures on a server. On a system that is not fault tolerant, a hard-drive failure will crash the server, damage data, and stop applications. With a fault-tolerant RAID array, the system will continue to function, and the damaged drive can be replaced at a scheduled time.

A damaged drive should be replaced as soon as possible. Once a drive has quit functioning, the system is no longer fault tolerant. A second drive failure **will** result in data loss.

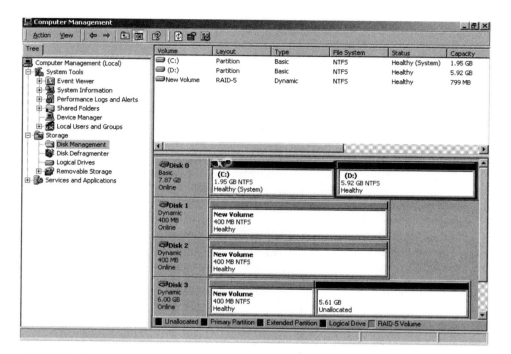

Figure 20–12   *RAID 5 volumes shown in Disk Management console.*

Mirrored Volume Recovery

If a physical drive fails in a mirror set, the remaining disk will continue to function. To repair the mirror set, it is necessary to break the mirror, replace the physical drive, and recreate the mirror set.

To recover from a damaged drive, follow these steps:

1. Physically remove and replace the damaged disk.
2. Within the Disk Management console, remove the missing physical drive.
3. Select the remaining member of the mirror volume and choose *Add Mirror* from the context or action menu.
4. Add the new drive to the mirror set. The system will automatically resync the mirrored volume set.

RAID 5 Recovery

A server with a RAID 5 array can survive a single hard-drive failure without an issue. The read times will be slightly slowed, as the system has to recreate the missing data from the parity information of the RAID array. To repair a RAID 5 array, replace the physical drive and regenerate the RAID configuration.

To recover from a damaged drive, follow these steps:

1. Physically remove and replace the damaged disk.
2. Within *Failed Redundancy*, right-click the volume and select *Repair Volume*.
3. Select the new disk as the new member of the volume. The system will automatically resync the RAID volume.

Emergency OS Repair

While Windows 2000 is a robust operating system, there may be times when it will need emergency maintenance. As with other operating systems, Windows 2000 can be rendered unstable by physical disk corruption, incorrect drivers, poorly written third-party software, or lack of maintenance. A good network administrator will recognize this possibility and be prepared to recover a damaged Windows 2000 installation.

There are three primary methods of recovering a malfunctioning installation. These methods are starting in Safe Mode, running the Recovery Console, or using the Emergency Repair Disk to rebuild the OS.

Safe Mode

Safe mode launches a Windows 2000 system with a minimal set of device drivers and services. This can be useful if an incorrect or corrupted device driver is preventing the system from booting. By booting into safe mode, a technician can replace the damaged or incorrect drivers, run diagnostics on a system, or recover valuable data. Safe mode cannot recover a system with corrupted system files or failed physical drives. To start safe mode, press F8 during the boot screen, and then select one of the following options:

SAFE MODE • Basic files and drivers only. The system will load nonserial mouse drivers, VGA video, keyboard drivers, storage subsystem drivers, and default system services. Safe mode does not load network drivers or drivers for accessories. If the system will not boot in safe mode, an Emergency Repair Disk (ERD) may be required to restore the system.

SAFE MODE WITH NETWORK SUPPORT • Safe mode as described above, plus network drivers and connections.

SAFE MODE WITH COMMAND PROMPT • Very basic Windows 2000 drivers and services. Displays a command prompt rather than a graphical user interface. Command-prompt mode is useful when resolving video driver issues.

ENABLE BOOT LOGGING • This is a normal boot, but the system logs each driver and service used by the operating system. The log name is nbtlog.txt. This log file is useful for troubleshooting boot problems.

VGA MODE • Windows 2000 boots using the basic VGA mode driver. This choice is often used when a new video driver has caused issues. Booting in VGA mode allows a technician to replace the video driver. All Windows 2000 Safe Mode modes use the VGA driver.

LAST KNOWN GOOD CONFIGURATION • This mode uses the registry information that Windows 2000 stored at the last shutdown. This mode can correct issues caused by incorrect configuration, but cannot correct issues created by corrupted drivers or missing files. Changes made since the last successful boot will be lost.

DIRECTORY SERVICE RESTORE MODE • This mode is used in restoring the SYS-VOL directory and the Active Directory directory service on a domain controller.

Debugging Mode: Sends debug information through a serial cable to another computer.

Windows 2000 Recovery Console

The Recovery Console provides an administrator with command-line tools that can be used to repair a damaged Windows 2000 installation. A technician can stop and start services; read and write data to local drives, both NTFS and FAT; write a new Master Boot Record to a local disk; manipulate files, and more.

The Recovery Console is often used to repair systems by replacing a file within the operating system with one from a floppy disk or CD-ROM. Another common use is disabling services that may be preventing the system from booting.

The Recovery Console may either be installed on a Windows 2000 or run from the boot CD. In either case, administrative rights are required to use the Recovery Console.

INSTALLING RECOVERY CONSOLE

The Recovery Console can be installed on a Windows 2000 server, so that it is always available during the boot process. After the Recovery Console is installed, it will be listed in the list of available operating systems. To install the Recovery Console, insert the Windows 2000 CD into the CD-ROM drive and type *<CD-ROM>\i386\winnt32.exe /cmdcons* at a command prompt. Follow the prompts to install the Recovery Console.

RUNNING RECOVERY CONSOLE FROM CD

If a system will not boot, or does not have the Recovery Console installed, the program can be run from the Windows 2000 CD. To run the Recovery Console from CD, insert the Windows 2000 CD or the first setup diskette into the system and boot the computer. After the system boots to the setup screen, select the option to repair the Windows 2000 installation, and then launch the Recovery Console.

RECOVERY CONSOLE COMMANDS

The Recovery Console offers the standard file-manipulation commands such as attrib, copy, delete, rename, and others. In addition, several commands that are unique to the Recovery Console are detailed below:

LOGON • Logs into an installation of Windows 2000 or Windows NT 4.0 as the local administrator. The *Logon* command will show all local installations of Windows NT or 2000. Logging in as the local administrator is required to run the Recovery Console.

DISABLE {SERVICE_NAME] | [DEVICE_DRIVER_NAME} •
service_name   The name of the system service to disable.
device_driver_name   The name of the device driver to disable.
      The *disable* command sets the startup type to SERVICE_DISABLED for the service or driver specified. When a device driver or service is disabled using the *Disable* command, the current startup type is shown on the console screen. This type should be recorded in case the driver or service needs to be restored

ENABLE {SERVICE_NAME | DEVICE_DRIVER_NAME} [STARTUP_TYPE] •
service_name   The name of the system service to enable.
device_driver_name   The name of the device driver to enable.
startup_type   The startup type for the service or device driver.
      Enables a Windows 2000 or Windows NT 4.0 system service or a device driver. When used without a startup type, the command lists the current startup type for the selected driver or service. When a device driver or service startup type is changed using the *Enable* command, the current startup type is shown on the console screen. This type should be recorded in case the driver or service needs to be restored (Table 20.2).

Table 20.2	Startup Types
Enable Startup Type	**Equivalent to**
SERVICE_AUTO_START	Automatic
SERVICE_DISABLED	Disabled
SERVICE_DEMAND_START	Manual
SERVICE_BOOT_START	System Boot
SERVICE_SYSTEM_START	Windows 2000 Startup

FIXBOOT [DRIVE] • The *Fixboot* command writes a new partition boot sector to the system partition. If a drive letter is specified, a boot sector will be written to that drive.

FIXMBR [DEVICE_NAME] • The *Fixmbr* command writes a new master boot record to a hard drive. The device name can be specified in either Advanced RISC Computing (ARC) format or as a Windows 2000 device name. The device name of the desired hard drive can be determined via the Map command, detailed below.

MAP [ARC] • The *Map* command displays a mapping of physical device names to drive letters, for use with the *Fixboot* and *Fixmbr* commands (Table 20.3). If the *arc* parameter is used, the output is in Advanced RISC Computing (ARC) device names rather than Windows 2000 device names.

Table 20.3	Device Name Output
Advanced RISC Computing (ARC)	**Windows 2000**
multi(0)disk(0)rdisk(0) partition(1)	\Device\HardDisk0\Partition1

EXIT • Exits the Recovery Console and reboots the system.

Emergency Repair Disk

The Emergency Repair Disk (ERD) feature helps you repair problems with system files, your startup environment (if you have a dual-boot or multiple-boot system), and the partition boot sector on your boot volume. Before you use the Emergency Repair Disk feature to repair your system, you must create an Emergency Repair Disk. You can do this using the Backup utility. Even if you have not created an Emergency Repair Disk, you can still try to use the Emergency Repair Disk process; however, any changes you have made to your system, such as Service Pack updates, may be lost and may need to be reinstalled.

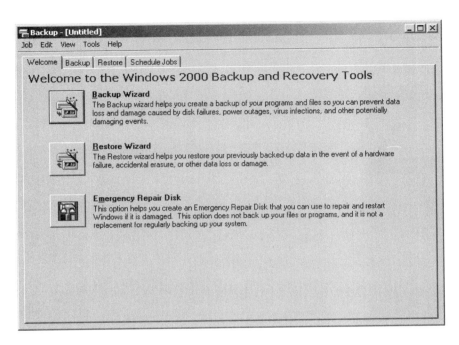

Creating a Windows 2000 ERD.

CREATING AN ERD

An Emergency Repair Disk is created via the backup software bundled with Windows 2000. To start the backup software, select Start, Programs, Accessories, System Tools, and then Backup. Selecting the *Emergency Repair Disk* button (Figure 20.13) will start an ERD mini-wizard. A blank 1.44-MB floppy disk is required to create an Emergency Repair Disk.

Choosing *Also back up the registry to the repair directory* (Figure 20.14) will back up the current registry files to a folder within the *systemroot/* repair folder. Backing up the registry is highly recommended. The repair process relies on information that is saved in the *systemroot*\repair folder. This folder should not be deleted or modified.

Emergency Repair Disks should be stored in a safe location (Figure 20.15). Many administrators maintain multiple copies of repair disks in separate locations. If a service is installed, drive arrays are changed, or patches are applied to the system, a new ERD is required.

USING AN ERD

The Emergency Repair Disk can be used to correct problems with a Windows 2000 system. The recovery process can correct damaged registries, environ-

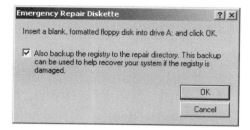

Figure 20–14   *Backing up the Registry.*

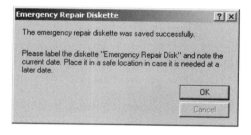

Figure 20–15   *Successful ERD.*

ment issues, and boot partition problems. The ERD should be kept current in order to increase the chances of recovery. If an ERD is not available, some steps of the recovery process may not available. To recover using an ERD, use the following steps:

• Boot the system from the Windows 2000 Setup diskettes or the CD.

• Select the repair option during setup. To repair a damaged or corrupt system, select R. Select R again to repair the system using the emergency repair process.

• Select the repair type. The fast repair option restores the registry, system files, boot sector and startup environment without intervention from the technician. The fast repair option will use a backup copy of the registry that was created the first time the Windows 2000 setup program was run. If you choose this option, settings or preferences may be lost. The manual option allows the technician to repair only the desired element, such as replacing only system files. However, the manual method cannot restore the registry of the system.

• Run the repair process. This will require the 1.44-MB ERD created via the Backup utility and a Windows 2000 CD. If there is no ERD for the system, the emergency repair process will attempt to repair the Windows 2000 installation, but may not be able to.

- Reboot the server. On a successful repair, the system will be functional after the restart.

REINSTALLATION

If a system is heavily damaged, recovery techniques may not be effective. In this situation, a reinstall of the operating system may be required. A reinstallation places a new copy of Windows 2000 over the damaged version. Unfortunately, reinstallation usually requires reinstalling OS patches and may require a reinstall of applications that store .dll or other files in Windows 2000. A reinstallation should be considered only as a last resort.

Chapter Summary

In this chapter we discussed some of the causes of computer disasters and how best to prepare for them. Disaster Recovery is the process of planning for and counteracting events that will result in an inoperative server. A system that can survive most common disasters is considered a *fault-tolerant* server.

The most common problem facing administrators is the loss of power to the server. Many companies manufacture devices that contain batteries and can power a system from those batteries. These uninterruptible power supplies (UPS) protect the system from an unplanned outage and provide a buffer in which to shut the system down. Early UPS devices were basically batteries, but modern UPS devices can communicate with a server and initiate a controlled shutdown when the battery is nearly drained.

Hard drives contain the most moving parts of any computer component, and thus fail relatively often. Server systems can be built so that the loss of a drive does not crash the system or lose data for the users of the system. Fault tolerance on hard drives is created via RAID (Redundant Array of Inexpensive Disks) arrays. A RAID array writes and reads data from several physical drives. The loss of any one drive will not result in data loss. If the system loses two or more drives, then the data will need to be restored from backup media.

There are several different implementations of RAID, and they are numbered to represent the different levels of fault tolerance. RAID arrays can be created either via hardware controllers or via Windows 2000 software. Hardware RAID tends to be faster and usually offers the ability to change drives while the system is functional. Software tends to be much cheaper than hardware RAID and is not proprietary. Windows 2000 supports RAID levels 1 and 5.

In the event that a server is unable to boot, there are several disaster recovery options. The first involves Safe Mode, which offers a wide range of boot options. These options include reverting to the last known good partition, starting with the lowest common video driver, and booting to a command prompt,

In the event that a safe mode boot does not correct the issue, a repair using an Emergency Repair Disk (ERD) may correct the problem. A repair can use an ERD to correct problems with the registry, boot partition, and environment settings. An ERD is created using the backup program and a blank 1.44-MB floppy.

The Recovery Console is a specialized command-line utility that allows reading and writing drive partitions (including NT File System) and provides the ability to manipulate files while the system itself is unresponsive. In addition, the Recovery Console can be used to enable or disable device drivers and services for troubleshooting.

Installing and Configuring Network Protocols

*W*indows 2000 is designed as a network operating system, and it requires network connectivity to perform at its ultimate potential. Necessarily, this involves installing and configuring network cards, drivers, and protocols. Installation of the network hardware is performed via the Control Panel and the Add/ Remove Hardware applet. For the purposes of this chapter, we will assume that the network interface card is installed properly in the server. If this is not the case, please see Chapter 5 for information on installing hardware in a Windows 2000 system.

Network protocols are the common language that allows disparate hardware and operating systems to speak to each other. More formally, a protocol is a mutually agreed upon format. Many differing protocols exist within the networking realm, but not all are in widespread use. Windows 2000 supports many major ones natively: TCP/IP, NWlink, NetBEUI AppleTalk, and DLC. To ensure communication between computers, all machines must be running the same protocol or protocols. Windows 2000 supports multiple protocols (or bindings) on the same computer.

21.1 Transmission Control Protocol/Internet Protocol

Transmission Control Protocol/Internet Protocol suite (TCP/IP) is the de facto standard protocol for computers that need to communicate over the Internet. TCP/IP was first developed by Defense Advanced Research Projects Agency (DARPA) in 1969. Since that point in time, the use of this protocol suite has spread worldwide, due to the innate advantages of its addressing schemes and through support by most network operating system vendors.

The TCP/IP Protocol Suite

TCP/IP is actually a combination of protocols that work together to ensure packets' reliable travel from one host to another. Transmission Control Protocol is a connection-oriented protocol, which means that before data can be transmitted, a reliable connection must be established and acknowledged. TCP guarantees delivery via sequencing information and checksums to validate header information and the data in the packet. Internet Protocol handles the routing of the data packets from one host to another, and any necessary fragmentation and reassembly of the packets. Together, they can route data from one host to another, verify that the data arrived intact, and reassemble the packets into the correct order.

TCP/IP ARCHITECTURE

The TCP/IP protocol suite consists of four architecture layers, within which the various protocols operate. The four-layer model does not map directly to the "standard" seven-layer OSI model. The layers in TCP/IP are the Network Inter-

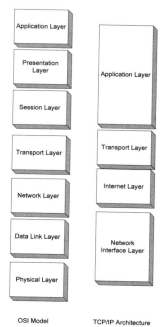

OSI Model   TCP/IP Architecture

Figure 21-1   *Architecture layers.*

face Layer, the Internet Layer, the Transport Layer, and the Application Layer (Figure 21.1).

The Network Interface Layer places the TCP/IP packets on the wire, regardless of what type of wire is involved. This layer is designed to interface with a variety of networking technologies and can connect to almost any modern networking medium. This layer is roughly analogous to the Data Link and Physical Layers of the OSI model.

The Internet Layer handles addressing, packaging, and routing. It is roughly the same as the network layer in the OSI model. It is comprised of a combination of protocols, the most important of which are ARP, ICMP, IGMP, and IP.

- **ARP (Address Resolution Protocol)** resolves an IP address to a physical network interface layer address, also known as a MAC address. MAC addresses are in the form 00-A0-C9-DD-64-C3.
- **ICMP (Internet Control Message Protocol)** reports errors, unsuccessful IP packet delivery attempts, and diagnostic functions.
- **IGMP (Internet Group Management Protocol)** is responsible for IP multicasting capabilities.
- **IP (Internet Protocol)** handles routing functions, addressing, and fragmenting and reassembling of data packets.

The Transport Layer is responsible for communicating between the Application Layer and the lower layers. This layer consists of two separate protocols with differing characteristics. TCP (Transmission Control Protocol) is designed for reliable connection-oriented communications. The protocol is responsible for establishing communication, verifying packet integrity, and sequencing. TCP uses a three-step handshake to establish a reliable connection and to end the connection (Tables 21.1 and 21.2). This method ensures that both hosts have compatible window buffer sizes and that both are aware of the end of the transmission.

Table 21.1		TCP Handshake
Client	**Server**	**Function**
SYN		Starts the connection with a sequence number and the window buffer size on the client.

Table 21.1		TCP Handshake (Continued)
	ACK, SYN	The remote computer acknowledges the connection and buffer information and sends its beginning sequence number.
ACK		The client acknowledges the sequence number of the remote computer and finishes establishing the connection.

Table 21.2		TCP Disconnect
Client	**Server**	**Function**
FIN, ACK		Sends an ending command and the sequence number for the connection.
	ACK	The remote computer acknowledges the sequence number of the connection and closes the session.
	FIN, ACK	Because a TCP connection is duplex, the remote computer must also end the connection—thus, the FIN and ACK packets.
ACK		The client acknowledges the sequence number of the connection and closes the session.

The second protocol in the Transport Layer is UDP (User Datagram Protocol), a connectionless and unreliable communication service that is used for both one-on-one connections and one-to-many communication. UDP is used in cases where the overhead required in a TCP connection is not desired, especially in cases where only small amounts of information are being passed.

Because the protocol is inherently unreliable, applications that use UDP are responsible for verifying delivery.

The Application Layer allows applications operating on the computer to receive data from the IP stack. Application Layer protocols include FTP (file transfer protocol), HTTP (hypertext transport protocol), DNS (domain name system) and many others. The Application Layer in TCP/IP performs many of the functions of the session, presentation and application layers of the OSI model.

TCP/IP ADDRESSING

Each computer on a TCP/IP interconnected network requires a unique identifier. While each network interface card has a unique physical address, the IP address is a unique logical address that is not dependent upon the MAC address. An IP address consists of a network ID and a host ID, and each machine requires a unique address. The network ID defines physical networks that are bordered by routers. Each machine on the same network must have an identical network ID, and each network ID must be unique. The host ID identifies a particular machine on the physical network; each host ID on a network must be unique.

IP addresses are 32 bits long, and the standard notation for writing an IP address is *dotted decimal notation*. The 32-bit address is separated into four eight-bit segments, and then each segment is converted to a binary number. The binary number for each segment will range between 0 and 255. IP addresses are written in the format *w.x.y.z*; as an example, the IP address for www.Microsoft.com is 207.46.131.137.

The network number is the part of the IP address that refers to the network ID, and the host ID refers to the computer or other device. Network IDs originally were separated into five address classes to allow for networks of various sizes. The original address classes were identified as A–D. Class A addresses had subnet masks of 255.0.0.0 and used the first 8 bits as a network address. Class B addresses had subnet masks of 255.255.0.0 and the first 16 bits of the IP address were used to identify the network. Class C addresses used the first 24 bits as a network address and had a 255.255.255.0 subnet. Class D is used for multicast addresses, and Class E is reserved for future use (see Table 21.3).

Table 21.3	Classful Addressing				
Class	Network	Position	Host Position	Number of Networks	Number of Hosts
A	1–126	*w.*	*x.y.z*	16	16,777,214
B	128–191	*w.x*	*y.z*	16,384	65,534

Table 21.3	Classful Addressing (Continued)				
C	192–223	*w.x.y.*	*z*	2,097,152	254

The problem with this addressing scheme is that the number of networks quickly expanded beyond the ability of classful addressing to support them. Additionally, there was an enormous waste of IP addresses in the larger networks; after all, few networks have 16 million hosts in them! As a result, Classless Inter Domain Routing (CIDR) was developed to enable more efficient use of IP addresses. CIDR requires more granular subnet masking than the traditional A, B, or C usage. The subnet mask is used to separate the host address from the network address within an IP address. The subnet mask tells the IP stack when a destination address is part of the local network, or whether the packet will need to be routed outside the local network. CIDR subnetting is expressed in *Network Prefix Notation* (see Table 21.4), which denotes the network address and the number of bits that define the network.

Table 21.4	Network Notation	
Binary	**Dec**	**CIDR**
00000000000000000000000000000000	0.0.0.0	/0
10000000000000000000000000000000	128.0.0.0	/1
11000000000000000000000000000000	192.0.0.0	/2
11100000000000000000000000000000	224.0.0.0	/3
11110000000000000000000000000000	240.0.0.0	/4
11111000000000000000000000000000	248.0.0.0	/5
11111100000000000000000000000000	252.0.0.0	/6
11111110000000000000000000000000	254.0.0.0	/7
11111111000000000000000000000000	255.0.0.0	/8 (class A)
11111111100000000000000000000000	255.128.0.0.	/9
11111111110000000000000000000000	255.192.0.0.	/10
11111111111000000000000000000000	255.224.0.0	/11
11111111111100000000000000000000	255.240.0.0	/12
11111111111110000000000000000000	255.248.0.0	/13
11111111111111000000000000000000	255.252.0.0	/14
11111111111111100000000000000000	255.254.0.0	/15
11111111111111110000000000000000	255.255.0.0	/16 (class B)

Table 21.4	Network Notation (Continued)	
11111111111111111000000000000000	255.255.128.0	/17
11111111111111111100000000000000	255.255.192.0	/18
11111111111111111110000000000000	255.255.224.0	/19
11111111111111111111000000000000	255.255.240.0	/20
11111111111111111111100000000000	255.255.248.0	/21
11111111111111111111110000000000	255.255.252.0	/22
11111111111111111111111000000000	255.255.254.0	/23
11111111111111111111111100000000	255.255.255.0	/24 (class C)
11111111111111111111111110000000	255.255.255.128	/25
11111111111111111111111111000000	255.255.255.192	/26
11111111111111111111111111100000	255.255.255.224	/27
11111111111111111111111111110000	255.255.255.240	/28
11111111111111111111111111111000	255.255.255.248	/29
11111111111111111111111111111100	255.255.255.252	/30
11111111111111111111111111111110	255.255.255.254	/31
11111111111111111111111111111111	255.255.255.255	/32 (single host)

IP addresses are assigned by the Internet Assigned Numbers Authority in blocks that vary in size depending upon the need of the receiving organization. For all intents and purposes, companies receive IP addresses from their ISPs (Internet Service Provider) today. Even with the advent of CIDR, the number of available network addresses still cannot meet the demand. As a result, the IETF created private range IP addresses that are not routable over the Internet. With network translation software now able to hide an entire network behind a single public IP address, private addresses allow companies to develop their internal network infrastructure to meet their business needs. RFC 1918 defines the following private addresses:

10.0.0.0–10.255.255.255 (10/8 prefix)
172.16.0.0–172.31.255.255 (172.16/12 prefix)
192.168.0.0–192.168.255.255 (192.168/16 prefix)

Companies can use these address ranges without fear of addressing conflicts and without having to obtain the addresses through the IANA.

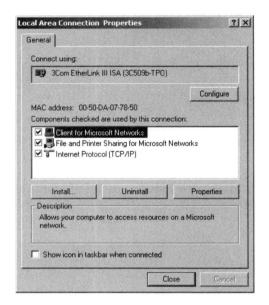

Figure 21-2   *Property sheet for LAN connection.*

Configuring TCP/IP on Windows 2000

The TCP/IP protocol is installed by default on a Windows 2000 server and cannot be removed. However, there are many configurable options with TCP/IP. As with most other configuration changes in Windows 2000, network protocols are configured with the Control Panel. To modify the TCP/IP properties, open the *Network and Dial-up Connections* applet and right-click on the *Local Area Network* connection (Figure 21.2). Selecting properties will bring up the information regarding that connection, including adapter type, bound protocols and clients, and other elements of that LAN connection.

Select the Internet Protocol (TCP/IP) entry and click on the *Properties* option. This brings up the TCP/IP properties sheet and will allow you to modify many of the TCP/IP configuration settings.

CONFIGURING TCP/IP WITH STATIC ADDRESSING

Each computer on a TCP/IP network needs to have a unique IP address associated with it. This IP address supplies routing information to the network infrastructure and identifies the machine to the other computers on the network. Addresses are assigned within the TCP/IP properties sheet, as are the related information: gateways, subnet masks, DNS and WINS servers, and the like.

Many times, you will want to assign a particular IP address to a system. A permanent address that is assigned to a particular machine is called a *static address*, and assigning permanent IP addresses is called *static addressing*. In most cases, a static address is assigned to a server, router, or other network resource that client machines need to access. Using static addresses on these kinds of resources ensures that the server, router, or other piece will always be available at the address expected by the clients.

In some smaller networks, the client PCs will each also be assigned a particular IP address. While this is workable in smaller environments, there are several problems with static addressing for clients in large environments. First, since each machine needs to be configured individually, the chances for a misconfiguration rise as the number of client PCs rises. A client that is configured incorrectly may cause conflicts on a network, may not function correctly, or may interfere with traffic bound to another device on the network. The second major problem is the logistics involved in tracking both the hardware and the IP addresses assigned to each piece of hardware. Every time there is a change in IP addresses, that change must be accurately recorded in some central list or database. If this list is not kept current, new machines may be accidentally assigned IP addresses that are already in use. The third major problem is the need to reconfigure each machine individually if the DNS, WINS, or gateway addresses change. This can be a large strain on the resources of your MIS department.

To assign an IP address to a Windows 2000 system, bring up the properties sheet and enter the IP address, subnet, and gateway (if applicable). The general properties sheet will also allow you to enter the IP addresses of the primary and alternate DNS servers on your network for name resolution (Figure 21.3).

It is important to maintain a record of the IP addresses that have been assigned on your network. While it is possible to obtain a listing of some of the addresses from the DNS services, a well-organized record will help prevent IP addressing conflicts and assist in troubleshooting connectivity issues.

CONFIGURING TCP/IP WITH DYNAMIC ADDRESSING

As mentioned earlier, each computer on a network must have a unique IP address. As the size of a network increases, maintaining unique addresses becomes more difficult. Each new computer on the network must be configured with an address that is not in use; otherwise, communications on both the new computer and the one that originally owned the address are likely to be disrupted. Some network administrators use large spreadsheets to keep track of IP addresses, while others use other techniques such as pinging the desired address and checking to see if another machine responds. While static addressing has its uses, there are alternate methods of supplying IP addresses.

Dynamic Host Configuration Protocol is a method of assigning addresses to computers automatically. A client machine that is configured to use DHCP broadcasts a request for an address when it boots. A Windows 2000 server run-

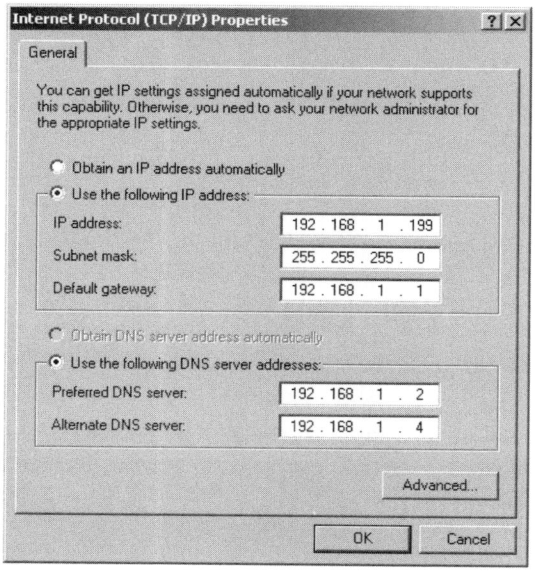

Internet Protocol (TCP/IP) Properties   ? X

General

You can get IP settings assigned automatically if your network supports
this capability. Otherwise, you need to ask your network administrator for
the appropriate IP settings.

○ Obtain an IP address automatically
◉ Use the following IP address:

IP address: 192 . 168 . 1 . 199

Subnet mask: 255 . 255 . 255 . 0

Default gateway: 192 . 168 . 1 . 1

○ Obtain DNS server address automatically
◉ Use the following DNS server addresses:

Preferred DNS server: 192 . 168 . 1 . 2

Alternate DNS server: 192 . 168 . 1 . 4

Advanced...

OK   Cancel

Figure 21–3   *Configuring static IP address.*

ning the DHCP server service receives this broadcast and responds to the client machine with the configuration information. This configuration information will include an IP address and subnet at a minimum, and can optionally include a default gateway, DNS and WINS server addresses, broadcast mode types, and more. DHCP server configuration and the various options will be discussed in an upcoming chapter.

To configure a Windows 2000 server to be a DHCP client, open the TCP/IP properties and select *Obtain an IP address automatically.* This setting will require the computer to broadcast the DHCP request on boot. A client machine can also be instructed to obtain DNS server information directly from the DHCP server by selecting *Obtain DNS server address automatically* (Figure 21.4). This is selected by default when the DHCP client is configured.

The advanced selections will allow the client to determine whether to receive NetBIOS name resolution settings from the DHCP server. As with static addressing, the WINS and DNS configuration can be set at the client. However, it is not possible to bind multiple DHCP addresses to a single NIC, nor can a static address and a DHCP address be assigned to a single NIC.

tip   TCP/IP configuration settings that are specified on the client computer will override settings sent from a DCHP server.

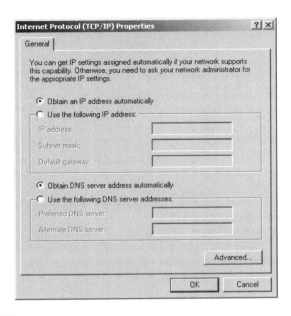

Figure 21—4   *Configuring DHCP IP address.*

ADVANCED TCP/IP CONFIGURATION

The advanced options within the TCP/IP properties sheet provide a network administrator the ability to fine-tune the configuration to best work with his or her network. The IP address tab allows the addition of IP addresses to the installed NIC card. The use of multiple IP addresses allows for multiple domains on a Web server, can create a one-legged firewall, or can allow a single NIC server to function as a low-usage router. Multiple IPs may also be bound to a single NIC to allow for access to two or more separate networks at the same time, or to allow mobile computers to attach to networks at multiple locations. It is important to note that a gateway must be defined for each network the computer is accessing.

Multiple DNS servers may also be defined within the advanced options. The standard setup allows for the definition of two DNS servers, a primary and an alternate. Within the advanced options many more DNS servers can be defined, and the order of use configured. In addition, several important DNS search parameters can be established. By default, Windows 2000 will make an attempt to locate remote computers via DNS and will expand the parameters on a name that is not a fully qualified domain name (e.g., Win2k.example.org). If you were searching for a computer named Corpserv, and your computer was in the homeoffice.example.org domain, Windows 2000 would look for corpserv.homeoffice.example.org and corpserv.example.org before declaring the desired machine unavailable. This behavior can be modified, however, by changing the settings on the DNS properties sheet. Unselecting the *Search the parent domains of the primary DNS domain* would result in Windows 2000 searching only the local DNS domain of homeoffice.example.org.

It is also possible to define the domains that Windows 2000 is allowed to search. Selecting *Search these DNS domains* will result in Windows 2000 searching only those DNS domains for the servers. For example, a network administrator could set the search domains to be servers.example.org and homeoffice.example.org, and Windows 2000 would search in servers.example.org first, then homeoffice.example.org, and then return an error. These search domains can also be other second-level domains; the administrator could set the search order to be example.org and anotherexample.org, and the operating system would search example.org first and then anotherexample.org.

The next option on the page is the entry for the domain name of the computer. By default, Windows 2000 will convert the name of the computer to a DNS-compliant name. This involves changing non-RFC compliant characters such as the underscore to a hyphen. Thus, a computer named Mary_Beth in the example.org domain would translate to mary-beth.example.org. However, the computer name and the DNS name do not have to be identical or even related. If a different name is desired, enter the fully qualified domain name in the domain name field.

Windows 2000 now uses DNS as the default in resolving computer names, rather than the previous WINS implementation. To provide the same automatic updated name and IP information that was available in WINS, Microsoft has implemented the Dynamic Domain Naming System in Windows 2000. Client computers can now register themselves automatically in the DNS system and change the information related to that particular machine. By default, this ability is enabled. To prevent this behavior, unselect the *Register this connection's addresses in DNS* option

Windows Internet Naming Service (WINS) is a legacy method for providing IP resolution for NetBIOS names. A WINS server maintains a database of NetBIOS names and their corresponding IP addresses and provides the IP addressing information to WINS clients. The database of names and IPs is dynamic, so that if the addressing changes on a WINS client, the WINS server reflects the updated information.

The WINS service is no longer required in a homogenous Windows 2000 networking environment, but networks that include legacy operating systems such as Windows NT 4.0 or the Windows 9x family will require a WINS server on the network.

To configure WINS on a Windows 2000 client, select the WINS tab in the advanced TCP/IP configuration options. Enter the IP addresses of the primary and secondary WINS servers, in the order in which you would like them accessed. Note that the first WINS server is the one with which the client computer will register.

Windows 2000 and previous versions of the Windows operating systems have alternate methods of resolving NetBIOS names to IP addresses. One method is the use of the LMHOSTS file. Located in the%systemroot%/system32/driver/etc., this text file can contain a listing of computer names, domains, and IP addresses. If an entry for a computer name is included in the LMHOSTS file, the addressing information used in the file will be used, and the WINS server will not be queried.

The use of LMHOSTS files does have several advantages. First, it marginally increases the speed of name resolution for those computers that are included in the file. Second, it allows name resolution for computers that, for security or technical reasons, are not included in a WINS database. However, these advantages are countered by the management difficulties inherent in maintaining a distributed name-resolution system. The LMHOSTS file needs to stay consistent on all clients within a network. While this can be overcome with login scripts that verify the existence and version of the LMHOSTS file, or be worked around with a #include statement, the centralized database is a more efficient approach.

The use of an LMHOSTS file can be enabled via selecting the *Enable LMHOSTS lookup* on the WINS tab of the advanced TCP/IP property sheet. This option is enabled by default. A sample Windows 2000 LMHOSTS file is included here for those administrators who must implement this form of name resolution.

SAMPLE LMHOSTS FILES

```
# Copyright (c) 1993-1995 Microsoft Corp.
#
# This is a sample LMHOSTS file used by the Microsoft TCP/IP for Windows
# NT.
#
# This file contains the mappings of IP addresses to NT computernames
# (NetBIOS) names. Each entry should be kept on an individual line.
# The IP address should be placed in the first column followed by the
# corresponding computer name. The address and the computername
# should be separated by at least one space or tab. The "#" character
# is generally used to denote the start of a comment (see the exceptions
# below).
#
# This file is compatible with Microsoft LAN Manager 2.x TCP/IP lmhosts
# files and offers the following extensions:
#
#     #PRE
#     #DOM:<domain>
```

```
#     #INCLUDE <filename>
#     #BEGIN_ALTERNATE

#     #END_ALTERNATE
#     \0xnn (nonprinting character support)
#
# Following any entry in the file with the characters "#PRE" will cause
# the entry to be preloaded into the name cache. By default, entries are
# not preloaded, but are parsed only after dynamic name resolution fails.
#
# Following an entry with the "#DOM:<domain>" tag will associate the
# entry with the domain specified by <domain>. This affects how the
# browser and logon services behave in TCP/IP environments. To preload
# the host name associated with #DOM entry, it is necessary to also add a
# #PRE to the line. The <domain> is always preloaded although it will not
# be shown when the name cache is viewed.
#
# Specifying "#INCLUDE <filename>" will force the RFC NetBIOS (NBT)
# software to seek the specified <filename> and parse it as if it were
# local. <filename> is generally a UNC-based name, allowing a
# centralized lmhosts file to be maintained on a server.
# It is ALWAYS necessary to provide a mapping for the IP address of the
# server prior to the #INCLUDE. This mapping must use the #PRE directive.
# In addition the share "public" in the example below must be in the
# LanManServer list of "NullSessionShares" in order for client machines to
# be able to read the lmhosts file successfully. This key is under
#\machine\system\currentcontrolset\services\lanmanserver\parameters\nullsessionshares
# in the registry. Simply add "public" to the list found there.
#
# The #BEGIN_ and #END_ALTERNATE keywords allow multiple #INCLUDE
# statements to be grouped together. Any single successful include
# will cause the group to succeed.
#
# Finally, non-printing characters can be embedded in mappings by
# first surrounding the NetBIOS name in quotations, then using the
# \0xnn notation to specify a hex value for a nonprinting character.
#
# The following example illustrates all of these extensions:
#
# 102.54.94.97    rhino        #PRE #DOM:networking  #net group's DC
# 102.54.94.102   "appname \0x14"              #special app server
# 102.54.94.123   popular      #PRE          #source server
# 102.54.94.117   localsrv     #PRE          #needed for the include
#
# #BEGIN_ALTERNATE
# #INCLUDE \\localsrv\public\lmhosts
# #INCLUDE \\rhino\public\lmhosts
# #END_ALTERNATE
```

```
#
# In the above example, the "appname" server contains a special

# character in its name, the "popular" and "localsrv" server names are
# preloaded, and the "rhino" server name is specified so it can be used
# to later #INCLUDE a centrally maintained lmhosts file if the "localsrv"
# system is unavailable.
#
# Note that the whole file is parsed including comments on each lookup,
# so keeping the number of comments to a minimum will improve performance.
# Therefore it is not advisable to simply add lmhosts file entries onto the

# end of this file.
```

The Options tab contains the configuration for IP security and IP filtering. TCP/IP filtering prevents Windows 2000 machines from passing or accepting packets on particular TCP ports, UDP ports, and IP protocols. This can be very useful when securing a server for public access. For example, an Internet Web server may be configured to accept traffic only on default HTTP, HTTPS, and FTP ports. This would help block malicious activity against the server. Windows 2000, like previous versions of NT, will accept traffic on all ports by default. To restrict traffic, select TCP/IP security on the options tab, choose the Properties button, and enable "Modify the settings as desired." If TCP/IP filtering is enabled or disabled, the settings affect all network adapters.

IP security is Microsoft's implementation of the IPSec (Internet Protocol Security) open standard developed by the IETF. IPSec is designed to provide an encrypted connection between two computers, so that sniffing, spoofing, data modification, and other attacks on the datastream can be foiled. The data is encrypted using a negotiated key and is checked against a checksum at the receiving end to verify that the packet has not been corrupted. IPSec can be deployed on a computer-by-computer basis or integrated into the Windows 2000 Active Directory policies. IPSec implementation can be controlled at the domain or organizational level, thus providing security without our having to implement it on each individual computer. Windows 2000 ships with the IPSec Policy Management administrative tool.

To enable IPSec on an individual computer, select the Options tab in the TCP/IP advanced property sheet and highlight IP security. Select Properties, and then choose the IP security policy from the dropdown menu.

Automatic Private IP Addressing

As mentioned previously, Windows 2000 supports both static IP addressing and dynamic IP addressing. DHCP tends to be a more easily managed and centrally configurable addressing scheme. However, this method requires a DHCP server on the network to service the client requests for IP addresses. If a DHCP server is unreachable, then the clients do not receive their IP addresses and are unable to function on the network.

Beginning with Windows 98, Microsoft introduced an extension of DCHP client functionality. The Automatic Private IP addressing extension allows a DHCP client that cannot reach a DHCP server to assign itself an address. This automatic addressing enables some limited network functionality to those clients. This DHCP extension is also included in all versions of Windows 2000. Thus, Windows 2000 clients can also assign addresses to themselves.

The range of addresses available to the automatic addressing feature is 199.254.0.0 to 169.254.255.255. These addresses have been reserved by the Internet Assigned Numbers Authority (IANA) for the automatic addressing feature. They are not routable and thus will not conflict with any other company's IP addressing scheme. A computer running the Windows 2000 or Windows 98 operating system will generate a random address within this range and broadcast the address to the network. If this address does not conflict with an existing assignment, the computer will assign the address to itself. The computer will use this information until it can contact a DHCP server, at which point it will pull its configuration information from the DHCP server.

The addresses in the automatic addressing range have a subnet mask of 255.255.0.0, but the automatic addressing feature does not define a gateway. This is understandable, because the client operating system does not have the infrastructure information necessary to determine the location of the gateway, and in any case the nonroutable addresses would be rejected at any router. As a result, computers using the automatic addressing scheme can only communicate with other machines using the automatic addressing. In a large routed enterprise network, the automatic addressing is unlikely to provide the network functionality needed by the users. However, in a smaller nonrouted environment, automatic addressing may fill the needs perfectly. As an example, a small business that is interconnected via a hub would only require setting the clients to DHCP, and the computers would negotiate IP addressing and be able to communicate via TCP/IP with little or no intervention from the users.

As mentioned previously, automatic addressing may not be appropriate for larger networks and may not be desired by some network administrators. By default, the functionality is enabled in Windows 2000 computers. To disable this behavior, the registry must be edited. To do so, add a DWORD value to *HKEY_LOCAL_MACHINE\SYSTEM\CurrentControlSet\Services\Tcpip\Paramaters\Interfaces\(Adapter GUID)* subkey. The DWORD value is IPAutoconfigurationEnabled and should be set to 0 to disable the function. If the entry is set to 1 or if the DWORD value is missing, the automatic addressing feature is enabled.

TCP/IP Utilities

Windows 2000 includes a full suite of TCP/IP utilities to provide client functionality and to provide troubleshooting capabilities (Table 21.5):

Table 21.5	TCP/IP Utilities
Utility	**Function**
ARP	Displays MAC addresses for IP addresses and allows editing of the local ARP table.
Finger	Retrieves user and system information from remote servers that support finger functionality.
FTP (file transfer protocol)	File transfer functionality between the local computer and a server running a FTP service. Windows 2000 can function both as a client and as a server.
Hostname	Prints the local computer host name.
IPconfig	Displays the local computer's current TCP/IP configuration.
Nbtstat	Displays netbios connections, cache, and other information
Netstat	Displays connection information for the local computer.
Ping	Verifies connectivity with remote hosts.
Remote Copy Protocol (RCP)	Copies files between a client and a RCP host.
Remote Execution (REXEC)	Runs a process or program on a remote host.
Remote Shell (RSH)	Runs commands on a remote UNIX host.
Route	Modifies and displays routing tables on the local host.
Telnet	Terminal emulation used to attach to remote computers running the telnet service. Windows 2000 can function as both a telnet client and server.
Tracert	Tests the route between the local host and a remote computer.
Trivial File Transfer Protocol (TFTP)	File transfer functionality between the local computer and a server running a TFTP service.

Using TCP/IP Utilities for Troubleshooting

It's an unfortunate fact of networking that issues will arise and result in computers that refuse to talk to the world. The TCP/IP utilities included with Windows 2000 can assist in troubleshooting network connectivity issues.

21.1.5.1 IPCONFIG

This command allows you to check the TCP/IP configuration on the local machine. The output shows the IP address, gateway, and subnet mask. The *ipconfig* command must be run from a command line. If additional information is needed, such as DHCP servers, DNS servers, MAC addresses, and the like, the command is *ipconfig/all*. The output of that command is shown below:

```
Windows NT IP Configuration

        Host Name . . . . . . . . . : WIN2KLAPTOP
        Primary Domain Name . . . . : FortWorth.local
        Node Type . . . . . . . . . : Hybrid
        IP Routing Enabled. . . . . : No
        WINS Proxy Enabled. . . . . : No

Ethernet adapter Local Area Connection:

        Adapter Domain Name . . . . :
        DNS Servers . . . . . . . . :
        Description . . . . . . . . : Xircom CreditCard
Ethernet 10/100 + Modem 56
        Physical Address. . . . . . : 00-10-A4-FD-BC-39
        DHCP Enabled. . . . . . . . : Yes
        Autoconfiguration Enabled . : Yes
        IP Address. . . . . . . . . : 172.16.3.22
        Subnet Mask . . . . . . . . : 255.255.0.0
        Default Gateway . . . . . . : 172.16.0.1
        DHCP Server . . . . . . . . : 172.16.1.4
```

PING

Ping is the basic IP connectivity troubleshooting. Run from a command line, the syntax is *Ping <address* or *computer name>*. The *ping* command uses ICMP packets to verify connectivity with a remote computer. The response, or lack thereof, from the ping can give a lead on a connectivity issue. For instance, if a computer cannot ping another by name, but receives a response when pinging to an IP address, then the problem lies somewhere in the name-resolution system: DNS, WINS, or perhaps in the *hosts/lmhosts* files.

```
C:\>ping ftp.prenhall.com

Pinging ftp.prenhall.com [63.69.110.64] with 32 bytes of data:

Reply from 63.69.110.64: bytes=32 time=50ms TTL=240
Reply from 63.69.110.64: bytes=32 time=50ms TTL=240
Reply from 63.69.110.64: bytes=32 time=50ms TTL=240
Reply from 63.69.110.64: bytes=32 time=50ms TTL=240

Ping statistics for 63.69.110.64:
    Packets: Sent = 4, Received = 4, Lost = 0 (0% loss),
```

```
Approximate round trip times in milli-seconds:
    Minimum = 50ms, Maximum = 50ms, Average = 50ms
```

ICMP is designed to provide diagnostic information on network connectivity issues. As such, there are several error messages that are typically received when packets do not reach their destination. The most common are listed in Table 21.6:

Table 21.6	ICMP Messages
Message	**Meaning**
Host Unreachable	The destination host on a remote network was not found. This message will not be generated for a host on the local network.
Network Unreachable	The route to a remote network was not found.
Destination Unreachable	The datagram could not be delivered to the destination host.

TRACERT

Tracert is a utility that, as the name suggests, traces the route between the local computer and a remote host. This tool can help in determining whether connectivity problems are occurring inside your network, and if so, where those problems lie. *Tracert* is run from the command line, and the syntax is *tracert <address* or *computer name>*.

```
C:\>tracert ftp.prenhall.com

Tracing route to ftp.prenhall.com [63.69.110.64]
over a maximum of 30 hops:

  1 10 ms <10 ms <10 ms   172.16.0.1
  2 <10 ms <10 ms 10 ms   204.0.11.53
  3 <10 ms  10 ms <10 ms  204.0.11.49
  4 <10 ms  10 ms <10 ms  core0-fa0-0-0.ftwo.tx.verio.neT.
[199.1.144.5]
  5 10 ms <10 ms 10 ms   border2-h0-0.dlls.tx.verio.net.
[206.50.192.10]
  6 <10 ms 10 ms 10 ms  g6-0.dfw2.verio.net. [129.250.31.49]
  7 <10 ms 10 ms 10 ms   serial3-0-1.br1.dfw7.ALTER.NET.
[137.39.21.121]
  8 <10 ms 10 ms 10 ms   106.at-6-0-0.XR1.DFW7.ALTER.NET.
[146.188.241.178]
  9 <10 ms 10 ms 10 ms   191.ATM3-0.TR1.DFW4.ALTER.NET.
```

```
[146.188.241.226]
 10 51 ms 50 ms 50 ms    108.ATM6-0.TR1.EWR1.ALTER.NET.
[146.188.136.242]
 11 50 ms 50 ms 50 ms    100.ATM7-0.XR1.EWR1.ALTER.NET.
[146.188.176.69]
 12 50 ms 50 ms 50 ms    193.ATM9-0-0.GW1.EWR1.ALTER.NET.
[146.188.176.41]
 13 51 ms 60 ms 50 ms    headland-mediagw.customer.ALTER.NET.
[157.130.19.86]
 14 60 ms 60 ms 60 ms    63.69.110.64

Trace complete.
```

If the trace does not reach the destination, you will see a result like the one below:

```
C:\>tracert strahan.tj


Tracing route to strahan.tj [63.68.134.114]
over a maximum of 30 hops:

<Removed for clarity>

 10 10 ms <10 ms <10 ms   directlink-ds3-gw.customer.alter.net.
[157.130.133.226]
 11 10 ms  10 ms 10 ms   rback2-ds3.directlink.net. [207.239.163.15]
 12     *         *          *      Request timed out.
 13     *         *          *      Request timed out.
 14     *         *          *      Request timed out.
```

This result indicates that there is a connectivity issue somewhere between your host and the destination computer. If this connectivity problem lies outside of your network, you may have to contact the administrator of the destination site or the engineer responsible for the network the destination site is located upon. This problem usually manifests itself locally as being able to reach some destination sites, but not a certain percentage. Network outages on major backbone providers can bring down large sections of the world's networks.

Sometimes connectivity problems can be a result of loops in the routing tables. In this case, the packets are swapped back and forth between two routers until the time-to-live (TTL) expires. This behavior will look like the following:

```
10 51 ms 50 ms 50 ms    108.ATM6-0.TR1.EWR1.ALTER.NET.
[146.188.136.242]
11 50 ms 50 ms 50 ms    100.ATM7-0.XR1.EWR1.ALTER.NET.
[146.188.176.69]
10 51 ms 50 ms 50 ms    108.ATM6-0.TR1.EWR1.ALTER.NET.
```

```
[146.188.136.242]
12 50 ms 50 ms 50 ms   100.ATM7-0.XR1.EWR1.ALTER.NET.
[146.188.176.69]
13 51 ms 50 ms 50 ms   108.ATM6-0.TR1.EWR1.ALTER.NET.
[146.188.136.242]
14 50 ms 50 ms 50 ms   100.ATM7-0.XR1.EWR1.ALTER.NET.
[146.188.176.69]
```

If the loop is occurring outside your network, contact the technical contact for the network that is suffering from the loop. In many cases the engineers will already be aware of this issue, but it never hurts to bring it to their attention. If it is local, verify the routing tables and configurations on both routers.

NWlink

NWLink is the Microsoft implementation of the IPX/SPX (Internetwork Packet Exchange/Sequenced Packet Exchange) protocol made popular by Novell during the 1980s. The IPX/SPX protocol was included as the default protocol in the popular NetWare networking product. Computers running Windows 2000 can connect as clients to NetWare servers and can provide file and print services on a NetWare network with the File and Print Services for NetWare (FPNW) add-on. In addition, a small Windows 2000 network can function using the NWLink protocol to connect various Microsoft operating systems.

Brief History and Uses of NWLINK

IPX/SPX was actually developed by a consortium of companies, but its inclusion as the default protocol in Novell's Netware products resulted in the protocol being linked in the minds of many primarily with Novell. IPX/SPX fit well in the network architecture of the 1980s and early 1990s, because it combined relatively high performance with the routing capabilities needed as PC networks expanded beyond simple workgroups. When Microsoft began entering the network operating system arena in earnest in the early 90s, Netware and the IPX/SPX protocol suite were well established. In order to provide connectivity with the established market leader at the time, Microsoft developed the NWLink implementation of the suite. With the appropriate client software installed, NWLink will allow a Windows-based PC to connect with Netware file shares and printers. In addition, an add-on product for Microsoft servers allows them to offer file and print services to Netware clients. Not surprisingly, this add-on is called File and Print Services for Netware (FPNW). FPNW is not included as part of Windows 2000 but is instead a separate product. NWLink also functions to provide NetWare clients access to BackOffice applications like

SQL server and SNA server. In these cases, the FPNW add-on is not required, because the BackOffice application handles any needed client interaction.

ARCHITECTURE OF NWLINK

Just as with TCP/IP, IPX/SPX is a suite of protocols that has both connection-oriented and connectionless capabilities. The complete suite consists of the proto-

Table 21.7	IPX/SPX Protocols
Protocol	**Function**
Internetwork Packet Exchange (IPX)	Provides routing capabilities and handles logical network addressing. This is a connectionless protocol.
NetWare Core Protocol (NCP)	Provides connectivity to client applications. NCP also runs over TCP/IP.
NetWare Link Services (NLSP)	Provides a centralized routing database for IPX/SPX routers.
Routing Information Protocol (RIP)	Passes routing information from one router to another via IPX.
Sequenced Packet Exchange (SPX)	Connection-oriented protocol that provides assured delivery via checksums and sequencing.
Service Advertising Protocol (SAP)	Tracks the services available on various hosts. IPX/SPX routers maintain a list of these services via the SAP agent.

cols shown in Table 21.7.

IPX ADDRESSING

IPX/SPX addressing differs from TCP/IP, but many of the concepts are the same. Each host needs to know where it is located in the network and where to find other host servers. The IPX/SPX protocol handles this issue through the implementation of four naming elements.

IPX Network Address: This is a unique identifier for each network segment. Roughly analogous to the network address in IP, this hexadecimal number identifies the network segment to which the hosts are attached. Two segments on the same network cannot have the same IPX network address, or communication will be disrupted. The address must be eight numbers long and cannot include all zeros, all Fs, or FFFFFFFE. In order to prevent conflicts when multiple NetWare networks are interconnected, Novell has developed the Novell Network Registry. For more information on globally unique network addresses, contact Novell.

NOVELL NETWORK REGISTRY

E-mail: registry@novell.com
Fax:(408)577-7605
Voice Mail: (408) 577-7506
Postal Address:
The Novell Network Address Registry
Mail Stop F4-71
2180 Fortune Drive
San Jose, CA 95131 USA

Internal IPX Address: This is a unique eight-digit address for each server on an IPX/SPX network. It is generated automatically during the install of the server software. Just as with TCP/IP, each server must have a unique address, or communication problems will occur. While this address can be set manually, it is not recommended.

Station IPX Address: This is a unique 12-digit address for each device on an IPX/SPX network. This identifier is the same as the physical address (MAC address) on the host.

Socket Identifier: Much like TCP/IP port numbers, each service on an IPX/SPX network has a related socket identifier. This number is normally not changed by the administrator.

Installing NWLink

NWLink is installed in the same manner as other network protocols. Open the property sheet for the LAN connection, and choose Install. When prompted for the type of installation, choose Protocol.

In the next dialog box (Figure 21.5), select the NWLink IPX/SPX/NetBIOS Compatible Transport Protocol and click OK. The system will copy files and install the protocol. It is not necessary to reboot the server.

Configuring NWLink

Configuration of NWLink is less involved than configuring the TCP/IP protocol. There are only three elements: internal network number, frame type, and network number. NWLink supports multiple frame types, but the operating system attempts to autodetect the frame type when the protocol is installed. If multiple frame types are detected, NWLink defaults to the newer 802.2 frame type (Figure 21.6).

802.3 is the default frame type for NetWare 2.x and 3.11 Ethernet networks, NetWare 3.12, and later defaults to 802.2 on Ethernet networks. Token Ring networks use frame type 802.5. In addition, all the above support the SNAP (Sub Network Access Protocol) frame type.

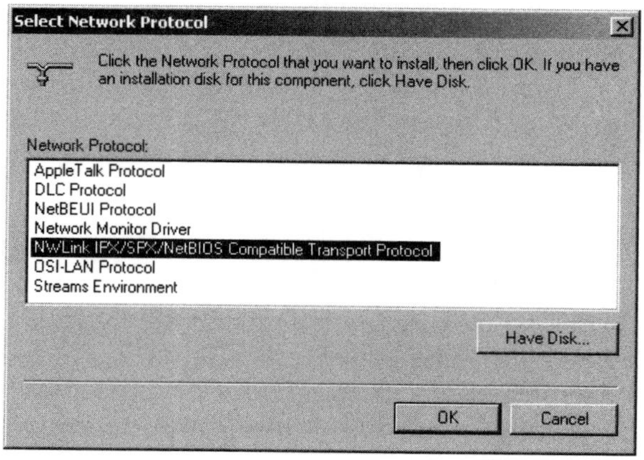

Select Network Protocol

Click the Network Protocol that you want to install, then click OK. If you have an installation disk for this component, click Have Disk.

Network Protocol:
- AppleTalk Protocol
- DLC Protocol
- NetBEUI Protocol
- Network Monitor Driver
- NWLink IPX/SPX/NetBIOS Compatible Transport Protocol
- OSI-LAN Protocol
- Streams Environment

Have Disk...

OK   Cancel

Figure 21–5 *Installing NWLink.*

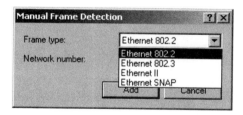

Manual Frame Detection

Frame type: Ethernet 802.2

Network number:
- Ethernet 802.2
- Ethernet 802.3
- Ethernet II
- Ethernet SNAP

Add   Cancel

Figure 21–6 *Supported frame types.*

The internal network number defaults to 00000000. In most cases this will be sufficient, but in three cases the internal network number would need to be modified:

1. File and Print Services for NetWare is installed on a Windows 2000 server and is bound to multiple adapters within the server.
2. File and Print Services for NetWare is installed, and multiple frame types are bound to a single adapter.
3. SAP (NetWare Services Advertising Protocol) is being used by an application.

To modify the internal network address of the adapter, enter a unique eight-digit hexadecimal number in the box labeled Internal Network Number (Figure 21.7).

The network address for the segment itself should be detected automatically by Windows 2000 when the NWLink protocol is installed. Normally, this number should not be changed. If for some reason the values need to be changed, Registry

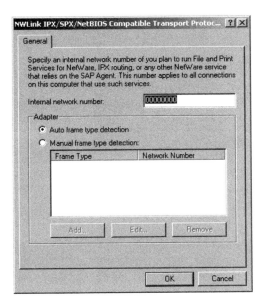

Figure 21-7 *Modifying the internal network number.*

changes are required. To manually set the network number, open *HKEY_LOCAL_MACHINE\SYSTEM\CurrentControlSet\Services\Nwlnkipx\Parameters\Adapters\<Adapter ID>* (Figure 21.8). Within this key there are two values that concern us. The first is Network Number, which specifies the network number for the adapter. This number is a hexadecimal eight-digit value. The default of 00000000 indicates an auto-detection configuration. To modify this value, open the *Regedt32* and modify the REG_MULTI_SZ value.

Regedit does not support the REG_MULTI_SZ value type.

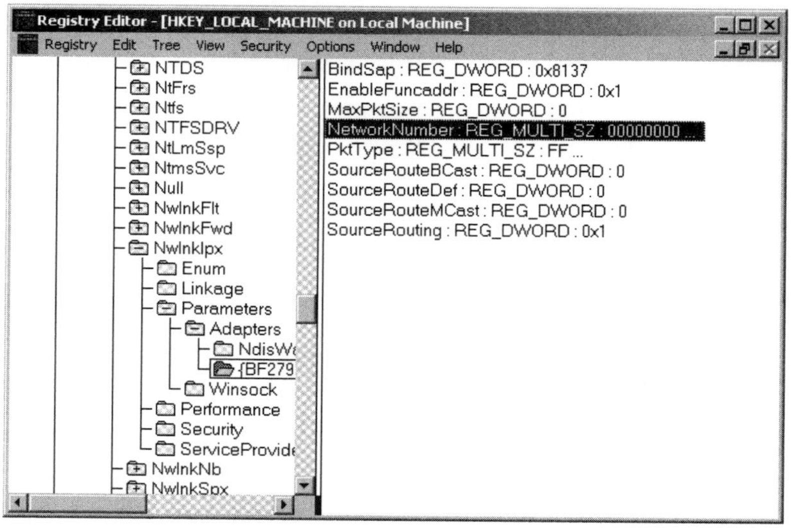

Figure 21-8   *Modifying network-number and packet-type values.*

Table 21.8	PktType Values
Value	**Packet Type**
0	Ethernet_II
1	Ethernet_802.3
2	802.2
3	SNAP
4	ArcNet
FF	Auto Detect

Modifying the network number for an adapter may require manually setting the packet time. Within the same subkey, there is a PktType value. This value is also a REG_MULTI_SZ value type and will also require Regedt32 to correctly modify the value. The default value if FF, which indicates an auto-detect mode. Allowed variables for the PktType value are listed in Table 21.8.

Other Supported Protocols

NetBIOS Extended User Interface (NetBEUI)

NetBEUI is a fast and efficient protocol designed for use in small workgroup networks. It is broadcast-based, which means it has inherent limitations that prevent it from being easily used in a routed LAN or WAN environment. First developed in the early 80s, the protocol has been at the core of Microsoft operating system name resolution through Windows NT 4.0, first via broadcast and later via WINS.

NetBEUI has many advantages for the smaller, nonrouted network environment. First, it is self-configuring and self-tuning. Other than ensuring that all the computers have unique names, there is almost no configuration to be done on a NetBEUI system. In fact, on a Windows 2000 system, there are no properties to configure at all!

In addition to being easy to install, the protocol requires very little overhead in terms of system resources. While that is less of a factor in these days of high-powered computers, system resources were a great concern when the protocol was first developed.

NetBEUI does have some inherent disadvantages. As mentioned before, the protocol cannot be routed, and so a network dependent upon NetBEUI cannot be segmented. This is coupled to the fact that the NetBEUI protocol is primarily broadcast based. Therefore, as networks grew larger, the "chattering" of the protocol began to reduce the efficiency of the network.

Installing NetBEUI is accomplished in the same manner as installing any other protocol. Open the connection properties, select Install, choose Protocol, and select NetBEUI protocol. The system will prompt for a reboot after the installation.

Data Link Control (DLC)

The DLC protocol was originally designed for communication with mainframe computers, and it still provides that functionality in many environments. The DLC protocol allows a Windows 2000 server to connect with terminal emulation to mainframes, and it also enables products such as the SNA server to function correctly. However, the primary use of the DLC protocol in many environments is connectivity to Hewlett-Packard JetDirect network adapters.

The DLC protocol is required on a Windows 2000 print server to allow network clients to print to a DLC JetDirect adapter. It is not necessary for the printing clients to have the protocol installed.

Installing DLC is accomplished in the same manner as installing any other protocol. Open the connection properties, select Install, choose Protocol, and select DLC protocol. The system will not prompt for a reboot after the installation.

AppleTalk

The AppleTalk protocol is by Apple Macintosh clients. This protocol must be installed on a Windows 2000 server if it is providing file or print services to Macintosh clients.

Installing the AppleTalk protocol is accomplished in the same manner as installing any other protocol. Open the connection properties, select Install, choose Protocol, and select the AppleTalk protocol. The system will not prompt for a reboot after the installation.

Understanding Network Bindings

Purpose of Network Bindings

Network Binding is the term used to describe the communication patterns between network protocols, services, and adapters. Services use the bound protocols to communicate with particular network adapters. Multiple protocols can be bound to a single adapter, and likewise, multiple adapters can be running the same protocol. In Figure 21.9, the network adapter used by the default LAN connection is bound to the TCP/IP protocol, and the TCP/IP protocol is bound to File and Printer Sharing for Microsoft Networks and the Client for Microsoft Networks. To check the bindings on a system, open Network and Dial-up Connections in the Control Panel, and select Advanced Settings from the Advanced toolbar menu.

Windows 2000 automatically handles the binding configuration when network protocols or services are installed. However, there may be times when the bindings need to be manually adjusted. Bindings can be removed from a particular service by simply removing the check from the selected box. Please note that you must have administrator rights to change bindings on a Windows 2000 system.

The Importance of Binding Order

The binding order refers to the order in which the operating system will use the network binding to provide services or attach to network resources. If a network adapter has multiple protocols bound to it, the first protocol will be the first used by the operating system to establish a connection to another computer. This can be quite significant in terms of network performance. Assume for a moment that a remote server is running only TCP/IP, and the protocols on the client machine are bound in the order of NWLink and TCP/IP. A connection to that remote server is first attempted via NWLink, and naturally fails. The connection is then attempted over TCP/IP, and should be successful. The problem

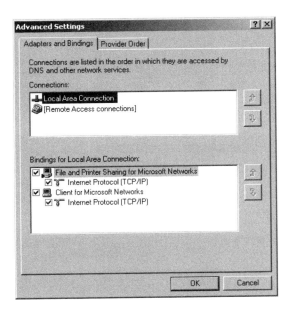

Figure 21-9   *Viewing network bindings.*

with that scenario is that the computer has to wait for the NWLink connection attempt to fail, and that may take some time.   Depending upon the ordering and number of the protocols in the binding order, the performance may be dismal indeed.

The solution to this issue is to modify the binding order so that the most frequently used protocol is bound first. This will allow the operating system to make the remote connections without having to wait through a timeout period. Given the example above, if the client computer had TCP/IP bound before the NWLink protocol, the first connection would be made via the correct protocol and network access times on the client would be improved.

From a server perspective, binding order initially seems less important. A server responds to a client request for information or access. The server is going to respond based upon the protocol the client uses: a TCP/IP response to a TCP/IP request, and a NWLink response to a NWLink request. If the server is not equipped with the requested protocol, obviously it is never going to see the initial client request. Therefore, from a server perspective, there is not a delay while a protocol times out.

This may lead some to believe that binding order on a server is unimportant. However, often a server requires a connection to another, such as a domain controller, application server, or another file server. In this case, the binding order once again affects the speed of the connection, because the

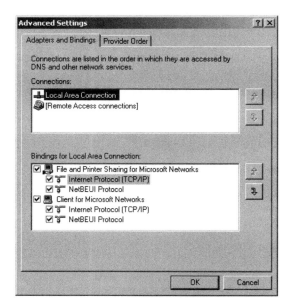

Viewing binding order.

server is now a client machine. If there is a protocol mismatch, the server must wait while the protocol times out.

Viewing Binding Order

To view the bindings order on a Windows 2000 system, open Network and Dial-up Connections in the Control Panel, and select Advanced Settings from the Advanced toolbar menu. The lower window shows the available protocols and the order of the bindings for each service. In the case shown in Figure 21.10, the computer has both the TCP/IP protocol and the NetBEUI protocol loaded. The TCP/IP protocol is first in the binding order and will be the default protocol for network connections.

Changing Binding Order

The binding order can be adjusted to optimize the client's access speeds on the network. As mentioned earlier, the first binding for a service will be the default choice for the operating system. If this binding is not the correct one, then the client will suffer from a timeout and then eventually use the next binding. To optimize client performance, the primary binding should be the one most often used to access network resources.

To change the binding order, select the Advanced Settings from the Advanced toolbar menu. This will bring up an applet that shows the current bindings and binding order of services on the computer. To move a protocol up in the binding order, select the appropriate protocol and then click on the up arrow located to the right (see Figure 21.10). To move a protocol down in the binding order, select the protocol and choose the down arrow button. To remove a protocol or service from the binding list, uncheck the box to the left of the protocol or service.

Chapter Summary

In this chapter we have discussed some of the network protocols that Windows 2000 supports. Windows 2000 is capable of functioning in a heterogeneous network consisting of multiple operating systems, protocols, and clients. The default protocol for Windows 2000 is TCP/IP, which stands for Transmission Control Protocol/Internet Protocol. TCP/IP is the de facto standard protocol for most network operating systems and is a required protocol for communication with and across the Internet.

TCP/IP adressing requires that each host be assigned a unique address. Windows 2000 supports both static addressing and DHCP (Dynamic Host Configuration Protocol). DHCP is a method in which a central server assigns IP addresses and other IP configuration information to client operating systems. It is recommended that servers use static addressing, while client computers on a network use DHCP to obtain the addressing. This is due to the enormous administrative load required to keep an accurate record of statically assigned addresses within a large environment, and the potential for rogue addresses. DHCP also allows for centralized control of IP configurations such as DNS servers, WINS servers, gateways, and similar information.

With the adoption of TCP/IP as the default protocol in Windows 2000, Microsoft has also implemented automatic private IP addressing. This automatic addressing is activated when a DHCP client is unable to reach a DHCP server. In this circumstance, the client will assign itself an IP address within the 199.254.0.0 to 169.254.255.255 range with a subnet of 255.255.0.0. This nonroutable IP address contains minimal configuration information; only the address and subnet are configured on the PC. Since there is not a gateway configured, the computer can only speak to others within the same 199.254.0.0 to 169.254.255.255 range. This functionality is designed to allow small hub-connected workgroups to function with minimal user configuration, similar to the way the NetBEUI protocol allowed for workgroup functionality in previous versions of Windows NT and Windows client operating systems.

Another protocol supported by Windows 2000 is NWLink. NWlink is Microsoft's implementation of the IPX/SPX protocol popularized by Novell with its NetWare product. The primary purpose of the NWLink protocol is to provide connectivity with NetWare servers and clients. It is also installed when the File and Print Services for NetWare add-on is installed on a Windows 2000 server. While a homogenous Windows 2000 network can function using NWLink as the primary protocol, it is not recommended.

AppleTalk is a protocol that will allow a Windows 2000 server to connect to Macintosh clients. Windows 2000 ships with the ability to function as a file and print server for Macintosh client computers. This functionality is not installed by default.

DLC is used primarily to communicate with Hewlett-Packard JetDirect print servers, which are commonly used to connect printers directly to a network. This protocol also can be used to communicate with some mainframes and similar equipment. This protocol is not recommended for general communication purposes.

NetBEUI is a fast, nonroutable protocol designed for small workgroup networks. The NetBEUI protocol was used extensively to provide name-resolution and connectivity functions in earlier versions of Microsoft operating systems. With the adoption of TCP/IP as the default protocol, NetBEUI is no longer required on a Windows 2000 network. However, to allow for transition and communication with legacy operating systems, NetBEUI is a supported option within Windows 2000.

Network protocols are associated with services and adapters (network cards) within the Windows 2000 operating system. These associations are called bindings. A protocol can be bound to multiple network adapters, and likewise, multiple protocols can be bound to a single adapter. Services are also bound to particular protocols and adapters. In a network environment that relies on a single protocol, bindings do not usually need to be adjusted on a system. However, in an environment that supports multiple protocols, the binding order may have an impact on network performance. The binding order is the order in which a computer will use network protocols to connect to a remote computer. A computer will attempt to make a connection with a remote machine with the first protocol in the binding order, and then with the next. If the remote computer is not running the same protocol that the client machine is attempting to use, the client has to wait for that protocol to time out before trying with the second protocol in the binding order. Depending upon the protocols in use, this may take some time. The user will perceive this timeout as a slow network response. To improve the response times on the client, move the most frequently used protocol to the top of the binding order. To view and modify the binding order, select Advanced Settings from the advanced toolbar menu within the network applet.

In the next few chapters we will discuss some of the network-centric services available within Windows 2000. These services include the Domain Naming System (DNS), the Dynamic Host Configuration Protocol (DHCP) server, and the legacy Windows Internet Naming Service (WINS).

Dynamic Host Configuration Service (DHCS)

With the widespread adoption of the Internet and routed networks, TCP/IP (Transmission Control Protocol/Internet Protocol) has become the de facto standard network protocol. TCP/IP provides for a robust connection and interoperability between most major operating systems. However, TCP/IP also requires that each computer on a network have a unique IP address. Originally, TCP/IP addresses were assigned manually to each host and configured locally on each computer. When networks were small, this was not much of an issue, but as networks grew larger and began to interact, maintaining accurate records of the IP addresses and configurations on the multitude of computers became a logistical problem. Fortunately, DHCP (Dynamic Host Configuration Protocol) helps solve some of these issues.

22.1 Understanding DHCP

DHCP is Microsoft's implementation of the BOOTP protocol. The BOOTP protocol was originally designed to allow workstations to automatically be configured when they booted within a network environment. The workstations contained just enough code to allow them to contact a server and pull down the configuration information. Microsoft uses an extension of BOOTP to enable automatic TCP/IP configuration for workstations on a network. The DHCP service enables centralized control and configuration of TCP/IP within a network. When a DHCP client contacts the DHCP server, the client is given an IP address and other configuration information automatically. The DHCP server contains one or more ranges of IP addresses, appropriate subnet masks, and optional information such as DNS and WINS entries. The client is granted the IP address for a specific amount of time, which is known as the lease time. At the end of that time, if the client has not renewed the lease, the client releases the IP address.

Advantages of DHCP

Strictly speaking, a client computer will have precisely the same functionality whether it is configured manually or via DHCP. If it is configured correctly, the client computer will be able to communicate on the local network and, if available, to remote networks. However, there is a greater chance of misconfiguration with the manually configured computer. Consider for a moment the steps required:

- First, whoever is configuring the computer must know the correct addressing scheme for the network. While this is not a major issue for most technicians, problems can arise when unqualified personnel change the settings, or if a setting is typed incorrectly.
- Second, an IP address must be assigned to the computer. In an environment that consists of static addresses, there must be some form of centralized tracking of IP addresses. This often takes the form of large spreadsheets or databases, with IP addresses being assigned by a system administrator or other personnel. However, if addresses have not been properly tracked, then the potential for conflict is high. Worse, an IP address may be changed or entered incorrectly, causing conflicts or other networking issues.
- The addresses for the default gateway, DNS servers, and WINS servers must be entered manually. Once again, an error here will generate networking issues for the client computer.
- If the computer is moved from one subnet to another, the IP information must be changed, the changes tracked, and errors corrected.

Now, let us consider what is involved in configuring a DHCP client, assuming that a DHCP server is running and is configured properly:
- Plug the client computer into the network.
- Turn it on.
- If the client moves to a new subnet, repeat the above two steps.

As you can see, the advantages on the client side are tremendous. Naturally, though, the server setup time needs to be considered. Within a small, non-routed network, manual configuration may be a better option. Additionally, a network that consists of computers running Windows 2000 and Windows 98 can use automatic private IP addressing to assign themselves an address within the 169.254.x.x range. However, automatic private IP addresses are not routable and thus are appropriate only on very simple networks that are not connected to external systems or the Internet.

DHCP Server Requirements

The DHCP service requires a computer capable of running Windows 2000 Server, and the system must be using the TCP/IP protocol. This server can be either a domain controller or a standalone server.

The DCHP server must be configured with a static IP address, subnet mask, default gateway and other TCP/IP settings. It is worth noting that TCP/IP configuration settings on the server itself do not pass to the clients.

The DHCP server must be configured with at least one scope. A scope is a range of addresses that the DHCP server can assign to the client computers. TCP/IP configuration settings for the DHCP clients are set by the scope.

DHCP Client Requirements

DHCP clients can run a variety of operating systems. Microsoft supports the following operating systems as DHCP clients:

- Windows 2000, Windows NT 4.0 Server, Windows NT 4.0 Workstation, Windows 3.51 Server, and Windows NT Workstation 3.51
- Windows 95 and Windows 98
- Windows for Workgroups 3.11, if the client is running the Microsoft TCP/IP-32 protocol stack. The TCP/IP-32 stack is included with Windows 2000 Server and also is included with some earlier versions of Windows NT.
- MS-DOS, when running Microsoft Network Client version 3.0 with real-mode drivers. This DOS client is included with Windows 2000 Server and also is included with some earlier versions of Windows NT.
- LAN Manager version 2.2c, which is bundled with Windows 2000 Server and is included with some earlier versions of Windows NT.

Additionally, many UNIX-based operating systems are capable of functioning as a DHCP client. However, Microsoft does not support these operating systems as clients.

DHCP Address Assignment

The DHCP process is the method by which the client receives an IP address from the server. DHCP uses a four-step process to assign IP configuration information to a client. The four steps are DHCPDISCOVER, DHCPOFFER, DHCPREQUEST, and DHCPACK. This process can be invoked by any of three conditions.

The first condition is a TCP/IP stack initializing on a DHCP client for the first time. In most cases, the client computer booting will generate this condition, but certain clients may have the ability to unload and reload the TCP/IP stack.

If a client computer requests a certain IP address and is denied, the DHCP process will be invoked and the client will be assigned a new address.

The third condition occurs if a client releases the assigned IP address and requests a new one, triggering the DHCP process (see Table 22.1).

Table 22.1	DHCP Process	
Client	**Server**	**Function**
DHCPDISCOVER		Broadcast with MAC address to locate DHCP server.
	DHCPOFFER	All available DHCP servers offer IP configuration information to client.
DHCPREQUEST		Broadcast to all DHCP servers, indicating desired IP offer. All others withdraw their offers
	DHCPACK	DHCP server acknowledges the client and sends the lease information to the client.

DHCPDISCOVER

When a DHCP client initializes, it begins with a very limited version of TCP/IP. The function of this version of TCP/IP is to broadcast a DHCPDISCOVER message to the local subnet. Because the client is unaware of the addresses of any DHCP servers, the broadcast is sent to IP address 0.0.0.0 with a subnet mask of 255.255.255.255. In a routed environment, the broadcast will be received by the router and, if configured as a DHCP helper, redirected to the segment on which the DHCP server is located.

The DHCDISCOVER packet contains the client's MAC address and computername.

DHCPOFFER

All DHCP servers that receive the DHCPDISCOVER respond to the client with a DHCPOFFER message. The offer includes the client's MAC address, an offered IP address, the subnet mask, the lease length, and the IP address of the DHCP server as an identifier. This packet is sent as a broadcast, since the client does not yet have an IP address. The DHCP server will reserve the address to prevent potential conflicts.

DHCPREQUEST

Once the client receives at least one DHCPOFFER, the client accepts one of the offers. In practical terms, the client will accept the first offer that it receives. Once the client accepts an offer, it broadcasts a DHCPREQUEST packet to all DHCP servers. The DHCPREQUEST packet includes the identifier of the accepted DHCP server. All other servers withdraw their offers and release the reservation.

DHCPACK

The selected DHCP server broadcasts a successful acknowledgment to the client. The acknowledgement includes the IP address for the client and other TCP/IP configuration information. This message has to be a broadcast, because the client does not yet have a complete TCP/IP stack initialized. Once the client receives this DHCPACK message, TCP/IP completes the initialization process, and the client can function normally on the network.

DCHPNACK

In some cases, the DHCP server will respond with a negative acknowledgment. The DHCPNACK will be broadcast to a client only during a renewal, when the requested IP address is unavailable or invalid. In the case of a DHCPNACK, the client begins the lease process again from the DHCPDISCOVER phase.

DHCP Lease Release and Renewal

IP addresses are issued on a temporary basis and expire after a certain period of time. This is known as the lease duration, and the administrator of the DHCP server determines its length. DHCP client computers must renew their leases before the end of the lease, or they will no longer have an IP address and network connectivity.

A DHCP client will attempt to renew its current lease when half of the lease has passed. The DHCP client sends a DHCPREQUEST to the DHCP server that granted the lease originally. If the server is contacted and the IP address is available, the DHCP server will send a DHCPACK to the client and renew the lease for another duration. If the IP configuration information has changed, the changes will be passed down to the client with the new lease.

If the server is available but the requested IP address is unavailable or invalid, the DHCP server sends a DHCPNACK packet to the client, informing it that the requested IP address is unavailable. The client will then reinitialize the DHCP process with a DHCPDISCOVER broadcast in order to procure a new address.

If the DHCP server that originally issued the lease is unavailable, the client computer will continue to use the IP address until the end of the lease. The client will broadcast another DHCPREQUEST message when 87.5% of the lease duration has expired. Any DHCP server can respond with either a DHCPACK or DHCPNACK to the broadcast. If the server responds with a DHCPACK, the client renews the IP address for another lease duration. In the event that the client receives a DHCPNACK, the client immediately releases the current IP address and initiates the DHCP lease process with a DHCPDISCOVER message.

If the client does not receive either a DHCPACK or a DHCPNACK, the lease for that IP address will expire. When a lease expires, the client releases the IP address and reinitiates the DHCP lease process. Until the client can contact a DHCP server and receive a new IP address, network connectivity will be impacted.

MANUAL RELEASE AND RENEWAL

From time to time, the need to manually release or renew a DHCP lease will arise. Modifications to TCP/IP configuration, movements of a client to a new subnet, or simple troubleshooting are several reasons a manual release or renewal would be required. Fortunately, Windows clients offer this ability.

A Windows 2000 DHCP client can use the *ipconfig* command from a command line to manipulate the DHCP process. *Ipconfig /renew* forces the client to send a DHCPREQUEST broadcast to the DHCP server that provided the lease. If the server is available, the lease is renewed. If any changes have been made to the TCP/IP configuration information served by the DHCP server, the client is updated with those changes. In the event that the DCHP server is not available, the client will continue to use the current IP address until the end of the lease.

The command *ipconfig /release* forces a manual release of the lease. The client sends a DHCPRELEASE message to the DHCP server and releases the IP address. When the server receives the DHCPRELEASE message, the IP address is returned to the pool of available addresses. It is important to note that Microsoft DHCP clients do not send a DHCPRELEASE message when they are shut down. This behavior helps maintain the same IP address on the client across boots.

Windows 9x clients offer the same functionality, but the process is handled via the *winipcfg* command. The *winipcfg* command is graphical interface, which allows the release and renewal of a lease by pressing a button. Windows NT clients follow the Windows 2000 use of *ipconfig*.

```
C:\>ipconfig /all

Windows 2000 IP Configuration

Host Name. . . . . . . . . . . . : WIN2K
Primary DNS Suffix  . . . . . . . : internal.pinball.nu
Node Type . . . . . . . . . . . . : Hybrid
IP Routing Enabled. . . . . . . . : No
WINS Proxy Enabled. . . . . . . . : No
```

```
DNS Suffix Search List. . . . . . : internal.pinball.nu

Ethernet adapter Local Area Connection :

Connection-specific DNS Suffix  . :
Description. . . . . . . . . . :3Com EtherLink III ISA (3C509b-TPO)
Physical Address. . . . . . . . : 00-50-DA-07-78-50
DHCP Enabled. . . . . . . . . . : No
IP Address. . . . . . . . . . . : 192.168.1.199
Subnet Mask . . . . . . . . . . : 255.255.255.0
Default Gateway . . . . . . . . :
DNS Servers . . . . . . . . . . : 192.168.1.2
                                  192.168.1.4
Primary WINS Server . . . . . . : 192.168.1.199
```

Installing the DHCP Server Service

To install the DHCP service on a Windows 2000 server, begin by opening the Windows Component Wizard. This can be accessed by opening the Control Panel, selecting Add/Remove Programs, and choosing Windows Components from the left-hand column. Scroll down and select Networking Services (Figure 22.1).

Select the Details button to open the Networking Services applet. Network services that are currently installed will be indicated by check marks. Select the option labeled Dynamic Host Configuration Service (DHCP). Then, select the OK button (Figure 22.2).

After you select the desired service and select OK, the Windows Component Wizard will return to the previous screen. Select Next to install the service. The system may ask for the installation CD or a path to the installation files at this point. Once the CD is inserted or the installation path is chosen, Windows 2000 will copy the necessary files for the DHCP service to the system. After this step, the service is installed and ready to be configured.

 Unlike previous versions of Windows NT, the system will not require a reboot after installing the DHCP Server service.

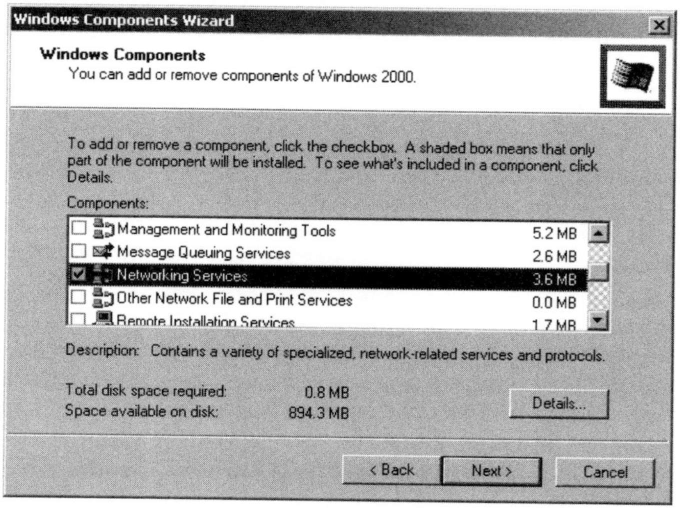

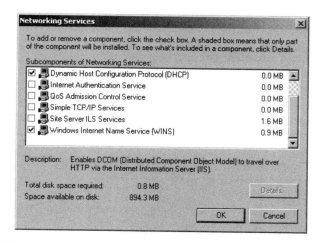

Figure 22–1

Modifying network services with the Windows Components Wizard.

Select the DHCP service from the networking options.

Figure 22–2

Configuring the DHCP Service

The DHCP server service begins running automatically when the server boots and after installation. However, the service cannot communicate with DHCP clients until after at least one scope has been created. A scope is a pool of IP addresses that a DHCP server can lease to DHCP clients. A DHCP server can have multiple scopes defined, but only one scope can be assigned to a subnet.

Installing and Configuring DHCP Scopes

A scope is a pool of addresses that the DHCP server can assign to clients. A DHCP server must have at least one DHCP scope defined before clients can receive IP addresses. There are several elements to consider while defining a scope:

- Every DHCP server must have at least one scope.
- If the range of IP addresses in the scope overlaps static addresses, the static address must be excluded from the scope.
- In many environments, DHCP servers will serve multiple subnets. A DHCP server can have multiple scopes created on it, but only one scope can be assigned per subnet.
- If DCHP servers are integrated into Windows 2000 security, each server must be authorized before the DHCP service will start.
- If there are multiple DHCP servers in the environment, beware of overlaps on scopes between the servers. DCHP servers do not share scope information or lease information, and an overlapping scope may generate IP conflicts and unusual network behavior.

INSTALLING A SCOPE

As with most other services in Windows 2000, DHCP is controlled via the Management Console. To launch the console, select DHCP from the Administrative Tools in the start menu, or through the Control Panel (Figure 22.3).

To install a new scope on the server, first select the DHCP server from the list shown on the left pane, and then select *New Scope* from the action or context menu. This will launch the Create Scope Wizard, which will lead you through the process of creating a scope.

The first step is to define the scope name and, if desired, enter a description for the scope. A descriptive name will help ease administration of the DHCP services (Figure 22.4).

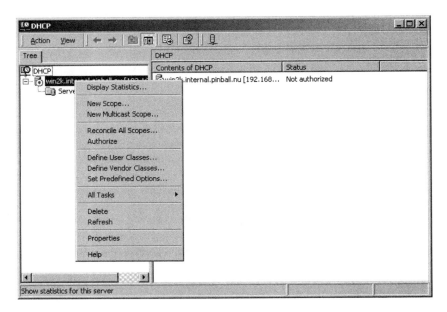

Figure 22–3   *DHCP Management Console.*

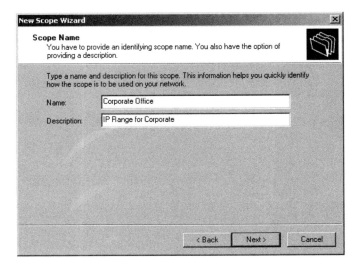

Figure 22–4   *Creating a new scope for the Corporate office.*

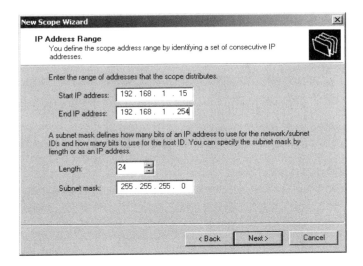

Figure 22–5   *Setting the IP range for a scope.*

Once the scope has been named, then the IP range for the scope is defined. Enter the beginning and ending address of the IP range. In addition, the subnet mask of the range can be modified if necessary (Figure 22.5).

In some situations, it may be necessary to remove a certain IP address or set of IP addresses from the pool of available addresses to avoid conflicting with hosts with static addresses. In the case of the Corporate scope defined in our example, there are two servers with static addresses within the range. In order to avoid network connectivity problems, we use *exclusions* to remove those two addresses from the pool (Figure 22.6).

The next screen will prompt for the duration of the lease. The default length of the lease is eight hours. While this value is appropriate for many environments, it may be adjusted to fit your specific needs. For example, a corporate environment that consists primarily of desktop computers would benefit from a much longer lease time. The increased length of the lease would help reduce the DHCPREQUEST and DHCPACK messages generated every time a lease is renewed. In contrast, a highly mobile routed environment would benefit from shorter lease times, because the DHCP server would release IP addresses back into the pool of available addresses more quickly, and the pool could be made smaller as a result.

There are optional values that can be defined while a scope is created. Each of these values can also be adjusted after the scope is active on the server.

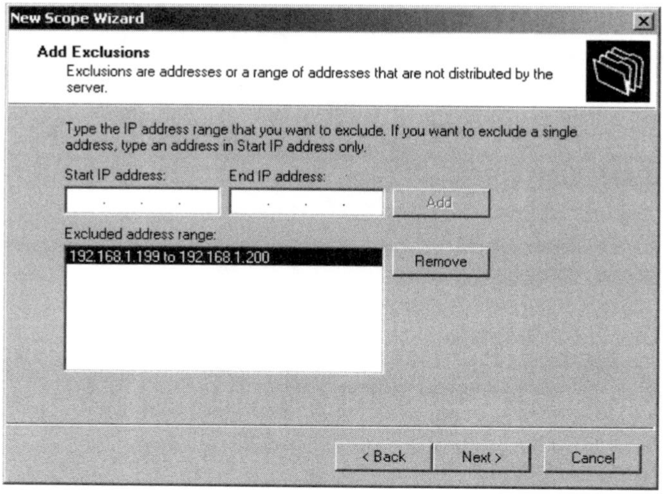

Figure 22–6   *Excluding addresses from the scope.*

SCOPE PARAMETERS

Before a scope can be created, some parameters must be defined. These parameters are required information that will be needed to set up the scope.

Name: The name of the scope, as shown in the Management Console.

Comment: Comment about the scope, if any.

Beginning IP Address: The first IP address that can be assigned to a client.

Ending IP Address: The last IP address that can be assigned to a client.

Subnet Mask: The subnet mask of the IP pool.

Exclusion Addresses: Any IP address or range of IP addresses that should not be assigned to clients.

Lease Length: The duration of the lease assigned to the client.

Configuring a Scope

After a scope is installed on the DHCP server, an array of options can be configured for the scope. Each of these options is passed to the client leasing an address within the scope. However, a locally configured setting will override the value sent by the DHCP server. While literally dozens of options can be configured per scope, this section will focus on the ones most commonly used. To configure these options, open the scope within the Management Console, then select *Scope Options* (Figure 22.7). Choose Configure Options from the context or action menu to modify the options. Some of the most commonly used options are:

- *003 Router*: This option defines the IP address of the router or default gateway for the scope. While listed as an option, this is a required value in a routed LAN or WAN environment. This value can be overridden by a locally configured default gateway.
- *006 DNS Servers*: This option defines the Domain Name System (DNS) servers the clients should use. If the client is configured locally for different name servers, the local configuration will override the DHCP-assigned DNS servers.
- *015 DNS Domain Name*: This option defines the DNS domain for the client.
- *044 WINS/NBNS Server*: This option defines the WINS servers for the client. If the WINS servers are defined locally on the client, that will override the DHCP-supplied addresses.
- *046 WINS/NBT Node Type*: This option defines the node type used for NetBIOS name resolution. In almost every case, the correct node to be used is Hybrid or H-node, which queries the WINS servers first, then attempts to resolve the address via broadcast methods. The node type for H-node is 0x8. Other methods are B-node (broadcast) at 0x1; P-node (peer) at 0x3; and M-node (mixed) at 0x4.
- *047 NetBIOS Scope ID*: If the network is using NetBIOS Scope IDs, clients will be able to communicate only with hosts using the same scope ID. This method is falling out of favor as switched VLANS become more popular.

Managing the DHCP Service

After the DHCP service is installed and scopes are configured, then DHCP becomes a matter of maintenance and management. Like other Windows 2000 services, DHCP is controlled via the Management Console. The DHCP portion is reached via the Administrative Tools options in the Control Panel or in the Start menu.

Reservation Within a Scope

A DHCP reservation is a method of ensuring that the DHCP server will always assign a particular host the same address. While the same functionality could be achieved by assigning a static address to the host, a reservation has two advantages. First, there is no need to track the static address separately or to create an exclusion for the IP address. Second, if TCP/IP configuration changes are made to the scope, those changes are propagated to the host automatically.

To create a reservation, the hardware address of the host's network card must be known. Also known as a MAC address, this is a hexadecimal address

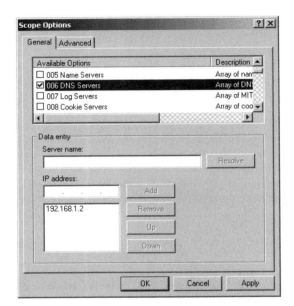

Figure 22–7 *Modifying scope options.*

that will appear similar to 00-50-DA-07-78-50 when using *ipconfig* or *winipcfg* to gather information.

Once this MAC address is known, open the management console and then open the scope in which you wish to make a reservation. Select the *Reservations* object, and then choose *New Reservation* from the context or action menu. The DCHP server will prompt for the IP address, hardware address, reservation name (which is not the computer name), and a description if desired (Figure 22.8).

The Add button will add the reservation to the DHCP scope and will limit the listed IP address to only the computer that matches the MAC address. Likewise, any DHCPREQUEST from that hardware address will receive the only specified address.

To delete a reservation, highlight the reservation and press the Delete key. The system will prompt for confirmation before deleting the entry.

Viewing Current Leases

If necessary, the Management Console can be used to view the current clients of the DHCP server. Selecting *Address Leases* under the desired scope will show all current leases within the right-hand pane of the Management Console (Figure 22.9). The listing can be sorted by IP address, the computer name, or the lease expiration. Additionally, an individual entry can be deleted from the

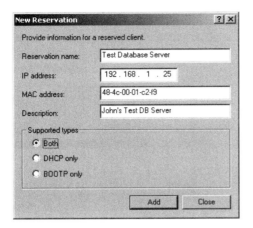

Figure 22–8   *Creating a reservation within a scope.*

listing. However, this merely releases the address back into the pool of available addresses. Because the client computer will still be using that address until the current lease expires, there is a possibility of IP numbering conflicts. The recently released IP address may be assigned to another client, thus causing networking problems for both hosts.

If a reserved address is deleted via this window, the reservation is removed from the DHCP server. If the reservation is still required, it will have to be entered a second time.

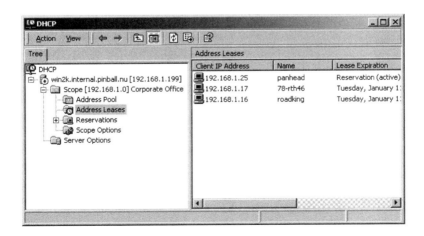

Figure 22–9   *Viewing active leases.*

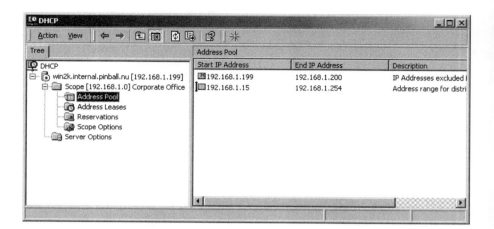

Figure 22–10 *Managing exclusions within a scope.*

Managing Exclusions

Exclusions are addresses within the IP range that the DHCP server cannot assign to a client. Exclusions are generally used to protect a host or range of hosts that have statically assigned IP addresses.

Exclusions are listed within the *Address Pool* folder of the scope. Selecting this folder will show the current address pool and any exclusion in the right-hand pane (Figure 22.10). To create a new exclusion range, select *New Exclusion Range* from the context or action menu. The system will prompt for the beginning and ending address of the exclusion range. If the range is a single address, enter that address in the *Start IP Address* field only.

Exclusion ranges can also be removed from a DCHP scope. Select the desired exclusion range and press the Delete key. The system will prompt for verification before removing the exclusion range.

Disaster Recovery and DHCP

While DHCP removes much of the administrative overhead of managing IP addresses, it does create a major failure point for the network. In the event that the DHCP server is unavailable for an extended time, the clients will begin to release their IP addresses. In most environments, the clients would then be without network connectivity. Fortunately, there are really only two ways for the service to fail: a corrupted database; or unavailability of the server due to hardware failure, network problems, or similar issues.

Backing Up the DHCP Database

The DHCP service automatically backs up the DHCP database every 60 minutes. The backup is stored at%systemroot%\WINNT\system32\dhcp\backup\Jet\new\dhcp.mdb. Adjusting the value of the BackUpInterval that is located in the registry can modify the timing of this backup. The value of this key is set in the number of minutes between backups. The full path to the entry is:

HKEY_LOCAL_MACHINE\CurrentControlSet\Services\DHCPServer\Parameters

Restoring the DHCP Database

If the DHCP database suffers from corruption, the DHCP service will automatically try to restore from the backup database when the service is restarted. In many cases this will be sufficient to resolve the issue.

There are two manual methods to restore the database, should the automated method fail. In both cases the DHCP service has to be stopped before attempting a restore, and restarted after restoration.

The first method is to manually force the service to restore from backup. To do so, stop the DHCP service. Then change the value for RestoreFlag in the registry to 1. Restart the service to force the restore. The registry key is located at:

HKEY_LOCAL_MACHINE\CurrentControlSet\Services\DHCPServer\Parameters

A manual copy of the files in the*%systemroot%\system32\dhcp\backup\jet* directory to*%systemroot%\system32\dhcp* will also replace the DHCP database. This copy must take place while the service is stopped.

Redundant Servers

If the DHCP server suffers from some form of hardware or network failure, or is otherwise unavailable, the clients will be unable to renew their leases. This will eventually lead to the systems dropping off the network as the computers release their IP addresses. Given a long enough lease time, there may be time to repair the server before the leases expire.

One method to overcome the single point of failure that DHCP creates is to split the IP range over two or more servers. This involves installing the DHCP service on multiple servers, then defining scopes such that both machines are serving the same subnet. The key to this method is enduring that the scopes do not overlap. Because DHCP servers do not share scope or lease information, overlapping addresses within the scopes would inevitably result in address conflicts.

It is not necessary to split the scopes evenly. In fact, Microsoft has recommended a 75/25 split on IP addresses. The reasoning is that the server with the

25% scope would not be activated unless the primary DHCP server are disabled. At that time, the backup scope on the 25% server would be enabled, and that server could renew leases for clients.

While the server with the smaller scope was handling renewals, the primary server would be repaired and brought back on line. The DHCP service would then be stopped on the redundant server. Clients that had renewed against the redundant server would receive a DHCPNACK on renewal and get an address in the original scope from the primary DHCP server.

Command-Line Tasks

Windows 2000 offers many more command-line tools than previous versions of Windows NT. One extended feature is the ability to control the WINS server from a command prompt. Combined with the telnet daemon included in Windows 2000, the service can be managed even if no traditional management tools are available.

The DHCP management tool is actually a subset of the this utility. To launch the net shell utility, open a command prompt and enter NETSH. After the net shell is running, typing DHCP will enter the DHCP context. To connect to the local server, type the SERVER command. Typing *SERVER <IP ADDRESS>* can access a remote server. Once the connection is made, several command line options are available to manipulate the service, the tables, and the individuals within these records. A summary of those commands is given in Table 22.2.

Table 22.2	Command Line Options	
Command	**Parameter**	**Function**
List		Lists all the commands available
Dump		Dumps configuration to the output
Help,?		Displays help
Add		Adds a configuration entry to a table
	Class	Adds a class to the server
	Mscope	Adds a multicast scope to the server
	Option	Adds a new option to the server

Table 22.2		Command Line Options (Continued)
	Scope	Adds a scope to the server
Delete		Deletes a configuration entry to a table
	Class	Deletes a specific class from the server
	Mscope	Deletes a multicast scope from the server
	Optiondef	Deletes an option from the server
	Optionvalue	Deletes an option value from the server
	Scope	Deletes a scope from the server
	Superscope	Deletes a superscope from the server
Initiate		Begins a process
	Auth	Initiates retry authorization with the server
	Reconcile	Checks and reconciles the database for all
Set		Sets the value of a configuration entry in a table
	Auditlog	Sets the audit log parameters for the server
	Databasebackuppath	Sets the database backup path for the server
	Databasecleanupinterva	Sets the database clean-up interval
	Databaseloggingflag	Sets/resets the database logging flag
	Databasename	Sets the name of the server database file
	Databasepath	Sets the path of the server database file

Table 22.2		Command Line Options (Continued)
	Databaserestoreflag	Sets/resets the database restore flag
	Databasebackupinterval	Sets the database backup interval of the current server
	Detectconflictretry	Sets the number of conflict-detection attempts by the DHCP server
	Dnsconfig	Sets the Dynamic DNS configuration for the server
	Optionvalue	Sets the global option value for the server
	Server	Sets the current server in the server mode
	Userclass	Sets the global user class name for subsequent operation
	Vendorclass	Sets the global vendor class name for subsequent operation
Show		Displays information about a set or a particular entry in a table
	All	Displays all information for the server
	auditlog	Displays the audit log settings for the server
	bindings	Displays binding information for the server
	class	Displays all available classes for the server
	detectconflictretry	Displays the detect conflict retry settings
	dnsconfig	Displays the dynamic DNS configuration for the server

Table 22.2	Command Line Options (Continued)	
	mibinfo	Displays MIBInfo for the server
	mscope	Displays all multicast scopes for the server
	optiondef	Displays all options for the server
	optionvalue	Displays all option values that are set for the server
	scope	Displays all available scopes under the server
	server	Displays the current server
	dbproperties	Displays server database configuration
	serverstatus	Displays the current status for the server
	userclass	Displays the currently set user class name
	Recbyversion	Displays records owned by a specific server
	vendorclass	Displays the currently set vendor class name
	version	Displays the current version of the server
Scope	scope <scope-ip-address>	To switch to the scope identified by the IP address
Mscope	mscope <mscope-name>	To switch to the mscope identified by the MScope name

After you are finished managing the DHCP server from the command line, you can either exit the net shell completely or exit the DHCP context and return to the shell. To exit the DHCP context and remain within the net shell, enter the command. (two periods). To exit the net shell completely, type *exit*.

Chapter Summary

Dynamic Host Configuration Protocol (DHCP) is Microsoft's implementation of the BOOTP protocol. The DHCP client requests an IP address and other Transmission Control Protocol/Internet Protocol (TCP/IP) configuration information from a DHCP server at boot. The DHCP client uses a four-step process to communicate with the DHCP servers on the network.

DHCP centralizes control of the IP addressing within a network and also allows centralized control of TCP/IP configuration information such as DNS servers, WINS servers, and the default gateway.

The range of IP addresses available to the clients is called a scope. Every DHCP server must have at least one scope defined before the service will function. Certain IP addresses or ranges of addresses within a scope can be excluded from the pool of addresses for the clients. These exclusions enable a DHCP admin to protect systems with static IP addresses. A reservation is almost exactly the opposite. A reservation pulls an IP address out of the pool and associates it with a particular hardware address. Only the host with that machine address can obtain the reserved IP.

The DHCP database is automatically backed up every hour. This timing can be adjusted via editing the registry. A corrupt database should be repaired automatically, but the administrator can force a reload of the database from the backup. As a last resort, the backup files can be copied directly into the DCHP subdirectory to replace the corrupted files.

An important new tool in Windows 2000 is the ability to control DHCP via a command line. Coupled with the telnet server shipping with Windows 2000 server, a DHCP server can be controlled remotely from almost any location and from almost any operating system. The DHCP commands are a subset of the net shell utility.

Windows Internet Naming Service (WINS)

*W*indows 2000 is designed to utilize Domain Name System (DNS) name resolution to locate both Internet resources and resources on the local network. Within a homogeneous Windows 2000 network, DNS servers alone are sufficient to provide name resolution to client machines. However, earlier Microsoft client and server operating systems do not have the capability to use DNS for NetBIOS name resolutions. These operating systems used WINS (Windows Internet Naming Service) to provide name resolution for local network resources. To provide compatibility with pervious operating systems such as Windows NT, Windows 9x, and the Windows 3.x family, Windows 2000 has the capability to function as both a WINS server and a WINS client.

Microsoft refers to earlier Microsoft operating systems as "downlevel" operating systems.

23.1 Uses of WINS within a Windows 2000 Network

23.1.1 Why Use WINS?

WINS provides many benefits within a mixed-level network environment. As mentioned earlier, a pure Windows 2000 environment will not require a WINS server; the 2000 Professional and Server operating systems are designed to use DNS for all name resolution. However, if your network environment includes earlier operating systems such as Windows NT, Windows 9x, Windows 3.x, or DOS, NetBIOS name resolution is required to access network resources. Within this environment, WINS provides many advantages over other methods of Net-BIOS name resolution.

One of the main advantages is the centralized dynamic database of name registrations maintained by the WINS servers. This database maintains a list of current computer name registrations and the IP address associated with that computer name. This database is dynamic, which means that it is updated as new computers come online and as older registrations expire.

The use of a centralized server eliminates the need to distribute LMHOSTS files to each client and also eliminates the headaches involved in maintaining those files on each client. In addition, use of a WINS server helps minimize NetBIOS name resolution broadcasts on the network; the client will broadcast a request only if the name is unavailable within the central database. Downlevel Windows and DOS clients on your network can use WINS to browse for remote Windows domains without requiring a domain controller on each subnet.

Clients that are unable to use NetBIOS name resolution can still use the WINS database to locate remote computers, provided that the DNS servers are integrated with the WINS servers. This option is easily enabled within Windows 2000 Server.

Is WINS Required?

Networks that are running Windows 2000 exclusively do not require Windows Internet Naming Service. Homogenous Windows 2000 networks can and should use DNS for name resolution. However, many network environments are going to include Windows 9x and Windows NT operating systems for the foreseeable future. Some of the following questions may help you decide whether WINS will be required for your environment:

1. Are there any computers running downlevel operating systems on the network? All older Microsoft operating systems require the use of NetBIOS to access network resources. These clients will require some method of resolving NetBIOS names to IP addresses. While LMHOSTS files will provide the functionality, the more efficient approach is a WINS server.

2. Do all applications support the use of DNS name resolution? In many cases, applications may not be able to support accessing remote computers by DNS resolution. In these cases, the WINS servers will be required.

3. Are all the clients on your network configured for an alternate name resolution system, such as DNS? If the Windows Internet Naming Service is removed from the network, client operating systems will need an alternate method to resolve names. This will require either the adoption of DNS within your network, broadcast resolution, or widespread use of

LMHOSTS and HOSTS files. Practically speaking, the removal of WINS can be accomplished only after a DNS system is implemented.

4. Is the network environment subnetted, or is it a flat network? As discussed earlier, NetBIOS clients can use a broadcast to locate network resources if there is no response from a WINS server. However, this broadcast cannot cross the routed networks that are common in the larger corporate environments. If the network is relatively small and comprises a single network segment, the use of broadcast name resolution may be an effective solution.

New WINS Features in Windows 2000

The Windows 2000 WINS server has been significantly enhanced over previous versions. While its essential functionality has not changed, there have been many improvements in manageability, client interaction, and search capabilities. Some of the newer features are detailed within this section.

DATABASE MANAGEMENT

Many of the enhancements included in the WINS service involve managing the database. Previous versions of Windows NT allowed for the manipulation of the entries within the database, but suffered from some deficiencies. Some of the new features include the ability to remove dynamic entries within the database; the tombstoning of records so that they are not replicated back to the WINS server; consistency checking among multiple WINS databases; export functionality, and more.

One enhancement is the ability to delete a dynamic entry. Previously, a dynamic entry would remain in the database until it expired. Static entries could be manually deleted, but dynamic entries could be deleted only via command-line resources kit utilities. Windows 2000 now allows both static and dynamic entries to be manually deleted from the Management Console. In addition, multiple entries can be selected and deleted at the same, and entries that contain nonalphanumeric characters can be manually deleted.

Manual tombstoning is perhaps one of the most useful enhancements within Windows 2000. Previously, a deleted record could be, and frequently was, replicated back to the original WINS server by one of its partners. Manually tombstoning an entry will replicate that deletion to the replication partners, thus removing the entry from all WINS servers.

One problem with WINS servers is maintaining consistency between replication partners. While earlier versions of the WINS server had database tools to remove expired or outdated entries, they lacked the ability to verify database consistency between WINS servers. This deficiency is corrected with Windows 2000. Record consistency and version numbers can now be checked from the Management Console.

New filters are now in place to sort the record entries within the WINS database. Previous versions of the WINS service allowed sorting by name and IP address, and allowed filtering by owner, but the updated version allows much more specific searches, including searching by name or part of a name. In addition, the entire WINS database can now be exported to comma-delimited text file.

SERVER MANAGEMENT

Just as the WINS record management has been enhanced, so has the management capability of the WINS servers themselves. Many advanced functions are now available through the Management Console, rather than registry edits. Additionally, Windows 2000 offers higher security and increased replication speed. New command-line capabilities can be teamed with the included telnet server to allow management of WINS servers from any telnet client.

The WINS service uses the shared Microsoft Management Console to provide for a more administrator-friendly environment and to integrate with other Windows 2000 management tools. One advantage that the Management Console provides is the ability to block certain WINS replication partners or owners and to allow overriding of static mappings. Both features required registry changes in previous versions of the WINS service.

One enhancement is the ability to create persistent connections between WINS replication partners. This persistent connection can increase the speed of replication between the servers, eliminating the overhead associated with opening, controlling, and closing replication sessions.

One security enhancement is the existence of a new user group, the WINS Users group. This local group has read-only access to the WINS Console. This group is automatically installed when the WINS service is installed on a server. Users in this group can view WINS-related information but cannot modify, delete, or add information to the database. WINS read-only access can be controlled on a per-server basis.

One of the most interesting enhancements is the inclusion of command-line tools that can control all the functions of a WINS server. This additional functionality will be discussed in some depth later in this chapter.

CLIENT ENHANCEMENTS

While most of the enhancements for WINS are server based, several enhancements within the Windows 2000 Professional client increase the functionality and fault tolerance of WINS. Both Windows 2000 and Windows 98 have the ability to include more than two WINS servers within their search lists. While the additional servers will not be used unless both the primary and secondary fail to respond, up to 12 servers can be included.

Windows 2000 and Windows NT clients running SP4 or later now can release and refresh their WINS entries without having to reboot the client computer. The *nbtstat-RR* command forces a release of the name entry within the primary WINS server, and then reregisters the local NetBIOS name with the WINS server.

WINS Name Resolution Process

WINS Registration

WINS name resolution begins with a client computer registering itself with the WINS server. The server registers the NetBIOS name, IP address, and physical address (MAC address) of the client computer. The server responds with an acknowledgment of the registration and records the entries within the WINS database. The acknowledgment also includes the length of time that the name will remain registered, known as the Time To Live or TTL. WINS entries are dynamic, meaning that they will expire after a certain amount of time and be removed from the database. The reason for this behavior is to accommodate the changing IP addresses common in a DHCP-enabled environment. Within such an environment, a computer may change addresses but still need to be accessed by name.

If a client PC tries to register a name that already exists within the database, the WINS server will try to resolve the conflict. It does so by querying the computer that currently has the registration and checking to see if it responds. If the currently registered machine does not respond, then the WINS server removes the older registration and allows the new machine to register that name and its IP address. The request time varies somewhat: As a general rule, the WINS server will send a request three times at 500-millisecond intervals. However, if the registered name represents a multihomed computer (one with multiple network adapters with TCP/IP bound to each adapter), the WINS server will query each of the IP addresses until it receives a response or until it has exhausted the addresses.

Name Resolution

When a downlevel operating system requests a resource by computer name, it is requesting a NetBIOS connection. NetBIOS name resolution can be performed in many different ways. The downlevel client performs the following steps to resolve a NetBIOS name:

1. The client first checks its own NetBIOS name, to verify whether the requested resource is a local resource on the client.
2. The client then checks its cache to see if the NetBIOS name is stored there. If a client has resolved that name within the last 10 minutes, the name and IP address should be located within the cache. The cache can be viewed by using the *nbtstat -c* command.

3. If the name is not located within the cache, the request is forwarded to its primary WINS server. If the name is located within the WINS database, the IP address is returned to the client. If the WINS server does not have an entry for the requested name, the client will contact other WINS servers in the order in which they are listed on the client.

4. In the event that no WINS server can resolve the name, the client then tries to resolve the name via a NetBIOS broadcast to the local subnet.

5. If the client does not receive a response from the broadcast, it will then search the LMHOSTS and HOSTS files for the requested name and its related IP address. The Use LMHOSTS Lookup option must be enabled for this step.

6. As a last resort, the client will attempt to use a DNS server for name resolution, if one is configured on the client.

Windows 2000 client or server computers do not resolve NetBIOS names in the same fashion as earlier operating systems. If a Windows 2000 machine is configured to use a WINS server, it will use hybrid node (h-node) name resolution by default. However, the name resolution sequence begins with a DNS method, as detailed below:

1. The client first checks its own NetBIOS name to verify whether the requested resource is a local resource on the client.

2. If the resource name exceeds 15 characters or includes periods, the client will begin by querying its DNS servers for the IP address.

3. The client then checks its cache to see if the NetBIOS name is stored there. If a client has resolved that name within the last 10 minutes, the name and IP address should be located within the cache. The cache can be viewed by using the *nbtstat -c* command.

4. If the name is not located within the cache, the request is forwarded to its primary WINS server. If the name is located within the WINS database, the IP address is returned to the client. If the WINS server does not have an entry for the requested name, the client will contact other WINS servers in the order in which they are listed on the client.

5. In the event that no WINS server can resolve the name, the client then tries to resolve it via a NetBIOS broadcast to the local subnet.

6. If the client does not receive a response from the broadcast, it will then search the LMHOSTS and HOSTS files for the requested name and its related IP address. The Use LMHOSTS Lookup option must be enabled for this step.

7. The client will then contact the DNS servers that are listed within the client TCP/IP properties.

Installing the WINS Service

To install the WINS service on a Windows 2000 server, begin by opening the Windows Component Wizard. This can be accessed by opening the Control Panel, selecting Add/Remove Programs, and choosing Windows Components from the

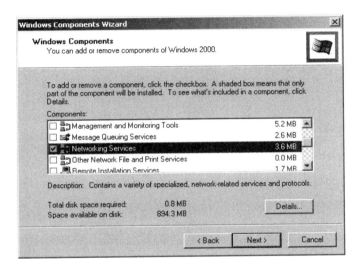

Figure 23-1

Modifying network services with the Windows Components Wizard.

left-hand column. Scroll down and select Networking Services (Figure 23.1).

Select the Details button to open the Networking Services applet. Network services that are currently installed will be indicated by check marks (Figure 23.2). Select the option labeled Windows Internet Naming Service (WINS). Then, select the OK button.

After selecting the desired service and selecting OK, the Windows Component Wizard will return to the previous screen. Select Next to install the service. The system may ask for the installation CD or a path to the installation files at this point. Once the CD is inserted or the installation path is chosen, Windows 2000 will copy the necessary files for the WINS service to the system. After this step, the service is installed and ready to be configured.

Unlike previous versions of Windows NT, the system will not require a reboot.

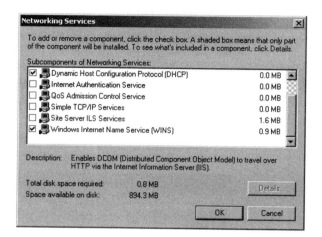

Select the WINS service from the networking options.

Managing the WINS Service

The WINS service is managed via the Windows Internet Naming Service Management Console Figure 23.3).The snap-in provides a centralized management point for one or more WINS servers. The WINS Management Console is installed during the installation of the WINS service. It is opened by choosing the WINS option from the Administrative Tools in the Programs on the Start Menu. Additionally, the WINS Console can be launched through the Control Panel within the Administrative Tools options.

Overview of the Management Console

Once the Management Console is started, the left pane will show the list of known WINS servers and the status of those servers. Functioning servers are indicated by a green arrow pointing upward. Servers that are down or stopped are marked with an X in a red circle. Inaccessible servers are also marked with an X.

The console will open with the current server selected and opened. The right-hand panel will list folders for active registrations and replication partners for the current server. Two menu items are listed on the tool bar: Action and View. The features in these menus will change depending upon the selection within the console. In general, the Action and View menus will include the same options as the right-click menu on each selected item. For our purposes, we will use the context menu for most of this chapter.

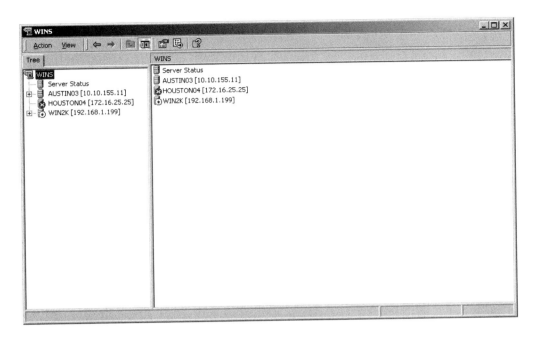

Figure 23–3   *WINS Management Console.*

The left-hand pane includes a Server Status icon, which is used for an overview of the WINS environment and then lists any individual WINS servers. The currently selected WINS server will be expanded and will include the folder structures for Active Registrations and Replication Partners. Please note that these are the same folders listed in the right-hand pane.

Managing Servers

The WINS Management Console allows for the control of all the WINS servers within an enterprise from a single point. The Management Console shows all known WINS servers and allows for the addition or deletion of WINS servers from the Console.

Adding a WINS Server to the Management Console

To add a WINS server to the list of servers shown within the Management Console, right-click on the Server Status icon within the left pane. One of the options that will appear is *Add Server* (Figure 23.4). After this option is selected, the system will prompt for the IP address of the remote WINS server (Figure 23.5). If the system can be contacted, it will appear within the left pane

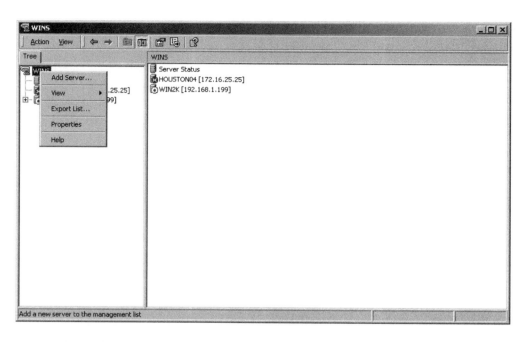

Figure 23–4 *Managing WINS Servers.*

of the Management Console. If the remote system is unreachable, unavailable, or otherwise unresponsive, the Management Console will prompt for the name of the remote WINS server. It will then be added to the Management Console but will be marked as down until communication is established.

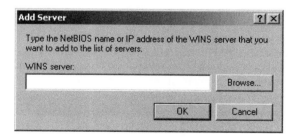

Figure 23–5 *Adding a WINS Server.*

Removing a WINS Server from the Management Console

Removing a WINS server from the list of servers shown within the Management Console is performed on a per-server basis. To remove a server, select it from the list in the left-hand pane of the Management Console. After right-clicking to bring up the context menu, select *Delete*. This will remove the server from the Management Console.

Please note that this does not remove the WINS service or the entries owned by the server. This action merely removes the WINS server from the list of servers controlled via that Management Console. In order to remove all entries related to a WINS server, the server must be decommissioned, as discussed below.

Decommissioning a WINS Server

In order to turn off the WINS services on a WINS server, it is vital that any related entries be purged from the WINS databases that have been replicated to other servers. In addition, any clients that are configured with the decommissioned server as either a primary or secondary WINS resource must be redirected to another WINS server.

To begin the process, open the appropriate server within the left-hand pane of the Management Console and right-click on the Active Registrations folder. From the context menu, select Delete Owner. The records for the selected WINS server will load, and then the system will prompt whether to tombstone the records on the replication partners. Select the *Replicate deletion to other WINS servers* option and select OK.

The Management Console will prompt to confirm the tombstoning of the records. Select YES to continue the action.

In order to complete the decommissioning of the server, right-click the Replication Partners folder associated with the server within the left-hand pane. From the context menu, select *Replicate Now*. This will force a replication of the deleted records to the replication partners. Once these records have replicated, then the server is ready to be decommissioned, and the WINS services can be stopped and uninstalled from the server.

Exporting WINS Server Information

WINS server lists can be exported to a comma-delimited text file for use in reporting tools, statistics, record keeping, and similar functions. To export a list of the WINS servers, right-click on the Server Status and choose *Export*. The system will prompt you for the destination directory.

Managing a Particular Server

The WINS Management Console allows for administration and manipulation of individual WINS servers. All of the tools available to the administrator are accessible via the context (right-click) menu, as well as the Action menu located near

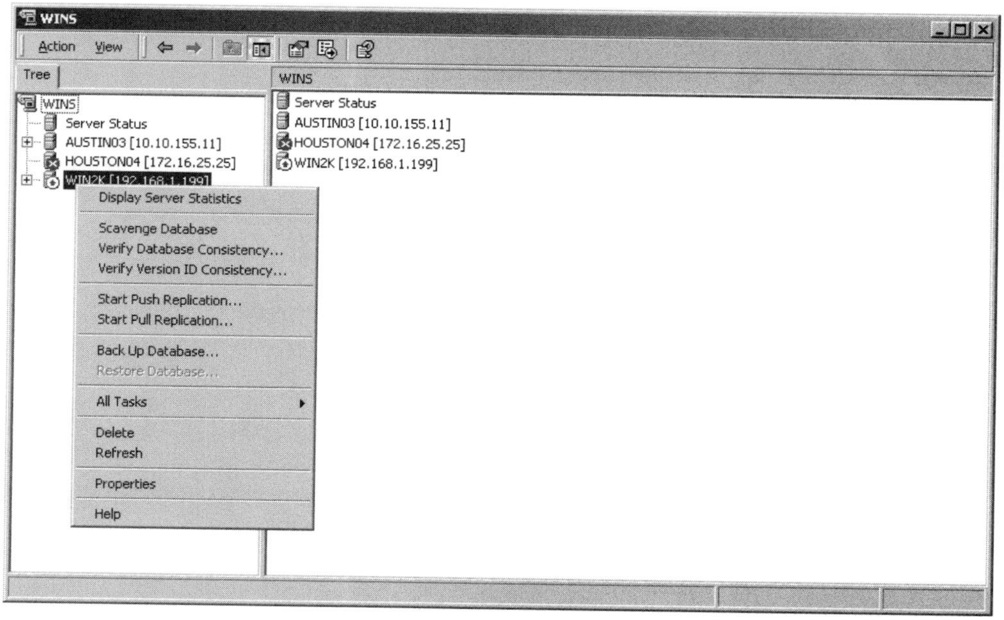

Figure 23–6 *Managing a single WINS server.*

the top of the MMC. As before, we will be using the context menu as our default interface in this section.

The WINS Management Console allows for database manipulation, database backup and restoration, forced replication, adjustments to the properties of a particular server, and more (Figure 23.6). Each element will be discussed shortly.

Server Statistics

The WINS server allows an administrator to view very detailed statistics concerning the usage and functions of a particular WINS server. These statistics are viewed by selecting *Display Server Statistics* from the context or action menus. Selecting this option will bring up a dialog box with the server statistics within it (Figure 23.7).

Some of the statistics available for the WINS server include the server start time; last replication time; the number of queries, both resolved and unresolved; registrations and conflicts; and last database scavenging time.

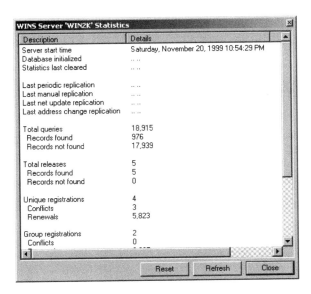

Figure 23–7   *Statistics for a WINS server.*

Database Management

The WINS database contains the entries for each registered computer on the network. This database is the core of the WINS service; if it is damaged, inaccurate, or otherwise inconsistent, name resolution on the network may not function correctly. Windows 2000 contains several integrated tools to maintain the WINS database.

SCAVENGING DATABASES

Every database needs periodic maintenance, and the WINS database is no exception. Removing outdated and expired entries from a WINS database is performed via a process called scavenging. Selecting *Scavenge Database* from the action or context menu can force this process manually for the desired server. However, in most environments, an automated scavenging is preferred. WINS will automatically scavenge the database at the intervals specified in the server properties.

Scavenging a database only removes outdated information that has been replicated from other WINS servers. Local entries that are released are eliminated automatically from a WINS server via the normal extinction process. If a WINS server is using default settings, this process takes 36 hours. The times involved in the extinction process can be modified via the properties sheet of the WINS server (Figure 23.8).

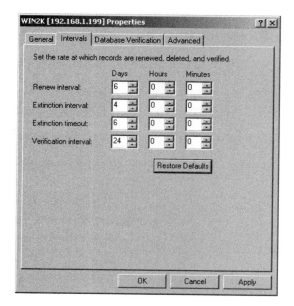

Figure 23-8   *Adjusting extinction intervals.*

Scavenging also compacts the WINS database, which minimizes the storage needs of the service and improves performance. If the WINS service is running during automated scavenging or manually initiated scavenging of the database, then the WINS database is dynamically compacted. While this is fairly efficient, better compaction can be achieved via *offline compaction*.

Weekly or monthly, the WINS service should be stopped on the server and a manual scavenging initiated. This will compact the WINS database, which is located at *%systemroot%\system32\wins\wins.mdb*. Monitoring the size of this file both before and after offline compaction should allow an administrator to determine the optimal offline scheduling for his or her environment.

VERIFYING DATABASE INTEGRITY AND VERSION NUMBER

WINS database consistency checking is performed by running an integrated utility. The utility checks the current local WINS database against other WINS servers. However, consistency checking will place a load on the network and should not be routinely performed during normal business hours.

To initiate a database consistency check, select Verify Database Consistency from the action or context menu. The system will prompt you to verify this action. Once the choice is verified, the WINS server will get the Owner-to-Highest-Version-ID mappings from other WINS servers and verify that the local server has the highest-version ID for any owned records.

Integrity checking can and should be scheduled for a low-usage time on the network. To schedule integrity, select the *Database Verification* tab on the property sheet for the WINS server. Verification options include setting the start time of verification, frequency between verifications, and whether to verify against the original owners of a record or a randomly selected server (Figure 23.9).

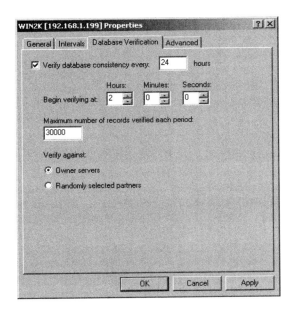

Figure 23–9 *Scheduling automated database verifications.*

BACKING UP AND RESTORING THE DATABASE

The WINS database is stored in *%systemroot%\system32\wins\wins.mdb* by default, although that path can be modified in the *Advanced* tab of the server property sheet. This database should be backed up on a regular basis to provide protection against corruption or other problems with the database. The WINS service provides for a method to back up the database while the server is online.

A manual backup can be forced by selecting *Backup Database* from the context or action menu. When this option is selected, the system will prompt for the location at which to store the backup database. After the location is selected, the backup file is created. The file path is *<selected location>\wins_bak\new\wins.mdb*.

As with many other administrative functions, WINS database backups can and should be automated. To do so, open the property sheet for the WINS server. Define the default backup path for the WINS database and, if desired, set the server to automatically back up the database when the service is stopped

(Figure 23.10). Once this default path is set, the database will be automatically backed up every three hours. As with a manual backup, the file path is *<selected location>\wins_bak\new\wins.mdb*.

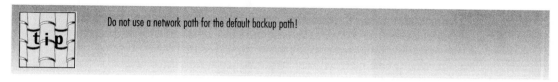

Do not use a network path for the default backup path!

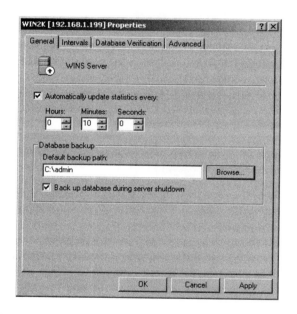

Figure 23–10   *Setting the default WINS backup path.*

In the event that a WINS database has to be restored from a backup, the WINS service must first be stopped. While the service can be stopped via the Services applet in the control panel or in the Administrative Tools program group, the preferred method is via the WINS Management Console. Select *All Tasks* from the context or action menu and then select *Stop*.

After the service is stopped, selecting Restore Database from the action or context menu can restore the database. The system will prompt for the location of the backup; this must be the same location as specified in the *General* tab of the server properties. After the database is restored, restart the service.

If the WINS database is corrupt, verify that the *Back up database during server shutdown* option is not selected in the General tab of the server properties. If this automatic backup is enabled, the corrupted database may overwrite the backup copy.

Managing Records

Ultimately, WINS management comes down to managing the individual entries within the database. Each of these entries is considered a record and can include a reference to a computer name, a domain name, the current logged-in user, a group, or a multihomed computer. Each entry must be unique within a particular WINS database.

Types of Records

Five types of records are supported by a WINS server. Each has a particular role within the WINS service. A short description of each and its uses follows.

Unique: A unique entry maps to a particular IP address. Each entry must have a unique name

Group: This is a name that references a group. Individual computers can be added to a group via the WINS Management Console. WINS does not place a limit on the number of entries within a group.

Domain Name: This maps a domain name to an IP address of a domain controller, with an 0x1C as the 16th byte. Only 25 computers can be part of a domain-name group. After that limit is reached, WINS will overwrite any duplicate entries or the oldest unique registration.

Internet Group: This is a user-defined grouping that groups resources for browsing purposes. An Internet group can contain up to 25 entries. It is important to note that a static entry cannot be replaced by a dynamic entry.

Multihomed: A computer that has multiple NICs will require a Registration as a multihomed entry to avoid conflicts. A multihomed computer can have up to 25 addresses registered to it. After that limit is reached, WINS will overwrite any duplicate entries or the oldest registration.

Viewing Records

Just as with most other WINS-related tasks, records are viewed via the WINS Management Console. In most cases, the administrator is going to be interested in records that are owned by the selected server, but the Management Console will also allow the entire database to be viewed, if necessary. To view records, first expand the WINS server within the Management Console, then select the Active Registrations folder to access the server database.

SHOWING ALL RECORDS

In order to show all records in the database, first select Active Registrations from the console tree. Then select *Find By Owner* from the action or context menu. When prompted to select servers to display records for, select *All Owners*. The entire WINS database will then appear in the details pane on the right side of the Management Console.

This task can be resource intensive and can impact server performance.

SHOWING LOCAL RECORDS

In order to show only local records in the database, first select Active Registrations from the console tree. Then select *Find By Owner* from the action or context menu. When prompted to select servers to display records for, select *This Owner*. The WINS database will then be filtered so that only the locally owned records will appear in the details pane on the right side of the Management Console.

This task can be resource intensive and can impact server performance.

FINDING A PARTICULAR RECORD

To view the details on a particular record, first select Active Registrations from the console tree. Then select *Find By Name* from the action or context menu. When prompted, enter the leading characters for the name(s) you wish to view (Figure 23.12). The WINS database will then be filtered so that only records that match that character sequence will appear in the details pane on the right side of the Management Console. To view the details of that entry, either select properties from the action or context menu or double-click on the record

FINDING A PARTICULAR RECORD TYPE

To filter for a particular record type, first select Active Registrations from the console tree. Then select *Find By Owner* from the action or context menu. Next, switch to the *Record Type* tab and unselect the record types that you do not wish to view (Figure 23.13). The WINS database will then be filtered so that only records that match that record type will appear in the details pane on the

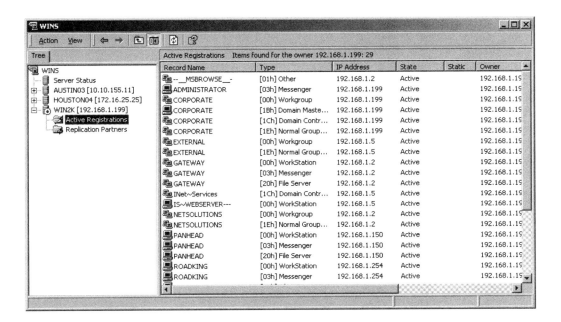

Viewing records by owner.

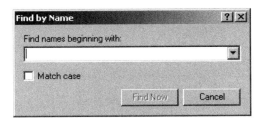

Finding records by name.

right side of the Management Console. To clear the filter, choose the *Record Type* tab and either unselect each type individually or click the *Clear All* option.

Manipulating Records

ADDING A STATIC MAPPING ENTRY

Most Microsoft operating systems include the capability to dynamically register with a WINS server, so that as a new computer joins the network, an entry is

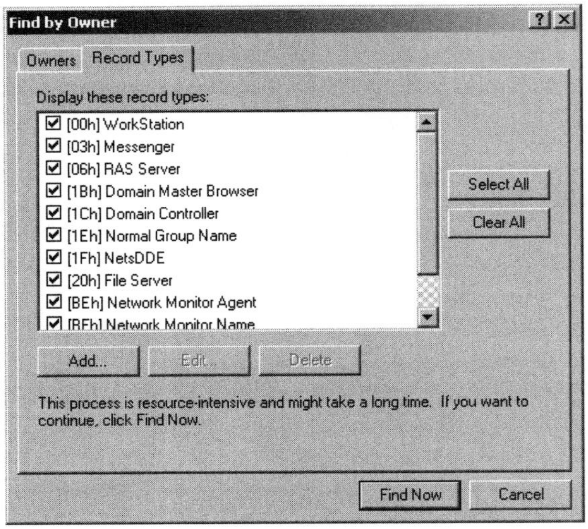

Figure 23–13   *Filtering records by type.*

automatically added to the WINS server. For these clients, little to no manual intervention is required. However, some operating systems are not designed in this manner. Because they do not automatically register with a WINS server, WINS clients will not be able to resolve the computer's name. This can be remedied by manually entering the necessary information into the WINS server. These manual entries are called static mappings.

To add a static entry within a WINS server, first select Active Registrations from the console tree. Select *New Static Mapping* from the action or context menu, and a New Static Mapping dialog box will appear (Figure 23.14). A static entry requires the following information:

Computer Name: This is the NetBIOS name of the computer

NetBios Scope: This is an optional field for the NetBIOS scope identifier. In many cases, it will be left blank.

Type: Select the record type associated with this computer.

IP Address: This is the IP address for the entry.

After entering the required information, select Apply to add the entry to the database. When all static entries have been added, select Cancel to close the dialog box. If there is an entry error in a static mapping, delete the mapping and create a new mapping. The only elements that can be modified after the entry is added are the IP address and, for certain group types, the order of addresses.

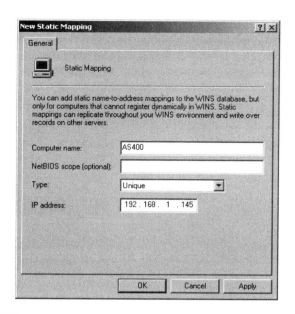

Figure 23-14   *Adding a static mapping to WINS.*

IMPORTING LMHOSTS ENTRIES

One useful feature of WINS in Windows 2000 is the ability to import the contents of an LMHOSTS file as static entries in the WINS database. This is very useful if a large number of hosts need to be added, or to support legacy network elements. In order to import the LMHOSTS file, first select **Active Registrations** from the console tree. Then select *Import LMHOSTS File* from the action or context menu.

Browse to the LMHOST file that you wish to import and select **Open**. By default, the LMHOSTS file is located at *%Systemroot%/winnt/system32/drivers/etc/LMHOSTS*. Once the file is selected, WINS will begin importing the entries into the WINS database. When all records are imported, a dialog box will inform you that the operation is complete.

DELETING RECORDS

From time to time, the need to delete a record will arise. In previous versions of Windows NT, only static entries could be manually deleted. This sometimes led to issues that prevented computers from reregistering themselves with the WINS server. Windows 2000 server offers several improvements that help resolve these issues. Windows 2000 WINS now offers support for the following:

Simple deletion: This allows for deleting WINS database records that are stored on a single server database. This is best used for static entries

Tombstoned deletion: This allows for deleting both the local WINS database records and those replicated to databases on other WINS servers. This is vital in a complex WINS environment.

Multiple-group selection: This allows for selection of multiple-displayed database records when performing either a simple or a tombstoned deletion. This improvement allows for more efficient record management.

To perform a simple deletion, first open the Active Registrations and filter to find the record or records that you wish to delete. After selecting the desired record(s), open the context or action menu. Selecting *Delete* from the menu will open a dialog box. Choose *Delete the record from only this server,* and the record or records will be deleted. Both static and dynamic entries can be deleted in this manner.

Simple deletion is effective with simple WINS environments and static entries, but in more complex environments there is the possibility that the deleted record will be replicated back to the WINS server from one of its partners. In order to eliminate this problem, the WINS server has the ability to delete a record and tombstone it in the same operation. Tombstoning is the process of marking a record for deletion and replicating that deletion to other WINS servers. As mentioned earlier, a record that has been tombstoned by other servers will be removed from the local WINS database during scavenging.

To perform a tombstoned deletion, first open the Active Registrations and filter to find the record or records that you wish to delete. After selecting the desired record(s), open the context or action menu. Selecting *Delete* from the menu will open a dialog box. Choose *Replicate deletion of the record to other servers (tombstone),* and the record or records will be deleted. In addition, notice of the deleted record will be sent to the server's replication partners, and the records will be marked as tombstoned on those servers. The records will be deleted from the remote systems after they expire.

Command-Line Tasks

Windows 2000 offers many more command-line tools than previous versions of Windows NT. One extended feature is the ability to control the WINS server from a command prompt. Combined with the telnet daemon included in Windows 2000, the service can be managed even if no traditional management tools are available.

The WINS management tool is actually a subset of the net shell utility. To launch the utility, open a command prompt and enter *NETSH*. After the net shell is running, typing *WINS* will enter the *WINS* context. To connect to the local server, type the *SERVER* command. Typing *SERVER <IP ADDRESS>* can access a remote server. Once the connection is made, the following line will be displayed on the console:

```
***You have Read and Write access to the server [SERVERNAME]***
```

After this prompt, several command-line options are available to manipulate the service, the tables, and the individuals within these records, as summarized in Table 23.1.

Table 23.1		Command-Line Options
Command	**Parameter**	**Function**
List		Lists all the commands available.
Dump		Dumps configuration to the output.
Help?		Displays help.
Add		Adds a configuration entry to a table.
	Name	Adds a name record to the server.
	Partner	Adds a replication partner to the server.
	PNGServer	Adds a list of Persona Non Grata Servers for the current server.
Check		Checks the integrity of a table.
	Database	Checks the consistency of the database.
	Name	Checks a list of name records against a set of WINS servers.
	Version	Checks the consistency of the version number.
Delete		Deletes a configuration entry from a table.
	Name	Deletes a registered name from the server database.
	Partner	Deletes a replication partner from the list of replication partners.
	Records	Deletes or tombstones all or a set of records from the server.
	Owners	Deletes a list of owners and their records.
	PNGServer	Deletes all or selected Persona Non Grata Servers from the list
Init		Initiates an operation for the table.
	Backup	Initiates backup of WINS database.

Table 23.1	Command-Line Options (Continued)	
	Import	Initiates import from an LMHOSTS file.
	Pull	Initiates and sends a pull trigger to another WINS server.
	PullRange	Initiates and pulls a range of records from another WINS server.
	Init Push	Initiates and sends a push trigger to another WINS server.
	Replicate	Initiates replication of database with replication partners.
	Restore	Initiates restoring of database from a file.
	Scavenge	Initiates scavenging of WINS database for the server.
	Search	Initiates search on the WINS server database for the specified record.
Reset		Resets a configuration entry in a table.
	Statistics	Resets the server statistics.
Set		Sets the value of a configuration entry in a table.
	AutoPartner-Config	Sets the automatic replication partner configuration info for the server.
	BackupPath	Sets the backup parameters for the server.
	Burstparam	Sets the burst-handling parameters for the server.
	DefaultParam	Sets the default values for the WINS server configuration parameters.
	Logparam	Sets the database and event-logging options.
	MigrateFlag	Sets the migration flag for the server.
	NameRecord	Sets Intervals and Timeout values for the server.
	PeriodicDB-Checking	Sets periodic database checking parameters for the server.
	Pullpartner-config	Sets the configuration parameters for the specified pull partner.

Table 23.1	Command-Line Options (Continued)	
	Pushpartner-config	Sets the configuration parameter for the specified push partner.
	PullParam	Sets the default pull-partner parameters for the server.
	PushParam	Sets the default push-partner parameters for the server.
	ReplicateFlag	Sets the replication flag for the server.
	Startversion	Sets the start version ID for the database.
Show		Displays information about a set or a particular entry in a table.
	Browser	Displays all active-domain master browser [1Bh] records.
	Database	Displays the database and records for all or a list of specified owner servers.
	Info	Displays server configuration information.
	Name	Displays the detail information for a particular record in the server.
	Partner	Displays all or pull or push partners for the server.
	Partnerproperties	Displays default partner configuration.
	Pullpartner-config	Displays configuration information for a pull partner.
	Pushpartner-config	Displays configuration information for a push partner.
	Reccount	Displays number of records owned by a specific owner server.
	Recbyversion	Displays records owned by a specific server.
	Server	Displays the currently selected server.
	Statistics	Displays the statistics for the WINS server.
	Version	Displays the current maximum version counter value for the WINS server.
	Versionmap	Displays the owner ID to Maximum Version Number mappings

After you are finished managing the WINS server from the command line, you can either exit the net shell completely or exit the WINS context and return to the shell. To exit the WINS context and remain within the net shell, enter the command. .(two periods). To exit the net shell completely, type *exit*.

Chapter Summary

WINS (Windows Internet Naming Service) is a method to map NetBIOS names to IP addresses. This mapping enables WINS clients to resolve NetBIOS names to a particular computer, and thus to connect to network resources. NetBIOS communication formed the core of earlier Windows networking, and thus Windows 3.x, 9x, and NT clients require a WINS server on a routed network. Windows 2000 clients are designed to use DNS (Domain Naming System) resolution and thus do not require WINS. In most business environments, legacy client operating systems will require a WINS server.

The WINS service maintains a database of computer names and IP addresses. WINS clients first check their local cache and then query the WINS server for the IP address of remote computers. WINS clients register themselves with the WINS server, and these registrations are dynamically updated when the IP address of the client computer changes, the client is removed from the network, or additional clients join the network.

The WINS database consists of various types of entries. These entries represent either single hosts (Unique), groups of computers (Domain Name, Group, Internet Group), or computers with multiple addresses (Multihomed). These entries represent every WINS-aware host that has registered with the server. If necessary, non-WINS-aware hosts can be represented in the database via a static mapping.

WINS is managed via the WINS Management Console. This console allows for the control of individual WINS servers, creation of replication relationships, viewing and manipulation of individual records, and stopping/starting the service itself. The Management Console is reached via the Administrative Tools applet in the control panel, or via the Administrative Tools program group in the Start menu.

An important new tool in Windows 2000 is the ability to control WINS via a command line. Coupled with the telnet server shipping with Windows 2000 Server, a WINS server can be controlled remotely from almost any location and from almost any operating system. The WINS commands are a subset of the net shell utility.

Domain Name
Server Service

*T*he Domain Name System, commonly referred to as DNS, is a distributed namespace used on TCP/IP networks and is typically associated with the Internet. DNS is a name resolution system often bypassed on networks that only used Windows- based operating systems in favor of Microsoft's proprietary WINS technology. However, with the advent of Windows 2000, DNS becomes a required element of an Active Directory environment. With that in mind, we will discuss the following topics in this chapter:

- Understanding DNS
- The Name Resolution Process
- Installing DNS on a Windows 2000 Server
- Administering the DNS Service
- Configuring DNS on a Client
- Troubleshooting the DNS Service

We will learn a lot of theory throughout the first half of the chapter, and then get to apply that theory in hands-on exercises during the last half.

24.1 Understanding DNS

Like WINS from the preceding chapter, DNS is a name resolution system that translates friendly names to nonfriendly IP addresses. With WINS, the friendly names are NetBIOS names. With DNS, they are DNS names such as *www.InsideIS.com*, *www.inside-corner.com*, *ftp.microsoft.com*, or *my.yahoo.com*. DNS is the choice for pure TCP/IP networks, whereas WINS in Windows 2000 exists primarily for backwards ompatibility with legacy Windows NT networks.

Unlike WINS, which is a proprietary Microsoft technology designed for use on Microsoft networks, DNS is an open standard that has been through the Internet Draft process and accepted by the IETF (Internet Engineering Task Force) as the standard method of resolving names to IP addresses on the Internet. DNS is defined primarily in RFCs (Requests for Comment) 1034 "Domain names—concepts and facilities," and 1035 "Domain names—implementation and specification," though there are additional RFCs related to DNS that propose additional functionality or advice on DNS use and troubleshooting. There is also a nice RFC archive and search engine at *http://sunsite.br/rfc/*.

DNS was originally accepted as a standard in 1987 to deal with the shortcomings of the old name resolution process on the Internet. Before the explosive growth of the Internet, records of all name-to-IP address mappings were kept in a single text file called *HOSTS*. Administrators familiar with TCP/IP probably are aware of *HOSTS* files and their use for static mappings on TCP/IP networks that do not use DNS. The *HOSTS* file in Windows 2000 is a text file located in the *systemroot\system32\drivers\etc.* directory. You can open and edit it with any text editor, such as Notepad, though the file should be saved as *HOSTS* with no extension. The major drawback to using a *HOSTS* file was that, the more the number of systems on the Internet grew, the larger the *HOSTS* file became, and the more time-consuming it became to keep it updated across all of the networks connected to the Internet through manual updates. The master *HOSTS* file was maintained by Stanford Research Institute's Network Information Center, from where systems administrators would FTP the latest copy of the file to update their name servers.

The advantages to using DNS are numerous. Some of them are:

• DNS is the standard for Internet name resolution. When private companies employ DNS, they are able to seamlessly integrate internal and external resources from the end-user perspective.

• Users are able to connect to internal and external network resources using the same naming conventions, reducing confusion and simplifying network use.

• DNS names such as *www.phptr.com* are much easier to remember than IP addresses such as 192.168.2.64.

• DNS names tend to remain more permanent than IP addresses. Especially in environments that use DHCP, server and workstation IP addresses can change on a regular basis, whereas the DNS name of the resource remains the same.

• DNS is a practical choice for heterogenous networks that have a mixture of Windows- and non-Windows-based servers and workstations.

• Active Directory uses a similar hierarchical type of structure, making it a perfect fit for use with DNS.

Defining the Domain Namespace

Many of the concepts of DNS will seem very familiar, since they are what Active Directory is based upon. The DNS namespace is based on a hierarchical tree structure, as shown in Figure 24.1.

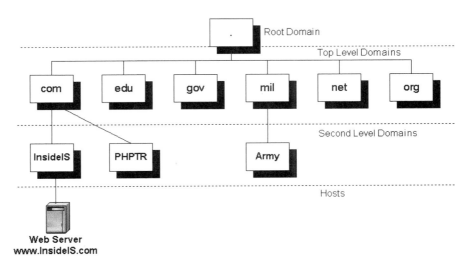

Figure 24-1   *The hierarchical namespace of DNS.*

DNS is a distributed database, which means no one server has the entire database on it and no one company is responsible for the entire DNS namespace (unlike the original *HOSTS* file that was maintained by a single organization). At the top of the namespace is the root domain, which is represented only by a period. The Internet root domain is managed by several organizations. Below the root domain are the top-level domains, which are recognizable as the extensions seen at the end of Websites, email addresses, and other Internet resources. Top-level domains are either two or three characters long and are codes to help organize Internet resources into logical groupings. *.com*, for example, used to represent commercial organizations, and *.net* representing providers of network resources on the Internet. We say "used to" because the lines have been largely blurred between *.com*, *.org*, and *.net*. Network Solutions (the primary registration service for those three top-level domains) no longer requires the entity that is registering a domain name to specify its purpose in order to control which top-level domain a person or company can register a domain name in. Table 24.1 lists the generic top-level domains with which most people are familiar.

Table 24.1	Top-level Internet Domain Names
Top Domain	**Description**
com	Commercial organizations
edu	Educational institutions
gov	United States government
mil	United States military
net	Network providers
org	Nonprofit organizations

SECOND-LEVEL DOMAINS

The *edu*, *gov*, and *mil* domains still have strict requirements for registering domain names. The *com*, *net*, and *org* domains, however, are basically open to anyone who wants to pay the money to register a name in that namespace. When you register a name with a registration authority such as Network Solutions, you are registering a second-level domain name. Second-level domain names, such as *Microsoft.com*, *InsideIS.com*, or *Whitehouse.gov*, are made up of a standard top-level name and a second-level name that is unique to that namespace.

Top-level domains are partitioned namespace, similar to domain trees in Active Directory. Names must be unique within a namespace, so while there can be a *domain1.com* and a *domain1.net*, there can only be one *domain1* second-level domain under a given top-level domain.

SUBDOMAINS

Second-level domains can be further divided into subdomains. However, the subdivisions are not called third-level domains. There can be as many unique subdomains as you want to have within a second-level domain. Examples of these would be *marketing.microsoft.com* or *sales.phptr.com*.

Host Names

Below the second-level domains are the hosts. A host is a network resource that has an IP address and, therefore, a DNS name. A host can be a server, workstation, router, printer, or anything that can have an IP address. In Figure 24.1 the server *WWW* is a host in the *InsideIS.com* domain. DNS namespace is written from left to right, host to top level. The entire name from host to root domain is referred to as the Fully Qualified Domain Name, or FQDN. In our example, *www.InsideIS.com.* is an FQDN (including the period after the *com*, which signifies the root domain). An example of an FQDN for a subdivided second-level domain would be *server1.support.microsoft.com.*.

Host names will not be the same as the computer name. Specific requirements for host names are spelled out in RFC 1035, and some of the characters that are valid for Windows 2000 computer names, such as the underscore character _, are not valid for DNS host names. By RFC specifications DNS names can consist of the English alphabet characters a–z and A–Z, numbers 0–9, and the hyphen.

Windows 2000 DNS also supports the Unicode character set, as defined in RFC 2044. Unicode supports characters not found in the English language that are required for languages such as Spanish, French, and German. The Unicode character set should be used only if all DNS servers in your organization support it.

Naming Guidelines

The following are some general guidelines for domain naming.

• Use standard DNS characters, and use Unicode only if all DNS servers support it. NetBIOS allowed many characters that are invalid in DNS names.

• Keep names simple and precise. Simple descriptive names are easier for users to remember and use.

• Keep names short. While an FQDN can be up to 245 characters, longer names are more cumbersome to work with.

• Remember that DNS names are not case-sensitive.

• Keep the domain structure as flat as possible. Going beyond three to four levels increases the administrative burden as well as introducing performance problems as the name resolution requests have to be referred to higher-level name servers.

• Names must be unique within a namespace.

• Plan your namespace carefully; once implemented, it is difficult to change later.

• The Internet Engineering Task Force (IETF) has published several Requests for Comment (RFC) documents that cover best practices for DNS, as recommended by various DNS architects and planners for the Internet. It is useful to review these RFCs, particularly if you are planning a large DNS design, such as for a large Internet service provider (ISP) that supports the use of DNS name service. Current RFCs that cover Internet DNS best practices include 1912 "Common DNS Operational and Configuration Errors," 2182 "Selection and Operation of Secondary DNS Servers," and 2219 "Use of DNS Aliases for Network Services."

Understanding Zones

The Domain Name System (DNS) allows a DNS namespace to be divided up into zones, which store name information about one or more DNS domains.

For each DNS domain name included in a zone, the zone becomes the authoritative source for information about that domain.

UNDERSTANDING THE DIFFERENCE BETWEEN ZONES AND DOMAINS

A zone is the smallest administrative unit for a name server and can cover a small or large range of the domain namespace. However, a zone starts as a storage database for only a single DNS domain name. For example, a zone could cover *Inside-Corner.com*, but could *not* cover both *Inside-Corner.com* and *InsideIS.com*. If other domains are added below the domain used to create the zone, these domains can either be part of the same zone or belong to another zone. For example, consider the *Inside-Corner.com* domain with subdomains *sales.Inside-Corner.com*, *engineering.Inside-Corner.com*, *development.Inside-Corner.com*, and *finance.Inside-Corner.com*. Any or all of those subdomains could be included in the same zone as *Inside-Corner.com*. Alternatively, additional zones could be created in order to divide the administrative responsibilities. For example, there might be separate administrators for the MIS units *development.Inside-Corner.com* and *engineering.Inside-Corner.com* and the business units *sales.Inside-Corner.com* and *finance.Inside-Corner.com*. The four subdomains could be split into two zones, administered by the respective systems administrators. To reiterate, once a subdomain is added, it can then either be:

- Managed and included as part of the original zone records, or
- Delegated away to another zone created to support the subdomain.

Multiple zones in the DNS namespace provide a means to delegate administrative responsibilities. A zone can only contain contiguous namespace, therefore a single zone could not be authoritative for both *Microsoft.com* and *InsideIS.com*. However, a single zone could be authoritative for both *sales.InsideIS.com* and *marketing.InsideIS.com* domains. In addition, *sales.InsideIS.com* and *marketing.InsideIS.com* could be split off into different zones. Figure 24.2 illustrates the concepts of zones.

ZONE REPLICATION AND TRANSFERS

Because of the important role that zones play in DNS, it is intended that they be available from more than one DNS server on the network to provide availability and fault tolerance when resolving name queries. Otherwise, if a single server is used and that server is not responding, queries for names in the zone can fail. For additional servers to host a zone, zone transfers are required to replicate and synchronize all copies of the zone used at each server configured to host the zone. When a new DNS server is added and configured as a secondary server for an existing zone, it performs a full initial transfer of the zone to obtain and replicates a full copy of resource records for the zone. Resource records are discussed later in this chapter. For most earlier DNS server implementations, this same method of full transfer for a zone is also used when the

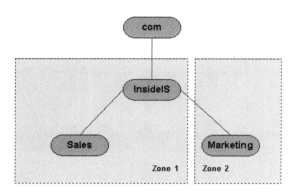

Figure 24-2 *DNS namespace subdivided into zones.*

zone requires updating after changes are made to the zone. For Windows 2000, the DNS service supports incremental zone transfer, a revised DNS zone-transfer process for intermediate changes.

Incremental zone transfers are described in RFC 1995 as an additional DNS standard for replicating DNS zones. When incremental transfers are supported by both a DNS server acting as the source for a zone and any servers that copy the zone from it, it provides a more efficient method of propagating zone changes and updates.

Windows 2000 Server supports incremental zone transfer through IXFR query. For earlier versions of the DNS service running on Windows NT Server 4.0 and for many other DNS server implementations, incremental zone transfer is not available and only full-zone (AXFR) queries and transfers are used to replicate zones. IXFR allows the secondary server to pull only those zone changes it needs in order to synchronize its copy of the zone with its source, rather than having to replicate the entire zone file.

With IXFR zone transfers, differences between the source and replicated versions of the zone are first determined. Each zone file has a start-of-authority (SOA) record for the zone, which has a serial-number field. If the zones are determined to be the same version by that serial number, then no transfer takes place. If the serial number for the zone at the source is greater than at the requesting secondary server, a transfer is made of only those changes to resource records (RRs) for each incremental version of the zone. For an IXFR query to succeed and changes to be sent, the source DNS server for the zone must keep a history of incremental zone changes to use when answering these queries. The incremental transfer process requires substantially less traffic on a network, and zone transfers are completed much faster.

THE PURPOSE OF NAME SERVERS

DNS name servers exist to provide name resolution services to client requests. To fulfill that role, DNS servers store the zone database files that allow client requests to be serviced, and they can store zone files for one or more zones. One name server contains the primary zone database file, which is the master copy for a zone. Conversely there must be at least one name server for a zone. Without a name server a zone cannot exist, since there would be no way to resolve DNS names to IP addresses.

A zone can have multiple DNS servers, which serves the following purpose:

• Provide fault tolerance—if the server containing the primary zone database file fails, a secondary server can provide name resolution without an interruption in service.

• Improve performance—Placing DNS servers on either side of a slow WAN link allows name resolution requests to be resolved locally rather than passing the requests over the slow connection. The reduction in network traffic can also improve the performance of other applications that need to use the WAN link.

• Reduce the load on the primary name server—systems can be configured to use secondary name servers to balance the name resolution load.

The Name Resolution Process

The process of name resolution involves translating, otherwise known as resolving, DNS names into IP addresses. When a user requests an Internet resource, such as *www.mycompany.com*, DNS resolves the name to an IP address, such as 192.168.1.21. Computers communicate with each other through numbers, not names. Humans communicate better with easy-to-remember names rather than long strings of numbers. If we have to look up our Aunt Sadie's phone number every time we want to call her, how can we remember or keep track of the IP addresses for every network resource we need to access? That is the thrust of DNS; it allows us humans to work within a context we're familiar and comfortable with in a world where raw numbers rule.

Speaking of remembering phone numbers, name resolution is a very similar process to looking up phone numbers. When you go to the phone book you usually look for the person's name as the basis for your search, in order to find the phone number with which the name is associated. The same process is used with DNS, and the DNS zone database file is the name server's phone book. In DNS terms you either perform a forward lookup query or a reverse lookup query, and a DNS server can cache query results for future use.

Defining Forward Lookup Query

A forward lookup query is the most common name resolution process, where names are resolved to IP addresses. A DNS name server can resolve names only for zones in which it has authority, so if a server cannot resolve a query, it passes the query to other name servers until it is completely resolved. At that time the results are passed back to the client. In the name resolution process DNS name servers can function as DNS clients, since when they cannot resolve the query request themselves, they in turn query other name servers. The following example steps through the process of a forward lookup query to access *www.microsoft.com*.

1. The end user types *www.microsoft.com* into her Web browser and presses *<Enter>*.
2. Since computers communicate by numbers and not names, the query for *www.microsoft.com* gets passed to the local DNS server as configured in the client's TCP/IP properties.
3. The local DNS server checks the zone database file to determine whether or not it has the name to IP address mapping for *www.microsoft.com*. It finds that it does not have authority for the *Microsoft.com* domain.
4. The local DNS server then queries the root domain, for resolution of the query.
5. The root domain refers the local server to the com name servers.
6. The local DNS server then queries a com server, which in turn refers the local server to the Microsoft name servers.
7. The local DNS server sends the name resolution query to a *Microsoft.com* name server. The Microsoft name server has authority for the zone that contains the server named *www*, so it responds to the client request with the IP address for *www.microsoft.com*. If the Microsoft name server had not had authority for the correct zone, the referral process would have continued as the query would have been passed to a Microsoft DNS server that did have authority for the zone containing *www*.
8. The local DNS server returns the IP address for *www.microsoft.com* to the client that originally made the request.
9. With the name resolution complete, the client can successfully access *www.microsoft.com*.

Name Server Caching

The name resolution process generates a lot of DNS traffic. When processing a query a name server will potentially have to send out several requests to get the name resolved to an IP address. With each query the name server makes, it discovers other DNS servers that have authority for particular zones. Rather than having to repeat the same processes every time a query is made, a name server can cache the query results locally. For our example above, the next time a client attempted to access *www.microsoft.com*, the name server would not repeat the process of querying the root, *com*, and ultimately the Microsoft name servers for name resolution. The local DNS server had already completed the request once and cached the results. It would already have the name to IP address mapping for *www.microsoft.com* stored, and would simply pass the IP address to the client. This not only speeds up the name resolution process, since repeat queries do not have to go through the entire name resolution process again, but it also has the benefit of reducing network traffic. That makes the bandwidth that repeat queries would have taken available for other applications.

The results of a query, however, are not cached forever. A configurable setting referred to as Time to Live, or TTL, determines how long the server will cache the result. The default value is 3600 seconds (1 hour), but this can be configured through the DNS Manager console. Having TTLs expire quickly will help ensure that the database is kept current; however, it will also generate more network traffic. TTLs are configured by right-clicking on the zone in the DNS Manager console and selecting Properties. Select the Start of Authority (SOA) tab to review and modify the TTL settings if necessary.

Caching is particularly beneficial for environments where the local DNS server links to the rest of the world (the Internet or other LANs in the corporate network) through a slow WAN link. In this instance, caching greatly reduces the amount of network traffic over the slow connection. Windows 2000 also supports caching-only servers that do not have any authority for any zone, but merely cache results for local use. They contain only the information they have received while processing client name resolution requests.

Defining Reverse Lookup Query

A reverse lookup query, as you might expect, is the opposite of a forward lookup query. Looking back at our phone-book example, a reverse lookup query would be the equivalent of having a phone number and trying to find out the name with which it was associated. Obviously our phone books are not organized in such a way that you can easily look up a phone number without knowing the name. The DNS distributed database is the same way; it is indexed by name and not by IP address. Without some other process in place, a reverse lookup query would require searching the entire database of every domain name to find that record, much as you would have to start at the front of the phone book and look at every single record to find the phone number, and then see the associated name.

To get around this problem and create a more efficient way to perform reverse lookup queries, a special second-level domain was created called *in-addr.arpa* (*arpa* is an exception to the standard two- and three-character top-level domain names). The *in-addr.arpa* domain follows the same type of hierarchical structure as the rest of the DNS namespace. However, it is indexed by IP address rather than by name. Subdomains in the *in-addr.arpa* domain are named after the dotted decimal IP address structure, except they are reversed. For example, if a company were assigned a class C network address of 192.168.1.0, their reverse lookup zone would be *1.168.198.in-addr.arpa*.

Organizations administer the subdomains of *in-addr.arpa* based upon their registered IP addresses and subnet masks.

Installing the DNS Service on a Windows 2000 Server

With much of the background theory of DNS out of the way, it's time to roll up our sleeves and install the DNS service on a Windows 2000 server. A couple of preinstallation tasks must be completed prior to actually running the installation, so we will examine those first.

Server Prerequisites

In order to use DNS, the adapter that the DNS service will bind to on the server must have a static IP address. A static IP address can be configured in the Internet Protocol (TCP/IP) properties dialog, which is accessed through the properties of the network interface. Figure 24-3 shows this configuration window.

In addition to configuring a static IP address, you need to configure the advanced TCP/IP properties to specify the IP address of the DNS server, as shown in Figure 24.4. Click the Advanced button in TCP/IP properties and then select the DNS tab.

Performing the Installation

The DNS service can be installed under a couple of different scenarios. The first we covered previously in the book when installing Active Directory. During the DCPROMO process, you can have the DNS service automatically set up and configured with the settings you specify. The DNS service can also be installed manually at any time after Windows 2000 Server has been installed. This manual installation is what we will focus on here.

When you install the DNS service, in addition to setting up the service, the setup process performs the following functions:

- Installs the DNS Manager and adds a shortcut to the console to the Administrative Tools folder on the Start menu. You use the DNS Manager Console for most DNS configuration tasks.
- Adds Registry keys for the DNS service underneath the following branch: *HKEY_LOCAL_MACHINE\System\CurrentControlSet\Services\Dns*.
- Creates a Dns folder under the *systemroot\System32* directory structure, where *systemroot* is the drive and directory where the Windows 2000 sys-

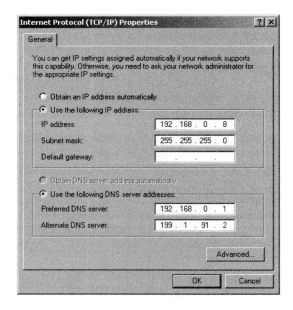

Figure 24–3   *Configuring a static IP address in Windows 2000 is done through Internet Protocol properties.*

tem files were installed, such as *C:\WINNT.*This folder stores the DNS database files, which are described in Table 24.2.

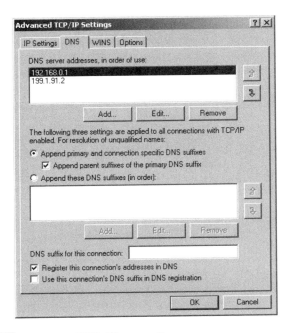

Figure 24–4   *Advanced TCP/IP properties.*

Table 24.2	DNS Database Files
Filename	**Description**
Domain.dns	The zone database file. *Domain* will be the name of the DNS domain, for example, Microsoft's DNS server would have a file called *Microsoft.com.dns*.
d.c.b.a.in-addr.arpa	The reverse lookup file, which maps IP addresses to DNS names. As previously mentioned, the *d.c.b.a* portion is the reverse-dotted decimal network ID. A subnet of 192.168.1.0 would have a filename of *1.168.192.in-addr.arpa.dns*.
Cache.dns	The cache file that stores information for resolving names outside of authoritative domains. By default, the file contains records for all of the root servers on the Internet.

Table 24.2	DNS Database Files (Continued)
Boot	This is an optional file that contains specifications controlling how the DNS service starts. The same information is stored in the Registry, and this file exists primarily for compatibility with BIND (Berkeley Internet Name Daemon) name servers, which make up the majority of the Internet.

PRECONFIGURING TCP/IP FOR DNS

The first step in setting up the DNS service is to preconfigure TCP/IP, as we discussed earlier in this section. You must assign a static IP address to the network card that DNS will bind to, and under advanced TCP/IP properties configure the DNS IP address. Since this server is where we are installing the DNS service, the DNS server IP address will be the same as the IP address specified for the server NIC.

You also have to configure the DNS domain name of the computer if you have not done so already. This is done as follows:

1. Open System Properties by right-clicking on My Computer and selecting Properties.
2. Click the Network Identification tab and click the Advanced button. If you are on a domain controller, you won't have this option and will be advised of it on the Network Identification property sheet. In this case, you can skip this step, because your server already belongs to a domain.
3. Specify a DNS domain name if necessary (if you aren't on a domain controller) and click OK. Reboot when prompted.

   Once the system reboots, you will be ready to install the DNS service.

INSTALLING DNS

You must be logged in as a user with administrator privileges on the server in order to install DNS. Once logged in, open Control Panel and launch the Add/Remove Programs wizard. Click on Add/Remove Windows Components. This will bring up the topmost window, as shown in Figure 24.5. Select Networking Services and click Details, which is illustrated in the bottom window of Figure 24-5.

Click OK and then Next and follow the prompts to install the DNS service. Click Finish to exit the wizard, once the file copying is complete, and close out of Control Panel. In the next section we will administer the DNS service, performing the actual configuration.

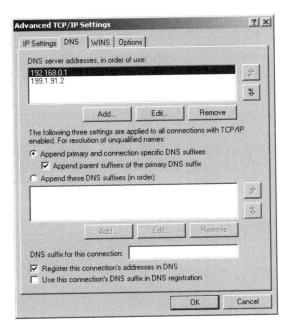

Figure 24–5

Adding the DNS service is completed through the Windows Components Wizard.

Administering the DNS Service

Now that we've installed the DNS service on our Windows 2000 server, we are ready to start configuring it. The first time you open the DNS Manager Console you will be able to configure your DNS server as a root server (if this is the first DNS server in your domain). You will also be able to create forward and reverse lookup zones.

In addition to creating zones, you can add resource records to the zone database file. Resource records are discussed in depth later in this chapter. Windows 2000 also supports Dynamic DNS, which allows the automatic updating of zone files by clients and services that support it.

In this section we will look at the following topics:

- Configuring a DNS Server
- Creating Zones
- Adding Resource Records
- Setting Up Dynamic DNS

Configuring a DNS Server

As we mentioned previously, the first time you start the DNS Manager Console, you will have the option of configuring your server as a root server. From our discussion earlier in this chapter, you know that the root domain is the topmost domain in the DNS namespace. It has authority over all of the top-level domains—which, if you remember from the Internet name pace are *com*, *edu*, *gov*, *net*, *org*, etc.

Because of the nature of root domain servers, there are issues to consider regarding their setup. The first is that you should not configure your DNS server as a root server if you are connected to the Internet. For obvious reasons you are not going to be able to add your very own root server to the public Internet that has authority over all top-level domains. If you configure your intranet DNS server as a root server, it will not be able to participate on the Internet, since it cannot be configured as a forwarder. A forwarder is what allows the server to forward queries that it cannot resolve to other servers. Root servers have absolute authority for the namespace they are in, so there cannot be a query that they could not resolve. If you configure a root server on your intranet, it will only be able to resolve queries on your intranet, and not queries for external resources.

If you do set up a root server on your intranet, ensure that LAN clients are going through a proxy server to gain access to the Internet. The proxy will do the necessary Network Address Translation (NAT) to connect to external resources, allowing your internal clients to use the internal DNS server for local name resolution while the proxy handles translating Internet resources by connecting to external DNS servers. Don't forget, there can only be one primary DNS server for a system. It is important to note, **if the primary DNS server cannot resolve a name, the secondary DNS server will not be attempted. A secondary DNS server is utilized only if the primary server is unavailable/not responding to queries**.

Creating Zones

Earlier in the chapter we discussed forward and reverse lookup queries. In order for your DNS server to process these queries, you must first configure forward and reverse lookup zones for the queries to be resolved.

FORWARD LOOKUP ZONES

As would be expected, a forward lookup zone allows the name server to process forward lookup queries. You must have at least one forward lookup zone for your DNS server to function. The first time you launch the DNS Manager you are presented with the "Configure the DNS server" dialog shown in Figure

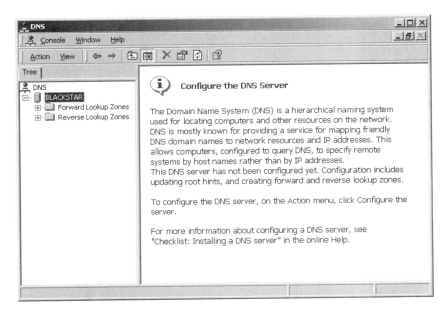

Figure 24–6   *Beginning to configure a DNS server.*

24.6. Alternatively, once a server has been configured, right-clicking the Forward Lookup Zones folder and clicking New Zone adds a new zone.

Once the new zone wizard starts, you will have a welcome dialog box. Click next to reach the window shown in Figure 24.7.

You will see Figure 24.7 only if this is the initial time you are launching DNS Manager. If you create a zone afterward, you will be greeted with a slightly different welcome screen. Whichever way you enter into creating a new forward lookup zone, you will reach the windows illustrated in Figure 24.8.

From Figure 24.8 you can see there are three choices for the type of zone to create. They are as follows:

• *Active Directory-integrated*—This option stores the zone database within the Active Directory. Integration within Active Directory provides an additional measure of security since the zone database is not stored in a text file, and allows DNS updates to be replicated alongside Active Directory data.

• *Standard Primary*—The Standard Primary option is used primarily for compatibility in environments where you have non-Windows 2000 DNS servers. Since other types of DNS servers are not Active Directory aware, this option maintains the zone database in a standard text file that can be read and updated by these other servers.

• *Standard Secondary*—The Standard Secondary option creates a copy of an existing zone. This option cannot be used unless there is already a stan-

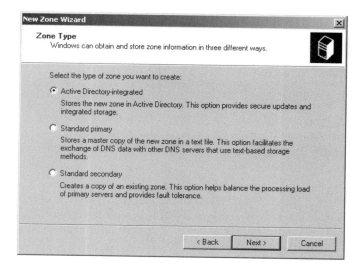

Figure 24–7   *Creating a new forward lookup zone.*

Figure 24–8   *Determining the type of zone to create.*

dard primary zone. When creating a Standard Secondary zone, you will be prompted for the name of the existing DNS server that will be used as the master to transfer zone information to the server on which you are creating the secondary zone. The idea behind a secondary zone is to provide fault tolerance in case the primary is not available, and load balancing since you can point some clients to the primary and some to the secondary for name resolution requests.

If you have only Windows 2000 DNS servers in your environment, you will want to use Active Directory-integrated. If you will have your Windows 2000 DNS server coexisting with non-Windows 2000 DNS servers, choose Standard Primary. Once you have decided on a zone type, click Next.

The next step is to assign a name for your zone. If you have a domain name registered with an Internet naming authority, you can configure your zone to use it. Otherwise, use your intranet zone and continue, as shown in Figure 24.9.

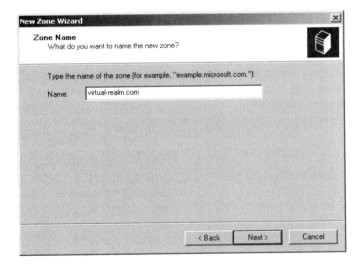

Figure 24–9   *Naming your zone.*

After naming your zone, you have to specify your zone database file name, if you are creating this zone after the initial setup. The zone file typically is the name of the zone with the addition of a *.dns* extension. Alternatively, you can copy an existing zone file from another computer to the *system-root\system32\dns* folder and specify it for use with this zone. This option is used for situations where you are migrating a zone from another name server.

If you choose Active Directory-integrated, you are not prompted for a zone file name. Windows 2000 automatically creates the zone database within the Active Directory. At this point click Finish, and your zone is complete.

REVERSE LOOKUP ZONES

As discussed previously, reverse lookup queries resolve names from IP addresses. This technique is used mostly for diagnostic purposes; tools like *nslookup* perform reverse lookups. Some Websites use reverse lookups as a security mechanism to ensure that the client making a request is in fact who they claim to be. Reverse lookup zones allow the processing of reverse lookup queries. There are several options with nslookup; the easiest way to see them is to type *nslookup* and press *<Enter>* from a command prompt, and then type help and press *<Enter>*. Most commonly you will simply type something like:

```
nslookup 192.168.1.1 <enter>
```

The above command will perform a reverse lookup against the IP address and return name information.

Reverse lookup zones are not required for a DNS server to function, so creating one is optional. Unless you have a reason not to create a reverse lookup zone, however, it is a good idea to have one if just for troubleshooting purposes. Creating a reverse lookup zone is very similar to creating a forward lookup zone. If you are going through the initial DNS configuration as we were above, once you create a forward lookup zone you are automatically given the opportunity to configure a reverse lookup zone. This is illustrated in Figure 24.10.

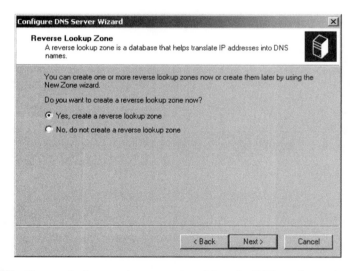

Figure 24-10   *Reverse lookup zones are optional, but the DNS configuration wizard gives you the opportunity to choose whether or not to create one.*

The DNS configuration wizard will ask you to specify what type of zone you want to create. This is the same as when creating a forward lookup zone; the options are Active Directory-integrated, Standard Primary, and Standard Secondary. As with forward lookup zones, the type of zone you will want to create will depend on your environment. If you are using only Windows 2000 DNS servers in an Active Directory environment, then Active Directory-integrated provides the best choice for security, performance, and ease of management. If your network environment requires compatibility with non-Windows 2000 name servers, or does not use Active Directory, then you will want to choose a Standard zone type.

The next step, as shown in Figure 24.11, is to configure the Network ID. The easiest way is to enter the octets of your network ID in the first field. You will be able to enter three octets, which is the maximum a network ID could be. If you have configured a standard class C IP network ID of 192.168.1.0 with a subnet mask of **255**.255.255.0 in Internet Protocol (TCP/IP) properties, the Network ID will fill the first three octets. If you have a class B network ID such as 169.254.0.0 with a subnet mask of 255.255.0.0, you will enter only the first two octets (which make up the network ID).

If you notice, as you are typing in the network ID, the reverse lookup zone name is automatically filling in with the correct name for your zone. Instead of entering the network ID in the first field, you can type the name of the zone directly by selecting Reverse lookup zone name. As previously discussed, the format of the reverse lookup zone name is the network ID in reverse order with a *.in-addr.arpa* domain extension. Our 192.168.1.0 network ID would have a reverse lookup zone name of *1.168.192.in-addr.arpa*.

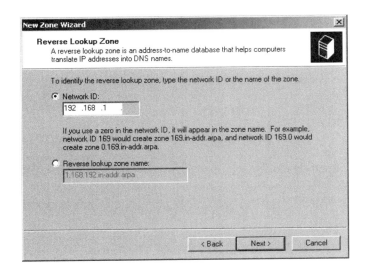

Figure 24–11   *Defining a reverse lookup zone.*

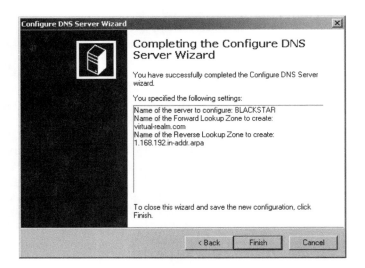

Figure 24-12
Confirming zone settings and finishing the DNS configuration wizard.

It is important to note that zeros are not left out if they are part of the network ID. If our class C network ID was 192.168.0.0, then the reverse lookup zone name would be *0.168.192.in-addr.arpa.*

As with creating a forward lookup zone, if you chose a Standard zone type you will be prompted for a *.dns* file name for the zone database file. This configuration setting is not required for Active Directory-integrated, since the zone database is stored within the Active Directory and not in a text file.

The last part of configuring zones on your name server is to confirm your settings, as illustrated in Figure 24.12, and click Finish.

Adding Resource Records

After creating your zones, you can continue with the configuration of your name server by adding resource records, which are entries in the zone database you add in order to provide name resolution for specific services. The most common types of resource records are:

• *Start of Authority (SOA)*— This record is automatically added when a zone is created. The SOA record identifies the name server that is authoritative for a zone as well as containing a few administrative details. This record is listed as a Start of Authority type in the DNS Manager.

• *Name Server (NS)*—The name server record is also added automatically upon the creation of a new zone. It specifies the name servers that are responsible for a domain name. Each zone should have at least two servers, one as a primary and one as a secondary to serve as a fault-tolerant backup and provide load balancing. This record is listed as a Name Server type in the DNS Manager.

• *Address (A)*—Basic static mapping that lists the IP address for a host name in a forward lookup zone. This record is listed as a Host type in the DNS Manager.

• *Canonical Name (CNAME)*—A CNAME is an alias for a particular host name. An example would be running Internet services *http* and *ftp* on a server named *blackstar.inside-corner.com*. You would have an A record for that host, plus you could have CNAME records for *www.inside-corner.com* and *ftp.inside-corner.com* to reflect the Internet services being provided. It would be possible to have multiple A records, one for each of the services. However, it is considered good practice to use a single A record and to use CNAME aliases for additional records. This record is listed as an Alias type in the DNS Manager.

• *Pointer (PTR)*—A Pointer associates a host name with an IP address and is used in reverse lookup zones. This record is listed as a Pointer type in the DNS Manager.

• *Mail Exchange (MX)*—A Mail Exchange record defines SMTP mail servers that are configured for a domain, as well as the order in which to use each mail server. This record is listed as a Mail Exchanger type in the DNS Manager.

This is by no means an exhaustive list of resource record types. In DNS Manager, click the Action menu and select Other New Records. As you can see from Figure 24.13, there is a large list of resource record types with descriptions. Any of these can be added to your zone.

Setting up Dynamic DNS

We have not yet mentioned one significant drawback of DNS, which is its static nature. Standard DNS servers do not support any kind of automatic updating or registering of clients with them, so new resource records must be manually added and maintained. Windows 2000, however, provides support for Dynamic DNS, which is a proposed standard outlined in RFCs 2136 and 2137. If a server supports Dynamic DNS, clients that also support the standard can register their addresses with the name server automatically at the time they receive an IP address from a DHCP server. It is important to note that clients using static IP addresses and not DHCP-assigned addresses cannot dynamically update the zone database file. Dynamic DNS works with DHCP to maintain the dynamically updated records. DHCP allows clients to register their A records at the time they receive an IP address, and DHCP adds a PTR record to the reverse lookup zone if one exists.

Windows 2000 Dynamic DNS is currently supported only on Windows 2000 DNS clients. Downlevel clients, such as those running Windows 98 or Windows NT 4.0, cannot participate in Dynamic DNS. Resource records for those clients must still be added manually.

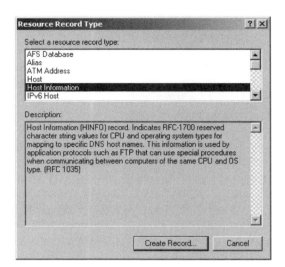

Figure 24–13 *There are many types of Resource Records that can be added to your domain.*

Configuring a Windows 2000 name server for Dynamic DNS is easy. First, click the View menu and ensure that Advanced is selected. Next, right-click on the forward or reverse lookup zone you wish to configure. Click the General tab, which will show information similar to that in Figure 24.14.

When you click the dropdown list next to "Allow Dynamic Updates?" you will have the following options:

- *NO*—Do not allow dynamic updates. Disables DDNS.
- *YES*—Enables dynamic updates
- *Only Secure Updates*—This option appears if you are using an Active Directory-integrated zone. It allows dynamic updates to take place only if they are done using the secure DNS update protocol.

Configuring DNS on a Client

Once the DNS service is installed and configured on the name server, you must configure clients to use your new name server. In order to be a DNS client, a computer must have the TCP/IP protocol installed. Windows NT and Windows 9x systems can be configured to use a Windows 2000 name server, even though they cannot participate in Dynamic DNS. Even Unix, Linux, and Macintosh clients can utilize a Windows 2000 DNS server. However, configuring those types of clients is outside the scope of this chapter, where we will focus exclusively on configuring Windows 2000 clients.

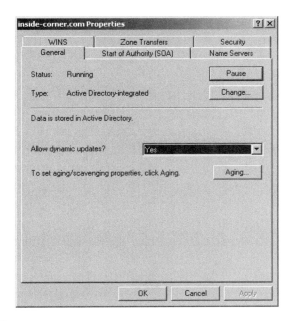

Figure 24–14 *Configuring Windows 2000 DNS to allow dynamic updates.*

To configure a Windows 2000 system to access a DNS server, we first have to get into the properties of TCP/IP. This is done easily by right-clicking on the My Network Places icon and clicking Properties. Next, right-click Local Area Connection (or the connection you want if you have multiple network connections configured), and click Properties. Then, select Internet Protocol (TCP/IP) and click Properties.

Once we're into the TCP/IP properties window, you will be able to see a dialog such as that in Figure 24.15 that allows you to specify name server addresses or obtain them from a DHCP server.

It is worth reiterating here that Windows 2000 clients can register themselves automatically with a Windows 2000 name server, if Dynamic DNS has been enabled, at the time they receive an IP address from a DHCP server. For that reason, you will want to consider using DHCP to assign IP addresses whenever possible. You can use DHCP to assign the name server addresses, and you should in environments that utilize DHCP. DNS servers must be explicitly configured though if you are not using DHCP or if you want the client computer to use a different DNS server than the DHCP server is configured to provide.

After typing in the IP addresses of the preferred and alternate DNS servers (also referred to as primary and secondary), click the Advanced button and then the DNS tab. As you can see in Figure 24.16, the DNS servers are listed in the order in which they will be queried. Only if the primary name server is

Configuring specific name server addresses is done through
Internet Protocol (TCP/IP) properties.

unavailable or not responding will the client attempt to use a secondary name server. If the primary server responds but is unable to resolve a name, the client will *not* try to use the secondary server. In an environment where there are two name servers for a given zone, it is helpful to configure some clients to use one server as their primary, and others to use the second server as their primary. This distributes the load across both servers, rather than having a heavily utilized primary server with no activity on the secondary server.

On this screen, you can optionally configure DNS suffixes that are added when attempting to resolve names. By adding additional suffixes to the list, you can search for short, unqualified computer names in more than one specified DNS domain. Remember from earlier in the chapter that a Fully Qualified Domain Name (FQDN) consists of the host through the root domain, including a "." on the end that represents the root domain. If a DNS query fails, the DNS Client can use this list to append other name suffix endings to your original name and repeat DNS queries to the DNS server for these alternate FQDNs.

For Windows 2000 computers, the following default DNS search behavior is used when completing and resolving short, unqualified names.

• When the suffix search list is empty or unspecified, the primary DNS suffix of the computer is appended to short unqualified names and DNS query is used to resolve the resulting FQDN. The primary DNS suffix is configured through the Network Identification tab of System Properties. If this query fails,

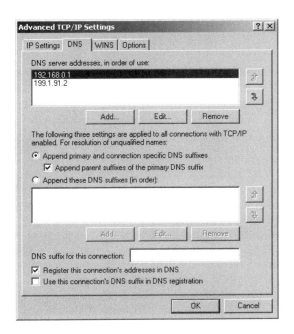

Figure 24—16   *Configuring DNS settings under Advanced TCP/IP properties.*

the computer can try additional queries for alternate FQDNs by appending any connection-specific DNS suffix configured for network connections.

- If no connection-specific suffixes are configured, or queries for these resultant connection-specific FQDNs fail, the client can then begin to retry queries based on systematic reduction of the primary suffix.

This all sounds complicated, but maybe an example would make it easier. If the primary suffix were *domain1.inside-corner.com*, the process would be able to retry queries for the short name by searching for it in the *inside-corner.com* and *com* domains if it failed in the *domain1.inside-corner.com* domain.

When the suffix search list is not empty and has at least one DNS suffix specified, attempts to qualify and resolve short DNS names are limited to searching only those FQDNs made possible by the specified suffix list. If queries are unsuccessful for any FQDNs formed as a result of appending and trying each suffix in the list, the query process fails, producing a "name not found" result.

The default choice is shown in Figure 24.16. You can optionally control which DNS suffixes are searched by clicking "Append these DNS Suffixes (in order)" and entering your desired settings. You can also disable the client from participating in Dynamic DNS by deselecting the "Register this connection's addresses in DNS" check box.

Troubleshooting the DNS Service

There are several troubleshooting steps to take if you have trouble getting your DNS server to work. In this section we will discuss monitoring a DNS server, configuring logging options, and using the nslookup utility.

Monitoring a DNS Server

The DNS Manager console gives you the ability to monitor the DNS service to ensure trouble-free functionality. To monitor a name server, open the DNS console, right-click on the server you want to monitor, and click Properties. When you click the Monitoring tab, you will see a screen similar to that in Figure 24.17.

Either or both of the following types of queries can be used to monitor the DNS service.

• *Simple Query*—The simple query is a basic iterative name resolution request. An iterative request from a client tells the DNS server that the client expects the best answer the DNS server can provide immediately, without contacting other DNS servers. This query, therefore, is purely local. The DNS client on the server machine contacts the DNS server service located on the same machine.

• *Recursive Query*—This type of test specifies that the DNS server perform a recursive query. This test is similar in its initial query processing to the Simple Query test in that it uses the local DNS resolver (client) to query the local DNS server, also located on the same computer. In this test, however, the client asks the server to use recursion to resolve an NS-type query (the NS resource record type was previously discussed in Section 24.4.3) for the root of the DNS domain namespace. This type of query typically requires additional recursive processing and can be helpful in verifying that server root hints or zone delegations have been properly set.

Once you have selected the tests to be used, either you can click the "Test Now" button to manually perform the tests immediately, or you can perform automatic testing at a specified time interval. Automated tests are performed according to the duration specified in "Test Interval," which is enabled by selecting the "Perform automatic testing at the following interval" check box. Results of all selected tests, whether manually or automatically performed, are displayed in the Test results list box at the bottom.

Configuring Logging Options

By clicking on the Logging tab in the name server properties, you can configure the DNS service to log specific types of activity. This is illustrated in Figure 24.18.

The logging options are as follows:

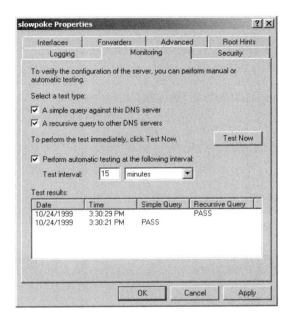

Figure 24–17 *Monitoring the DNS service.*

• *Query*—Logs queries received by the DNS Server service from clients.

• *Notify*—Logs notification messages received by the DNS Server service from other servers.

• *Update*—Logs dynamic updates received by the DNS Server service from other computers.

• *Questions*—Logs the contents of the question section for each DNS query message processed by the DNS Server service.

• *Answers*—Logs the contents of the answer section for each DNS query message processed by the DNS Server service.

• *Send*—Logs the number of DNS query messages sent by the DNS Server service.

• *Receive*—Logs the number of DNS query messages received by the DNS Server service.

• *UDP*—Logs the number of DNS requests received by the DNS Server service over a UDP port.

• *TCP*—Logs the number of DNS requests received by the DNS Server service over a TCP port.

• *Full packets*—Logs the number of full packets written and sent by the DNS Server service.

• *Write through*—Logs the number of packets written through by the DNS Server service and back to the zone.

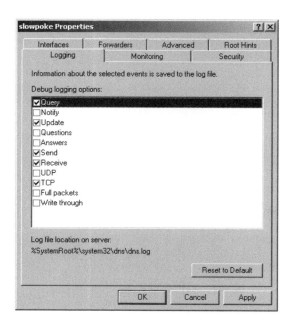

Figure 24–18

The Windows 2000 DNS service has many logging options that can be configured.

By default, all debug logging options are disabled, because they can be resource intensive, which affects overall server performance and consumes disk space. When selectively enabled, the DNS Server service can perform additional trace-level logging of selected types of events or messages for general troubleshooting and debugging of the server. Because logging can be resource intensive, it should only be used temporarily when more detailed information about server performance is needed.

Using Nslookup

The primary DNS service diagnostic tool is the nslookup command, which is installed along with other TCP/IP utilities at the time the TCP/IP protocol is installed. Nslookup is a commandline utility that performs a reverse lookup query against a name server (therefore, a reverse lookup zone must already be configured), resolving a host name from a supplied IP address. There are two modes: noninteractive and interactive.

NONINTERACTIVE NSLOOKUP

Noninteractive nslookup is used whenever you only want a single query to be resolved. You just type the syntax for a valid nslookup command, and data is returned. Figure 24.19 illustrates a noninteractive nslookup command.

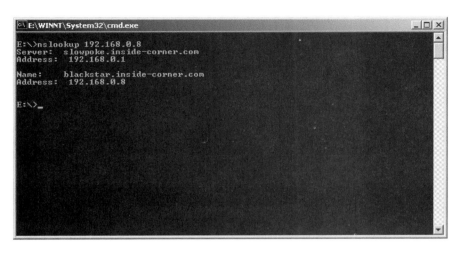

Figure 24–19

Performing an nslookup to determine the host name associated with a given IP address.

There are options that you can add to gain further control over the behavior of nslookup. By default, the command will use the default name server as specified in DNS properties. This, along with other options, can be configured as described below.

INTERACTIVE NSLOOKUP

Interactive mode is used when you want to perform multiple nslookup commands consecutively. To enter interactive mode, simply type *nslookup* at a command prompt and press Enter.

Interactive mode is also used when you want to view the help file. The nslookup help, as illustrated in Figure 24.20, provides all of the options available to control the behavior of the nslookup command.

Chapter Summary

In this chapter we covered the Windows 2000 DNS service. Starting out, we discussed the theory behind how DNS works and how to understand namespace, host names, and zones. We then looked at the name resolution process itself and how forward and reverse lookup zones were used to resolve names.

With the theory covered we moved into installing the DNS service on a Windows 2000 server and then configured and administered the DNS service. In doing so, we learned about creating zones and adding resource records, the

```
E:\WINNT\System32\cmd.exe - nslookup                                    _ □ ×

E:\>nslookup
Default Server:  slowpoke.inside-corner.com
Address:  192.168.0.1

> ?
Commands:    (identifiers are shown in uppercase, [] means optional)
NAME                    - print info about the host/domain NAME using default server
NAME1 NAME2             - as above, but use NAME2 as server
help or ?               - print info on common commands
set OPTION              - set an option
    all                     - print options, current server and host
    [no]debug               - print debugging information
    [no]d2                  - print exhaustive debugging information
    [no]defname             - append domain name to each query
    [no]recurse             - ask for recursive answer to query
    [no]search              - use domain search list
    [no]vc                  - always use a virtual circuit
    domain=NAME             - set default domain name to NAME
    srchlist=N1[/N2/.../N6] - set domain to N1 and search list to N1,N2, etc.
    root=NAME               - set root server to NAME
    retry=X                 - set number of retries to X
    timeout=X               - set initial time-out interval to X seconds
    type=X                  - set query type (ex. A,ANY,CNAME,MX,NS,PTR,SOA,SRV)
    querytype=X             - same as type
    class=X                 - set query class (ex. IN (Internet), ANY)
    [no]msxfr               - use MS fast zone transfer
    ixfrver=X               - current version to use in IXFR transfer request
server NAME             - set default server to NAME, using current default server
lserver NAME            - set default server to NAME, using initial server
finger [USER]           - finger the optional NAME at the current default host
root                    - set current default server to the root
ls [opt] DOMAIN [> FILE] - list addresses in DOMAIN (optional: output to FILE)
    -a                      - list canonical names and aliases
    -d                      - list all records
    -t TYPE                 - list records of the given type (e.g. A,CNAME,MX,NS,PTR etc.)
view FILE                   - sort an 'ls' output file and view it with pg
exit                    - exit the program

>
```

Figure 24–20   *Nslookup provides numerous configuration options that allows you to control how the command works.*

"meat and potatoes" of DNS management. We came to understand the implications of the different types of zones, and when to use Active Directory-integrated versus Standard zones. We learned that Windows 2000 supports Dynamic DNS on both the client and server ends, which allows DNS clients to automatically add their A records to the zone database at the time they receive an IP address from a DHCP server.

With the server configuration complete, we discussed configuring Windows 2000 clients to use DNS services. Windows 2000 DNS servers can also resolve names for NT, Windows 9x, UNIX, Macintosh, or any other clients that support the DNS standards, though we did not specifically cover configuring client services on those platforms. Lastly, we looked at some of the troubleshooting options that can be used if the DNS service iis not functioning correctly.

DNS plays a major role in Windows 2000 Active Directory, so feel free to refer to this chapter again if you have any DNS-related questions while planning your Active Directory infrastructure.

Auditing

*O*ne of the foremost concerns on computer networks these days is security. While computer hackers have been around as long as there have been computers and networks to hack into, it seems that with each passing week there are more and more network security breaches making the mainstream news. This chapter won't help you keep potential intruders out of your network, however, it will show you how to force a would-be hacker into leaving an audit trail that might provide you with the information you need in order to catch him and to later shore up network weaknesses. In this chapter we will discuss the following issues related to auditing.

- Understanding Auditing
- Designing an Audit Policy
- Applying an Audit Policy
- The Windows 2000 Event Viewer

25.1 Understanding Auditing

Auditing, as we have already said, allows an administrator to track security-related events as they happen on the network. Auditing is not a process that allows an administrator to control access to network resources; rather, it enables the administrator to determine through log files what types of activities are happening on the network. This can be useful in determining if there has been a security breach and where the breach came from. The clues from an audit trail can be useful in fixing a security problem as well. At the point in which a security breach has been detected, other tools and utilities can be utilized to prevent the problem from recurring.

In Windows 2000, activities that are monitored by auditing are referred to as events. Windows 2000, like previous versions of Windows NT, includes an Event Viewer administrative tool that provides a GUI interface to reading log files. Later in this chapter we will discuss the Event Viewer in depth, but for now let's just say that when an audited resource triggers an event, the security log provides the following information:

- The action that was performed
- The time and date of the event
- The user account that was used to perform the action
- Whether the action was successful or if it failed (useful in determining if other security policies are working effectively)

Applying an Audit Policy

In Windows 2000, we use the term *audit policy* to describe the conditions under which we want security events to be logged. When an event occurs that meets the criteria specified in the audit policy, the event is written to the security log on the Windows 2000 computer on which it occurred. The security log is what allows you to track the events you have configured.

Since Windows 2000 writes security events to the security log on the machine on which they occurred, you might wonder how that makes for very efficient administration. Fortunately, Microsoft includes a feature that allows you to open the security logs (and other Event Viewer logs) from a single administrative console. This requires administrator privileges on the systems you wish to view, however.

For example, suppose a user attempted to access a shared folder on a server in which she did not have sufficient access rights. The security event would be written to the security log on the server rather than on the computer the user attempted the action from, since it was at the server that the authentication failed and therefore the security event was generated.

Audit policies can be set for both the success and failure events. It might seem odd to track successful security events, but they can be indicators of someone inappropriately accessing network resources or making unauthorized changes. Failure events are important to track for obvious reasons. They can show internal network users who might be randomly browsing network resources in order to see what they can get into, as well as show any attempts to log in or access network resources from unauthorized sources. Failure events can often form patterns of behavior that point out trouble spots or potentially troublemaking for users on the network.

Designing an Audit Policy

If you take away only one thing from this book, it should be the importance of effective planning before just diving in and implementing some feature of Windows 2000. The same holds true for designing an audit policy. There are several considerations to take into account as you are planning your strategy. In addition to the design guidelines presented in the next section, you will want to consider the resource usage of the logging. At first glance it might seem like a good idea to just log everything. However, log files take up disk space and can quickly grow unmanageable. Additionally, you still have to sort through all of the logs, which can be burdensome if there is too much information. Auditing also consumes system resources such as processor time and memory, which can increase the load on a server.

Guidelines for Designing an Audit Policy

Since auditing does increase the load on a system as security events are checked and logged upon occurrence, it is disabled by default. It is important to carefully plan what systems you want to enable logging on, and especially what specific types of events to log. Windows 2000 will allow you to log the success and/or failure of the following types of events:

- *Account logon events*—Logons and logoffs by user accounts
- *Logon events*—Logons and logoffs to a system, different from Account Logon events
- *Account management*—Changes to user accounts and groups
- *Directory Service access*—Access to Active Directory resources
- *Object access*—Access to network resources, such as shared folders and printers
- *Policy change*—Changes made to policy settings, typically used to ensure that unauthorized administrative changes are not being made
- *Privilege use*—The use of user rights that have been granted; ensures the tracking of a user who is simply poking around the network looking at what she can get into.
- *Process tracking*—Process creation, execution, and deletion. Whenever a program performs an action, a process event would be logged. Process tracking is very resource intensive and will generate a significant number of events. Logging of this item should be done only for a short time to fulfill a specific purpose.
- *System events*—System events that take place on a workstation or server, such as a user logging on or off, or restarting the computer.

As we have mentioned, you can audit both successes and failures for the above events. You can log either or, both, or neither. You should determine what exactly your goal in auditing will be. Are you trying to see what resources are the most popular on your network, thereby establishing usage patterns?

Success events will provide you with this type of information. Are you trying to ensure that if someone breaks into your systems you'll know about the attempt and whether or not they were successful? Failure events are very good at showing this type of information.

There are other questions that must be considered as you plan your audit policy. Some of them are:

- Whom am I auditing?
- How often will I be able to review the security logs?
- Is my proposed audit policy both useful and manageable?
- Will I need to archive old events or simply overwrite them?

WHOM AM I AUDITING?

Is your goal to audit resource usage by everyone or just a selection of users? If it is everyone, apply the policy to the Everyone group rather than to just Domain Users. In doing so, events will be generated whenever anyone connects to a resource, not just an authenticated user.

HOW OFTEN WILL I BE ABLE TO REVIEW THE SECURITY LOGS?

While the more time you can spend on security the better, you should take a realistic look at the amount of time you will be able to spend. Understanding time constraints will have a bearing on how much information you should log. If you log much more information than you can reasonably go through, the loss of an important security event among many not-so-important events becomes more likely.

IS MY PROPOSED AUDIT POLICY BOTH USEFUL AND MANAGEABLE?

This question goes hand-in-hand with the previous one. As mentioned, initially it seems like a great idea to just log everything. After all, if you log every event, you will capture any significant security event, right? While true in theory, in practice information glut can be almost as bad as no information at all. Not only is it difficult to navigate through security logs full of irrelevant information, but recording all of that information increases the overhead on the server. Audit policies should be used on important network resources, and care needs to be taken to ensure that the events being logged will provide you with useful information about network usage. There's no sense in auditing for events that have little relevance to your environment, or that will make it more likely that you will miss an important event hidden in the clutter.

WILL I NEED TO ARCHIVE OLD EVENTS OR SIMPLY OVERWRITE THEM?

Later in this chapter we will discuss managing event logs, but for now let's point out that the log files are preallocated disk space that can fill up. When a log fills up, it can either start overwriting the oldest events in the log or stop logging events until an administrator intervenes. The administrator can choose to archive event logs to a separate file and purge the existing logs, or simply delete old events.

Archiving logs gives the administrator the ability to do trend analysis— that is, look at network usage patterns over time to see what changes, if any, have occurred.

Applying an Audit Policy

Now that we have planned an audit policy, and know what resources we are going to audit and why, we are ready to implement the policy. In this section we will get our hands dirty with the following topics:

- Configuring Auditing
- Setting an Audit Policy
- Auditing Data Access

The section on auditing data access will include auditing files, folders, Active Directory objects, and printers. After completing this section we will be able to audit any Windows 2000 resource on our network.

Configuring Auditing

How we configure auditing is dependent on the role of the Windows 2000 system we are configuring. That means that auditing is configured differently, depending on what type of system we are configuring it on.

The types of systems can be divided into two camps, domain controllers and non-domain controllers. Non-domain controllers include both member servers and Windows 2000 Professional workstations.

- *Domain Controllers*—For domain controllers, an audit policy that is created on one applies to all domain controllers in the domain. So configuring an audit policy for events that take place on domain controllers (such as the access of Active Directory objects) is done through Group Policy.

- *NonDomain Controllers*—For nondomain controllers, which can be either standalone servers, member servers, or Windows 2000 Professional workstations, audit policies must be created on each individual machine. The policies created on a nondomain controller do not apply to any system other than the one that has auditing configured, so if you want to audit events on multiple machines you will need to configure them individually.

- It is important to note that the differences in how auditing is configured on a Windows 2000 system depending on whether or not it is a domain controller, do not affect the types of events that can be configured. In other words, the type of events that you can choose to audit are the same on domain controllers and nondomain controllers. To illustrate this, Figure 25.1 is taken

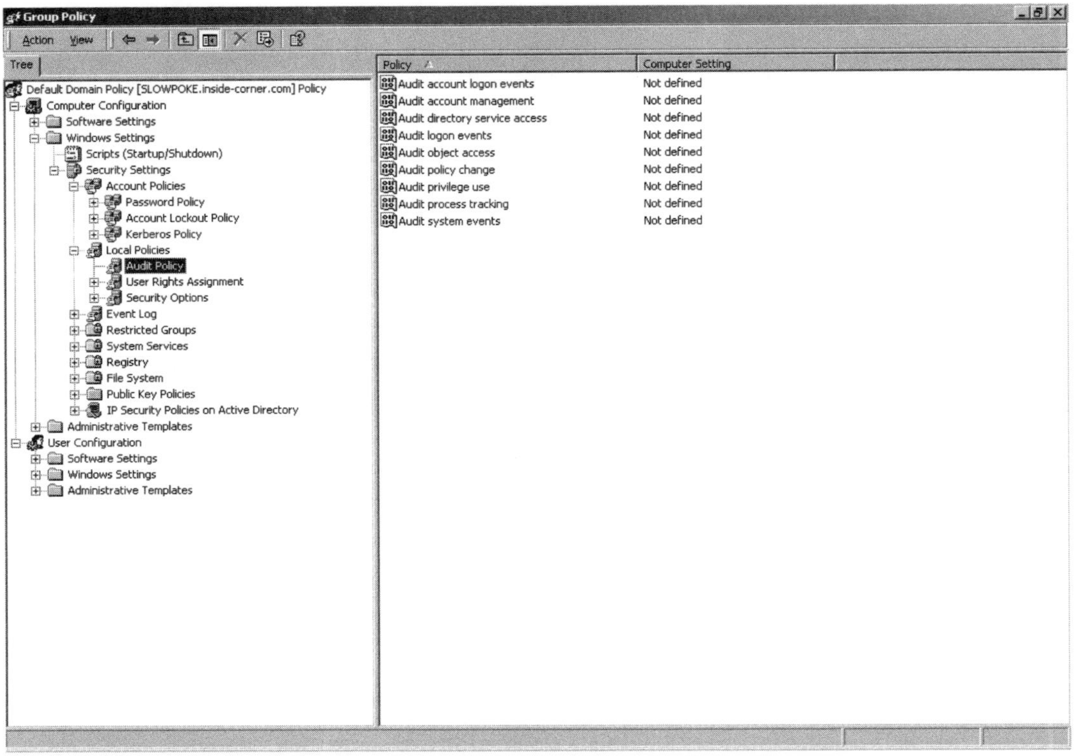

Figure 25–1   *The types of events that can be configured on a Windows 2000 domain controller.*

from a Windows 2000 domain controller and Figure 25.2 from a Windows 2000 Professional workstation that is a member of the same Active Directory domain.

AUDITING REQUIREMENTS

There are a couple of requirements to meet in order to be able to configure an audit policy on a system. The first is that the resources to be audited, such as files and folders, must be located on an NTFS partition. The FAT file system does not support directory- and file-level security like NTFS.

The second requirement is permissions. If you are logged in as an administrator, there should not be a problem, because by default the Administrators group is granted the necessary permissions for auditing. However, if you are using a regular user account on a domain controller, your account must be a member of the Group Policy Creator Owners group, as shown in Figure 25.3.

By default, the administrators group is a member of Group Policy Creator Owners. That means that any user account belonging to the administrators

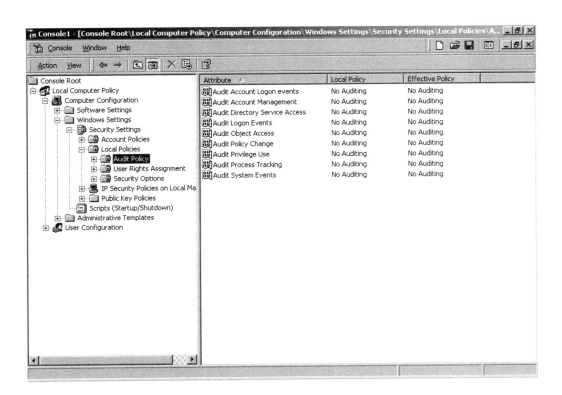

Figure 25–2

The types of events that can be configured on a Windows 2000 Professional workstation.

group will automatically have the requisite permissions. On nondomain controllers, such as our Windows 2000 Professional system from Figure 25.2, there is no Group Policy Creator Owners group. To make audit policy changes on these machines you must simply be a member of the local Administrators group.

SETTING UP AUDITING

Setting up auditing is a simple two-step process as follows:

1. Enable auditing of types of events through the appropriate Group Policy MMC snap-in. This enables auditing, but does not start tracking specific events.
2. Enable auditing of specific events in Windows 2000. Here is where you specify what files, folders, printers, etc., you want to track events for. Once this step is taken, Windows 2000 will start tracking events for the audited resources and logging them for your later viewing.

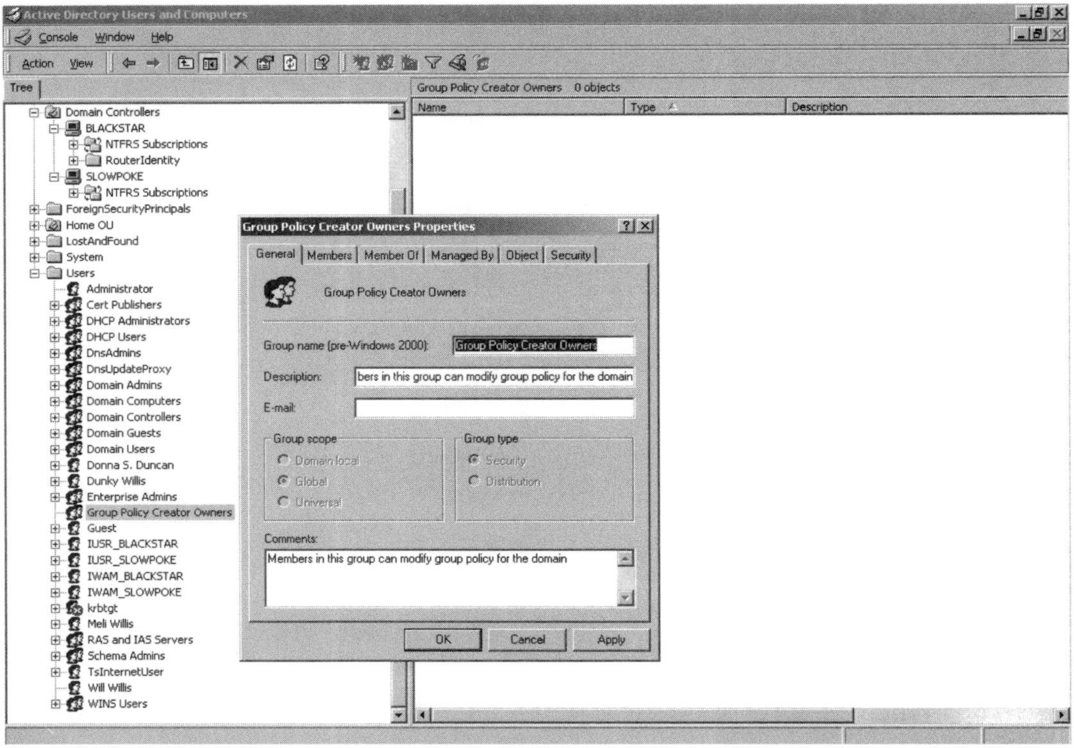

Figure 25–3

A user must be a member of the Group Policy Creator Owners group in order to make changes to audit policies.

Setting an Audit Policy

Setting an audit policy, as discussed previously, is a two-step process. The first step is enabling the different types of events to be audited. We know from earlier in the chapter that Windows 2000 can track the following types of events:

- Account Logon Events
- Account Management
- Directory Service Access
- Logon Events
- Object Access
- Policy Change
- Privilege User
- Process Tracking
- System Events

For each type of event that can be audited you can choose whether to audit successes, failures, or both. On Domain Controllers, audit policies are created either through the Domain Controller Security Policy MMC snap-in, accessible through the Administrative Tools program group shown in Figure 25.4, or through Group Policy in Active Directory Users and Computers by viewing the properties of the Domain Controllers container, clicking on the Group Policy

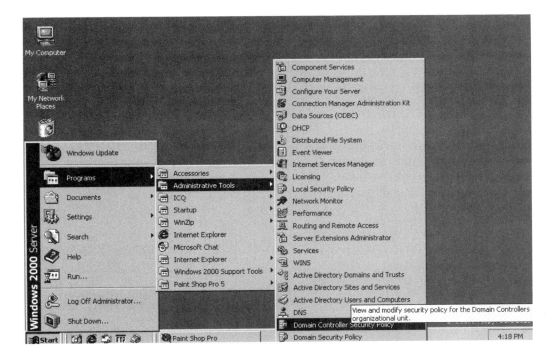

Figure 25–4   *Starting the Domain Controller Security Policy MMC.*

tab, and clicking Edit.

As you can see in Figure 25.5, even though the title bar says Group Policy instead of Domain Controller Security Policy, shown in Figure 25.6, both consoles allow you to get to Security Settings\Local Policies\Audit Policy, which is where auditing is enabled.

Enabling auditing on a nondomain controller is largely the same as on a domain controller. However, getting to the Group Policy snap-in takes a little effort. Windows 2000 does not make the Group Policy snap-in readily available in the form of an icon through Administrative Tools or through the Computer Management MMC. You can create an MMC Console for yourself so that you can configure audit settings, as follows:

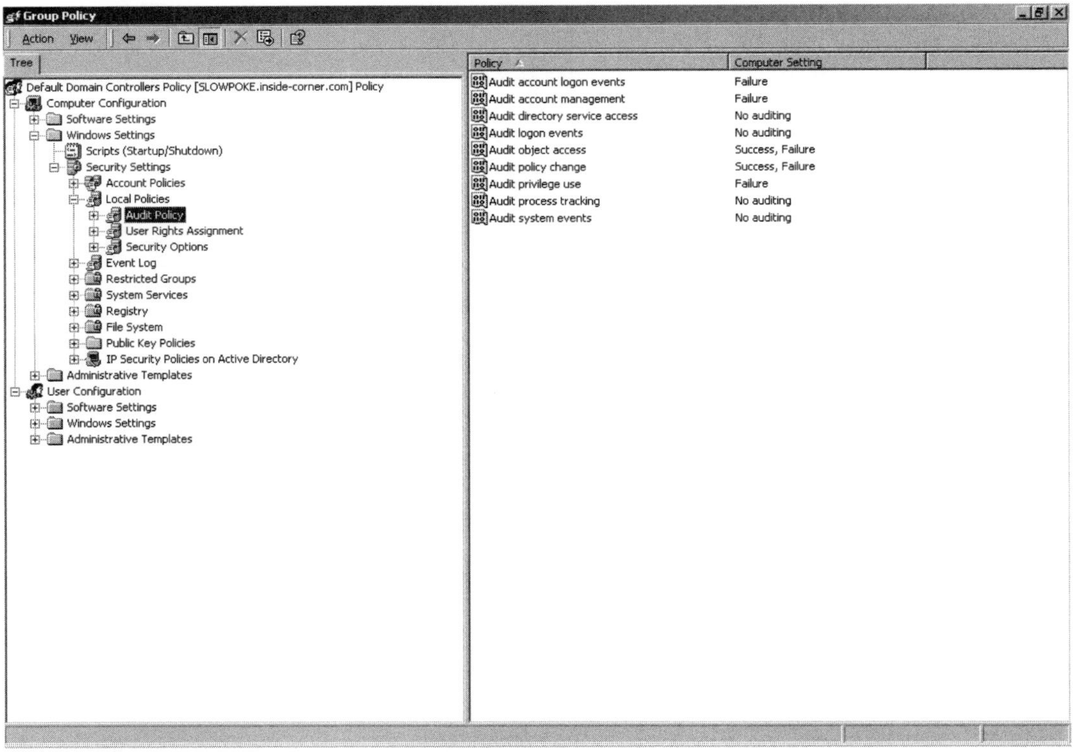

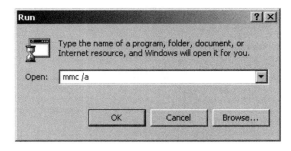

Figure 25-5   *The Group Policy MMC snap-in allows you to configure audit policy settings.*

1. Click Start->Run and type: *mmc /a,* as shown in Figure 25.7.

Figure 25-6   *Launching a new, empty MMC console.*

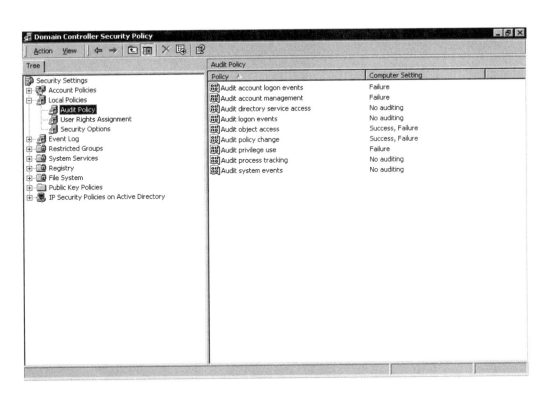

Figure 25-7

Like the Group Policy MMC, the Domain Controller Security Policy MMC allows you to configure audit policy settings.

2. When the new console opens up, click the Console menu and select Add/ Remove Snap-in, as shown in Figure 25.8.
3. Next, the window shown in Figure 25.9 will appear. Note that it is currently blank. Click Add to bring up the list of available snap-ins.
4. In Figure 25.10 you can see the list of available snap-ins on your Windows 2000 system. Scroll down and select the Group Policy snap-in and click Add.
5. When you add the Group Policy snap-in, a dialog shown in Figure 25.11 will be displayed. This is informing you that you can store Group Policy Objects on a local computer (the default) or within Active Directory. Click Finish.
6. When you click Finish, Windows 2000 will return you to the Add/Remove Snap-in dialog. Notice in Figure 25.12 that there is now a snap-in for Local Computer Policy listed, whereas previously the list was empty. At this point you could either repeat steps 3 and 4 to add additional snap-ins to your console, or click OK to finish. For our purposes, click OK.

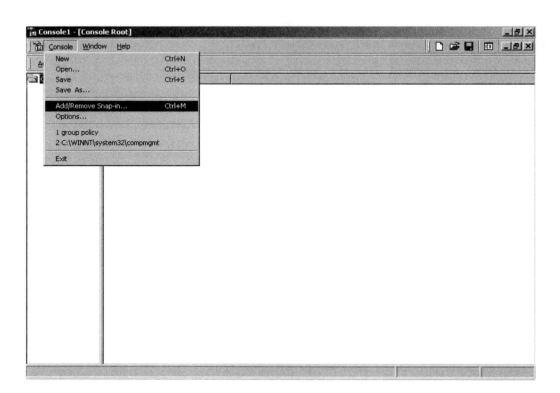

Figure 25–8   *Selecting the Add/Remove Snap-in option to bring in the Group*
Policy snap-in.

7. Now we have our Local Computer Policy snap-in, shown in Figure 25.13. You will probably want to save the console so you won't have to repeat this process every time you want to make changes or review settings. Simply click the Console menu and Save As to save the console.

By default, each type of event is configured for No Auditing. To enable auditing, either double-click the specific event type or highlight the event and select Security from the Action menu of the console. The dialog shown in Figure 25.14 will appear.

Auditing Data Access

We have completed step one and enabled auditing for different types of events, but even with that done, Windows 2000 has nothing specific to audit—in other words, nothing to *do*. So now we must move to step two, specifying specific objects to be audited. In this section we will discuss auditing of:

• Files and Folders

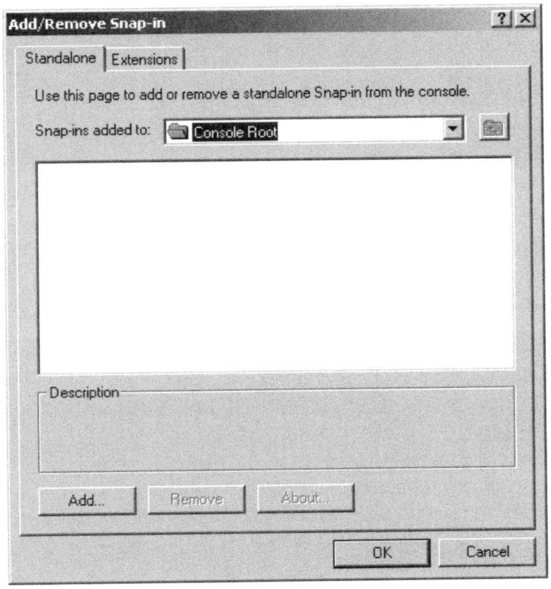

Figure 25–9 *The Add/Remove Snap-in page shows what snap-ins will be added to or removed from the current console.*

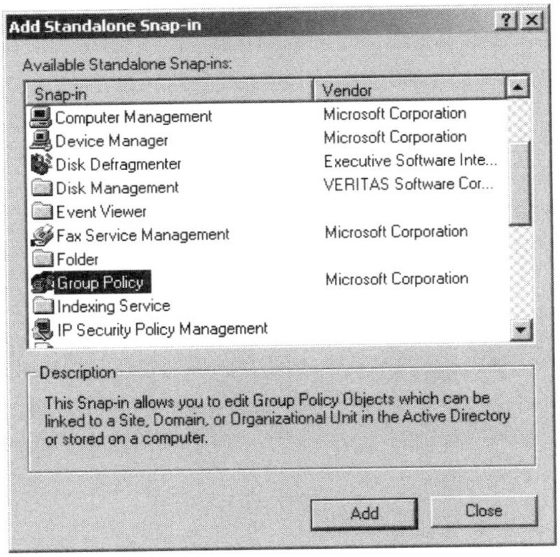

Figure 25–10 *Selecting the Group Policy snap-in to add to our current MMC console.*

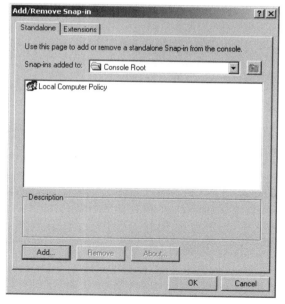

Figure 25–11 *Determining whether Group Policy Objects should be stored on a local computer or within Active Directory.*

Figure 25–12 *The Local Computer Policy snap-in now appears in our list of snap-ins to be added to the current console.*

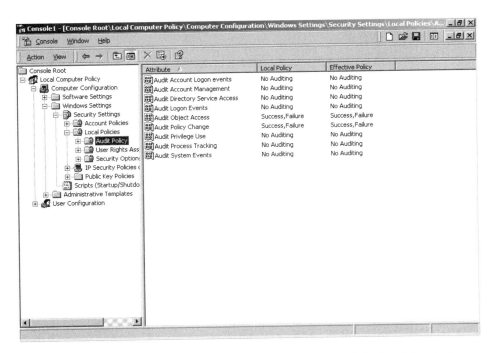

Figure 25-13

A custom MMC console with the addition of the Local Computer Policy snap-in.

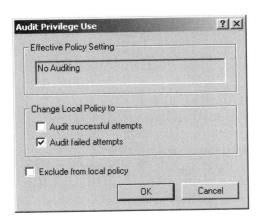

Figure 25-14

The Audit dialog where you can change the local policy settings.

- Active Directory Objects
- Printers

AUDITING FILES AND FOLDERS

For many companies, the security of network files is an important issue. Windows 2000 responds to those concerns by allowing you to audit specific files on a system. In order to audit files, the Audit Object Access policy setting must have already been configured. If object access is being audited, you can enable auditing of a specific file by right-clicking on it in My Computer or Windows Explorer, and clicking Properties. When the properties of the file appear, click the Security tab, as shown in Figure 25.15.

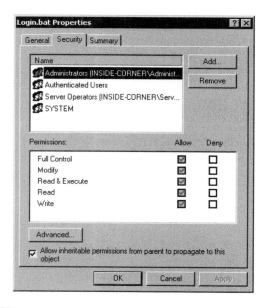

Figure 25–15   *The security properties of a* login.bat *file.*

Click the Advanced tab to see the Access Control Settings for the file. As you can see in Figure 25.16, by default the auditing entries are blank. You will have to click the Add button to add entries to the list. When you click Add, you will see the dialog shown in Figure 25.17, where you select the user, computer, or group you want to audit.

After selecting someone to audit, in this example the Guests group, you will see a window similar to that in Figure 25.18.

As you can see, there are many settings to configure with regard to this one specific file. Since our example is auditing the Guest group, it makes sense to enable all of the failure events to ensure that any failed attempt by someone in the Guests group to manipulate this file is logged. With the successful access section we have selected to log whenever the file is written, modified, or exe-

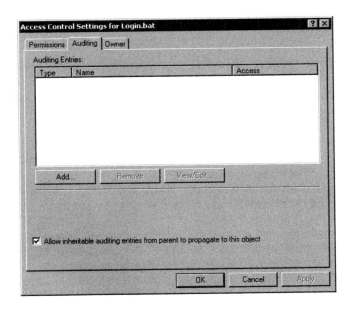

Figure 25-16   *Access Control Settings for* login.bat.

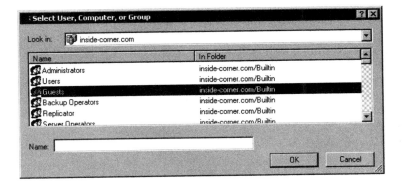

Figure 25-17   *Selecting a user, computer, or group to audit.*

cuted by the Guests group, but we do not care if the file is read successfully. What settings you choose will depend on the file that is being audited and what group you are auditing. For example, if we were auditing the Authenticated Users group, we would not want to audit the successful execution of the file. The reason is that *login.bat* is a login script, so it executes whenever a user logs into the domain. You would have a security log full of meaningless events,

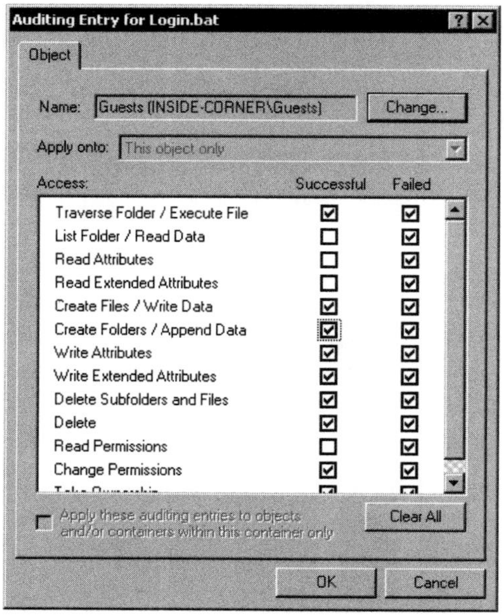

Figure 25-18

Configuring audit settings for the Guest group on the login.bat
file.

that a user successfully logged in and executed *login.bat*. So plan carefully
what types of access are important to audit and what are not.

After configuring the success and failure events for file auditing, click OK.
Now you see in Figure 25.19 that auditing entries are listed with the types of
access that are to be audited. Click OK to return to file properties and click OK
again to save the settings.

The process is identical for configuring auditing on folders. When you
configure auditing for a folder, the settings apply to all files in that folder unless
you override them by configuring individual files separately within the folder.

AUDITING ACTIVE DIRECTORY OBJECTS

Configuring auditing on Active Directory objects is very similar to configuring
it for files and folders. The easiest way is through the Active Directory Users and
Computers snap-in, which can be launched on a domain controller though the
Administrative Tools program group.

1. On the View menu of the console, select Advanced Features (if there is not
   already a check mark by it).
2. Right-click the Active Directory object you want to set auditing for, such as
   the Users container, and click Properties.
3. Click the Auditing tab.

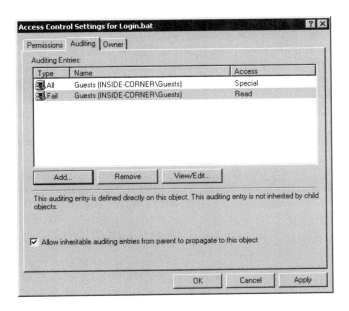

Figure 25-19   *Audit entries shown for Guest access to* Login.bat.

4. Click Add.
5. Select the user, computer, or group you want to audit and click OK.
6. Configure the audit settings for the Active Directory object. Figure 25-20 illustrates an example of configuring auditing on the Users object for access by the Guests group.

Some of the key Active Directory object events are as follows:
- *Full Control*—Any type of action performed on the object
- *List Contents*—Viewing the contents/objects within an object that is being audited.
- *Read All Properties*—Viewing any property of the audited object
- *Write All Properties*—Modifying any properties of the audited object
- *Delete*—Deleting any objects within the audited object
- *Read Permissions*—Viewing the permissions of an audited object
- *Modify Permissions*—Changing the permissions of an audited object
- *Modify Owner*—Changing the owner of an audited object

If you scroll through the list on your computer of available configuration options, you will see many more attributes than what is listed above. However, those are the major events to consider. The other options exist to provide a higher level of granularity for circumstances where the basic settings are not specific enough. In most cases, sticking with configuring the settings above will be adequate.

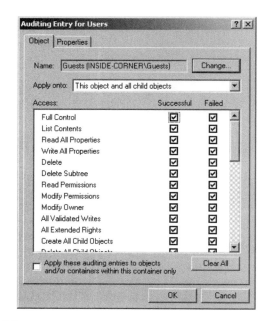

Figure 25–20
Configuring auditing on the Users object for access by the Guests group.

AUDITING PRINTERS

Auditing printers is basically the same as the auditing we have done up to this point. Open the Printers folder, right-click on the printer you want to configure, and select Properties. Click the security tab and click Advanced, and then click the Auditing tab. Click Add and select the user, computer, or group you want to audit, and click OK. You will see a dialog similar to that in Figure 25.21.

The settings that can be configured for printer auditing include:

- *Print*—The obvious, printing a file on the printer
- *Manage Printers*—Things like changing print settings, pausing or resuming a printer, sharing or unsharing a printer
- *Manage Documents*—Managing documents includes changing job settings, pausing or resuming a job, or purging documents from the queue
- *Read Permissions*—Viewing a printer's properties
- *Change Permissions*—Modifying a printer's properties
- *Take Ownership*—Taking ownership of a printer

Printer auditing is probably not something many people think of when it comes to security policies. In most cases it is not necessary to audit printers; however, some departments have printers that print sensitive documents on a regular basis. In those cases, it is important to ensure that only authorized users

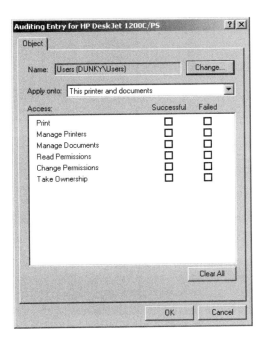

Figure 25–21   *Configuring audit settings for a printer.*

are able to manage documents or printer settings. As always, careful planning of the security needs for your organization will dictate whether or not you need to audit printers or any other resources.

The Windows 2000 Event Viewer

All of this auditing is great, but how do you view the results of the logging you have set up Windows 2000 to do? The answer lies in the Event Viewer, a Windows 2000 utility that allows you to view a variety of logs and events. In this section, we'll discuss the following topics related to the Event Viewer.

- Understanding Logs
- Using the Security Log
- Managing Logs
- Archiving Logs

Understanding Logs

By default in Windows 2000, certain types of events are logged automatically. Other types of events, specifically security-related events, are not logged unless the administrator enables auditing. So, if we were to look at the security log before we went through the steps in the preceding sections, we would find the log to be empty. The Event Viewer is the GUI tool that lets you look at the contents of the log files, because the logs are not text files that can be viewed directly with Notepad or some other text viewer.

The Event Viewer can be accessed through the Administrative Tools program group on the Start menu. When you open the Event Viewer, there will be at least three log files listed, as summarized in Table 25.1.

Table 25.1	Log File Descriptions
Log	**Description**
Application	The Application Log contains information, warnings, and errors about programs and services running on the system. The developers of the individual programs specify the events that are recorded.
Security	The Security Log contains information about the success and failure of audited events. The events you choose to audit affect what information is recorded in this log.
System	The System Log contains information, warnings, and errors generated from Windows 2000 itself. Such information may include system services that failed to start at boot, or a system process such as replication that could not contact another system. The system events that Windows 2000 records have been hard-coded by the developers at Microsoft.

We said that there would be *at least* three logs listed. Those listed above will be on every system, from Windows 2000 Professional through Windows 2000 Datacenter Server. However, in many instances you will have more than three logs listed. Figure 25.22, for example, shows a Windows 2000 Server system that is an Active Directory domain controller and is running the DNS Server service. Notice that because of its additional roles there are three additional logs listed for Directory Service, DNS Server, and File Replication Service.

Using the Security Log

In this chapter the security log is our primary focus, because it relates to the auditing we have previously configured. Once you have opened the Event Viewer, click on the Security Log icon on the left side of the window. If you have enabled auditing and generated some security events, they will be listed. In our example security log from Figure 25.22, we notice there are many

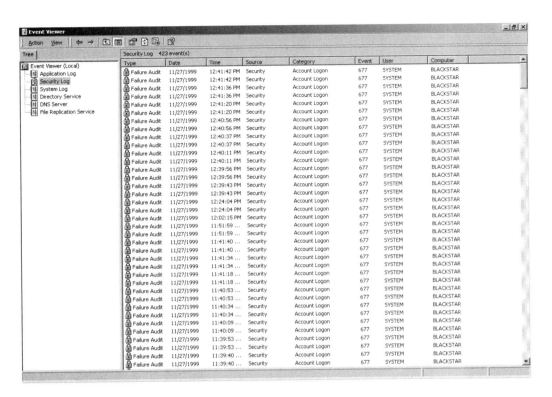

Figure 25–22

The Event Viewer on a Windows 2000 domain controller that is running the DNS Server service adds additional logs to the listing.

repeated failure audits. If we double-click on one of the events, Windows 2000 will give us more detail, such as in Figure 25.23.

Examining the detail, we see the date and time that the event occurred, an important detail for a security event. The type is failure, so we know it was a failed audit rather than a successful audit. For the security log the source will always be security, and we see that the category is Account Logon. From this detail we know that we had a failed account logon event take place at a given date and time. The user account used to attempt the action was the system account, and we are told the computer where the action was attempted. The description provides additional information about what specifically was being attempted when the failed audit occurred. In our example, the system account was attempting to log on to the LDAP service and failed. The Event ID and Failure Code can be useful if you need to contact Microsoft's technical support for assistance, and often you can search the TechNet knowledge base on those codes and find additional information about the origin of the problem.

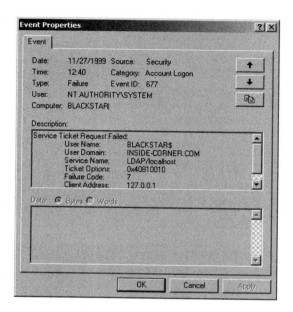

Figure 25–23 *Double-clicking on an event will bring up additional information regarding that event.*

Looking at our security log as a whole, we notice the same error repeated over and over at regular intervals. Given that the errors are at regular intervals and not random, we would suspect a system configuration problem rather than a security problem in the sense of someone trying to break in. Further investigation on this system revealed just that, a configuration problem. Once resolved, the account logon errors ceased.

LOCATING SIGNIFICANT EVENTS

By default, when you launch the Event Viewer, all events are displayed. In our example where we have a lot of repeating events, which we know are meaningless as far as security monitoring goes, we might want to filter out the clutter or search for specific events. To do this we use the Filter and/or Find commands, both available from the View menu on the Event Viewer console. Figures 25.24 and 25.25 show examples of the Filter and Find dialogs, respectively.

To filter or find, simply fill in the blanks with the information you want as your criteria, such as an event ID or a user name. In the case of the find command, Events that match the criteria are displayed and you can navigate forward and back through the results. For the Filter command, only the events that match the filter are displayed in the main events window. So, while the

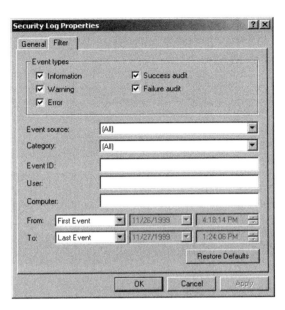

Figure 25-24

The Filter window of the Event Viewer is used to filter the view to show only the events you want to see.

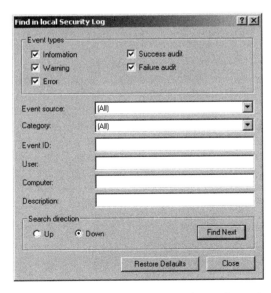

Figure 25-25

The Find window of the Event Viewer is used to find specific events in the log.

two tools are similar, they have slightly different purposes and present the results in different ways.

Managing Logs

Over time, log files will grow and eventually fill up to a maximum size. What happens when the log reaches the maximum size, however, can be configured. Figure 25.26 shows the properties of the security log with the default settings.

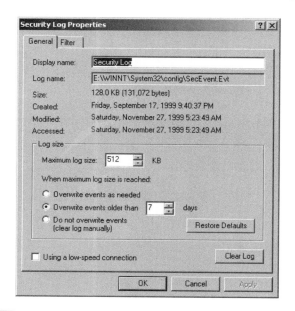

Figure 25-26 *The default properties of the security log.*

Viewing the properties, we see that the maximum log size by default is 512 KB, and that Windows 2000 will overwrite security events older than 7 days, once the log reaches its maximum size. The log file size can be decreased or increased, with the valid range being from 64 KB to 4 GB. In most cases, 512 KB is sufficient. However, when Windows 2000 does reach the maximum log size, you have these choices:

• *Overwrite Events as Needed*—Windows 2000 will simply start overwriting the oldest events in the log. The advantage of this is that it does not require any kind of administrator intervention when the log reaches its maximum. The disadvantage is that this option makes it difficult to analyze event trends over time, since old events are constantly being replaced by newer events.

• *Overwrite Events Older than X Days*—Windows 2000 will overwrite events older than the number of days you specify, which by default is 7 days.

This option has the same advantages and disadvantages as overwriting events as needed, with the exception that if the log reaches its maximum size and there are no events older than the days specified, logging will stop and administrator intervention will be required.

- *Do Not Overwrite Events (Clear Log Manually)*—This option provides the best choice for being able to track event trends over time. However, when the log fills to the maximum, logging will stop until an administrator intervenes. This option requires administrator maintenance periodically in the form of archiving, discussed next.

Archiving Events

Archiving security logs allows you to save a history of the events for trend analysis. In order to archive a log file, you click the Save Log File As command from the Action menu on the Event Viewer Console.

As a general practice, I like to name my archive files with the dates the log encompasses, as well as the type of log, such as *SEC091199-112999.evt*. That way, if I want to review past log files at a later date, I will know at a glance the dates each saved log file includes. The file name above would refer to a security log that spanned Sept. 11, 1999 through Nov. 29, 1999.

Once you have saved the log file, you can clear the events in the current log through the Action menu. Windows 2000 will generate an event into a new log that shows that the log has been cleared. That is a security measure, so that no one can simply clear a log to cover their tracks without you as the administrator knowing the log was cleared.

To view an archived log file, select Open Log File from the Action menu. Select the log file you want to open and choose the type of log, as in Figure 25.27.

The reason for specifying the type of log in the log file, as discussed in the previous tip, is that, as you can see in the figure, Windows 2000 requires us to specify what type of log we are opening. Once you have archived many logs, it becomes difficult to know just by looking what the saved file actually is. Therefore, it is important to use a standard naming convention, which includes the type of log and the dates the log includes.

Chapter Summary

In this chapter we learned about auditing, starting with what auditing is and moving into guidelines for designing an audit policy. Once we had discussed guidelines for auditing, and emphasized that proper planning was important, since just auditing everything was not a good idea, we started configuring and applying an audit policy to our network. We discussed the differences between

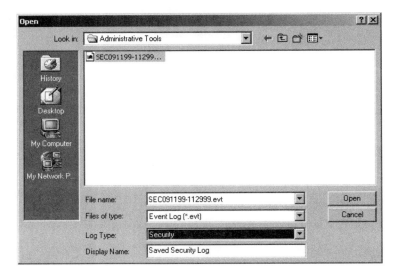

Figure 25–27   *Opening an archived log file*

audit policies on domain controllers and nondomain controllers, and the auditing of specific objects like files and folders, Active Directory objects, and Printers.

After configuring and implementing our audit policies, we discussed the Event Viewer and how to view, manage, and archive our event logs. At this point, you should feel comfortable developing an audit policy for your own network and managing the results of your audit policy through the Event Viewer. In the next chapter we will continue our discussion of network security by moving into monitoring network resources.

Monitoring Network Resources

*A*s we just learned, auditing access to network resources is nice …but what if we want to view what is happening on our network in real time? The major limitation of auditing is that it will only tell you what has happened after the fact, you have little way to know what resources are currently in use. Consider a case where an unauthorized person copied files from a confidential folder on a server. Auditing would tell you the files were copied and when, but network monitoring would show you that a folder was being accessed inappropriately at the time it was occurring. Fortunately, there are utilities that provide a real-time view of your network. In this chapter, we will discuss the following topics related to monitoring network resources:

- Overview of Monitoring Network Resources
- Monitoring Access to Shared Folders
- Monitoring Network Users

26.1 Overview of Monitoring Network Resources

In Windows NT version prior to Windows 2000, monitoring access to network resources was accomplished primarily through the Server Manager administrative utility. In Windows 2000, however, the functionality of Server Manager has been absorbed into other MMC snap-ins. For monitoring network resources, we now have the Shared Folders snap-in, which will also allow you to send administrative alerts to users. Before we get into using the Shared Folders snap-in, though, it will be helpful to have an understanding of why we should monitor network resources in real time and what the requirements are to monitor network resources.

Why Monitor Network Resources?

The Shared Folders snap-in allows you to monitor network resources on either a local computer or a remote system. There are several reasons why we would want to monitor network resources using the Shared Folders snap-in, which are listed below.

- *Preventive vs. Reactive Administration*—Auditing, as we discussed in the previous chapter, only allows you to determine what resources were accessed *after the fact*. This is an important consideration. While auditing is important, it will only allow you to react to a security problem that has already taken place, which can potentially be too late. Monitoring network resources in real time through Shared Folders allows you to discover problems as they might be occurring, and to cut them off before damage is done.
- *Security*—Along the lines of preventive administration, the Shared Folders snap-in enables the administrator to ensure that resources are being accessed appropriately.
- *Capacity Planning*—By seeing what resources are commonly used and by what users, the administrator is able to plan for future growth. Heavily used resources can be replicated or otherwise adjusted to provide more efficient access to users.
- *Maintenance*—At times you might need to make a resource unavailable, possibly to move it to a different drive or server, or to change permissions. The Shared Folders snap-in allows you to see if a resource is in use, and if it is, you can send an administrative alert to the users currently using the resource. You can also forcibly disconnect a user from a resource through this utility.

Requirements Before Monitoring Network Resources

For obvious reasons, not everyone is able to monitor network resources with the Shared Folders snap-in. To monitor computers across an Active Directory domain, the user account attempting to perform the monitoring by default must be a member of the Administrators or Server Operators group. However, another possibility is to utilize the granularity Windows 2000 offers when configuring user accounts. A specific user account can be given only the requisite permissions to use the Shared Folders utility. Assigning specific permissions to user accounts was discussed previously in the chapter on administering user accounts.

For Windows 2000 Professional workstations, a user belonging to the local Power Users group can also use the Shared Folders snap-in. However, their ability to monitor access to network resources will be restricted to the local machine. In other words, they cannot monitor a remote machine.

Monitoring Access to Shared Folders

One of the most common monitoring tasks is monitoring access to shared folders. Using the Shares folder of the Shared Folders snap-in provides a view of the shared folders on a system and how many times they are currently being accessed. This information is useful in capacity planning and in seeing how your server is being used. Figure 26.1 shows the Computer Management administrative tool, which contains the Shared Folders snap-in.

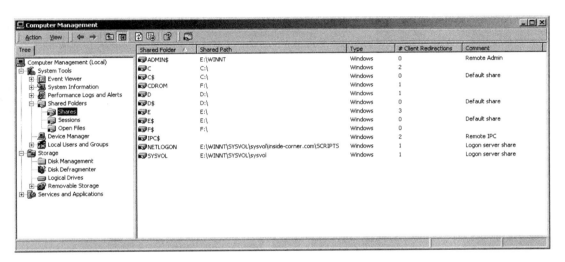

Figure 26-1   *The Shared Folders snap-in allows the administrator to see what folders are being accessed.*

If you notice, within the Shared Folders snap-in portion of Computer Management there are three different categories. They are Shares, Sessions, and Open Files. We will discuss all of them in this chapter, starting with Shares.

Shared Folders

From Figure 26.1, we saw the list of folders shared on this server and the number of times they have been accessed. We can tell the number of times the folder has been accessed under the heading of "# Client Redirections." The fields that make up the Shares detail are as follows:

- *Shared Folder*—the name by which the folder was shared.
- *Shared Path*—The physical path on the system to the shared folder. This is the actual location of the folder on a hard drive.
- *Type*—This displays the type of system that shared the folder, for example Windows, NetWare, or Macintosh.

- *# Client Redirections*—The number of current connections to a shared folder.

- *Comment*—A description of the folder that was given at the time the folder was shared. Windows 2000 has default comments to go along with the default shared folders. If you do not supply a comment when you share a folder, the comment field will appear blank.

It is important to note that this screen is not dynamic; it is a snapshot in time of the current activity. You will need to refresh the view by clicking Refresh from the Action menu or by pressing the <F5> function key in order to get the most current view.

USER LIMITS

At times it may be desirable to limit the number of users that can simultaneously access a shared folder. The folder could be located on a server across a slow WAN connection and you don't want too much bandwidth used by users accessing a particular share. Or, the shared folder might be on an underpowered server that can handle only a certain amount of users. Or, it might be on a server that performs a more critical function such as running a SQL Server database, in which case you would not want so many users accessing files in the shared folder simultaneously that it would bog down users working with the SQL Server. All of these are potential reasons to impose a limit on the number of users who can access a shared folder at the same time.

By default, Windows 2000 (like Windows NT before it) does not limit the amount of simultaneous connections to a shared resource. The only caveat to this statement is Windows 2000 Professional, which like Windows NT Workstation has an operating-system-imposed limit of 10 simultaneous connections to a system. However, even on a Windows 2000 Professional system, if you look at the properties of a shared folder it will say "Maximum Allowed" by default and not identify a specific number. Figure 26.2 shows the properties of a shared folder, which is accessed by right-clicking on the shared folder name in the Shares detail pane and clicking Properties.

If you want to specify a maximum number of users who can access a shared folder, click the Allow radio button and either type in the number of users you want or click the up and down arrows to specify the number of users. Once you select the number of users you'd like, click OK to finalize the settings.

MODIFYING PERMISSIONS

When you initially share a folder, you have the opportunity to assign access permissions to it. By default, Windows 2000 gives the Everyone group full control of a folder. Full control means just that; they can read, write, change, and delete files within the folder. Figure 26.3 shows the Share Permissions of a shared folder, accessible through the properties of the shared folder.

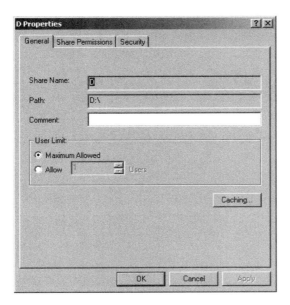

Figure 26–2

You can impose a user limit on shared folders through the folder's properties.

Figure 26–3

The Share Permissions of a shared folder show the level of access different users and groups have.

You use the Share Permissions property page to add or remove users, groups, or computers to the permissions list, or to simply view the current settings. In most cases, Everyone having full control to a shared folder is not appropriate. So, you will want to modify the default permissions when you share a folder.

In addition to being able to configure the share permissions, you can also review and modify the NTFS permissions of the physical folder on the hard drive (not the share mapping). This is done under the Security properties page, as shown in Figure 26.4.

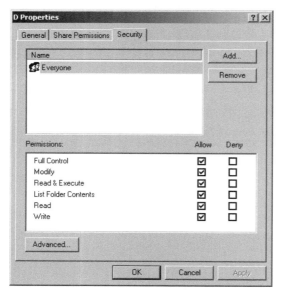

Figure 26–4 *The Security properties page allows an administrator to configure the NTFS permissions for a folder.*

SHARING FOLDERS

Besides monitoring shared folders, the Shared Folders snap-in can also be used to create new shares. In fact, it is the only way in Windows 2000 to create a share on a remote system without having to be physically sitting at that machine. In this section we will go through the process of sharing a folder with this snap-in.

1. First, right-click on a blank part of the Shares window and click New File Share. Alternatively, click the Action menu and then New File Share.

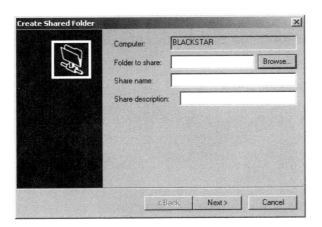

Figure 26–5

Creating a new shared folder through the Shared Folders snap-in.

2. You will see the dialog shown in Figure 26.5. Type the path to the folder you want to share, or click Browse to search for it. For practice, click Browse, which will bring up the dialog shown in Figure 26.6.

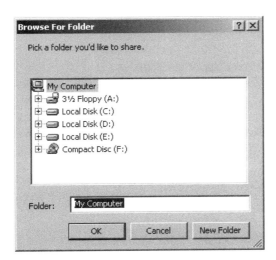

Figure 26–6

Browsing for the folder you wish to share.

3. Select the folder you want to share and click OK. You will be returned to the window shown in Figure 26.5, which will now show the name of the folder to share. Fill in the rest of the information, similar to that in Figure 26.7, and click Next.

Figure 26-7   *Completing the information necessary to share a folder.*

4. Next we define the security settings we want the folder to have. By default, as we have said, Windows 2000 will assign full control to all users (the Everyone group). A very nice feature of Windows 2000 as compared to Windows NT 4.0 is the addition of some typical security settings that you can select. In NT 4.0 you had to go through the process of changing the permissions of the Everyone group and then adding users or groups with the permissions you wanted them to have—a cumbersome system if you were sharing multiple folders at a single sitting. You can customize the settings to whatever granularity you would like by clicking the "Customize share and folder permissions" radio button and then clicking the Custom button. Once you have configured the permissions you want for your shared folder, similar to that in Figure 26.8, click Finish.

5. Windows 2000 will ask you if you want to create another shared folder, as shown in Figure 26.9. If you want to share another folder, click Yes, and the wizard will restart. Otherwise, click No to exit back to the Computer Management Console.

Monitoring Access to Open Files

Another feature of the Shared Folders MMC snap-in is the ability to view files that are currently open. Figure 26.10 shows an example of the Open Files detail, where you can see the shared files and folders that are currently open on this server.

In addition to the obvious security benefits of being able to see who is using what files, this utility is also useful if you need to disconnect a resource. For example, if you modify access permissions to a shared folder, the changes do not affect a user until they have disconnected and attempt to reconnect to a resource. If you wanted to invoke the security permissions immediately, you

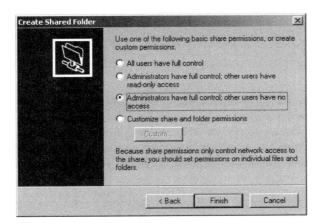

Figure 26–8   *Assigning security permissions to the shared folder.*

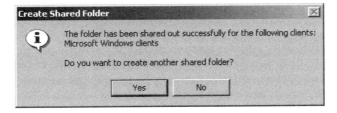

Figure 26–9   *Windows 2000 allows you the option to create additional*
shared folders or to exit the wizard.

would have to disconnect all users from the shared folder. With the Open Files utility you can see who has files open so that you can send them an administrative message (discussed later in this chapter) warning them to save their work before you disconnect them.

DISCONNECTING USERS FROM OPEN FILES

As we previously said, in order for changes you make to security settings to take place immediately, you must disconnect users from the open files. It is **extremely important** to note that when you disconnect a user from an open file, **any unsaved changes to that file will be lost.** Great care should be taken before disconnecting an open file to ensure that the user has her file and been given the opportunity to close the file herself.

To disconnect an open file, simply right-click the file from the list of open files and select Close Open File. Windows 2000 will confirm your decision by asking if you are sure. When you click "Yes," Windows closes the file.

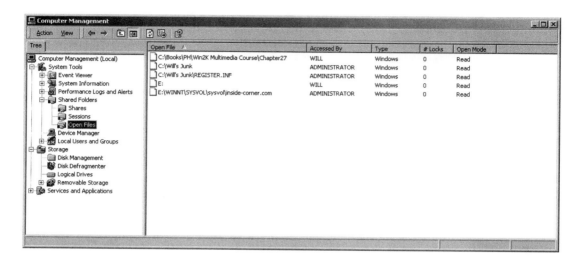

The Open Files portion of the Shared Folders snap-in allows you to view the files currently open through network connections.

Monitoring Network Users

You might have wondered if we had skipped the Sessions utility of the Shared Folders snap-in, since we jumped from Shares straight to Open Folders. Fear not, we haven't skipped it and will cover it here.

By using the Sessions utility, shown in Figure 26.11, you can view information about network connections that Shares and Open Files does not provide.

Like the Open Files utility, Sessions shows the user account that has established the connection to the system. It also shows the computer name or IP address of the system the user is establishing the connection from, and the number of open files they have in use. Additionally, you can see the length of time they have been connected as well as the idle time, and whether the connection has been authenticated or whether they are connected with the Guest account. The idle time can be an important parameter to monitor, especially if you have set a maximum user limit on your shared folders, and users are being denied access because the connection limit has been reached. You can disconnect users that have excessive idle times, such as in our example where a user has had a file open for over a day. Obviously, they have not been using the file continuously, most likely it was forgotten.

DISCONNECTING USERS

Disconnecting a user session is very similar to disconnecting an open file. Simply right-click on the session you wish to disconnect, and select Close Session.

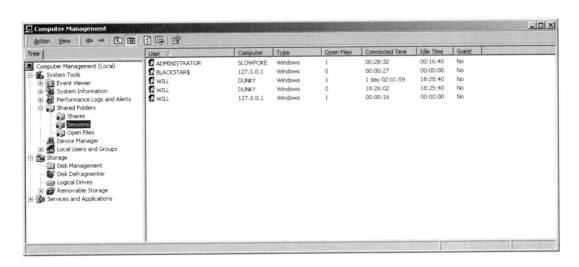

The Sessions window of the Shared Folders snap-in provides a view of network connections to your system.

The user's network connection will be disconnected at that point. Note that the user can immediately attempt to reestablish that session, and Windows-based clients will attempt to reconnect without user intervention. The only way to prevent this is to change the permissions so that the user does not have access to the share. It may not be an issue, though, if you are disconnecting a user simply to update the share or NTFS permissions, that will be accomplished even if they reconnect.

You can disconnect all sessions simultaneously by right clicking on the Sessions folder and selecting Disconnect All Sessions.

Administrative Messages to Users

Before disconnecting users from resources, it is good practice to warn them. Fortunately, rather than having to call everyone up on the phone, Windows 2000 provides you with the ability to send out administrative messages from the server console. Other occasions on which you would want to send out an administrative message are when you are shutting down/rebooting the server or performing any action that could interrupt users' work, such as restoring files from backup or upgrading software.

An administrative message is also known as a console message, since it is sent from the server console. Sending console messages is done from the Shares window of the Shared Folders snap-in. Right-click on the Shares folder, select All Tasks, and click Send Console Message. You will see a dialog similar to that shown in Figure 26.12.

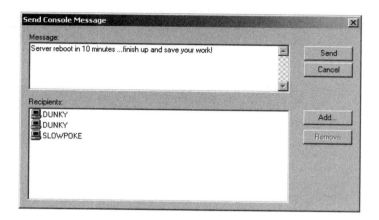

Figure 26–12   *The dialog to send a console message to users.*

The console message dialog shows the list of computers with open connections that are currently capable of receiving administrative messages. Windows 2000 and Windows NT systems are capable of receiving console messages without any user intervention. Windows 9x clients, however, must be running the Win popup utility (found in the Windows installation directory if TCP/IP is installed) in order to receive console messages.

Chapter Summary

In this chapter we looked at monitoring network resources currently in use on a server. The primary tool to do this is the Shared Folders MMC snap-in, which can be easily accessed through the Computer Management administrative tool. We discussed the purposes of monitoring network resources and the requirements to perform these functions. We learned that the Shared Folders snap-in has three main components, as follows:

- Shares
- Sessions
- Open Files

In addition to discussing the components of the Shared Folders snap-in, we learned how to disconnect open files and sessions, and what issues surround those tasks. We also learned how to share folders using the Shared Folders snap-in and that it can be used to share folders on remote machines as well as on the local machine. Lastly, we covered sending console messages to users, warning them before they are disconnected from network resources.

With the knowledge from this chapter and the last, you now have a foundation for understanding basic Windows 2000 security administration.

Introduction to Windows 2000 Printing

*P*rinting is one of the most important network-related activity for most companies, second only to sharing files and data. A well-planned and well-executed printing strategy can help a company work more effectively, while simultaneously reducing the workload on the network administrator. Windows 2000 printing is very similar to that in earlier versions of the Windows NT operating system and offers some interesting additional capabilities. This chapter will explain Windows 2000 printing terminology and discuss planning and implementation of a network printing strategy, installing and configuring network printers, and installing shared printers on network clients.

27.1 Printing Terminology

There are four elements within Windows 2000 printing process, and the terminology is not quite that one might normally expect. The four elements are as follows:

Printer: The software process between the operating system and the physical printing device that actually generates the document. This process controls the destination of the document, priorities among documents, timing, queues, and other elements of the printing process

Print Server: The server on which the print queues reside and to which the print devices are attached. Print devices can be physically attached to the print server, or can be networked devices attached via TCP/IP or other network protocol.

Print Device: The physical device that actually generates the output. A print device can be physically attached to a print server or attached via a network connection.

Printer Drivers: The software that allows the operating system to convert printer commands to the specific output on a print device. Printer drivers are written specifically for combinations of operating systems and print devices, and the use of an inappropriate driver can generate garbled printing or even no output.

Prerequisites for Network Printing

Network printing within a Windows 2000 environment has certain requirements. The precise requirements will, of course, be dictated by the network environment and business needs, but the essentials are described below.

Print Server: A Windows 2000 computer functioning as a network print server. This computer may run Windows 2000 Server or Windows 2000 Professional. If Professional is used as a print server, there may be no more than 10 concurrent connections to the print server at any time.

Network Connectivity: While obvious, the underlying connectivity is often overlooked when installing or troubleshooting network printing. Verify connectivity to networked print devices before installing print services.

RAM: Printing can be a RAM-intensive process, depending upon the number and complexity of the print jobs submitted to the server. It is recommended to install additional RAM in a print server, in addition to the minimum required to run the Windows 2000 operating system. Insufficient RAM can result in poor printing performance.

Hard-Drive Space: Print jobs are queued on the print server, and as such are temporarily stored on the hard drive while processing or while waiting for the print device to become ready for printing. Depending on the size and number of print jobs submitted by the network clients, this might require extra space, in addition to that required for the operating system.

Planning a Network Printing Environment

Planning is the key to a successful implementation of a network printing environment. While technical issues are important to the planning process, there are other elements to consider as well. These include client usage, locations, cost, and more. The technical issues are fairly straightforward: the capabilities of the print server, the capabilities of the print devices, bandwidth issues, and other similar issues. The human issues involve access, placement, and similar issues. Each of these elements is discussed further in this chapter.

Technical Considerations

PRINT SERVER HARDWARE

As mentioned earlier, the print server needs to be a computer that has sufficient RAM and hard-drive space to support the type of printing performed by the users of the network. The print server need not be dedicated solely to printing; many networks have servers that perform both file-sharing and print-server functions. The printing load on the network should determine whether the print server should be a standalone machine or even multiple machines. As an example, a publishing company is more likely to need multiple dedicated print servers, while an e-commerce firm is more likely to conduct its business electronically.

PRINT DEVICES

Other technical issues relate to the printing devices themselves. A printing device (the physical hardware that generates the final print) will generally be under a greater load as a network-attached, rather than a stand-alone device. While it may be tempting to place printing devices designed for personal or home use on a network, they will generally perform poorly in terms of speed and reliability. Long-term planning should include purchasing print devices designed for high levels of use in a network environment. While the initial cost will likely be higher, a properly designed and maintained network print device will outlast and outperform the personal-use devices.

BANDWIDTH

Bandwidth is another element to take under consideration when designing a network printing solution. While this is unlikely to be an issue within a local 100-Mbit LAN, it does begin to become important over a WAN. Consider the case of a remote office connected to the corporate office via a 56-KB ISDN connection: any print jobs submitted to a centralized print server would have to cross the ISDN connection, be processed by the print server, and then cross the ISDN link again. If this remote office typically prints a large number of documents, a bottleneck may develop at the WAN link. In this scenario, a local print server may be a logical solution to the bottleneck, and could possibly be implemented with Windows 2000 Professional if there were 10 or fewer concurrent connections to the server.

CLIENT WORKSTATIONS

One last element to consider is the type of clients that will be connecting to the print server. Clients running Microsoft operating systems can connect to either Windows 2000 Server or Professional print servers. Clients that are using Macintosh systems can connect only to a print server operating on Windows

2000 Server with Print Services for Macintosh installed. Clients running a UNIX-based operating system can connect to a print server operating on Windows 2000 Server or Professional with Print Services for UNIX installed.

WINDOWS 2000 SERVER OR PROFESSIONAL?

Determining the Proper Print Server

Both the Professional and Server version of Windows 2000 offer print-server capabilities. However, the Professional version is appropriate only in the following environment:
Ten or fewer concurrent connections to the print server
Microsoft clients are fully supported
Macintosh clients are not printing to the print server
Netware clients are not printing to the print server
UNIX clients are supported if Print Services for UNIX are installed
In summary, Windows 2000 Professional may be appropriate for smaller offices or remote properties, but larger networks will require Windows 2000 Server.

Nontechnical Considerations

Network design is only partially a technical discussion; often, there are nontechnical elements that must be considered when implementing a plan. Network printing is no exception to this rule. Some elements that should be considered when designing printing solutions are ease of use, locations, supportability, political considerations, cost, and security.

SUPPORT

Ease of use and supportability are interconnected concepts. The print device that is implemented should meet the needs of the users printing to it and should not require highly technical skills to perform basic maintenance, such as changing toner cartridges and adding paper. Obviously, trained personnel must support some specialty printing solutions, such as plotters and high-end color devices, but the majority of the print devices should not require these skills. Many print devices intended for network use are designed in a modular fashion, so that repair becomes a matter of replacing a particular module, rather than a myriad of complicated parts.

LOCATION

Location is always a prime concern when developing a printing solution, and it is the single element that is most obvious to the end users. A properly implemented print solution will prevent users from walking across a floor on a regular basis but will avoid excess printing devices. Often, departmental print devices are implemented, and confidential documents like performance reviews or contracts are printed on a local print device. Cost also plays a significant role in the design: few companies have unlimited resources for print servers and print devices.

POLITICS

Political considerations and security also work hand in hand in most environments. Usually these come into play when discussing specialty printing devices, such as color printers, large plotters, or transparency printers. Access to these devices is normally limited to those who have a legitimate business need, in order to prevent misuse of the resources (such as printing 300 color copies of one's resume). The political considerations begin when determining which users have a "legitimate business need." It is highly recommended that the network administrator receive a written policy from upper management defining business needs, so that one can avoid unpleasant situations.

Creating Network Printers

Network printers are created upon the print server and shared to the network users. The print server can set up and share print devices that are connected locally and those that are connected via network interface devices. In most cases, network printing devices are not directly connected to the print server.

This section will describe setting up and sharing a network printing device, connecting a client machine to a shared print device, driver planning and installation of drivers for both the print server and the client computers, and centralized driver installation

Adding and Sharing Network Printers

Print devices are added via the *Add Printer Wizard*, which is available through the Printers folder on the Start Menu. Click on Start → Settings → Printers to access the Printers folder, or access it through the Control Panel. Clicking on the Add Printer Wizard begins a process that will walk one through the installation of a printing device, sharing and naming the device, and installing the correct drivers. The wizard will also allow a network administrator to add a port to the print server, such as a TCP/IP port for a network device.

BEGINNING THE PRINTER INSTALL PROCESS

After beginning the Add Printer Wizard, select Next to continue into the process itself. The first screen thereafter will ask if one is installing a local or a network printer. This may be slightly confusing: On a print server, one must select Local Port, even if connecting to a network print device (Figure 27.1). The network option is used to connect as a client to printers already shared on the network.

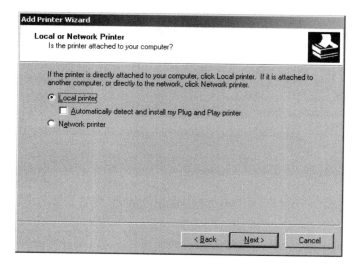

Select Local Port to install a printer on a print server.

The next screen will ask you to select the proper port for the print device you are installing (Figure 27.2). While a print server may have a printing device connected to a local LPT or serial port, most implementations will involve creating a network port. Select *Create a New Port* and choose the proper protocol for your network. By default, Windows 2000 loads TCP/IP printing only. If your network includes Macintosh or UNIX-based machines, additional print services must be installed on the print server. For the purposes of this example, we will be installing a TCP/IP-based Hewlett Packard Jet Direct device.

A JetDirect device is a small piece of hardware that allows a printer to communicate with a network. A JetDirect device can communicate via standard network protocols with other devices on the network and can be directly addressed by those other devices. Some printers attach to JetDirect equipment via the printer's parallel port, while other models are designed specifically to accept JetDirect cards. Other manufacturers also produce similar devices that perform the same function.

If the proper network port has already been installed, it will be selectable in the upper window.

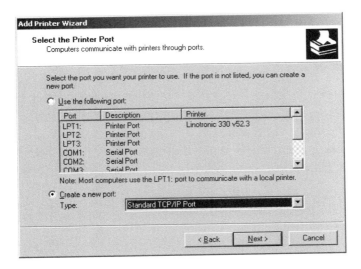

Figure 27–2   *Select a preexisting port or create a new network port.*

After selecting the default TCP/IP protocol, one must enter the IP address of the network printing device and the port name on which to connect (Figure 27.3). The IP address will be determined by the numbering scheme in use on your network. It is advisable either to set a static IP address on the network printing devices or to use reserved leases within DHCP to ensure that the IP address of the print devices does not change. The port name may be important, depending on the type of network print device to which one is connecting. The name is unimportant on a Jet Direct connected device, and can be customized to assist when troubleshooting and tracking. By default, Windows 2000 uses an *IP_<ip address>* format for the port.

After inserting the IP address and the port, one must select the type of network printing device. Windows 2000 offers options ranging from the Axis

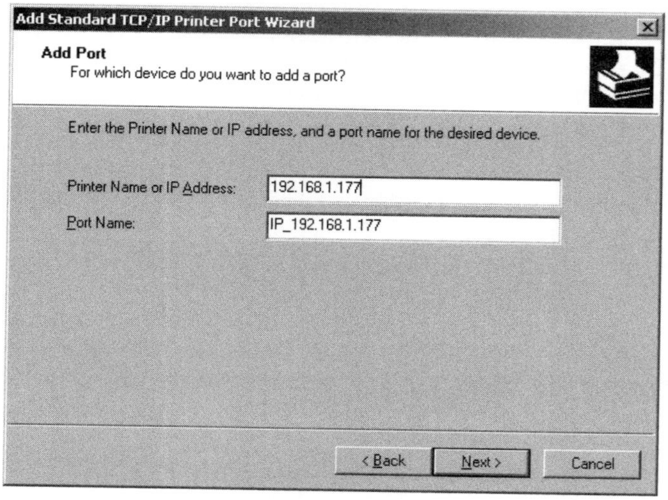

Figure 27-3   *Enter the IP address and port of the selected network printing device.*

devices to Xerox devices. For our purposes, we will choose Hewlett Packard Jet Direct. If the proper selection is not available, one can select *Custom* and enter the proper port numbers and other elements for the print device.

The next screen will be a summary of the selections thus far. Verify that the IP address, port name, and adapter type match the print device. If the settings are correct, continue by selecting *Finish* to install the port on the print server.

INSTALLING THE PRINT DEVICE

After the port is installed on the print server, one can add the print device. The print device is the physical hardware that generates the output and is the portion of the printing process that the end user generally refers to as a "printer." The second portion of the Add Printer Wizard appears after a port is installed or selected, and it controls the installation of the print device and drivers.

The first screen on the wizard will offer a selection of manufacturers and print devices (Figure 27.4). Windows 2000 ships with drivers for each of these listed devices. If your device is not available as a selection, you will need a driver from the manufacturer in order to use the print device correctly. To install a manufacturer's driver, select the *Have Disk* option and direct Windows 2000 to the proper file location.

If the device is listed, simply select that manufacturer and device, and choose Next.

At this point Windows 2000 will either install the drivers for the print device, or prompt you to keep the existing drivers if another identical device is

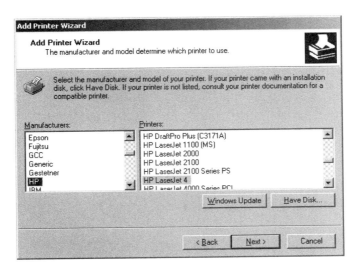

Figure 27-4

Select the proper print device or install drivers for an unlisted device.

previously installed. After the drivers are installed, the next screen will prompt for a printer name (Figure 27.5). Each printer must have a unique name. Please note that this name is only used locally on the print server; clients will see the share name, which we will discuss below. This screen also prompts whether to set this printer as the default printer. This will only affect printing from the print server itself.

Descriptive names such as Finance_LJ4_Rm7220 help when troubleshooting printing issues.

The next step is to determine the shared name of the printing device. This is the name that the client computer will see if they browse to the printer or enter a path to the printer. If the printer is shared, Windows 2000 will automatically default to an 8.3 format on the share name. Most newer Microsoft client operating systems can connect to a printer path of up to 31 characters, but DOS and Windows 3.x clients, as well as some non-Microsoft operating systems, will require the 8.3 naming convention. If your network will support the longer naming convention, a more descriptive share name can be used. Note that each share name on a print server must be unique to that server, but duplicate share names on different servers are acceptable.

The next step is simply adding the description and comments to the printer to help the clients determine which printer is appropriate for their

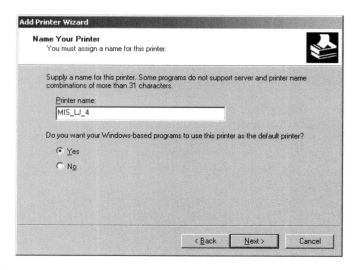

Figure 27-5

Enter the name of the printer as it will appear locally on the print server.

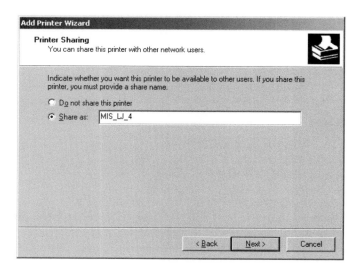

Figure 27-6

Enter the share name for the print device.

needs. After entering these comments, clicking Next will bring you to the final screen for the printer installation. Verify on this screen that the settings, adapter type, name, share name, and other elements are correct, and then select Finish. The printer is then installed and will show up in the Printers folder. The open hand under the printer name indicates that it is now shared.

Configuring Client Computers

By this point we have configured the print device, shared it, and verified that the system is functioning correctly. The next step is the most important, though often overlooked: connecting the client machines to the shared printer. Several elements need to be considered at this point: management of print drivers, installing the printers, and how to best present the printers to the client machines.

Installing Printers Using the Add Printer Wizard

Just as on the print server, the Add Printer Wizard is used to connect client machines to the shared printers. The procedure begins in much the same way, but varies at the Port Selection screen. Unlike the print server, on which the ports were local, the client machine will select Network Printer to connect to a remote port. After selecting Network Printer, a screen appears that will allow you to find the network printer in three separate ways (Figure 27.7).

The options available to the client machine are finding a printer within the Directory, connecting by name, and connecting via URL. If a client selects the first option and clicks the next button, they can search via name, features, contact information, or many other elements. The printers within the directory that match the desired features appear on a search results list, and can then be selected. Pressing OK installs the printer on the system and prompts whether to set the printer as the default.

Selecting the second option will connect the client to the specified printer or, if no printer is specified, will generate a list of computers. The client can browse that list and find the printer. Selecting that printer and choosing OK will install the printer and prompt whether to set the printer as the default.

The third option will allow a connection via a URL (Universal Resource Locator) path. The specific path must be entered in the *URL*: field, as this option does not support browsing. Once again, the wizard will prompt for the default printer.

Installing Printers via a Web Browser

Client computers running Windows 2000 can now connect to a Windows 2000 print server via a Web browser. This method of connection will install drivers, allow control of documents, and show the properties of the printer. The printers are accessible at *http://<print server name>/printers*, or *http://<print*

Options for finding network printers.

server name>/<printer share name>. Clients with other operating systems will not be able to connect in this manner.

Driver Management

As mentioned earlier, printer drivers are the software that allows a certain operating system to communicate correctly with a particular print device. Every computer that needs to print to a particular printer requires that the correct printer drivers be installed. Driver installation, however, can be troublesome in a large-enterprise environment. Traditionally, printer drivers are installed locally on the client machines via diskette or CD-ROM. The problems with installing drivers manually are threefold:

Availability: Obtaining the drivers when installing the printer may be difficult, especially on unusual print devices.

Consistency: It is difficult to ensure that every client on the network is using the correct drivers, which may result in unnecessary issues and troubleshooting.

Updates: Often, printer drivers are updated with bug fixes and additional features. Localized printer drivers will require that each machine individually receive the updates.

Previous versions of Windows NT offered a form of centralized print drivers, but required that the CD-ROMs for each client operating system be available while installing the print device on the print server. Windows 2000 takes this concept a bit further by offering the client printer drivers as an integral part of the installation process. With the centralized print drivers, Microsoft

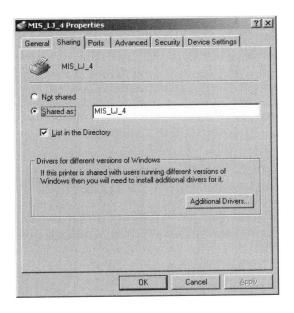

Figure 27–8   *Selecting* Additional *Drivers will install client printer drivers.*

Windows-based clients will automatically install the correct drivers when they are connected to the print device. If the network printer drivers are updated, Windows 2000 and NT clients will also automatically update, while Windows 95 and 98 clients simply have to choose to update the drivers from the server.

Installing the additional printer drivers is a simple matter. Select the printer properties and choose the *Sharing* tab. Select the *Additional Drivers* button as shown in Figure 27.8:

Once that option is selected, a screen will appear that will allow you to install drivers for Windows 2000 (Intel only), Windows NT 4.0 or earlier (Alpha, Intel, MIPS, and PPC chips), Windows 98, and Windows 95 (Figure 27.9). Selecting a client OS will install the requested drivers onto the print server, and they will be automatically downloaded to the clients when they attach to the printer. The Windows 2000 client drivers are automatically installed when the print device is installed on the print server.

Chapter Summary

This chapter has discussed printing terminology, planning network printing solutions, creating network printers, and connecting client computers to the shared printers. Windows 2000 printing terminology defines a printer as the software process that connects operating systems to the print devices and con-

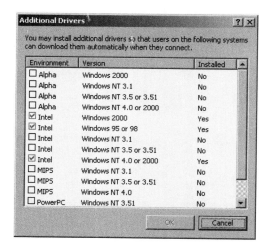

Figure 27–9   *Selecting client printer driver for automatic installation*

trols queuing, timing, and the like. A print device is the physical device that actually generates the output of the print job. A print server is the computer on which the print queues and the printing process reside. Both Windows 2000 Server and Professional can perform this function, but Professional is limited in terms of concurrent connections and additional capabilities. A printer driver is the software that allows communication between the operating system and the print device and is specific to an operating system/print device combination.

Planning a network printing solution requires an understanding of the number of clients, their printing habits, available resources, bandwidth, and the types of client computers. A properly implemented network printing solution will allow a company to work efficiently without consuming excess resources. When a specialty printer is located upon a network, it is a good practice to define in advance access rights to that device, and to have that access definition approved in writing.

Client machines attach to print devices shared from print servers. The clients may find available printers in a number of ways: searching the directory tree, browsing via the network, or by URL if the exact name is known. Windows 2000 clients can attach to printers via a Web browser, by attaching to *http://<print server name>/printers* or by attaching to *http://<print server name>/<print share name>*. Other clients do not have this ability.

Client machines require device drivers to print to shared printers. Device drivers may be loaded locally, but this is not recommended due to problems with availability, consistency, and updates. Windows 2000 can store the client drivers on the print server and download them automatically to the clients when they first connect. Windows 2000 and NT clients will update automatically if the drivers on the print server are changed, but Windows 95 and 98 require manual updates.

Windows 2000 offers a powerful and flexible printing system with centralized management features to ease administration duties. In the next chapter we will investigate administration and troubleshooting of network printing.

Administering Windows 2000 Printing

Configuring and installing network printers is only the first step in providing an efficient and effective printing solution for a company or enterprise. Printing must also be administered on a regular basis, and a network administrator must also be able to troubleshoot issues with printing when they arise. In this chapter we will discuss controlling documents and queues, setting security permissions on specialty print devices, the use and configuration of printer pools, and troubleshooting common network printing problems.

28.1 Managing the Print Process

The network administrator can manage the printing process on several levels. The first level is at the printers themselves. The administrator can assign certain paper sizes to particular paper trays and can require the use of a separator page for print jobs. The second level of administration lies at the document level, where an administrator or print operator can manipulate, redirect, or kill print jobs while they are in the queues.

28.1.1 Managing Print Devices

There are basically two elements to managing the print devices: assigning forms to particular paper trays, and determining which, if any, separator page is appropriate for the printing device and the needs of the clients.

FORMS AND PRINT DEVICES

Print devices often have multiple paper trays so that the print jobs can be printed on different paper sizes or use extra capabilities such as envelope printing. By assigning a particular *form* to a paper tray, the administrator can ensure that jobs are printed to the correct paper trays (Figure 28.1). To set the form preferences, perform the following:

1. Open the properties page for the desired print device
2. Select the Device Settings tab
3. Associate the paper trays with their respective forms by selecting each tray and choosing the paper size
4. Select Apply and OK to save the settings for the print device.

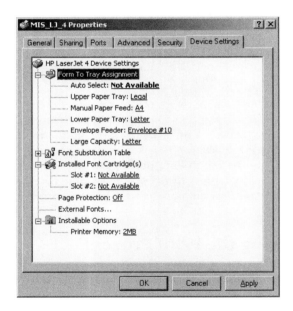

Figure 28–1   *Assigning paper trays to forms.*

SEPARATOR PAGES

A separator page is a file that can send commands directly to a print device. Separator pages can perform two functions. The first is to generate banner pages, which are pages that print before each print job. Separator pages can include the computer name that generated the print job, job number, date, and other options. The second function of a separator page is to switch a print device between print modes. This functionality can be used to change a printer from PCL (Printer Control Language) to Postscript. It offers added flexibility on hardware that can print with both. By default, separator pages are not installed on a print device. If the network administrator chooses to install a separator page, either default Windows 2000 separator pages or custom separator pages are available.

The preinstalled separator pages are located in the *%systemroot%/ system32* directory with a *.sep* extension. Three separator pages are of interest to most network administrators: *sysprint.sep*, *pcl.sep*, and *pscript.sep*. The fourth preinstalled separator page is *sysprtj.sep*, which uses Japanese characters.

Sysprint.sep: Postscript-compatible separator page that prints a separator before each print job.

PCL.sep: PCL-compatible separator page that prints a separator page before each print job.

Pscript.sep: Postscript-compatible separator page that switches a PCL/Postscript HP printer to Postscript format. This does not print a banner page.

Copying and editing the existing *sep* files can create custom separator pages. The *.sep* files can be opened in any text editor, and modified to meet the needs of the users. The escape codes are interpreted by the separator-file interpreter to generate the proper behavior at the printer. The codes are listed in Table 28.1; @ is assumed to be the escape character.

Table 28.1	Escape Codes
Escape Code	**Purpose**
@	The escape character. This needs to be the only character on the first line.
@N	Prints the computer name that generated the print job.
@D	Prints the date the job was submitted.
@I	Prints the job number.
@Lxxxx	Prints all the characters following the code until the next escape code.
@T	Prints the time the job was submitted.
@Fpathname	Prints the requested file directly to the print device, beginning on an empty line. The print server does not process the file.
@Wnn	Sets the maximum width of the separator page. The default is 80, and can be as large as 256 characters. Any additional characters are ignored.

Table 28.1	Escape Codes (Continued)
@Hnn	Sends a printer control code directly to the print device. The *nn* variable is a hexadecimal ascii code that will be specific to a particular print device.
*@B@*S	Prints in single-width mode until the *@U* escape code.
*@B@*M	Prints in double-wide mode until the *@U* escape code.
@E	Ejects the page from the printing device.
@n	Skips 0–9 lines. Setting this to 0 moves the text to the next line.
@U	Turns off block-mode printing.

To install a separator page, open the printer properties and choose the Advanced tab. There is a button for Separator page on the Advanced settings page. Selecting this option will allow you to enter the filename for the desired separator page, or you can browse to the preferred Separator-page file. Select Apply, and the Separator page is installed on that printer. This procedure will have to be performed on each printer that will use a separator page.

Managing Documents

Documents are the core of the network printing process. The ultimate goal of a network administrator should be reliable, consistent printing. However, even in the best-designed systems, occasional issues may prevent a document from processing correctly. In these cases, a print operator or the equivalent may have to manually manipulate a document to restart it, redirect it, or delete it entirely. This section will discuss the proper methods to control and manage documents within a network printing environment.

DOCUMENT HANDLING

Documents are controlled via the Printers folder within the Control Panel by selecting the desired printer and either double-clicking on it, or selecting *Open* from the context menu. Once the printer is opened, the individual documents queued on that printer are visible and can be manipulated. This view will also allow an individual to check the status of jobs in the print queue. This can be extremely useful when troubleshooting printing problems.

Manipulating the documents is handled through the *Documents* menu item on the toolbar. Options within that menu will allow individual documents to be paused, resumed, and canceled as needed. The properties of the document are also available via this menu and may be used to change the priority of the print job and the allowed printing times.

PAUSING DOCUMENTS • Often, a document will need to be paused while it is still within the queue. There are many reasons why an administrator would pause printing: The printer may be damaged or off-line, there may be problems with the paper selection, or the job simply may be of less importance than something behind it in the queue. There are actually two separate ways to pause printing. The first is to pause the document, and the second is to pause the entire printer.

To pause the entire printer, select the *File* menu and choose *Pause printing* from the menu. This will halt all printing to the printer, though the queue will still accept new jobs. To resume printing, select the *File* menu again and remove the check mark next to the *pause printing* option.

To pause a single document, select the document, then click on the *Documents* menu item. Choose *Pause* from the document menu to halt the printing of the selected document. This will prevent that particular document from printing, while allowing those behind it in the queue to print normally. Selecting *Resume* from the document menu will allow the job to proceed.

CANCELING DOCUMENTS • Print jobs may sometimes need to be cancelled before they finish printing. This may be due to runaway print jobs (usually caused by incorrect drivers), massive print jobs, or sometimes just a simple mistake. As with pausing documents, there are two ways to clear a print job from the queue. Regardless of the method chosen, it is a good idea to pause either the printer or that particular print job before canceling the document.

To clear an individual document, select the desired document in the queue. Once that job is selected, choose the *Documents* menu from the toolbar, then select *Cancel*. The job will then be removed from the queue.

In some cases it may be desirable to clear the entire queue on a particular printer. To do so, select the *File* menu from the toolbar, then choose *Cancel all documents*. This will clear all print jobs in the queue.

RESTARTING DOCUMENTS • In some cases, there may be a need to restart a print job that is in the queue. Restarting a print job will force the document to start printing again from the beginning of the document. This can be useful when a document requires a certain type of paper such as letterhead, or when the printer device has been reset during a print job. Note that this differs from restarting a paused printing job, because in that case the printing resumes from the next page of the document.

REDIRECTING PRINT QUEUES

From time to time, it may be useful to redirect a print queue from one print device to another. Perhaps the print device is broken or unavailable, or perhaps the print device has been replaced with an upgraded unit. In any case, redirecting a print queue is relatively simple, and if performed correctly, the clients would never even notice (with the exception of their print jobs arriving at the "wrong" printer!).

To redirect a printer queue, first verify that an alternate port is available on the print server. If not, create one as discussed in the previous chapter. Next, pause all print jobs to that queue, using the administrative functions on the printer. At this point, enter the printer properties and select the *Ports* tab. This will bring up a list of the possible printing ports. Simply select the desired port and select *Apply*. This will associate the printer queue with that particular port and automatically restart the print jobs in the queue.

Note that redirecting a print queue requires that the new print device be identical to the print device on the previous port. Redirecting print jobs to a different type of print device may result in garbled or no printing, especially if the printer drivers are incompatible.

This is a very useful troubleshooting tool that will allow the users to continue to print while the administrator works on repairing a damaged or nonresponsive printer.

SETTING NOTIFICATIONS

Often, clients on a network would like notification when a document has printed successfully. Windows 2000, like the previous versions of NT, offers this capability. However, the capability is set on a per-server basis, so that one cannot have only particular users or those who use a particular printer notified.

To enable notification of printing success, enter the Printers folder, select File, and Server Properties, and the Advanced tab (Figure 28.2). Select the box labeled *Notify when remote documents are printed*. After making the change, the spooler services must be stopped and restarted on the print server for it to take effect. One can also choose to have the computer that sent the print job to be alerted, rather than the username. The reasoning behind this is to allow the notice to be received, even if the user is no longer logged into the network.

SETTING PRIORITIES ON NETWORK PRINTERS

Priority is a method of measuring the relative importance of a particular print job within a queue. Priority can range from 1 to 99; by default, all print jobs print at a priority of 1. It is possible to raise the priority of a particular job within a queue in order to force it to the top of the queue. There are several reasons why one might want to do so; for example, there may be a small job in line behind a very large one, or perhaps the VP of the company needs a special report printed quickly. In both of these cases, raising the priority of the individual job would accomplish the goal.

To raise the priority of a document, first select the document in the queue. Then, on the Documents menu, select properties. In the General tab, there will be a slider for priority. As mentioned earlier, this defaults to 1. Raising

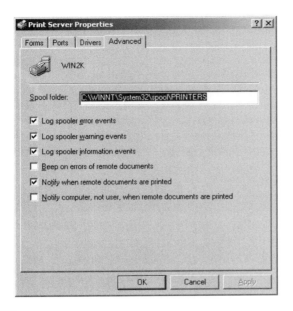

Enabling notifications of network printing.

this number and pressing OK will move the document to the head of the queue.

This method is fine for the occasional document boost, but consider the situation where a particular person or group always requires a higher priority in the queue. Very few administrators have the time or inclination to watch the queue constantly and manually adjust the priorities on each print job. Fortunately, there is a technique that will automatically raise the priority for those individuals.

The secret lies in the fact that the administrator can define multiple printers that are directed toward the same print device. Creating a second identical printer and associating it with the same port on the print server creates a second queue. This second printer can then be adjusted so that any print job submitted to it automatically gains a priority boost. To set the priority on a per-printer basis, open the printer properties sheet and set the priority to the desired level (Figure 28.3). This will automatically raise the value of the documents in this print queue versus the original print queue and will ensure that jobs submitted to the second printer output first.

To prevent everyone from printing to the new higher-priority printer, the default security permissions on the printer will have to be modified. This will be discussed in more detail a little further in this chapter, but the essentials are that the Everyone would be removed from the printer, and the specific group

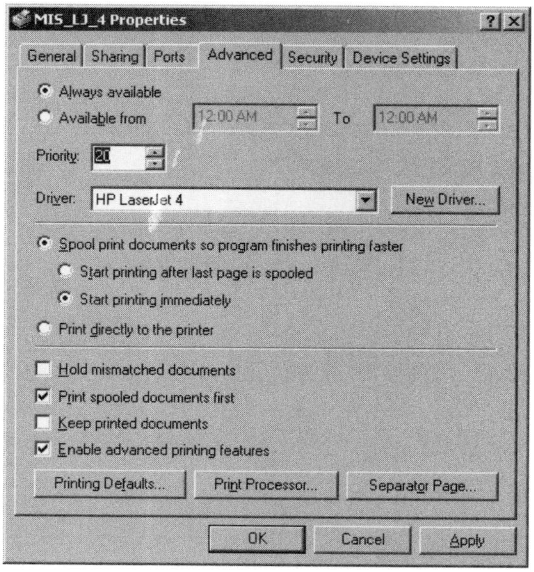

Figure 28-3
Setting priority for a printer.

added with print rights. This would then require that the client be a member of the specific group to print to the high-priority printer.

SETTING PRINTING TIMES

In many network environments, printers are set for 24-hour operation. However, there may be situations where restricting the availability of a printer may increase the effectiveness of the business. Take, for example, a situation in which two departments must share a particular print device, and one department routinely prints very large reports for the next morning's meetings. If a print job from the second department enters the queue behind the report, it may take a very long time to be processed. Creating multiple printers with different priorities may ease the problem, but the second department's jobs will still be interspersed with the reports.

One way to resolve the issue and still provide functionality to both departments is to arrange for the reports to be printed off-hours. This will still allow the first department to have their reports for the morning meetings, while increasing availability to the second department. If the printer is set to 24-hour operation, however, someone must manually send the reports to the printer during the off-hours. Clearly this is an unacceptable solution.

Fortunately, though, there is a more elegant answer. One simply needs to create a second printer pointing to the same print device, and adjust its availability to be between the desired hours. Creating the printer in this way will allow it to accept print jobs throughout the day and queue them. When the proper time arrives, the print server will release the queue, and the jobs will print to the print device. This method allows the printer to be used at night without intervention and leaves the original printer queue intact for normal daily printing or emergency reports.

Restricting the time for a printer is accomplished by selecting the printer properties, choosing the Advanced tab, and entering a starting and ending time for the print device (Figure 28.4). Once this change is applied, the print server will automatically hold jobs in the queue until those specific times.

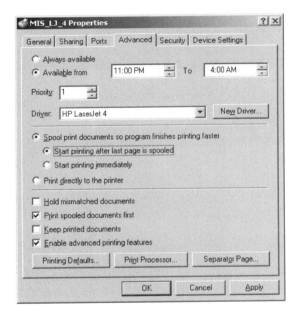

Figure 28–4   *Setting time constraints for a printer.*

Managing Printer Pools

In a high-volume printing environment, there may be times when a print queue is backed up to the point of delaying jobs for a substantial length of time. In these environments, users often have to search through alternate printers to find one with a shorter queue, and then redirect their print job to that printer. This leads to productivity loss and frustration on the part of the network users.

Printer pooling can provide an alternative to this scenario. Two or more identical print devices are assigned to the same print queue. The print server will automatically redirect the print job to the print device that is available. This results in shorter print queues and a more satisfied user community. Printer

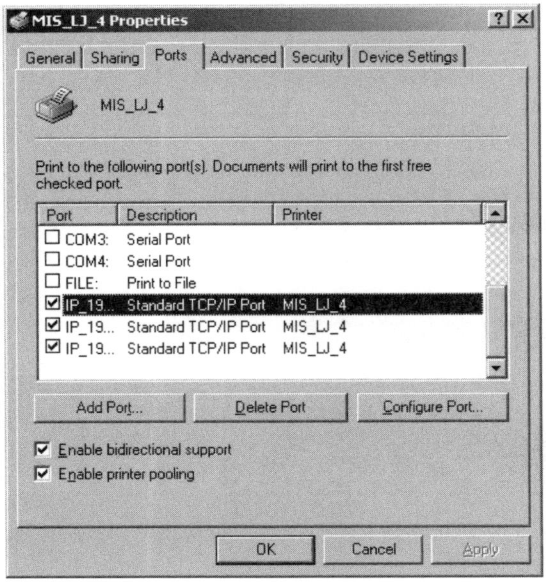

MIS_LJ_4 Properties

General | Sharing | **Ports** | Advanced | Security | Device Settings

MIS_LJ_4

Print to the following port(s). Documents will print to the first free checked port.

Port	Description	Printer
☐ COM3:	Serial Port	
☐ COM4:	Serial Port	
☐ FILE:	Print to File	
☑ IP_19...	Standard TCP/IP Port	MIS_LJ_4
☑ IP_19...	Standard TCP/IP Port	MIS_LJ_4
☑ IP_19...	Standard TCP/IP Port	MIS_LJ_4

Add Port...   Delete Port   Configure Port...

☑ Enable bidirectional support
☑ Enable printer pooling

OK   Cancel   Apply

Figure 28–5   *Creating a printer pool.*

pooling also allows an administrator or print operator to manipulate multiple physical print devices from a single printer.

Because the print job can be sent to any print device within the pool, they should all be located near each other.

CREATING PRINTER POOLS

To create a printer pool, begin by selecting the desired printer in the printers folder. Open the properties of the printer and select the *Ports* tab. At this point check the *Enable Printer Pooling* option, then choose the ports on which the pooled print devices reside (Figure 28.5). If the additional ports do not exist, they can be added at this time.

Printer pools allow an administrator to easily add printing capability or remove a defective printer without requiring the client machines to change their printer configurations. If additional capability is needed, add another print device and port to the printer pool. In the event that a print device breaks down or is otherwise unavailable, remove the related port from the printer pool, and the remaining devices continue to process jobs.

It is important to note that all print devices attached to a printing pool must be able to use the same printer drivers. The devices do not have to be identical, but it is recommended that as similar a device as possible be used. If a printing device that is not compatible is added to a printing pool, garbled or no output is the likely result.

PRIORITIES AND PRINTER POOLS

Earlier, we discussed setting priorities on printers, so that documents were printed in order of importance rather than queue order. Setting printer priorities involves creating a second printer that is directed to the same printing device, and assigning a higher priority to that second printer. Print jobs sent to the higher-priority printer will print before those sent to the lower-priority printer.

Printer pools can also have the capability to handle various priority levels for print jobs. The procedure for creating a second-priority queue is very similar to creating one for a single-print device. To create a high-priority printer pool, create a second printer and enable printer pooling on the printer. Attach the printer to the print devices by associating the printer with the ports connected to the devices. At this point, you have created a second printer pool. Assign a higher priority to this printer pool in the *General* tab, and select OK. Print jobs sent to the new printer pool will now print before those sent to the original pool, even though they are printing to the same physical devices.

It is not possible to set priority between physical devices in the same printer pool.

Permissions and the Printing Process

Windows 2000 uses permissions to control printing on network devices and the administration of printers. The default permissions on a network printer allow everyone to connect to a printer, print to the printer, and control his or her own documents. Print Operators, Server Operators, and Administrators have more advanced rights that allow them to control all documents, clear print queues, change permissions on printers, and delete printers entirely.

Printer permissions are broken into three categories: Print, Manage Documents, and Manage Printers. The various permission categories allow ranges of control over the printers and the documents. The differences are listed in Table 28.2.

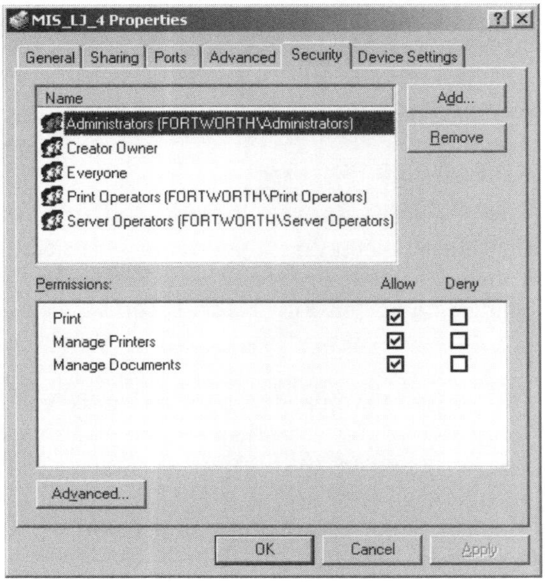

Figure 28–6 *Managing printer permissions.*

Permissions are managed through the security tab on the printer properties (Figure 28.6). The default permissions grant Print permissions to the Everyone group, Manage Documents to the Creator Owner group, and Manage Printers to the Administrators, Print Operators, and Server Operators. Additional group or individual user permissions can be modified from this tab.

Note that the permissions can be allowed and denied. If a particular permission is denied, that overrides any allowed permission. For example, if a particular user is denied access to print to a printer, that denial will override the print permissions allowed to the Everyone group.

Table 28.2	Printer Permissions	
Print	**Manage Documents**	**Manage Printers**
Connect to the printer	Connect to the printer	Connect to the printer
Print	Print	Print
Pause, Resume, Cancel, and Restart own documents	Pause, Resume, Cancel, and Restart own documents	Pause, Resume, Cancel, and Restart own documents
	Pause, Resume, Cancel and Restart others' documents	Pause, Resume, Cancel, and Restart others' documents
	Adjust print-job settings	Adjust print-job settings
		Adjust printer properties
		Change permissions
		Clear the print queue
		Share printer
		Delete printer

Securing Printers via Permissions

Access to printers on a Windows 2000 network is controlled by the security permissions on the printers. While the default permissions are often appropriate for general-use printers, there may be situations in which a more secured printer is desired. This is often the case with specialty printing devices, such as high-end color printers or check printers. Windows 2000 offers the ability to control access to a printer by groups or even by an individual user.

CONTROLLING ACCESS VIA GROUPS

In most cases, controlling printing via groups is the most logical method from a network administrator's viewpoint. Rather than granting and revoking individual rights on printers, an administrator can simply move the user accounts into the proper groups to grant permission, or remove them to revoke permission. Managing via groups also makes it easier to replicate a particular user's printer permissions; simply duplicate the group membership.

To control permissions on a printer, select the Security tab from the printer properties. Choose Add and select the proper group (Figure 28.7).

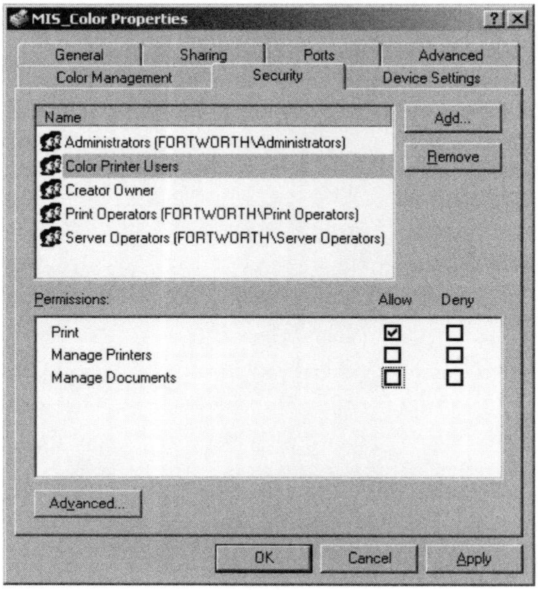

Figure 28-7

*Limiting a color printer to Color Printer Users via group permis-
sions.*

Once the proper group is added, adjust their permissions as appropriate. To
deny a group access to a printer, select the group and check the Deny box
under Print permissions. To allow a group access to a printer, select Allow for
Print permissions.

Remove the Everyone group from the permissions to limit it to a particular group. If the Everyone group still has Print privileges,
that will allow any network user to print to the printer.

CONTROLLING ACCESS VIA USER RIGHTS

Despite the advantages of controlling access via groups, there may be times
when access must be granted or denied on an individual basis. Windows 2000
can control access down to the individual user. As with the groups, select Add
on the Security tab, and locate the proper user ID (Figure 28.8). After adding
the user, adjust the permissions appropriately. In this particular case, Michelle
Hill has been denied access to the printer in MIS. Note that the Everyone group
still has Print permissions, but the Deny on the individual access overrides
those permissions.

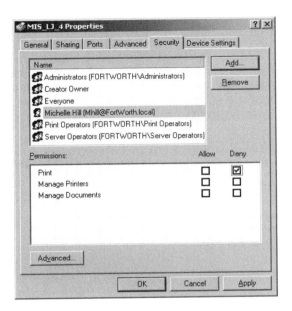

Figure 28-8 *Limiting access via individual permissions.*

TAKING OWNERSHIP OF A PRINTER

A printer is associated with the user ID of the account that creates the printer. In most cases, this will be an administrator account, print operator, or the like. However, if changes are made in the security and permissions on a printer, it is possible that a printer may end up orphaned when unused accounts are disabled or deleted. In this case, the printer can no longer be administered.

Fortunately, an administrator can take ownership of a printer. This procedure will allow the administrator to control the printer and either delete it or correct the permissions issues that created the orphan. To view ownership of a printer, choose the Security tab on the printer properties, then press the Advanced button. This will bring up the Advanced properties sheet (Figure 28.9). Choosing the Owner tab will reveal the current owner of the printer. To take ownership of the printer, choose the new owner from the list of eligible user accounts and groups, then choose Apply. The ownership information will change to the selected user.

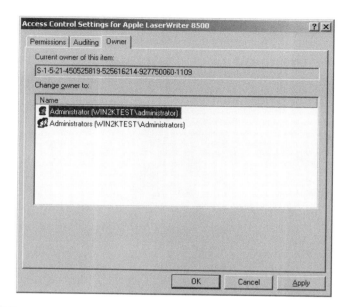

Figure 28–9   *Taking ownership of an orphaned printer.*

Accessing Printers for Administration

Administrators and Print Operators must access printers to control printers, queues, and documents. Under earlier Windows NT operating systems, printers were accessed and controlled via the Control Panel. This capability is still present in Windows 2000. All printers and their properties can be reached via the Control Panel, or via the standard shortcut from the Start Menu under Settings. However, Windows 2000 now offers additional printer control capabilities.

Windows 2000 now offers control of shared printers via a Web browser. All shared printers are visible on a single Web page and can be controlled by administrators or print operators from any other computer running the Windows 2000 operating system. The Web interface allows an authorized person to pause and resume the printer; clear the queue; pause, restart, resume and cancel documents; and view the properties of the printer (Figure 28.10). Properties of the printer cannot be changed from the Web interface.

The web interface allows an operator to monitor multiple printers from a single point, greatly easing printer administration duties. The web interface is listed at *http://<servername>/printers*, and individual printers are available at *http://<servername>/<sharename>*.

The Windows 2000 print server must be running Internet Information Server to enable Web access to the printers.

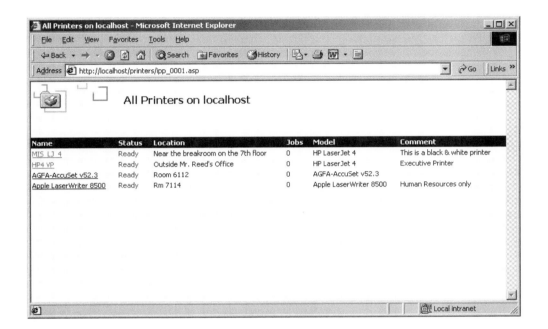

Figure 28-10   *Web interface to shared printers on a Windows 2000 server.*

Troubleshooting Network Printing

Network printing can be very reliable, if properly planned and configured. Unfortunately, issues will arise in even the best networks, and printing is no exception. Troubleshooting is a skill that a network administrator develops over time, but many issues have similar causes. This section is designed to assist in beginning the troubleshooting process, but each network environment and situation is somewhat different. These tips can help but cannot guarantee success on any particular printing issue.

Nobody Can Print to a Particular Network Printer

This situation can result from several situations. Think connectivity and permissions in a case where no one can reach a particular printer. Items to check include the following:

Connectivity: Is the print device connected to the network? Are the cables connected correctly? Is the print device online? Are the protocols the same on the print server and the NIC on the printer? If the network is IP based, will a ping to the printer return a response? Many times, a symptom of connectivity problems to the printer is multiple jobs building up in a queue.

Permissions: Can Administrators or Print Operators print to the printer? If so, there's probably a permissions issue. If the clients are receiving an "Access Denied" error, check to ensure they have print permissions on the printer. Verify that the Everyone group has Print permissions on general-use printers.

Configuration: Verify the port that attaches the printer to the print device. If the port is incorrectly selected, the print jobs may be printing elsewhere. Do the print jobs stay in the queue, or do they appear to process and vanish? The latter case can indicate a redirected printer.

Power: As simplistic as it sounds, power problems cause a large number of printing issues. Verify the printer is plugged in and turned on.

Everyone's Print Jobs Are Garbled

In this case, drivers are a good place to begin. Additionally, a hardware failure in the network interface cards on the printer or on the print server can cause issues.

Drivers: The normal culprit in garbled printing is a corrupted or inappropriate driver. If printer drivers are stored centrally, a corrupted driver could be passed to multiple machines. Try manually updating the drivers on a client machine and printing to the print device. If that clears the problem, the centralized drivers may need to be updated or changed.

Connectivity: As mentioned in the previous section, verify the network connectivity to the printer and, if possible, run diagnostic routines against the NIC cards both in the server and in any printer interface. Failing but still semi-functional NIC cards can corrupt data passing through them. One way to test for this issue is to attach a client machine directly to the print device and check the output. If the job prints correctly, the problem probably lies in the network connection.

Print Server: Verify that the print server has sufficient hard-drive space and RAM to handle the print jobs. If it is lacking in either department, slow, no, or garbled printing may result.

One Person Cannot Print

Usually a single incident of a problem points toward a configuration problem on the client operating system or permission problems with the user ID.

Permissions: Begin by logging out the user and logging in with a new ID. Can the new user print to the printer? If so, check permissions on the printer and group membership.

Connectivity: Can the client print to any other printers? Do they have access to any other network resources such as shared directories?

Printer Configuration: Is the client mapped to the correct printer? Are the correct printer drivers loaded?

One Person Receives Garbled Output

This is almost always a driver issue. Verify that others are printing to the printer correctly, and then verify the drivers that are installed on the client machine. Updating or replacing the drivers will usually cure this type of issue.

Best Practices for Printer Administration

Printer administration is often overlooked by network administrators due to other, higher-priority maintenance issues. However, several practices may ease the day-to-day administration of network printing.

1. Create a descriptive naming convention, and use it consistently. One large company this author worked for had printers named after science-fiction characters. Unfortunately, few people could remember how the names related to the physical print devices. The result was many calls to the support organization to verify printer mappings, and a support organization that had to keep lists of printer names and locations at hand. Changing to a less creative but more descriptive naming convention based on building code, floor, nearest room or cubicle, and printer type reduced the support load greatly.

2. Grant Help Desk personnel Print Operator rights. This will allow trouble calls involving document management to be handled quickly and improve responsiveness to the network users.

3. Use group membership to control access to secure printers, rather than assigning permissions to individual user IDs. This will allow easier duplication of printing rights and more efficient management of printer rights.

4. Centralize printer drivers. This will ensure that client machines are using correct printer drivers for print devices and ease the process of updating drivers.

Chapter Summary

In this chapter we discussed administering a network printing solution under Windows 2000. Printer management includes preassigning particular paper sizes to particular paper trays and using separator pages to provide information about each print job. The separator-page information can include the username, the date and time of the print job, and other elements as determined by the administrator.

Document management is the process of controlling the flow of print jobs through a queue. Documents can be paused, resumed, restarted, or cancelled by the user who created the job. Print operators and administrators can perform all four actions on others' print jobs and have additional abilities over the printer itself. Print operators and administrators can pause the printer and clear the entire queue if desired.

Queue management can involve creating additional printers for high-priority documents, redirecting queues around disabled print devices, or setting time restrictions on printers. Multiple print devices can be attached to a single print queue to create a printer pool, which will distribute documents to the next available printing device. All devices in a printing pool must use the same device drivers to ensure proper output.

Permissions control the ability of users to control their own and others' print jobs. Default permissions grant everyone the right to print to a printer and control his or her own jobs. Printer operators have the ability to control all aspects of a printer. Permissions can be used to control access to printers and can be assigned on a user or group basis. Administrators can take ownership of printers if needed and can control all aspects of a printer.

Administration of network printers can be accomplished through the Control Panel on the print server, or via a Web interface that is a new feature in Windows 2000. Internet Information Server must be installed on the print server to access the printers via a Web browser.

Troubleshooting network printing can be difficult, but the main areas to check are connectivity, print drivers, and permissions. Proper network printing practices can reduce the support load for network printing and can free MIS resources to work on other issues.

Network Administration

A primary focus of any Network Administrator should be to develop a network that runs well, is designed logically, and can be easily understood by others if the current administrator is unavailable. Many times, a network will run fine until the administrator leaves. At that time, the accumulated knowledge that is required for understanding even a simple environment is gone, and his or her successor is in for a rocky ride.

This chapter will focus on two areas in which many network environments can be improved: documentation and change control.

29.1 Documentation

People tend to fall into one of two categories when it comes to documentation. Either one loves to document an environment, or one hates it. Love it or hate it, there's no denying that there is a very real need to maintain a current paper record of the network environment and to keep a copy of the documentation off-site. Some would argue that documentation can be maintained in an electronic form only, but if the goal is both understanding the network environment and providing the capability to recreate that environment after a disaster, then a paper backup to the electronic form is vital.

29.1.1 Password Documentation

The cardinal rule of password security is often "write nothing down." Unfortunately, the strategy of committing all the passwords to memory does little good if the only people who know them just left the company or the country. Having multiple people memorize the passwords mitigates the danger somewhat, but it is not unusual to lose multiple administrators to the competition at the same time. Most IT professionals are professional enough in their duties to ensure a reasonable transition to the next caretaker, but sometimes unforeseeable situations may not allow for that transition.

One method of providing emergency access to passwords is to use a safe deposit box. Safe deposit boxes are provided by financial institutions to protect valuables. Most financial institutions will allow only authorized individuals to access a safe deposit box. Current passwords can be stored within the safe deposit box, either in an electronic format or on paper (or both!). Access to the box should be limited to the CIO or similar upper management of the company.

Server Documentation

Server documentation should be one of the top priorities of any administrator. If a system has to be rebuilt or recreated, as in the case of a disaster, thorough documentation can save many hours and much frustration. Additionally, documentation of serial numbers and the hardware installed in a server can be very useful when speaking with vendor technical support or when trying to resolve a warranty claim on server products.

At this author's place of employment, we have a Red Book for each server. Within this book, which is really a three-ring binder, is the documentation for each machine. Each binder is labeled with the server name. Multiple copies of these binders exist, with at least one copy being kept off-site. While every environment will require slightly different documents, a general list of elements that should be included in a Red Book follows:

- Hardware documentation
- Operating System documentation
- Application documentation
- Shared Resources documentation
- User information
- Printer documentation

Each of these elements will now be discussed in detail.

HARDWARE DOCUMENTATION

Think about your server farm for a moment. Can you name the manufacturer, model, and serial number of each machine off the top of your head? Unless you have either an amazing memory or a small server environment, there's probably a machine or two you missed. Now consider the various hardware that has been added to those servers, such as RAID controllers, multiport serial cards, tape units, etc. As you can see, there's quite a bit of information that needs to be collected on each of these machines.

At an absolute minimum, each server's binder should include the manufacturer, model number, serial number, and date of purchase. In addition, any additional hardware installed inside or attached to a server should be individually listed with model, part number, and purchase date. If you have to call a manufacturer for technical support or for warranty support, this will be the first information that the vendor will request. Having the information readily available will help shorten the length of time to resolve any issue.

Speaking of the warranty, the binder should also include any warranty information you have, including coverage periods, exceptions, contact numbers, renewal dates, and similar information.

Hardware documentation should also include any hardware RAID configuration information.

OS DOCUMENTATION

Regardless of the network operating system used within your environment, similar elements need to be documented for each server. Some of the most important information to document includes any customized installation parameters, network protocol information, software RAID configuration, licensing information, any service-specific settings, and similar information.

This section should also include installation instruction and software for any third-party hardware drivers. If the media for the drivers is not available, at the very minimum a list of locations from which the drivers can be downloaded should be included.

Essentially, it is the variations from the normal NOS install that should be well documented. The underlying assumption here is that whoever is using the documentation will be familiar with a generic NOS install and needs to know only the specific modifications related to a particular server.

APPLICATION DOCUMENTATION

Years ago, servers were exactly what the name suggested: machines that stored files in a centralized location and offered them to clients. However, today's networked environment often includes many application servers in addition to the traditional file and print servers. These application servers can offer anything from HTTP servers to fax services to a database backend. Naturally, as the complexities of the services grow, so does the need to document the installation and configuration of those services. There's little worse than inheriting a network, only to discover that the company is dependent upon an undocumented third-party application that you've never even seen before that moment.

All third-party applications or services that impact a server should be fully documented. At a bare minimum, documentation should include the following:

- Vendor contact information.
- Technical support information.
- Serial numbers, licensing information, and any activation codes.

- Installation instructions, including information on any changes made to the OS.
- Removal instructions, including information on any changes made to the OS.
- Operation and maintenance instructions for the application or service.
- Any known information about interoperability with other services/applications on the same server. This may prevent a fatal interaction.
- Configuration settings, both server based and client based.
- Lists of the current users of the application, and the use of the application.
- How business-critical a certain application or service is to the company. This information could be useful when determining the order in which to restore services after a disaster.

SHARE DOCUMENTATION

File sharing is still the core of network systems, though other uses are making headway (streaming audio office memos, anyone?). In most network settings there will be multiple shares for departmental information, companywide file sharing, individual network home directories, application shares, and much more. Access to each of these shares is likely to be controlled based on group or individual share rights. As the size of the network environment grows, the number of shares and the associated rights also rises.

Records of all shares and the user rights associated with those shares should be kept in a paper form, and at least one copy should be kept off-site for archival purposes.

Data from a crashed server can be restored to another machine rather quickly, assuming some form of disaster recovery plan is in place and the data files are being backed up on a regular basis. Recreating shares and the associated rights takes much longer. As an example, one of the servers at this author's place of employment has over 800 individual user home directories. Assuming that a home directory share can be created and the access rights modified in only 1 minute, that's a total of over 13 hours of constant effort to recreate those shares. Admittedly, there are methods of using line commands and batch files to create the shares much more quickly, but even this requires planning, good knowledge of command-line utilities, and a record of the preexisting shares on the server.

Fortunately, there is a way to export the shares on a server to a registry file and then simply import that key on the new server. As long as the directories themselves exist, the server will recreate the shares the next time it is rebooted or the server service is restarted. The registry key is:

HKEY_LOCAL_MACHINE\SYSTEM\CurrentControlSet\Services\LanManServer\Shares

To export this key to a file, select the *Export Registry File* option from the *Registry* dropdown menu, then enter a filename and a location. The share information and the associated security information will be exported to a *.reg* file.

To import this information into another server, simply import the *.reg* file by selecting *Import Registry File* from the *Registry* menu. The registry file will be written into the registry entries. At that point, either rebooting the server or restarting the server service will create the original shares on the replacement server.

USER DOCUMENTATION

User information is generally the easiest information to maintain. Whether using Windows 2000 in the older NT domain model or with the new Active Directory method, domain user information is normally replicated to multiple servers within the organization. Because of this replication, paper documentation of individual user accounts is not really necessary.

Documentation of the local groups, domain groups, and any templates is strongly recommended, however.

PRINTER DOCUMENTATION

Although the entire business world seems to be working toward a paperless environment, few companies have actually accomplished a truly paper-free workplace. One reason may be the mindset that paper documentation is somehow more official than an email or intranet posting. An additional factor is the inherent distrust of computers that some people still seem to possess.

In any case, it seems that printers continue to provide more capabilities and more services than ever. These added capabilities are adding complexity to the printing environment. In most environments that this author has managed, the number of printers easily entered triple digits. Obviously, once the printing environment reaches this level, even the best administrator will not be able to remember every detail on each queue and print device.

Printer documentation is often included within the book of the server that hosts the print queue, but a separate printer documentation binder may be a better choice for your situation. In any case, printer documentation should contain at least the following information:

- Make, model, and serial number for each physical print device
- Device drivers for each model of print device or, at a minimum, information about download locations for the drivers
- Physical locations of each print device
- Name of printer queues
- Access rights, if any are enforced
- Network protocols, including TCP/IP address if any
- Share names

• Recreating printer shares on a replacement server is a painstaking job, if it has to be done manually. Fortunately, we can use a shortcut much like the one used earlier for recreating shares. Printer information is stored in the *Registry*. As with the share information, this key can be exported using the *Export Registry Key* entry in the *Registry* menu and imported into another server via the *Import Registry Key* entry in the *Registry* menu. The key that manages printer shares and ports is

HKEY_LOCAL_MACHINE\SYSTEM\CurrentControlSet\Control\Print\Printers

This key includes the port information, share name info, access rights, and the type of printer driver. However, there is one important element to this technique: printer drivers are not transferred from one machine to another. If all of your client machines are using their own printer drivers, this is not a big issue. If you have Windows 2000 clients on the network, they automatically receive their drivers from the server, and thus these clients will not be able to print to the print queues.

To resolve this issue, a printer driver must be installed for each model of printer that exists on the network.

Network Documentation

The overlap between a network server administrator's duties and support for the network infrastructure itself is likely to be a function of the size of the network environment. If you work for a very large company, the LAN/WAN infrastructure is likely to be handled by a separate infrastructure group. In a smaller firm, the lines tend to blur, and the infrastructure may very well end up being handled by the server administrator.

The level of documentation for a network will naturally vary depending upon its design. At a minimum, the network needs to be as well documented as the servers. The goal of the documentation is to be able to replace or repair the network in a timely manner if any of the pieces fail. Some elements that should be documented are:

• Make, model, MAC address, and serial numbers of all LAN/WAN equipment
• Purpose of each piece of equipment, especially in an inherited network
• Configuration information for each piece of equipment
• The interconnections between equipment (network diagram)
• Location of the TFTP server and the system configuration files
• WAN connection information and WAN provider information
Some of these elements are discussed in further detail below.

HARDWARE DOCUMENTATION

Network hardware includes anything that is used to transfer data from one machine to another, with the exception of the servers and the wire itself. This can include hubs, switches, routers, remote access equipment, firewalls, and much more.

Each piece of equipment should have its make, model, MAC addresses (if applicable), serial number, and date of purchase recorded in a master list. This information is relatively easy to maintain when buying new equipment. If you have to document a network that you've inherited, the situation can be much tougher. Some equipment may not have visible markings and may have to be unmounted from the equipment racks so that you can find all the information. If there is no previous documentation, determining the date of purchase may be nearly impossible.

Once the makes, models, and serial numbers are determined for the network infrastructure, you can start to find out about warranty and specification information. Specification sheets for much equipment can be printed from manufacturer sites on the World Wide Web. To find out if the equipment is under warranty or maintenance contracts, call the manufacturer of each piece. In many cases, the manufacturer will be able to search its records for your company's information. In other cases, the manufacturer may be able to direct you to the vendor or distributor that originally sold the equipment to your company. In either case, you are sure to be informed about their new maintenance contract offerings!

CONFIGURATION INFORMATION

Documenting the configuration information on network equipment is even more vital than documenting the physical hardware. Physical hardware is easily replaced, but a lost custom configuration can be impossible to recreate, especially if the original configuration isn't known.

Some network hardware uses configuration files that are essentially a series of text-mode commands. Often, these configuration files can simply be printed from a terminal emulator and included within the documentation, in addition to keeping electronic copies of the configuration files. Other hardware uses menu-driven or graphic-based interfaces to set the configurations. Usually, with this hardware, the configuration file can be exported to a floppy or a network server. In any case, make absolutely sure you have a copy of these configuration files. From personal experience, there's nothing worse than watching a router come up from a planned or unplanned power outage, only to find that it does not have its previous configuration any more.

TFTP SERVERS

As you start inventorying and saving the configurations of the network hardware, you will probably discover that much of the equipment does not have any removable media. Most network hardware is completely solid state, with no provision for hard drives, floppy drives, and similar media. This raises the obvious question: how does one save the configuration elsewhere?

In general, network infrastructure hardware is capable of communicating with *a TFTP server* to write and read configuration information. TFTP is an acronym for Trivial File Transfer Protocol. TFTP is a lightweight file transfer protocol that does not use authentication or any other form of security. Instead, a TFTP server will accept any request for a download, if it has the file available. In addition, if a TFTP server is configured for uploads, any upload request will be accepted.

Network hardware will often look to download configuration information from a particular TFTP server if it cannot find its startup configuration files. Likewise, network hardware can upload their configuration information to a particular TFTP server. Most network hardware saves the default IP address of the TFTP server in nonvolatile memory, so that it can find the TFTP server after a reboot.

The manual for your network hardware should indicate how to configure the hardware to upload and download from a TFTP server. The procedure will vary depending upon the hardware.

 It is vital that you verify the IP address of the default TFTP server. Otherwise, incorrect or no configuration information may be loaded on the network hardware.

TFTP server software for Windows-based computers is available from most major network systems manufacturers, in addition to the many freeware or shareware servers available from the various Internet download sites.

Vendor Documentation

In today's Information Technology world, many of the day-to-day operational tasks are outsourced to external organizations. This makes perfect sense from a business and technology point of view, because the core organization can focus on the business, while the external organization can focus on its particular role. Outsourcing can take many forms, but some of the most common are telecommunication providers, specialty hardware maintenance, printer maintenance and repair, software design and implementation, and similar functions. Essentially, any role that requires very specialized skills, has extremely high-cost equipment requirements, or functions at various workload levels throughout the year is a good candidate for outsourcing. Outsourcing can help an understaffed IT department respond to the demands of the current business world, without having to hire staff devoted to specialized needs.

However, outsourcing has its fair share of problems, and most of them relate to communication with and accountability to the corporate organization. Issues arise when each side believes that the other is responsible for a particular aspect of a project or a service. From an administrator's point of view, communication and coordination with an outside vendor is vital.

SERVICE PROVIDER PLANS

It is impossible to evaluate the quality of a service provider if you are unaware of their responsibilities and requirements. It is vital that you possess, read, and understand the current contract between the service provider and the corporate offices. Service provider plans should be in place for each outsourced activity and should explicitly state the roles and responsibilities of both your company and the service provider. Quite often the formal contract between the companies is explicit enough to be used as the basis of this document.

RESPONSE TIMES

A quick response to a problem or request is always a positive when dealing with any outside vendor. However, the definition of "response" needs to be clearly understood by each party. Some vendors use the term to refer to the time to have someone on site, while others use the term to refer to the time when they acknowledge a problem and begin to work on the issue. Thus, a two-hour response time from one vendor might be a "better" response than a 30-minute time from another vendor.

Because of these kinds of differences, we advocate a three-tier system for determining and monitoring response times to problems. The three-tier method divides the response into three discrete segments:

1. **Acknowledgment Time**: This is the length of time that the vendor has to acknowledge the problem or request, assign someone to the problem or request, and contact your company with the assignment information. In some cases, the vendor will be able to acknowledge and assign a problem to the proper personnel during the initial problem report.
2. **Response Time**: Response time is the length of time it takes before the assigned personnel begin working on the issue. Depending upon your contracts, this may be on-site support, or may be remote support.
3. **Resolution Time**: Time until the issue is corrected to the customer's satisfaction.

ESCALATION PROCEDURES

All vendors should provide detailed procedures for escalating issues within their support organization, including time-to-escalation and the contact individuals for those who control the escalation process. Few things are more annoying than being stuck between the end users and the outsourcing vendor during an issue.

CONTACT INFO

Current and complete contact information for each vendor is a vital part of the documentation. Contact information should include both the front-line and escalation personnel, as well as any nontechnical contacts. At a minimum, contact information should include the following:

- Names of primary and secondary technical contact at the vendor
- Name of primary and secondary nontechnical contact at the vendor
- Mailing address of the vendor
- Physical address of the vendor, if different from the mailing address
- Main telephone number
- Backup telephone numbers, if any
- Main fax number
- Backup fax numbers, if any
- Email addresses for primary and secondary technical contacts
- Email addresses for primary and secondary nontechnical contacts

note   All contact information should be kept in both electronic and paper form.

Change Control

Network environments are constantly evolving as technology advances. New services, additional servers, and updated software all impact the current environment. Poorly planned or implemented changes can adversely affect the network and result in unplanned downtime or even data loss. To manage the changes, many companies have implemented a change-control process.

A change-control process helps prevent problems from entering the network environment by increasing awareness of changes, reviewing the changes and the plans, and managing the implementation of these changes. A change-control process should be a formalized process, though the actual process will vary depending upon a company's needs.

The Change-Control Process

The goal of the change-control process is to invite review of proposed changes before they are put into production. In addition, a change-control process ensures that the change is communicated to the affected end users, and also that the relevant groups within MIS are aware of the changes. Creating and maintaining communication between MIS and the end-user environment can help foster a better understanding of the challenges that each group faces and will help minimize the business impact of any network system changes.

The change-control process begins with a request for a network system modification. This request should include the needed modifications and the justification for the changes. The request is directed to a Change Control Coordinator, who is responsible for reviewing and approving the changes. The request is then sent to those who will implement the change.

This process obviously demands that certain roles and responsibilities be fulfilled. These roles and related responsibilities are discussed below. Please note that the actual name of the role may vary between organizations; these labels are used as examples. In addition, many times a person or group may actually fill several roles in the process.

INITIATOR

The Initiator is the person or group who is requesting a change in the production environment. This person or group is responsible for creating the change request, justifying the changes to the satisfaction of the committee, monitoring the change, communicating with the end-user population before, during, and after the change, and taking a leadership role in regards to the network modifications. The Initiator also communicates with the implementer of the change to ensure that the proper resources are available. It is important that the Initiator thoroughly understand both the business and technical implications of the request.

CHANGE CONTROL COORDINATOR

The Change Control Coordinator receives the request from the Initiator. The Coordinator may be a single individual or, more likely, a committee of senior technical and managerial people. The Change Control Coordinator handles timing and procedural issues, routes the request to the Reviewer and Approver, and coordinates interaction between the Initiator of the request and the Implementer of the request. Two of the main functions of the coordinator are to manage the scheduling of change requests, especially when multiple change requests are under consideration, and to verify that company policy is followed in relation to the requests. It is important that the Coordinator thoroughly understand both the business and technical implications of any requests, and how multiple changes will interact.

REVIEWER

The Reviewer is responsible for reviewing the request and the implementation plan for the request. The review should take into consideration the business impact of the change, the technical requirements of the change, available resources for the change, and other scheduled events that might impact the success of the change. If there are any issues with the request or if anything needs additional clarification, then the Reviewer should send the request back to the Initiator for more information. If the Reviewer accepts the request and the implementation plan, the request is sent back to the Coordinator for further action.

APPROVER

The Approver has the final say on whether the project moves ahead. This person will usually be in upper management, either in the IS department or on the business side of the company. The Approver should base his or her decision on information from the Initiator, feedback from the Reviewer, and input from the Coordinator. This person needs to fully understand the business implications of any change and should have enough technical background to comprehend the implementation plan.

IMPLEMENTER

The Implementer is the person or group that actually performs the changes requested. In many cases, the Implementer and the Initiator are overlapping positions. If the two positions do not overlap, the Implementer should work with the Initiator to develop a workable implementation plan and a rollback plan for the requested change.

The Change Request

In order to maintain a consistent change-control process, it is important that the change request be standardized. Many companies create a standard form that must be filled out by the initiator of any change request. This form can exist in either hard copy or electronic format, depending upon the needs of the company. Regardless of the format, the content can usually be boiled down into the six elements that any journalist would instantly recognize: who, what, when, where, why, and how (Figure 29.1).

WHO?

This element of the change request actually has multiple meanings: whom will the change affect, and who will be producing the change? Who bears ultimate responsibility for the results of the change? Who is the contact for the request?

WHAT?

This element answers the question, what is being changed? Is the change related to hardware, software, configurations, or something else? This needs to be very specific.

WHEN?

Scheduling is always an issue when making changes to a business-critical system. Changes must be scheduled so that necessary IS resources are available. In addition, any scheduling should include input from the affected end users, so that their business functions are not impaired by the changes.

WHERE?

Which locations will be affected by the proposed change? This may be a particular floor, one server, or an entire state WAN, depending upon the scope of the project. This element becomes more important if there are security access controls for the location. If there are security problems, then the changes must be coordinated to allow the technicians or other personnel access to the systems during the changes.

WHY?

This is the most important element of the change request. Why is this change taking place? What benefits arise from the change, or what problems will the change correct? Any change to a production environment should have a legitimate justification. If the justification cannot be clearly stated, perhaps the need for a change should be reevaluated.

HOW?

This is the implementation plan for the change, and the rollback plan if the change does not function as expected. Implementation plans should always include a listing of required personnel, required resources, detailed steps in making the changes, specific testing procedure and the measurement metrics for those tests, and a timeline for the change. The rollback plan should include a listing of events or problems that will trigger a rollback, required personnel, required resources, detailed steps for bringing the system back to its original state, testing procedures to determine if the system is back to its original state, and an estimated timeline for a rollback. For most projects, lack of a rollback plan should immediately draw scrutiny from the Reviewer and the Approver.

Chapter Summary

Documentation of a network environment is often an overlooked or ignored aspect of network administration. Any network needs to be documented so that another administrator could manage the network on an emergency or replacement basis. Documentation should be in both electronic and hard-copy form, in order to provide some redundancy.

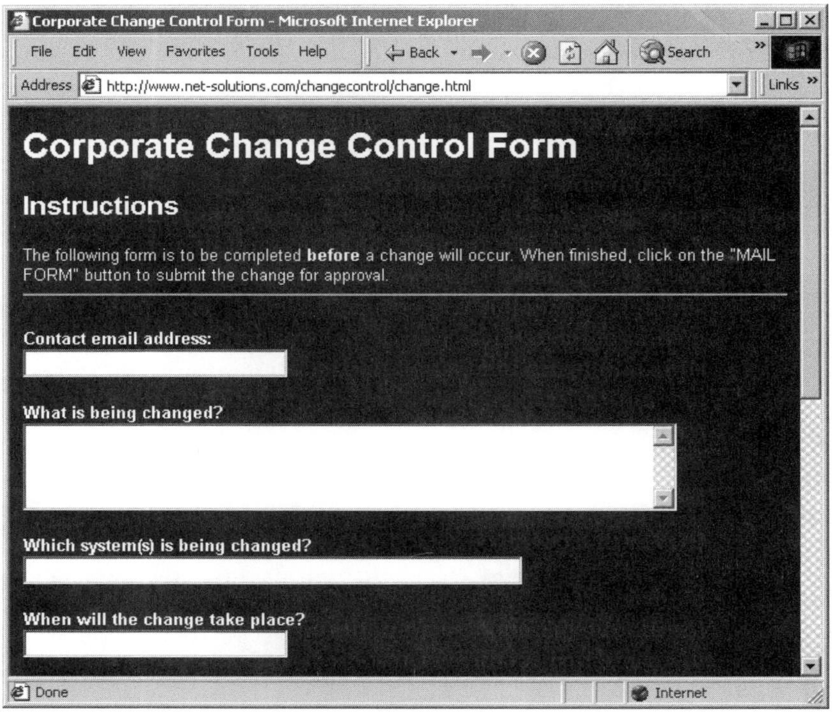

Figure 29–1　*Submitting a change request via a Web form.*

Administrative passwords should remain on a strict need-to-know basis, but there should be a method to recover those passwords. One method is to use a safe deposit box to store a current copy of the passwords. While this is technically insecure, the safe deposit box should be limited to a very small group of people, such as the CIO or IS director.

Each server should be thoroughly documented, so that a replacement system can be brought online quickly in the event of a disaster. Server documentation should include details on hardware specifications, operating-system configuration, applications and services, shared resources, system user information, and printers.

Network infrastructure elements should also be documented and the configuration information for each piece recorded or stored off-site. Documentation on network systems should include make, model, and serial number for each piece; purpose of each piece of equipment; configuration information for each piece of equipment; location of the TFTP server and configuration files; and WAN configuration information, if appropriate.

Vendor relations are often a major element of a network administrator's function. Communication with external vendors is vital in order to reduce or eliminate downtime and user frustration. To ensure that the vendor and the administrator are communicating clearly, all elements of the relationship between the two companies should be detailed. Some elements that should be clarified and documented are response times, escalation procedures, multiple methods of contacting the vendor, and the overall role of the vendor within the IT environment.

Change management is a method of controlling the changes to the production environment. Planning, rollback plans, and a concern for the needs of the end user characterize controlled changes. The change-management process itself involves submitting a detailed change request, receiving the proper review, approval, and schedule, and then implementing that change. The details of a change-management procedure vary from company to company, but the general concepts remain constant. The goal of change management is to avoid introducing problems into a network environment as a direct result of a change in the environment.

INDEX